For Gilbert Cruz,
With Great Admiration
& with Thanks for
Putting Books on
A Pedestal

George Fisher

Beware Euphoria

Beware Euphoria

The Moral Roots and Racial Myths of America's War on Drugs

GEORGE FISHER

OXFORD
UNIVERSITY PRESS

OXFORD
UNIVERSITY PRESS

Oxford University Press is a department of the University of Oxford. It furthers the University's objective of excellence in research, scholarship, and education by publishing worldwide. Oxford is a registered trade mark of Oxford University Press in the UK and certain other countries.

Published in the United States of America by Oxford University Press
198 Madison Avenue, New York, NY 10016, United States of America.

Library of Congress Cataloging-in-Publication Data
Names: Fisher, George, 1959– author.
Title: Beware euphoria : the moral roots and racial myths of America's war on drugs / George Fisher.
Description: Cambridge, United Kingdom ; New York, NY : Oxford University Press, 2024. |
Includes bibliographical references and index.
Identifiers: LCCN 2023030162 (print) | LCCN 2023030163 (ebook) |
ISBN 9780197688489 (hardback) | ISBN 9780197688496 (updf)| ISBN 9780197688502 (epub) |
ISBN 9780197688519 (digital-online)
Subjects: LCSH: Drugs of abuse—Law and legislation—United States—History. |
Narcotic laws—United States—History. |
Drugs of abuse—Law and legislation—United States—Criminal provisions. |
Drugs—Moral and ethical aspects—United States. | Drug control—United States. |
Drug legalization—United States. | Marijuana—Therapeutic use—United States.
Classification: LCC KF3890 .F57 2024 (print) | LCC KF3890 (ebook) |
DDC 178.0973—dc23/eng/20231002
LC record available at https://lccn.loc.gov/2023030162
LC ebook record available at https://lccn.loc.gov/2023030163

DOI: 10.1093/oso/9780197688489.001.0001

Printed by Integrated Books International, United States of America

Note to Readers
This publication is designed to provide accurate and authoritative information in regard to the subject matter covered. It is based upon sources believed to be accurate and reliable and is intended to be current as of the time it was written. It is sold with the understanding that the publisher is not engaged in rendering legal, accounting, or other professional services. If legal advice or other expert assistance is required, the services of a competent professional person should be sought. Also, to confirm that the information has not been affected or changed by recent developments, traditional legal research techniques should be used, including checking primary sources where appropriate.

(Based on the Declaration of Principles jointly adopted by a Committee of the American Bar Association and a Committee of Publishers and Associations.)

You may order this or any other Oxford University Press publication
by visiting the Oxford University Press website at www.oup.com.

For my mother,
who taught perseverance first of all.

Contents

Illustrations

Figures

Tables

Acknowledgments

Some books take a village; this one took an army. Without the dozens of dogged student researchers and dedicated librarians who helped track down and dig out endless sources, this book would have remained forever a line on my to-do list. In footnotes scattered throughout the book, I have called out specific students and librarians for brilliant discoveries and heroic efforts. Here I list them in the order of their service, beginning with those who first helped shape unformed musings and ending with proofers and indexer.

Among my indispensable student researchers were Eileen O'Pray, Jessica Lowe, Hollie Day Downs, Leslie Meltzer Henry, Simon Stern, Zoe Scharff, Duane Pozza, Stephen Mansell, Jake Gardener, Elena Saxonhouse, Muhammad Shahzad, Micah Myers, Manish Kumar, Helen Kim, Mamei Sun, Sang Ngo, Matt Buckley, Blair Hornstine, Kelly Finley, Kathryne Young, Aidan McGlaze, David Crandall, Justin Barnard, Stephanie Alessi, Doru Gavril, Billy Abbott, Luke Weiger, Yonathan Arbel, Sara Mayeux, Rani Gupta, Alethea Sargent, Alisa Philo, Lisa Goodman, Matthew Miller, Gabriel Schlabach, Michael Morillo, Nicholas Standish, Taylor Davidson, Katie Bies, Abbee Cox, Jason Despain, Zehava Robbins, Jordan Orosz, David Oyer, Akansha Dubey, Hai Jin Park, Brett Diehl, Tyler Jones, Sydney Kirlan-Stout, Nathan Tauger, Jenny Moroney, Hayden Henderson, and Jack Gleiberman.

The librarians and archivists, all magnificently talented, included Sonia Moss, Kate Wilko, Richie Porter, Alba Holgado, Rachael Samberg, Leizel Ching, Sean Kaneshiro, George Wilson, Alex Zhang, Birgit Calhoun, Kevin Rothenberg, Katie Siler, Shay Elbaum, Taryn Marks, Grace Lo, Alan January, Alex Bainbridge, Paul Donovan, Lauren Roberts, Lynn Calvin, and David Pleiss.

My generous and learned academic colleagues supported me in myriad ways. Some offered ideas or expertise, some cautioned against mistakes or morasses, and some showed me the charity of honest criticism. Again I've offered thanks for specific insights in footnotes throughout the book. Here I list colleagues chronologically in order of their contributions: Bill Simon, Kenji Yoshino, Bill Eskridge, Barbara Fried, Dan Kahan, Stephen Carter, Ian Ayres, Judith Resnick, Denny Curtis, Rob Gaudet, Avi Soifer, Morton Horwitz, Andy Koppelman, Ariela Dubler, John Cavadini, William Klingshirn, Mark Vessey, Jim Baumohl, Keith Humphreys, and Frank Herrmann. I owe special thanks to Lawrence Friedman, Don Herzog, and Amalia Kessler, who read the entire manuscript and lent me honest and clear-eyed guidance.

I owe thanks as well to several students who took part in a legal theory workshop at Yale Law School and mounted thoughtful challenges: John Amash, Steve Hessler, Rob Mikos, Michael Moreland, Patrick Raulerson, Marcela Sánchez, Jennifer Saulino, and Jonathan Witmer-Rich.

Then there are the good people who helped guide the manuscript to publication. Jack Rakove introduced me to Don Lamm, who shared the wisdom of long experience. Alex Flach and Brian Stone gave the manuscript a home at Oxford University Press and steered me past bureaucratic shoals. Lane Berger and Getsy Deva Kirubai managed the endless challenges of preproduction and production and ensured a polished and elegant volume. And Mary Rosewood cast a perfectionist's eye over every word and comma.

Finally I want to thank three family members—my aunt Lu Koeppe, who at age eighty-two ventured with me on a tour of Denver's still young cannabis dispensaries; my uncle Richard Koeppe, who for years clipped and mailed me cannabis news from Denver's local press; and my mother, without whose never-quit attitude I would have quit long ago.

G.F.
San Francisco
September 2023

Prologue

Why are we married to alcohol?

More to the point, why have we stayed faithful? Since time out of mind, alcohol has reigned almost everywhere as our lone legal intoxicant. Countless rivals have beckoned our affections, whispering promises of elegiac dreams or fantastic visions or the bliss of suspended awareness. Yet forswearing all others, we have held true to alcohol.

This book aims to explain why. Today, with so much in flux, with legalized cannabis advancing across the land, it's time to ask why we've remained wedded to alcohol so long. Though I hope to explain this long devotion and our stubborn rejection of other recreational drugs, I won't defend our war on drugs. Instead, I'll ask how it came to pass. Like many others, I question the wisdom of our national drug-law regime. Our struggle to suppress recreational drugs has spawned a thriving street trade marked by extortionate prices, extravagant profits, violent turf wars, and abusive police tactics. Accused drug offenders, too often young men of color, bloat our prisons. By waging a war with such faint prospects for victory, we perhaps have blinded ourselves to better ways to attack the evils of drugs.

But the policies of the present are not the focus of this book. Instead, I look backward for the roots of a regime that has embraced alcohol, if only warily, while spurning its recreational rivals.

Alcohol Monogamy

Why then have we been married to alcohol?

The answer is scarcely seen in scholarly assaults on the drug war and hardly heard in the rhetoric of policymakers who prop up our laws against change. Ask those academics who deride our drug bans how such wayward policies took hold. Many will say racism, so often the virus of injustice, spread its worm here. We banned opium, they say, because Chinese miners and railroad workers brought it here; cocaine because African Americans made it their drug of choice; and marijuana because migrant Mexicans cast its seeds north of the border. Or, they say, our drug laws arose because early factory owners feared drug-hazed workers would drag down output. Rooted in racism and class conflict, they charge, drug bans claim no legitimacy as law.

Ask instead those officeholders who defy change how our drug laws came to pass. Most reply in utilitarian tones, speaking a calculus of harms and risks. The dangers of addiction, they say, and of overdose and death proved weightier than the rapture of escape. Alcohol, they admit, is a pestilence too—but it is the devil we know. Alcohol has survived despite its evils because we have learned how to keep them in check.

Attractive or plausible as these claims may be, they all miss the mark. Why have we banned recreational intoxicants? The answer is almost too plain to see.

We have banned recreational intoxicants because they *intoxicate*—they disable our reason and self-command, if only for a while—with no better excuse than recreation. We have banned recreational intoxicants not because they harm us or give pleasure to groups we despise, but because of our cultural *euphoria taboo*—an old and deep and essentially moral aversion to pleasures that numb the mind.

But doesn't alcohol too befuddle the brain? Surely it can, but only when taken in excess. Used in moderation, alcohol leaves reason intact and acuity almost undimmed. It delivers not the mindless rapture of escape, but the pleasure of minds meeting, engaged with each other and the now more manageable cares of this world. Yet if alcohol came only as a ten-shot swallow, so one couldn't drink but get drunk, we would ban it too. Alcohol may be the devil we know, but if it served *only* to intoxicate, slurring conversation without brightening it, alcohol too would face the prohibitionist's ax.

Of course at times we *have* banned drink. Maine and a trail of copycat states outlawed alcohol in the mid-nineteenth century, and the Eighteenth Amendment turned America dry decades later. Americans' exuberant resistance to national prohibition has made that era of moonshine and speakeasies irresistible material for modern historians and storytellers. But the prominence of these episodes in our historical memory obscures the reality of our relationship with alcohol. Save for a few years here or a dozen years there, alcohol has survived for millennia as a routine, widely condoned if often reviled fixture of Western culture.

More precisely, alcohol has thrived as our lone *recreational* drug. Alcohol has other uses—as sacramental wine, say, or a substrate for some medicines. Other drugs, too, have *non*-recreational uses that don't offend the law. Hence opium and cocaine and their kin deaden physical pain, and peyote enables the spiritual rituals of native peoples. Prozac, Xanax, and their ilk aim to restore normal moods and coping mechanisms. Such non-recreational drug use, however, is not the topic of this book on our cultural euphoria taboo. Instead my focus is on drugging to pleasure and disable the mind and on the role old moral notions have played in banning such drug use.

Drugs' Dangers

But aren't the *real* sins of banned drugs that they kill by overdose and addict? Surely if a drug kills even when used with care, it should and will be banned. So too should thalidomide and other drugs that cripple users or disfigure their offspring. Yet the case against opium, cocaine, and cannabis in the early days of our drug war rarely focused on their ravages to the body. Instead, early lawmakers banned these drugs because they blight our brains, if only briefly, blotting out reason with base pleasure.

Addiction in this light is not a stand-alone cause of antidrug lawmaking but an aggravator of moral ills. People confess addiction to caffeine, yet no one thinks this dependency shameful, and no lawmaker deems it cause for a ban. For caffeine sharpens rather than deadens the mind and delivers no euphoric escape from reality. Even nicotine, though fiercely addictive, is lawful throughout the land. Cigarettes' hazards to health have put them off limits to minors, and their danger to bystanders has exiled them from public spaces. Someday, maybe, their distortion of the health marketplace will trigger a broader ban. But addictiveness alone has prompted no bar. Because nicotine, like caffeine, concentrates the mind, it escapes the clamor of moral condemnation that falls on any drug daring to call itself Ecstasy.

Still, the addictive power of many drugs figures in our drug war's moral history. Though addictiveness alone will not prompt the ban of a *non*-euphoric drug, *adding* addictiveness to a euphoric drug's stupefying power spurs an even stricter ban. For addiction aggravates the moral offense of capitulating to base pleasure by making that collapse enduring and complete. The addictive quality of many intoxicants magnifies the loss of self-control and makes the addicted, in the words of Saint Thomas Aquinas, "a slave to pleasures."

Race-Hued Morality

Race too plays a role in this history of our drug war, but not the role commonly claimed.

At certain times and in certain places racial biases have warped the timing and severity of our drug bans—and over time, the racism that pulses through our culture has contorted our drug-law regimes. Seen in rearview across decades of racial strife, our earliest antidrug laws seem grown from soil soaked in racism. Drug war historians have projected onto this earlier era the dynamics of today's race-infused justice system, in which police officers' biases—and those of prosecutors, judges, jurors, and lawmakers—skew outcomes against Black and Brown persons. Against this modern backdrop, claims that early drug bans arose from bigotry toward Chinese newcomers, African Americans, and Mexicans seem compelling.

Such accounts are not simply mistaken—they are exactly wrong. For our earliest antidrug laws were not about the Chinese, African Americans, or Mexicans sometimes linked with opium, cocaine, and marijuana. *These were laws about whites.* The lawmakers who erected America's earliest drug bans acted first and foremost to protect the morals of their own racial kin. And because the morals of *most* importance to white lawmakers were those of white women and their own offspring, they acted fastest and most forcefully when a drug took white women and white youth—and especially *respectable* women and youth—in its clutches.

Police officers, too, often trained their drug-enforcement zeal on white users and those who sold to whites. Nor was this focus on the morals of white users merely a feint to cover a more devious design—say, to criminalize and imprison *non*-white *sellers.* We'll see that when Chinese den keepers sold opium to other Chinese, they suffered little police interference—yet when whites opened opium dens for other whites, police hauled them in. Later, when laws against cocaine and cannabis first took form, the sellers in question were often white, and perhaps mostly so.

Here then was racism, but not the same breed of racism fingered by many historians as the force behind early antidrug laws. These laws arose not out of hatred of non-whites linked with certain drugs and not with intent to oppress them. Instead, lawmakers acted to protect the morals of their own kind while disregarding the morals of others.

Defining Morality

Any study that looks to moral attitudes to explain historical trends first must say *whose* moral code is at issue. Ultimately, this book aims to explain how the American legal regimes governing alcohol and other recreational drugs took form. That goal compels a focus on the Western, largely Christian moral tradition, especially that of England and America, for English law helped shape much of our own.

And because elected representatives crafted our antidrug laws, the morals that matter most are those of the cultural mainstream, to which successful politicians pay fealty. So I'm not writing about *my* moral attitudes or yours. Not everyone shares mainstream values—or we'd have no need for drug laws—and those who don't will not recognize themselves here. They may, however, recognize their neighbors. In some places—Berkeley, say, or Boulder or Greenwich

Village—even one's neighbors may fall outside the mold. But I am writing about the broad middle of American society, not its bluest extremities.

In defining *moral*, I prefer to set dictionaries aside. *Moral* has many meanings, but here I mean only one: we have deemed moral what befits decent and essentially *human* conduct. And we have deemed essentially human the shared pleasures of the mind, including love, learning, conversation, wit, and fellow feeling. Not all else is *immoral*. But those things that undermine or disable what is essentially human, that render us appetitive or base or insensitive to the world about us, risk condemnation. Hence our cultural aversion to intoxication stems mostly from the nature of intoxication itself—its heedless suspension of self-control, its abdication of rational functioning, its indulgence in mindless pleasure.

These phrases may call to mind the stupefying euphoria of opium smoking or drunkenness. They also may call to mind sex. For sex, like drug intoxication and drunkenness, suspends self-control, abdicates rationality, and indulges in mindless pleasure. Sex is our original euphoriant, our ur-pleasure. In the Western moral tradition, lust and drunkenness have stood side by side in the dock, accused of robbing us of our godlike reason and transforming us into beasts. So the Church's regulation of sex in early Christian times set the moral template for the regulation of alcohol in Puritan times and of drugs still later. This similarity among the old moral regimes governing sex and alcohol and drugs is some evidence of the primacy of moral objections in shaping the regulation of substance abuse. For while sex and intoxicants are bad in many ways, only along the moral dimension are they bad in the same way.

Tempering all three moral regimes is the moral excuse of *necessity*. From the days of Plato onward, a plausible claim of need has suspended the usual strictures against euphoric conduct or substance abuse. Necessity weaves in and out of this narrative, sometimes setting the terms of lawful indulgence in sex or alcohol or drugs and sometimes supplying a tempting excuse to cross the lines of the law for those who claim to be moral but wish to indulge.

The Path Ahead

This book traces a long path across time and space. I will make stops along that path, digging into debates about conduct or substances in specific eras and locales. At times the reader may wish to linger, digging deeper at one spot or exploring diverging trails. Yet only by taking broad steps between stops, sometimes traversing swaths of time and space, can we see the shared beliefs driving sexual strictures, drunkenness taboos, and drug bans.

Our journey begins in San Francisco in the mid- to late nineteenth century, where a recent ban on opium dens stood alongside a thriving saloon culture. Here we face the paradox of monogamy: Why have we banned only one of these vices, not obviously the worse of the two?

To resolve that paradox, we step back in time and seek in Chapter 1 the seeds of this moral regime in early Christian strictures against sex. The old Church Fathers, and most prominently Saint Augustine, condemned recreational, nonprocreative sex, which indulges our beastly appetites and suspends our god-like reason. But however troubling sex might be as a moral matter, the Church Fathers saw our survival required it. Here we have the mediating force of necessity. The demands of marriage and procreation excused indulgence in the mindless, uncontrolled pleasure of sex—but only as necessary.

Moralists of medieval and early modern times condemned drunkenness in terms strikingly like Saint Augustine's condemnation of sex. They too recognized the moral excuse of necessity. Alcohol claimed to serve several needs—as a dietary staple, a sanitary beverage, an all-purpose nostrum against pain and winter's dank cold. As with sex, necessity did not grant unconditional license to indulge. One could use alcohol only as necessary—and never to intoxicate. In exploring the realm that lay between alcohol's necessary use and its inebriating abuse, Saint Thomas Aquinas and later moralists defined *temperance*, or drinking in moderation, as a moral safe harbor.

These three principles—the sinfulness of drunkenness, the moral excuse of necessity, and the safe harbor of moderation—largely defined the terms of temperance debates raging in England and America in the seventeenth through twentieth centuries. As set out in Chapters 2 and 3, these principles helped shape the making and unmaking of England's brief eighteenth-century gin ban and the rise and fall of American national prohibition.

The temperance wars finally subsided as combatants came to terms around a moral accommodation of alcohol. The regime that rose in prohibition's place embraced a new view of the *social necessity* of alcohol—a concept that happily required a web of rules, legal and social, ensuring that "social drinking" always fell shy of drunkenness. This is the alcohol regime we inherit today, one that tolerates moderate drinking as a social lubricant—a facilitator of fellowship and good cheer. In this moral regime, drink makers broadcast their products' power to spark conversation, but never their power to intoxicate.

Alcohol monogamy captures the essentially exclusive nature of this moral accommodation of moderate alcohol use. That most people do not call alcohol a "drug" suggests we box it separately in our minds from other intoxicants. Our elaborate moral rationalization of drinking has sustained our bond with alcohol even as it has shut out rival intoxicants—for the terms of this moral arrangement have proved hard for other drugs to meet.

The difficulty emerged when alcohol's first real recreational rival reached American shores in the late nineteenth century. Opium dens newly arrived from China did not fit the moral framework that had sustained alcohol use. Smoked opium served no apparent need—doctors thought it useless as medicine—and permitted no subintoxicating use. Unlike alcohol, opium did not enliven but narcotized conversation. Worse, it acted (or was thought to act) as a sexual stimulant, driving respectable young women to ruin. The result, detailed in Chapter 4, was that opium dens and opium smoking met ready legislative condemnation. So did other recreational drugs as they came on the scene. Legislators distinguished necessary—and hence legitimate—medical *use* from recreational *abuse* simply by criminalizing sales not made by prescription. This legislative stratagem spurred a social revolution, as lawmakers across the land passed law after endless law targeting recreational drug abuse.

These early laws against opium dens and—somewhat later—cocaine and cannabis rarely had roots in racial strife. Overwhelmingly, they sprang from the traditional moral censure of intoxication for intoxication's sake. Above all, these laws responded to the moral threat posed by euphoric, mind-disabling drugs to respectable white women and youth. Chapters 5, 6, and 7, which address opium dens, cocaine, and cannabis, advance two missions. They aim first to show how fully the evidence refutes traditional claims that early antidrug laws took rise from racial hatred. Even the most familiar claim of all—that in banning opium dens, white lawmakers acted in horror of racial mixing in the dens—proves false, at least in the early years of our drug war. These chapters document instead how lawmakers focused on women and youth of their own ilk. Most of our early laws against opium, cocaine, and cannabis therefore targeted white users and those who sold to them.

By the time our journey arrives at the present in Chapter 8, the racial dynamic of the drug war had grown vastly different and distressingly familiar. Even as economic realities consigned the drug trade to poorer, often non-white sellers, the law's seeming inability to suppress the trade drove lawmakers toward ever harsher penalties. As prisons swelled with mostly non-white dealers, the entire apparatus of antidrug law enforcement suffered attack as a tool of racial oppression. And as these attacks sharpened and spread, they helped tip the balance of public opinion toward legalizing recreational marijuana.

So we arrive in the end at this historical irony: though racial biases did not drive our drug laws' early rise, racial biases may speed those laws' demise.

Introduction

Monogamy's Paradox

One night in 1891 or 1892, two unlikely figures strode down a gray and gritty alley in San Francisco's Chinatown. White men often found their way to Chinatown, but rarely at this hour, and when they did, their business was rarely good. Yet here was a minister, cane in hand. The Reverend Frederick J. Masters was on a mission—and had brought a man with a camera to record it.[1]

Down "an alley of execrable squalor," with "sickly fumes" rising from every cellar, the men found a door that opened to a stair that dropped to a cramped and lightless passage that ended at last at another door. Masters rapped with his cane.

The door opened slightly, showing a sliver of a man—a face and a hand. The face was Chinese, the hand raised in a gesture of *procul este profani*—the "take your trouble elsewhere" of an earlier age.[2] Addressing the man in Chinese, Masters overcame his feigned innocence and won entry to the world within. "Nose, eyes and ears soon tell us," he recalled, "we are in the presence of the dusky tyrant."

Opium.

That such a place existed in 1892 may seem odd. Seventeen years before, in 1875, San Francisco wrote the nation's first ban on opium dens. The board of supervisors made it a crime punished by up to six months in jail to keep such a den or visit one to smoke opium. But that ordinance, driven in part by the supervisors' distress that young "WHITE MEN AND WOMEN . . . of respectable parentage" had begun to indulge in what most thought a Chinese vice, seemingly had little impact on dens kept by and for the Chinese. San Francisco police largely left such dens unmolested as long as whites dared not enter.[3] As an

---

[1] I've drawn this description of Masters's visit to the den from Frederick J. Masters, "Opium and It's [*sic*] Votaries," 1 *California Illustrated Magazine* (May 1892), pp. 631–38.

[2] *Procul este profani*—literally, "Be gone, unholy ones"—is from Virgil's *Aeneid*, bk. 6/258. Masters uses the expression in "Opium and It's Votaries," p. 633.

[3] The ordinance and a brief account of its passage are printed in "The Opium Dens," *San Francisco Chronicle*, Nov. 16, 1875, p. 3, and "Board of Supervisors," *Daily Alta California*, Nov. 16, 1875, p. 1; "Board of Supervisors," *id.*, Nov. 23, 1875, p. 1. I thank my research assistant Helen Kim for persevering in a difficult hunt for the text of the ordinance, which does not appear to survive in any San Francisco public document. Latimer and Goldberg's uncited claim that San Francisco passed an ordinance against opium smoking "as early as 1874" appears mistaken. Dean Latimer & Jeff Goldberg, *Flowers in the Blood: The Story of Opium* (1981), p. 208; *see also* Kathleen Auerhahn, "The Split Labor Market and the Origins of Antidrug Legislation in the United States," *Law and Social*

Beware Euphoria. George Fisher, Oxford University Press. © Oxford University Press 2024.
DOI: 10.1093/oso/9780197688489.003.0001

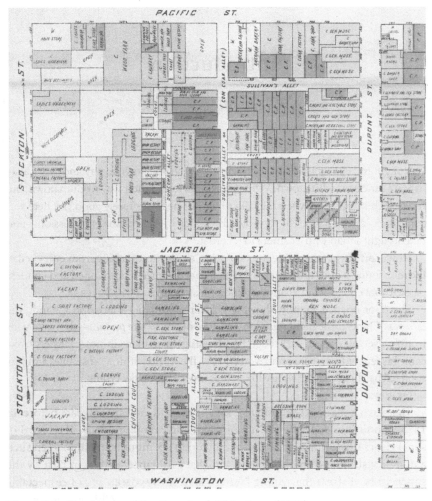

Figure I.1: Two blocks of San Francisco's Chinatown (1885).

1885 map of Chinatown shown in Figure I.1 suggests, the district remained pocked with dens (colored yellow in the map) long after the ban took hold.

Masters did not go to the little establishment off Jackson Street to smoke opium. Instead, he went to investigate opium smoking among the Chinese and seek some remedy. As superintendent of the city's Methodist Chinese Mission and a one-time missionary to China, he perhaps harbored two biases on his descent into the den.[4]

Inquiry, vol. 24 (1999), p. 422 (repeating Latimer and Goldberg's claim). I present the evidence that police targeted mainly white smokers in Chapter 5.

[4] Masters noted his role as the superintendent of the Chinese mission in "Opium and It's Votaries," p. 631. In a later article he reported he had spent "twenty-two years . . . among the Chinese

Figure I.2: A San Francisco Opium Den (c. 1892).

Unlike so many others of his day, he may have borne no hatred toward the Chinese, often victims of open and vicious racism. But as a Methodist minister, he perhaps held a dim view of opium smoking. During much of the nineteenth century, Methodists had championed American and British temperance movements and had fought for strict limits and ultimately a total ban on alcohol. Having rejected one recreational intoxicant, Methodists hardly seemed likely to embrace another.

We can merely guess at Masters's opinions as he stepped down into the den, for he didn't disclose his thoughts. Fortunately, he recorded what he saw, richly detailed in the pages of *California Illustrated Magazine*. Alongside prose descriptions, he printed pictures of the den and its denizens caught in the glare of "flash light photographs" that burst into the den's "Stygian darkness."

The resulting images convey nothing so much as a scene of stifling banality. Far from the hoped-for den of exotic depravity, the reader discovers a sooty hovel with forlorn smokers lying almost hidden beneath cluttered shelves and hat hooks (see Figure I.2). Disappointed by these photos, the reader turns instead to Masters's ornate Victorian prose, which impresses more potent images on the mind.

in Kwangtung and the United States." Frederick J. Masters, "The Opium Traffic in California," *The Chautauquan*, vol. 24 (n.s. 15) (1896–97), p. 55.

The darkness strikes us first. Descending into the den, Masters passed three or four Chinese patrons "crawling out into the light." Feeling his way along a narrow passage, he emerged into the dusty, sultry haze of the den. There a "stupefying smoke fills the hovel, through the gloom of which the feeble yellow light of three or four opium lamps struggles hopelessly to penetrate." Other writers of the day had ventured into the underground of the dens, and they too wrote of the smoky darkness. Over and over we read of "dens shut out from air and sunlight," of the futile efforts of a "sickly, guttering tallow candle" or a "dull red light that illuminates nothing," and of "the hesitating dusk" of the "low, black, . . . cave-like hole underneath the sidewalk."[5]

What strike us next are the den's spartan furniture and the smokers' recumbent poses. The sole furnishings were three or four matted wooden bunks, on which the den's patrons curled, their faces turned toward the proprietor's hissing pipes. In one after another contemporary description of a squalid den, we read of smokers lying on "greasy benches" or "a filthy pallet," their bunks stacked "one above the other, like the berths on shipboard," their "swollen, nerveless lips . . . glued" to the pipe. "Many persons suppose that opium is used in the same way that tobacco is," wrote one observer. "This, however, is a mistake. Tobacco can be smoked standing, walking, and at business. The opium smoker always lies down when indulging his habit, and gives all his attention to the process of inhaling the fumes of the drug." Sometimes an author would add the notable detail that male smokers shared a bunk with indifferent females, who "manifest no bashfulness in smoking with strange men, and . . . usually remove the shoes, loosen the corsets, and remain for hours on the hard wooden bunks." And sometimes, it seemed, an author added to this threat of promiscuity the haunting specter of miscegenation—"the sickening sight of young white girls from sixteen to twenty years of age lying half-undressed on the floor or couches, smoking with their 'lovers.' Men and women, Chinese and white people, mix indiscriminately in Chinatown smoking houses."[6]

---

[5] David T. Courtwright, *Forces of Habit: Drugs and the Making of the Modern World* (2001), p. 177 (quoting from "Death in the Pipe," *San Francisco Chronicle*, Feb. 23, 1877, p. 3) ("dens shut out . . ."); Mark Twain, *Roughing It* (Hartford: American Publishing Company, 1872) (reprint Oxford University Press, Shelley Fisher Fishkin ed., 1996), p. 395 ("sickly, guttering . . ."); [Dan De Quille,] "A Cave of Oblivion," *Daily Territorial Enterprise*, July 28, 1874, p. 3 ("dull red light . . ."); George Parsons Lathrop, "The Sorcery of Madjoon," *Scribner's Monthly*, vol. 20 (1880), pp. 416, 418 ("hesitating dusk . . ."); "A Growing Evil," *San Francisco Chronicle*, July 25, 1881, p. 3 ("low, black . . .").

[6] Thomas J. Vivian, "John Chinaman in San Francisco," *Scribner's Monthly*, vol. 12 (Oct 1876), pp. 862, 870 ("greasy benches"); "Topics in the Sagebrush," *New York Times*, Feb. 21, 1881, p. 1 ("filthy pallet"); Dan De Quille, *The Big Bonanza* (New York: Alfred A. Knopf, 1947) (1876 ed. reprint), p. 295 (". . . like the berths on shipboard"); "A Growing Evil," *San Francisco Chronicle*, July 25, 1881, p. 3 ("swollen, nerveless . . ."); "Chinese in New-York: How They Live, and Where," *New York Times*, Dec. 26, 1873, p. 3 ("Many persons suppose . . ."); H.H. Kane, *Opium-Smoking in America and China: A Study of Its Prevalence, and Effects, Immediate and Remote, on the Individual and the Nation* (New York: G.P. Putnam's Sons, 1882), p. 74 ("manifest no bashfulness . . ."); "The Opium Habit in

Then there is the silence. "We had been in this den about five minutes," Masters wrote, "and no one had spoken a word. It was like being in a sepulcher with the dead. The noise of the street could not reach us there, and nothing could be heard but the sputtering of opium pipes. What a contrast to the glare and glitter of the saloon, or the hilarious shouts and drunken orgies of the dive! . . . No wild frenzy and excited mirth are here," he concluded. "It is a place of shades and sleep and dreams; the hush of the grave . . . ." Far removed from frenzy or mirth, the satisfied smoker, struck literally dumb by the den's narcotic fumes, "sinks back, the pipe slips from his hand, and oblivious of everything around him, he drops off to sleep."

A decade before, when George Parsons Lathrop wrote in *Scribner's Monthly* of his visit to an opium den in an unspecified "cosmopolis," he reported with almost identical imagery the contrast between the den's ghostly silence and the saloon's convivial din. "What most impresses us, now," he said, "is the silence of the scene. . . . [N]ot a word is spoken; everything proceeds in a wicked, ominous hush, which becomes oppressive. How unlike the prodigal gas of the barrooms, with their silver-mounted taps, their glittering, vari-colored bottles, their seductive air of social re-union, are the hesitating dusk of this gloomy interior, the motionless forms and the silence! In the bar-room," he continued, "there is bewildering brilliance; here, no concealment or palliation is attempted— everything is in harmony with the work of death that is being done . . . ." Or as Nevada journalist Dan De Quille wrote after visiting a Virginia City den in 1874, it was a "Cave of Oblivion."[7]

Gloomy and silent as the den might have been when set against the glare and glitter and excited mirth of the saloon, Masters wondered whether the "terrible curse" of opium smoking was truly worse than the vice of drunkenness. Opium, he said, caused nothing like "the appalling amount of crime that results from the use of alcoholic liquors. . . . Opium does not brutalize and inflame human passions but soothes and finally destroys them. In an opium den one never hears a brawl, or a curse, or sees men fighting like infuriated demons." Nor did the opium smoker, like so many drunks, "go home to drag his wife out of bed by the hair of her head." And opium, he said, posed no substantial risk to health. "[U]sed moderately and with proper bodily nourishment opium smoking

San Francisco," *Medical and Surgical Reporter*, vol. 57 (1887), p. 784 (quoting San Francisco doctor Winslow Anderson) ("the sickening sight . . .").

[7] Lathrop, "Sorcery of Madjoon," pp. 416–18; [Dan De Quille,] "A Cave of Oblivion," *Daily Territorial Enterprise*, July 28, 1874, p. 3. This newspaper account, published without byline, is reprinted in De Quille, *The Big Bonanza*, pp. 295–96. De Quille's real name was William Wright. *See* ibid., p. viii.

is . . . not attended by any immediate debilitation or any visible physical infirmity as is generally supposed."[8] At first glance, then, the balance of evils favored the den.

Monogamy's Paradox

Masters was hardly the first to note that alcohol fuels more crime and far more violence than opium or any of its derivatives. Half a century earlier the Reverend Walter Colton had written of opium that "[i]t allows a man to be a gentleman; it makes him visionary, but his visions create no noise, no riots; they deal no blows, blacken no one's eyes, and frighten no one's peace." Nor was Masters the first to see that opium's comparatively mild health effects, while hardly benign, make alcohol look like a major public health threat. Masters and others repeated tales of hopeless opium addicts who nonetheless displayed astonishing physical stamina, lived out ample spans, and executed exacting tasks with consummate skill.[9]

Yet at the time Masters wrote, opium dens had been banned in San Francisco for seventeen years and had been unlawful across California for more than a decade. Between 1877 and 1907, twenty-four states and territories made it a crime to keep an opium den or visit such a place to smoke opium. By 1914, another fourteen states and territories had criminalized any distribution of opium not authorized by a doctor's prescription. That year the federal government effectively banned opium sales nationwide.[10]

Meanwhile alcohol and alcohol-serving saloons remained in most states perfectly legal unless banned locally. Not till after the Eighteenth Amendment to the US Constitution took effect in 1920 did California act to end alcohol consumption. And no sooner was the prohibition amendment repealed in 1933 than

---

[8] Masters, "Opium and It's Votaries," p. 638.
[9] Walter Colton, "Turkish Sketches," *Knickerbocker*, vol. 7 (1836), p. 421; Kane, *Opium-Smoking in America and China*, p. 90 (questioning reports by patients and others of the health hazards of opium); Masters, "Opium and It's Votaries," p. 638 (discussing feats of endurance by opium smokers); Alonzo Calkins, "Opium and Its Victims," *The Galaxy*, vol. 4 (1867), pp. 25, 27 (describing feats of endurance and long lives). Later Calkins reported contrary evidence of persistently short lifespans. *See* ibid., pp. 29–30.
[10] "An Act . . . Relating to the Sale and Use of Opium," 1881 *Calif. Stats.* ch. 40 (Act of Mar. 4, 1881), § 1, p. 34 (making it a misdemeanor to keep an opium den or to visit one to smoke opium); Table 4A (listing state and territorial opium den bans); Table 4C (listing state and territorial opium bans). In counting early state laws against opium dens, I do not include Hawaii, which banned all opium sales not authorized by prescription in 1874, when it was still an independent kingdom. *See* "An Act to Restrict the Importation and Sale of Opium . . ." (Act of Aug. 8, 1874), *reprinted in Compiled Laws of the Hawaiian Kingdom* (Honolulu: Hawaiian Gazette Office, 1884), pp. 571–72. I count Hawaii in the second group of fifteen states, as it became a territory of the United States in 1900. I discuss the 1914 Harrison Narcotic Act in Chapter 4.

the state restored lawful alcohol sales. Since prohibition's repeal, there has been no serious debate about a nationwide alcohol ban. Today every state permits liquor sales, and but for those nations influenced by Islamic law, every nation does too. Yet opium dens were and remain strictly off limits, and our broader war on drugs rages on. Despite some recent softening toward cannabis and the use of psychedelics in therapy, the drug foes' flanks have held firm on all other fronts.

Why then are we married to alcohol? The search for an answer leads back through the centuries to the roots of America's drug-law regime. But we begin here, with Frederick Masters's visit to the little den off Jackson Street, because San Francisco is where America's drug war began. The city's 1875 ban on opium dens seems to have been the nation's first law criminalizing use of a recreational intoxicant other than alcohol. The country was then engaged in a struggle over alcohol, one that alcohol ultimately won. Perhaps we may find in the meeting of these epic conflicts clues to why two so similar wars ended so differently.

The Evil of the Dens

The perceived evil of the dens took many forms. First and foremost was the matter of race. We have seen already the San Francisco supervisors' vexation that the city's Chinese kept "eight opium-smoking establishments . . . for the exclusive use of WHITE MEN AND WOMEN." One easily could multiply venomous quotes linking the dens with the hated Chinese. Politicians and newspapers of the day spoke of the "swarms of Chinamen, thick as maggots in cheese, smoking opium" in "the vilest dens of Mongol depravity." We read of "the noisome salival drippings of coolie bawds"—of "those soulless human reptiles" and "pigtailed rat[s]" and their "blighting vice." Even the urbane George Parsons Lathrop wrote in *Scribner's* of the den's "suitably Asiatic [air], poisoned by too many Chinese lungs" and of its "tigerish little proprietor" who went "crawling about his work."[11]

Seizing on such rhetoric—and on a good deal more dealing with drugs other than opium—a generation of drug war historians has cast the nation's early drug laws as a response not to the evils of the drugs, but to the race of those who used them. Richard Bonnie and Charles Whitebread triggered this scholarly onslaught

[11] "The Opium Dens," *San Francisco Chronicle*, Nov. 16, 1875, p. 3 ("eight opium-smoking establishments . . ."); *Speech of Hon. Aaron A. Sargent, of California, in the Senate of the United States* (Washington: Government Printing Office, May 2, 1876), p. 3(quoted in Diana Lynn Ahmad, "'Caves of Oblivion': Opium Dens and Exclusion Laws, 1850–1882" (Ph.D. Dissertation, University of Missouri-Columbia, 1997), p. 76) ("swarms of Chinamen . . ."); "Death in the Pipe," *San Francisco Chronicle*, Feb. 23, 1877, p. 3 ("vilest dens of Mongol depravity . . ." and "noisome salival drippings . . ."); "Opium Smoking: The Hideous Heathen Vice in Our Midst," *Reno Evening Gazette*, Feb. 21, 1879, p. 3 ("soulless human reptiles . . ." and "blighting vice"); Vivian, "John Chinaman in San Francisco," p. 865 ("pigtailed rat"); Lathrop, "Sorcery of Madjoon," pp. 417, 418.

when they wrote in 1970 that lawmakers sought to suppress those drugs that had "achieved a significant degree of 'street' use . . . especially when 'street' use is identified with the poor and with racial minorities." Three years later, David Musto spoke of the role of miscegenation panic—the terror of white women's seduction by Chinese demons in the dens. As for other drugs, Musto observed that "cocaine was supposed to enable blacks to withstand bullets which would kill normal persons and to stimulate sexual assault," and "Chicanos in the Southwest were believed to be incited to violence by smoking marihuana." Other historians followed in Bonnie and Whitebread's and Musto's trail, adopting almost unaltered their thesis that racial bias lay at the roots of the nation's early drug bans.[12]

Beyond the problem of race were the health risks of opium. Though Frederick Masters and several experts looked on opium's hazards with complacency, many others viewed them with alarm. In 1867 Dr. Alonzo Calkins quoted one authority's warning "that the youth who begins [smoking opium] at twenty must not calculate on passing thirty-six." A decade later, the *San Francisco Chronicle* reported that sharing a pipe, especially with the Chinese, could cause leprosy. A Nevada newspaper told in 1879 of an apparent fatal overdose in an opium den and warned readers of the habit's lethal risks. Even Frederick Masters felt compelled in 1896 to note that "where opium is smoked there is a marked deterioration physically, mentally, and morally."[13]

In time I will return to race-based accounts of the drug war and to theories that turn on health risks and other harms. Despite their intuitive appeal,

---

[12] Richard J. Bonnie & Charles H. Whitebread II, "The Forbidden Fruit and the Tree of Knowledge: An Inquiry into the Legal History of American Marijuana Prohibition," 56 *Virginia Law Review* 971 (1970), p. 984; David F. Musto, *The American Disease: Origins of Narcotic Control* (New York: Oxford University Press, 3d ed. 1999) (1973), pp. 294–95; Courtwright, *Forces of Habit*, p. 171 (One source of opposition to nonmedical drug use "is the association of a particular drug with deviant or disliked groups. . . . [O]pium smoking [was associated] with Chinese laborers; . . . and cocaine with out-of-control black men."); Steven B. Duke & Albert C. Gross, *America's Longest War: Rethinking Our Tragic Crusade Against Drugs* (New York: G.P. Putnam's Sons, 1993), p. 83 ("This early American [antidrug] legislation superficially appears to have been motivated by white communities' fears that use of specific drugs might inspire minority males to act violently or express sexual interest in white women."); Lisa McGirr, *The War on Alcohol: Prohibition and the Rise of the American State* (New York: W.W. Norton & Company, 2016), p. 253 ("Other narcotic drugs were . . . more closely associated [than was alcohol] with minority populations—Chinese in the west, African-Americans in the south, Mexicans in the southwest—making a broad consensus for their criminalization . . . easier to maintain."); Carl Erik Fisher, *The Urge: Our History of Addiction* (New York: Penguin Press, 2022), pp. 124–30, 141–42, 184; Michael M. Cohen, "Race, Coca Cola, and the Southern Origins of Drug Prohibition," *Southern Cultures*, vol. 12, no. 3 (2006), pp. 55, 56 ("At the root of the drug-prohibition movement in the United States is race, the driving force behind the first laws criminalizing drug use . . . .").

[13] Calkins, "Opium and Its Victims," pp. 29–30; Ahmad, "Caves of Oblivion," pp. 105–06 (citing *Chronicle* report of February 28, 1877); "Died in an Opium Den," *Virginia City Territorial Enterprise*, Mar. 28, 1879, p. 3; "Really Dead," *Virginia City Territorial Enterprise*, Mar. 29, 1879, p. 3; "Opium Smoking," *Virginia City Territorial Enterprise*, Mar. 29, 1879, p. 3 (all cited in Diana L. Ahmad, *The Opium Debate and Chinese Exclusion Laws in the Nineteenth-Century American West* (Reno: University of Nevada Press, 2007), p. 44); Masters, "The Opium Traffic in California," p. 56.

I believe all such theories crumble in the face of sustained scrutiny and empirical evidence. That analysis must wait till more of our story is told. For now I ask this: Subtract from Masters's image of the Jackson Street den any hint of the race of the occupants. Subtract as well any thought that opium could harm health or shorten life or spur even a small increase in crime. Subtract finally the risk of addiction—so that nothing remains but the den, the drug, the smokers, and the drug's present impact on them. Would San Francisco's supervisors have tolerated what remained—a place where citizens went to smoke themselves senseless? Would such a place be lawful today?

I believe not. For the fundamental evil of the den—the thing that distinguished it from the saloon—was not race or crime or health risks.

It was the silence.

What was the nature of that silence—that sepulchral hush so unlike "the prodigal gas of the barrooms," the "excited mirth," and "seductive air of social re-union"? At first one might understand the den's silence as a simple function of the task of smoking. The inebriate whose "swollen, nerveless lips were glued" to the pipe could not talk, at least in the moment. But the true source of the den's eerie quiet was not the act of smoking but the smoke—the narcotic vapors of the pipe. For the smoke, as we learn time and again from almost every scribe who stooped into a den, was "stupefying," its consumers "stupefied" or simply "stupid," and their sought-for state either "stupor" or "stupefaction."[14] As Dan De Quille wrote after visiting his "Cave of Oblivion" in 1874, "These fellows are silent as dead men and seem unconscious of our presence. . . . To a looker-on it is all vapid, vacuous stupefaction." Or as the *New York Times* reported in 1873, "scores of persons . . . spend hour after hour, never ceasing until they drop off into the death-like stupor which is the aim of all opium smoking."[15]

The death-like stupor that was the aim of all opium smoking. This was the business of intoxication. No one entered an opium den save to render himself "senseless." Once there, the visitor went about his business: "The opium smoker . . . gives all his attention to the process of inhaling the fumes . . . ." Then, "stretched out at full length . . . , gazing into vacancy with fixed, staring eyes, unconscious of

---

[14] "The Opium Habit," *San Francisco Chronicle*, Feb. 1, 1886, p. 2 ("stupefying"); Masters, "Opium and It's Votaries," pp. 633–34 ("stupefying" and "stupefaction"); "A Growing Evil," *San Francisco Chronicle*, July 25, 1881, p. 3 ("stupefied"); Lathrop, "Sorcery of Madjoon," p. 417 ("stupefied"); "Chinese in New-York," *New York Times*, Dec. 26, 1873, p. 3("stupid"); "Opium and the Lottery," *Sacramento Daily Record-Union*, Feb. 23, 1876, p. 1 ("stupid"); Willard B. Farwell et al., "The Report of the Special Committee of the Board of Supervisors of San Francisco, on the Condition of the Chinese Quarter of that City," *in The Chinese at Home and Abroad* (San Francisco: A.L. Bancroft & Co., 1885), p. 17 ("stupefaction"), p. 26 ("stupor"); [Dan De Quille,] "A Cave of Oblivion," *Daily Territorial Enterprise*, July 28, 1874, p. 3 ("stupor"); "The Opium Dens," *San Francisco Chronicle*, Nov. 16, 1875, p. 3.

[15] [De Quille,] "Cave of Oblivion," p. 3; "Chinese in New-York," p. 3.

AN UNDERGROUND OPIUM DEN BY FLASH-LIGHT.

Figure I.3: An Opium Smoker (c. 1896).

all that is passing around" him, he slips into the desired "dreamy oblivion."[16] The opium smoker pictured in Figure I.3, who appeared in a second article by Frederick Masters, wears the very image of stupefaction: he lies sprawled on his bunk, awake but unseeing, still clutching his pipe.

Stupor was not merely one of many opium-induced effects. It was instead the drug's defining feature, the root source of opium's classification as a "narcotic."

---

[16] "A Growing Evil," p. 3 ("senseless" and "dreamy oblivion"); "Chinese in New-York," p. 3 ("The opium smoker . . ."); Auerhahn, "The Split Labor Market," p. 421 (quoting Albert S. Evans, "A Cruise on the Barbary Coast," *in A la California: Sketch of Life in the Golden State* (San Francisco: A.L. Bancroft, 1873) ("stretched out at full length . . .")).

The 1895 edition of *Webster's Academic Dictionary* supplies "[s]tupefying" as the first definition of *narcotic*. The 1890 *Century Dictionary* renders *narcotic* as "[h]aving the power to produce stupor." Together, the two books' definitions of *narcotic* yield five uses of some form of the word "stupor." And the stupor of the opium, more than the race of the participants, seems to have prompted the San Francisco Board of Supervisors' 1875 ordinance. The dens that most aggrieved the board were not those in which Chinese smoked, or even those in which white smokers intermingled with Chinese, but rather those kept *"for the exclusive use of* WHITE MEN AND WOMEN." The supervisors fretted that such "young men and women of respectable parentage . . . inhale[d] the fumes from the opium pipes *until a state of stupefaction is produced.*"[17]

Given all this focus on opium's stupefying power, it seems likely that somewhere in the nature of stupor lies a clue to our worldwide ban on opium.

Stupefaction's Vice

The opium stupor is merely one variety of intoxication. *Webster's Academic Dictionary* defined "intoxicate" in 1895 as "[t]o make drunk; to excite *or stupefy* by strong drink or by a narcotic."[18] The perceived vice of intoxication supplies the driving force behind the evolutionary story that lies ahead. For in this retelling of the origin of our drug laws, the evil of drugs arose first and foremost from their use as intoxicants for intoxication's sake. The primary force behind our laws against recreational drugs was therefore neither racial nor utilitarian, but moral.

The nature of *stupor* helps explain the broader moral objection to intoxication. To be *stupefied* is to abandon one's faculties or—in older moral tones—to abdicate one's God-given reason. But one needn't be a theist to appreciate the moral objection to stupefaction for stupefaction's sake. Something about a lolling, vegetative escape from life's concerns and realities seems vaguely but powerfully awry.

The evil of the dens was that they served precisely to help patrons abandon all command of their faculties, all reason. Worse, patrons gave up their reason to *pleasure*—and in particular to that brand of mindless pleasure implied by the emphasis on stupor. That is, the dens served as houses of intoxication. And because visitors to the dens soon grew hopelessly dependent on their drug, hopelessly addicted, they became in the eyes of the community *slaves to pleasure.*

---

[17] *Webster's Academic Dictionary: A Dictionary of the English Language* (New York: American Book Company, 1895), p. 375; *The Century Dictionary of the English Language* (New York: The Century Co., 1890), Part 14, p. 3934; "The Opium Dens," *San Francisco Chronicle*, Nov. 16, 1875, at 3 (emphasis added).

[18] *Webster's Academic Dictionary*, p. 304 (emphasis added). This was the second definition given of the transitive form of the verb "intoxicate." The first definition was "[t]o poison; to drug."

For opium was notoriously pleasurable and notoriously addictive. Alonzo Calkins, the first prominent American expert on opium, wrote in 1867 of the mindless, senseless ecstasy of the opium high: "The reasoning faculty, that intellectual balance-wheel, reels out of equipoise, and the imagination, now swinging loose from its moorings, bounds away on buoyant wing to luxuriate upon the hallucinative raptures of a paradise." The smoker abandoned not merely his reason, but the concerns of life itself. Opium "puts out of sight the real and unpleasant crudities of daily life," wrote Dr. Harry Hubbell Kane in 1882, "and magnifies and elevates into view a pleasant bubble, whose play of colors and misty outlines are born of the pipe alone." In Frederick Masters's eyes, the opium smoker "float[ed] away into a state of revolting enjoyment."[19]

And what at first was pleasure soon became habit. George Parsons Lathrop, who introduced us to the den of his "cosmopolis," told of "the pleasure that allures to a continuance of [opium's] use, until the dependent upon it is morally manacled." The lesson was nearly as old as the Christian age. In the fourth century after Christ, Saint Augustine lamented his "lust [had] yielded to become habit, and habit not resisted became necessity. These were like links hanging one on another—which is why I have called it a chain—and their hard bondage held me bound hand and foot."[20]

Though the image is religious, the consequence was legal. Many state drug laws of the late nineteenth and early twentieth centuries supplied definitions of addiction, inebriation, and like terms that emphasized above all the narcotics user's *loss of self-control*—an expression that seems to capture both the abandoned reason and the manacled will of the addicted. Hence, in what appears to be the earliest law of this variety, Connecticut declared in 1874 that any person "so far addicted to the intemperate use of narcotics or stimulants as to have *lost the power of self-control*" was to be committed to an inebriate asylum for a minimum of four months. A Massachusetts law of 1909 tracked the quoted language almost exactly, as did a California law of 1911 and an Idaho law of 1913.[21]

Meanwhile a Colorado act of 1895 defined "drunkard" as a "person who has acquired the desire of using alcoholic or malt drinks, morphine, opium, cocaine or other narcotic substance used for the purpose of producing intoxication, to

[19] Calkins, "Opium and Its Victims," pp. 25, 26; Kane, *Opium-Smoking in America and China*, p. 61; Masters, "The Opium Traffic in California," p. 56.
[20] Lathrop, "Sorcery of Madjoon," p. 419; St. Augustine, *Confessions* (Books i–xiii) (F.J. Sheed trans., Indianapolis: Hackett Publishing Company, 1993), 8.5, p. 135.
[21] "An Act Concerning Inebriates, Dipsomaniacs, and Habitual Drunkards," 1874 *Connecticut Public Acts*, ch. 113 (Act of July 25, 1874), § 1, p. 256 (emphasis added); "An Act to Revise and Codify the Laws Relating to Insane Persons," 1909 *Massachusetts Acts*, ch. 504 (Act of June 16, 1909), §§ 50, 56, pp. 695, 697; "An Act . . . Relating to Arrest, Hearing and Commitment of Inebriates and Drug Habitués . . . ," 1911 *California Statutes*, ch. 214 (Act of Mar. 21, 1911), p. 396; "An Act . . . Providing for the Arrest, Examination and Commitment of Persons Addicted to the Intemperate Use of Narcotics or Stimulants . . . ," 1913 *Idaho General Laws*, ch. 56 (Act of Mar. 4, 1913), § 1, p. 166.

such a degree as to deprive him or her of *reasonable self-control.*" The previous year, Louisiana and Maryland had adopted similar language, as did Oklahoma and North Dakota in 1895 and Michigan in 1907. Colorado later added to its law the words "or stupor" after the word "intoxication." Even today the concept of intoxication embraces both stupor and loss of self-control. *Webster's Third New International Dictionary* defines "intoxicate" as "to excite *or stupefy* by alcohol or a drug *especially to the point where physical and mental control is markedly diminished.*"[22]

Surely it would make no sense to condemn opium dens as houses of intoxication, where young men and women went to abandon their self-control, while sparing saloons the same judgment. Yet both George Parsons Lathrop and Methodist minister Frederick Masters cast drinking establishments in a far more attractive light. For Masters, a visit to the den "was like being in a sepulcher with the dead," a world removed from the "glare and glitter" and "excited mirth" of the saloon. For Lathrop, the "ominous hush" of the den compared gloomily with the "prodigal gas" and "bewildering brilliance" of the barroom. The distinction, as both men saw, was that in the best of its forms, the saloon was a consummately social place, abuzz with the "seductive air of social re-union." And if the saloon was to take this social form, its patrons could not drink themselves stupid. The saloon, unlike the den, was not a house of stupefaction.

The Paradox of the Saloon

Why then was the saloon banished—if not from California and New York, where Masters and Lathrop wrote, then from the nation as a whole in 1920? And why was alcohol delivered from exile less than fourteen years later? The same nation that hailed the Eighteenth Amendment in 1920 and spread prohibition across the land gustily greeted its repeal by the Twenty-First Amendment in 1933. Why did the same forgiving nation that returned drinking holes to our social fold lock out opium dens for good? For even as barkeeps threw open the speakeasy's blackout blinds, the den remained shuttered forever.

---

[22] "An Act to Provide for the Treatment and Cure of Habitual Drunkards . . . ," 1895 *Colorado Laws*, ch. 74 (Act of Apr. 13, 1895), § 6, p. 174 (emphasis added); "An Act to Provide for the Treatment and Cure of Habitual Drunkards . . . ," 1894 *Louisiana Acts*, No. 157 (Act of July 12, 1894), § 4, p. 197; "An Act to Provide for the Treatment and Cure of Habitual Drunkards," 1894 *Maryland Laws*, ch. 247 (Act of Apr. 3, 1894), § 5, p. 326; "An Act to Provide for the Treatment and Cure of Habitual Drunkards . . . ," 1895 *Oklahoma Sessions Laws*, ch. 29 (Act of Mar. 8, 1895), § 4, p. 158; "An Act to Provide for the Treatment and Cure of Habitual Drunkards . . . ," 1895 *North Dakota Laws*, ch. 68 (Act of Mar. 6, 1895), § 3, p. 101; "An Act to Authorize . . . Contracts for the Cure of Drunkenness . . . ," 1907 *Michigan Acts*, No. 68 (Act of Apr. 30, 1907), § 3, p. 72; 1911 *Colorado Statutes Annotated*, vol. 2, § 2134, at 1312; "Intoxicate," *Merriam-Webster.com* (Sept. 24, 2016) (emphasis added).

I ask these questions in the historical sense: *How did these things come to pass?* Seeking answers, we must take a long step back in time and then trace forward the forces that made the drinking spot redeemable but the den a perpetual outcast. The calculus—the *moral* calculus—that distinguished the saloon from the den proves to have three variables. One we have seen already—the perceived immorality of reason-depriving, stupefying, self-abandoning pleasure. The second was the role of *necessity* and the moral excuse it could give for indulging in otherwise forbidden pleasures or for tempting the bounds of temptation. The third was the moral safe harbor of *moderation*.

In search of these moral forces—and of the moral roots of our monogamy with alcohol—we must step far back in time. Indeed, we must return to the very beginning.

And in the beginning there was sex.

PART I
MORAL ROOTS

1

Sex, Drunkenness, and the Euphoria Taboo

How is it we arrive at Eden? The path backward is neither straight nor moonlit. Whatever metaphors may lurk in that garden, its forbidden fruit means neither alcohol nor opium nor any other fiendish drug.

Instead the path backward stops first at a more natural destination—Boston, the seat of American Puritan thought, from which we later travel back to Paradise. We arrive at Boston about a half-century after the Puritan settlement of New England, during an age of strident rhetoric against the evils of drunkenness. Here we might hope to uncover clues to the nation's modern ambivalence toward alcohol and our insistent rejection of other drugs.

Having reached Boston, we naturally might seek out its Second Church—the North Church—and the pulpit of Increase Mather, the church's famed pastor and later president of Harvard College, who in 1673 delivered what appears to be at least his second sermon against drunkenness, ominously titled *Wo to Drunkards*.[1] "Who hath woe?" the Scripture asks. "[W]ho hath sorrow? . . . who hath redness of eyes? They that tarry long at the wine . . . ." (Prov. 23:29, 30.)

In this rambling, catchall condemnation of drunkenness, Mather fell insistently on two themes. The first was that drunkenness robbed the drinker of his God-given reason. "Drunkenness is injurious and *wofully* prejudicial as to the Soul . . . *In that it darkeneth the Light of Reason*. That noble Faculty of the Soul is as it were overwhelmed and drowned by this Vice . . . ." By drowning our reason, we forsake not only our souls, but our earthly liberty too: "Sometimes [drunkenness] is so gross and notorious, as that the wholesome Laws of men take hold of it and punish it; namely, when a man is so *overcome with wine*, as that he can neither speak nor act like a rational Creature, when reason is disturbed thereby . . . ."[2]

Mather's second theme joined with his first: by depriving the drinker of his noble faculty of reason, drunkenness reduced him to a beast. "Whilest a man is under the actual power of this Evil, he is like a Reasonless Creature, devoid of all judgement and understanding . . . . Reason is that whereby a man excels a Beast,

---

[1] Increase Mather, *Wo to Drunkards: Two Sermons Testifying Against the Sin of Drunkenness* (Cambridge: Marmaduke Johnson, 1673). Mather complained that nine years before, "I had occasion to Preach a whole Sermon, that I might testifie against the sin of Drunkenness," apparently to no effect. Ibid., p. 27.

[2] Mather, *Wo to Drunkards*, pp. 3, 10.

Beware Euphoria. George Fisher, Oxford University Press. © Oxford University Press 2024.
DOI: 10.1093/oso/9780197688489.003.0002

but this sin depriveth him of his excellency." Indeed the drinker's sin was yet greater: "Drunkenness is worse than a bruitish sin; for a Beast will drink no more th[a]n shall do him good, and therefore a Drunkard is worse than a Beast. . . . How woful is that Evil which shall deprive a man of the Image of God, and debase him below a Beast?"[3]

Each of Mather's themes echoed throughout the anti-drunkenness screeds of his day. A decade later and an ocean away, Matthew Scrivener, vicar of Haslingfield, sounded Mather's core charges of disabled reason and defaced godliness. In his 1685 *Treatise Against Drunkennesse*, Scrivener wrote that God "made Man after his own Image, and indued him with Understanding and Divine Reason, [yet] these are commonly wasted [by the drunkard, who] . . . defac[es] the Image of God himself, in himself." A year earlier, the anonymous author of *The Great Evil of Health-Drinking*—a work commonly credited to Charles Morton, who later served under Increase Mather as vice president of Harvard College—struck similar themes in similar terms: "I will still marvel, why Men, endued with so noble and divine a Faculty as Reason . . . deface [God's] Image in themselves and others by Intemperance[.]" Or as Shropshire minister Edward Bury wrote in 1676, drunkards "lose not only Gods Image, but the use of Reason also."[4] Tract after anti-drunkenness tract drummed these same themes.

Other authors also echoed Mather's refrain that those who paralyzed reason through drink reduced themselves to beasts. Scrivener defined a "Sot" as one who, "indulging to his senses, degenerates from that stately . . . Posture God hath to man given, boweth down his Reason to his Senses, and hangs down his Head to the Earth, after the manner of Beasts." Bury said drunkards "live the very lives of Swine, drinking in their swill, and wallowing in the mire." He asked what distinguishes "a Man from a Beast but the use of Reason, but if Reason be drowned, as it is in the *Drunkard* where lies the difference[?]" John Hart wrote in 1663 that "[d]runkards rather resemble bruit beasts th[a]n men." Rendering this theme in the language of stupefaction that later would become so common, Colchester preacher Owen Stockton said drunkenness "stupifies the Soul." Wine

---

[3] Mather, *Wo to Drunkards*, pp. 10–11.

[4] Matthew Scrivener, *A Treatise Against Drunkennesse* . . . (London: Charles Brown, 1685), p. 100; [Charles Morton?], *The Great Evil of Health-Drinking* . . . (London: Jonathan Robinson, 1684), p. 5; Edward Bury, *England's Bane, or the Deadly Danger of Drunkenness* (London: Thomas Parkhurst, 1677), p. 6. On Charles Morton, *see* William Prideaux Courtney, "Morton, Charles (1627–1698)," in *Dictionary of National Biography* (Sidney Lee ed., New York: Macmillan & Co., 1894), vol. 39, pp. 149–50; Sara Schechner Genuth, "From Heaven's Alarm to Public Appeal: Comets and the Rise of Astronomy at Harvard," in *Science at Harvard University: Historical Perspectives* (Clark A. Elliott & Margaret W. Rossiter eds., Cranbury, N.J.: Associated University Presses, 1992), pp. 28, 33 (noting that Morton was vice president of Harvard College from 1697 to 1698, the year of his death). Morton left England for Massachusetts in 1686, two years after publication of *The Great Evil of Health-Drinking*.

"stupifieth the mind, it blinds and darkens the understanding, and maketh men sottish . . . ."[5]

More surprisingly—because the image springs less naturally to mind—three of these authors mimicked Mather in arguing that animals, in drinking only what they need, prove wiser than drunkards, who drink themselves silly. In Hart's words, "the bruit creatures all, unless dogs or swine, will neither eat nor drink more th[a]n what serves to satisfie nature . . . ; But drunkards they drink not to satisfie, but to surfeit nature. . . . The Horse and the Ass may teach the drunkards wit . . . ." Or in Stockton's words: "[Y]ea this sin makes a man worse than a beast. The Ass is a silly beast, yet the Asses will not drink to excess, they drink no more than will quench their thirst." Or in Bury's: "[T]he *Drunkard* is fitly compared to a Swine for nastiness, for I know not any other Creature that will drink till he Burst . . . ."[6] This theme, too, found many imitators.

The Spurious Augustine

We first begin to see the link between these seventeenth-century teachings on drunkenness and the matter of sex in Eden when we go in hunt of the source of Mather's lesson that "a Beast will drink no more than shall do him good, and therefore a Drunkard is worse than a Beast." Mather supplied no citation for the passage. But elsewhere, when making a different point, he named two plausible but unexpected sources: "*August. Serm. de Temp.* 231, 232."[7]

That two Augustinian sermons on temperance might have supplied Mather's bestial imagery seems plausible enough. Saint Augustine's fourth- and fifth-century writings are teeming with animals in the posture of fallen humans. And Augustine was among those to whom Mather and other Puritan preachers most often appealed for moral authority. During the twelve centuries spanning the works of Saint Paul the Apostle and Saint Thomas Aquinas, Augustine stood far above other expositors of Church teachings and remains perhaps the most

---

[5] Scrivener, *Treatise Against Drunkennesse*, p. 66; Bury, *England's Bane*, pp. 4, 6; [John Hart,] *The Dreadfull Character of a Drunkard* (London: for Eliz. Andrews, 1663), p. 19 (my pagination); Owen Stockton, *A Warning to Drunkards . . .* (London: J.R. for Thomas Parkhurst, 1682), pp. 18, 20. In an unpaginated preface to Stockton's work, John Fairfax wrote that Stockton died before he had "put to it *ultimam manum*." It is unclear whether Fairfax merely published Stockton's manuscript or penned words he remembered hearing Stockton deliver (as Fairfax said) *viva voce*. Stockton died in 1680. "Stockton, Owen (1630–1680)," in *Dictionary of National Biography* (Sidney Lee ed., London: Smith, Elder, & Co., 1898), vol. 54, p. 393.

[6] [Hart,] *Dreadfull Character of a Drunkard*, p. 12 (my pagination); Stockton, *Warning to Drunkards*, p. 19; Bury, *England's Bane*, p. 5.

[7] Mather, *Wo to Drunkards*, p. 31 n.z. Mather also cited the first of these sermons elsewhere. *See* Increase Mather, *A Testimony Against Several Prophane and Superstitious Customs* (London: n.p., 1687, University of Virginia Press reprint, 1953), Text, p. 3.

influential of all. It's true that Mather and most Protestant prelates of his day were virulently anti-Catholic, but the ancient Church Fathers escaped this prejudice. Augustine commanded broad authority on a great variety of topics, and many in Mather's day displayed intimate knowledge of his works. Mather himself repeatedly drew on Augustine's writings, anglicizing his name and recalling his words in the offhandedly familiar way usually reserved for citations to Scripture: "*Austine* I remember confesseth, that . . . ."[8]

Still, Mather's reference to these sermons on temperance prompts surprise because no modern compilation of Augustine's works bears trace of them. Combing through dozens of volumes of Augustine's writings and hundreds of published sermons, a modern researcher finds only scattered references to drunkenness. Some few of these exceed a paragraph; many more are fleeting, merely listing drunkenness among other condemned pleasures.[9] Perhaps Augustine said little of drunkenness because he suffered from *other* weaknesses of the flesh: he obsessed about sex and the burden of celibacy, and sometimes he overate. "Drunkenness is far from me," he wrote in his *Confessions*, an open letter to God, "and Thou wilt have mercy that it may never come near me, but overeating has sometimes crept up on Thy servant . . . ."[10]

Frustrated by Mather's false lead to these purported Augustinian sermons, the modern researcher begins to smell a ruse. Yet if Mather fronted a faked Augustine in his crusade against drunkenness, he was not alone. Other tract writers before and after Mather cited Augustine's two supposed sermons on drunkenness to support indictments of that vice.[11] The last of these writers, Matthew Scrivener, proves our most valuable source. At the end of his 1685 *Treatise Against*

---

[8] Mather, *Wo to Drunkards*, p. 33. For other citations to Augustine (some spurious), *see* ibid., p. 25 n.q.; Mather, *Testimony Against Prophane Customs*, Preface, pp. 14, 15, 16; Text, pp. 3, 8, 14, 17.

[9] *See, e.g.*, Sermon 225, "On Easter Day; to the *Infantes*," in *The Works of Saint Augustine: A Translation for the 21st Century*, vol. III/6 (Edmund Hill trans., Hyde Park: New City Press, 1993), ¶ 4, p. 250 ("[T]he apostle says, *Do not get drunk on wine, which leads to all kinds of debauchery*."). Augustine's two most extensive discussions of drunkenness, in Letters 22 and 29, addressed parishioners' drunkenness in church and in the cemetery. *See* St. Augustine, Letter 29, "A Letter of a Priest of Hippo Regius to Alypius, Bishop of Thagaste . . . ," in *The Works of Saint Augustine: A Translation for the 21st Century*, vol. II/1 (Roland Teske trans., Hyde Park: New City Press, 2001), ¶ 2, p. 95 ("I commented, therefore, on dogs and pigs in such a way that those arguing against the commandments of God with an obstinate barking and devoted to the filth of carnal pleasure were forced to be ashamed. . . ."). Letter 22 is similar in substance and tone but less detailed. *See* St. Augustine, Letter 22, "Augustine, a Priest, Sends Greetings to Bishop Aurelius," in *The Works of Saint Augustine*, vol. II/1, p. 58. My thanks to research assistants Matt Buckley and Luke Weiger, who helped confirm Augustine never wrote more extensively about drunkenness.

[10] St. Augustine, *Confessions (Books i–xiii)* (F.J. Sheed trans., Indianapolis: Hackett Publishing Company, 1993), 10.31, p. 195.

[11] *See, e.g.*, [Morton], *Great Evil of Health-Drinking*, pp. 16–17, 89–90, 121–22; William Prynne, *Healthes: Sicknesse. Or a Compendious and Briefe Discourse; Proving, the Drinking and Pledging of Healthes, to Be Sinfull . . .* (London: n.p., 1628), pp. 17 n.b., 29–32 & n.n., 35 n.*, 65 n.a.; George Gascoyne, *A Delicate Diet, for Daintiemouthde Droonkardes* (London: Richard Jhones, 1576), pp. 5–6, 10–22 (my pagination). I thank Matt Buckley and Luke Weiger for their exhaustive searches for references to Sermons 231 and 232.

Drunkennesse, Scrivener appended both of the elusive Augustinian sermons, unabridged and "Faithfully Translated" into English by Scrivener himself.[12] Here indeed we find the likely source of the argument made by Mather and others that drunkards are more foolish than beasts. It appears in the first of the two sermons, numbered 231 and titled "*De Tempore*, of Shunning Drunkennesse":

> [W]hen Beasts are led to the watering, so soon as they have satisfied their
> Thirst, ... they neither will, nor can drink at all. Let Drunken men consider, whether
> they be not worse than Beasts: For seeing Beasts will not drink more than is requi-
> site, they take down twice, yea thrice as much Drink as is expedient for them.[13]

The wonder is not that this argument found imitators. With so noble a provenance, issued from the hand of the great saint himself, it bore the weight of his celebrity. The wonder is rather that these sermons almost melted into history—for Scrivener appears to be the last English writer to rely on their authority.

Tracking a Fraud

It turns out the sermons were not Augustine's at all. *Someone* had co-opted the saint's enormous prestige to condemn drunkenness, a vice that rarely engaged his attention. Yet Scrivener was not our forger. It's true he betrayed some doubt of authenticity: "[I]f any man shall endeavour to weaken, by calling in question the Genuinesse of those Sermons, I shall not here enter into dispute about them ...." And Scrivener's name screamed imposture—a pen name almost by definition. But "Scrivener" had been his family's title for generations and offers no cause for mistrust.[14] By tracing these sermons back in time, moreover, we can prove his innocence.

For the first of the two sermons had turned up at least a century earlier—in the 1576 tract, *A Delicate Diet, for Daintiemouthde Droonkardes*, by poet and satirist George Gascoyne (usually Gascoigne).[15] Like Increase Mather and others of the Puritan era, Gascoigne argued that a drunkard, by robbing himself of his godlike reason, "transform[ed] him self ... from a man to a Beast." Rather abruptly, he

---

[12] Scrivener, *Treatise Against Drunkennesse*, title page and pp. A5, 157–93. I thank Leslie Meltzer for her discovery of Scrivener's version of these sermons.

[13] *The Two Hundred and One and Thirtieth Sermon of St. Augustine: De Tempore, of Shunning Drunkennesse*, appended to Scrivener, *Treatise Against Drunkennesse*, pp. 159, 166–67.

[14] Scrivener, *Treatise Against Drunkennesse*, p. A5. According to the *Dictionary of National Biography* (Sidney Lee ed., London: Smith, Elder, & Co., 1897), vol. 51, pp. 126–27, Scrivener "was probably descended of the family of Scrivener of Sibtoft."

[15] Gascoyne, *Delicate Diet*, pp. A.ii; "George Gascoyne," *in The Cambridge History of English Literature* (Cambridge University Press, 1909), vol. 3, pp. 201–10.

linked this theme to Augustine: "And since God hath made none other so notable difference betweene Man and Beast, as that he hath endewed the one, and
deprived the other of reason and understanding: I thought meete . . . to translate
the foresayde . . . Epistle of S. Augustine . . . ." What follows is a slightly abridged
version of Scrivener's Sermon 231. Gascoigne's translation differs, but includes
the now-familiar lesson that drunkards may be "worse then brute Beastes: for
wheras brute Beastes wyll drinke no more then that which shall suffise them,
[drunkards] wyl yet drink fowre tymes more then behoveth . . . ."[16]

Yet Gascoigne was *not* our Augustinian forger, for the trail of these sermons
continues back another quarter-century, to what appears to be the first English
printing of either sermon—a 1553 collection by Thomas Paynel (usually Paynell)
titled *Twelve Sermons of Saynt Augustine*. A one-time chaplain to Henry VIII,
Paynell included in this collection yet another version of Scrivener's Sermon
231.[17] Having now seen three different translations of this sermon—Paynell's in
1553, Gascoigne's in 1576, and Scrivener's in 1685—even a cynic must conclude
that a Latin original exists *someplace* and that, even if not Augustine's work, it
seemed genuine enough to have fooled three accomplished men of letters.

Indeed there is a Latin text. The trail leads from Paynell to various Continental
compilers and from them to archives scattered across Europe. And then it leads a
millennium back in time to the apparent source of our two so-called Augustinian
sermons against drunkenness—the sixth-century Gallic bishop, Saint Caesarius
of Arles.[18]

Born just forty years after Augustine's death, Caesarius wrote in the master's
looming shadow and often in open imitation of him. Given the eagerness of later

[16] Gascoyne, *Delicate Diet*, pp. 9–10 (my pagination) ("And since God hath made . . ."), p. 16
("worse then brute Beastes . . ."), p. 31 ("transform[ed] him self . . . from a man to a Beast . . .").
Several passages in Scrivener's version of the first sermon have no counterpart in Gascoigne's. *See,
e.g.*, Scrivener, *Treatise Against Drunkennesse*, pp. 162, 163–64, 165–66, 167–69, 171, 171–73.
[17] "Of Eschuynge and Avoydyng of Ebrietie and Dronkennes," in *Twelve Sermons of Saynt
Augustine, Now Lately Translated into English by Thomas Paynel* (London: John Cawood, [1553])
(pages not numbered). For more on Paynell and his translation, *see* Mark Vessey, "English
Translations of the Latin Fathers, 1517–1611," in *The Reception of the Church Fathers in the West
from the Carolingians to the Maurists* (Irena Backus ed., 1997), vol. 2, pp. 775, 789, 799–801;
Geoffrey Eatough, "Paynell, Thomas (d. 1564?)," in *Oxford Dictionary of National Biography* (Oxford
University Press, 2004), vol. 43, pp. 225–26.
[18] The sermons appear as numbers 46 and 47 in Dom Germain Morin's collection of Caesarius's
works. *See Sancti Caesarii Arelatensis: Sermones*, vol. 1 (*vol. 103 of Corpus Christianorum: Series
Latina* (D. Germani Morin ed., 1953)), pp. 205–15. For English translations, *see Saint Caesarius of
Arles: Sermons*, vol. 1 (*vol. 31 of The Fathers of the Church: A New Translation* (Mary Magdeleine
Mueller trans., 1956)), pp. 231–43. By far the most complete
modern work on Caesarius's life and work is William E. Klingshirn's *Caesarius of Arles: The Making
of a Christian Community in Late Antique Gaul* (New York: Cambridge University Press, 1994).
Klingshirn discusses the two sermons against drunkenness in some detail at pages 196 to 199.
I am grateful to Mark Vessey of the University of British Columbia, Bill Klingshirn of the Catholic
University of America, and John Cavadini of the University of Notre Dame for their generous guidance in tracing these two sermons to their apparent source.

compilers to claim newfound works for Augustine, many of Caesarius's writings inevitably found their way onto Augustine's rolls. Of the twelve "Sermons of Saynt Augustine" in Paynell's 1553 edition, nine are now claimed for Caesarius and not one for Augustine.[19] Caesarius may have encouraged such misattribution. He "did not hesitate to place at the head of his sermons, even of those which were really his own, the name of some Doctor or Father of the Church by whom he had been more or less inspired."[20]

We likely never will know whether Caesarius issued the sermons against drunkenness in his own name or Augustine's, for no manuscript survives from his day. We do know Caesarius made a notable mistake, one Augustine did not make. Caesarius—but not Augustine—slyly misquoted Scripture to highlight the affinity between the sins of drunkenness and illicit sex.

Misquoting Paul

Caesarius's contrivance dealt with a familiar warning by the Apostle Paul in the first book of Corinthians. Augustine, in a letter touching on drunkenness, quoted Paul faithfully: "*Make no mistake. Neither fornicators, nor idolators, nor adulterers, nor the effeminate, nor sodomites, nor thieves, nor the greedy, nor the drunken, nor slanderers, nor robbers will possess the kingdom of God.*"[21] (1 Cor. 6:9–10.) Caesarius employed this same injunction in his second sermon against drunkenness, but dropped from Paul's list several sinners whose offenses touched neither sex nor drunkenness—the thieves, slanderers, and robbers. Matthew Scrivener's 1685 translation of Caesarius's words captured the elision: "*Neither Fornicators, nor Idolaters* (saieth [Paul]) *nor effeminate, nor abusers of themselves with mankinde, nor Covetous, nor Adulterers, nor Drunkards, shall inherit the Kingdom of God.*" Then, as though to emphasize Paul's magnified focus on sex, Caesarius added (in Scrivener's rendering): "*See, he joyneth here Drunkards with Fornicators and Idolaters, and Sodomists, and Adulterers.*"[22] Elsewhere Caesarius made his meaning even plainer by leaving out the idolaters and the covetous: "'Neither fornicators, nor the effeminate, nor sodomites will possess

---

[19] Vessey, "English Translations of the Latin Fathers," pp. 800–01 & n.49.

[20] Dom Germain Morin, "The Homilies," in *Orate Fratres* (1939–1940), vol. 14, pp. 485–86, *quoted in* Mueller, *Saint Caesarius of Arles, Sermons*, vol. 1, p. xxii.

[21] St. Augustine, Letter 29, ¶ 5, p. 96. But for a few grammatical adjustments, Augustine's Latin original of this passage is a word-for-word rendition of the corresponding passage in the *Vulgate*, Saint Jerome's Latin translation, which Augustine sometimes cited. *See, e.g., De Doctrina Christiana, in The Works of Saint Augustine: A Translation for the 21st Century*, vol. I/11 (Edmund Hill trans., Hyde Park: New City Press, 1996), § 4.7.15, p. 210 & n.22.

[22] "Scrivener, *Treatise Against Drunkennesse*, p. 184 (quoting "The Second Sermon of St. Augustine: *Of Avoiding Drunkennesse*"). For Caesarius's Latin originals of these passages, *see* Morin, *Sancti Caesarii Arelatensis: Sermones*, vol. 1, ¶ 4, p. 213.

the kingdom of God'; moreover: 'neither adulterers nor drunkards will possess the kingdom of God.'"[23]

By the time Scrivener translated Caesarius's sermons in 1685, it was faddish for anti-drunkenness tract writers to prune Paul's words as Caesarius had done. In his 1682 *Warning to Drunkards*, preacher Owen Stockton lopped off most of Paul's warning, baring the link between sex and drunkenness: "*Be not deceived, Neither Fornicators—nor Drunkards—shall inherit the Kingdom of God.*" Several years earlier, in a tract against the twin sins of drunkenness and whoremongering, preacher Richard Garbutt reduced the entire scriptural passage to a seven-word fragment: "Be not deceived, neither Fornicators nor Drunkards." But the masterwork of editing came from the hand of William Thompson and his coauthor, Richard Mather, father of Increase Mather, who cropped both Corinthians and Paul's similar exhortation in Galatians. (Gal. 5:19–21.) Thompson and Mather melted together a combined list of twenty-seven sins, ranging from envy to witchcraft to murder, and kept only those that truck in sex or drink: "neither whoremongers nor adulterers, nor drunkards, nor any that walk in such waies and works of the flesh, shall have any inheritance in the kingdome of God."[24]

If called to account for their selective quotation of Scripture, all these authors could have defended their course by reference to the great Saint Augustine himself, whose spurious sermons took similar liberty with the words of the Apostle. Perhaps that's why these sermons proved so popular among Puritans—they linked Augustine's famed reproofs of illicit sex with later injunctions against drunkenness. Perhaps that explains Matthew Scrivener's stubborn publication of the sermons under Augustine's name. For in 1683, two years *before* Scrivener published his *Treatise Against Drunkennesse* and the translated sermons, both sermons had been authoritatively exposed as the work of Caesarius.[25]

Maybe Scrivener had not heard this scholarly verdict. Or maybe his near confession of the sermons' inauthenticity shows he knew of the verdict but preferred

---

[23] Saint Caesarius of Arles, "A Reproof of Married Men Who Do Not Blush or Fear to Commit Adultery . . . ," in Mueller, *Saint Caesarius of Arles, Sermons*, vol. 1, Sermon 42, p. 208, ¶ 2, p. 209.

[24] Stockton, *Warning to Drunkards*, pp. 33, 174; Richard Garbut[t], *One Come from the Dead, to Awaken Drunkards and Whoremongers* (London: Francis Smith, [1675?]), p. 87; Richard Mather & William Thompson, *An Heart-Melting Exhortation . . .* (London: A.M., 1650), p. 27 (citing Gal. 5:20–21; 1 Cor. 6:9–10). The collection of Garbutt's sermons was published long after his death in 1630.

[25] In a massive reconstruction of Augustine's work, the Benedictines of Saint Maur credited Caesarius with more than a hundred sermons once claimed for Augustine. They relegated our two sermons, listed as numbers 231 and 232 in an earlier edition of Augustine's work, to an appendix and assigned them two new numbers, 294 and 295. See Mueller, *Saint Caesarius of Arles, Sermons*, vol. 1, pp. xxiii–xxiv; Morin, *Sancti Caesarii Arelatensis: Sermones*, vol. 1, pp. xiv, xviii, 205, 211. As early as 1669 Stephan (Etienne) Baluze had identified both sermons as the work of Caesarius and published them in a small collection of his sermons. Stephanus Baluzius, *Sancti Cæsarii Episcopi Arelatensis: Homiliæ xiv* (Paris: Franciscum Muguet, 1669), pp. 31–48 (Homiliæ v & vi); Morin, *Sancti Caesarii Arelatensis: Sermones*, vol. 1, pp. xiii, 205, 211. I thank John Cavadini and Mark Vessey for pointing me to the Maurists' work.

to ignore it. Either way, the lasting prominence of the spurious Augustinian sermons reflected an enduring bond between Augustine's views of illicit sex and the perceived immorality of drunkenness.

And so in a misquotation of Paul by a mimic of Augustine, we spy an essential link in the minds of seventeenth-century moralists between their own strident condemnations of drunkenness and Augustine's far more probing disquisitions on sex.

On to Eden

Augustine roamed his youth haunted by lust. In later life, long after he had followed God in celibacy, he called forth the fever that once plagued him—"the hot imagination of puberty mists [that] steamed up to becloud and darken my heart." Memories of youthful torments—or fond fantasies of a middle-aged moralist?—spill across the pages of his *Confessions*. His was the original confessional, startlingly modern in its frankness, jarring in its sexual imagery: "But when I rose against You in my pride . . . , those lower things became greater than I and . . . bore in upon me, massed thick . . . . [A]nd I was separated from You by my own swollenness . . . ." Only Joyce's *Portrait of the Artist as a Young Man*, written a millennium and a half later in the master's mold, presents so sulfurous an image of youthful guilt. For Augustine as for Joyce, the image was bestial and low. Now Augustine: "Arrived now at adolescence I burned for all the satisfactions of hell, and I sank to the animal in a succession of dark lusts . . . ." Now Joyce: "Like a beast in its lair his soul had lain down in its own filth . . . ."[26]

The sin of sex in Augustine's eyes was to part us from our reason, the faculty that casts us in God's image and sets us above beasts of the field. "Mating and begetting is something animals do too; reasoning and understanding are proper to human beings." In his world view, the upper realm always should rule over the lower—humans over animals, reason over appetite, the mind over the lower members: "[W]e see man, made to Your image and likeness, dominating all the irrational animals by reason of that same image and likeness, that is by the power of reason and understanding . . . ."[27]

Just as human reason should rule over beasts that crawl the earth, so it should master our most bestial parts: Man "subordinates to the peace of the rational

---

[26] St. Augustine, *Confessions*, 2.1–2.2, p. 23; 7.7, p. 115; James Joyce, *A Portrait of the Artist as a Young Man* (New York: Viking Press, 1964 (1916)), p. 115. Augustine's word for sinking to the animal is *silvescere*—literally to run to wood or to run wild.

[27] St. Augustine, Sermon 8, "On the Plagues of Egypt and the Ten Commandments of the Law," in *The Works of Saint Augustine: A Translation for the 21st Century*, vol. III/1 (Edmund Hill trans., Brooklyn: New City Press, 1990), ¶ 8, p. 245 ("Mating and begetting . . ."); St. Augustine, *Confessions*, 13.32, p. 283 ("we see man, made to Your image . . .").

soul all that part of his nature which he shares with the beasts, so that he may engage in deliberate thought and act in accordance with this thought . . . ." Hence our "reason, which presides in the mind, ought like a king in control to restrain the impulses of the lower flesh . . . ." Shakespeare's Iago, with a villain's unwonted wisdom, saw the point: "[W]e have reason to cool our raging motions, our carnal stings, our unbitted lusts . . . ." Or as Joyce's priest warned his young protagonist, "Sin . . . is a base consent to the promptings of our corrupt nature to the lower instincts, to that which is gross and beastlike; and it is also a turning away from the counsel of our higher nature . . . ."[28]

Borrowing from Saint Paul, Augustine alleged that sex upsets the hierarchy of the mind by setting "the law in the members . . . *at war with the law of the mind*." (Rom. 7:23.) "So intense is the pleasure that when it reaches its climax there is an almost total extinction of mental alertness; the intellectual sentries, as it were, are overwhelmed." A man's disabled reason unleashes his inner beast—he "refuses to tame in himself a certain appetite of the flesh which we have in common with animals."[29]

This liberation of the lower members and the impotence of reason are not mere figures of speech. During sex the genitals move quite literally at the volition of lust, not reason: they "become as it were the private property of lust, which has brought them so completely under its sway that they have no power of movement if this passion fails . . . ." Our failure of physical control punctuates our loss of moral self-control—when consumed by lust, we are masters of neither our passions nor our lower selves. The result, as David Richards reads Augustine, is "a degrading loss of self-control."[30]

It did not have to be this way. Before the Fall, Augustine said, human reproduction required no such abandoned reason. "[L]ust did not yet arouse those members independently of [Adam and Eve's] decision. The flesh did not yet, in a fashion, give proof of man's disobedience by a disobedience of its own." Had they not eaten of the fruit and passed from grace, Adam "would have sowed the seed and the woman would have conceived the child when their sexual organs had

---

[28] St. Augustine, *Concerning the City of God Against the Pagans* (Henry Bettenson trans., London: Penguin Books, 1984), 19.14, p. 873 ("subordinates to the peace . . ."); St. Augustine, "On the Plagues of Egypt," ¶ 8, p. 245 ("reason, which presides in the mind . . ."); *Othello*, I, iii., 329–31; Joyce, *Portrait of the Artist*, p. 127.

[29] St. Augustine, *The Literal Meaning of Genesis* (John Hammond Taylor trans., New York: Newman Press, 1982), vol. 2, 11.31.40, p. 163 ("the law in the members"); St. Augustine, *City of God*, 14.16, p. 577 ("So intense is the pleasure . . ."); St. Augustine, "Plagues of Egypt," ¶ 8, pp. 244–45 ("refuses to tame . . .").

[30] St. Augustine, *City of God*, 14.19, p. 581; David A. J. Richards, *Sex, Drugs, Death, and the Law: An Essay on Human Rights and Overcriminalization* (Totowa, N.J.: Rowman and Littlefield, 1982), p. 169.

been aroused by the will, at the appropriate time and in the necessary degree, and had not been excited by lust."[31]

The point is not that Augustine thought pleasure bad or asceticism a virtue. Rather he aimed to show that *reason*—and its mastery over flesh—is what casts humans in God's image and sets us apart from beasts. So the sin of sex was not its "natural delight," but its giving rein to that delight "up to the point of unreasoning and wicked lust." Reason's abandonment during sex and lust's triumph over our lower parts render us ungodly, inhuman, bestial, low. We feel shame at our nakedness and hide during sex because our nakedness and lust expose us as beasts. "The sexual act . . . shuns the public gaze. A natural sense of shame ensures that even brothels make provision for secrecy . . . ." Even procreative marital sex seeks privacy: "It is lawful and respectable certainly; but does it not require a private room and the absence of witnesses?"[32]

On this foundation Augustine sought to explain one of the mysteries of Eden—why Adam and Eve were shamelessly naked before the Fall, but covered themselves afterward. Scripture says before they sinned, "they were both naked," yet they "were not ashamed." (Gen. 2:25.) Augustine asked, "Why would they be ashamed"? They had as yet "experienced no motion of the flesh of which they would be ashamed. They did not think that anything had to be covered, because they did not feel that anything had to be restrained." The couple then ate from the tree—the tree of knowledge of good and evil—and "the eyes of them both were opened, and they knew that they were naked . . . ." (Gen. 2:17, 3:7.) They cast "their eyes on their bodies, [and] felt a movement of concupiscence which they had not known." They discovered "the law in the members *was at war with the law of the mind*," and their bodies became "subject to the same drive by which there is in animals a desire to copulate . . . ."[33]

---

[31] St. Augustine, *City of God*, 14.17, p. 578 ("lust did not yet arouse . . ."); 14.24, pp. 587–88 ("would have sowed the seed . . ."); *accord* St. Augustine, *Literal Meaning of Genesis*, vol. 2, 9.10.18, pp. 81–82 (suggesting that Adam and Eve moved their reproductive organs "in the same way that one commands his feet when he walks").

[32] John J. Hugo, *St. Augustine on Nature, Sex and Marriage* (Chicago: Scepter, 1969), pp. 75–76, 84–87, 114–15 (rejecting the suggestion that Augustine condemned all bodily pleasures); St. Augustine, "The Good of Marriage," in *Treatises on Marriage and Other Subjects (vol. 27 of The Fathers of the Church: A New Translation)* (Charles T. Wilcox et al., trans., New York: Fathers of the Church, Inc., 1955), § 16.18, pp. 9, 33 ("natural delight" and "up to the point . . ."); St. Augustine, *City of God*, 14.18, p. 579 ("The sexual act . . ." and "It is lawful . . ."). In arguing that Augustine condemned the reasonless pleasure of lust but not the "natural delight" inhering in procreative sex, I follow Saint Thomas Aquinas's interpretation of Augustine. *See* St. Thomas Aquinas, *Summa Theologica* (Fathers of the English Dominican Province trans., San Francisco: Benziger Brothers, Inc., 1947), vol. 1, 1.98.2, p. 494.

[33] St. Augustine, *Literal Meaning of Genesis*, vol. 2, 11.1.3, p. 135 ("Why would they be ashamed . . . ?"), 11.31.40, p. 163 ("the law in the members . . ."), 11.31.41, p. 164 ("Casting their eyes on their bodies . . ."), 11.32.42, p. 165 ("subject to the same drive . . .").

Figure 1.1: *Adam and Eve* (late third century).

Adam and Eve felt shame at the animality of their parts—and "in this troubled state they hastened to get fig leaves, they sewed aprons together, and . . . they hid what was to their shame." Less than a century before Augustine's time, a tomb artist captured on a Roman catacomb wall the primal couple's shock at their nakedness. Shown in Figure 1.1, the pair reflexively cover themselves, heads bowed.[34]

---

[34] St. Augustine, *Literal Meaning of Genesis*, vol. 2, 11.32.42, p. 165. I draw the date and site of the painting in Figure 1.1 from Margaret R. Miles, *Carnal Knowing: Female Nakedness and Religious Meaning in the Christian West* (Boston: Beacon Press, 1989), p. 27.

Necessity's Excuse—And Necessity's Elasticity

Augustine acknowledged, as he had to, the necessity of sex. We must multiply. And humans—men at least—cannot multiply without the mindless loss of control of the climax. "[S]uch pleasure is a necessary accompaniment of . . . sexual intercourse with a view to procreation." It may be that the holy among us "would prefer, if possible, to beget children without lust of this kind" and to move our parts "at the bidding of the will."[35] But we can't—and our need to multiply justifies our indulgence in animal lust.

Hence the imperative of *need* excuses otherwise forbidden conduct. Even incest in Eden was "a completely decent procedure," Augustine allowed, "under the pressure of necessity." Later this stopgap became "completely reprehensible"—but that "change had to be made when it became possible . . . as there came to be a supply of possible wives . . . ." From then on, "[n]ot only was there no necessity for unions between brother and sister; such unions henceforth were banned."[36]

The lesson of incest in Eden is that the morality of bestial pleasures depends on the *needs* those pleasures serve. Procreation is a human need, so "[t]he intercourse necessary for generation is without fault" if in marriage. Food and drink are human needs, and because "pleasure is a necessary accompaniment of eating and drinking in order to live," this "carnal pleasure" likewise is faultless. Happily Augustine did not confine human needs to the obvious (and narrow) necessities of life. Beyond *life* were other desirable ends—"wisdom, health, friendship." He excused the pleasures needed to secure these ends:

> God gives us some goods which are . . . necessary for something else, such as learning, food, drink, sleep, marriage, sexual intercourse. Certain of these are necessary for the sake of wisdom, such as learning; others for the sake of health, such as food and drink and sleep; others for the sake of friendship, such as marriage or intercourse, for from this comes the propagation of the human race in which friendly association is a great good.

By stretching the proper ends of carnal pleasure beyond the strict necessities of life, Augustine vastly widened the realm of permitted or at least pardoned pleasures. Hence he justified marriage among those too old to bear children by valuing "the natural companionship between the two sexes." The "pardonable intercourse in spouses," young or old, even when children are not in view,

---

[35] St. Augustine, *City of God*, 14.16, p. 577 ("would prefer, if possible . . ." and "at the bidding of the will"), 19.1, p. 844 ("such pleasure is . . .").

[36] St. Augustine, *City of God*, 15.16, p. 623–24.

is therefore no greater an offense than the "immoderate appetite for . . . lawful food."[37]

Augustine expanded the bounds of excusable pleasures in yet another way. Here his reasoning was admittedly sloppy and self-serving. He confessed that when the border between necessity and self-indulgence is fuzzy, a little rationalization can excuse a lot of pleasure. Augustine never needed this expedient for sex, as he had sworn a bright-line vow of celibacy. But eating and drinking were "not the kind of thing[s] I can resolve once and for all to cut off and touch no more, as I could with fornication." We all have to eat, and "the necessity is sweet to me"—and ill defined. "For the reins of the throat are to be held somewhere between too lightly and too tightly":

> [O]ften it is not at all clear whether it is the necessary care of my body calling for more nourishment, or the deceiving indulgence of greed wanting to be served. Because of this uncertainty my wretched soul is glad, and uses it as a cover and an excuse, rejoicing that it does not clearly appear what is sufficient for the needs of health, so that under the cloak of health it may shelter the business of pleasure.

"Who is he, Lord," Augustine pled, "that is not carried somewhat beyond the limits of the necessary?"[38]

Augustine's Platonic Roots

Just as Matthew Scrivener and his contemporaries fortified their moral aversion to drunkenness with appeals to Augustine's authority, Augustine grounded much of his moral analysis of sex in Plato's teachings. Pagan though Plato may have been, he deployed against mindless pleasures many of the same arguments and images Augustine embraced over seven centuries later. Their intellectual kinship suggests that while Augustine's words bore the Church's seal, there was nothing peculiarly Christian about his censure of unreasoning pleasure for pleasure's sake.

Confined by his poor Greek to Latin translations, Augustine may have read only a single Platonic text—Cicero's incomplete translation of Plato's later-life dialogue, the *Timaeus*. Augustine made the most of the *Timaeus*. In a single work, *City of God*, he credited or openly borrowed from Cicero's translation over

---

[37] St. Augustine, "The Good of Marriage," 3.3, p. 12 ("the natural companionship between the two sexes"), 9.9, pp. 21–22 ("wisdom, health, friendship" and "God gives us some goods . . ."), 10.11, p. 24 ("[t]he intercourse necessary for generation . . ."), 16.18, p. 32 ("carnal pleasure"; "pardonable intercourse in spouses"; "immoderate appetite for . . . lawful food"); St. Augustine, *City of God*, 19.1, p. 844 ("pleasure is a necessary accompaniment . . .").

[38] St. Augustine, *Confessions*, 10.31, pp. 195–97.

a dozen times. And though he likely never read the *Republic* or other Platonic texts, Augustine surely had heard of them and often invoked them in his own vast writings.[39]

Augustine allowed that Plato had erred in worshiping "a plurality of Gods."[40] But when Plato wrote of human morals, the primacy of reason over appetite, and the mediating role of necessity, he offered a moral template Augustine could adopt. Hence we find in Cicero's translated fragment of the *Timaeus*, which presented a comprehensive theory of human morality, the same high-low hierarchy that framed Augustine's writings: humans over animals, reason over appetite, the mind over the lower members.

When Plato's Creator brought forth humans, he built first their souls, housed in their heads, fitted with eyes to give light. Humans "carry[] on high the dwelling-place of the most sacred and divine part of us," the "lord of all that is in us." Beasts by contrast never ponder "the nature of the heavens" and so have "their front legs and their heads resting upon the earth." And serpents, "the most foolish" beasts of all, "trail their bodies entirely upon the ground."[41]

Guiding readers on a tour of the human body downward from the head, Plato stopped to note those "things which come into being through necessity." Crouching near the belly lies our inner beast, "which desires meats and drinks and the other things of which it has need by reason of the bodily nature." Tied down "like a wild animal which was chained up with man, [he] must be nourished if man was to exist." He had "no part in opinion or reason or mind, but only in feelings of pleasure and pain and the desires which accompany them." Lower still stirred "the organ of generation." To prod us to "the love of procreation," it

---

[39] *See, e.g.*, St. Augustine, *City of God*, 13.16, p. 525 (openly quoting Cicero's translation of the *Timaeus*). After extensive analysis Gerard O'Daly concluded, "The one extended portion of Plato's writings that Augustine read is the section of the *Timaeus* (27d–47b) translated by Cicero." James O'Donnell added that it appears Augustine restudied the *Timaeus* shortly before writing *City of God*. Gerard J.P. O'Daly, *Augustine's City of God: A Reader's Guide* (New York: Oxford University Press, 1999), pp. 255–56; James J. O'Donnell, "Augustine's Classical Readings," in *Recherches Augustiniennes*, vol. 15, pp. 144, 156–57 (Paris: Étude Augustiniennes, 1980). Frederick Van Fleteren concluded that Augustine knew the *Republic* "though encyclopedias, doxographies, or other authors." Despite his limited reading of Plato, Augustine managed to refer to him a lot. Van Fleteren reported that " 'Plato' and its cognates occur 252 times in Augustine's works." Frederick Van Fleteren, "Plato, Platonism," in *Augustine Through the Ages: An Encyclopedia* (Allan D. Fitzgerald ed., Grand Rapids: William B. Eerdmans Pub., 1999), p. 651. I thank Luke Weiger for his adroit guidance in tracking Augustinian themes to Plato, Plato's followers, and other classical authors.

[40] St. Augustine, *City of God*, 8.12, p. 316.

[41] Plato, *Timaeus* (Benjamin Jowett trans., New York: Macmillan Publishing Company, 1985), 41–45, pp. 24–27 ("carrying on high" and "the lord of all . . ."), 90, p. 73 (God's creation of the soul and why humans stand upright), 91–92, p. 75 (concerning wild beasts and serpents). Introducing this volume, Glenn Morrow explained that the concept of a "cosmic craftsman," rendered "God" in this translation, is "no doubt a metaphor and should not be pressed too closely." Glenn R. Morrow, *Introduction*, in ibid., pp. vii, xi, xiv–xv. I've drawn all quotes of the *Timaeus* from Benjamin Jowett's translation from the Greek text.

"becom[es] rebellious and masterful, like an animal disobedient to reason, and maddened with the sting of lust, seeks to gain absolute sway."[42]

So our physical beings sack us with a struggle for dominion of reason over appetite. Plato wrote in the *Republic* that "the soul is composed of at least two distinct parts. One is the reasoning part. The other is appetite or desire, where hunger, thirst, and sexual passion have their abode along with other irrational drives." The "temperate man" is one in whom "[t]here are no quarrels among the parts because there is agreement among them that the rational element should govern the whole" and reason should dominate base appetite. Such a man "is praised for being master of himself."[43]

This struggle for self-mastery totters always on defeat. "After all, we know that extreme pleasure drives a man out of his mind no less than extreme pain." Even if by day our reason dominates our appetites, by night "rationality slumber[s]," and our "wild and brutish part, sated with food and drink, becomes restless and goes on the prowl in search of anything that will satisfy its instincts." As Kleinias said in Plato's *Laws*, in words both Scripture and Augustine later echoed, "there is a war going on in us, ourselves against ourselves"—and the "first and best of all victories [is] the victory of oneself over oneself."[44]

Plato's scheme of "*necessary* and *unnecessary* pleasures," laid out in his *Republic*, likewise anticipated Augustine. Both the philosopher and the saint judged necessary not only what sustains life—food, shelter, a little sex—but also those pleasures that enable a *good* life. "Necessary," Plato wrote, "are those pleasures which by our natures we cannot do without, *as well as those pleasures from which we benefit*. Nature, in effect, *compels us* to desire both kinds." We have appetite not only for bread, without which we die, but also "the appetite for meat if it could be shown to sustain good health." Unnecessary pleasures are those "desires that do the soul no good and might in fact be harmful. . . . These are the

---

[42] Plato, *Timaeus*, 47–48, p. 30 ("things which come . . ."); 70, p. 54 ("which desires meats and drinks . . ."; "like a wild animal . . ."), 77, p. 60 ("no part in opinion or reason or mind . . ."), 91, p. 74 ("the organ of generation," and "the love of procreation," and "becom[es] rebellious and masterful . . .").

[43] Plato, *The Republic* (Richard W. Sterling & William C. Scott trans., New York: W.W. Norton & Company, 1985), 4.430e–4.431a, p. 126 ("is praised for being . . ."), 4.439d, p. 134 ("the soul is composed . . ."), 4.442c–d, p. 136 ("temperate man" and "There are no quarrels . . ."). There is also a third part to the soul, Plato wrote—"the spirited part," which generates anger and indignation. Ibid., 4.439e–4.441a, pp. 134–35. When discussing the *Republic*, unless otherwise noted, I attribute to Plato himself words he assigned to Socrates, his chief expositor in that work.

[44] Plato, *Republic*, 3.402e, p. 100 ("After all, we know . . ."), 9.571b–9.572b, pp. 262–63 ("rationality slumber[s]" and "wild and brutish part . . ."); *The Laws of Plato* (Thomas L. Pangle trans., New York: Basic Books, Inc., 1980), 626e, p. 5. As noted earlier, Augustine wrote of Adam and Eve that "the law in the members *was at war with the law of the mind." Literal Meaning of Genesis*, vol. 2, 11.31.40, p. 163 (quoting Rom. 7:23). Similar phrases appear elsewhere in the New Testament. Jas. 4:1 ("From whence come wars and fightings among you? come they not hence, even of your lusts that war in your members?"); 1 Pet. 2:11 ("[A]bstain from fleshly lusts, which war against the soul . . . .").

ones that undermine moderation in the soul and bodily good health . . . ." A man governed by unnecessary pleasures is simply "a drone, buzzing with appetites and desires."[45]

Whether Augustine knowingly co-opted Plato's moral scheme or merely reasoned his way to the same end seems past our power to know. Either way the lesson holds: the moral superiority of reason over appetite and the moral excuse of need were fixtures of Western thought long before Augustine gave them a peculiarly Christian cast. We should not expect their influence to have spread only within the Church's domain. Though Augustine lent them his pedigree, these concepts remained for centuries—and remain today—far more prominent than Augustine's dimming shadow.

Sex and Drunkenness as Moral Siblings

Plato fills another gap in this moral history. Because Augustine wrote little of drunkenness, we must cobble his views on drink from what he said about sex. Here Plato proves a useful guide, for he decried drunkenness and appetitive sex in the same moralized strains.

Like Caesarius and later Puritans, Plato found rhetorical force in human and animal drinking habits. He stressed the supremacy of human sobriety, declaring in the *Republic* that human reason should regulate the desire to drink. "[I]f a thirsty man refrains from drinking, it must be due to a part of him different from the thirsty part that pulls every animal to water." There must be something in temperate persons "that bids them abstain, something that overpowers and inhibits the initial urge. . . . And what is the inhibiting agent? Is it not reason and reflection?"[46]

These themes and images are so purely Augustine's—which is to say Augustine's are so purely Plato's—that we may take Plato's drinking norms as a rough guide to what Augustine's might have been. Plato set out his views in surprisingly prudish detail in the *Laws*. His concern was not "the drinking or non-drinking of wine in general, but . . . getting drunk." He allowed that those who shared wine together, if properly governed and "communing with friends in peace and with goodwill," would "part from one another closer friends than they had been before." But a drunken man was "least the master of himself"

---

[45] Plato, *Republic*, 8:558d–8.559d, pp. 250–51 (emphasis added). Elizabeth Belfiore adds useful insights to Plato's discussion of necessary and unnecessary pleasures. Elizabeth Belfiore, "Wine and *Catharsis* of the Emotions in Plato's *Laws*," *Classical Quarterly*, vol. 36 (1986), pp. 421–23.

[46] Plato, *Republic*, 4.439b–4.440b, 4.442c–d, pp. 133–34, 136.

and therefore "most wicked," for "prudent thoughts . . . abandon anyone who becomes thoroughly soused."[47]

Hence children under age eighteen should have no wine, for their bodies are already afire and want no more fuel. Young men aged eighteen to thirty may "taste wine with due measure," but for them "drunkenness and copious wine drinking will be totally forbidden." Only men nearing forty may indulge in Dionysian tributes. For them wine is "a drug that heals the austerity of old age"—"a medicine given . . . to put awe in the soul and health as well as strength in the body."[48]

Plato's moralized wine-drinking regime—holding that drink in moderation smooths conversation and social exchange, while drunkenness suspends reason and unleashes base appetites—grew cliché, rehearsed in religious and secular tomes till the dawn of the twentieth century. True, Plato differed from later Puritans in some particulars. Puritan moralists spurned his view that drunkenness might salve bodily ills and even character deficiencies. Though Puritans agreed medical need justified some alcohol use, they thought it never absolved *drunkenness*, for medical authorities of the day saw no need to get drunk to gain alcohol's healing powers. On most other fronts, however, Plato's drinking laws survived in mainstream moral discourse two millennia later.

Yet the reception of Plato's views on both sides of the Atlantic typically came stripped of attribution. As we follow through time his preference for temperate wine drinking, Plato's name surfaces only rarely. Instead it was Augustine and other Church Fathers who prominently sponsored such views in the West and ushered them through history. In Augustine's rendering all these themes—the beastliness of base appetite, the exaltation of godly reason, the virtues of temperance, in which our lower members submit to reason's command, and the excuse of necessity—compose a code of *sexual* morality. Their application in Puritan England and America to drink required an act of reverse translation. Matthew Scrivener's and Increase Mather's embrace of Caesarius's sermons against drunkenness, wrongly thought Augustine's, composed part of that translation process.

Aquinas and Moderation

Behind the similarities between the moral regimes governing sex and alcohol lies a major difference. In the case of sex, sin begins almost exactly where need leaves off. That's because the pleasure of sex commonly renders us reasonless: "So

[47] Plato, *Laws*, 637d, p. 17 ("the drinking or non-drinking . . ."), 640b, p. 20 ("communing with friends in peace . . ."), 645e–646a, p. 26 ("least the master of himself"; "most wicked"; "prudent thoughts . . ."), 671e–672a, p. 54 ("part from one another closer friends . . .").

[48] Plato, *Laws*, 666a–b, p. 47 ("taste wine with due measure"; "drunkenness and copious wine drinking . . ."; "a drug that heals . . ."), 672d, p. 55 ("a medicine given . . .").

intense is the pleasure," Augustine said, "that when it reaches its climax, there is an almost total extinction of mental alertness . . . ." Or in Aristotle's words, "no one could have any thoughts when enjoying *that* . . . ."[49] Sex therefore avoids sin only when justified by necessity, however broadly defined. Drinking is different. The alcoholic sin lies principally in *drunkenness* and drowning one's reason. Drinking short of this mark avoids the principal evil—and while the strictest Puritan moralists might have faulted all drinking for tempting the boundaries of true sin, none deemed the temptation as bad as the sin.

Hence we encounter a question Augustine never faced in the context of sex: What is the moral status of drinking that ventures past the limit of need but falls well short of drunkenness? In this twilight zone between sin and safety lies the realm of *moderation*. Augustine rarely examined this zone, perhaps because he perceived no such realm in the context of sex.[50] The task of exploring moderation fell instead to another great expositor of Church doctrine, Saint Thomas Aquinas. In his monumental *Summa Theologica*, Aquinas undertook in the thirteenth century to apply Augustine's moral analysis of sex to the sins of drink.

Readily observing that Augustine's teachings on sex applied outside that realm, Aquinas identified in drunkenness the same evils Augustine saw in sex. He wrote generally of *intemperance*, which embraced the various "*sins of the flesh*":

[I]ntemperance is most disgraceful for two reasons. First, because it is most repugnant to human excellence, since it is about pleasures common to us and the lower animals . . . . Secondly, because it is most repugnant to man's clarity or beauty; inasmuch as the pleasures which are the matter of intemperance dim the light of reason from which all the clarity and beauty of virtue arises . . . .

Temperance, in contrast, "repels that which is most disgraceful and unbecoming to man, namely animal lusts." And drunkenness begets lust—for "the use of too much wine affords an incentive to venereal pleasure." On this score Aquinas found ample authority in Scripture, including the admonition in Ephesians 5:18, "Be not drunk with wine wherein is lust."[51]

---

[49] Augustine, *City of God*, 14.16, p. 577; Aristotle, *Nicomachean Ethics* (Christopher Rowe trans., New York: Oxford University Press, 2002), 7.11.1152b17–1152b18, p. 204.

[50] Kissing "was seldom mentioned by Augustine." Peter Brown, *Augustine of Hippo: A Biography* (Berkeley: University of California Press, 1967), p. 73. In an online search of Saint Augustine's writings my research assistant Jason Despain confirmed Brown's observation, finding only passing mention of kissing, almost never of romantic kissing.

[51] St. Thomas, *Summa Theologica* (Fathers of the English Dominican Province trans., San Francisco: Benziger Brothers, Inc., 1947), vol. 2, II.II.142.4, p. 1775 ("intemperance is most disgraceful . . ."); II.II.145.4, p. 1783 ("repels that which . . ."); II.II.153.1, p. 1811 ("the use of too much . . ."); II.II.153.3, p. 1812 ("Be not drunk . . .").

Though intentional drunkenness is among the gravest of sins—indeed a mortal sin because the drunkard "willingly and knowingly deprives himself of the use of reason, whereby he performs virtuous deeds and avoids sin"—not all drink is sinful. Like other pleasurable vices, drink sometimes can claim the justification of need: "Now nature has introduced pleasure into the operations that are necessary for man's life. Wherefore the natural order requires that man should make use of these pleasures, in so far as they are necessary for man's well-being, as regards the preservation either of the individual or of the species." In particular, wine could claim necessity as medicine. Here Aquinas quoted the advice of Paul the Apostle: "Do not still drink water, but use a little wine for thy stomach's sake, and thy frequent infirmities . . . ." (1 Tim. 5:23.)[52]

Yet permission to indulge in wine and other pleasures extended *only so far as* their necessary use: "In order to avoid sin, pleasure must be shunned, not altogether, but so that it is not sought more than necessity requires." Necessity therefore defined the bounds of temperance, which "takes the need of this life, as the rule of the pleasurable objects of which it makes use, and uses them only for as much as the need of this life requires." So Aquinas rejected the medicinal use of wine to induce vomiting: he reasoned that as "drinking lukewarm water" also makes one vomit, there was "no need for intoxicating drink."[53]

At this point Aquinas's only-as-necessary moral regime governing drinking looks even more rigid than Augustine's regime governing sex. But just as Augustine moderated his regime by recognizing as necessary certain goods— "wisdom, health, friendship"—that aren't strict necessities of life, Aquinas defined the bounds of need generously:

> The need of human life may be taken in two ways. First, it may be taken in the sense in which we apply the term *necessary* to that without which a thing cannot be at all; thus food is necessary to an animal. Secondly, it may be taken for something without which a thing cannot be becomingly. Now temperance regards not only the former of these needs, but also the latter.

Having broadened the class of "necessary" goals to include one's "becoming" existence, Aquinas expanded on the content of this concession: "[T]emperance regards need according to the requirements of life, and this depends not only on the requirements of the body, but also on the requirements of external things, such as riches and station, and more still on the requirements of good conduct."[54]

---

[52] St. Thomas, *Summa Theologica*, vol. 2, II.II.150.2, p. 1800 ("willingly and knowingly . . ."), II.II.142.1, p. 1772 ("Now nature has introduced . . ."), II.II.149.3, p. 1798 ("Do not still drink water . . .").

[53] St. Thomas, *Summa Theologica*, vol. 2, II.II.142.1, p. 1772 ("In order to avoid sin . . ."), II.II.141.6, p. 1769 ("takes the need of this life . . ."), II.II.150.2, p. 1801 ("drinking lukewarm water" and "no need for intoxicating drink").

[54] St. Thomas, *Summa Theologica*, vol. 2, II.II.141.6, p. 1770.

The upshot of this very broad definition of "necessary" goods is that a person may use a broad range of pleasant things "*moderately, according to the demands of place and time, and in keeping with those among whom one dwells*"—where using something "*immoderately . . . mean*[s] going beyond the bounds of reason." Later Aquinas referred to "moderation" again, this time in response to an argument that "wine is altogether unlawful." After rebutting this claim with Paul's permission to use wine "for thy stomach's sake," he added a second scriptural quote: "*Wine drunken with moderation is the joy of the soul and the heart.*"[55]

This latter dictum grants generous license for wine drinking. The notion that one may drink moderately with no better excuse than "the joy of the soul and the heart" comes close to saying we may drink without sin *and without need* if we do so moderately, keeping a wide berth from the mortal sin of drunkenness. Nor was this the only time Aquinas endorsed so liberal a standard of permissible pleasures. Elsewhere he quoted Aristotle (who invoked Plato) to similar effect: "Hence the Philosopher says that the *temperate man also desires other pleasant things*, those namely that are not necessary for health or a sound condition of the body, *so long as they are not prejudicial to these things.*" In yet a third place, Aquinas wrote that to be "sufficient for salvation . . . it is required . . . not that a man abstain altogether from wine, but that he abstain from its immoderate use."[56]

Aquinas relied as well on Augustine's words. He quoted Augustine's injunction that "[i]n both Testaments the temperate man finds confirmation of the rule . . . commanding him to avail himself of [the things of this life] with the moderation of a user, not the attachment of a lover, in so far as they are requisite for the needs of this life and of his station."[57] Here we see in Augustine some of the same ambivalence Aquinas later expressed concerning the scope of "moderate" use. On the one hand, Augustine defined the concept narrowly to comprehend only *necessary* pleasures: one may use the things of this life moderately, "in so far as they are *requisite* for the *needs* of this life . . . ." On the other hand, one's needs encompass "the needs of . . . his *station*," affording a potential sinner a broad margin of moral error.

Caesarius's sermons against drunkenness, long attributed to Augustine, captured this ambivalence. His unflattering comparison of humans to beasts

---

[55] St. Thomas, *Summa Theologica*, vol. 2, II.II.141.6, p. 1770 ("*moderately, according . . .*" (emphasis added)); vol. 1, I.I.98.2, p. 494 ("immoderately . . . means . . ." (emphasis in original)); vol. 2, II.II. 149.3, p. 1798 ("*Wine drunken with . . .*"). As the source of the last quote Aquinas cited "Ecclus. xxxi 36." The reference is to Ecclesiasticus, also known as the Book of Sirach. Though Sirach chapter 31 of the King James Bible has only 31 verses, there are 42 verses in Ecclesiasticus chapter 31 of the Vulgate Bible.

[56] St. Thomas, *Summa Theologica*, vol. 2, II.II.141.6, p. 1770 ("Hence the Philosopher . . ."), II.II.149.3, p. 1798 ("sufficient for salvation . . .").

[57] Augustine, *De. Morib. Eccl.* xxi, *quoted in* St. Thomas, *Summa Theologica*, vol. 2, II.II.141.6, p. 1769.

suggested one could drink properly only what one needed: "Let Drunken men consider, whether they be not worse than Beasts: For seeing Beasts will not drink more than is requisite, they take down twice, yea thrice as much Drink as is expedient for them." Yet Caesarius endorsed a rather generous zone of permitted moderate drinking, apparently bound only by the overriding command to avoid drunkenness. Scrivener's 1685 translation captured this tension: "If you drink Wine moderately, you may be sober. . . . Wine drunk moderately, exalts the mind and body, and is healthful for body and soul. Wine much drunk, is the stoutnesse of Drunkennesse . . . ."[58]

This ambivalence was not Caesarius's fault—or Augustine's or Aquinas's. Rather it inheres in the properties of alcohol. Between necessary drinking and drunkenness lay a vast realm where drinking exceeded what was requisite yet fell far short of drunkenness and served to lighten the heart. One could imagine a rule that all drinking that exceeds *need* needlessly tempts toward the mortal error of drunkenness. At times, Aquinas seemed to endorse such a rigid standard. At other times, he stood ready to tolerate a more liberal rule, one that permitted some drinking that exceeds necessity as long as it stops short of drunkenness. For "[w]ine measurably drunk and in season bringeth gladness of the heart, and cheerfulness of the mind." (Ecclus. 31:28.)

The ambivalence of these great thinkers infected scores of lesser-known moral authorities and lawmakers who in later centuries shaped real-world English and American alcohol and drug policy. Hence lawmakers have condemned that part of alcohol and drug use that is genuinely intoxicating, robbing us of our reason and our power to govern our lower instincts. But they generally have tolerated the *sub*intoxicating use of alcohol because it fills a variety of perceived needs. And lawmakers have suffered the *risk* that subintoxicating drinking will stray past the boundary to drunkenness because alcohol, when used moderately, leaves us in command of our reason and makes more bearable the cares of this world.

The Path from Eden

As we journey from Eden back to Puritan times, we find a moral regime fixated on appetitive sex but now turning its condemnatory zeal against drunkenness. Both vices roused contempt as pointless pleasures that numbed the mind, disabled self-control, and goaded humans to act like animals. And these twin evils conspired in vice. By suspending our reason and disabling those intellectual

---

[58] Scrivener, *Treatise Against Drunkennesse*, pp. 166–67, 169 (purporting to quote Augustine, De Tempore, *Of Shunning* Drunkennesse (Sermon 231)). This passage largely consists of a series of rough quotations from Sirach, the Apocrypha's version of Ecclesiasticus. Ecclus. 31:27–30.

Figure 1.2: Peter Paul Rubens, *Lot and His Daughters* (c. 1613–1614).

sentries that Augustine said should "tame" the "appetite of the flesh which we have in common with animals," drunkenness tempts us toward the untamed, unconstrained sex of animals. For lust is the passion most likely to rule when reason is down.

That the road to lust was paved by drunkenness supplied endless inspiration for anti-drunkenness writers of the Puritan era. Almost every script sounded some variation on the theme, and almost all claimed Biblical authority. Writing in 1576, George Gascoigne invoked the story of Lot and his daughters. (Gen. 19:31–38.) Gascoigne branded them "Beasts, who in theyr droonkennesse, committed abhominable incest in the sight of God . . . ." John Hart's 1663 version was pithier: "When Lot was filled with wine, then was he fit for incest."[59] As cast by Peter Paul Rubens a half-century earlier, the women and the wine mingled their seductive charms (see Figure 1.2). One daughter, with bared breast, offered a cup of the same shape; the other, deceptively demure, tipped the lapping tongue of her carafe toward her father's groin.

Gascoigne told also of Noah, whose son Ham found him in a drunken stupor. (Gen. 9:20–22.) Noah was "through this beastly vice, so Metamorphosed," Gascoigne wrote, "that he lay in his Tent uncovered, and shewed thereby the

---

[59] Gascoyne, *Delicate Diet,* p. 26; [Hart,] *Dreadfull Character of a Drunkard*, p. 8 (my pagination).

Figure 1.3: Giovanni Bellini, *Drunken Noah* (c. 1500–1515).

secrets which shame and nature forbyd us to disclose[.]"[60] In Giovanni Bellini's portrayal, predating Gascoigne by some seventy-five years, a grinning Ham leers at his father's nakedness, delighting in his degradation, as a nearly empty wine cup tips again toward the father's groin (see Figure 1.3).

A century later, Increase Mather called down the proverbs of Solomon: "Look not thou upon the wine when it is red . . . . Thine eyes shall behold strange women" (Prov. 23:29–33). Several others cited the same lines, including Edward Raban, who ruined their rhythm even as he amplified their meaning: "It is to bee marked," he wrote in 1622, "that the wise king Salomon often joyneth Whoredome, with Drunkennesse; strong drink, with strange women, &c. as unseparable companions." Mather also cited the Apostle Paul—"Let us walk honestly . . . not in rioting and drunkenness, not in chambering and wantonness" (Rom. 13:13)—as did John Hart in 1663, Charles Phelpes and Edward Bury in the 1670s, and William Assheton in 1692.[61]

Next to the Scriptures in order of authority were the words of the early saints. Here Bury rehearsed two vivid examples. He translated the words of Saint

---

[60] Gascoyne, *Delicate Diet*, p. 25 (my pagination).
[61] Mather, *Wo to Drunkards*, p. 13; Edward Raban, *Rabans Resolution, against Drunkennes and Whoredome* (St. Andrews: E. Raban, 1622), p. 7; [Hart], *Dreadfull Character of a Drunkard*, p. 8; C[harles] P[helpes], *A Caveat against Drunkenness, Especially in Evil Times* (London: Tho. Parkhurst, 1676), pp. 102–03; Bury, *England's Bane*, pp. 19; William Assheton, *A Discourse Against Drunkenness, Swearing & Cursing* (London: Tho. Braddyll, 1692), p. 19.

Ambrose, a contemporary of Augustine, as "The first evil . . . of Drunkenness is the hazzard of Chastity . . . ." And he rendered Saint Jerome's counsel in the sly maxim, "Drunkenness is the Gallery that leads to Letchery."[62]

But these authors proved most creative when they left Scripture and saints behind and applied their own aphoristic craft to the theme that drunkenness begets lust. Raban alleged "[d]runkenness . . . bringeth us forwarde unto Whoredome." Mather said the "vile sin of Uncleanness . . . is the fruit of Drunkenness . . . ." Hart riffed off the genealogies of Genesis: "Fulness of drink breeds fulness of sin and fulness of lust; intemperancy begets incontinency . . . ." Matthew Scrivener blended sexual theme with sexual allusion in a playful bit of free verse: "Intemperance . . . cuts the chords of Discipline erected in the Soul, asunder, and throws open the doors for all Lusts to sally out at pleasure." And Bury offered a deftly efficient play on the Augustinian themes of abandoned reason, consequent bestiality, and lapse of control over our animal appetites: "[W]hen a Man or Woman hath no more reason than a Beast, why should they not act as Beasts?"[63]

Bury's last aphorism exposes the irreducible moral offense of intoxication: in robbing us of our reason, it strips us of the faculty that distinguishes us from beasts and reduces humans to a bundle of unconstrained appetites—quaffing, pissing, fornicating at will. Then as now, the reaction of many (sober) onlookers to such drunken bestiality was disgust. And those who inveighed against drunkenness exploited this power of disgust to rouse moral condemnation. "[H]ow monstrouse a thyng it is to beholde a man dronken," declared an unnamed author in 1545; "how he stumblith, tumbleth, waloweth; . . . his nose droppeth . . . ; his breth stynketh . . . ."[64]

Drink's Necessity

Though they tumbled one over another in decrying the spewing and vomiting and wallowing of drunken human swine, not one of these sixteenth- and seventeenth-century tract writers proposed to ban drink. Most never bothered to address the issue, as though the very possibility never crossed their minds. Instead, over and over, these writers condemned the unlawful *abuse* of alcohol but acknowledged its lawful *use*—and even its *necessity*. "Drink is in it self a good

[62] Bury, *England's Bane*, pp. 19–20.

[63] Raban, *Resolution, against Drunkennes*, p. 1; Mather, *Wo to Drunkards*, p. 13; [Hart], *Dreadfull Character of a Drunkard*, pp. 8, 11 (my pagination); Scrivener, *Treatise Against Drunkennesse*, p. 65; Bury, *England's Bane*, p. 19.

[64] *An Invective ageinst Glotony and Dronkennes* (London: Richard Lant and Richard Bankes, 1545), pp. 17–18 (my pagination). For more grotesque portraits of drunken human swine, *see* Bury, *England's Bane*, pp. 4–6; Phelpes, *Caveat against Drunkenness*, p. 10.

creature of God, and to be received with thankfulness," Increase Mather wrote, nodding to Paul's injunction that "every creature of God is good, and nothing to be refused . . . ." (1 Tim. 4.4.) Only "the *abuse* of drink is from Satan." Decades earlier the Massachusetts General Court had lamented that "much drunkennes[s]" and "wast[e] of the good creatures of God" prevailed in the colony's inns. Those words borrowed in turn from the earliest English act "for repressing the odious and loathsome Sin of Drunkenness," adopted by Parliament in 1606 to keep subjects from "abusively wasting the good Creatures of God."[65]

Mather read and occasionally cited the works of moralist Robert Bolton, who offered the adage, "Distinguish between drinking measurably, as you *need* it, and unmeasurably, when you *need* it not." Bolton's message was that necessity served as the benchmark dividing moderate—or "measurabl[e]"—drinking from immoderate drinking. Hence Mather allowed that "no sober Minister will speak against the Licensing of" taverns and alehouses, for these places become an evil only when their number exceeds their necessity: "I know that in such a great Town as this, there is *need* of such Houses, . . . but I wish there be not more of them th[a]n there is any *need* of."[66]

Borrowing his father's words, Cotton Mather insisted in a 1708 essay that he too condemned not the use of drink but its abuse: "I would be so understood, that the ABUSE and EXCESS of the Liquor, is all that is complained of. It is a *Creature of God* . . . [and] has a claim to that Allowance . . . ." He acknowledged legitimate *uses* of alcohol—indeed of rum, the worst sort of alcohol—as medicine and to ward off heat and cold. Apologizing for even mentioning rum by name, the younger Mather explained, "When I did but now take the *Name*, it was as the *Thing* ought to be taken; of meer *Necessity*." Rum has a "manifold use, both as a *Medicine*, and a *Cordial*. Some Diseases have been relieved by it, when it has been employ'd no otherwise than it ought to be." And "[i]t may not be amiss for many Labouring men, especially when Extream *Heat* or Extream *Cold*, Endangers them in their Labours, moderately this way to fortify themselves."[67]

Others of the day admitted alcohol's medical necessity. "[I]n some cases . . . it may be needful," Charles Phelpes said, "as the Apostle saith to Timothy: *Drink no*

[65] Mather, *Wo to Drunkards*, p. 4 (emphasis added); *Records of the Governor and Company of Massachusetts Bay in New England*, vol. 1 (1628–1641) (Nathaniel B. Shurtleff ed., Boston: William White, 1853), p. 213; "An Act for Repressing the Odious and Loathsome Sin of Drunkenness," 4 Jac. 1, c. 5, § 1 (1606). Massachusetts first banned drunkenness in the home in 1636. Mark Lender, "Drunkenness as an Offense in Early New England," *Quarterly Journal of Studies on Alcohol*, vol. 34, pp. 353, 360 (1973).

[66] Robert Bolton, *Christian Directory*, Tom. 1, ch. 8, p. 388, *quoted in* [Morton?], *Great Evil of Health-Drinking*, p. 31 (emphasis added); Mather, *Wo to Drunkards*, pp. 4, 29 (emphasis added); Mather, *Testimony Against Several Prophane and Superstitious Customs*, Text, p. 8 (citing "Mr. Bolton" on another point).

[67] [Cotton Mather,] *Sober Considerations, on a Growing Flood of Iniquity* (Boston: John Allen, 1708), p. 5.

longer Water, but use a little Wine for thy Stomacks sake, and for thy oft infirmities,
1 Tim. 5.23. So again, *Give Strong Drink to him that is ready to perish, and Wine to
those that be bitter of Soul, or heavy of heart,* Prov. 31.6, 7, 2 Sam. 16.2." Quoting
the same two passages, Owen Stockton conceded alcohol may be used as medicine but only—he stressed again and again—if taken in moderation. He expanded on the last-cited proverb and the excuse it supplied for drinking by those
who are "heavy of heart": "[W]ine and strong drink moderately taken, are usefull
for such as are of a sorrowfull spirit, for they are of a cheering nature . . . ."[68]

Medical authorities of the sixteenth, seventeenth, and eighteenth centuries put
their professional seal on medical theories contemporary moralists drew from
Scripture. Writing a century before Stockton, Dutch physician Levinus Lemnius
anticipated the use of wine to treat the heavy of heart. His family medical treatise,
published in English in 1576, endorsed "measurable drinking of Wyne" for those
who "are of Nature, sorowfull [and] lumpish." Decades later Thomas Coghan
invested spiced and herbed wines and ales and distilled *Aqua vitae* with a colorful
array of healing powers. His 1636 *Haven of Health* proposed one or another alcoholic decoction to soothe the stomach, rouse the appetite, cleanse the bladder,
and unblock the bowels; to stanch diarrhea, kill worms, and clear phlegm; to cure
toothaches and bad breath; to prompt sleep, improve eyesight, forestall palsies,
warm the aged, and aid conception. Wary of such promiscuous alcohol use, physician George Cheyne warned in 1724 of the risk of addiction: "People . . . ought
to tremble at the first *Cravings,* for such poisonous Liquors." Yet he too approved
the use of strong drink "by the *Direction* of a *Physician,*" especially for those
"under an actual *Fit* of the *Gout,* or *Cholick* in the *Stomach.*"[69]

Even those observers who scorned claims of medicinal need as phony pretexts
saw that such excuses cloaked indulgence with a moral purpose. Hence the
anonymous author of *The Occasional Monitor* of 1731 condemned those "volup-
tuous Persons" who "pretend . . . *they are of a moist cold Constitution;* and so for
a Remedy . . . precipitate themselves into all Manner of Excess in *Wine* [and]
Strong-Water . . . . Such Men are not *sincere,*" the author continued, and "would
gladly cover this Vice of theirs by an honest Pretext." So they "plead, *That they are
always sick,* and be daily drunkening, by *Necessity,* as they call it, because they
cannot live without it . . . ."[70]

[68] [Phelpes,] *Caveat against Drunkenness,* p. 8; Stockton, *Warning to Drunkards,* pp. 13–14, 112.
[69] Levine Lemnie *[Levinus Lemnius], The Touchstone of Complexions . . .* (Thomas Newton trans.,
London: Thomas Marsh, 1576), p. 139; Thomas Coghan *[sometimes Cogan], The Haven of Health*
(London: Anne Griffin, 1636), pp. 61, 239–40, 244–45, 247–49, 262; George Cheyne, *An Essay of
Health and Long Life* (London: George Strahan, 1724), p. 50. John French's *Art of Distillation* of 1651
followed Coghan in prescribing various alcoholic mixtures for a range of maladies. *See* Camper
English, *Doctors and Distillers: The Remarkable Medicinal History of Beer, Wine, Spirits, and Cocktails*
(New York: Penguin Books, 2022), pp. 55–56, 59–61.
[70] *The Occasional Monitor* (London: H. Cooke & E. Cooke, 1731), pp. 6–7.

While many doctors and moralists deemed wine and distilled alcohol essential medicines, laypeople saw the softer fermented drinks—beer and ale—as essential *foods*. Thomas Coghan granted beer "the virtue of nourishing, which it hath of the corne whereof it is made." If taken moderately, he said, beer "increaseth strength." Matthew Scrivener was more skeptical, deriding claims that "Ale . . . hath its name, *Ab Alendo*, from nourishing." Yet fermented drinks contributed a large part of most people's caloric intake—and took a form less readily spoiled than milk, meat, or bread. In the late seventeenth century, the average person of all ages and sexes drank as much as a quart of beer a day, and laboring men perhaps a great deal more. The beer was maybe weak—2 or 3 percent alcohol—but at some five hundred calories a quart, it counted as a small meal in itself.[71]

Widely thought an indispensable substitute for water, beer was the standard beverage at every meal. Despite a few lonely advocates of the superiority of water, suspicion of contamination and other concerns tilted public opinion decidedly toward beer. "[W]ater is not holsome, sole by it selfe, for an Englysshe man," advised dietician Andrewe Boorde in the sixteenth century. "If any man do [u]se to drynke water with wyne, let it be purely strayned; and then se[e]th[e] it . . . ." Nor could milk substitute for beer. Not till the late nineteenth century was decent milk generally available in urban centers. Per capita consumption at the end of the seventeenth century appears to have lagged a quart of milk a week.[72]

Of course a simple hankering for "a pot of good Ale" may explain the ubiquity of fermented drinks. "Would you believe it," a French visitor asked in 1726, "though water is to be had in abundance in London, and of fairly good quality, absolutely none is drunk? . . . In this country nothing but beer is drunk, and it is . . . what everyone drinks when thirsty . . . ."[73] But even if claims of need

---

[71] Coghan, *Haven of Health*, p. 251; Scrivener, *Treatise Against Drunkennesse*, p. 30; [Charles Davenant,] *An Essay upon Ways and Means of Supplying the War* (London: Jacob Tonson, 2d ed. 1695), p. 136 (estimating the per capita consumption of beer in London as a quart per day); Peter Clark, *The English Alehouse: A Social History, 1200–1830* (New York: Longman, 1983), p. 209 (noting that in the 1690s John Houghton assumed an average figure of a quart per head per day and citing reports from the 1730s that some laboring men drank as much as a gallon of strong beer daily); Andrew Barr, *Drink* (New York: Bantam Press, 1995), p. 250 & n.* (estimating caloric content and alcohol content of contemporary beer). *See also* [Thomas Wilson,] *Distilled Spirituous Liquors the Bane of the Nation* (London: J. Roberts, 1736), p. 20 ("We will suppose a labouring Man or Woman will drink of Strong Beer or Ale and Small Beer all together a Quart a Day . . . .").

[72] Sidney & Beatrice Webb, *The History of Liquor Licensing: Principally from 1700 to 1830* (1903, Archon Books, 1963), p. 4 (noting beer was the standard beverage); Andrewe Boorde, *A Dyetary of He[a]lth* (1542?) (F.J. Furnivall ed., London: Early English Text Society, 1870), pp. 252–53; Barr, *Drink*, pp. 264–65 (discussing milk consumption). Among the few who advocated the superiority of water was physician George Cheyne, who observed that those who drank nothing but water "have lived in *Health, Indolence*, and *Chearfulness*, to a great Age." Cheyne, *Essay of Health and Long Life*, p. 43.

[73] [Peter Mews], *The Ex-ale-tation of Ale, the Anciant Lickquor of this Realme* (London: T. Badger, 1646), p. 1; Cesar de Saussure, *A Foreign View of England in 1725–1729: The Letters of Monsieur Cesar de Saussure to His Family* (Madame van Muyden trans. (1902), London: Caliban Books, 1995), pp. 98–99.

rationalized a simple craving for alcohol, appeals to necessity suggest the vigor of the Augustinian moral order, in which such claims could justify pleasures otherwise deemed sinfully self-indulgent.

Beyond professing that alcohol met medical and dietary needs, some moralists argued that *taverns*, which invariably served alcohol, filled a separate, *institutional* need. Both Increase and Cotton Mather acknowledged that some tradesmen had no other place to transact business: "It is not unlawful," Increase Mather wrote, "for a Church-Member to go into the Tavern, when the Business of his Civil Calling does *necessarily* Call him thereunto."[74] In a sermon Cotton Mather co-wrote with other ministers in 1726, he warned against converting the demands of business into an all-purpose excuse for cavorting at the alehouse: "Some it may be will plead *Necessity*, or at least great *Conveniency* in the Case, with regard to the Ends of their *Calling* & *Business* . . . ." Yet "there are Others among us, Merchants, Shop-keepers, Tradesmen, &c. that have perhaps as much Business & as good Success as you; who yet don't attend your Evening Conversations at the Tavern, and do but seldom, if ever, transact any Business there. Now these are Witnesses against you, and must stop your Mouths, as to the Plea of Necessity . . . ."

The ministers allowed that *travelers* might find "Publick Houses to be necessary or at least convenient." But "it do's not follow," they insisted, addressing their neighbors, "that you may go thither, when Necessity do'sn't compel . . . . For that may be innocent & lawful, when done occasionally & transiently, upon some particular & extraordinary Emergence; which becomes criminal & scandalous, when it grows to a Custom, and is done unnecessarily. . . . [W]e fear," the ministers concluded, "Taverns are multiply'd among us, beyond the bounds of real Necessity . . . ."[75]

In many ways, then, the moral regime governing drink in early modern England and Puritan America looked very much like Augustine's moral framework governing sex. Because drunkenness like sex strips us of our godlike reason and lowers us to the state of brute beasts, drunkenness was a grave sin. Like sex, however, alcohol often was necessary. And just as sexual intercourse was without fault if procreation was the goal, so drinking carried no blame if the end was to heal an ailing body or salve a downcast mind, to warm or nourish the body, to supplant or disinfect unsanitary water, or even perhaps to smooth a balky business transaction.

[74] Increase Mather, Appendix to Several Ministers, *A Serious Address to Those Who Unnecessarily Frequent the Tavern* (Boston: S. Garrish, 1726), p. 29.
[75] Several Ministers, *A Serious Address*, pp. 22–23. For other uses of some form of *necessity* in this sermon, *see* pp. i, 1, 7, 8, 14, 17.

Incontinence and Its Vices

These links between sex and drunkenness may help explain the several meanings given *incontinence*. Augustine most often applied *continentia* to "the purity that is exercised in controlling the reproductive organs," which separates humans from those beasts that have sex wherever they can as long as the season is right. The principal and earliest definition of *incontinence* in the *Oxford English Dictionary* similarly addresses a lack of control over the bodily appetites in general and sexual passion in particular. Used in this sense, *incontinence* appeared in English by 1382. At times, however, Augustine invested *continentia* with broader meaning, comprehending a general curbing of bodily appetites. Hence he claimed "the function of continence is to be on the watch to restrain and heal any enjoyment of pleasures that are in conflict with the pleasures of wisdom."[76] When later moralists applied "incontinence" to drunkenness, they likewise traded on older images of sexual licentiousness and dyed drunkenness in the same moral hue.

But the most common usage of *incontinence* today, traced by the *Oxford English Dictionary* only to the mid-eighteenth century, relates to an entirely different loss of self-control, the one that most clearly reduces humans to the level of barnyard animals.[77] Here we come almost full circle back to Increase Mather and his obsession with the beastliness of drunkenness. For as it happens, Mather's son left a vivid testimonial to the horror of our own bestiality. A Puritan preacher himself, Cotton Mather reprised his father's denunciations of drunkenness, sometimes in even more strident tones. "There is a Sin," he wrote in a 1708 tract, "which turns a *Man* into a *Brute*; & because of that, it makes him worse than a *Brute*. It is the Sin of DRUNKENNESS," which "defac[es] the *Image* of God in his *Reason*." The title page bears a pithy Latin quote Mather credited to Augustine. Translated it declares, "DRUNKENNESS is the mother of all evil deeds, the cause of faults, the root of crimes, and the origin of vices."[78]

[76] St. Augustine, "Continence," in *Marriage and Virginity*, in *The Works of Saint Augustine: A Translation for the 21st Century*, vol. I/9 (Ray Kearney trans., Hyde Park: New City Press, 1999), § 2.5, p. 194 ("the purity that is exercised . . ."), § 13.28, p. 212 ("the function of continence . . ."); *Oxford English Dictionary* (2d ed. 1989), vol. 7, p. 820 ("Want of continence or self-restraint; inability to contain or retain: a. With reference to the bodily appetites, esp. the sexual passion: Unchastity.").

[77] The *OED* lists as the second definition of incontinence the "[i]nability to retain a natural evacuation, esp. incontinence of urine." It quotes a mid-eighteenth-century midwife's handbook as the earliest use of incontinence in this sense. *Oxford English Dictionary* (2d ed. 1989), vol. 7, p. 820. To test my sense that the most common modern use of the word relates to bowel or urine control, I surveyed a year's issues of the *New York Times* between August 9, 2008, and August 9, 2009. Of thirty-six uses of some form of *incontinent* (advertisements not included), thirty-two referred to lack of bowel or urine control. One dealt with financial profligacy; three others were ambiguous.

[78] [Mather,] *Sober Considerations*, pp. 7, 13. The quote assigned to Augustine—"EBRIETAS, est Flagitiorum omnium mater, culparumque materia, Radix criminum, et Origo vitiorum"—does not come from the Latin text of either of Caesarius's sermons. Professor Frank Herrmann, in correspondence with the author, reports that the quote comes from a work of no known authorship,

One day the younger Mather found himself suddenly confronted with an image of his bestiality. His diary records his revulsion at yielding to the "*Necessity of Nature*" and the "Condition of the *Beast*": "I was once emptying the *Cistern of Nature*, and making *Water* at the Wall. At the same Time, there came a *Dog*," he wrote, "who did so too, before me. Thought I; 'What mean, and vile Things are the Children of Men, in this mortal State! How much do our *natural Necessities* abase us, and place us in some regard, on the same Level with the very *Dogs!*' "[79]

The lesson spanning all three meanings of *incontinence* is this: we perceive self-control as an essentially human attribute and its loss—incontinence—as essentially bestial. This belief has proved as pervasive in the contexts of sex and drinking as in that of urinating and defecating. Hence drunkenness renders humans bestial in two related ways. It deprives us of self-control generally. And it robs us in particular of those forms of *continence* that are so distinctively human. For the drunkard is prey to lust—and he pisses against walls.

Animality and Disgust

The several meanings of incontinence and the younger Mather's disgust at his animal nature carry a broader lesson: to travel from the perceived animality of appetitive sex and drunkenness to their perceived immorality, we need not call on Plato or Augustine or even theism. For the moral dynamic that drives this story was neither Plato's creation nor Augustine's. Rather the aversion to bestial behavior they expressed so vividly may reach beyond theism and the Christian tradition and take rise from more broadly human instincts. Augustine may have cloaked these instincts in the language of Christian theology—and his immense influence no doubt fortified these ideas among early Christians and the later Puritans who embraced his tradition. But the link between perceived animality and perceived immorality seems to exist naturally and outside of faith.

For as Paul Rozin and his research colleagues have written, "Anything that reminds us that we are animals elicits disgust." A long chain of studies of the human emotion of disgust has led them to conclude, in distinctly Augustinian tones, that "[i]nsofar as humans behave like animals, the distinction between humans and animals is blurred, and we see ourselves as lowered, debased . . . ." They report a need common to many human cultures to carve clear distinctions

"De sobrietate et Castitate," which probably originated in southern Gaul or northern Italy in the sixth century. The work appears in *Patrologiæ Latina* (J.-P. Migne ed., Paris, 1861), vol. 40, col. 1106. I thank Birgit Calhoun of the Crown Law Library for her translation.

[79] *Diary of Cotton Mather 1681–1708* (Boston: Massachusetts Historical Society, 1911), 7th ser., vol. 7, p. 357; ibid., *1709–24* (Boston: Massachusetts Historical Society, 1912), 7th ser., vol. 8, p. 69.

between human and animal behaviors. To conceal our bestial kinship, we cloak our animal acts, especially eating, mating, and excreting, in specifically human trappings. Complicated and exacting customs govern time, place, and manner and emphasize hygiene and cleanliness. "Each culture prescribes the proper way to perform these actions—by, for example, placing most animals off limits as potential foods, and all animals and most people off limits as potential sexual partners. People who ignore these prescriptions are reviled as disgusting and animal-like." They offend against what Norbert Elias called the "civilizing process," in which people "have sought to suppress in themselves everything that they feel to be of an 'animalic character.'"[80]

Yet try as we might to deny our animal origins, our bodies "confound us," for we "still eat, excrete, and have sex." As Kant wrote, "Sexuality . . . exposes mankind to the danger of equality with the beasts." More discerningly, Aristotle distinguished the bodily pleasures unique to humans—those of sight (colors and painting), of sound (singing and drama), and sometimes of smell (flowers and incense)—from those "shared in by all the other animals." These bestial pleasures—eating, drinking, sex—are indulgences of touch and sometimes taste. They "belong[] to us not in so far as we are human beings but in so far as we are animals." *Taste* of course can be a matter of refinement, as when a person knows fine wines. But when taste simply drives *appetite*, it is bestial.[81]

In his sweeping study of the *Anatomy of Disgust*, William Ian Miller recognizes this human "concern to claim ourselves superior to animals and our horror that we are assimilable to them." But disgust must respond to *more* than reminders of our animal origins, he says, for some animals rouse no disgust. After all, we admire gazelles and jaguars for their superhuman speed and agility. The animal trait that troubled Plato and Augustine, however, was *appetite*. Just as Aristotle distinguished bodily pleasures that seem appetitive and therefore bestial from others that seem more refined, we must distinguish appetitive from refined animals. When Plato wrote of beasts that never ponder "the nature of the heavens" and rest "their front legs and their heads . . . upon the earth," he was not thinking of cougars, their noses to the wind. He meant instead the appetitive beasts—cows,

[80] Paul Rozin, Jonathan Haidt, & Clark R. McCauley, "Disgust," in *Handbook of Emotions* (Michael Lewis & Jeannette M. Haviland-Jones eds., New York: The Guilford Press, 2000), pp. 637, 642; Norbert Elias, *The Civilizing Process: Sociogenetic and Psychogenetic Investigations* (Edmund Jephcott trans., Oxford: Blackwell Publishers, 2000 (1939)), p. 102. The cited study supplies in my view the best and most comprehensive summary of Rozin's and his collaborators' work.

[81] Jonathan Haidt, Paul Rozin, Clark McCauley, & Sumio Imada, "Body, Psyche, and Culture: The Relationship Between Disgust and Morality," *Psychology and Developing Societies*, vol. 9 (1997), pp. 107, 112; Immanuel Kant, "Duties Towards the Body in Respect of Sexual Impulse," *in Lectures on Ethics* (Louis Infield trans., New York: The Century Co., 1930), pp. 162, 164; Aristotle, *Nicomachean Ethics* (Christopher Rowe trans., New York: Oxford University Press, 2002), 3.10.1118a1–1118b4, pp. 138–39.

swine, jackasses—which drop their heads from the heavens and snouts to the ground and feed and make dung the day long.[82]

Rozin and Miller agree that an onlooker's disgust at the behavior of others can spur *moral* censure. "We perceive what disgusts," Miller writes, "and tend to imbue it with defective moral status for that reason alone." They agree, too, that those acts that most readily spark disgust and moral condemnation are (in Miller's words) "moral issues that involve the body" or (in Rozin's) those that "involv[e] some reminder of our animal nature." Miller says "all manifestations of disgust [have] a moral dimension," but the badge of immorality appears to attach most readily to those disgusting behaviors that surrender to *appetite*. These he labels "offen[ses] against some idea of moderation and temperance."[83] Hence a man said to "feed at his trough" seems immoral for having abdicated reason to base appetite, a verdict that follows whether his trough is literal and the appetite hunger or figurative and the appetite lust.

James Joyce saw how disgust at bowing to the base cravings of our animal nature urged a verdict of immorality. In a series of sermons pitilessly devoted to hell's eternal agonies, Joyce's priest warned guilty youth of the fate awaiting those who "yield to the promptings of your lower nature, [who] live like the beasts of the field, nay worse than the beasts of the field for they, at least, are but brutes and have not reason to guide them." Such sinners would endure the derision of hell's fallen angels: "Such is the language of those fiendish tormentors, words of taunting and of reproach, of hatred and of disgust. Of disgust, yes! For even they, the very devils, . . . must turn away, revolted and disgusted, from the contemplation of those unspeakable sins by which degraded man outrages and defiles . . . and pollutes himself."[84]

And long before Joyce, Augustine leveled a similar charge. After lamenting those who go "crazy in their foul, perverted pleasures," he wrote, "When they have caught sight of themselves they will find the sight repulsive . . . . A drunken man does not find himself disgusting, but a sober person is revolted by the sight."[85]

---

[82] William Ian Miller, *The Anatomy of Disgust* (Cambridge: Harvard University Press, 1997), p. 49; Plato, *Timaeus*, 91, p. 75.

[83] Miller, *Anatomy of Disgust*, p. 106 ("all manifestations of disgust . . ."), p. 121 ("offen[ses] against some idea . . ."), p. 180 ("We perceive what disgusts . . ."), p. 205 ("moral issues that involve . . ."); Rozin et al., "Disgust," p. 643.

[84] Joyce, *Portrait of the Artist*, pp. 123–24.

[85] St. Augustine, "Exposition of Psalm 98: A Sermon to the People," in *The Works of Saint Augustine: A Translation for the 21st Century*, vol. III/18 (Maria Boulding trans., Hyde Park: New City Press, 2002), pp. 466, 471.

Drunkenness, Drug Abuse, and the Euphoria Taboo

When aimed at drunkenness and drug intoxication, the moral censure of our cultural euphoria taboo typically has taken two forms. The first focuses on the drunkard's or drug user's *abandoning essentially human standards of behavior*. Here we find the same epithets lobbed at substance abusers that Joyce's glowering priest spewed at his schoolboy Sybarites—degraded, defiled, debased, degenerated, debauched—all alleging descent beneath human dignity. Such words underscore the drunkard's or drug addict's revolting display of raw appetite unregulated by higher reason or self-control. They bear the same image Plato conjured when he rebuked those who "look down with their heads bent to the table. Like cattle, they graze, fatten, and copulate."[86] Such grazing and copulating is *low* in three ways—in rejecting the reason that makes us godlike, in appeasing the appetites of our lower members, and in mimicking those beasts that hang low their heads or slither on their bellies.

The second accusation of bestiality takes less literal form: it addresses how drunkards and drug users have *quit the task of living in human society* by avoiding "all the troubles, pains, and responsibilities of life."[87] Here the common epithets target the user's withdrawal from society. Hence we hear accusations of escape from reality, mind alteration, and tuning out.

Set against both images of bestiality is the person who maintains appropriately human standards of behavior—who has domesticated and refined the bestial appetites. For such a person, sex serves as one component of an affective, often familial relationship that is itself part of the human community; drinking is one of the rituals of social interaction and dining; and appropriate drug use heals the body or sharpens the mind. All enable more competent functioning within human society.

Our course now is to follow forward the history of alcohol and drug regulation, weighing as we go the role played by the language of Christian condemnation and the moral condemnation of disgust. For now, our focus remains on drunkenness, as the problem of recreational drugs remains down the road. The next chapter, therefore, explores how the moral reproach of appetitive conduct, the excuse of necessity, and the safe harbor of moderation helped shape the legal regulation of alcohol. We begin in 1736, a half-century after Matthew Scrivener published his translations of the spurious Augustinian sermons against drunkenness, when the English Parliament enacted the common-law world's first national prohibition of an alcoholic drink. Here we spy our first chance to observe on the ground and up close how the long-evolving moral regime governing alcohol use and abuse helped give form to earthly laws.

---

[86] Plato, *Republic*, 9.586a–b, p. 277.
[87] Charles Warrington Earle, "Opium-Smoking in Chicago," 52 *Chicago Medical Journal and Examiner*, 104 (Feb. 1886), p. 112.

2

The Gin Crisis

For seven brief years almost three hundred years ago, the British Parliament largely banned the retail sale of gin. Fleeting as they were, the years of the gin ban have claimed a place in our historical imagination. Their enduring allure traces in part to their grand chronicler, William Hogarth, who captured the moral economy of the gin craze in his preachy woodcuts, "Gin Lane" and "Beer Street."[1] Though not published till 1751, fifteen years after the ban first took hold, these engravings stand as the canonical images of the crisis that moved Parliament to act.

Neither subtle in their message nor famous for their craft, "Gin Lane" and "Beer Street" excel as historical artifacts—as reminders of a time when gin and beer were not simply different strengths of the same drug, but carried entirely different moral meanings. Only the more pernicious of these meanings resonates today. To our jaded twenty-first-century eyes, the portrait of Gin Lane in Figure 2.1 fits comfortably within the iconography of our modern drug war. Here we see the sort of histrionic imagery common in mainstream media accounts of drugs' depredations. Gin Lane is a place of poverty, bestiality, and licentiousness. But for the gin cellar that undergirds a thriving pawnshop and the distillery and coffin maker across the way, the lane lies in ruins. In one corner a man who pawned his clothes for gin slumps in stupor, shamelessly naked, clutching his bottle. Another stoops to the level of a brute beast, with which he fights for a bone. And foreground center a ragged woman—a ruined whore?—lolls in the dreamy satiety of her twin addictions, gin and snuff, baring her swollen breasts and syphilitic legs as her child tumbles from impious pietà to untimely death.[2]

Less familiar to modern eyes is Hogarth's view of "Beer Street." Here we find nothing like the boozy rowdiness of a modern ballgame or frat party. Beer Street instead is a scene of bustle and prosperity, where cobbler and blacksmith, pavers and porter, vegetable monger and fishwives turn their trades in convivial cheer, nourished by bubbling tankards of brew. As Hogarth wrote of this scene, shown in Figure 2.2, "Industry and Jollity go hand in hand."[3] The denizens of Beer

---

[1] *Engravings by Hogarth: 101 Prints* (Sean Shesgreen ed., 1973), plate nos. 75 ("Beer Street") and 76 ("Gin Lane") (1751).

[2] I am grateful to Monique Westra, who spied Hogarth's pietà imagery.

[3] *Engravings by Hogarth*, text accompanying plate no. 75 (quoting Hogarth).

Beware Euphoria. George Fisher, Oxford University Press. © Oxford University Press 2024.
DOI: 10.1093/oso/9780197688489.003.0003

Figure 2.1: William Hogarth, "Gin Lane" (1751).

Street are a well-dressed, well-fed lot, brimming with vigor, as sturdy as the prosperous establishments that rise behind them. A verse penned under the image promises that beer—the "Genius of Health"—"Can sinewy Strength impart." Only the pawnshop has gone to seed, its proprietor cowering behind a locked door through which he draws his beer.

To understand the gin crisis and gin ban, we must begin by asking what made gin a poison while beer was the stuff of life. This question foreshadows another we encounter later: What makes alcohol a valued social lubricant and other intoxicating drugs an evil?

Figure 2.2: William Hogarth, "Beer Street" (1751).

Gin as a Drunkenness Agent

Beer, ale, and fermented cider were the traditional beverages of the English working class. Gin was a relative unknown. Other than French brandy, largely an upper-class drink, distilled alcohol remained scarce in England till the late seventeenth century. When war with France led to punitive duties on imported brandy, Parliament threw open the domestic distilling industry, which produced mainly gin. Hefty excise duties on beer and ale made gin comparatively cheap, and official control over alehouse licenses, together with regulatory constraints on beer sellers, made gin selling comparatively easy. Hawkers sold gin from houses, street stalls, and wheelbarrows. By the 1730s London had a reported 1,500 distillers and at least 7,000 retailers, all serving a city of some 800,000 people—or about one gin seller for every 114 people. In the words of a 1733 observer, "one half of the Town seems to set up to furnish *poyson* to destroy the other half."[4]

As cheap gin won over the lower classes, consumption of British spirits swelled from about half a million gallons reported in 1688 to 6.4 million in 1735. The result, wrote Beatrice and Sidney Webb, was "a perfect pandemonium of drunkenness." Tobias Smollett's classic portrait in prose, issued a decade or two after the crisis had passed, supplied the voice-over for Hogarth's "Gin Lane": "[T]he populace of London were sunk into the most brutal degeneracy, by drinking to excess the pernicious spirit called gin, which was sold so cheap that the lowest class of the people could afford to indulge themselves in one continued state of intoxication, to the destruction of all morals, industry, and order." Recounting one of the era's most infamous images, Smollett reported "that the retailers of this poisonous compound set up painted boards in public, inviting people to be drunk for the small expense of one penny; assuring them they might be dead drunk for two-pence, and have straw for nothing."[5]

Smollett explained his reference to straw in terms hinting of both bestiality and sex. Gin retailers, he said, "provided cellars and places strewed with straw, to which they conveyed those wretches who were overwhelmed with

---

[4] Sidney & Beatrice Webb, *The History of Liquor Licensing: Principally from 1700 to 1830* (Hamden, Conn.: Archon Books, 1963 (1903)), p. 4, pp. 24–26 (noting beer's traditional role and tracing the onset of the gin crisis); Peter Clark, "The 'Mother Gin' Controversy in Early Eighteenth-Century England," *Transactions of the Royal Historical Society*, vol. 38 (1988), pp. 63–68 (supplying the number of retailers and explaining the obstacles to beer and ale sales); William Kennedy, *English Taxation, 1640–1799* (London: Frank Cass & Co. Ltd., 1913, Augustus M. Kelley, Publishers reprint, 1964), pp. 137–38 (detailing the difference in excise taxes imposed on imported and domestic spirits); *The Parliamentary History of England from the Earliest Period to the Year 1803* (London: T.C. Hansard, 1812) [hereinafter cited as *Hansard's Parliamentary Debates*] (Commons), vol. 9, p. 1039 (1736) (remarks of William Pulteney) (observing that the high duties placed on brandy and rum "have raised the price so high, that the lower sort of people cannot afford to make a constant and excessive use of them"); "Theophilus," *The Gentleman's Magazine*, vol. 3 (Feb. 1733), pp. 88, 89 ("one half of the town . . ."). The figure of 7,000 retailers comes from *The Report of His Majesty's Justices of the Peace, at Hick's-Hall, January-Sessions, 1735-6, appended to* [Thomas Wilson,] *Distilled Spirituous Liquors the Bane of the Nation* (London: J. Roberts, 1736), App. pp. 14, 15. The justices reported that within the Bills of Mortality, excluding London and Southwark, there were "7044 Houses and Shops wherein *Geneva* and other *Distilled Spirituous Liquors* are publickly sold by Retale." This number did not, however, include many "*Garrets, Cellars,* back Rooms, and other Places not publickly exposed to View, and which therefore escaped the Notice of our Officers."

[5] Clark, "'Mother Gin' Controversy," pp. 64, 67 (supplying consumption figures); Webbs, *History of Liquor Licensing*, p. 26; Tobias Smollett, *The History of England, from the Revolution to the Death of George the Second* (London: Longman, Brown, Green, and Longmans, 1848 (1756–57)), vol. 2, p. 430. The Webbs warn against relying too strictly on figures of gin consumption, as they are based on revenue commissioners' reports and therefore exclude unlicensed production and smuggled drink. *See* Webbs, *History of Liquor Licensing*, p. 42 n.3.

intoxication. In these dismal caverns they lay until they had recovered some use of their faculties . . . in hideous receptacles of the most filthy vice . . . . Such beastly practices . . . would have reflected disgrace upon the most barbarous community."[6]

Whether any sign promising drunkenness for a penny and oblivion for two-pence ever hung in Georgian London is past proving. One tireless advocate of the gin trade insisted in 1736 that despite reports of such a sign outside a distiller's shop in Southwark, his own "diligent Enquiry" had turned up no reason to credit these accounts. The story nonetheless found legs. In 1743 Thomas Secker, Bishop of Oxford, warned that after repeal of the 1736 gin ban, "new invitations will be hung out to catch the eyes of passengers, who will again be enticed with promises of being made drunk for a penny."[7] Hogarth also picked up the reference and included the sign among the clutter of Gin Lane (see Figure 2.1). Over the door to the gin cellar, where Dante might have warned visitors to abandon all hope, Hogarth beckoned:

> Drunk for a penny
> Dead drunk for two pence
> Clean straw for nothing.

Even if such a sign never hung, its imagined boasts claimed some truth: gin swillers could drink themselves drunk for just a few pence. In the early eighteenth century, when beer was fetching threepence a quart, a Londoner could buy a quartern of gin—or four ounces—for three halfpence.[8] A modern shot is about an ounce and a half of liquor. As gin of the era was about as potent as London Dry gin today, a drinker of 1736 could swig the equivalent of three and a half modern shots for the very modest sum of twopence. A drunk's worth of gin was therefore well within budget for London laborers earning between eighteen pence and

---

[6] Smollett, *History of England*, vol. 2, p. 430.

[7] *A Supplement to the Impartial Enquiry into the Present State of the British Distillery* (London: J. Roberts, 1736), p. 13; *Hansard's Parliamentary Debates* (Lords), vol. 12, p. 1328 (1743) (remarks of Thomas Secker, the Bishop of Oxford).

[8] Jessica Warner states three halfpence as the typical price of a quartern of gin throughout this period. In the first edition of his 1736 anti-gin tract, *Bane of the Nation*, Thomas Wilson suggested the price of gin was "Three-farthings a Quartern"—or half Warner's price, as a farthing was a quarter-penny. But Wilson deleted this reference from the second edition of his work, published later in 1736—and in newly added text put the retail price of gin at "three Half-pence *per* Quartern." Moreover, in a report printed shortly after the 1736 gin ban took effect, the *Northampton Mercury* wrote of a new gin substitute. "[T]he Price too is upon a Par with Geneva , , , and sold for . . . Three Half pence the Quartern . . . ." Jessica Warner, *Craze: Gin and Debauchery in an Age of Reason* (New York: Four Walls Eight Windows, 2002), pp. 35–36; [Wilson,] *Bane of the Nation*, p. 13; [Thomas Wilson,] *Distilled Spirituous Liquors the Bane of the Nation* (London: J. Roberts, 2d ed. 1736), p. 24; "Domestick Occurrences," *Northampton Mercury*, Dec. 20, 1736, p. 141. I thank Kevin Rothenberg of the Crown Law Library for helping me confirm this calculation.

two shillings (or twenty-four pence) a day. In the words of an anonymous 1736 pamphleteer, "The Distillers Art, (which may justly be called A *Master-Piece* of the DEVIL) has put Drunkenness within the Reach of Poverty, by Making these Liquors so very CHEAP." Or as Lord Hervey said during parliamentary debates, the distillers had made "drunkenness the cheapest of all vices."[9]

For supporters of the gin ban, the sign's reference to free straw and all it conjured proved as disturbing as the gin. In his famed 1736 tract calling for abolition of the gin trade, Thomas Wilson charged that one retailer "has a large empty Room backward, where as his wretched Guests get intoxicated, they are laid together in Heaps, promiscuously, Men, Women, and Children, till they recover their Senses . . . ." Seven years later, as the House of Lords debated repeal of the gin ban, Thomas Secker recalled—and magnified—similar images: "[T]hey tell me, every one of these gin-shops had a back shop or celler, strowed every morning with fresh straw, where those that got drunk were thrown, men and women promiscuously together: here they might commit what wickedness they pleased . . . ."[10]

While gin rendered drinkers quickly and cheaply drunk and hence casual in their morals, beer was a different matter. In contemporary eyes, beer simply wasn't a drunkenness agent. For one thing it acted too slowly. One speaker argued in Parliament in 1736 that "before a man becomes flustered with beer or ale, he has time to reflect, and to consider the many misfortunes to which he exposes himself and his family, by idling away his time at an alehouse . . . ." Secker later echoed the point: "But the difference between spirituous and other strong liquors [such as beer] lies in this: of all other strong liquors a man must drink a large quantity, and must be at it a long time, before he is quite deprived of his reason: he has time to reflect what he is about . . . ." Then there was the matter of stomach space. As Secker put it: "I am told, even the liquor itself becomes nauseous before a man can be quite fuddled; so that a man must put a sort of force upon himself, before he can swallow down so much of any other sort of strong liquor [such as beer] as to deprive himself of all sense and reason."[11]

[9] Patrick Dillon, *Gin: The Much-Lamented Death of Madam Geneva* (Boston: Justin, Charles & Co., 2002), p. 168 (comparing gin of the era to modern London Dry); *A Hole to Creep Out at from the Late Act of Parliament Against Geneva, and Other Spirituous Liquors* (London: J. Hughs, 1736), p. 4 (my pagination); *Hansard's Parliamentary Debates* (Lords), vol. 12, p. 1311 (1743) (remarks of Lord Hervey). The information about London wages comes from a comment by Lord Hervey in 1743 Parliamentary debates. *Id.*, p. 1261 ("[B]ut to a man who earns his 18*d.* or 2*s.* d day, as many labouring men do here about London . . . ."). Lord Hervey attributed his reference to "the cheapest of all vices" to his peer Dr. Thomas Sherlock, bishop of Salisbury, who had lamented in a sermon that "so much *Art* and *Skill* has been shewn of late Years, to make *Drunkenness* the *Cheapest of all Vices.*" [Wilson,] *Bane of the Nation*, p. 27 (quoting Sherlock's address).

[10] [Wilson,] *Bane of the Nation* (2d ed.), p. vi; *Hansard's Parliamentary Debates* (Lords), vol. 12, p. 1206 (Feb. 22, 1743) (remarks of Dr. Thomas Secker, the Bishop of Oxford).

[11] *Hansard's Parliamentary Debates* (Commons), vol. 9, p. 1088 (1736) (remarks of an unidentified speaker); ibid. (Lords), vol. 12, p. 1205 (Feb. 15, 1743) (remarks of Thomas Secker, the Bishop of Oxford).

Gin stood out, then, as a peculiarly potent drunkenness agent, both quick and efficient. "[W]ith spirituous liquor the case is vastly different," Secker said, for "a small quantity, no more perhaps than a man can swallow down at a draught, deprives him of all reason and reflection . . . ." "[F]ew could keep themselves within any Bounds," argued another Parliamentary speaker, "because a small Quantity deprived them of their Reason . . . ." "[A] quarter of a pint," claimed a third, "is sufficient to intoxicate the brain." But the words that best captured how gin changed the very nature of drinking were those of the Earl of Cholmondeley, who pronounced gin drinking "the new art of sudden intoxication."[12]

Not only was gin-based drunkenness quick, it was somehow "a new Kind of Drunkenness," as magistrate and novelist Henry Fielding called it in 1751, "unknown to our Ancestors." Unlike beer and ale and other fermented drinks, gin was said to addict. Many observers lamented those persons "addicted to the Drinking of Spirits"—those "addicted to *Drams*"—or "the lower Kind of People addicted to this Vice." Arguing to retain the gin ban in 1743, Lord Lonsdale alleged that "if any of the gin-shop-keepers themselves are honest enough, they will tell you, that when poor creatures fall once into the habit of gin-drinking, they never leave it off as long as they have a rag to wear, or a leg to crawl on." And gin's addictiveness, wrote Stephen Hales, justified a ban: "Now since it is found by long Experience, extremely difficult, for the unhappy habitual *Dram-Drinkers* to extricate themselves from this prevailing Vice; so much the more it becomes the Duty of the Governors of the Nations, to withhold from them so irresistible a Temptation . . . ."[13] Despite this multitude of voices indicting gin as addictive, however, none leveled a similar charge at beer.

The Moral Evil of Gin-Based Drunkenness

The tumultuous disputes surrounding the 1736 Gin Act and its 1743 repeal consumed hundreds of pages of Thomas Hansard's *Parliamentary Debates* and endless reams of newsprint and pamphlet paper. At the center of the storm stood

---

[12] *Hansard's Parliamentary Debates* (Lords), vol. 12, p. 1205 (Feb. 15, 1743) (remarks of Thomas Secker, the Bishop of Oxford); ibid. (Commons), vol. 9, p. 1042 (Mar. 8, 1736) (remarks of an unidentified speaker) ("[F]ew could keep themselves . . ."); ibid. (Lords), vol. 12, p. 1373 (Feb. 24, 1743) (remarks of Lord Lonsdale) ("[A] quarter of a pint . . ."); ibid. (Lords), vol. 12, p. 1338 (Feb. 22, 1743) (remarks of the Earl of Cholmondeley).

[13] Henry Fielding, *An Enquiry into the Causes of the Late Increase of Robbers* (London: A. Millar, 1751), p. 27; [Wilson,] *Bane of the Nation*, p. 32 ("addicted to the Drinking of Spirits"); Stephen Hales, *A Friendly Admonition to the Drinkers of Gin, Brandy, and other Distilled Spirituous Liquors* (London: B. Dod, 5th ed. 1754 (1733)), p. 27 ("addicted to *Drams*"); *The Presentment of the London Grand-Jury* (undated), *appended to* [Wilson,] *Bane of the Nation*, App. pp. 3, 4 ("the lower Kind of People addicted to this Vice"); *Hansard's Parliamentary Debates* (Lords), vol. 12, p. 1246 (Feb. 24, 1743) (remarks of Lord Lonsdale); Hales, *Friendly Admonition* (5th ed.), p. 31.

the question of prohibition, for the crux of the controversy was whether to regulate gin's sale or forbid it altogether. Beneath the swirling invective stirred by the prohibition debate lay a broad social consensus about the need for *some* measure to address the evil at hand. None but the occasional bawdy balladeer defended gin-based drunkenness. One anonymous pamphleteer who campaigned heatedly against prohibition nonetheless allowed there was one point on which reformers "were never yet contradicted, that the immoderate Use of Spirituous Liquors produces bad effects . . . ."[14]

Those who advocated the cause of prohibition floated a raft of allegations against gin, both moral and pragmatic. The moral allegations included of course promoting promiscuity—those reported promises of "straw for nothing" and Thomas Secker's fitful image of fetid cellars where last night's drunks "commit[ted] what wickedness they pleased." Gin's opponents invoked as well the fundamental moral claim that drunkenness robbed drinkers of their reason and their capacity to govern their lower instincts—ancient themes that survived intact into the eighteenth century. One author had declared in *The Spectator* in 1714 that "[t]he sober man, by the strength of reason, may keep under and subdue every vice or folly to which he is most inclined; but wine . . . gives fury to the passions . . . ." Another, writing in *The Tatler* a few years earlier, stressed the loss of self-control: "Were there only this single consideration, that we are less masters of ourselves, when we drink in the least proportion above the exigencies of thirst . . . it were sufficient to make us abhor this vice. . . . As for my part, I ever esteemed a *drunkard* of all vicious persons the most vicious: for . . . what can we think of him, who . . . incapacitates himself for the duties and offices of life, by a suspension of all his faculties?"[15]

These themes of suspended reason and unleashed passions figured boldly in what was perhaps the most influential publication urging adoption of the 1736 gin ban—Thomas Wilson's *Distilled Spirituous Liquors the Bane of the Nation*, which made a sensation when published in London early that year. Sir Joseph Jekyll, the chief legislative sponsor of the 1736 act, financed the first edition of Wilson's tract, effectively anointing it the official manifesto of the gin ban. Deemed "a very learned Divine" by Henry Fielding, Wilson was a leading

---

[14] *An Impartial Enquiry into the Present State of the British Distillery* (London: J. Roberts, 1736), p. 2.

[15] *The Spectator*, vol. 8, no. 569, pp. 68, 70 (July 19, 1714) (unsigned and untitled entry); *The Tatler*, no. 241 (Oct. 24, 1710), *in The Tatler and the Guardian: Complete in One Volume* (Edinburgh: William P. Nimmo & Co., 1880), p. 427 (unsigned and untitled entry). The *Tatler* entry was ascribed to editor Isaac Bickerstaff, a fictive form assumed by Richard Steele. *See The Tatler*, no. 252 (Nov. 18, 1710), *in The Tatler and the Guardian*, p. 442 (reprinting a letter to "Mr. Bickerstaff" referring to "[y]our discourse against drinking" of October 24, 1710). As Steele and Joseph Addison wrote both *The Tatler* and *The Spectator*, these essays may have sprung from the same hand.

member of the Society for Promoting Christian Knowledge, a loose collection of London intellectuals that helped fire the propaganda campaign against gin.[16]

Wilson concluded his famous work with a long peroration borrowed from a 1724 sermon of Edward Chandler, Bishop of Litchfield and Coventry, who spoke repeatedly of the drunkard's loss of reason:

> While [strong liquors] insensibly *abate* and *intoxicate* the Vigour of Reason, they *inflame* the Blood, and *heighten* the Passions, and so make People ready for any Kind of Wickedness . . . .
>
> What should hinder Men or Women under the Influence of so powerful an *Opiate* to their Understanding, from proceeding to lewd and immodest Actions . . . [?]

Seven years later, as Parliament debated repeal of the Gin Act, Lord Hervey called up the same imagery in the gin ban's defense: "[W]ith regard to the morals of the people," he said, "it is well known that drunkenness of every kind inflames all the passions of mankind, and at the same time deprives them of that which is designed by nature as a check upon our passions, I mean our reason."[17]

And eight years after that, in 1751, as Parliament prepared once again to take up the question of the gin trade, Henry Fielding invested his considerable talents in a campaign for tighter regulation. He spelled out the moral objection against drunkenness in much the same terms used twelve centuries before by our Augustinian mimic, Caesarius of Arles. Hence we see the familiar unfavorable comparison of man to beast: "Creatures of the animal or brutal Kind, which have nothing but their Senses to gratify, . . . yet never eat or drink to Excess, but will quit both their Food and Water as soon as their Hunger and thirst are satisfied. . . . Whereas Man," Fielding continued, "who boasts of his high and celestial Endowments, the Dignity of his Nature, and his Superiority to all other Creatures, is subject . . . to every Gust of Passion, is a Slave to his Appetite, and follows the Dictates of his Senses . . . ."[18]

---

[16] Clark, "'Mother Gin' Controversy," pp. 67, 74–76; Lee Davison, "Experiments in the Social Regulation of Industry: Gin Legislation, 1729–1751, *in Stilling the Grumbling Hive: The Response to Social and Economic Problems in England, 1689–1750* (Lee Davison et al. eds., 1992), pp. 25, 33; Fielding, *Enquiry into the Increase of Robbers,* p. 30 n.*.

[17] [Wilson,] *Bane of the Nation,* pp. 59–60 (quoting Edward Chandler, *A Sermon Preached to the Societies for Reformation of Manners on January 4th 1724* (London: James Knapton, 1724), p. 16); *Hansard's Parliamentary Debates* (Lords), vol. 12, p. 1194 (1743) (remarks of Lord Hervey).

[18] [Henry Fielding,] *A Dissertation on Mr. Hogarth's Six Prints Lately Publish'd* (London: B. Dickinson, 1751), pp. 3–4. Jessica Warner identifies Fielding as the author of this work, published anonymously. Warner, *Craze,* p. 194.

The Worry over Women

Though Fielding fretted that "Man" was slave to his passions, gin drinking roused the greatest moral concern when the drinkers were women. "My Mind is wounded," Thomas Wilson wrote in the second edition of his anti-gin tract, "but to think of imputing any share of this Depravity to them. But, alas! 'tis too well known to be concealed . . . ." Women appeared in Hogarth's Gin Lane in several guises, all compromised by gin. There were the pawnbroker's suppli-cant tendering her pots for gin money; the heedless mother with bared breasts pinching at her snuff; and another mother at center right, pouring gin down her infant's throat (see Figure 2.1). Two troubling figures appear more subtly, almost innocently obscure. Standing to the right under the distillery's eaves, un-disturbed by the drunken brawl nearby, two young women sip gin with studied nonchalance, hoping none will notice the shoulder patches that betray them truants from St. Giles parish school.[19]

His delivery was blunt, but Hogarth's message was valid, for a great number of both gin drinkers and gin sellers were women. The monikers "Mother Gin" and "Madam Geneva" were more puns than metaphors, marks of a distressing social reality. Peter Clark reports that in 1735 and 1736 almost a quarter of London's gin sellers were women—and women perhaps accounted for even more of the city's unlicensed sellers, who tended to be poorer. Of gin sellers imprisoned for failing to pay fines assessed under the 1736 Act, fully three-quarters may have been women. Clark speculates that women who migrated to the city may have turned to selling gin when they found themselves locked out from licensed victualing. Other women may have started *drinking* gin when they found them-selves shut out from alehouses. "[I]t was thought disgraceful for a woman to be seen in a public-house," wrote London-area magistrate Patrick Colquhoun, "and those who would venture to sit down among men in a taproom were considered as infamous prostitutes." But women drinkers could visit gin sellers, often con-cealed behind the doors of such legitimate businesses as butchers, cobblers, and tailors.[20]

And most notoriously chandlers. The chandlers of old England sold more than candles. They were the general storekeepers of their day—"partly Cheesemonger, Oil-Man, Grocer, Distiller," in one contemporary's words—and "the most obnoxious Dealer[s] in and about London." Thomas Wilson lamented how readily women could sneak unsuspected into a chandler's shop for a drink. "[O]ur *Female Servants*," he said, "would be asham'd to go to a *Brandy-Shop* or

---

[19] [Wilson,] *Bane of the Nation* (2d ed.), p. xi; *Engravings by Hogarth*, plate no. 76 (editor's note).
[20] Clark, "'Mother Gin' Controversy," p. 70; [Patrick Colquhoun,] *Observations and Facts Relative to Public Houses in the City of London and Its Environs* (London: Henry Fry, 1794), p. 17, *quoted in* Andrew Barr, *Drink* (New York: Bantam Press, 1995), p. 181.

an *Ale-House*, because it would appear at once for what they went thither; but the *Chandlers-Shop* furnishes so many little Necessaries to a Family, that there they can unsuspected resort and indulge themselves . . . ." Some years later Henry Fielding struck the same theme. "Go to any Chandler's Shop," he warned, "and tho' you shall see Nobody in it, yet if you pass thro' it into an adjoining Room, you will seldom fail of seeing half a Dozen or half a Score . . . refreshing their Spirits with a Glass of Juniper [gin]; these are generally Females, Servant-Maids, and the Wives of midling Sort of People . . . ."[21]

Anxieties over drinking women, as Rod Phillips has written, traverse eras and cultures and turn on the twin threats to women's sexual purity and the health of their broods. Both threats prompted handwringing among those who feared gin. First were worries about youth—and therefore the nation's posterity, its laboring strength, and the vigor of its men in arms. Screed after anti-gin screed called up chilling images of "Pigmy Size[d]," "goggle-ey'd" offspring, "born weakly and sickly," "half burnt and shrivelled," "deform'd, and discolour'd." And beyond those children who absorbed gin in the womb or at their mothers' breasts were those fed the poison directly. Fielding echoed many in lamenting those "tender Mothers, [who] to stop their [children's] little gaping Mouths, . . . will pour down a spoonful of their own delightful Cordial . . . ." The consequence for the rising generation, Stephen Hales wrote in 1754, appeared in tallies of christenings and child mortality. Since 1724, "when the Use of *Spirituous Liquors* became so common," christenings had "continually *decreased*." And those children "that *are born*, come into the World with such *bad Constitutions*, that . . . they die in prodigious Numbers under *Five* Years old." Hale's figures were numbing. Of an annual average of 14,457 christenings in London, 10,590 children died by age five.[22]

Women's gin drinking led as well to moral decline. "How often do we see Women, as well as Men," a London-area grand jury asked, "lying in the very Channels and Corners of Streets like dead Carcasses generally without Cloaths to . . . cover their Nakedness and Shame?" A committee of magistrates added "[t]hat by inflaming their blood, and stupifying their Senses, [gin-drinking women] expose themselves an easy Prey to the Attacks of vicious Men." And in a

[21] R. Campbell, *The London Tradesman* (London: T. Gardner, 1747), p. 280; [Wilson,] *Bane of the Nation* (2d ed.), p. vii; [Fielding,] *Dissertation on Mr. Hogarth's Six Prints*, p. 9. Peter Clark reports that chandlers accounted for over 40% of gin sellers in London in 1735–1736. Clark, " 'Mother Gin' Controversy," pp. 68–69, 84.

[22] Rod Phillips, *Alcohol: A History* (Chapel Hill: University of North Carolina Press, 2014), p. 318; [Stephen Hales,] *A Friendly Admonition to the Drinkers of Brandy, and Other Distilled Spirituous Liquors* (London: Joseph Downing, 1733), p. 13 ("Pigmy Size[d] . . ."); [Fielding,] *Dissertation on Mr. Hogarth's Six Prints*, p. 14 ("goggle-ey'd"), p. 16 ("tender Mothers . . ."); *Report of His Majesty's Justices*, appended to [Wilson,] *Bane of the Nation*, App. pp. 14, 18 ("born weakly and sickly"); *The Presentment of the Middlesex Grand-Jury*, appended to [Wilson,] *Bane of the Nation*, App. pp. 7, 8 ("half burnt and shrivelled"); [Wilson,] *Bane of the Nation* (2d ed.), p. xii ("deform'd, and discolour'd"); Hales, *Friendly Admonition* (5th ed. 1754), App. III, pp. 40–42 (supplying childbirth and child mortality figures).

pamphlet commenting on Hogarth's newly published "Gin Lane," Henry Fielding worried about the "Woman [who] accustoms herself to Dram-drinking, . . . for so sure as she habituates herself to drinking so sure it is she will never be satisfied without it . . . ." After she has pawned all she has to feed her habit, she will thieve from her parents or master. Then "thro' mere Necessity [she] becomes a Street-walker, and at last an abandon'd Prostitute."[23]

Long before the gin crisis, moral authorities had warned of drink's temptation to female promiscuity. Aquinas wrote that "sobriety is most requisite in . . . women, because . . . in women there is not sufficient strength of mind to resist concupiscence." Increase Mather declared that "[f]or *a man* to love to be drunk is horrible impiety; but if this be true concerning *a woman*, there's a *daughter of Belial* indeed." Or as Matthew Scrivener said, "it is as odious for a Woman to be Drunk once a year, as for a Man once a week . . . ."[24]

The concerns of the gin era—of drunken Hogarthian "*Women* throwing off all Shame and Modesty in the open day," as a London grand jury put it—followed in this well-worn path.[25]

The Worldly Evils of Gin-Based Drunkenness

Beyond hazarding children's health and their elders' morals, gin faced a litany of more prosaic accusations. Gin ravaged the body, fueling "Chronical Distempers . . . Consumptions, Dropsies, Jaundice." Gin left the workforce "too feeble for labour, too indolent for application, too stupid for ingenuity." It drained the nation of "strong and lusty *Soldiers*" and a vigorous defense. It robbed the drinker's family of scarce funds and left his wretched children, "whose blood is tainted with inveterate and accumulated maladies, . . . an additional burden to the community."[26]

---

[23] *The Presentment of the Grand-Jury of the Tower-Hamlets* (1735), *appended to* [Wilson,] *Bane of the Nation*, App. pp. 11, 12; *Report of His Majesty's Justices, appended to* [Wilson,] *Bane of the Nation*, App. pp. 14, 18–19; [Fielding,] *Dissertation on Mr Hogarth's Six Prints*, pp. 11–12.

[24] St. Thomas, *Summa Theologica* (Fathers of the English Dominican Province trans., San Francisco: Benziger Brothers, Inc., 1947), vol. 2, II.II.149.4, p. 1799; Increase Mather, *Wo to Drunkards: Two Sermons Testifying Against the Sin of Drunkenness* (Cambridge: Marmaduke Johnson, 1673), p. 9; Scrivener, *Treatise Against Drunkennesse*, p. 48.

[25] *Presentment of the Middlesex Grand-Jury, appended to* [Wilson,] *Bane of the Nation*, App. pp. 3, 5.

[26] [Wilson,] *Bane of the Nation*, p. 31 ("Chronical Distempers . . ."); *Hansard's Parliamentary Debates* (Lords), vol. 12, p. 1194 (1743) (remarks of Lord Hervey) ("too feeble for labour . . ."); *Presentment of the London Grand-Jury, appended to* [Wilson,] *Bane of the Nation*, App. pp. 3, 4 ("strong and lusty Soldiers"); *Hansard's Parliamentary Debates* (Lords), vol. 12, p. 1309 (1743) (remarks of Lord Hervey) (noting that because "the drunkard's work is little and his expences are great . . . , he must soon see his family distressed . . ."); ibid., p. 1347 (remarks of Lord Lonsdale) ("whose blood is tainted . . .").

And gin, critics said, caused crime. For it was now "in the Power of every Miscreant to inflame his Blood, and fit himself for the most horrible Barbarities for Two–pence . . . ." Indeed drinkers had little choice but to thieve, for "the intoxicating Draught itself disqualifies them from using any honest Means to acquire it." So there followed a "vast Increase of *Thieves* and *Pilferers*" and "High-way and Street Robberies, attended sometimes with most cruel, unheard of Murthers," most of which "have been laid and concerted at Gin-Shops."[27]

The anti-gin forces even had a poster killer—Judith Defour, whose gin-hazed inhumanity made her an iconic villain of the reform movement. A single working mother, Defour had surrendered her two-year-old to the care of parish authorities. One Sunday in January 1734 she took her daughter from the parish residence for a late-morning outing and never returned. Later, wracked with grief and guilt, she led witnesses to a frigid field where little Mary lay in a ditch, naked and lifeless. Defour confessed she and another woman had stripped the girl to pawn her new clothes, donated days before by parish authorities. The women meant only to strand the girl, Defour said, but strangled her to stop her crying. Then they sold her clothes for sixteen pence, divided the money, "and join'd for a Quartern of Gin." Two years later Thomas Wilson recounted this episode, still "fresh in every body's Memory," to buttress his case against gin.[28]

The Pragmatic Politics of the Gin Ban

So the anti-gin reformers recruited every possible argument to the cause of prohibition. They stoked fears about health to persuade those who cared little of morals and concerns about crime to convince those who cared little of health. As Caesarius had written in the spurious Augustinian sermons more than a millennium before, "let them at least be afraid of Bodily distempers, who have no regard to the Salvation of their Souls . . . ."[29] By attacking gin along all possible fronts, Wilson and his cohort set the standard for every future temperance movement, including our modern drug war with its multipronged rationales.

---

[27] *Letter from a Gentleman in the Country to His Friend in Town*, appended to Hales, *Friendly Admonition* (5th ed.), pp. 31–33 ("in the Power . . ."); Fielding, *Enquiry into the Increase of Robbers*, p. 29 ("the intoxicating Draught . . ."); *Report of His Majesty's Justices*, appended to [Wilson,] *Bane of the Nation*, App. pp. 14, 19 ("vast Increase . . ."); *The Trial of the Spirits: or, Some Considerations upon the Pernicious Consequences of the Gin-Trade to Great-Britain* (London: T. Cooper, 2d ed. 1736), p. 5 ("High-way and Street Robberies . . ."); *Presentment of the London Grand-Jury*, appended to [Wilson,] *Bane of the Nation*, App. pp. 3, 4 ("have been laid and concerted . . .").

[28] *The Proceedings at the Sessions of the Peace, and Oyer and Terminer, for the City of London* (Feb. 27–Mar. 1, 1734), no. 3, pp. 82–83; [Wilson,] *Bane of the Nation*, p. 9. Patrick Dillon discusses (and elaborates on) the Defour case at some length. Dillon, *Gin*, pp. 93–97.

[29] I quote here from Scrivener's translation of Caesarius's second sermon against drunkenness, which Scrivener attributed to Augustine. Scrivener, *Treatise Against Drunkennesse*, p. 185.

Despite obvious strategic benefits, this scattershot strategy of reform can madden the modern researcher who seeks to unravel real rationales from makeweight rhetoric.

Gin's opponents made little attempt to array their charges from bad to worst. Nor did they distinguish those allegations that persuaded *them* to oppose gin from those they mouthed merely to persuade others. Proponents of the ban simply staked out a range of rationales, charging that free consumption of gin would blight morals, health, public order, the public fisc, industry, men in arms, and the posterity of our race. At first glance there is no way to know how greatly each rationale added to the impetus for reform.

Still, there is reason to doubt that the worldly evils gin wrought—sickness, poverty, inattentive workers, dissipated soldiers, and crime—played prominently in spurring the gin ban. The chief advocates of the 1736 ban were all members or associates of the Society for Promoting Christian Knowledge (SPCK), a group founded in 1699 to "counteract the growth of vice and immorality" through charity schools and improving literature. Members included both tract-writer Thomas Wilson and Thomas Secker, the Bishop of Oxford, who later spoke so vigorously against gin in the House of Lords. They included, too, clergyman Stephen Hales, author of an earlier and widely famed anti-drunkenness tract, and anti-gin zealot Sir John Gonson, who as chief magistrate of the Tower Hamlets supervised a gin-trashing report by the grand jury published only weeks before Parliament took up consideration of the gin ban. It was Gonson's report that told of women "lying in the very Channels and Corners of Streets . . . without Cloaths to . . . cover their Nakedness and Shame."[30]

By winning the Parliamentary sponsorship of Sir Joseph Jekyll and deftly managing the propaganda war sparked by Wilson's influential tract, this claque won passage of the 1736 ban over minimal legislative opposition. Jekyll, though not a member of the SPCK, was a fellow traveler in its moral mission, having devoted himself to suppression of lotteries and lewd stagecraft, among other moral causes. With a "Face . . . like a Winter's Day," rigid with age and wealth, Jekyll may have been insufferable in his piety, but he seems to have been sincere. Even Queen Caroline, the group's most illustrious ally, appears to have been roused by moral—or at least moralistic—motives. Jekyll reported "[t]hat he had seen the Queen who seemed to be an hearty enemy to distilled and spirituous liquors. Said she had seen a great deal of Bestialities and Indecencies as she has gone by in the streets."[31]

---

[30] Dillon, *Gin*, pp. 98–99, 103, 106; Warner, *Craze*, pp. 105, 109–11; *Presentment of the Grand-Jury of the Tower-Hamlets, appended to* [Wilson,] *Bane of the Nation*, App. pp. 11–14.

[31] [Charles Hanbury Williams,] *S-S and J-L: A New Ballad* (London: W. Webb, 2d ed. 1743), p. 3, *quoted in* Warner, *Craze*, p. 109 ("Face . . . like a Winter's Day"); *The Diaries of Thomas Wilson, D.D., 1731–37 and 1750* (C.L.S. Linnell ed., London: Society for Promoting Christian Knowledge, 1964), p. 143 ("[t]hat he had seen the Queen . . ."); Dillon, *Gin*, p. 107 (noting the Queen's support). On

The task of discerning the true motives of this coterie of moral reformers must confront their self-conscious efforts to curtail their moral mission. Shortly before publication of his anti-gin monument, *Bane of the Nation*, Thomas Wilson solicited Jekyll's opinion of the work. Though Jekyll "approved it in the Maine," Wilson wrote in his diary, he asked "that its Moral Reflections might be kept to the last and not intermixt in the Body of the Treatise." As Lee Davison writes of this passage, Jekyll "felt neither Parliament nor the public needed to be convinced of moral decay, but it was indispensable to prove that regulation would not lead to economic decline."[32] That is, advocates of the gin ban realized their stiffest opposition would come from those with vested economic interests in the gin trade, chiefly the distillers and powerful landholders whose grain the distillers consumed.

Wilson's tract therefore ended—but did not begin—by quoting Edward Chandler's very Augustinian indictment of alcohol: "While [strong liquors] insensibly *abate* and *intoxicate* the Vigour of Reason, they *inflame* the Blood, and *heighten* the Passions, and so make People ready for any Kind of Wickedness . . . ." The tract *began* by quoting a very different, nonmoralizing work titled *An Essay upon Ways and Means*, which Wilson deployed to prove that gin drinking "hinder[s] the *Consumption* of *Flesh* and *Corn*"—and hence shrinks farm income. Yet it seems clear the tract's moral peroration touched more closely on the reformers' deepest motives than did its economic overture, which Wilson included to defuse likely enemies rather than inspire likely friends.[33]

In his own famous tract against drunkenness, Stephen Hales likewise withheld his most strident moralizing language till the end. After stressing in the first and longest section of his pamphlet the health hazards and addictiveness of distilled liquors, he suddenly cut himself short: "BUT let us consider the spiritual, as well as temporal Evils, that Men bring upon themselves by the Sin of Drunkenness." Only in his closing paragraphs did he roll out his most potent moral weapon against drunkenness—the image of man's bestiality: "In a Word, If all these Considerations will not deter Men from this odious Vice, they must still wallow in their Vomit, and continue in this sottish, senseless Condition, till the Flames of Hell rouse them . . . ."[34]

A quarter-century later Samuel Johnson commented on this tendency of moral reformers to couch their anti-drink advocacy in amoral tones. One day

Jekyll and his character, *see* Dillon, *Gin*, pp. 104–05; Warner, *Craze*, 105–09; Clark, " 'Mother Gin' Controversy," pp. 75–76.

[32] *Diaries of Thomas Wilson*, pp. 146–47; Davison, "Experiments in the Social Regulation of Industry," p. 31.

[33] [Wilson,] *Bane of the Nation*, pp. 2, 60.

[34] [Hales,] *Friendly Admonition*, pp. 17, 22.

in 1763, the young James Boswell spoke with Johnson "of preaching, and of the great success which those called Methodists have." Johnson replied in his usual declamatory style: "Sir, it is owing to [Methodists'] expressing themselves in a plain and familiar manner, which is the only way to do good to the common people . . . . To insist against drunkenness as a crime, because it debases reason, the noblest faculty of man, would be of no service to the common people: but to tell them that they may die in a fit of drunkenness, and shew them how dreadful that would be, cannot fail to make a deep impression."[35] Folks already given to drunkenness, Johnson apparently thought, had slipped past the reach of moral appeals but not past appeals to their pocketbooks or health.

I suggest we seek the most potent motives behind the gin ban by focusing not on the 1736 ban, but on its 1743 repeal. As was true of alcohol prohibition in the United States almost two centuries later, the ultimate lesson of the gin ban is that it failed. And both movements failed for the same reason: they overreached public sentiment and mainstream morality on the alcohol question.

The Pragmatic Politics of Repeal

The 1736 act adopted the most basic of strategies: it sought to price gin out of existence. The act imposed a gargantuan annual license fee of fifty pounds (about $10,000 in today's money) on every retailer of gin or other distilled alcoholic drinks and a duty of twenty shillings (or about $200) on every gallon of spirits sold at retail. No one in Parliament pretended to call the act a revenue-raising measure. As William Pulteney said, it "will amount to a total prohibition."[36]

Despite early claims of success in convicting a great number of illegal gin sellers, enforcement of the ban soon broke down. In those days before regularized police forces, enforcement depended on private drinker-informants who bought from illegal sellers and then turned them in. Entitled to a reward per conviction of five pounds (about $1,000 today), informants naturally became "detested as the oppressors of the people." At least four were killed by mobs.[37]

---

[35] *Boswell's Life of Johnson* (R.W. Chapman ed., New York: Oxford University Press, 1953), pp. 324–25.

[36] "An Act for Laying a Duty upon the Retailers of Spirituous Liquors, and for Licensing the Retailers Thereof," 9 Geo. 2, ch. 23, §§ 1–3 (1736); *Hansard's Parliamentary Debates* (Commons), vol. 9, p. 1039 (1736) (remarks of William Pulteney).

[37] Jessica Warner & Frank Ivis, "'Damn You, You Informing Bitch.' *Vox Populi* and the Unmaking of the Gin Act of 1736," *Journal of Social History*, vol. 33, pp. 299, 306, 318–19 (1999) (reporting official figures reflecting over 12,000 convictions by August 1738); Davison, "Experiments in the Social Regulation of Industry," pp. 36–37, 39–40 (arguing that "reported totals of convictions under the Excise were . . . dramatically overstated"); *Hansard's Parliamentary Debates* (Lords), vol. 12, p. 1323 (1743) (remarks of Lord Bathurst) ("detested as the oppressors . . ."); Warner & Ivis, "'Damn You,'" p. 309 (four killed by mobs); *The Speech of Nathaniel Blackerby, Esq.* (London: J. and J. Fox, 1738), pp. 8–9 (complaining of "the mobbing, beating, and evil treating" of informants).

The mobs, Lord Bathurst explained, saw those targeted by the law "as persons under unjust persecution, whom every one was obliged by the ties of humanity to encourage, reward, and protect . . . ." Parliament responded by boosting informants' rewards, but by 1741 enforcement effectively ceased. By 1742, British gin production stood at an all-time high of over seven million gallons. Virtually no one bothered to take out the license required by the 1736 act: throughout the law's seven-year reign, only twenty retailers were so honest (or foolish) as to pay the fifty-pound fee. The mob "drank gin in defiance of the law," the Earl of Ilay argued in 1743, "rais[ing] among the people . . . a contempt of law, order, and government."[38]

Yet it was not this spectacle of impotence that sparked the Gin Act's repeal, but the government's clamoring need for funds. In one respect the 1736 act had worked as planned: it effectively ended the *legal* trade in gin and thereby stanched what had been a rich flow of duties and licensing fees. Seven years later, those lost funds looked newly tempting to a cash-strapped government suddenly embroiled in a far-flung European war. So the ministry proposed to replace the 1736 act with a far more modest set of duties and licensing fees that effectively re-legalized the traffic. A retail license now would cost but a pound a year and the duty on a gallon of simple English spirits just a penny. Small as they were, these assessments stood to generate an expected annual revenue of £140,000.[39]

Having cruised through the House of Commons, the repeal act met indignant opposition in Lords, where some peers found its naked expediency too grasping to bear. "What name we are to give this new fund I know not," the Earl of Chesterfield said, "unless we are to call it the Drinking Fund." Others put the point with less finesse. "This is really like a tradesman's mortgaging the prostitution of his wife or daughter," Lord Hervey charged, "for the sake of raising money to supply his luxury or extravagance." And Lord Talbot said simply, "[M]oney! . . . To gain money . . . they are now about to sacrifice the health and virtue of the people . . . ." Yet despite the united resistance of the bishops in the House of Lords, who voted in a solid wall against repeal, the gin ban fell to history's dustbin.[40]

---

[38] *Hansard's Parliamentary Debates* (Lords), vol. 12, p. 1323 (1743) (remarks of Lord Bathurst) ("as persons under unjust . . ."); 10 Geo. 2, ch. 17, § 9 (1737); 11 Geo. 2, ch. 26 (1738); Warner & Ivis, "'Damn You,'" p. 306; Webbs, *History of Liquor Licensing*, p. 31 (putting production of gin in 1742 at 7,160,000); Davison, "Experiments in the Social Regulation of Industry," p. 35 (noting only twenty licenses were issued between 1736 and 1743); *Hansard's Parliamentary Debates* (Lords), vol. 12, p. 1243 (remarks of Lord Ilay).

[39] *An Act for Repealing Certain Duties on Spirituous Liquors . . .* , 16 Geo. 2, ch. 8, § 2 (1743); Dillon, *Gin*, pp. 219–23.

[40] *Hansard's Parliamentary Debates* (Lords), vol. 12, p. 1220 (1743) (remarks of the Earl of Chesterfield); ibid., p. 1193 (remarks of Lord Hervey); ibid., p. 1391 (remarks of Lord Talbot); ibid., p. 1291 (remarks of the Earl of Chesterfield) ("I do not find, that any one of [the bishops] will advise or consent to" the bill.); ibid., p. 1426 n* (noting passage of the repeal bill and the opposition of all the

The Moral Dynamic of Repeal

Whether from expediency or conviction, many of those advocating repeal claimed more principled grounds than money lust. Their argument embraced two concepts long familiar to the moral discourse of alcohol regulation: necessity and moderation. Oddly, this moral dynamic lay couched in the language of tax policy.

All parties agreed the repeal measure, if passed, would amount to a tax on gin. They agreed too about certain fundamental principles of taxation. When laying a consumption tax, the government first had to determine if the commodity targeted was a *necessity, luxury*, or *vice*. "We ought never," the Earl of Chesterfield said, "to tax any thing that nature or custom has made *necessary* for supporting the industrious poor . . . ." The principle was familiar to all present. Almost half a century earlier, Charles Davenant had advised in his *Essay upon Ways and Means* that "[i]t should be the Care of all Governments" to make "all the Necessaries of Life" affordable to the poor. Davenant apparently had the welfare of the poor at heart—he hoped to render "the Necessaries of Life . . . cheaper to the Poor, that they might . . . enjoy more Ease and Plenty . . . ." But by 1743, when Parliament debated repeal of the gin ban, tax theorists staked the principle on the less charitable basis that a tax on necessities inevitably must hike the cost of labor.[41]

All parties agreed with a second dictum laid down by the Earl of Chesterfield: it was wrong to raise revenues by taxing *vices*. "Would you lay a tax upon a breach of the ten commandments?" he asked. "Would not such a tax . . . imply an indulgence to all those who could pay the tax?" Vice was "not properly to be taxed, but suppressed; and heavy taxes are sometimes the only means by which that suppression can be attained."[42]

If the government should tax neither necessities nor vices, all consumption taxes must fall on *luxuries*. "The proper Commodities to lay Excises upon, are those, which serve meerly to Luxury," Davenant explained, "because that way the Poor would be least affected." Chesterfield agreed, but stressed the goal of deterrence: "Luxury, . . . or the excess of that which is pernicious only by its excess, may

---

bishops present); Smollett, *History of England*, vol. 2, p. 431 (noting that "the whole bench of bishops voted against" repeal).

[41] *Hansard's Parliamentary Debates* (Lords), vol. 12, p. 1290 (1743) (remarks of the Earl of Chesterfield) (emphasis added); [Charles Davenant,] *An Essay upon Ways and Means of Supplying the War* (London: Jacob Tonson, 2d ed. 1695), p. 129; William Kennedy, *English Taxation, 1640–1799* (Augustus M. Kelley reprint, 1968 (1913)), pp. 108–11, 113–15 (quoting contemporary writers and speakers advocating against taxes on necessities because they would hike labor costs). William Kennedy reported that as early as 1608 there was "general acceptance" of the principle that in imposing import duties, "the necessaries of the people should be spared." Ibid., p. 13.
[42] *Hansard's Parliamentary Debates* (Lords), vol. 12, pp. 1219, 1345 (1743) (remarks of the Earl of Chesterfield).

very properly be taxed, that such excess, though not strictly unlawful, may be made more difficult." As William Kennedy noted, by the time of the gin debates the understanding that taxes on luxuries were "the one satisfactory kind of tax" was very "much part of the common stock of ideas."[43]

All parties therefore endorsed the tripartite tax scheme. They disagreed only about whether gin was a necessity, luxury, or vice. Gin clearly *could* be a vice. No one defended drunkenness, and even the most dogged advocates of repeal agreed with the Duke of Newcastle that "when a man drinks so much of these liquors at a time as to make himself drunk, or so often as to impair his health, this is a *vicious* use which ought to be prohibited and punished . . . ."[44] Disagreement between supporters and opponents of repeal focused, then, on whether gin sometimes was also a necessity—and whether it ever was merely a luxury and not a vice.

Gin as a Necessity of Life

No one called gin a necessary *food*. Among alcoholic drinks, only beer counted in contemporary eyes as an essential part of the diet. Hence a 1647 writer on tax policy enjoined the government to take "tender care . . . of the fundamentalls . . . of Man's life, namely Bread, Flesh, Salt, *Small-beere*, &c." A few decades later the Brewers Company of London argued against extension of the beer excise on the grounds that it fell "only upon victuals"—and that "beer and ale, next to bread, are the stay and staff of the poor."[45]

Gin's claim of necessity, like that of other distilled liquors, lay in its use as medicine and a hedge against cold weather. All save the most strident gin antagonists acknowledged its medicinal value. Indeed Parliament took care to provide that the duties and fees imposed by the 1736 gin ban and 1743 repeal measure "shall not extend to any Physicians, Apothecaries, Surgeons, or Chymists, as to any Spirits or Spirituous Liquors, which they may use in the Preparation or making up of Medicines for sick, lame, or distempered Persons only."[46]

---

[43] [Davenant,] *Essay upon Ways and Means*, p. 129; *Hansard's Parliamentary Debates* (Lords), vol. 12, p. 1345 (1743) (remarks of the Earl of Chesterfield); Kennedy, *English Taxation*, p. 129. Kennedy argued that the understanding that taxes should fall upon luxuries was in place at least a generation before Davenant published his treatise. Kennedy, *English Taxation*, pp. 29–30, 76–78. I thank Barbara Fried for pointing me to Kennedy's work.

[44] *Hansard's Parliamentary Debates* (Lords), vol. 12, p. 1272 (1743) (remarks of the Duke of Newcastle) (emphasis added).

[45] *The Standard of Equality, in Subsidiary Taxes and Payments* (London: D.H., 1647), p. 16, *quoted in* Kennedy, *English Taxation*, p. 76 (emphasis added); *S. P. Dom.*, Chas. 2, vol. 1, no. 146, *quoted in* Kennedy, *English Taxation*, p. 77.

[46] George Cheyne, *An Essay of Health and Long Life* (London: George Strahan, 1724), p. 43; 16 Geo. 2, ch. 8, § 12 (1743); 9 Geo. 2, ch. 23, § 12 (1736) (containing the same language but for the addition of the word "other" in the phrase "spirits or other spirituous liquors").

This exemption inevitably spurred suspicion that druggists sold duty-free gin under cover of mortars and pestles. Days before the 1736 ban took hold, the *Northampton Mercury* reported rumors that "[s]everal Distillers are going to set up Apothecaries Shops." Weeks later the paper lamented that "whilst the Distiller is depriv'd of the Benefit of his lawful Calling, the Apothecary, through the Indulgence of the Legislature, . . . shall have full Liberty to defeat the Intention of Parliament." Looking back on these times a century and a half later, temperance scholar Henry Wheeler reported that the word "dram," commonly used to refer to a serving of gin, originated in druggists' attempts to evade the English gin acts—"a dram, or drachm, being an apothecary's measure for the spirituous liquors which he sold."[47]

Still, lawmakers sought to preserve access to medicinal gin. During debates on the 1743 repeal bill, Lord Bathurst argued that in setting duties on distilled liquors, the government ought to "raise the price so, as to put it out of the power of the meaner sort of people to purchase too great a quantity . . . without putting it out of their power to have a single dram when it is *absolutely necessary* for the support of nature . . . ." Such necessity may arise often, Bathurst said, "in this cold climate, especially in damp foggy weather, or in marshy or fenny parts of the country." Likewise the Duke of Newcastle urged that "[a] small dram of spirituous liquors may sometimes be *necessary*, in a very cold day, or when a man is become faint with hard labour, and it would be cruel to raise the price of them so high as to put even this use out of the reach of the poor." And Lord Hervey noted that a properly laid duty would make it apparent to even the poorest people "that if they or any of their family wanted a single dram *upon an emergency*, they might, and could afford to purchase it at the next ale-house . . . ."[48]

As vigorously as some in Parliament proclaimed gin's necessity to health, others denied it. "[N]o climate, no temperature of the air, can make a dram of spirituous liquors *necessary* to a person in full health and vigour," said Bishop Secker. "Even in our most foggy weather, or in the most fenny parts of the country, . . . a draught of good warm beer would have a better effect against the inclemency of the weather, than a dram of any kind . . . ." So, too, the Earl of Sandwich insisted that "the liquor called gin is not a *necessary* . . . of life; for when a dram of any spirituous liquor happens to be absolutely necessary, which,

---

[47] "Domestick Occurrences," *Northampton Mercury*, Sept. 20, 1736, p. 91; "Domestick Occurrences," ibid., October 11, 1736, p. 103; Henry Wheeler, *Methodism and the Temperance Reformation* (Cincinnati: Walden and Stowe 1882), p. 18.

[48] *Hansard's Parliamentary Debates* (Lords), vol. 12 (1743), p. 1202 (remarks of Lord Bathurst) (emphasis added); ibid., p. 1272 (remarks of the Duke of Newcastle) (emphasis added); ibid., p. 1198 (remarks of Lord Hervey) (emphasis added).

I believe, is seldom, if ever the case, even the poorest person may get one single dram of brandy or rum . . . ."[49]

Secker and the Earl of Sandwich, however, spoke in the minority. Most in the House of Lords, like most in the country, believed medical need sometimes justified gin drinking. Any tax scheme therefore had to exempt medicinal use or impose a tax modest enough to permit even the very poor to buy the occasional dram of gin.

Gin Drinking as a Luxury

The question of gin's necessity was the less important—and less controversial—dispute concerning the tax treatment of gin. Members of the House of Lords invested far more time and passion debating whether gin, when drunk as a beverage, ever qualified as a simple *luxury* or always amounted to *vice*. At bottom the moral dispute over gin and the debate about proper tax policy reduced to one question: Must *any* gin drinking inevitably tend toward *excessive* gin drinking? The answer turned on the old moral notion of moderation.

Those who supported the repeal measure, together with its milder, less prohibitive table of duties and licensing fees, believed gin drinking needn't always be a vice. The Duke of Newcastle stated their case most eloquently and couched it most neatly in the language of tax. In spirituous liquors "there is a necessary, a luxurious, and a vicious use," he began. "When a man takes a larger dram than is necessary, or oftener than is necessary, but never so much at a time as to make himself drunk, it is a luxurious use, and luxury ought to be taxed in the poor as well as the rich." On these principles Newcastle defended the fees and duties imposed by the repeal bill, for they put "the purchase of a large dose of spirituous liquors . . . out of the power of a poor man . . . . [H]e must content himself with what is necessary, perhaps he may sometimes launch out into a little luxury, but he will seldom or never be able to launch out into a vicious use of such liquors."[50] Hence Newcastle cast gin's luxurious use as what Aquinas and seventeenth-century moralists called *moderate* use, permitted by both Puritanism and tax policy.

Other leading advocates of repeal likewise distinguished between the luxurious or moderate use of gin, which they aimed to regulate and tax but not ban, and its vicious use to induce drunkenness, which they condemned. "[E]xcessive

---

[49] *Hansard's Parliamentary Debates* (Lords), vol. 12, pp. 1207–08 (1743) (remarks of Thomas Secker, the Bishop of Oxford) (emphasis added); ibid., pp. 1276–77 (1743) (remarks of the Earl of Sandwich) (emphasis added).

[50] *Hansard's Parliamentary Debates* (Lords), vol. 12, pp. 1272–73 (remarks of the Duke of Newcastle).

use," Lord Bathurst said, "is the only grievance complained of, for I never heard that a single moderate dram, even of the pernicious liquor called gin, was either a crime or a sin . . . ." "The moderate use of spirituous liquors" the Earl of Cholmondeley agreed, "is not what is, or ought to be complained of: it is the excessive use that is attended with all those fatal consequences which have been mentioned."[51]

Opponents of repeal, in contrast, believed moderate gin drinkers would follow temptation into drunkenness and luxury into vice. They staked this conviction partly on the intoxicating potency of gin. There is with gin no window between moderate and excessive use, Bishop Secker said. "[A] small quantity, no more perhaps than a man can swallow down at a draught, deprives him of all reason and reflection . . . ." And Lord Hervey alleged the government would be complicit in tempting drinkers to drink too much. "The duty proposed is not near so high as to . . . prevent the excessive use of . . . [gin]; it is not designed as such," he said. "[I]t is designed as a fund for bringing money into the king's exchequer: and therefore we may depend upon it, that the use of this commodity, and even the excessive use of it, will be encouraged, or at least connived at by the king's ministers . . . ." Embracing this theme, the Earl of Chesterfield challenged his colleagues to "declare openly and freely, that you hereby intend to encourage and promote the excessive drinking of gin, in order to encrease his majesty's revenue . . . ."[52]

The Reign of Moderation

Despite such skepticism about moderate gin use, the repeal bill passed, returning England to a regime of legalized but regulated gin sales. Here there's no cause for surprise. Repeal of the 1736 gin ban would have followed soon enough had not a continental war and consequent money crunch forced the issue in 1743. For by outlawing even moderate gin drinking and putting even occasional necessary use beyond the means of the poor, the 1736 law had overreached mainstream morality. No substantial Christian authority from Aquinas onward had condemned necessary alcohol use or even unnecessary use within the bounds of moderation. Virtually all authorities explicitly condoned such drinking. Augustine himself had done so, albeit in the voice of his alter ego, Caesarius. Even gin's most strident opponents in Parliament faulted moderate gin drinking only on the theory that condoning it risked drunkenness. To Lord Carteret's claim that "no man will

[51] *Hansard's Parliamentary Debates* (Lords), vol. 12, p. 1203 (remarks of Lord Bathurst); ibid., pp. 1215–16 (remarks of the Earl of Cholmondeley).

[52] *Hansard's Parliamentary Debates* (Lords), vol. 12, p. 1205 (1743) (remarks of Bishop Secker); ibid., p. 1199 (remarks of Lord Hervey); ibid., p. 1220 (remarks of the Earl of Chesterfield).

say, there is any vice in drinking a single dram even of gin itself," the backers of the gin ban offered no answer beyond their raw insistence that one dram always leads to the next.[53]

Such grim predictions could not stand in the face of a stubborn reality: though the 1736 gin ban had failed in the long run to suppress gin drinking, this empty gesture of a law had stripped a cash-strapped government of a rich and badly wanted revenue source. Lord Carteret therefore triumphed with cold pragmatism: "[T]he people will indulge themselves in this vicious habit; and since there is no preventing it, the government ought to avail themselves of it . . . ." In a concession to the command of moderation, Carteret added that the government should gather gin revenues "in such a manner as by degrees to put a stop, at least to the excessive use of this pernicious liquor." This gesture hardly sounded genuine, and Carteret's opponents readily dismissed his bill as "nothing but a money job"—"an experiment to discover . . . how much the court may be enriched by the destruction of the subjects."[54]

But by and by, Carteret's prediction that careful regulation and shrewdly imposed excises could moderate gin consumption proved true. For as it turns out, gin consumption in Britain likely never again matched the heights it hit in 1743, the year the gin ban fell.[55]

This denouement of the gin crisis resembled in broad strokes the downfall of American prohibition almost two centuries later. In each case a fairly brief term of prohibition marked by halfhearted enforcement and increasing public alienation gave way to overwhelming sentiment for repeal. In neither case did repeal mean bacchanal. Instead, once all parties settled on the understanding that there would be no ban and that the vice lay chiefly in the excess, lawmakers committed themselves to the cause of moderation. Their efforts exploited the convenient reality that the alcohol trade rests on substantial businesses—manufacturers and licensed retailers—that the law can regulate and penalize and enlist in the cause of moderation.

Even the hurriedly passed repeal act of 1743 reflected a dawning awareness of the means to achieve moderation. Lawmakers saw that the "new art of sudden intoxication" that had plagued London was a function not only of gin but of the manner of its sale. The most despised gin sellers were the street dealers

---

[53] *Hansard's Parliamentary Debates* (Lords), vol. 12, p. 1226 (remarks of Lord Carteret).

[54] *Hansard's Parliamentary Debates* (Lords), vol. 12, p. 1225 (1743) (remarks of Lord Carteret); ibid., p. 1231 (remarks of Lord Lonsdale) ("nothing but a money job"); ibid., p. 1430 (remarks of Lord Hervey) ("an experiment to discover . . .").

[55] Dillon, *Gin*, p. 228 (noting that the gin craze peaked in 1743 and that spirit production declined for the next forty years); Warner, *Craze*, p. 3 (similar); J.S. & G.D., "High Spirits," *The Economist* (June 17, 2013), *online at* http://www.economist.com/blogs/graphicdetail/2013/06/daily-chart-9 (reporting that yearly per person gin consumption in Britain in 2012 was only 0.4 liters (or 0.11 gallons) as against 2.2 gallons in 1743).

who hawked from wheelbarrows and baskets and offered neither means nor motive to linger. Even in banning gin generally, the 1736 law specifically targeted
those who sold "about the Streets, Highways, or Fields, in any Wheelbarrow or
Basket . . . ." The 1743 repeal act therefore restricted retail licenses to "Taverns,
Victualling Houses, Inns, Coffee Houses, or Ale Houses," establishments that
offered patrons not just a drink but a place to gather. Moreover, lawmakers hoped
to leverage proprietors' sizeable investments to compel compliance with laws
against keeping unruly houses and serving drunken patrons.[56]

At least in the immediate aftermath of repeal, licensing authorities apparently enforced the new law's restrictions. The *London Evening Post* reported a
week after the repeal took effect that "when many applied for Licences not within
the said Act, . . . they were absolutely refus'd, and put entirely out of Hopes of
obtaining any." And gin consumption promptly fell, dropping 19 percent in the
first year. As duties began to creep higher, annual consumption of gin and other
cheap spirits trended lower—from a high of 2.2 gallons per person in 1743 to just
1.2 gallons in 1752.[57]

Yet the real triumph of gin regulation did not arrive till 1751, when lawmakers
gathered the wisdom gained in long years of gin legislation and crafted the last
major gin act of the era. Beyond doubling license fees and increasing duties by
half, the new act established a web of enforcement mechanisms to thwart any
escape from the regulatory scheme. Like the 1743 law, the new statute imposed
duties on distillers rather than elusive retailers—and added a mechanism for
registering each cask of every distiller to frustrate evasion. And like its prede-
cessor, the 1751 act limited licenses to taverns and similar establishments—but
also specified that any London licensee "shall occupy a tenement or tenements
of the yearly value of ten pounds or upwards," a rule that disqualified many less
substantial retailers. The act provided, moreover, that any unlicensed seller
would forfeit its entire stock of distilled goods. The act hiked the penalties for
second offenders and made third offenders felons, subject to seven years' ser-
vitude in America. It authorized warrants to search the homes and businesses
of suspected offenders. And it forbade distillers to sell knowingly to unlicensed
retailers. Then, to spur others to inform against lawless distillers, the act allotted
half of any assessed fine or costs to the responsible informant *even if* that informant happened to be the same unlicensed retailer who received the liquor in
question, in which case the informant would receive the reward *and* immunity
from prosecution.[58]

---

[56] 9 Geo. 2, ch. 23, § 13 (1736); 16 Geo. 2, ch. 8, § 10 (1743).

[57] Dillon, *Gin*, p. 229–31 (noting stringent enforcement of statutory limits on licensing and 19%
drop in production in 1744); *London Evening-Post*, March 29, 1743, p. 2, *quoted in* Dillon, *Gin*, p. 230
("When many applied . . ."); Warner, *Craze*, p. 3 (supplying per capita consumption figures).

[58] *An Act for Granting to His Majesty an Additional Duty upon Spirituous Liquors* . . . , 24 Geo. 2,
ch. 40, § 1 (1751) (increasing duties payable by the distiller); § 5 (doubling license fee); § 8 (imposing

The verdict of history is that this new law worked. Within a year, gin production had fallen from over seven million gallons to less than four and a half million. By 1757, annual consumption stood at just 0.6 gallons per person—half what it had been five years before—and held more or less steady for another two decades.[59] So the evidence suggests we may trace the happy close of the gin crisis to the 1751 law.

Though some modern readers will view this tidy ending skeptically, the law's success should not shock. The acts of 1743 and 1751 restored the law to rough conformity with mainstream morality, which condemned drunkenness but tolerated necessary or moderate alcohol use. The failed ban of 1736 had strived to impose a rigid moral standard held only by an impassioned few. Moderate drinking, even of distilled alcohol, was the moral norm. The 1751 law, which imposed exactly that, was not doomed to fail.

Looking back in 1795 across the intervening four decades, Edmund Burke appraised and sought to defend gin's moral status. "Undoubtedly there may be a dangerous abuse in the excess of spirits," he wrote, "and at one time I am ready to believe the abuse was great. When spirits are cheap, the business of drunkenness is atchieved with little time or labour . . . ." Here Burke called to mind the fear that had impelled the anti-gin reformers. "[B]ut that evil I consider to be wholly done away. Observation for the last forty years, and very particularly for the last thirty, has furnished me with ten instances of drunkenness from other causes, for one from this." With gin-based drunkenness no longer threatening the social order, gin and other spirits could serve with safety their traditional moral roles rooted in necessity: "Ardent spirit is a great medicine, often to remove distempers—much more frequently to prevent them, or to chase them away in their beginnings. . . . It invigorates the stomach for the digestion of [a] poor meagre diet, [and] . . . it is a medicine for the mind."[60]

---

minimum value on licensed establishments); § 9 (providing for forfeiture and increasing penalties on second and third offenders); §§ 9, 32 (providing for payment to informants even when defendants failed to pay fines); § 10 (authorizing search warrants); § 11 (making it an offense for distiller knowingly to sell to unlicensed retailer and indemnifying and rewarding those unlicensed retailers who inform against their supplier); § 18 (requiring distillers to register casks).

[59] Dillon, *Gin*, p. 263; Warner, *Craze*, p. 3.

[60] Edmund Burke, *Thoughts and Details on Scarcity (1795), in Select Works of Edmund Burke* (Indianapolis: Liberty Fund, 1999), vol. 4, pp. 49, 87–88. My thanks to Don Herzog for pointing me to this passage.

Looking Westward

This sketch of the moral dynamic of the gin ban preludes much of what lies ahead. The rise and fall of American alcohol prohibition replayed many of the same moral themes and raised many of the same questions of public policy, even if the longer timeline and broader geographical reach of that movement demand a more complicated telling.

To begin that story, we cross the Atlantic to America and journey to Philadelphia, where we find the words and thoughts of those who banished English gin just taking root.

3

Prohibition's Rise, Its Fall, and the Reign of Social Drinking

Three months after Parliament voted the 1736 Gin Act into law, news of the ban hit American shores. Benjamin Franklin devoted the first three pages of his *Pennsylvania Gazette* to the story, reprinting in full a London magistrates' report that detailed the city's runaway gin trade and helped spur the reforming spirit in England. Many of Franklin's readers must have lingered over those details that struck near their American homes. Americans, too, knew the "fatal Effects" of liquor on "Morals and Religion." Americans lamented how liquor rendered victims "incapable of hard Labour" and "bold and daring in committing Robberies, and other Offences" and how it drew fathers and sometimes mothers into drinking shops, leaving their children "starv'd and naked at Home." And they deplored how, "with respect to the Women themselves, [liquor] has this further ill Effect, that by inflaming their Blood, and stupifying their Senses, they expose themselves an easy Prey to the Attacks of vi[c]ious Men."

But the liquor that concerned Americans of that era was not gin but rum. As Franklin's correspondent observed in prefacing the magistrate's report, "our RUM does the same Mischief in proportion, as their GENEVA."[1]

America's First Prohibition

Franklin was not the first to color American rum in the same villainous shade as English gin. Among Thomas Wilson's cohorts in England's anti-gin campaign was James Oglethorpe, a fellow member of the Society for Promoting Christian Knowledge. An Oxford dropout who later claimed his father's parliamentary seat, Oglethorpe fought to reform London's prisons. In 1732 he turned his reforming passion westward and sailed for Savannah to found a new colony for "poor Subjects" beset by "Misfortunes and Want of Employment."

Worried his settlers were falling prey to rum's allure, Oglethorpe returned to England and in April 1735 secured the King's and Privy Council's approval of an "Act To [P]revent the Importation and Use of Rum and Brandies in the Province

---

[1] *Pennsylvania Gazette*, July 22–Aug. 2, 1736, pp. 1–3.

Beware Euphoria. George Fisher, Oxford University Press. © Oxford University Press 2024.
DOI: 10.1093/oso/9780197688489.003.0004

of Georgia." While in London, Oglethorpe joined Wilson at a strategy session with Sir Joseph Jekyll, the Gin Act's parliamentary champion, whose earlier support of Oglethorpe's Savannah settlement had won him the fame of Georgia's Jekyll Sound and Jekyll Island. This strategy session bore fruit, for Parliament approved the Gin Act in early 1736—but by then Oglethorpe had returned to Georgia with his own statute and had put in force the Western world's first governmental prohibition of an alcoholic drink.[2]

Like England's Gin Act, Oglethorpe's rum ban survived just seven short years. His settlers despised it—and not just those whose past "Misfortunes and Want of Employment" hinted at old habits of dissipation. Also aggrieved were the strikingly literate settlers whose scathing *Narrative of the Colony of Georgia*, printed in 1741, aired a litany of grievances against Oglethorpe's rule. One of their bitterest complaints targeted Oglethorpe's rigid rum ban. Here the authors anticipated arguments that those demanding repeal of England's gin ban would make two years later. Rum was *necessary*, they said—medically so—and its use *in moderation* was no vice.[3]

That the *Narrative*'s lead author, Patrick Tailfer, was a physician no doubt added weight to the claim of medical need, rooted in worries of impure water. Georgia water, the *Narrative* alleged, did not bear drinking unless purified with alcohol: "[T]he Experience of all the Inhabitants of America will prove the Necessity of qualifying *Water* with some *Spirit*, . . . and the Usefulness of this Expe[di]ent has been sufficiently evident to all the Inhabitants of Georgia who could procure *it*, and use *it* with Moderation." Oglethorpe had heard this advice before. His fellow colonial leader, Thomas Penn, son of Pennsylvania's founder,

---

[2] Andrew Barr, *Drink* (New York: Bantam Press, 1995), p. 288 (noting Oglethorpe's 1732 voyage and 1734 return to England); Patrick Tailfer et al., *A True and Historical Narrative of the Colony of Georgia in America* (Charles-Town, S.C.: P. Timothy, 1741), p. 3 (quoting the King's charter for the colony of Georgia, which hailed it as a haven for the down and out); Peter Clark, "The 'Mother Gin' Controversy in Early Eighteenth-Century England," *Transactions of the Royal Historical Society*, vol. 38 (1988), pp. 63, 74–75 (noting Oglethorpe's membership in the S.P.C.K. and his participation with Wilson in the strategy session with Jekyll); Charles C. Jones, *The History of Georgia* (Boston: Houghton, Mifflin and Company 1883), vol. 1, p. 163 (reporting that Oglethorpe named Jekyll Island in honor of his friend, Sir Joseph); Thomas Hart Wilkins, "Sir Joseph Jekyll and His Impact on Oglethorpe's Georgia," *Georgia Historical Quarterly*, vol. 91, no. 2 (Summer 2007), pp. 119–22, 134; [Thomas Wilson], *Distilled Spirituous Liquors the Bane of the Nation* (London: J. Roberts, 1736), pp. 53–54 (reporting that the Georgia Trustees "have this last Year made an Act *To prevent the Importation and Use of Rum and Brandies in the Province of Georgia*; which Act his Majesty thought proper to . . . receive His Majesty's Royal Approbation, which with the Advice of his Privy Council he was pleased to give accordingly, April 3, 1735"). On Oglethorpe, *see* Edwin L. Jackson, "James Oglethorpe (1696–1785)," *New Georgia Encyclopedia* (2003), *online at* https://www.georgiae ncyclopedia.org/articles/government-politics/james-oglethorpe-1696-1785.

[3] Mark Edward Lender & James Kirby Martin, *Drinking in America: A History* (New York: The Free Press, 1987), p. 34 (noting the 1742 demise of Oglethorpe's rum ban); Tailfer et al., *Narrative of the Colony of Georgia*, pp. 28–29 (complaining of the rum ban).

William Penn, had warned him that "the moderate use of [rum] mixed with Water in the very hottest Weather is very necessary."[4]

Indeed Oglethorpe never intended his settlers to subsist on water alone. In a concession to the need for some other drink, his early plans for Savannah included extensive vineyards for winemaking. And a surviving ration sheet issued to the settlers of Frederica, who sailed with Oglethorpe to Georgia in 1735, promised each adult a quart of molasses a week "for brewing Beer." Older children were allotted half a quart for the same purpose, younger children a third of a quart, and working men an extra pint of "Strong-beer" a day.[5]

Plans for winegrowing and brewing, however, ended in either failure or silence. Tailfer and his coauthors chronicled abortive efforts to cultivate decent grapes. About brewing beer from molasses they said nothing—possibly because the expected trade with the sugar-growing islands of the West Indies never materialized. Though one historian of the colony reported that a Savannah store stocked both beer and wine, Oglethorpe himself complained, "We want Beer here extreamly." Tailfer and his cohort wrote that settlers were put to the "insupportable" task of tilling fields in "the sultry Heat of the Sun," having only "*Water* without any Qualification [as] the chief Drink . . . ." The consequence was "*inflammatory Fevers* of various kinds . . . which brought on to many a Cessation both from Work and Life . . . ."[6]

Taking such complaints to Parliament in 1742, Oglethorpe's sullen settlers won prompt satisfaction. Thomas Stephens, son of the president of Savannah County, presented a petition on behalf of the People of Georgia that described in broad terms "the Failure of [the colony's] Scheme, which has been found to be utterly impracticable." Barely two months later, the full House of Commons resolved in response "[t]hat it will be an Advantage to the Colony of Georgia,

---

[4] Tailfer et al., *Narrative of the Colony of Georgia*, pp. 28–29; Thomas Penn to James Oglethorpe (Aug. 4, 1734), Egmont Papers, 14200, pt. 1, p. 91. On the title page of the *Narrative*, Tailfer styled himself an M.D., and Oglethorpe referred to him as "an Apothecary Surgeon who gives Physick." *The Colonial Records of the State of Georgia* (Allen D. Candler ed., Atlanta: Chas. P. Byrd, 1913), vol. 22, pt. 2, p. 178 (letter from Oglethorpe to the Georgia trustees, July 16, 1739). I thank my research assistant Jason Despain for tracking down the Penn quote.

[5] Tailfer et al., *Narrative of the Colony of Georgia*, p. 27 (noting the intention to establish vineyards); Francis Moore, *A Voyage to Georgia, Begun in the Year 1735* (London: Jacob Robinson, 1744), pp. 4–5 (quoting the ration sheets for the settlers of Frederica). *See also* Lender & Martin, *Drinking in America*, p. 34 (reporting that Oglethorpe and the London trustees of Georgia encouraged settlers to drink "English beer" rather than rum).

[6] Tailfer et al., *Narrative of the Colony of Georgia*, pp. 28–29 (noting the lack of trade with the Sugar Islands); ibid., p. 31 (complaining of field work with no drink but water); ibid., pp. 36–38 (recounting abortive winegrowing attempts); Jones, *History of Georgia*, vol. 1, p. 189 (noting beer and wine at the trustees' store in Savannah); *Colonial Records of Georgia*, vol. 22, pt. 1, p. 275 (letter from Oglethorpe to the Georgia trustees, Oct. 7, 1738) (complaining of beer shortage). In a 1736 letter to the Georgia trustees, Paul Jenys wrote of "the misfortune [that] there has been no Mellasses to be bought in [your] Collony . . . to make Spruce Beer." *Colonial Records of Georgia*, vol. 21, p. 209.

to permit the Importation of Rum into the said Colony from any of the other British Colonies."[7]

Oglethorpe's renegade followers were not the first New World settlers to declare life without rum insupportable. Even Cotton Mather, who stood second to none in his enmity to rum-based drunkenness, acknowledged rum's "*Necessity* . . . both as a *Medicine*" and to protect workers "when Extream *Heat* or Extream *Cold*, Endangers them in their Labours." Mather's words preceded Oglethorpe's Savannah landing by a quarter-century, and for almost half a century after that landing, no prominent voice challenged Mather's injunction "that the ABUSE and EXCESS of the Liquor, is all that is complained of."[8]

The "Liquor" in question was not always rum. British blockades during the Revolutionary War choked off imports of molasses and rum, and even after the war a scarcity of molasses left many rum stills dry. With rum prices rising, rum lost market share to relatively cheap whiskey distilled from grain. Whiskey did not overtake rum as the nation's favorite spirit till the early nineteenth century, but by war's end, the trend lines were fixed. Whether the spirit in question was whiskey or rum or some other, however, the notion of its necessity seemed secure. Hence when Congress dared tax whiskey and like beverages in 1791, latter-day residents of Oglethorpe's Georgia colony agitated to exempt peach brandy—a "necessary of life," one Georgian said, as "all the physicians tell us . . . in this warm climate."[9]

Enter the Philadelphians

Like England's gin ban, Oglethorpe's Georgia experiment foundered in the face of a general popular belief in alcohol's necessity. Over the next century and a half, as the American temperance movement grew from scratch into one of the largest popular crusades in our history, shifts in attitudes toward alcohol centered not

---

[7] *The Annals of Europe for the Year 1742* (London: T. Astley, 1745), pp. 201–03; *The History and Proceedings of the Third Parliament of King George II* . . . (London: Richard Chandler, 1743), pp. 271–72; George Whitefield, *A Continuation of the Account of the Orphan-House in Georgia* . . . (Edinburgh: T. Lumisden & J. Robertson, 1742), p. 18 ("The last Parliament have resolved to support the Colony of Georgia: They have altered the Constitution in [that] . . . [t]hey have allowed the Importation of Rum . . . ."); Jones, *History of Georgia*, vol. 1, pp. 416, 420–21 (supplying Thomas Stephen's identity as son of Savannah President William Stephens).

[8] [Cotton Mather,] *Sober Considerations, on a Growing Flood of Iniquity* (Boston: John Allen, 1708), p. 5.

[9] W.J. Rorabaugh, *The Alcoholic Republic An American Tradition* (New York: Oxford University Press, 1979), p. 53 (noting Georgians demanded exemption from an excise law for peach brandy); ibid., pp. 64–66 (recounting difficulties with molasses importation); ibid., pp. 61, 67–69 (chronicling whiskey's gains on the rum trade); Philanthropos, Letter to Editor, *Augusta Chronicle and Gazette of the State*, vol. 6, no. 268 (Nov. 26, 1791), p. 2 (printing Georgian's letter seeking an excise exemption for peach brandy).

on the perceived immorality of drunkenness—here opinions remained largely unmoved—but on alcohol's perceived necessity. The driving force behind the American temperance movement was therefore not merely moral but scientific. Only as doctors and scientists swept away timeworn dogmas embracing alcohol as a necessity of life could temperance advocates demand first a ban on all distilled liquors and at last full-scale alcohol prohibition.

A different temperance movement, proceeding parallel to the one I chart here, arose from very different tensions. Across colonial America and the early Republic, native tribes beseeched their white occupiers to forbid sale or barter of whiskey and other spirits to Native Americans. Both white traders and government agents had exploited the ferocity of these foreign drugs to gain goods and ground on disastrous terms for the tribes. "My people barter away their best treasures for the white man's miserable firewater," one chief lamented. The prohibitions that resulted, narrowly directed at trade with native tribes, sometimes had moral motives but expressed as well the tribes' economic and territorial anxieties.[10] These bans are a critical component of a shameful chapter in American history, but proceeded separately from the movement among European newcomers to constrain their own drinking. *That* movement could advance only so far while old notions of alcohol's need held firm.

To find the first sustained attacks on the claimed necessity of distilled spirits, let us return to Franklin's Philadelphia and his broad intellectual circle. There we find the earliest standard bearers of this newly scientific assault on alcohol—a mostly forgotten Quaker schoolmaster and abolitionist, Anthony Benezet, and his illustrious and long-celebrated friend, Dr. Benjamin Rush. Despite his lesser fame, Benezet claims first billing, for his 1774 anti-alcohol manifesto may have been the first American publication to call for an all-out ban of distilled alcoholic drinks.

Like Oglethorpe, Benezet drew inspiration from the English anti-gin campaign of the 1730s. His pamphlet's ominous title, *The Mighty Destroyer Displayed*, alluded awkwardly to Stephen Hales's condemnation of "those mighty destroyers and debasers of the human species, *fermented distilled spirituous liquors*."[11]

---

[10] Mark Lawrence Schrad, *Smashing the Liquor Machine: A Global History of Prohibition* (New York: Oxford University Press, 2021), p. 260 (quoting Miami Chief Mihšihkinaahkwa), pp. 257–78 (recounting tribes' advocacy for bans on liquor trade to Indigenous persons); Carl Erik Fisher, *The Urge: Our History of Addiction* (New York: Penguin Press, 2022), pp. 33–36, 40–41 (describing the temperance work of Mohegan minister Samson Occom, Seneca preacher Handsome Lake, and other Native advocates).

[11] Anthony Benezet, *The Mighty Destroyer Displayed, in Some Account of the Dreadful Havock Made by the Mistaken Use as Well as Abuse of Distilled Spir[i]tuous Liquors* (Philadelphia: Joseph Cruikshank, 1774), p. 4 (quoting Hales); *Illustrations of the Literary History of the Eighteenth Century, Consisting of Authentic Memoirs and Original Letters of Eminent Persons* (John Nichols ed., London: Nichols, Son, and Bentley, 1817), vol. 2, pp. 809–10 (quoting a letter from Hales to Dr. William Stukeley, Sept. 25, 1758) (noting Hales's efforts "to rouse the attention and indignation

Hales, a London minister and courtier, served on the council of Oglethorpe's Georgia corporation and authored a 1733 tract on gin's depredations that informed Thomas Wilson's famous advocacy of an English gin ban. In the opening sentence of the *Mighty Destroyer*, Benezet confessed his debt to Hales's work. He likewise drew liberally from Dr. George Cheyne, whose 1724 *Essay of Health and Long Life* inspired Wilson and became a chief text of the English reform movement. And Benezet mimicked Wilson in branding drunkenness "the cheapest of all vices," an epithet echoed in Lord Hervey's anti-gin fusillade during Parliamentary debates about the Gin Act's 1743 repeal.[12]

Benezet led his assault on distilled drinks with a chilling account of the physical toll of those "caustic burning spirits." He reserved his harshest attack, however, for the moral ravages of drink, which he expressed in long-familiar terms of unleashed passions and disabled reason. Distilled liquor "heightens the passions of men and depraves their morals . . . ; the feelings of the mind are gradually benumb'd . . . ." And liquor's power to addict magnified its ills: "[T]here is very great danger of even sober people who use them, with what is termed moderation, becoming habituated . . . ."[13]

Benezet knew all such onslaughts on the liquor trade must fall short if people deemed distilled alcohol a necessity of life. He therefore sought to expose as mistaken two supposed needs for spirits. "It is pretended," he began, "that drams comfort, warm, and defend from the severity of weather" and without them men "should perish with cold." Benezet countered that "the false flash of a dram" warms not nearly so well as the "vital heat" of a sober person. After all, "men did not perish in the coldest countries for want of drams formerly, when they were not to be had."[14]

He challenged, too, the widespread belief that spirits were necessary to purify water. "Amongst the several prejudices in favour of the *mistaken use* of spirituous liquors, there is none gives it a greater sanction or support, than . . . that . . . a moderate quantity of rum mixed with water, is the best and safest liquor that can be drank; hence confirming it, that spirit in one form or other is *necessary*." Even if spirits make the water taste better, Benezet argued, "yet all the bad qualities of

---

of mankind against this mighty debaser and destroyer of the human species . . . those, worse than infernal, spirits . . ."). My thanks to Jason Despain for discovering the Stukeley letter.

[12] Tailfer et al., *Narrative of the Colony of Georgia*, p. 8 (identifying Hales as a councilmember); [Stephen Hales,] *A Friendly Admonition to the Drinkers of Brandy, and Other Distilled Spirituous Liquors* (London: Joseph Downing, 1733); Benezet, *Mighty Destroyer*, pp. 3–4 (citing Hales); ibid., pp. 5, 16–18, 30, 47 (citing Cheyne); ibid., p. 9 ("the cheapest of vices"); Wilson, *Bane of the Nation*, p. 27 ("the *Cheapest of all Vices*"); *Hansard's Parliamentary Debates* (Lords), vol. 12, p. 1311 (1743) (remarks of Lord Hervey) ("the cheapest of all vices").

[13] Benezet, *Mighty Destroyer*, pp. 4–5 (quoting "Dr. Hoffman") ("caustic burning spirits . . ."); pp. 14–15 ("heightens the passions of men . . ."); pp. 37–38 ("there is a very great danger . . .").

[14] Ibid., pp. 6–7.

the water will remain, to which will only be superadded the bad qualities of the spirit." He offered instead several techniques for purifying bad water.[15]

A few years later Benezet rejected two more claims of need for distilled liquors. At the back of his schoolmasterly *Pennsylvania Spelling-Book* of 1779, Benezet added a catechism on temperance and other topics. The imaginary catechist asked, "[A]re not spirituous liquors thought to be of service in many cases?" The pupil's prescribed response confined the legitimate medical use of alcohol to a very small compass: "A very small quantity, may be used for washing sores and such like purposes." Then, borrowing directly from Dr. George Cheyne, the pupil added that distilled liquors "were in former times, kept only in Apothecaries shops for sale, as other drugs . . . ."[16]

Unappeased, the catechist pressed the question of necessity: "Is it not a prevailing opinion, that hard labour could not be supported without the use of strong liquors?" Again the pupil's reply was negative: "But several physicians, particularly Doctor [William] Buchan, . . . tells us that this opinion, tho' common, is very erroneous; and that on the contrary, 'Men who never tasted strong liquor, are not only able to endure more fatigue, but also live much longer than those who use them daily.'" In yet a third publication Benezet restated his conviction that "very little or no strong liquor is *necessary* at those [harvest] times . . . . If such labour was carried on with steadiness and proper moderation, there would certainly be no *need* of a recruit of strength being sought for by that means . . . ."[17]

Rush's Anti-Rum Campaign

Benezet's schoolbook catechism, in which an invented American pupil quotes British doctors Cheyne and Buchan, confessed Benezet's limited authority on what was concededly a medical question. For while the sin of alcohol *abuse* was a moral matter, the claim of distilled alcohol's legitimate *use* was typically medical—and on such questions Benezet carried no portfolio. His limited influence on the course of the American temperance movement therefore may trace to his humble schoolmaster station. The enormous impact of his friend and townsman Benjamin Rush, in contrast, owed much to Rush's rank as the fledgling

---

[15] Ibid., pp. 27–28 ("Amongst the several . . .") (emphasis added); ibid., p. 29 ("yet all the bad qualities . . ."); ibid., pp. 29–30 (suggesting purification techniques).

[16] Anthony Benezet, *The Pennsylvania Spelling-Book or Youth's Friendly Instructor and Monitor* (Dublin: John Gough, 6th ed. 1800), pp. 119–20; George Cheyne, *An Essay of Health and Long Life* (London: George Strahan, 1724), p. 43 ("They were formerly kept in England, as other Medicines are, in *Apothecaries Shops*, and prescrib'd by Physicians . . . .").

[17] Benezet, *Pennsylvania Spelling-Book*, pp. 121–22; [Anthony Benezet,] *Remarks on the Nature and bad Effects of Spirituous Liquors* [Philadelphia: n.p., 1775?], pp. 5–6 (emphasis added).

nation's foremost physician and father of American psychiatry, whose image till recently graced the crest of the American Psychiatric Association.[18]

Historians portray Rush as a Revolutionary stock figure. Born to a family of middling means and fatherless at five, Rush succeeded by dint of distant family connections, who secured him a sound education, together with his own rich endowments: a strong mind, a fine pen, and a New World knack for winning fame and famous friends. He finished college by fifteen. By twenty-five he had befriended Franklin and taken a professorship. At thirty he won election to the Continental Congress and signed the Declaration of Independence. He was a correspondent of George Washington, John Adams, and Patrick Henry and a confidante of Thomas Paine. By thirty-five he had served as physician general of the Revolutionary Army; by forty-five he was the best-known doctor in America.[19]

This glittering Revolutionary resume obscures deep flaws and complex virtues. Rush resigned as surgeon general after falling out with Washington and largely withdrew from politics, keeping only Adams among his coterie of famous friends. He boosted himself and his work relentlessly but with mixed success, sometimes failing to publish and sometimes seeing published works ignored. And his fondness for purgatives and bloodletting, which he prescribed for a remarkable range of ills, prompted doubts of his curative wisdom. Yet if we may trust his own account, Rush walked mostly in the right path. Closed by his Presbyterian upbringing from the elite Episcopalian and Quaker circles of the city, he ministered instead to the poor, often without pay, picking lice from his clothes after sitting bedside by patients stricken with consumption or plague.[20]

---

[18]   David Freeman Hawke, *Benjamin Rush: Revolutionary Gadfly* (Indianapolis: The Bobbs-Merrill Company, Inc., 1971), p. 6 (calling Rush in his day "the foremost physician in the United States"); ibid., p. 291 (noting Rush has been titled the "father of American psychiatry"). The American Psychiatric Association announced in May 2015 that its logo no longer would feature Rush's image, though the old seal still will be used for ceremonial purposes. *See* American Psychiatric Association, "APA Unveils New Logo at Opening Session" (May 16, 2015), *online at* http://www.psychnews.org/update/update_AM_15_2_d.html.

[19]   Rush was born on January 4, 1746 (N.S.). His father died in July 1751. Samuel Finley, an uncle on Rush's mother's side, sponsored his early education. Rush took his bachelor's degree from what is now Princeton University in September 1760. He was appointed the College of Philadelphia's first professor of chemistry in 1769 and physician general of the Revolutionary Army early in 1777. Hawke, *Revolutionary Gadfly*, pp. 8, 11–12, 70, 86, 372; *The Autobiography of Benjamin Rush: His 'Travels Through Life' Together with His Commonplace Book for 1789–1813* (George W. Corner ed., Princeton: The American Philosophical Society, 1948), pp. 35–36, 55, 113–14, 119, 131; *Letters of Benjamin Rush* (L.H. Butterfield ed., Philadelphia: American Philosophical Society, 1951), vol. 1, pp. 152, 180, 182, 587.

[20]   *See* Rush, *Autobiography*, p. 79–80 (explaining religious rivalries in Philadelphia, Rush's exclusion from Quaker and Episcopalian circles, and his reasons for serving the poor); ibid., pp. 83–84 (describing his ministries to the poor); ibid., pp. 133–37 & n.13 (discussing his growing disaffection with Washington and resignation from the army); *Letters of Benjamin Rush*, vol. 1, pp. 182–84 & n.1; vol. 2, 1197–1208 (letter from Rush to Patrick Henry complaining of Washington and editor's appendix detailing Rush's relationship with Washington); Ron Chernow, *Alexander Hamilton* (New York: Penguin Press, 2004), p. 449 (suggesting Rush's purgatives and bloodletting debilitated yellow fever patients). Rush's "Directions for the Cure of Sundry Common Diseases" included

And whenever not working, he wrote. He wrote compulsively, and while he wrote on many topics outside his field—opposing the death sentence and slavery (though he owned a slave), backing prison reform and the proper education of girls—he wrote mostly in the spirit of reform.[21] Hence when Rush took up the matter of alcohol abuse, he did so as America's leading physician—but a physician of a peculiarly moralizing stripe.

Rush fixed his reforming zeal on the menace of distilled liquor. In 1772, at just twenty-six, he printed a broadside on that topic as one of three *Sermons to Gentlemen upon Temperance.*[22] He followed with a stream of pamphlets and lectures that ran forty years to his death. The overwhelming reception of one pamphlet—*An Enquiry into the Effects of Spirituous Liquors*, first printed in Philadelphia in about 1784—won him greater fame in his lifetime and for a century beyond than any other work, save perhaps his essays on the young science of psychiatry.[23]

Grasping the *Enquiry*'s potential, Rush financed an early printing, secured annual reprintings, and shipped copies to local friends and points abroad.[24] Between the first and second printings he scrubbed the pamphlet's parochial references to rum drinking in Pennsylvania and rendered them universally American. His efforts repaid him, for the *Enquiry* lived on. Before Rush's death in 1813 it had run through at least seven editions. By 1850, the American Tract Society had distributed a reported 172,000 copies, and in 1885 temperance forces

repeated recommendations for bleeding and purging. *See* Hawke, *Revolutionary Gadfly*, pp. 395–98 (reprinting Rush's "Directions").

[21] On Rush's purchase of a slave, see Hawke, *Revolutionary Gadfly*, p. 84.

[22] Benjamin Rush, *Sermons to Gentlemen upon Temperance and Exercise* (Philadelphia: John Dunlap, 1772). Parts of this essay had appeared in the *Pennsylvania Gazettes* of December 26, 1771 (page 1), and January 9, 1772 (page 1), and in the *Pennsylvania Packet* of February 17, 1772 (page 1). *See* Hawke, *Revolutionary Gadfly*, pp. 94–96 (discussing this essay).

[23] The first publication date of the *Enquiry* is uncertain, as its earliest versions are undated. It was in print at least by summer 1784, as a correspondent of Rush acknowledged receiving a copy that July. See the very helpful note of editor L. H. Butterfield in *Letters of Benjamin Rush*, vol. 1, pp. 272–73 n.1. For consistency's sake, I will refer to this pamphlet in my text as the *Enquiry*, though Rush titled most of the later editions the *Inquiry*.

[24] John A. Woods ed., "The Correspondence of Benjamin Rush and Granville Sharp 1773–1809," *Journal of American Studies*, vol. 1 (1967), pp. 1, 25 (reporting in a letter to English abolitionist Granville Sharp on June 5, 1785, that "[t]he tract upon the abuse of spirits, was printed at my own expence, and has had an extensive circulation."); *Letters of Benjamin Rush*, vol. 1, p. 272 n.1 (noting Rush had sent a copy to Rev. John King); ibid., pp. 272–73 n.1 (editor's note reporting over twenty different pamphlet printings of the *Enquiry*); ibid., p. 460 (claiming in a letter to Jeremy Belknap on May 6, 1788, that he had "every year for several years past republished the enclosed tract two or three weeks before harvest"); Rush, *Autobiography*, p. 290 (noting in 1810 he had "sent a copy of the 3rd edition of my inquiries to Jno. [Quincy] Adams Esqr. at Petersburgh . . . to be made public in Russia"); ibid., p. 296 (reporting he sent 1,000 copies to the Presbyterian General Assembly meeting in Philadelphia in 1811); Hawke, *Revolutionary Gadfly*, p. 277 (noting that London bookseller Charles Dilly, who occasionally served as Rush's publisher, had arranged a reprinting of the *Enquiry* in London's *Gentleman's Magazine* in 1786).

celebrated the centenary of its publication as the centenary of the American temperance movement. Even in 1919, on the brink of national prohibition, Elizabeth Tilton would write that "this voice from the medical profession probably did more than any one thing to lay the foundation of the temperance reform."[25]

Rush's Anti-Rum Morality

Rush shared Augustine's concern that "reason, which presides in the mind, ought like a king in control to restrain the impulses of the lower flesh . . . ." In a 1788 address for college students, he reflected on the personal morality of drunkenness in distinctly Augustinian and Puritan strains. "What dreadful catastrophe," Rush asked of an imaginary patient driven mad by drink, "has dethroned his reason, and converted this man, made originally in the image of God, into a beast of prey?"[26] Distilled liquors "impair the memory, debilitate the understanding, and pervert the moral faculties." They reduce the drunkard to a "state of langour and stupidity" and bestial mimicry: "In folly, . . . a calf,—in stupidity, an ass,—in roaring, a mad bull,—in quarrelling, and fighting, a dog,—in cruelty, a tiger,—in fetor, a skunk,—in filthiness, a hog,—and in obscenity, a he-goat." We can find such allusions centuries earlier: "[T]he[y] spue like dogges, howe grunte the[y] like hogges," wrote the unnamed author of the 1545 *Invective ageinst Glotony and Dronkennes*.[27]

Even Caesarius's parable—once thought Augustine's—about animals refusing to drink past their needs found its way into Rush's writing, albeit in an especially

---

[25]   Compare the *Enquiry* of 1784 (Philadelphia: Thomas Bradford), pp. 244, 249, with the *Inquiry* of 1790 (Boston: Thomas and Andrews), pp. 4, 10–11; *Letters of Benjamin Rush*, vol. 1, p. 273 n.1 (noting Rush's practice of reprinting the *Enquiry* before each harvest and the distribution by 1850 of 172,000 copies by the American Tract Society); Ernest H. Cherrington, *The Evolution of Prohibition in the United States of America* (reprint Montclair, N.J.: Patterson Smith, 1969 (1920)), p. 219 (noting an 1884 resolution by the General Conference of the Methodist Episcopal Church to celebrate the centennial of the *Enquiry* as the centennial of the American temperance movement); Elizabeth Tilton, "Landmarks in the History of Prohibition in the United States," in Raymond Calkins, *Substitutes for the Saloon* (New York: Houghton Mifflin Co., 2d ed. 1919), pp. 303, 304.

[26]   St. Augustine, Sermon 8, "On the Plagues of Egypt and the Ten Commandments of the Law," in *The Works of Saint Augustine: A Translation for the 21st Century*, vol. III/1 (Edmund Hill trans., Brooklyn: New City Press, 1990), ¶ 8, p. 245; [Benjamin Rush], "An Oration on the Effects of Spirit[u]ous Liquors upon the Human Body," *American Museum*, vol. 4 (Oct. 1788), p. 325. Though unsigned, the cited oration surely was Rush's work. On October 7, 1888, Rush wrote to Boston minister Jeremy Belknap, "I enclose you an oration which I composed for Dr Clarkson's youngest son against spirituous liquors." *Letters of Benjamin Rush*, vol. 1, pp. 489–90. L. H. Butterfield, who edited Rush's letters, reported that Rush intended to deliver the oration at Dr. Clarkson's son's graduation from Princeton. *See ibid.*, p. 491 n.5. The oration's full title, as printed in *American Museum*, makes reference to that event: "An oration on the effects of spirit[u]ous liqors upon the human body, and upon society; *intended to have been delivered at a late commencement.*" (Emphasis added.)

[27]   Rush, *Inquiry* (New-Brunswick: A. Blauvelt 1805), p. 5 ("state of langour . . ."); ibid., p. 6 ("In folly, . . ."); ibid., p. 10 ("impair the memory . . ."); *An Invective ageinst Glotony and Dronkennes* (London: Richard Lant and Richard Bankes, 1545), p. 19 (my pagination).

literal form. Rush told of a goat invited by his master into a tavern "and drenched with some of his liquor. The poor animal staggered home with his master, a good deal intoxicated," Rush wrote. "The next day he followed him to his accustomed tavern. When the goat came to the door, he paused: his master made signs for him to follow him into the house. The goat stood still. An attempt was made to thrust him into the tavern. He resisted . . . . His master," Rush concluded, "was so much affected by a sense of shame in observing the conduct of his goat to be so much more rational than his own, that he ceased from that time to drink spirituous liquors." Here again the author of the 1545 *Invective* anticipated Rush: "[T]he verie brute and unreasonable beastes have in this more reason then men."[28]

Like many moral authorities before him, Rush condemned the incontinence of drunkenness in part because it led so readily to sexual incontinence: "Hence the frequent transition from the bottle to the brothel!" he wrote. He followed Caesarius and a whole train of late medieval and Puritan writers in making the point with the story of Lot lying with his daughters: "The incestuous gratification of the sexual appetite . . . was the effect, we are told, of the intemperate use of wine." Rush sorely lamented how drunkenness prompted "immodest actions" in women, "who, when sober, are uniformly remarkable for chaste and decent manners."[29]

Beyond sexual incontinence, drunkenness led to the distinctive incontinence of barnyard animals: A drunk sometimes "falls into a profound sleep," Rush wrote, "with such a relaxation of the muscles which confine the bladder and the lower bowels, as to produce a symptom which delicacy forbids me to mention." The result was to render the drinker "an object of pity *and disgust* to his family and friends."[30]

Rush's Assault on Necessity

Just as schoolmaster Benezet held no portfolio as a doctor, Rush held none as a moralist. So while Rush's moral views may have animated his writings, his enormous influence traces to his place at the pinnacle of American medicine. True, Rush was not the first doctor to write of the physical evils of hard drink.

[28] Rush, *Inquiry* (New York: Cornelius Davis, 1811), pp. 28–29 ("A noted drunkard was once followed . . ."); *Invective ageinst Glotony and Dronkennes*, p. 11 (my pagination).

[29] Benjamin Rush, *Medical Inquiries and Observations upon Diseases of the Mind* (Philadelphia: John Grigg, 4th ed. 1830), p. 349; *Saint Caesarius of Arles: Sermons, vol. 1 (vol. 31 of The Fathers of the Church: A New Translation* (Mary Magdeleine Mueller trans., New York: Fathers of the Church, 1956)), p. 234 (quoting from sermon 46: "The extent of the evil of drunkenness is clearly shown in the case of Lot and his daughters. When he was drunk with wine, he lay with his daughters and was not aware of it."); Rush, *Inquiry* (1805 ed.), p. 4 ("immodest actions" and "who, when sober . . .").

[30] Rush, *Inquiry* (1805 ed.), p. 5 (emphasis added).

Dr. William Buchan, for one, had cataloged the consumptions, convulsions, gout, and gravel of heavy drinkers in his 1769 treatise, *Domestic Medicine*.[31] Rush's distinctive contribution to the rise of the temperance movement was his full-fledged, well-credentialed assault on long-unquestioned notions of the necessity of distilled liquors, which Buchan had left unexamined.

Like Benezet, Rush believed that absent the excuse of necessity, the distinction between the *use* and *abuse* of distilled liquors dissolved: "In order to put an end to the desolating effects of spirituous liquors, it will be proper for our ministers to preach against, not the *abuse* of them only, but their *use* altogether. They are never *necessary* but in sickness: and then they are better applied to the outside, than to the inside of the body."[32]

At the core of his famous *Enquiry*, therefore, Rush turned a newly skeptical eye on old notions of necessity. Writing with the portentous air of a manifesto, he announced he would "now take notice of the occasions and circumstances which are supposed to render the use of ardent spirits *necessary*, and endeavour to shew that the arguments in favour of their use in such cases are founded in error, and that in each of them, ardent spirits, instead of affording strength to the body, increase the evils they are intended to relieve." First he took aim at the common prejudice, often voiced in Parliamentary debates about the Gin Act, that spirits are "*necessary* in very cold weather." Rush's rebuttal anticipated the view of modern scientists that by raising blood to the skin, alcohol generates the illusion of warmth even as the body sheds heat more rapidly than before: "[T]he temporary warmth [spirits] produce, is always succeeded by a greater disposition in the body to be affected by cold." One can find real warmth, Rush said, in heavy clothes and a hearty meal.[33]

Turning next to the opposite prejudice—that spirits "are said to be necessary in very warm weather"—Rush wrote that one might as well throw oil on a burning house "as pour ardent spirits into the stomach, to lessen the effects of a hot sun upon the skin." Spirits "increase, instead of lessening the effects of heat upon the body, and thereby dispose to diseases of all kinds." Here Rush stood on shakier scientific ground, but his citation of similar conclusions reached by a recent study of rum use among British soldiers in the West Indies added apparent heft to his stance.[34]

---

[31] William Buchan, *Domestic Medicine; or, the Family Physician* (Philadelphia: John Dunlap, 1772), *Domestic Medicine*, p. 58.

[32] Benjamin Rush, "An Address to the Ministers of the Gospel of Every Denomination in the United States, upon Subjects Interesting to Morals" (June 21, 1788), in *Essays Literary, Moral and Philosophical* (Michael Meranze ed., Schenectady: Union College Press, 1988), pp. 67–68 (emphasis added).

[33] Rush, *Inquiry* (1805 ed.), pp. 12–13 (emphasis added).

[34] Rush, *Inquiry* (1805 ed.), pp. 13–14.

He treated with equal disdain the belief that "ardent spirits lessen the effects of hard labour upon the body." After all, look at the horse: "[W]ith every muscle of his body swelled from morning till night in the plough, . . . does he make signs for a . . . glass of spirits to enable him to cleave the ground . . . ?—No—he requires nothing but cool water, and substantial food." In a line that rang throughout the temperance debates of the nineteenth century, Rush declared simply, "There is no nourishment in ardent spirits." They may give the illusion of strength, but "weakness and fatigue" always follow.[35]

Indeed there were "only two cases . . . in which spirituous liquors are innocent or *necessary*"—and each involved the use of spirits as medicine. When exhaustion prompts faintness or blood stoppage, Rush said, "the sudden stimulus of spirits may be necessary." Here he appealed to "the advice of Solomon, who confines the use of 'strong drink' only to him 'that is ready to perish!' " (Prov. 31:6.) Then, too, "when the body has been long exposed to wet weather, and more especially if cold be joined with it, a moderate quantity of spirits is not only proper but highly useful to . . . prevent a fever." Rush made no attempt to reconcile this advice with his earlier denial that "spirituous liquors lessen the effects of cold upon the body."[36] It seems he deemed *wet* cold a different matter.

Yet even when using spirits as medicine, a wise doctor would use them sparingly: "So apprehensive am I of the danger of contracting a love for spirituous liquors, by accustoming the stomach to their stimulus, that I think the fewer medicines we exhibit in spirituous vehicles the better." Or, as Rush wrote to a friend, spirits "are safe in those medicines only which are given in *drops*."[37]

Though medical necessity excused occasional use of spirits, habitual use claimed no license. So when Rush and other members of the Philadelphia College of Physicians petitioned the young American Congress in 1790 to raise excises on distilled liquors, they argued without qualification that "the habitual use of distilled spirits, in any case whatever, is wholly unnecessary; that they neither fortify the body against the morbid effects of heat or cold, nor render labor more easy nor more productive . . . ." Besides, the petitioners said, "there are many articles of diet and drink, which are not only safe and perfectly salutary, but preferable to distilled spirits, for the above-mentioned purposes."[38]

---

[35] Rush, *Inquiry* (1805 ed.), p. 14.

[36] Rush, *Enquiry* (1784 ed.), pp. 244–45 (emphasis added). Rush retained the distinction between ordinary exposure to very cold weather and long exposure to wet, cold conditions in later editions of the *Inquiry*. Rush, *Inquiry* (1805 ed.), pp. 13–14.

[37] Rush, *Enquiry* (1784 ed.), pp. 247–48 ("So apprehensive am I . . . "); *Letters of Benjamin Rush*, vol. 1 (letter to John Coakley Lettsom, Aug. 16, 1788), pp. 479–80.

[38] "Deleterious Effects of Distilled Spirits on the Human System," in *American State Papers: Miscellaneous* (Washington: Gales and Seaton, 1834), vol. 1, no. 16, pp. 20–21 (Dec. 27, 1790), *quoted in* John Allen Krout, *The Origins of Prohibition* (New York: Alfred A. Knopf, 1925), p. 70; *Letters of Benjamin Rush*, vol. 1, pp. 479, 480 (letter to John Coakley Lettsom, Aug. 16, 1788) (mentioning the petition); ibid., p. 481 n.3 (editor's note quoting the petition and reporting

Rush and the Softer Alcohols

Among these "safe and perfectly salutary" drinks Rush counted the various fermented beverages—beer, alcoholic cider, and wine. Of these he spoke with an unguarded fondness that embarrassed the stricter temperance reformers of a later generation, who hailed Rush as their patron but apologized for his apostasy. It was "a sign of progress of our state in wealth and happiness," he wrote, "that a single brewer in Chester county sold above 1000 barrels of beer last year." He deemed cider—that "excellent liquor"—to be "perfectly inoffensive and whole-some." And of "good old wine," he declared, "It must be a bad heart indeed that is not rendered more chearful and more generous by a few glasses . . . ." Rush published recipes for homemade beers and wines and even cited the pleasant-ness of maple beer as a reason to extend legal protection to the sugar maple tree.[39]

While Rush can claim to have catalyzed the American temperance move-ment, therefore, the total-abstinence movement that swept the nation in the 1830s was never his brainchild. For him, fermented drinks stood apart from the despised ardent spirits because they raised no similar moral objection and made quite legitimate claims of need. On moral grounds they escaped fault by posing so little risk of intoxication. Rehearsing an argument made by Bishop Thomas Secker during Parliamentary debates about the Gin Act half a cen-tury earlier, Rush suggested a drinker could not stomach enough beer or wine to get drunk: "Fermented liquors contain so little spirit, and that so intimately combined with other matters, that they can seldom be drunken in sufficient quantities to produce intoxication . . . without exciting a disrelish to their taste, or pain, from their distending the stomach." Today getting drunk on beer is no great feat. But in a day when even the abstemious John Adams, who railed against "this degrading, beastly vice of intemperance," began each day with a tankard of

---

that "the substance and style attest BR's collaboration, and he was in fact on the committee appointed to prepare it").

[39] *Letters of Benjamin Rush*, vol. 1, p. 273 n.1 (editor's note: "[Rush's] nineteenth-century followers were obliged to apologize for his insidious recommendation of wine and beer as substitutes for spirits."); Rush, *Enquiry* (1784 ed.), p. 246 ("a sign of progress . . ."); ibid., pp. 245–46 ("excellent liquor"); ibid., p. 246 ("It must be a bad heart . . ."); [Benjamin Rush,] *Sermons to the Rich and Studious, on Temperance and Exercise* (London: Edward and Charles Dilly, 1772), p. 41 ("good old wine"); *Letters of Benjamin Rush*, vol. 1, pp. 587, 593, 595 (letter to Thomas Jefferson, July 10, 1791) (calling for protection of the sugar maple tree). Rush published recipes for maple beer and maple wine in Agricola [Benjamin Rush], "Advantages of the Culture of the Sugar Maple-Tree," *American Museum*, vol. 4 (Oct. 1788), pp. 349, 350, and two recipes for apple wine in Rush, *Inquiry* (1805 ed.), pp. 17–18. David Freeman Hawke has noted Rush once drank a quart of beer while stopping in his travels and sometimes had a pint and a half of Madeira after dinner. Hawke, *Revolutionary Gadfly*, pp. 300, 303. On Rush's authorship of the *American Museum* essay, *see Letters of Benjamin Rush*, vol. 1, pp. 490–91 n.2.

cider, the beverages were less potent, and the average person's alcohol tolerance greater.[40]

Even if beer, cider, and wine posed *some* risk of drunkenness, they escaped Rush's moral censure by staking credible claims of need. Beer and cider had little enough alcohol to serve as food. "It abounds with nourishment," Rush wrote of beer, "hence we find many of the common people in Great-Britain endure hard labour with no other food than a quart or three pints of this liq[uo]r, with a few pounds of bread a day." Wine, too, was "nourishing," though the principal service of this "sovereign antidote to disease and care" was medical. "In chronic diseases, which are accompanied with a languor of the whole system, which shows itself in a more especial manner in the *stomach*, wine is a sovereign remedy. It was to relieve a complaint of this kind that St. Paul prescribed it to his son Timothy." Then, too, wine differed from distilled spirits in serving a social function. "Unlike ardent spirits, which render the temper irritable, wines generally inspire cheerfulness and good humour." So wine drinkers rarely drank alone: wine "derives its relish principally from company, and is seldom like spirituous liquors drank in a chimney corner or in a closet."[41]

Beyond serving as food, medicine, and social salve, fermented drinks filled a final, far-reaching need: they supplied a safe daily beverage when water seemed risky. Over the years Rush's views on water's merits as a daily drink proved unstable. Indeed we may trace in his writings the same gradual embrace of water that a few decades later would characterize the broader temperance movement and help spark the fever for total abstinence.

Throughout the first two decades of his career, Rush warned against one particular form of water drinking—consuming too much cold water on a very hot day. He wrote that in some Philadelphia summers "four or five persons have died suddenly from this cause, in one day."[42] So grave was the danger that in 1770 he advised those who could not wait for their water to warm to spike it with spirits instead, for "this infallibly prevents the water doing any harm." Returning to the topic three years later, Rush dropped this endorsement of spirits and instead plugged laudanum, a solution of opium in alcohol, as an antidote to the

[40] Rush, *Inquiry* (1805 ed.), p. 3; Rorabaugh, *Alcoholic Republic*, p. 6 (quoting a letter from Adams to William Willis (Feb. 21, 1819), *in The Works of John Adams* (Charles Francis Adams ed., Boston: Little Brown and Company, 1856), vol. 10, p. 365, and noting Adams's cider drinking).

[41] Rush, *Enquiry* (1784 ed.), pp. 245–46 ("It abounds with nourishment . . ."); ibid., p. 246 (deeming wine "nourishing" and noting that it "derives its relish principally from company"); [Rush], *Sermons to the Rich*, pp. 30–31 ("In chronic diseases . . ."); ibid., p. 41 ("sovereign antidote . . ."); Rush, *Inquiry* (1805 ed.), p. 17 ("Unlike ardent spirits . . .").

[42] Benjamin Rush, "An Account of the Disorder Occasioned by Drinking Cold Water in Warm Weather, and the Method of Curing It," *in Medical Inquiries and Observations* (London: C. Dilly, 3d ed. 1789), p. 150 (reprinting a 1773 essay). David Freeman Hawke noted in his biography that Rush wrote this essay on the dangers of cold water in 1773, but left it unpublished till 1789. Hawke, *Revolutionary Gadfly*, p. 101.

deadly effects of cold water. In August 1780, he wrote John Adams that with temperatures in Philadelphia hitting ninety-five degrees, "[m]any have died from drinking cold water . . . ." By 1793 he could report with pride that after his essay on the dangers of drinking cold water had been posted about town, the city's death toll from that cause had plunged from twenty or thirty a year to just two persons in the previous two years.[43]

Nor did Rush much approve of drinking *hot* water, at least when brewed as tea or coffee. He wrote in 1773 that his revered teacher, Dr. William Cullen, "considers both Tea and Coffee as *deleterious*, and having mischievous effects on the nervous system." The next year Rush despaired of "the ravages which TEA is making upon the health and populousness of our country" and of the "complicated diseases" this "hydra" had introduced.[44]

Hence in the first edition of his famous *Enquiry*, printed in about 1784, Rush never counseled spirit drinkers to take up coffee or plain water instead. Rather, he recommended cider, beer, wine, or a concoction of vinegar or buttermilk mixed with sweetened water. Of tea he said grudgingly that while he was "no advocate for [its] general or excessive use," when drunk "in moderate quantities with sugar and cream or milk, I believe it is in general innocent, and at all times to be preferred to spirituous liquors." But of water he could muster no praise: "[T]he experience of all ages and countries, and even nature herself all seem to demand drinks more grateful and more cordial than simple water."[45]

Yet by the time Rush issued the third edition of his *Enquiry* in 1805, he had grown less rabid about water. Once, in an anomalous essay published years before, he had styled water "the most simple and wholesome drink." Now he returned to that theme. He gave "SIMPLE WATER" first billing among alternatives to distilled spirits and said he knew of many persons "who never drank any thing but water, and enjoyed uninterrupted good health." He likewise relented in his antipathy to coffee, which he deemed "agreeable and exhilarating." Sandwiched between his benedictions of water and coffee, however, was Rush's warm praise of cider, malt liquors, and wine, which he still extended as options to those "unable to relish" plain water.[46]

[43] X.Y.Z. [Benjamin Rush], "[no title]," *Pennsylvania Journal and the Weekly Advertiser* (Aug. 9, 1770), pp. 1, 4; Rush, "Drinking Cold Water in Warm Weather," p. 152 ("I know of but one certain remedy for this disease, and that is LIQUID LAUDANUM."); *Letters of Benjamin Rush*, vol. 1, pp. 254, 255 (letter to John Adams, Aug. 25, 1780); ibid., vol. 2, pp. 629, 630 n.2 (letter to the Humane Society of Massachusetts, Mar. 9, 1793).
[44] Philo-Aletheias [Benjamin Rush], [no title], *Pennsylvania Journal and the Weekly Advertiser* (Dec. 22, 1773), p. 1; Benjamin Rush, *An Oration . . . Containing an Enquiry into the Natural History of Medicine Among Indians in North-America* (Philadelphia: Joseph Cruikshank, 1774), pp. 69–70.
[45] Rush, *Enquiry* (1784 ed.), p. 245 (commenting on water); ibid., pp. 245–47 (recommending various drinks); ibid., p. 248 (commenting on tea).
[46] [Benjamin Rush,] *Sermons to the Rich and Studious, on Temperance and Exercise* (London: Edward and Charles Dilly, 1772), p. 53 ("the most simple . . ."); Rush, *Inquiry* (1805 ed.),

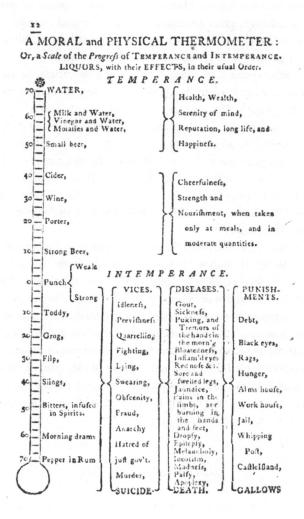

Figure 3.1: Benjamin Rush, "Moral and Physical Thermometer" (1790).

Rush's tenacious tolerance of fermented beverages appears in graphic relief on his "Moral and Physical Thermometer," conceived in about 1789 and republished in almost unchanged form for decades.[47] Figure 3.1 presents one of the thermometer's earliest versions, printed in the *Enquiry*'s 1790 edition.

p. 15 (praising "SIMPLE WATER" and addressing persons "who are unable to relish" water); ibid., pp. 15–18 (praising fermented drinks); ibid., p. 19 ("agreeable and exhilarating").

[47] *Letters of Benjamin Rush*, vol. 1, p. 501 n.2 (editor's note speculating that the thermometer first appeared in 1789 and noting various reprintings); ibid., p. 512 (opp.) (reprinting 1789 version of the thermometer).

Measuring not heat but degrees of temperance, the thermometer shows temperance rising as a drinker gives up strong beer for wine and wine for cider. Yet all these drinks bestow cheerfulness, strength, and nourishment "when taken only at meals, and in moderate quantities." Drinkers of small beer reap even the rewards of health, wealth, reputation, long life, and happiness. At the nether end of the scale, though, as drinkers descend through degrees of intemperance, they suffer worsening health, declining morals, and their just deserts.

An 1811 version of the thermometer, among the last printed in Rush's lifetime, reveals only two adjustments in his attitude toward fermented drinks. The thermometer promises only water drinkers the ultimate rewards of "health and wealth." And it permits only "small"—rather than "moderate"—quantities of cider, wine, and strong beer to those who seek "Cheerfulness, Strength, and Nourishment." But drinkers of small beer still gain "Serenity of Mind, Reputation, Long Life, and Happiness."[48]

Rush's thermometer reinforced the moral dynamic at the core of his analysis of alcohol drinking. Though water was the only perfectly temperate drink, his scheme condoned fermented beverages, for they posed little risk of intoxication and could claim the excuse of necessity. Distilled spirits found no such refuge. Because spirits typically served no need—either medical or nutritional or as a hedge against heat or cold—their sole purpose was self-gratification. Almost all spirit drinkers drank recreationally and therefore suffered the moral censure that befell those who disabled their reason in pursuit of pleasure. Rush's triumphant 1788 claim that "[s]pirituous liquors give way in every part of the United States to beer and cider" shows how readily he reconciled his scorn for spirits with his frequent fondness for fermented drinks.[49]

Rush and the Methodists

Early in his campaign against ardent spirits, Rush proposed attacking the rum traffic legislatively. He recommended in 1784 that Pennsylvania lawmakers consider "whether more laws should not be made to encrease the expence and lessen the consumption of spirituous liquors, and whether some mark of public infamy should not be inflicted by law upon every man convicted before a common magistrate of drunkenness." Five years later, frustrated by the Continental Congress's failure to lay a high tariff on molasses used for rum, Rush despaired to a friend that "[h]uman reason has been employed in vain, and . . . we have nothing to

---

[48] Rush, *Inquiry* (1811 ed.), faceplate.
[49] *Letters of Benjamin Rush*, vol. 1, p. 496 (letter to Jeremy Belknap, Nov. 5, 1788).

hope from the influence of *law* in making men wise and sober." He was now "disposed to believe that the business must be effected finally by religion alone."[50]

When a revised edition of the *Enquiry* appeared in 1805, Rush repeated his call for heavy duties on spirits and penalties for drunkards. Now, though, he suggested that "[t]o aid the operation of these laws, [it would] be extremely useful for the rulers of the different denominations of Christian churches to unite, and render the sale and consumption of ardent spirits a subject of ecclesiastical jurisdiction." And he appealed to the clergy directly: "Ministers of the gospel of every denomination in the United States!—aid me with all the weight you possess in society . . . to save our fellow men from being destroyed, by the great destroyer of their lives and souls."[51]

Happily two Christian denominations already had embraced the cause. "The Methodists, and society of Friends," Rush wrote, "have for some time past, viewed [ardent spirits] as contraband articles . . . ."[52] What Rush presented as a simple religious edict was in truth more complex. For while the Quakers had taken action without Rush's intercession, the far larger congregation of American Methodists did so only after hearing him plead his cause—and Methodists framed their edict in terms Rush might have urged.

Of all American Christian denominations, the Methodists stood most rigidly against alcohol abuse and ranked among the earliest to condemn the trade in distilled liquors. As Methodist minister Henry Wheeler wrote in his 1882 history of the church's role in the temperance movement, Methodists were the first to make "total abstinence from strong drink a part of [their] organic law and a test of Church membership." What's more, American Methodists wielded real force. In 1804 there were by one count 104,000 Methodists in America—more than in Britain, the church's birthplace.[53]

The church's leadership in the American temperance campaign traced to the rigid asceticism of founder John Wesley. As a young man in his native England, Wesley had read Dr. George Cheyne's *Essay of Health and Long Life* and adopted its prescription of a spare and temperate diet. Later, during a nearly two-year stint as the young pastor of James Oglethorpe's Georgia colony, Wesley proved too abstemious even for the residents of that officially rum-starved enclave. As one complained, he "drenched them with the physic of an intolerant discipline."[54]

[50] Rush, *Enquiry* (1784 ed.), p. 249; *Letters of Benjamin Rush*, vol. 1, pp. 520, 521 n.2 (letter to Jeremy Belknap, July 13, 1789).

[51] Rush, *Inquiry* (1805 ed.), pp. 28, 30.

[52] Ibid., pp. 30–31.

[53] Rorabaugh, *Alcoholic Republic*, p. 207 ("Although most denominations had long condemned public drunkenness as sinful, it was revivalistic Methodists who most vigorously opposed alcohol."); Henry Wheeler, *Methodism and the Temperance Reformation* (Cincinnati: Walden and Stowe, 1882), p. 203; Rush, *Autobiography*, p. 324 (noting a minister's report of the number of Methodists in the United States and putting the number in Britain at 94,000).

[54] A.G., "John Wesley," *Dictionary of National Biography* (Sidney Lee ed., New York: The Macmillan Company, 1899), vol. 60, p. 303 (citing a letter Wesley wrote to his mother at age twenty-one

Wesley's views on drunkenness tracked those of Puritan preachers of the late seventeenth century. He opened his 1745 "Word to a Drunkard" with long-familiar themes and phrases:

> Are *you* a Man? God made you a *Man*. But you make yourself a *Beast*. Wherein does a *Man* differ from a *Beast*? Is it not chiefly in *Reason*, in *Understanding*? But you throw away what *Reason* you have. You strip yourself of your *Understanding*.

A likely source of this imagery was Shropshire minister Edward Bury, author of *England's Bane* of 1677. "[W]hat is it that differenceth a Man from a Beast," Bury had asked, "but the use of Reason, but if Reason be drowned, as it is in the *Drunkard* where lies the difference[?]" Bury himself was a borrower, for the same cadences had appeared in the 1545 *Invective ageinst Glotony and Dronkennes*: "In what thyng doth man differ fro brute beastes? [I]s it not by the gift of wit, understandyng, reason, that he received of his master wherby we be lordes and rulers of other creatures? but he that disposeth hymself of his witte by dronkennes, is wurse then any beastes."[55]

In succeeding sentences Wesley's text shadowed Bury's. First Bury: "[T]he *Drunkard* is fitly compared to a Swine for nastiness, for I know not any other Creature that . . . doth delight so much in Swill, and wallowing in the mire . . . ." Now Wesley: "You do all you can to make yourself . . . a *Swine*, a poor, filthy Swine. Go and wallow with them in the Mire!" Again Bury: "[Drunkards] are worse than Beasts who . . . retain what God gave them in the Creation, but [drunkards] do not, they lose not only Gods Image, but the use of Reason . . . ." Now Wesley: "O, how honourable is a *Beast* of God's making, compared to one who makes himself a *Beast*!"[56]

But unlike Bury and so many Puritan tract writers who labored in near obscurity, Wesley broadcast his views on drunkenness to throngs of the faithful. Hence when he and brother Charles Wesley issued General Rules for the United Societies of Methodists on May 1, 1743, they transmuted the preachings of Bury and many others into church doctrine. The Wesleys enjoined followers to avoid evil of every kind, including "[d]runkenness,

---

describing Cheyne's work). Charles Jones details Wesley's ill-starred tenure as pastor of Oglethorpe's Georgia colony. *History of Georgia*, vol. 1, pp. 280–96 (quote from p. 287).

[55] [John Wesley,] *A Word to a Drunkard* ([Bristol,] 1748), p. 2; Edward Bury, *England's Bane, or the Deadly Danger of Drunkenness* (London: Thomas Parkhurst, 1677), p. 4; *Invective ageinst Glotony and Dronkennes*, pp. 16–17 (my pagination). For the original, 1745 publication date of Wesley's *Word to a Drunkard, see* Wheeler, *Methodism*, p. 21.

[56] Bury, *England's Bane*, pp. 5–6; [Wesley,] *Word to a Drunkard*, p. 2.

buying or selling spirituous liquors, or drinking them, *unless in cases of extreme necessity.*"[57]

Both the date and the doctrine are significant. Barely two months earlier, the Wesleys had seen Parliament repeal England's seven-year-old gin ban. Lawmakers had declared that in England's dank winters and fenny realms, gin sometimes was "*absolutely necessary* for the support of nature." The Wesleys agreed that spirits sometimes served real needs, but recognized only the seemingly narrower realm of "extreme necessity," a phrase they did not define. When John Wesley drafted directions in 1744 to govern Methodist Band Societies, formed for more intimate communion and counsel, he called on members "[t]o taste no spirituous liquor, *no dram* of any kind, unless prescrib'd by a physician."[58] It is unclear whether Wesley conceived this rule as stricter than the usual injunction against spirit drinking or instead as an interpretation of it. If an interpretation, the later rule confined the realm of "extreme necessity" to medicinal use of spirits, excluding their use merely to ward off cold.

Whatever the bounds of "extreme necessity," the Wesleys' views of appropriate drinking diverged from those of the 1743 Parliament in a second, far more substantial way. Most lawmakers had agreed with the Earl of Cholmondeley that "[t]he moderate use of spirituous liquors . . . is not what is, or ought to be complained of" and with Lord Carteret that "[t]he vice consists in the immoderate use of" gin.[59] They, unlike the Wesleys, were prepared to condone so much gin drinking as extended beyond the excuse of necessity but stopped short of the forbidden zone of drunkenness. The Wesleys, anticipating the total-abstinence campaigns of the nineteenth century, forbade *all* non-necessary use of spirits, however moderate. For Methodists, then, the bounds of permitted drinking would bloat or shrink depending on notions of liquor's need.

These principles followed Methodism west when the church took root in America in 1766. Soon American Methodists proved more rigidly austere than their forbears. In 1780 they elaborated on the Wesleys' original rule and resolved to "disapprove of the practice of distilling grain into liquor" and to "disown our friends who will not renounce the practice." Again in 1783 they asked, "Should our friends be permitted to make spirituous liquors, sell and drink them in drams?"—and answered emphatically, "By no means . . . ." When the Methodist

---

[57] Wheeler, *Methodism*, pp. 16–17 (quoting the Wesleys' rule (emphasis added)). The Wesleys' rule, word for word, remains church doctrine today. *See* United Methodist Church, "The General Rules of the Methodist Church," *online at* http://www.umc.org/what-we-believe/general-rules-of-the-methodist-church.

[58] *Hansard's Parliamentary Debates* (Lords), vol. 12, p. 1202 (1743) (remarks of Lord Bathurst) (emphasis added); "Directions Given to the Band Societies" (n.p., Dec. 25, 1744), *online at* https://archive.org/stream/rulesofbandsocie468wesl#page/2/mode/2up.

[59] *Hansard's Parliamentary Debates* (Lords), vol. 12, pp. 1215–16 (1743) (remarks of the Earl of Cholmondeley); ibid., p. 1226 (remarks of Lord Carteret).

Episcopal Church in America organized separately from the English Church in 1784, it retained the Wesleys' original injunction against distilled liquors as well as the 1780 and 1783 elaborations. That year the newly independent American church asked whether "our ministers or traveling preachers [may] drink spirituous liquors" and answered with an echo of Wesley's early direction for Band Societies: "By no means, unless it be medicinally."[60] Against the clarity of this rule governing clergy stood the ambiguity of the Wesleys' original rule for everyone else, permitting spirit drinking only "in cases of extreme necessity."

Now enter Dr. Rush, whose 1784 *Enquiry* aimed to debunk old claims about the need for distilled spirits and who declared in a 1789 letter that "religion alone" could mount the battle against spirits. When a conference of American Methodists met in Philadelphia in late September 1788, Rush appeared before them to plead his case against the necessity of distilled liquors. Sadly, Rush left little record of the event. A brief postscript in an October 7 letter noted merely that he and another physician "lately delivered a testimony against [spirituous liquors] in a public conference of the Methodists in this city ... ."[61]

Thankfully, however, Methodist ministers Jesse and Leroy Lee supplied lasting accounts of Rush's efforts to discredit the claimed necessity of spirits. First Reverend Leroy Lee:

> [D]uring the session of this Conference, the celebrated Dr. Rush visited it, and delivered an earnest and animated address on the use of ardent spirits .... He insisted that allowable cases requiring their use were very few, and seldom occurring, and when necessary, *but very little* ought, in any case, to be used; and he besought the Conference to use their influence in trying to put a stop to the use, as well as to the abuse of ardent spirits.

Reverend Jesse Lee added that Rush listed two permissible uses of spirits—the same two medicinal applications he had noted in his *Enquiry* about four years earlier: "[I]f a person was chilled with cold, or wet, or was ready to faint with fatigue, a little might be of service ... ."[62]

When writing of these events almost a century later, historian and minister Henry Wheeler speculated that before Rush's address, some Methodists may have "put a very liberal construction upon the phrase, 'unless in cases of extreme necessity,' and made that a cover under which moderate drinkers could

[60] Wheeler, *Methodism*, pp. 45, 47, 48, 51; *Minutes of the Methodist Conferences, Annually Held in America; From 1773 to 1813, Inclusive* (New York: Daniel Hitt and Thomas Ware, 1813), p. 41.

[61] *Letters of Benjamin Rush*, vol. 1, pp. 489, 490 (letter to Jeremy Belknap, Oct. 7, 1788).

[62] Leroy M. Lee, *The Life and Times of the Rev. Jesse Lee* (Louisville: John Early, 1848), p. 211; Jesse Lee, *A Short Account of the Life and Death of the Reverend John Lee, a Methodist Minister in the United States of America* (Baltimore: John West Butler, 1805), pp. 37–38. I thank Sang Ngo for helping to pin down Rush's participation at the 1788 conference.

hide themselves." His suspicion recalled Augustine's confession that "the necessity [of eating and drinking] is sweet to me," for "my wretched soul ... uses it as a cover and an excuse, rejoicing that ... under the cloak of health it may shelter the business of pleasure." If Methodists likewise smudged the borders of necessity to gratify indulgence, Wheeler said, "it would seem natural that the more stringent temperance men would wish to take away every subterfuge, and make the rule one of *absolute abstinence*."[63]

Strict temperance advocates perhaps found the ammunition they needed in the great Dr. Rush's attack on the purported needs served by distilled spirits. For it appears that during this same 1788 conference, American Methodists struck out the last six words of the Wesleys' rule—"unless in cases of extreme necessity"— and converted the rule's qualified injunction into an absolute ban against "buying or selling spirituous liquors, or drinking them." Though the date of the rule change is uncertain, it was in place by 1789, and Reverend Wheeler "suppose[d it] to have been made at the conference held in Philadelphia, September, 1788."[64]

Wheeler laid the change to Rush's influence. "Dr. Rush's known ability and wide celebrity would give his opinions great weight with the conference. . . . Is it not exceedingly probable that the address of this man produced such conviction, or enkindled such enthusiasm, as led to the change of the rule, thereby removing even the appearance of any indorsement whatever of the use of spirituous liquors[?]" Yet as Wheeler perhaps saw, nothing Rush said warranted this change. On the contrary, in his address to the conference Rush had specified two cases of "extreme necessity" that justified medicinal use of spirits. Hence even Wheeler, an abstaining Methodist minister of the late nineteenth century, could "see no good reason for thus tampering with the rules of the Church." Rather than reflecting any flaw in the Wesleys' original injunction, the change likely "arose from a growing laxity on the part of some, and a corresponding rigidness on the part of others."[65] That is, those Methodists who wished to drink had stretched the confines of strict necessity to forgive their lapses, and those who disapproved responded by forbidding spirits altogether, even when used as medicine.

The new rule was a bridge too far. Harsher still than the English gin ban of 1736, which had outstripped mainstream morality by forbidding even moderate use of gin, the Methodists' rule of 1788 stands among the few in American or British history to ban medically necessary uses. It met a quick fate. Wheeler reported that a 1790 amendment replaced the 1788 rule, which had proved "evidently too rigid for some of the preachers and people," with a gentler condemnation of "[d]runkenness, or drinking spirituous liquors, unless [in] cases

[63] Wheeler, *Methodism*, pp. 52–53; St. Augustine, *Confessions* (Books i–xiii) (F.J. Sheed trans., Indianapolis: Hackett Publishing Company, 1993), 10.31, p. 195.
[64] Wheeler, *Methodism*, pp. 52–53.
[65] Ibid., pp. 52, 54.

of necessity." The latter rule more than reversed the rigidity of 1788. By omitting the modifier "extreme" from the Wesleys' original formula, the 1790 amendment hinted that some lesser degree of "necessity" might justify use of spirits. And by omitting the Wesleys' reference to "buying or selling" spirits, the amendment seemingly condoned profiting from rum. Whether the drafters intended these omissions isn't clear. "By whose authority [the amendment] was done we can not ascertain," Wheeler reported; "no minute was made of the action."[66]

This new rule and its ambiguities survived almost four decades. Not till 1828 did American Methodists clarify that "to discountenance the *needless* use of ardent spirits . . . it is important that we neither drink ourselves (except medicinally), nor give it to visitors or workmen."[67] This interpretation of their 1790 rule at last paid homage to the message Dr. Rush had read at their 1788 conference and to Rush's rejection as *needless* all nonmedicinal use of spirits.

Fleeting as it was, Rush's encounter with the Methodists taught several enduring lessons about the course of the American temperance movement. First was the risk of overreaching mainstream morality. England's gin ban and Georgia's rum ban had fallen after seven short years in great part because the moral mainstream still condoned moderate drinking of spirits and condemned only drunkenness. The Methodists' 1788 rule reached further by denouncing even medicinal use—and hence fell faster. Second was the force of necessity. By challenging old claims that distilled liquors warmed, cooled, and fueled the body, Rush perhaps inspired the Methodists' ill-starred 1788 rule. Long after that rule fell to dust, arguments about alcohol's necessity gathered force, helping power and shape the nineteenth-century temperance debate. And third was the influence of science. For here was America's foremost physician scoffing at the physiological claims long made for spirits—and prompting not only doctors but divines to take heed.

Rush's Broader Influence

Rush lived till 1813—long enough to usher his 1784 *Enquiry* through seven editions and to see its message take hold in institutions that would outlive him. Among the many medical men who read his work was Billy J. Clark, a young doctor in the Hudson River Valley mill town of Moreau. Moved by Rush's arguments, Clark sought the aid of his local Congregational minister, and in 1808 they founded the Temperate Society of Moreau and Northumberland, among America's first temperance organizations. Sometimes called the

---

[66] Ibid., pp. 57.
[67] Ibid., pp. 46; ibid., p. 71 (quoting *Conference Journal* (1828), vol. 1, p. 359) (emphasis added).

Union Temperate Society, the group soon made Rush an honorary member. Subscribers pledged to use no "rum, gin, whiskey, wine, or any distilled spirits, or compositions of the same, . . . except by advice of a physician, or in case of actual disease," or—if wine—at public dinners. The society thereby followed Rush in permitting spirits only as medicine and in exempting beer and malt liquors from censure—and somewhat exceeded him in typically confining wine to its biblical sanction "for thy stomach's sake."[68]

Despite the pioneering role of Dr. Clark, whose society inspired formation of at least one other New York temperance organization, Rush's most influential follower carried not satchel but prayer book. Across the state from Moreau, the Presbyterian pastor of East Hampton, Lyman Beecher, had taken up Rush's *Enquiry* and begun preaching against intemperance as early as 1806. Two decades passed before Beecher, now in the Congregational pulpit of Litchfield, Connecticut, published his widely famous *Six Sermons on . . . Intemperance*, which would rank him second only to Rush among the early leaders of the American temperance movement. "Reprinted during the next decade by almost every temperance organization of consequence, the sermons were"—in historian John Allen Krout's words—"as widely read and exerted as great an influence as any other contribution to the literature of the reform."[69]

Where Rush had written in compact, often bloodless prose, filling a scant nine pages with the *Enquiry*'s first edition, Beecher splashed his florid portraits of the drunkard's fate across a hundred heated pages. He opened as did Increase Mather a century and a half before: "Who hath woe? who hath sorrow? . . . who hath redness of eyes?" But in structure and theme the *Six Sermons* flowed more directly from Rush's work. Hence Beecher took as true Rush's claim that distilled liquors served no need but as medicine. "The use of ardent spirits, employed as an auxiliary to labor," Beecher said, "is insisted on as necessary; but . . . is utterly useless . . . ." Echoing Rush without attribution, he declared, "THERE IS NO NUTRITION IN

---

[68] Though the earliest description of these events I have seen dates to 1833, a half-dozen local newspaper items document the society's existence as early as 1810. *American Quarterly Temperance Magazine*, vol. 1, no. 2 (May 1833), pp. 99–104 (reprinting correspondence from Lebbeus Armstrong, Feb. 4, 1833); Lebbeus Armstrong, *The Temperance Reformation: Its History* . . . (New York: Fowlers and Wells, 1853), pp. 18–23. Examples of early news items include "Union Temperate Society," *Independent American* (Ballston Spa, N.Y.), May 15, 1810, p. 3 (locating the society in Moreau); "An Oration at a Meeting of the Union Temperate Society . . . ," *Saratoga Advertiser*, May 22, 1810, p. 1. My research assistant Brett Diehl, aided by Saratoga County Historian Lauren Roberts and volunteer researcher Lynn Calvin, turned up the earliest of these sources.

[69] Krout, *Origins of Prohibition*, pp. 80–81 & n.16, 105–06; John Kobler, *Ardent Spirits: The Rise and Fall of Prohibition* (New York: G.P. Putnam's Sons, 1973), pp. 51–55; *Autobiography, Correspondence, Etc., of Lyman Beecher, D.D.* (Charles Beecher ed., New York: Harper & Brothers, 1865), vol. 1, p. 177 ("I had read Rush on intemperance . . . ."). The earliest surviving editions of Beecher's *Six Sermons* appear to date to 1827. But a footnote reports, "These Discourses were composed and delivered at Litchfield, in the year 1826 . . . ." Lyman Beecher, *Six Sermons on the Nature, Occasions, Signs, Evils, and Remedy of Intemperance* (New York: American Tract Society, 1827), p. 87 n.*.

ARDENT SPIRIT." Though Beecher allowed the utility of distilled liquor as medicine, he insisted it be kept "in the hands of the apothecary, to be sent for like other medicine, when prescribed."[70]

For all other purposes distilled liquor was needless and therefore properly banned. Hence Beecher posed a two-part syllogism: The "commerce in ardent spirits is unlawful, 1. Inasmuch as it is useless; and, 2. As it is eminently pernicious." Having embraced Rush's verdict on liquor's uselessness, Beecher devoted his labors to proving the syllogism's second premise. Spirits were pernicious in that they "generate[] a host of bodily infirmities and diseases"; they drive the drunkard to neglect his children and torment his wife; and they shackle the drinker in the slavery of addiction. Drunken criminals menace our communities; drunken voters threaten the body politic; and drunken workers will lay waste to our national industries. And the wages of this vice are paid by the virtuous—for sluggish drunkards thrust their "hands deep into your pockets" and "contrive to arrive [at the poorhouse] as early as idleness and excess will give them a passport to this sinecure of vice."[71]

The Necessity Debate: Alcohol for Warmth

Wesley's Methodists, together with Clark's Congregationalists and Beecher's Presbyterians, joined with other Protestant denominations in the evangelical revival movement now known as the Second Great Awakening. Historians of the nineteenth-century temperance movement often trace its strength and breadth to the fervor for social salvation and personal purification fed by this movement. Largely ignored is the force these denominations drew from Rush and others whose scientific advances lay the foundation for temperance reform. For unless congregants agreed with Rush that strong drink made no credible claim of need, the prohibition movement might have died at birth. Gradually over the course of the nineteenth century, advancing medicine, sanitation, and food preservation snapped the strained notions of necessity that for centuries had excused alcoholic indulgence. Suddenly, life without alcohol grew thinkable—and when it did, the old moral accommodation with alcohol broke down.

---

[70] Beecher, Six Sermons, p. 5 ("Who hath woe?"); ibid., p. 18 ("in the hands . . ."); ibid., p. 22 ("The use of ardent . . ."); Rush, Inquiry (1805 ed.), p. 14 ("There is no nourishment in ardent spirits.").

[71] Beecher, Six Sermons, pp. 15–16 (concerning addiction); ibid., pp. 11, 33–37 (discussing "bodily infirmities and diseases"); ibid., pp. 24, 69, 101–02 (discussing neglect of children); ibid., p. 53 (concerning the threat to industry); ibid., p. 54 ("contrive to arrive . . ."); ibid., p. 56 ("hands deep into your pockets . . ."); ibid., p. 57 (mentioning crime); ibid., pp. 57–59 (discussing the threat of drunken voters); ibid., pp. 69–70 (discussing drunkards' treatment of their spouses); ibid., p. 73 ("commerce in ardent spirits . . .").

Among the first of these strained notions to splinter was alcohol's purported power to warm the body. Rush's insistence that spirits "always render the body more liable to be affected and injured by cold" stood only on his stature, not on scientific investigation, and perhaps could not overcome the flush of warmth plainly felt by many drinkers.[72] So the controversy dragged on while doctors and others debated whether the calories shed by drink-swollen capillaries exceeded those added by alcohol.

A half-century after Rush's death the lead article in the September 1868 issue of London's venerable *Fraser's Magazine* declared the question closed and alcohol the loser. Titled "The Alcoholic Controversy," the article recalled that early in the century "it was unhesitatingly believed, here and in America, that brandy and other spirits kept a man warm in severe cold." But new evidence suggested otherwise. "A great shock to this belief came from the first Arctic voyage of Captain Ross, and from those of Parry which followed. Undeniable trial showed that spirits *chilled* men, and were most dangerous."[73] The author did not explain what made the adventurers' trials "[u]ndeniable," but the notoriety of Ross and Parry surely added force to the claim.

Since those Arctic voyages, the scientific evidence against alcohol's warming power had mounted. A simple thermometer placed under a drinker's tongue, the article noted, confirms "alcohol has *lessened* animal heat." To this evidence the author added the long experience of Russians, who knew something about cold and something about alcohol and held the same view. Then there was the opinion of Dr. Francis Anstie, who opposed teetotalism, but nonetheless "concede[d] it as proved ... that when the body is at its normal standard of temperature, a draught of alcohol *chills* it."[74]

Falling far short of today's scientific standards, this evidence found ready acceptance among many nineteenth-century temperance advocates—testimony, perhaps, more to their eagerness for scientific support than to the merits of the studies. Not everyone was persuaded. Five years after the *Fraser's Magazine* article, Henry Lake wrote that Londoners who travel to Scotland or Ireland "very soon recognise the *necessity* of fortifying themselves against the cold or damp with a glass of poteen or mountain dew"—slang for illicitly distilled whiskey.[75] Still the great majority of scientific commentators fell in with the modern view that alcohol lessens body heat.

The explosive popularity of tea and especially coffee likewise challenged claims of alcohol's necessity as a warming agent. "The Alcoholic Controversy"

---

[72] Rush, *Enquiry* (1784 ed.), p. 244.

[73] "The Alcoholic Controversy," *Fraser's Magazine for Town and Country*, vol. 78 (Sept. 1868), p. 294 ("it was unhesitatingly..."); ibid., pp. 294–95 ("A great shock...").

[74] "The Alcoholic Controversy," p. 295.

[75] Henry Lake, "A Drop of Good Beer," *Belgravia*, vol. 9 (Nov. 1872), pp. 62, 63 (emphasis added).

reported that Commodore Parry had replaced chilling spirits with coffee and tea on his polar expeditions and that English stagecoach drivers had made the same substitution, displacing the serial dram-drinking once thought indispensable on open-air winter rides. Coffee and tea were not new, of course. As early as 1724 Dr. George Cheyne had advised that "[a] Dish or two of *Coffee*, with a little *Milk* to soften it, in raw or damp Weather . . . is not only innocent, but a present *Relief.*" But Cheyne, like many of his day, regarded coffee as a novelty unsuited for daily use. Meanwhile tea's high cost and caloric deficit made it for many in Cheyne's day a pointless luxury. A London wag wrote in 1736 of "that EXPENSIVE NOTHING (as a *Great Physician* calls it) TEA" and of the "*Poor, Puny, Starv'd, Sickly, Pale Looking*, HALF-MADE, *Weakly*, TEA-BEGOTTEN Children" born to tea-drinking mothers.[76]

In the United States, tea drinking never gained the favor it found in Britain. Burdened by ties with British tyranny and heavy import duties lasting till the early nineteenth century, American annual tea consumption languished at less than a pound a head as late as 1832. Even so, before 1825 tea outsold coffee, which cost still more, and both cost more per cup than a glass of mixed whiskey. By 1830, the price of coffee had fallen sharply, and when Congress that year yielded to appeals by temperance reformers to abolish the coffee duty, consumption jumped—rising from less than two pounds per person in the 1820s to more than five pounds by about 1835. As a stamp of coffee's mainstream status, the *Baltimore American* deemed it in 1833 "among the necessaries of life."[77]

The Necessity Debate: Alcohol as a Safe Beverage

Greater consumption of coffee and tea helped wash away a second age-old justification for alcohol: its claimed need as a sanitary beverage. Till the mid-nineteenth century, the unhealthfulness of many local water supplies had posed a standing objection to anyone so visionary as to suggest an alcohol ban. When water was unfit, alcohol was the only safe, cheap, and ever ready alternative. Even doctors often agreed. As David Ramsay wrote in 1809 of life in his native South Carolina, "medical theories are made to bend to appetite. Accommodating professional men by their example and advice, recommend [spirituous liquors] as a corrector of the water."[78]

---

[76] "The Alcoholic Controversy," p. 295; Cheyne, *Essay of Health and Long Life*, p. 61; *A Hole to Creep Out at from the Late Act of Parliament against Geneva, and Other Spirituous Liquors* (London: J. Hughs, 1736), p. 2 (my pagination).

[77] Rorabaugh, *Alcoholic Republic*, pp. 99–100 (quoting *Niles Weekly Register*, vol. 44 (1833), pp. 390–91, which in turn quoted the *Baltimore American*) ("among the necessaries of life").

[78] David Ramsay, *Ramsay's History of South Carolina* (Newberry, S.C.: W.J. Duffie, 1858 (1809)), vol. 2, p. 218.

Anthony Benezet anticipated such pretexts in his 1774 pamphlet, *The Mighty Destroyer Displayed*. Inclining toward total abstinence, Benezet directed readers to plain water. *Not* water "made more palatable by mixing spirit with it," he insisted, but what Dr. Cheyne had called "the primitive original beverage." For those who claimed their water wasn't pure, Benezet suggested filtering it through "porous stones, or . . . an earthen vessel, in the bottom of which there is a quantity of sand." Or you could mix water with loam: when "well stirred and left to settle, the noxious parts will subside with the loam, and the water may be drawn off clear and fit for use." No doubt Benezet wrote in earnest, but readers perhaps balked at drinking sand-filtered or loam-soaked water. More plausible were Benezet's advice to boil water and his endorsement of coffee and tea, which "may be truly termed innocent and friendly to our natures."[79]

Though coffee and tea supplied sanitary substitutes for plain water and alcohol, they did not suit every thirst and were not always at hand. And well into the nineteenth century, as W. J. Rorabaugh has written, many Americans lacked a ready source of safe water. Generations of New Yorkers endured brackish wells, meager supply, and frequent epidemics, made worse when flush toilets arrived around 1820, spiking both water consumption and waterborne sewage. In Washington the only piped water in the 1820s was privately owned and served just two Pennsylvania Avenue blocks. And St. Louis residents simply let Mississippi River water stand before they drank it.[80]

Slowly, however, water supplies improved. New Yorkers heralded a new day in 1842, as dammed waters from the Croton River began flowing forty miles south to the City. When their teetotaling mayor filled a basin with iced Croton water at the city's July Fourth celebrations in 1844, he fulfilled the temperance ideal of substituting "Cold Water" for alcohol. Improvement wasn't uniform. Despite a new municipal water system finished in 1848, Boston water smelled strange and looked bad late into the nineteenth century, while smug New Yorkers mocked Chicago's water as a "mixed drink[]." Still the tide had turned, and by mid-century, fear of waterborne disease no longer gave much support to the claim of alcohol's necessity.[81]

---

[79] Benezet, *Mighty Destroyer*, pp. 29–30 ("made more palatable . . ." and "the primitive original beverage" and "porous stones, or . . ." and "well stirred and . . ." recommending boiling); ibid., p. 38 ("may be truly termed . . .").

[80] Rorabaugh, *Alcoholic Republic*, pp. 95–96; "The New York City Water Supply System," ch. 2 of National Research Council, Commission on Geosciences, Environment and Resources, *Watershed Management for Potable Water Supply: Assessing the New York City Strategy* (2000), pp. 45–46.

[81] Rorabaugh, *Alcoholic Republic*, p. 97 (describing the Croton River project); "New York City Water Supply System," pp. 47–48; Rod Phillips, *Alcohol: A History* (Chapel Hill: University of North Carolina Press, 2014), p. 190 (noting Boston's municipal water system); ibid., pp. 214–15 (discussing the importance of fresh water supplies to prohibition's progress); Perry R. Duis, *The Saloon: Public Drinking in Chicago and Boston, 1880–1920* (Chicago: University of Illinois Press, 1983), p. 95 (describing Boston's water and quoting "Very Mixed," *Puck*, vol. 32, no. 808 (Aug. 31, 1892), p. 21).

Even as one objection to plain water dissolved, a second proved stubbornly persistent. Benjamin Rush was hardly alone in warning of the lethal danger of drinking too much cold water on a hot day. As early as 1641, a pamphlet extolling the benefits of "Warme Beere" repeated several instructive anecdotes of "those who drinking cold drink being hot fall sick to the death." Over a century and a half later, Virginia statesman John Randolph cautioned his nephew, "I see by the papers, eight deaths in one week from cold water, in Philadelphia alone." The fear persisted as late as 1840, when a Massachusetts newspaper printed an arresting account:

Sudden Death.— On Friday afternoon, Mr. Theophilus Chase died very sud-denly, from drinking a large quantity of cold water when overheated by expo-sure to the sun.

Complicating the story's moral, the paper added that "Mr. Chase was addicted to the use of ardent spirits, and, we are told, had indulged himself very freely during the few intensely hot days, immediately preceding his death."[82]

Oddly persistent for centuries, this fear of cold water slipped from the scene sometime in the nineteenth century. By the 1830s, temperance reformers trumpeted their fidelity not merely to water but to *cold* water. A Mississippi temperance journal claimed the title *Cold Water Man*, as did a "pocket companion for the temperate" published in Albany in 1832 by one Dr. Springwater. The *Boston Temperance Songster* of 1844 included a ditty with the lyric, "Cold Water is king, cold water is lord . . . ." Most striking was the innovation of Presbyterian minister Thomas Poage Hunt of Virginia, who undertook in 1836 to assemble throngs of children into "Cold Water Armies" to sing the virtues of temperance. By 1841, a Boston publisher was producing the *Cold Water Army*, a children's weekly. That year almost a thousand boys and girls marched with the Cold Water Army at a temperance parade in Baltimore. And a year earlier in Lowell, Massachusetts, some sixteen hundred youths held a "temperance jubilee." Under the headline, "Cold Water Army," the Lowell *Courier* told how children sang to the tune of "Auld Lang Syne":

> Though others love their Rum and Wine,
>   And drink till they are mad,
> To Water we will still incline,
>   To make us strong and glad.

---

[82] F.W., *Warme Beere* (Cambridge: R.D. for Henry Overton, 1641), pp. 12–14; John Randolph, *Letters of John Randolph to a Young Relative* (Philadelphia: Carey, Lea & Blanchard, 1834), p. 91 (letter to Theodore B. Dudley, July 15, 1811), *quoted in* Rorabaugh, pp. 97–98; "Sudden Death," Lowell *Courier*, July 23, 1840, p. 2.

We love the clear Cold Water Springs,
Supplied by gentle showers;
W[e] feel the strength cold water brings,—
"The Victory is ours."[83]

The Necessity Debate: Alcohol as Food

By the mid-nineteenth century, two of the three props supporting the purported necessity of nonmedicinal alcohol had crumbled. The notion that spirits warmed the body on a cold day fell in the face of physiological facts and the fashion for coffee and tea. And alcohol's asserted need as a substitute for water, both purer and less lethal in the heat, gave way before advancing city sanitation and parades of small children. Yet the fact remained that neither coffee, tea, nor cold water could build strong bones. So even as other justifications for drinking fell away, alcohol's claim to serve as an essential nutrient held fast, sparing it from condemnation as pure indulgence in sensory pleasure.

To be sure, nobody deemed *spirits* an essential part of the diet. Distilled alcohol had served in popular belief to warm the body and purify water. The erosion of these notions in the first half of the nineteenth century helped set the terms of the early temperance movement, which largely followed Benjamin Rush in condemning nonmedicinal spirits even while condoning wine, beer, and other fermented drinks. The latter served properly as *foods*. As Rush's *Moral and Physical Thermometer* declared, fermented drinks supplied "[n]ourishment, when taken only at meals, and in moderate quantities" (see Figure 3.1). Or as the anonymous author of "The Alcoholic Controversy" wrote in 1868: "[A]mong the mass of medical men, . . . the prevalent doctrine concerning beer and wine, though not concerning spirits, was and is, that they are *nourishing*, add *force* as well as *warmth*, that they aid digestion, and in our climate may fairly be called necessaries."[84]

Perhaps for this reason, the earliest experiments with statewide alcohol prohibition reached only distilled liquor. The Massachusetts "fifteen-gallon law" of 1838 outlawed sales of distilled liquor in quantities less than fifteen gallons, effectively banning spirit sales in shops and taverns. By later standards the law was a

---

[83] Krout, *Origins of Prohibition*, p. 139 n.35 (noting the Natchez journal *Cold Water Man*); ibid., pp. 185–86 (noting 1841 Baltimore march); ibid., p. 186 n. 5 (describing Hunt's work); ibid., p. 243 n.40 (noting publication of the *Cold Water Army*); Doctor Springwater, *The Cold-Water-Man: or, A Pocket Companion for the Temperate* (Albany: Packard and Van Benthuysen, 1832); A.J. Locke, "A Song for Tea-Parties," in *The Boston Temperance Songster* (R.K. Potter ed., Boston: White & Potter, 1849 (1844)), p. 59, *quoted in* Rorabaugh, *Alcoholic Republic*, p. 198; Kobler, *Ardent Spirits*, pp. 69–70 (describing Hunt's work); "Cold Water Army," *Lowell Courier*, July 7, 1840, p. 2.

[84] "The Alcoholic Controversy," p. 294.

half-measure, for it imposed no restriction on beer or wine. But in 1838 it made Massachusetts the standard bearer, ahead of every state save Tennessee, which likewise banned retail spirit sales that year. Modest as it was, the Massachusetts law met pitched resistance. Repeal efforts began even before it took effect, and within two years a gubernatorial candidate rumored to oppose the law rode public disaffection into the State House and promptly signed a repeal. The Tennessee law lasted longer, but by 1846 it too was gone, an apparent victim of the need "to increase the Revenue"—the purpose expressed in the repeal act's title.[85]

Even as the conviction that fermented drinks delivered necessary nutrients helped stave off full-scale prohibition, advancing science began to eat away at old beliefs. After noting that "the prevalent doctrine concerning beer and wine . . . was and is, that they are *nourishing*," while spirits are not, the author of "The Alcoholic Controversy" announced the confounding verdict of laboratory trials: "*That all this is unscientific*, appears, the moment we learn that beer and wine *owe their characteristic properties only to the alcohol in them*." For "chemical inquiry [had shown] that *all* the liquors contained the very same element, AL- COHOL . . . ."[86]

The author apparently had in mind the work of chemist William Brande, whose investigations published in 1811 had dashed the long-held belief that only distilled liquors contained alcohol. Today it's hard to fathom that folks once failed to see beer and wine as alcoholic drinks, containing the same active ingredient as whisky, rum, and gin. Yet Brande's finding that the same poisonous compound infected all these drinks had come as startling news. And though beer and wine contained less alcohol per ounce than spirits, Brande delivered the shocking ver- dict that more than 20 percent of a glass of Madeira, America's favorite wine, was alcohol.[87]

Brande's discovery, said the author of "The Alcoholic Controversy," "drove the more eager philanthropists to the doctrine of *total* abstinence from alco- holic liquors as beverage." Lyman Beecher was among the first to respond. At

---

[85] "An Act to Regulate the Sale of Spirituous Liquors," 1838 *Massachusetts Laws*, ch. 157 (Act of Apr. 19, 1838), p. 442; "An Act to Repeal 'An Act to Regulate the Sale of Spirituous Liquors,'" 1840 *Massachusetts Acts*, ch. 1 (Act of Feb. 11, 1840), p. 179. For an excellent history of the Massachusetts law's passage and downfall, *see* Krout, *Origins of Prohibition*, pp. 262–71. On the Tennessee law, *see* "An Act to Repeal All Laws Licensing Tipling Houses . . . ," 1837–1838 *Tennessee Acts*, ch. 120 (Act of Jan. 26, 1838), pp. 186–87; "An Act to Tax and Regulate Tippling and Tippling Houses, and to Increase the Revenue," 1845–1846 *Tennessee Acts*, ch. 90 (Act of Jan. 23, 1846), pp. 154–58; Krout, *Origins of Prohibition*, p. 273 n.22.

[86] "The Alcoholic Controversy," p. 289 ("chemical inquiry . . ."); ibid., p. 294 ("the prevalent doc- trine concerning" and "That all this is unscientific . . .") (emphasis added).

[87] *See* Rorabaugh, *Alcoholic Republic*, pp. 100–02, 273 n.9 (discussing Brande's work, including his reference to Madeira, and its reception).

the outset of an 1827 printing of his *Six Sermons*, he added a footnote that made plain the force of Brande's finding:

> When the following discourses were written, alcohol in the form of ardent spirits, so called at that day, was the most common intoxicating beverage in use. But as the poison in every form is the same, and the effect the same, the argument against this form [of intoxicating beverage] applies alike to every form.

American Methodists likewise responded, though not till the *Edinburgh Review* published an endorsement of Brande's findings in 1828 and the American Temperance Society featured his work in its 1832 annual report. At that year's Methodist General Conference, a temperance committee embraced "*entire abstinence*." Its report drummed on Brande's conclusions, insisting over and over that "*alcohol* is the principle of all intoxication"—that "alcohol [is] found in all *spirituous* liquors, and in most of our *wines* and malt drinks"—and that "the essential constituent in all intoxicating liquors, producing inebriety, is alcohol . . . ." The committee repeated Brande's estimates of the alcohol content of brandy, Madeira, cider, porter, and ale and implored, "Who is not alarmed, not to say confounded, when he reflects upon the amount of this bewitching poison which is found in all our fashionable drinks?"[88]

By the mid-1830s, the vanguard of the temperance movement had recanted its early tolerance of beer, cider, and wine. In 1836 the newly named American Temperance Union, formed three years earlier in Philadelphia, endorsed a proposal by Lyman Beecher and Congregational minister Justin Edwards to replace its original pledge of "total abstinence from the use of ardent spirits" with a commitment to "total abstinence *from all that can intoxicate*." The new language was intentionally obscure, allowing radicals such as Beecher and Edwards to extend the ban to beer, cider, and wine, while letting others exempt these less potent drinks. Over the next several years the general, if uneven, trend among temperance societies was toward absolute bans on alcoholic drinks.[89]

The discovery that the same menacing compound infused both distilled and fermented drinks hiked the stakes of the debate about alcohol's food value. For if alcohol served no essential role in nourishing the body, *all* alcoholic beverages could face moral condemnation—not merely spirits, but beer, cider, and wine

---

[88] "The Alcoholic Controversy," p. 289; Beecher, *Six Sermons*, p. 5 n.*; *Address to the Young Men of Worcester County, by a Committee of the Young Men's Temperance Convention* (Worcester: S.H. Colton and Co., 1835), pp. 3–5 (urging abstinence from wine and beer because "*[a]lcohol exists in these liquors*" and noting that after the 1828 publication of an article in the *Edinburgh Review*, the correctness of Brande's views "is now undoubtedly settled"); Wheeler, *Methodism*, pp. 86–89 (quoting from 1832 report).

[89] Krout, *Origins of Prohibition*, pp. 132–33; 153–63.

too. On the other hand, if studies confirmed the age-old belief that beer "abounds with nourishment," as Rush put it, beer would find sanction though it contained the same "poison" as rum. The former result would offend those who condoned moderate consumption of alcohol; the latter would distress contenders for total abstinence. So the two moral camps warred over a physiological fact that was beyond their ken and perhaps past resolution. Even today the food value of beer eludes easy judgment: yes, as Rush said, a laborer could have nothing but "a quart or three pints of [beer], with a few pounds of bread a day." But no nutritionist would counsel that course.[90]

The food-value dispute slogged on through the nineteenth century and into the twentieth, sparking skirmishes till the very eve of national prohibition. Methodists set the terms of debate soon after Brande's findings gained notoriety. The church's 1832 temperance committee declared, "The mischievous *principle* of inebriety . . . can not be made to nourish and invigorate the body. . . . No alcoholic substance can be controlled, digested, or appropriated by the stomach."[91]

These views acquired scientific stature in 1860, when a team of French scientists led by Ludger Lallemand reported that except for a tiny portion exhaled in the breath, alcohol passes unchanged through the body. The result, as the anonymous author of "Does Alcohol Act as Food?" reported in 1862, was "that the holders of extreme anti-alcoholic views . . . profess to be able to establish the non-nutritive character of alcohol by chemical proofs, from which there is no appeal." The author questioned Lallemand's findings, however, and highlighted "unmistakable facts which we can see with our own eyes"—the many cases "among regular dram-drinkers, *of almost total abstinence, for years together, from any food except alcohol and water*." As alcohol "is capable, almost unaided, of supporting life for years," it must be a food, even if "a bad and insufficient food."[92]

The battle lines drawn, competing camps exchanged sallies over the next sixty years. In 1867 a British author challenged temperance zealots "to show that wine and beer . . . are not, if taken in moderation, as wholesome and nutritious as bread or beef." A year later, the author of "The Alcoholic Controversy" maintained that as alcohol "is never disintegrated [in the body], it cannot be food"—and claimed it reduces appetite for other foods only because it "makes the current of life more sluggish, and lowers vital power." Therefore, "no government should treat alcoholic drink as it treats potatoes, milk and honey; nor class it with foods; nor talk

---

[90]   Rush, *Enquiry* (1784 ed.), p. 246.

[91]   Wheeler, *Methodism*, pp. 86–87 (quoting 1832 committee report).

[92]   Ludger Lallemand et al., *Du Rôle de l'Alcool et des Anesthésiques dans l'Organisme: Recherches Expérimentales* (Paris: F. Chamerot, 1860); "Does Alcohol Act as Food?," *The Cornhill Magazine*, vol. 6 (July–Dec. 1862), pp. 319–24. Some measure of the impact of Lallemand and his colleagues' work is a long and appreciative 1861 review suggesting the authors had robbed the great chemist Liebig's imperial domain "of an entire province." "Reviews," *Medical Times and Gazette*, vol. 1, no. 2 (Jan. 12, 1861), p. 42.

of it as 'a necessary article' . . . ." Another English author answered in 1875 that "whether alcohol is, or is not, a species of food . . . no one would dispute the fact that it possesses a remarkable power of substituting itself for solid, wholesome aliments, at least for a time."[93]

And so it went. Toward the end of the nineteenth century those contending for alcohol's food value trumpeted the findings of Professor W. O. Atwater of Connecticut's Wesleyan College, who proved Lallemand mistaken in claiming the body never oxidizes alcohol. In a bitter rejoinder printed in 1900, Milwaukee physiologist John Madden mocked the public's unschooled reception of Atwater's news:

[T]here has existed in the minds of the laity a belief that this is a discovery of importance, far-reaching and revolutionary in its character. "Alcohol is a food" has been shouted from the housetops of the lay press; "Alcohol is a food" has been echoed . . . by the tens of thousands of bibulous humanity who are seeking for some legitimate or decent excuse to become intoxicated with a favorite form of alcoholic beverage.

It galled Madden that "one of the oldest and most conservative" medical journals had joined the bibulous public in concluding from Atwater's work that "alcohol taken in small and digestible amounts is a food." Madden dismissed such nonsense: "Alcohol, containing no nitrogen, is incapable of furnishing new tissue," nor can it be stored as fat or converted to glycogen. And even if the body can oxidize alcohol, the body can't live on it any more than the body could live on chloroform or ether. For if we replaced all the carbohydrates the average adult needs each day with alcohol, "[t]his quantity would approximate a quart of whiskey daily, and lead to a pretty prompt extinction of the human race."[94]

In the end, the argument that alcohol, if a food, is a very bad food carried the day. Whatever may have been true before canning and refrigeration and before railroads could speed unspoiled foods to far-flung markets, people no longer needed beer to fuel the body. In 1909 sociologist Harry S. Warner delivered this verdict in terms more economic than scientific. " '[T]o furnish heat equal to that obtained from a nickel's worth of flour requires the alcohol and solids of 29.6 glasses of beer, costing at five cents per glass, $1.48.' No workingman can afford to purchase heat-producing power at such a tremendous cost to say nothing of the [ill] effects of the alcohol as a drug." If beer is

---

[93] "Intemperance and Intolerance," *Blackwood's Edinburgh Magazine*, vol. 149 (Aug. 1867), pp. 208, 209–10; "The Alcoholic Controversy," pp. 296–97; "What We Drink," *All the Year Round*, vol. 15 (Oct. 23, 1875), pp. 77, 79.

[94] John Madden, "The Food Value of Alcohol," *The Independent* (May 31, 1900), pp. 1312–14.

a food, therefore, "it is an exceedingly costly, deceptive and vicious 'food.'"[95]

Still, Warner allowed that much of the lay public clung to traditional notions of alcohol's dietary role. "To large numbers of people beer is 'a liquid food,' apparently as necessary as bread . . . ." And who could blame them? Breweries battled stoutly to bolster old notions, advertising their wares in newspapers and streetcars as "life-giving" and "health-sustaining"—as "liquid food" and "the purest and best of all foods and drinks." They claimed, Warner alleged, that "beer is to the adult what milk is to the child."[96]

Looking back at this debate from the summer of 1918, University of Nebraska sociologist George Elliott Howard concluded, "Refuge after refuge of the liquor interest has been destroyed." Though Howard spoke of science and its clash with the liquor interests, the context of the conflict was moral. Scientific advances had undone the old need-based justifications that once spared alcohol from moral condemnation even as the liquor interests cannily, if vainly, tried to reassert those notions of need. Stripped of these "[p]et fallacies," alcohol emerged as a purely antisocial, immoral force that deprived drinkers of their reason and left them prey to brute passions. "Has not the scientific laboratory proved," Howard asked, "that the habitual use of alcohol, in whatever quantity, disintegrates the moral character? It impairs the judgment, clouds the reason, and enfeebles the will; while at the same time it arouses the appetites, inflames the passions, releases the primitive beast from the artificial restraint of social discipline."[97]

Here was the language of Augustine filtered down through the ages. If drink served no *need*, it served only to intoxicate, to suspend reason, to disable self-control, to abandon the drinker to animal lusts. What then could save it from moral condemnation?

Prohibition's First Waves

Less than a generation after the wider public learned of Brande's findings about the alcohol content of beer and wine, the movement toward full-scale prohibition crashed onto the American scene. Rising from the temperance fever of

[95] Harry S. Warner, *Social Welfare and the Liquor Problem* (Chicago: The Intercollegiate Prohibition Association, 1909), pp. 52–53 (quoting G.O. Higley, "Is Beer a 'Liquid Food?'" *American Issue*, vol. 15, no. 1 (Jan. 4, 1907), p. 3).

[96] Warner, *Social Welfare and the Liquor Problem* (1909 ed.), pp. 50–51 ("life-giving," "health-sustaining," "liquid food," "the purest and best . . ."); Harry S. Warner, *Social Welfare and the Liquor Problem* (Chicago: The Intercollegiate Prohibition Association, 2d ed. 1913), p. 80 ("To large numbers . . ."); ibid., p. 81 ("beer is to the adult . . .").

[97] George Elliott Howard, "Alcohol and Crime: A Study in Social Causation," *American Journal of Sociology*, vol. 24 (July 1918), pp. 61–62.

the early nineteenth century, this first prohibition movement ascended with the optimism that only moral righteousness can fuel. It took root statewide first in Maine, which in 1851 became the nation's first full-fledged prohibition state, barring all sales of intoxicating drinks. The fiery hero of this legislative triumph, Portland Mayor Neal Dow, had learned dislike of liquor from his Quaker rearing and the catalytic work of Benjamin Rush, whom Dow called "the pioneer of the temperance revolution."[98]

Dow's victory in Maine energized far-flung followers and sparked wildfire lawmaking across the Northeast and Midwest. In just four years, fourteen more states and territories had enacted full-scale alcohol prohibition. Illinois was the first to trail Maine, followed by Ohio, the Minnesota Territory, Rhode Island, Massachusetts, Vermont, Michigan, Indiana, Connecticut, Delaware, Iowa, Nebraska Territory, New York, and New Hampshire. But there the blaze abated. After New Hampshire barred alcohol sales in 1855, no other state did so for a quarter-century.[99] The causes of the cooling are uncertain. Perhaps the sectional tensions that presaged the Civil War distracted lawmakers and voters from the alcohol question. Or perhaps the prohibition movement had exhausted the states most receptive to its message. Or perhaps—and this seems likely—prohibition fever faded as reports of difficulties filtered back from those states that went dry.

For this alcohol prohibition movement, like all those before or since, failed. Not only did this drive fail to penetrate south past Delaware or west past Nebraska, but prohibition failed to endure in those states that tried it. Within just three years of the end of this burst of lawmaking—by 1858—at least seven of the fifteen new "Maine laws" had fallen or were substantially weakened. And when Massachusetts finally repealed its prohibition law in 1875, Maine and its two neighbors, New Hampshire and Vermont, stood alone atop the hill.[100]

---

[98] "An Act for the Suppression of Drinking Houses and Tippling Shops," 1851 *Maine Acts*, ch. 211 (Act of June 2, 1851), p. 210; Neal Dow, *The Reminiscences of Neal Dow* (Portland, Me.: The Evening Express Publishing Company, 1898), pp. 162–63.

[99] Cherrington, *Evolution of Prohibition*, pp. 136–39, 145–62, 184–207; Kobler, *Ardent Spirits*, pp. 88–91.

[100] Ernest Cherrington reported that Ohio's 1851 prohibition amendment "was never fully enforced." The Illinois act of the same year was repealed just two years later. The laws of Rhode Island, the Minnesota Territory, Massachusetts, and Vermont, all adopted in 1852, apparently survived (with occasional interruptions) till 1863, 1870, 1875, and 1902. The Indiana and Michigan laws of 1853 survived off and on till their repeals in 1858 and 1875. Connecticut's 1854 law was repealed in 1872. And of the five prohibition laws of 1855, those of Delaware, Iowa, the Nebraska Territory, and New York all met repeal or court rejection within three years. Only New Hampshire's survived, though it too fell in 1903. *See* Cherrington, *Evolution of Prohibition*, pp. 136–39, 146–62, 184–97. Maine's 1851 prohibition law gave way in 1856 to a local-option scheme permitting city and town authorities to license liquor retailers, but was reinstated in 1858. "An Act to Restrain and Regulate the Sale of Intoxicating Liquors . . . ," 1856 *Maine Acts*, ch. 255 (Act of Apr. 7, 1856), pp. 272–78; "An Act for the Suppression of Drinking Houses and Tippling Shops," 1858 *Maine Acts*, ch. 33 (Act of Mar. 25, 1858), pp. 31–43.

Soon the momentum shifted again toward prohibition, though only briefly. In 1880 Kansas became the first state since 1855 to adopt a Maine law. By the end of the decade Iowa, North and South Dakota, and (haltingly) Rhode Island would follow, though not all would keep their new laws for long. What has become known as the second wave of statewide prohibition laws proved even less durable than the first.[101] For while a "wave" of four Plains states joined a remote New England cluster, an anti-prohibition tsunami crashed across the land. Legislatures rejected prohibition initiatives in Minnesota, Wisconsin, Missouri, Arkansas, Illinois, Indiana, New Jersey, and Connecticut—and voters rejected them in Washington, Oregon, Nebraska, Texas, Michigan, Tennessee, West Virginia, Pennsylvania, North Carolina, and Massachusetts. When the waters cleared at decade's end, just six prohibition states remained—Kansas, North Dakota, South Dakota, New Hampshire, Vermont, and Maine.[102]

Moderation vs. Total Abstinence

Behind this ambivalence toward state-enforced prohibition lay a moral struggle that had convulsed the temperance movement for the previous half-century. Not till scientific and medical advances of the nineteenth century began dismantling old notions of alcohol's necessity did the concept of total abstinence, whether voluntary or imposed by government prohibition, become viable. Till then the nascent temperance movement had gathered largely in one body behind Benjamin Rush's standard, which demanded a ban on distilled alcoholic drinks unless used medically, but condoned the use of wine, beer, and other fermented drinks in moderation.

Once complete abstinence from nonmedicinal alcohol appeared possible, temperance leaders confronted the dilemma of moderation at which Saint Thomas Aquinas had hinted six centuries earlier: Where between the sin of drunkenness and the security of complete abstinence must the moral boundary lie? Some temperance leaders argued that alcohol, shorn of claims of need, must go. Others reached a different verdict: their moral rule was *moderation*, and their mantra was that measured use of alcohol was no vice. With the temperance

---

[101] On laws enacted in the second "wave," *see* Cherrington, *Evolution of Prohibition*, pp. 176–84, 206–36, and Raymond B. Fosdick & Albert L. Scott, *Toward Liquor Control* (New York: Harper & Brothers, 1933), p. 3. The three-stage division of state prohibition laws was apparently the creation of journalist George Kibbe Turner, who called the stages not *waves*, but *movements*. George Kibbe Turner, "Beer and the City Liquor Problem," *McClure's Magazine*, vol. 33 (1909), pp. 528, 538 (1909). Other, better-known prohibition historians borrowed the three-stage model and substituted the term *waves*. See, e.g., Cherrington, *Evolution of Prohibition*, pp. 135, 176; Fosdick & Scott, *Toward Liquor Control*, pp. 2–4.

[102] Cherrington, *Evolution of Prohibition*, pp. 176–80.

community torn between moderationists and cold-water warriors for full-scale prohibition, there followed a decades-long struggle between those who sought to suppress only abusive drinking and those who wanted to ban every drop. The dispute festered till the early decades of the twentieth century.

This was the bloodiest sort of ideological battle—a turf war among friends. For the warring factions in this moderation-versus-total-abstinence dispute all claimed the same position—in favor of self-control and against drunkenness. All agreed that those given to drunkenness should be forbidden to drink and that distilled liquors, which posed the greatest risk of drunkenness, should be banned except as medicine. They disputed a single question: Is it immoral for responsible drinkers with substantial self-control to indulge moderately in a substance sinful if overused? Moderationists exalted the self-control of moral autonomy. Total abstainers insisted on "absolute safety" and freedom from temptation, never daring to risk a drunkard's incontinence. It was a debate that had roiled the temperance community for half a century and would drag on for half a century more.

Presbyterian minister Howard Crosby framed the case for one camp. *Temperance*, he said in 1881, "signifies the moral quality of moderation" and "a grand moral subjection of the whole man to the sway of reason." It does not impose "a legalism that prohibits man from any drink that can intoxicate." Crosby insisted "true civilization is in the direction of personal self-control, and not in that of governmental prohibition." Whereas government regulation of liquor sales "is a help to self-control, . . . prohibition would be a hindrance."[103]

In the opposing camp stood one-time abolitionist firebrand Wendell Phillips, who voiced a concern shared by many total-abstinence advocates: that even those who drank moderately would fall prey to addiction. Phillips warned "how insidiously the habits of sensual indulgence creep on their victim, until he wakes to find himself in chains of iron, his very will destroyed[.]" As a Maine newspaper editor put it, "Most men become drunkards by trying to drink moderately, and failing."[104]

That alcohol could addict even when used in moderation was hardly news in the nineteenth century. For more than a millennium, prominent writers on the scourge of drunkenness foretold the irresistible thirst that followed regular use. In his spurious Augustinian sermons of the sixth century, Caesarius cautioned that men "gradually add one or two cups a day to the usual amount of drink" till "the passion of drunkenness takes such a strong hold on them that it makes them thirsty all the time." The word *addict* appeared in this sense as early as 1545, when

---

[103] Chancellor [Howard] Crosby, "A Calm View of the Temperance Question," *in Moderation vs. Total Abstinence; or, Dr. Crosby and His Reviewers* (New York: The National Temperance Society and Publication House, 1881), pp. 7–8, 111.

[104] Wendell Phillips, "A Reply to Dr. Crosby's 'Calm View of Temperance,'" *in Moderation vs. Total Abstinence*, p. 53; Lewiston (Me.) *Journal, quoted in Moderation vs. Total Abstinence*, p. 109.

the anonymous author of the *Invective ageinst Glotony and Dronkennes* told what "madnes" it is "to employe and addict ourselves to suche pleasure as bryngeth with it so many calamities . . . of bodi & soule." Owen Stockton wrote in the next century that "[d]runkenness is an enticing, bewitching sin, which is very hardly left by those that are addicted to it." And in 1708 Cotton Mather warned of addiction without using the word. Even those who are merely "*Sipping* at" rum, he wrote, "come to *Crave* after it; such a *Craving* they have, that they cannot go without it. They are never *Drunk*; 'tis true; But they become Enslaved unto the *Bottel* of *Drink*."[105]

From Caesarius onward, then, the tension between alcohol's necessary use and the danger of habitual abuse had backdropped virtually every serious discussion of drunkenness. Only in the nineteenth century, when life without alcohol first became thinkable, did total abstinence emerge as a potential escape from this ancient tension. Radical temperance reformers now were in a position to ask: If even moderate drinkers risk addiction and drunkenness, and if no necessity justifies alcohol's use as a beverage, what moral excuse can even moderate drinking claim?

In its rebuttal of Dr. Crosby's stance, the *Episcopal Recorder* put the case nicely. First the *Recorder* alleged the risk of addiction: "The evils of moderate drinking, as the inevitable precursor of intemperance, seem to us to be beyond contraindication." Then the editors addressed the lack of need: "If there was any necessity for the use of alcohol as a beverage we can understand that men should contend for the right to use it in moderation; but apart from its use in a medicinal point of view it cannot be shown to have ever been of benefit. It therefore passes our comprehension," the editors concluded triumphantly, "that any man can be found to defend its use in moderation even." Or as another of Crosby's opponents put it, when it came to alcohol's use as a beverage, "*total abstinence is the only ground of absolute safety*."[106]

The warring camps of the temperance movement sparred for decades as the political momentum swung first one way, then the other in an uneasy standoff. By 1880, the mass of the temperance movement had shifted toward complete abstinence, while momentum in the states had swung toward the moderationists. Crosby derided the "little success here and there" that the "total-abstinence crusade" had gained over the years. "A partial success in Maine has been proclaimed as proving the question against the painful failures everywhere else . . . ." In January 1881, when Dr. Crosby spoke, only four states banned the retail sale of

---

[105] *St. Caesarius, Sermons*, vol. 1, p. 236 (quoting from sermon 46); *Invective ageinst Glotony and Dronkennes*, p. 20 (my pagination); Owen Stockton, *A Warning to Drunkards* . . . (London: J.R. for Thomas Parkhurst, 1682), p. 35; [Mather,] *Sober Considerations*, p. 11.

[106] *Episcopal Recorder*, quoted in *Moderation vs. Total Abstinence*, pp. 110–11 (supplying no further citation); Foster, "A Reply to Dr. Crosby," p. 67.

alcohol. In Wendell Phillips's words, Maine reigned "far above all, set on a hill"—joined only by its small Northern neighbors, New Hampshire and Vermont, and the distant prairie outpost of Kansas.[107]

Yet in the late-century ruins of the statewide prohibitions lay the groundwork of future success—for women had assumed a newly prominent role among temperance forces. The Woman's Christian Temperance Union (WCTU) had emerged in 1874 in the aftermath of a Midwestern women's campaign to protest and shutter local saloons. Joined later by the even more powerful Anti-Saloon League, founded in 1893, the WCTU demonized the saloon as the blighted symbol of all that was wrong with liquor.[108] The saloon and the passion to ban it prove central to our story, for antagonism to the saloon helped break the ideological stalemate between moderationists and total abstainers. To see how, we need to take a long step back and examine the milieu in which the saloon thrived—the milieu of social drinking.

Old-Time Social Drinking Rituals

The expression *social drinking* seems to have entered common parlance only in the early nineteenth century. I've seen no American use of the term before 1803 and only widely scattered earlier uses in England.[109] Yet ritualized communal drinking dates back centuries. Early forms—in particular, "health-drinking" and the indulgence of feast days—drew the wrath of moralists who perhaps spied in social drinking the potential to excuse a broad swath of not strictly necessary drinking.

The metaphorical brilliance of the custom of *health-drinking* was its sly tailgating on the moral sanction given medically necessary alcohol use. The medical excuse dates at least to Plato's *Laws* and the license granted older men to take

---

[107] Crosby, "A Calm View," p. 13; Phillips, "A Reply to Dr. Crosby," p. 57; Cherrington, *Evolution of Prohibition*, p. 180 and throughout.

[108] On the Midwestern women's anti-saloon campaign, *see* Schrad, *Smashing the Liquor Machine*, pp. 368–75. On the founding of the WCTU and its role, *see* Cherrington, *Evolution of Prohibition*, pp. 170–71, 181–82, 190–92; Joseph R. Gusfield, *Symbolic Crusade: Status Politics and the American Temperance Movement* (Urbana: University of Illinois Press, 1963), pp. 88–89 Schrad, *Smashing the Liquor Machine*, pp. 375–84. On the Anti-Saloon League, *see* Cherrington, *Evolution of Prohibition*, pp. 253–54; Daniel Okrent, *Last Call: The Rise and Fall of Prohibition* (New York: Scribner 2010), pp. 34–42.

[109] The *Oxford English Dictionary*, third edition, lists an 1808 source as the first appearance of the term. But *social drinking* appeared in a poem titled, "From the Persian of Hafiz," first printed in Philadelphia in *The Port Folio* and reprinted in Samuel Saunter, "The American Lounger," *Hudson (N.Y.) Gazette*, July 12, 1803, p. 4. The term appeared in England as early as 1659 but only rarely for the next century and a half. John Gauden, *Hiera Dakrya, Ecclesiae Anglicanae Suspiria* (London: By J.G. for R. Royston, 1659), vol. 4, p. 656. My thanks to Taryn Marks of the Crown Law Library for tracing the term's lineage.

wine "as a drug that heals the austerity of old age" and "put[s] . . . health as well as strength in the body." The origins of ritualized toasts to one another's health are more obscure. Increase Mather, never an entirely reliable source on Augustine's teachings, attributed to him this condemnation of health-drinking: "That filthy and unhappy Custom (saith Au[gu]stin) of *Drinking Healths is a Relique of Paganism* and . . . the Poyson of the Devil." As his source, Mather listed "*De Tempore, Serm.* 131." This citation traces not to anything Augustine wrote, but to the first of Caesarius's sixth-century sermons on drunkenness, later attributed to Augustine. Yet even Caesarius said nothing of health-drinking. The drinking practice he decried as "pagan" was a sophomoric ritual in which "men . . . drink in great measure without measure, whether willingly or not, whenever they give a banquet for each other."[110]

If Mather's citation to Augustine says nothing about the origins of health-drinking, it does prove that by 1687, when Mather wrote, the practice alarmed Puritan moralists. "It has occasioned the Sin of Drunkenness more than a thousand millions of Times," Mather charged. "When wicked men intend a Debauch, they are wont to begin with an Health." Worse, as in most drinking rituals, even those who would prefer to abstain or stop while sober feel compelled to continue.[111]

The most insidious aspect of "healthing" was the pretended necessity it supplied for drunkenness. "Men could not be commonly cheated out of their Senses and Reason, but by a Ceremonious Mist, some goodly Pretence," wrote the anonymous author of *The Great Evil of Health-Drinking* in 1684. "The Form of Invitation among us is a Health." But "when that which is intended, is the gratification of the Flesh, and the Health is but a pretence for it, it cannot be excused nor defended." In his 1685 *Treatise against Drunkennesse*, which devoted thirty-odd pages to the dangers of health-drinking, Matthew Scrivener explained that "there is [w]hat they call a Moral Necessity upon [a drinker] to do as is required of him." Refusal to drink a health risks "offending the propounder, and disobliging the Person for whose sake [the health] is offered." Yet this supposed necessity was a cover, Scrivener argued, "prompted . . . rather from [drinkers'] Lusts than Loyalty so much pretended." Even Charles II felt obliged to expose the sham, declaring in 1660 his dislike of those "who spend their time in Taverns, Tipling-houses, and Debauches, giving no other evidence of their affection to us, but in Drinking our HEALTH."[112]

[110] *The Laws of Plato* (Thomas L. Pangle trans., New York: Basic Books, Inc., 1980), 666b, p. 47 ("as a drug that heals . . ."); ibid., 672d, p. 55 ("put[s] . . . health . . ."); Increase Mather, *A Testimony Against Several Prophane and Superstitious Customs* (London: n.p. 1687, University of Virginia Press reprint, 1953), Text, p. 3; St. Caesarius, *Sermons*, vol. 1, p. 237 (quoting from sermon 46). Mather meant to reference Sermon 231, not 131.

[111] Mather, *Testimony Against Prophane Customs*, Text, pp. 5, 6.

[112] [Charles Morton?], *The Great Evil of Health-Drinking* . . . (London: Jonathan Robinson, 1684), pp. 18, 40, 77–78, 89–90; Matthew Scrivener, *A Treatise Against Drunkennesse* . . . (London: Charles

Another custom hinting at later notions of social drinking was the ceremo-nial community bash. Such bashes may have spun off from older saints'-day celebrations, at which carousers indulged in the conceit that they drank healths in the saints' honor. Of this practice the genuine Augustine had something to say. He told a friend how he had scolded parishioners for their insistence on marking saints' days with drunken feasts in church. Augustine had borrowed a reading from Matthew: "Give not that which is holy unto the dogs, neither cast ye your pearls before swine . . . ." (Matt. 7:6.) Exploiting the bestial imagery, he "commented . . . on dogs and pigs in such a way that those arguing against the commandments of God with an obstinate barking and devoted to the filth of carnal pleasures were forced to be ashamed . . . ."[113]

Though Augustine scorned ritualized quaffing in church, ceremonial com-munity drinking endured at least another fifteen hundred years. As late as 1827, Lyman Beecher lamented the moral license the community claimed for its hol-iday bacchanals. "When any of these holidays arrive," he wrote, "and they come as often almost as saints' days in the calendar, they bring with them, to many, the insatiable desire of drinking, as well as a dispensation from the sin, as effi-cacious and quieting to the conscience as papal indulgences." Beecher perhaps intended his snide references to saints' days and papal indulgences to brand community drinking rituals as Catholic relics. Yet long before his day, such rituals had taken root in the colonial experience and lost any sectarian valence. Barn-raisings, church-raisings, fence-railings, baptisms, weddings, funerals, ordinations, musters, and elections all proved occasions for drinking in throngs. As Harry S. Warner wrote in 1909, such social forms were secular artifacts of the "the ninety-five saints days of old England, 'almost ear-marked for indulgence in alcoholic merriment.'"[114]

It is tempting to see health-drinking and feast days and similar social rituals as evidence of a bibulous past, when drunkenness was celebrated, not reviled, and carried no tedious moral freight. Perhaps Americans prefer to see our past this way, taking a roguish pride in our randy, rowdy national adolescence. In reality, the profusion of old drinking rituals bears evidence of a starchy moral code, albeit one compromised by a creative and high-spirited folk. After all, these drinking

---

Brown, 1685), pp. 122, 127–28; H[enry] J[essey], *The Lords Loud Call to England* (London: for Is. Chapman, 1660), p. 42 (quoting proclamation of Charles II, May 30, 1660).

[113] Letter 29, "A Letter of a Priest of Hippo Regius to Alypius . . . ," in *The Works of Saint Augustine: A Translation for the 21st Century*, vol. 2/1, p. 95 (Roland Teske trans., Hyde Park: New City Press, 2001).
[114] Lyman Beecher, *Six Sermons on the Nature, Occasions, Signs, Evils, and Remedy of Intemperance* (Boston, T.R. Marvin, 4th ed. 1828), pp. 26–27; Harry S. Warner, *Social Welfare and the Liquor Problem* (Chicago: The Intercollegiate Prohibition Association, 7th ed. 1916 (1909)), pp. 24–26 (supplying no citation for the internal quote). On Colonial drinking practices, *see* Krout, *Origins of Prohibition*, pp. 38–40, 62–63; Lender & Martin, *Drinking in America*, p. 51.

forms, whether rituals or holidays, were *pretexts*—and the need for pretexts betrayed an unwillingness to drink heavily without some sanction, whether civic custom or divine indulgence. And they were *social* pretexts. They confessed a reluctance to get drunk alone and an understanding that social cheer was a saving grace—a *use* that spared heavy drinking the ignominious label *abuse*. Still, these rituals sustained a relentless moral barrage. For at least in their cruder forms, they were excuses for *drunkenness*. And whatever the pretext and social benefit, incitement to drunkenness drew broad and sometimes furious moral censure.

The Emergence of Social Drinking, So Called

The anonymous author of *The Great Evil of Health-Drinking* compared that sodden ritual to a form of drinking that sounds downright wholesome: "Mutual, sober, communicative Drinking, is an expression of a Friendship and Confederacy . . . ." In these few words the author captured four aspects of a form of drinking that requires no moral apology. It must be *mutual* and hence social; *sober* and not drunken; *communicative* and not stupefying; and in pursuit of *friendship* and *confederacy*, not fleshly gratification. Eight years later, in 1692, Beckenham rector William Assheton endorsed a similar formula of conversational drinking. Though he insisted drinking "immoderate[ly] and in excess, is the ruin of good Society and the very bane of Conversation," Assheton allowed the usefulness of "prudent moderate Drinking." The latter, he said, may assist in the *"preserving of Friendship; and the maintaining good Neighbourhood."*[115]

A 1710 exchange in *The Tatler* suggests contemporary norms followed professional moralists in forgiving light drinking for the sake of good society and conversation. After declaring how abhorrent he deemed any drinking "above the exigencies of thirst" if it renders us "less masters of ourselves," the editor received several letters accusing him of excessive rigor. One correspondent insisted that "[t]hough I am as much against excess . . . as yourself," moderate drinking could cure a reticent wit and rescue a fine conversation. With the "enlivening aid" of a pint of beer or "a certain quantity" of wine, a bashful man "thinks clearer, speaks more ready," and "express[es] himself upon any subject with more life and vivacity [and] more variety of ideas." Chastened, the editor owned that "wine may very allowably be used, in a degree above the supply of mere necessity, by such as labour under melancholy, or are tongue-tied by modesty. It is certainly a very

---

[115] [Morton], *Great Evil of Health-Drinking*, p. 40; William Assheton, *A Discourse Against Drunkenness, Swearing & Cursing* (London: Tho. Braddyll, 1692), p. 26.

agreeable change, when we see a glass raise a lifeless conversation into all the pleasures of wit and good-humour."[116]

In medical literature, too, one finds warm indulgence of conversational drinking. In his 1724 *Essay of Health and Long Life*, a virtual manifesto of the English anti-gin movement and a favorite authority of Anthony Benezet, Dr. George Cheyne gave no quarter to drunkards. "[A] *Sot*," he wrote, "is the lowest Character in Life." Yet he disavowed any "Intention here to discourage the innocent Means of *enlivening* Conversation, promoting *Friendship*, comforting the *sorrowful* Heart, and raising the *drooping* Spirits, by the *chearful Cup*, and the *social Repast*."[117]

Such benevolent tolerance of light conversational drinking grew scarcer as the temperance movement of the late eighteenth and nineteenth centuries gathered force. A more severe ascetic than the sometimes rotund Cheyne, John Wesley trained a censorious eye on the social repast. In his 1745 "Word to a Drunkard" he challenged the imaginary offender: "Do you not rather drink, for the sake of Company? Do you not do it, to oblige your *Friends*? For *Company*, do you say? How is this? Will you take a Dose of *Ratsbane* for *Company*?"[118] Wesley's target in this essay was drunkenness, however, not the sort of modest, convivial indulgence we today would call social drinking. And his signature decree banned only "spirituous liquors . . . unless in cases of extreme necessity"—not all forms of the cheering cup.

Truly social drinking—what the *Oxford English Dictionary* today defines as "[m]oderate drinking on social occasions"—did not bear the scourge of a prominent moralist till Presbyterian minister Lyman Beecher and a few fellow travelers began turning the temperance tide toward total abstinence in the early nineteenth century. Beecher may have been the first notable commentator to use the term *social drinking* in print. Yet he wielded it so often in his *Six Sermons on . . . Temperance* of 1826, and with such vehemence, that the term must have had wide currency before he troubled to denounce the practice. At least four times by name and once by allusion, he attacked "that accursed resort of social drinking." His assault reduced to a single claim, the same claim deployed by total abstainers against all moderate drinking—that those who indulged soon would slip past the bounds of moderation and down a fast slope toward drunkenness. "Evening resorts for conversation," he warned, "have proved fatal to thousands. Though . . . all should seem only the 'feast of reason, and the flow of

---

[116] *The Tatler*, no. 241 (Oct. 24, 1710), *in The Tatler and the Guardian*, p. 427 (untitled entry); ibid., no. 252 (Nov. 18, 1710), p. 442.

[117] Cheyne, *Essay of Health and Long Life*, p. 51.

[118] [Wesley,] *Word to a Drunkard*, p. 3. On Cheynes's struggles with overweight, *see* "Cheyne, George, M.D.," *in Dictionary of National Biography*, vol. 10, p. 218 (Leslie Stephen ed., New York: MacMillan and Co., 1889).

soul,' yet . . . many a wretched man has shaken his chains and cried out . . . , oh! that accursed resort of *social drinking*; there my hands were bound and my feet put in fetters; there I went a freeman and became a slave, a temperate man and became a drunkard."[119]

In the face of this fearful warning, social drinking proved a sturdier foe than simple moderation. For three separate moral props helped shield social drinkers against sliding into drunkenness. First were the *norms* of social drinking, which demanded that drinkers never approach the sinful zone of intoxication. Because heavy drink dulls the mind, thickens the tongue, and coarsens behavior, one who hopes to engage in reasoned social conversation must stop far short of drunkenness. As Assheton put it, "that which is immoderate and in excess, is the ruin of good Society, and the very bane of Conversation."

Then, too, social drinkers *policed* one another's moderation. No one wanted a drunk at the dinner table. Temperance reformers fretted endlessly about the dangers of peer pressure. They hated health-drinking because participants deemed refusal to drink disrespectful of the person toasted. "[O]ur young Masters . . . swear you shall drink, or swear they'll run you through," charged *The Great Evil of Health-Drinking*.[120] But the peer pressure of social drinking ran the other way. Companions eager for reasoned conversation helped guard fellow drinkers against excess.

And social drinking was never *solitary* drinking. Of all forms of drunkenness, getting drunk alone was deemed most depraved. As one parliamentary speaker said during Gin Act debates in 1736, "very few persons were so ridiculously abandoned as to get drunk by themselves." In pleasuring himself, the lonely drunk seemed the moral equivalent of a masturbator: he did for mindless pleasure what could, in the right company, have had a moral purpose. By drinking in private, moreover, he disabled the social mechanisms that otherwise helped guard against drunkenness. Benjamin Rush grasped the point a half-century later in defending wine over spirits. Wine "derives its relish principally from company," he said, "and is seldom like spirituous liquors drank in a chimney corner or in a closet." In another half-century Lyman Beecher remained on theme. Much as he despised social drinking, Beecher saw the danger lurking in a drinker's withdrawal from society. A man who "finds himself disposed to drink oftener, and more than he is willing to do before his family and the world, and begins to drink slily and in secret places," soon "will hasten on to ruin." Social drinking could

---

[119] For Beecher's various references to social drinking, *see Six Sermons* (4th ed. 1828), pp. 18–19, 20, 44, 102, 103 (emphasis added).

[120] [Morton], *Great Evil of Health-Drinking*, p. 11. *See also* Scrivener, *Treatise Against Drunkennesse*, pp. 126–28 ("[T]he Drunken Dictator of mis-rule comes to him with his Glasse or Cup in his hand, his Sword many times by his side, . . . and offers, obliges, obtrudes, threatens the civil, modest, and moderate person . . . ."); Mather, *Testimony Against Prophane Customs*, Text, pp. 6–7 ("[I]t is no better when a man that is not athirst is required to Drink a Pint of Liquor for anothers Health.").

have protected him: "So long as the eye of friendship and a regard to public observation kept him within limits, there was some hope of reformation; but when
he cuts this last cord, and launches out alone with his boat and bottle, he . . . probably will never return."[121]

Social drinking stood morally above simple moderation for yet another reason.
It claimed the excuse of necessity—the *social necessity* of easing rational conversation. Augustine had written that beyond the strict necessities of life, there
were other desirable ends—"wisdom, health, friendship"—and that some carnal
pleasures were necessary for achieving these ends. Assheton saw social drinking
as "serviceable to [the] Ends" of friendship and "good Neighbourhood." For
Cheyne, "the *chearful Cup*, and the *social Repast*" were the "innocent Means of
enlivening Conversation, [and] promoting *Friendship*." And the more moderate
one's drinking—the further one stayed from the sinful realm of drunkenness—
the more reasonable and *useful* one's social conversation.

Social Saloons

Recall those oddly jovial saloons that George Parsons Lathrop and Frederick
Masters extolled over ghostly opium dens where patrons lay dumb with dope.
"What most impresses us, now, is the silence of the scene," Lathrop wrote of a
tomblike den. How unlike this "wicked, ominous hush" was "the prodigal gas of
the barrooms, with . . . their glittering vari-colored bottles, their seductive air of
social re-union." "It was like being in a sepulcher with the dead," Masters said of a
den. "What a contrast to the glare and glitter of the saloon," with its "wild frenzy
and excited mirth." No longer odd, these images of 1880 and 1892, which cast a
warm light on social saloons, now fit naturally in an age when the best excuse for
drink was conversation.

Yet the drinking places most admired in this era of growing anti-saloon
sentiment were not American-style saloons at all. They were "the Continental
type" of saloon, as Congregational minister Raymond Calkins called them in
1901—the German biergartens and Parisian boulevard restaurants and the little
Italian, Hungarian, and Polish establishments so unlike their tawdrier American
cousins. Whether on their native soil or in the foreign quarters of America's big
cities, these places served a "motive of sociability and amusement . . . as strong
in the patron as the desire for drink." They were the spots best suited to social

---

[121] *Hansard's Parliamentary Debates* (Commons), vol. 9, p. 1042 (Mar. 8, 1736) (statement of
an unidentified speaker); Rush, *Enquiry* (1784 ed.), p. 246; Beecher, *Six Sermons* (4th ed. 1828),
p. 31. Edward Slingerland has documented cross-cultural norms against solitary drinking and social
rituals that guard against drinking to excess. Edward Slingerland, *Drunk: How We Sipped, Danced,
and Stumbled Our Way to Civilization* (New York: Little, Brown Spark, 2021), pp. 239–43.

drinking, where a man could sit with his wife or a newspaper, whiling his time in the company of friends.

Calkins focused on four features of these social saloons—the furnishings, the pace of drinking, the talk, and the lack of drunkenness. "The drinking is done at tables," he said. "Very often there is no bar. The atmosphere is that of comfort and of sociability. There is much less intoxication, as a rule, than in the bar saloons. Distilled liquors are seldom called for . . . . More time is spent over the drink than in the 'stand-up' saloons. It is more of a loafing-place; the social element dominates." In these continental-style saloons, "the drinking is made the accompaniment of many varied forms of social activity." As an 1864 essayist, perhaps Charles Dickens, wrote about the drinking places of France, here "you are not expected to empty liquor into yourself as from one vessel into another . . . ."[122]

The biergarten and the café, even more than Lathrop's and Masters's glittering saloons, presented drinking in its most moral form. In these family-friendly establishments where friends met and lingered and where alcohol was an option, not a cover charge, the drinking almost always was moderate and almost always served social ends.

Stand-Up Saloons

Amid fond words for such continental drinking spots and their occasional American counterparts, sentiment against "the saloon" frothed and boiled over. One year Frederick Masters could speak of the glare, glitter, and excited mirth of America's social saloons. The next year—1893—the Anti-Saloon League would take form, vowing to reduce those temples of depravity to ashes. So we return to the paradox posed earlier: Why was the saloon banned—if not in California and New York, where Masters and Lathrop wrote, then in the nation as a whole in 1920? And why did drinking places rebound so readily when the Eighteenth Amendment, which had spread prohibition across the land, met resounding repeal less than fourteen years later?

The paradox largely dissolves when we distinguish two very different sorts of saloon. The best—those on the continental model—presented scenes of merry but sober social mirth, where drinkers lounged with friends and drank lightly to ease their chatter. The worst—those that fueled prohibitionists' fury—were the "stand-ups." For *stand-up* saloons resembled neither cafés nor biergartens, but the dens.

---

[122] Calkins, *Substitutes for the Saloon*, pp. 19–20; "You Must Drink!" *All the Year Round*, vol. 11 (1864), pp. 437, 438.

Like the dens, which lacked all furnishings beyond their spartan wooden bunks, stand-up saloons sported only a bar. Denied tables, chairs, and stools, patrons downed their drinks standing. An 1850s observer said most Americans "march up to the bar, pour out a drink, dash it down without the possibility of tasting it, toss the money over the counter, and rush out like an ignited sky-rocket"—all in "a quarter of a minute."[123]

The spectacle was not exclusively American. English observers too deplored the "rough-and-ready stand-up constituted drink-shop," where "the customer must come, like a bucket to a well, and fill himself and go away again." The lack of chairs conveyed the message, " 'Do not loiter, but drink.' . . . [Y]ou have no right to remain in the place another moment unless you renew your consumption." The unnamed author of "You Must Drink!" lamented in 1864 that in British drinking places, "you must stand up to your devotions, and get through them in a thorough business-like fashion." In London, men "swill their liquors like pigs. A London public-house is a trough."[124]

The American stand-up saloon pictured in a 1909 issue of *McClure's Magazine*, despite its tuxedoed tenders, resembles nothing so much as a drinking man's trough (see Figure 3.2). Stretching the length of an alley-shaped room lined with bottles, three servers at the ready, the bar is a model of efficiency, engineered to serve the maximum number in the minimum space in minimum time. "[E]ven the rudest sitting accommodation is being refused," an English observer wrote in 1877, "since drinking goes on faster and more profitably when the customers are kept standing round a bar."[125] With no place to sit or to look one's companion square in the face, drinkers had little inclination to dally and converse.

This image of trough-like efficiency was not unique to the metropolis, whether New York or London. In their massive 1900 study of the American temperance movement, Joseph Rowntree and Arthur Sherwell printed interior photos of five saloons in Portland, Maine, one of the first beachheads of liquor prohibition. Each photo shows a bar stretching the length of the room. Not one shows a table, chair, or even barstool. "The men came to drink," one Boston-area minister recalled; "they generally stood at the bar, and when the drinking was done they went away."[126]

---

[123] Warner, *Social Welfare and the Liquor Problem* (7th ed. 1916), p. 22 (describing the stand-up saloon); W.C., "American Jottings: Bars, Groggeries, Maine Law, and Other Things," *Chambers's Journal of Popular Literature Science and Arts*, vol. 3 (1855), pp. 42, 45 (quoting the *New York Tribune*).

[124] "You Must Drink!" pp. 437, 438–40. Mark Lawrence Schrad writes of nineteenth-century British dram shops in like terms: "no tables, no chairs, and no sociability—just drunken profits that extended the length of the bar." Schrad, *Smashing the Liquor Machine*, p. 147.

[125] Charles Graham, "Beer, and the Temperance Problem," *Contemporary Review*, vol. 30, no. 72 (June–Nov. 1877), p. 81.

[126] Joseph Rowntree & Arthur Sherwell, *The Temperance Problem and Social Reform* (7th ed. 1900), pp. 138A, 140A, 142A, 150A, 158A; G. Walter Fiske, "Prohibition and the Church," *in* Calkins, *Substitutes for the Saloon*, p. 349 (quoting a Boston-area minister).

THE SIMPLE OLD-STYLE LIQUOR SALOON

Figure 3.2: A Stand-Up Saloon (1909).

The specter of silent men in chairless bars downing drinks at quarter-minute intervals prompted reformers to scoff at the supposed social utility of saloons. "One of the alleged motives that lead men into the saloon is the desire to satisfy the social instincts," wrote Boston University sociologist John Marshall Barker in 1905. Grudgingly, Barker allowed that some saloons—those that most resembled Masters's and Lathrop's gaslit halls of mirth and social reunion—had "attractions as a social centre. A few of them are brilliantly lighted and furnished with warmth, free seats, and public conveniences, and seemingly are entitled to a measure of respect . . . ." But such saloons are "exceedingly rare," Barker said. "The average type of saloon is gross and vulgar. It has no tables, chairs, or accommodations. The things most in evidence are barrels, bottles, glasses, and a bare counter where men line up to drink." In such a saloon, it is "impossible . . . to satisfy any legitimate social instinct or necessity." Instead the saloon "becomes an instrument to make a man intoxicated."[127]

Barker and other reformers hated the stand-ups with their custom of "perpendicular drinking" because these saloons, like opium dens, served as little more

---

[127] John Marshall Barker, *The Saloon Problem and Social Reform* (Boston: The Everett Press, 1905 (Arno Press reprint, 1970)), pp. 37, 184–86.

than *houses of intoxication*. Or in the words of our English observer of 1864, their effect was "to promote excessive drinking, for drinking sake." Over a century earlier, the Earl of Cholmondeley had complained that gin introduced "the new art of sudden intoxication."[128] The stand-up saloons of the late nineteenth and early twentieth centuries sought to revive this art—and suffered the same moral condemnation.

Looking back in 1909, Harry S. Warner speculated on the forces that had transformed the typical American saloon from a semi-social center to a counter of consumption. He said "the more active life of the people," "tenser business competition," and "brewery control" had conspired with other factors to form "a distinct type—the stand-up saloon, with long bar and lines of men leaning over it." Warner's references to the people's active life and business competition cut the same way: stand-ups were good for both speed and profit because (as another had observed) "drinking goes on faster and more profitably when the customers are kept standing round a bar." Brewery control of vast numbers of saloons, which paid fealty to the beermakers that supplied their fixtures, signage, and license fees, aggravated the need for profits and the imperative of drinking fast and never lingering.[129]

As did "high-license" schemes, by which states hiked the fees of liquor sellers both to shrink their numbers and fill state coffers. High licenses had the perverse effect of converting social saloons into stand-ups. "The amount of furniture supplied depends largely on the license system that prevails," Raymond Calkins noted in 1901. "Where the license is low and the saloons are numerous, competition results in a larger attempt to provide for the physical comfort of patrons." Hence in St. Louis, where licenses were cheap, "[t]he great majority of saloons . . . are furnished with . . . tables and chairs for the convenience of their patrons. One who passes by can often see card-playing through the open door. Many of them also have billiard and pool tables . . . ." Where licenses were dear, however, such amenities were rare. To recoup heavy fees, proprietors scrimped on furniture and frills and encouraged patrons to drink fast and never dawdle. And scarce licenses meant proprietors could scrimp as they wished, for patrons often had no place more commodious to go. As Calkins put it, "Where the license

[128] Fiske, "Prohibition and the Church," p. 350 ("Some saloons are . . . given up wholly to 'perpendicular drinking.'"); Edward Huntington Williams, "Negro Cocaine 'Fiends' New Southern Menace," *New York Times Sunday Magazine* (Feb. 8, 1914), p. 12 ("[Prohibition] obliged [the drinker] to forego the pleasure of leaning against a bar and 'taking his drink perpendicularly' . . ."); "You Must Drink!" p. 439; *Hansard's Parliamentary Debates* (Lords), vol. 12, p. 1338 (1743) (remarks of the Earl of Cholmondeley).
[129] Warner, *Social Welfare and the Liquor Problem* (7th ed. 1916), p. 22; Graham, "Beer, and the Temperance Problem," p. 81 ("drinking goes on . . ."); Okrent, *Last Call*, pp. 29–30 (describing "tied house[s]").

is high and the saloons are limited in number, other attractions than the drink are not needed."[130]

Social Substitutes for the Saloon

Despite all the saloon's ills as a social institution, many social commentators wished to preserve much of what the saloon supplied. They saw that the better American saloons, like their French and German counterparts, gave poor and working-class men a social refuge from life's cares. Though references to saloons as "poor men's clubs" grew cliché, they had a measure of truth. Observers spoke of working men's "fundamental social instinct" and "vital human need" for the camaraderie of the saloon and of "a positive necessity for what the saloon has hitherto offered." Over and over contemporaries pointed to "the social instinct that demands and finds its satisfaction within the saloon," "the social craving which the saloon has been recognizing," and the "primal desire" and "imperative demand for human companionship and sociability."[131] This rhetoric did not all spring from prohibition's opponents. On the contrary, often it was the result of handwringing by prohibitionists about what they would have wrought once they won.

For the best saloons served as more than watering spots. They filled a profusion of social roles—from post office and business office to credit union and union hall, from employment agency and steamship agency to reading room and public restroom. "We cannot dodge the fact that [saloons] *have* served as the poor man's club," Oberlin theologian G. Walter Fiske wrote. "We cannot deny that they have furnished the only available social centre where men might gather, in many a community . . . ." There men can find "warmth and light and a welcome, and a sort of good cheer and a kind of comradeship."[132] To the army of

---

[130] Calkins, *Substitutes for the Saloon*, pp. 8, 28.

[131] "The Church's Temperance Duties," in *Prohibition: Its Relation to Temperance, Good Morals & Sound Government* (Joseph Debar ed., Cincinnati, n.p. [1910]), pp. 204, 207 (quoting Bishop Fallows of Chicago) ("The saloon is emphatically the 'poor man's club.'"); Fiske, "Prohibition and the Church," p. 351 ("vital human need" and "the social craving which . . ."); Warner, *Social Welfare and the Liquor Problem* (7th ed. 1916), p. 172 ("a fundamental social instinct"); James W. Johnson, *To Drink or Not To Drink? A Vital, Personal Problem Facing America Today* (n.p., n.d.), p. 5 ("a positive necessity for . . ."); Calkins, *Substitutes for the Saloon*, p. 5 ("the social instinct that demands . . ."); Francis G. Peabody, "Introduction" to Calkins, *Substitutes for the Saloon*, pp. xxvii, xxxi ("imperative demand for . . ."); ibid., p. xxxii ("primal desire").

[132] Calkins, *Substitutes for the Saloon*, pp. 9–11, 22 (union hall, cultural center, credit agency, post office, business space); Warner, *Social Welfare and the Liquor Problem* (7th ed. 1916), p. 230 (function hall, chapel, employment agency, reading room, steamship agency, political headquarters) (citing Charles Stelzle, *American Social and Religious Conditions* (New York: Fleming H. Revell Company, 1912), p. 111); Peabody, "Introduction" to Calkins, *Substitutes for the Saloon*, pp. xxi–xxii (news room, drinking fountain, lavatory); Fiske, "Prohibition and the Church," p. 350.

armchair sociologists who advocated prohibition, life without the saloon seemed as unthinkable as life with it.

The solution, as Raymond Calkins argued most prominently, was to establish an array of alternative, nonalcoholic meeting spots that would serve the saloon's social role but not its alcohol. The effort had been underway for half a century by the time Harvard theology professor Francis G. Peabody gave it a name in his 1896 essay, "Substitutes for the Saloon." Five years later Calkins borrowed the title for his famous manifesto of the movement, which detailed the need for saloon stand-ins and the forms they should take. The aim, Calkins said, was to plant such substitutes across the landscape long before prohibition took hold. It would be unjust "[t]o destroy the social functions of the saloon without making any provision for the social needs of the people." Of the institutions promoted as possible substitutes, lunchrooms, coffeehouses, and reading rooms were among the most promising, as were bowling alleys, YMCAs, and "moving-picture shows."[133] Long before the Eighteenth Amendment wiped out the legal liquor traffic, reform groups countrywide opened such places apace.

The Stalemate Broken: National Prohibition's Rise

In the end, of course, prohibition came and the saloon had to go. Moral aversion to the saloon—or to a particular image of the saloon, involving fast drinking, frequent drunkenness, and a dollop of prostitution—impelled the nation's ultimate embrace of the Eighteenth Amendment and its ban on traffic in intoxicating beverages. But other forces too were at work. Or more precisely, in certain regions of the country other factors aggravated antagonism toward saloons and snapped the stalemate that for over half a century had kept the nation tottering between drys and drinkers, between total abstinence and moderation, between prohibition and its repeal.

The pattern of state prohibition laws culminating in congressional approval of the Eighteenth Amendment holds clues to these other forces. The second prohibition wave of the 1880s had crested quickly and crashed, leaving only five prohibition states by century's end. By 1904, there were just three: Maine, Kansas, and North Dakota.[134] Three years later, prohibition's progress resumed, as Oklahoma, Georgia, and Alabama doubled the dry-state roster. Mississippi and North Carolina joined in 1908; then came Tennessee in 1909 and West

---

[133] Francis G. Peabody, "Substitutes for the Saloon," *The Forum*, vol. 21 (1896), p. 595; Calkins, *Substitutes for the Saloon*, pp. 25–26; Warner, *Social Welfare and the Liquor Problem* (7th ed. 1916), pp. 178–79 ("moving-picture shows"); Duis, *The Saloon*, pp. 197–202 ("The Search for Substitutes").

[134] Tilton, "Landmarks in the History of Prohibition," p. 312; Cherrington, *Evolution of Prohibition*, pp. 180–81.

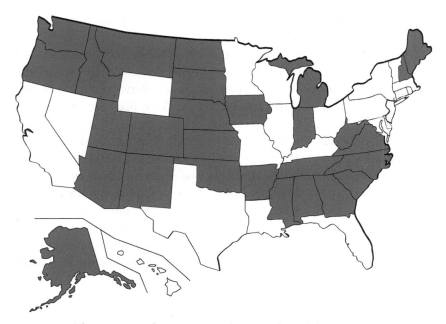

Figure 3.3: Those states or future states with statewide prohibition laws in place when Congress sent the Eighteenth Amendment to the states for ratification in December 1917.

Virginia in 1912. In 1914 this measured Southern advance suddenly gave way to metastatic growth, as prohibition also spread west. Virginia, Arizona, Colorado, Oregon, and Washington all went dry in 1914; South Carolina, Arkansas, Iowa, and Idaho in 1915. Four more states followed in 1916, then another four plus Alaska in 1917. In all, twenty-seven states and Alaska had embraced prohibition before Congress sent the Eighteenth Amendment to the states for ratification in December 1917. Of these, only Maine and New Hampshire fell northeast of Indiana. As the map in Figure 3.3 shows, they sat as lonely outposts in a region where prohibition once held sway sixty-odd years before.[135]

The course and speed of this third and last state-based prohibition movement suggest three prominent causes and one trigger. In the many Southern and occasional Midwestern states that embraced prohibition beginning in 1907, the suspicion of racist motives looms large. With increasing mobility and economic

---

[135] The best guide to this course of lawmaking is Ernest Cherrington's. I drew the critical dates from his exhaustive chronology of prohibition-related events. *See* Cherrington, *Evolution of Prohibition*, pp. 281–362; Tilton, "Landmarks in the History of Prohibition," p. 316. In my state tally, I have put a state in the dry column on the date its people or legislature voted to go dry, though the effective date of a new prohibition law sometimes was delayed as long as two years.

independence, African Americans were less in thrall of white landholders and more able to establish and patronize saloons than were the freedmen of a generation before. The specter of hard-drinking Black men carousing by night unsettled many whites. Shortly after Georgia's new prohibition statute took effect early in 1908, the leader of that state's dry forces, Seaborn Wright, claimed slavery's demise demanded prohibition in the South—not to oppress the freedman, Wright insisted, but to protect him. The states of the old South had forbidden liquor sales to slaves, "and this one thing, in spite of the grinding hardships of slavery, [had] made of the Negro the finest physically developed race on the continent . . . ." But after the Civil War, saloons "stretch[ed] their paralyzing arms to this semi-savage, child race," Wright said, "destroying all that was best in the Negro mind and heart and body." Prohibition laws now must rise as a bulwark against perdition: "[T]he development, the safety, aye, the very life of the Negro race of the South hangs upon his absolute separation from intoxicating liquors. Four-fifths of his crimes against our women come from this infernal source, it is behind nine-tenths of the race conflicts in the South."[136]

That same year, during a "crusade against the saloon," the Nashville *Tennessean* ran back-to-back front-page editorials claiming a drunken Black man had murdered a white fourteen-year-old named Margaret Lear in Louisiana. "Men of Tennessee," the paper asked, "Do you think the fate of Margaret Lear may not come to the innocent school girl or the virtuous woman of Tennessee? . . . [T]he negro fairly docile and industrious, becomes, when filled with liquor, turbulent and dangerous and a menace to life, property, and the repose of the community." Seven months later, just days into the next legislative session, the governor signed laws effectively banning alcohol sales and manufacture in Tennessee.[137]

In 1922, as prohibition reigned over a divided nation, journalist Fabian Franklin blamed the mess on "the desire of the South to keep liquor away from negroes." Franklin complained that "the people of New York are being deprived of their right to the harmless enjoyment of wine and beer in order that the negroes of Alabama and Texas may not get beastly drunk on rotgut whiskey." Historian Robert Binkley added that but for the constitutional requirement of equal treatment, Southern states would have barred African Americans alone from drinking. "Out of formal respect for the [Fourteenth] Amendment, the

---

[136] Seaborn Wright, "The Race Problem and the Liquor Traffic," *American Issue* (May 9, 1908), pp. 6, 7. To the same effect was John Temple Graves, "The Fight Against Alcohol: Third Article—Georgia Pioneers the Prohibition Crusade," *Cosmopolitan*, vol. 45 (1908), pp. 88–89. On the effective date of Georgia's prohibition law, *see* Cherrington, *Evolution of Prohibition*, p. 281.

[137] "Who Killed Margaret Lear?" [Nashville] *Tennessean*, June 16–17, 1908, p. 1, *reprinted in Columbia Herald*, June 19, 1908, p. 8; Paul E. Isaac, *Prohibition and Politics: Turbulent Decades in Tennessee, 1885–1920* (University of Tennessee Press, 1965), p. 148 (quoting from the *Tennessean*); "An Act to Prohibit the Sale of Intoxicating Liquors . . . ," 1909 *Tennessee Acts*, ch. 1 (Act of Jan. 13, 1909), p. 3; "An Act to Prohibit the Manufacture in this State of Intoxicating Liquors . . . ," ibid., ch. 10 (Act of Jan. 21, 1909), p. 21.

legislation had to take the form of general Prohibition . . . ." Even if many African American leaders in the South condemned the depredations of the liquor traffic, the triumph of prohibition in state after Southern state likely traces largely to whites' avowed fears of drunken Black men.[138]

Alongside racism, perhaps, lay nativism. Old-stock Protestants of the South, Midwest, and Plains, heirs to the Puritan tradition and its aversion to mind-numbing pleasures, looked northeastward with dread. They saw seaboard cities teeming with recently docked immigrants from harder-drinking and often Catholic homelands—Germany and especially Ireland in the nineteenth century, Southern and Eastern Europe in the twentieth. In Joseph Gusfield's 1963 analysis of the sociological rift of these times, the drive to ban drink nationwide was a "symbolic crusade" in which threatened natives asserted cultural primacy over less moralized newcomers. In Richard Hofstadter's words, prohibition expressed an aversion "not merely . . . to drunkenness and to the evils that accompanied it, but to the immigrant drinking masses, [and] to the pleasures and amenities of city life . . . ."[139]

Contemporary observers spotlighted this struggle between rural and urban, native and newcomer, Protestant and Catholic, South and East. Journalist George Kibbe Turner wrote in 1909 that the South distinctively "preserves the conditions, habits, and religious feeling of the . . . [era] of the great Protestant temperance movement in the early part of the [nineteenth] century." The South's traditionalism stemmed from its demographics, Turner said. For every Southern foreigner, he counted fifteen natives; for every city dweller, twenty farmers; for every non-Protestant, ten Protestant church members.[140]

That same year, Harry S. Warner fretted openly about the half-million immigrants of the previous two decades—the "Italians, Poles, Russians, Hungarians, Bohemians and Jews," who have proved unable to "break away from the long-existing social endorsement of alcohol." He quoted Dr. Alexander MacNichol's verdict that this "vast immigration of inferior peoples, . . . augmenting our drinking classes, furnishing additional soil from which

---

[138] Fabian Franklin, *What Prohibition Has Done to America* (New York: Harcourt, Brace and Company, 1922), pp. 72–73; Robert C. Binkley, *Responsible Drinking: A Discreet Inquiry and a Modest Proposal* (New York: The Vanguard Press, 1930), pp. 53–54. Binkley referred to the Fifteenth Amendment, which granted African Americans suffrage, rather than the Fourteenth Amendment, which guaranteed equal protection of the laws. I presume he meant to refer to the latter. Robert Post pointed me to Franklin's very interesting book. On the strident anti-liquor activism of Booker T. Washington and other prominent African Americans, *see* Schrad, *Smashing the Liquor Machine*, pp. 483–85.

[139] Gusfield, *Symbolic Crusade*; Richard Hofstadter, *The Age of Reform: From Bryan to F.D.R.* (New York: Alfred A. Knopf, 1955), pp. 289–90. For another take on this theme, *see* Peter H. Odegard, *Pressure Politics: The Story of the Anti-Saloon League* (New York: Columbia University Press, 1928), pp. 29–35.

[140] Turner, "Beer and the City Liquor Problem," pp. 538–39.

to propagate criminals, . . . renders more imperative the necessity for these movements which will alleviate and enlighten." With such comments swirling about, one observer declared, "This whole Anti-Saloon League movement is in reality a thinly veiled warfare on everything foreign . . . ."[141]

Though the South's peculiar demographics may help explain its rather sudden conversion to prohibition, demographics help far less in the West. The westward spread of prohibition fever beginning in 1914 reached states too remote to fear spill-off from Eastern immigrant cities. In the West, it appears different forces were at work—particularly women's suffrage and the immense power of the Woman's Christian Temperance Union. WCTU members pledged not merely "to abstain from all distilled, fermented and malt liquors," but "to employ all proper means to discourage the use of and traffic in the same."[142]

In the battle to ban the traffic by law, no weapon was as potent as the vote, and women had won the vote largely in the West. Sixteen states and future states gave women the vote before Congress proposed the Nineteenth Amendment with its grant of universal female suffrage in June 1919. Of these, only New York lay in the Northeast and only Michigan in the Midwest. All the rest fell in the Plains or westward (see Figure 3.4).[143] The West's embrace of suffrage likely traced to the lack of suitable partners for the men who went west in search of farmland and gold. Seeking to attract women settlers, Western states promised the vote. And having gained the vote, women won prohibition too. By the end of 1917, seven of the West's ten suffrage states had banned drink. All seven—Arizona, Colorado, Oregon, Washington, Idaho, Montana, and Utah—went dry after women gained suffrage, as did Alaska when Congress enacted prohibition in the territory in accord with a popular vote. Of the ten Far Western states and territories that submitted the prohibition question to an electorate that included women, only Nevada and Wyoming voted no.[144]

[141] Warner, *Social Welfare and the Liquor Problem* (7th ed. 1916), p. 26; ibid., p. 159 (quoting imperfectly T. Alexander MacNichol, "Alcohol and the Disabilities of School Children," *The National Advocate*, vol. 43, no. 2 (Feb. 1908), pp. 30–31); "Beer and the City Liquor Problem" (review essay), in Debar, *Prohibition: Its Relation to Temperance*, p. 249 ("This whole Anti-Saloon League movement . . .").

[142] Alan P. Grimes, *The Puritan Ethic and Woman Suffrage* (New York: Oxford University Press, 1967), p. 84 (quoting the WCTU pledge). On the role of the WCTU and women's organized resistance to the alcohol trade, *see* Lender & Martin, *Drinking in America*, pp. 88–92, 106–08; Okrent, *Last Call*, pp. 16–23.

[143] My research assistant Zoe Scharff hunted down the earliest suffrage acts and amendments in the various states. The resulting timeline is almost identical to that assembled by Alexander Keyssar in *The Right To Vote: The Contested History of Democracy in the United States* (New York: Basic Books, 2000), tbl. A.20.

[144] Compare Figures 3.3 and 3.4. My list of prohibition states relies especially on Cherrington, *Evolution of Prohibition*. My counts and comparisons largely align with those of Alan Grimes. Grimes, *Puritan Ethic and Woman Suffrage*, pp. 57–58, 86, 114–15, 131.

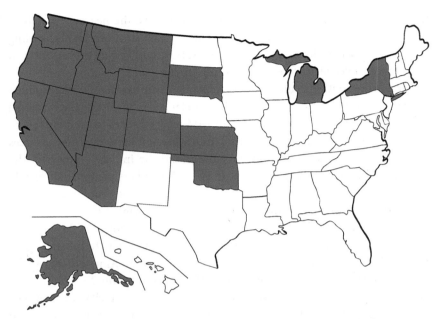

Figure 3.4: Those states or future states that granted women suffrage before Congress sent the Nineteenth Amendment to the states for ratification in June 1919.

Nor is the link between women's suffrage and prohibition a mystery. Women drank less than men; they found less solace than men in the saloon's musky milieu; and they alone knew the violence and abandonment of husbands who staggered home from saloons drunk, mean, and broke. "[W]e who are the innocent victims of the [liquor] license system," wrote Elizabeth Cady Stanton in 1852, "should [have] a voice in pulling it down." Or as Western suffrage activist Abigail Scott Duniway warned a generation later, "Let woman arm herself with the ballot, and we shall see if she cannot drive the liquor traffic to the abode of owls and bats." Wise to this dynamic, prohibition's friends and foes waged war over suffrage too. North Dakota Senator Asle J. Gronna—a friend—defended the suffrage amendment in 1914, arguing "all nations must ultimately, stamp out the liquor curse, if they are not to perish form the earth. And I believe that giving the women the vote will hasten the day when this is accomplished in the United States." Two years earlier, the president of the National Retail Liquor Dealers' Association—a foe—warned his members they "need fear the Woman's Christian Temperance Union and the ballot in the hands of women; therefore, gentlemen, fight woman suffrage!" Brewers,

Daniel Okrent recounts, staged repeated covert campaigns to crush suffrage at the ballot box.[145]

Empirical evidence of women's impact on suffrage votes is slender but suggestive. Drawing on county voting patterns in statewide prohibition contests between 1907 and 1919, Professor Michael Lewis found a mildly positive—but not statistically significant—correlation between women's voting rights and prohibition victories. A century earlier, suffrage advocate Ella Seass Stewart headlined stronger evidence of a link. Stewart analyzed local option elections in Illinois, where women's limited suffrage compelled officials to count their ballots separately from men's. Elections in 1913 and 1914 had turned 262 Illinois cities and towns dry. Women tipped the balance in over a hundred townships, Stewart reported, voting nearly two-to-one against saloons. In Jacksonville, Illinois, almost 82 percent of women voted dry; in Galesburg, 90 percent did so; in Atlanta and Benton, 96 percent; and in Virginia, a *hundred* percent of 395 women voters. In only four cities did most women vote wet. Trumpeting these results, one "Anti-Saloon League enthusiast" told the *New York Times*, "The spread of woman's suffrage is helping us materially. . . . In a few places where they voted last year they made the liquor interests gasp." And Western women promoted prohibition by means other than voting. In several Western campaigns for statewide prohibition, Stewart wrote, "the work of securing the signatures for the referendum is credited largely to women."[146]

Women's suffrage victories helped fuel the drive to prohibition in the West, as did racism and nativism in the South and Midwest. All three forces stood against the stand-up saloon and its role as a drinking trough for drinking's sake. As these

---

[145] Schrad, *Smashing the Liquor Machine*, p. 344 (quoting Stanton); [Untitled item,] *New Northwest* (Portland, Ore.), May 26, 1871, p. 2 (quoting Duniway); "The Inevitable Result," ibid., May 17, 1872, p. 2 (quoting Duniway: "Women must have a chance to vote and legislate whisky hells out of existence."); *Congressional Record*, vol. 51, pt. 5 (63d Cong., 2d Sess.), p. 5088 (Mar. 19, 1914) (remarks of Mr. Gronna), *quoted in* Grimes, *supra*, p. 131; Okrent, *Last Call*, pp. 64–66 (quoting NRLDA president). On the early link between suffrage and prohibition, *see* David E. Kyvig, *Repealing National Prohibition* (Chicago: University of Chicago Press, 1979), p. 118; Cherrington, *Evolution of Prohibition*, p. 334 ("The enfranchisement of women in Kansas is estimated to have added 300,000 voters to the Prohibition army."). Local laws often simply barred women from entering saloons. *See State v. Nelson*, 10 Idaho 522, 524–26, 529 (1905) (quoting ordinances forbidding saloons to admit women in Boise, Denver, and Middlesboro, Kentucky); "The Supervisors: A New Order to Exclude Women from Saloons at Night," *San Francisco Chronicle*, Sept. 1, 1874, p. 3. I am grateful to my former student Rae Woods for pointing me to the Duniway quotes.

[146] Michael Lewis, "Access to Saloons, Wet Voter Turnout, and Statewide Prohibition Referenda, 1907–1919," *Social Science History*, vol. 32, no. 3 (Fall 2008), pp. 393–94; Ella Seass Stewart, "Woman Suffrage and the Liquor Traffic," *The Annals of the American Academy of Political and Social Science*, vol. 56 (Nov. 1914), p. 143; p. 148 ("the work of . . ."); p. 150 (noting election results); p. 152; Edward Marshall, "Is National Prohibition Actually Close at Hand?" *New York Times Magazine*, Apr. 19, 1914, p. 10 (quoting William H. Anderson). I thank Kevin Rothenberg for pointing me to the Lewis and Stewart studies.

sentiments tipped the nation toward total abstinence, the trigger was war. At the outbreak of war in Europe in August 1914, there were ten prohibition states. By war's end in November 1918, there were thirty-two, as well as Alaska and Hawaii, which Congress had made dry—and five other states had ratified the Eighteenth Amendment's call for national prohibition.

In Congress, too, war seemed to harden prohibitionist sentiment. When a proposed prohibition amendment came before the House of Representatives in December 1914, it won by margins of 61 to 29 percent in the South and 57 to 35 percent in the West. But it met solid resistance among Eastern representatives, who rejected it by 60 to 28 percent. America's entry in the European conflict undercut resistance. Two days after President Woodrow Wilson asked Congress to declare war on Germany on April 2, 1917, Congress took up consideration of the Eighteenth Amendment. When the House voted on this new prohibition amendment in December 1917, ninety-nine Eastern representatives voted in favor, as against only fifty-nine in 1914. As journalist Ames Brown wrote in the *Atlantic Monthly* in 1915, "The Great War has had the effect of imparting to the anti-alcohol movement what is perhaps the greatest impetus it has received in all the ages."[147]

War smoothed the path to prohibition in part by deepening aversion to all things German. Suddenly beers named Busch, Blatz, Pabst, and Schlitz pricked patriotic sensibilities. "German brewers," one observer alleged in August 1917, "have rendered thousands of men inefficient and are thus crippling the Republic in its war on Prussian militarism." And war helped allay fears of prohibition by forcing the nation through a trial dry run. America's entry into the fray in April 1917 prompted grain shortages that gave alcohol abstinence a newly patriotic sheen. As Elizabeth Tilton wrote soon after the armistice, "the people felt that the Government could not with justice ask them to save every crumb and then proceed to allow the brewers to waste [grain] by the thousands of tons."[148] And not just grain: brewers and distillers consumed fuel, freight, and manpower too, all potential assets in the war effort.

So with battles raging in August 1917, Congress outlawed the manufacture and import of distilled drink for the conflict's duration and empowered

---

[147] Alan Grimes tallied House votes and reported the results in Grimes, *Puritan Ethic and Woman Suffrage*, pp. 133–34, 142. For the December 17, 1917, vote in the House to send the Eighteenth Amendment to the states for ratification, *see* the *Congressional Record*, vol. 56, pt. 1 (65th Cong., 2d Sess.), pp. 469–70 (Dec. 17, 1917); L. Ames Brown, "Nation-Wide Prohibition," *Atlantic Monthly*, vol. 115, no. 6 (June 1915), pp. 735, 736. I thank Robert Post for pointing out the coincidence of Wilson's war message and congressional consideration of the prohibition amendment.

[148] Peter H. Odegard, *Pressure Politics: The Story of the Anti-Saloon League* (New York: Octagon Books, 1966), p. 60 (quoting from *American Issue*, Ohio Edition, Aug. 3, 1917); Okrent, *Last Call*, p. 100 (quoting dry politician John Strange: "[T]he worst of all our German enemies . . . are Pabst, Schlitz, Blatz, and Miller."); ibid., pp. 98–103 (detailing the war's impact on the fight for prohibition); Tilton, "Landmarks in the History of Prohibition," p. 316.

President Wilson to extend the ban to beer and wine. On December 18, ten days after Wilson forbade brewing most malt liquors with more than 2.75 percent alcohol, lawmakers approved the Eighteenth Amendment with its full-fledged ban of all "intoxicating liquors." As the proposed amendment charged through the state ratification process and the Great War finally ground to a halt, Congress issued the War-Time Prohibition Act of November 1918, which likewise widened the wartime ban to all "intoxicating" beverages and held it in place till troops demobilized. Meanwhile, state after state ratified the proposed Eighteenth Amendment, which became part of the Constitution when the thirty-sixth state voted its approval in January 1919.[149]

National Prohibition's Onset and Demise

My aim in detailing these many forces—racism, nativism, suffrage, and war— that propelled the nation toward national prohibition is not to prove their lasting influence in the struggle against recreational intoxicants. On the contrary, I aim to show that national prohibition in America was a mistake—a historical fluke. A particular agglomeration of sectional forces joined briefly to push the nation past the bounds of mainstream morality on the alcohol question. Suddenly, the struggle between moderationists and total abstainers, stuck in stalemate for decades, tipped sharply the abstainers' way.

Very soon, however, it tipped back again. Hence the true lesson of national prohibition is not why it started, for the social and political patchwork that brought it in being proved fleeting. Instead, the lesson of this reform is that it ended—and did so with dispatch. For a stasis so far outside mainstream morality could not hold.

Yet on January 16, 1920, the day the saloons closed, the forces for reform saw themselves on the precipice of a new age. Already they had begun to put in place the post-saloon regime they so long had imagined. Among the most prominent monuments of this regime were the saloon substitutes Raymond Calkins had envisioned two decades before. By 1920, many saloon substitutes were open for business, and as prohibition took hold, reformers struggled to get others up and running.[150]

---

[149] Lever Food and Fuel Control Act, Act of Aug. 10, 1917, ch. 53, § 15, 40 Stat. 276, 282; J. Reuben Clark Jr. ed., *Emergency Legislation Passed Prior to December, 1917* . . . (Washington: Government Printing Office, 1918), pp. 151–52 (reprinting Wilson's proclamation); War-Time Prohibition Act, Act of Nov. 21, 1918, ch. 212, 40 Stat. 1045, 1046; Kyvig, *Repealing National Prohibition*, pp. 36–37 (reviewing some of these events); Tilton, "Landmarks in the History of Prohibition," pp. 316–17 (same).

[150] Duis, *The Saloon*, p. 199 (reporting the establishment of debating societies, folk arts and dance performances, gymnasiums, and social centers); Calkins, *Substitutes for the Saloons*, p. v (mentioning parks, playgrounds, benefit societies, and various agencies to reach men and boys in the city).

Some substitutes succeeded in attracting the saloons' former clientele. Others were thudding failures. Community lunchrooms, with their treacly aroma of charitable intermeddling, quickly lost the patronage of visitors who found their lunches served with a spoonful of proselytizing. Alcohol-free missionary saloons—among them New York's "Church Army Tea Saloon"—followed the same course to oblivion. As one Congregational pastor observed, the "type of man [who used to go to the saloons] does not want to be 'uplifted,' and I don't know that I blame him." Or in the words of a Los Angeles minister, "folks do not care to have a hand reached down to them from above." Among the few saloon substitutes that thrived were commercial movie houses. There, a former drinker could enter without meeting the "clammy hand-shake" of the well-meaning temperance missionary—and without that "uncomfortable sense of 'being done good to.'"[151] Indeed, of all saloon substitutes, the most successful were the least philanthropic.

And the least philanthropic of all were speakeasies, which mushroomed in every dark alley and dank cellar in every downbeat business district in downtown America. Home brewers flourished, too, and with them home distillers and vintners. That is, in the end prohibition mostly failed. Early years of falling drinking soon gave way to gains. Arrests for public drunkenness and deaths from liver cirrhosis and alcoholism plummeted between 1917 and 1920, as many state bans and then national prohibition took force. An upward trend began around 1920, wiping out most but not all earlier declines. Though alcohol consumption did not regain pre-prohibition levels till after World War II, the impression on the ground was of wide-scale disregard of the law. "[P]rohibition," wrote humorist Al Bromley in 1927, "is better than no liquor at all!"[152]

---

[151] Calkins, *Substitutes for the Saloon*, p. 222 (explaining the failure of the Church Army Tea Saloon: "[T]he benevolent and religious features [were] not helpful"); Fiske, "Prohibition and the Church," p. 355 (quoting Congregational pastor); ibid., p. 353 (quoting Los Angeles pastor); Adele F. Woodard, "The Motion-Picture Theatre as a Saloon Substitute," *in* Calkins, *Substitutes for the Saloon*, p. 358 ("No agency has furnished a stimulus [for patrons to abandon the saloon] so powerful as this form of entertainment."); Duis, *The Saloon*, p. 293 (noting that by 1908 there were 88 movie houses in Boston and 320 in Chicago); Kyvig, *Repealing National Prohibition*, p. 28 (reporting that by 1930 average sales hit 90 million tickets a week); James Peyton Sizer, *The Commercialization of Leisure* (Boston: Richard G. Badger, 1917), p. 47 ("clammy hand-shake"); Fiske, "Prohibition and the Church," p. 354 ("uncomfortable sense of 'being done good to'").

[152] Phillips, *Alcohol*, p. 266 (noting a 1931 police estimate of 32,000 speakeasies in New York City); Sean Dennis Cashman, *Prohibition: The Lie of the Land* (New York: The Free Press, 1981), p. 212 (reporting massive illicit production and importation of spirits); Lisa McGirr, *The War on Alcohol: Prohibition and the Rise of the American State* (New York: W.W. Norton & Company, 2014), pp. 52–53 (detailing home manufacture). On the temporary reduction of alcohol consumption during national prohibition, *see* Wayne Hall, "What Are the Policy Lessons of National Alcohol Prohibition in the United States, 1920–1933?" *Addiction*, vol. 105 (2010), pp. 1164, 1166–69; Snowshor Al, "Hot Pages frum My Diary," *Chicago Tribune*, Aug. 14, 1927, p. N3. I thank Keith Humphreys for pointing me to Hall's paper.

The reasons for this perceived failure were varied, but among the most potent was the sheer impossibility of consistent enforcement. As Senator David Walsh argued in 1932, "What is the reason for the agitation in America to-day against the eighteenth amendment? The illicit saloon or speakeasy; the inability of the Federal Government to . . . suppress the sale and transportation of intoxicating liquor." Senator William E. Borah of Idaho said it too: "The reason for advocating the repeal of the eighteenth amendment . . . is because the National Government can not enforce the liquor law." Writing from ground zero of the gangland alcohol wars, a *Chicago Tribune* editorialist warned in 1929 that "teetotalism is notoriously and inherently unenforceable by law." Truly banning drink "would necessitate a perpetual civil war in this country with half the population devoting most of its time to disciplining the other half." These voices perhaps claimed too much, Lisa McGirr writes, for in some places enforcement was vigorous—and indeed high-handed, biased, and abusive.[153] But the general point remains: the law held little claim on the nation's moral convictions.

And prohibition failed because of the speakeasies' irrepressible success. Prohibition failed for the same reason most saloon substitutes failed—because the critical ingredient in the saloons' success in salving the social man was not the setting but the drink. It was the drink, after all, that eased the speaking. Even Raymond Calkins, the most stalwart of all supporters of saloon substitutes, admitted "alcohol is a stimulant to sociability. It warms the cockles of the heart and promotes good cheer. Tea, coffee, and ginger ale in any quantity cannot rival in this respect a single glass of beer." In the end, Americans accepted that the critical social lubricant was alcohol.[154]

Prohibition failed, too, for several separate if related reasons. Widespread evasion bred bad liquor, poisoned patrons, government graft, invasive enforcement, and gangland rule. And the gangsters rarely paid taxes. When the Great Depression hit, the nation felt keenly the jobs and taxes lost to the drink ban—an echo of the monetary strain that helped doom England's 1736 gin ban. In fiscal year 1916, when most states still permitted alcohol sales, the federal government reaped 47 percent of internal revenues from taxes and duties on alcohol—against only 13 percent from personal income taxes. Then, between 1919 and 1929, federal tax receipts from spirits, wine, and beer crashed from $483 million to less than $13 million. In the Depression's depths in August 1931, the *New York Times*

---

[153] *Congressional Record*, vol. 75, pt. 14 (72d Cong., 1st Sess.), p. 15675 (July 16, 1932) (remarks of Mr. Walsh); ibid., p. 15676 (remarks of Mr. Borah); "A Prohibition Poser," *Chicago Daily Tribune*, Sept. 20, 1928, p. 10; McGirr, *War on Alcohol*, pp. 78–95, 121–38, 149–51.

[154] *Oxford English Dictionary* (Oxford: 2d ed. 1989), v. 16, p. 142 (noting the word "speakeasy" is derived from the verb "speak" and the adverb "easy"); Calkins, *Substitutes for the Saloon*, p. 217; Slingerland, *Drunk*, p. 190 (Alcohol "is the ideal social enhancer."). In truth the *easy* in speakeasy probably meant *softly*, so as to avoid the law's attention. Irving Lewis Allen, *The City in Slang: New York Life and Popular Slang* (New York: Oxford University Press, 1993), p. 72.

blamed prohibition for the loss of up to eighty thousand jobs in the beer and wine trades and repeated a congressman's estimate that permitting sales of these beverages would generate a billion dollars in new revenues. Meanwhile, income tax receipts plunged 60 percent in the three years after the 1929 market crash. "A large investment house in Wall Street goes so far," the *Times* wrote, "as to assert that 'the United States holds in its hands the means for rehabilitation of the world through the repeal of the Eighteenth Amendment.'"[155]

The point was not lost on Congress. Debating repeal in 1932, lawmakers itemized prohibition's costs and heralded the economic boon of repeal. Ohio Representative Arthur P. Lamneck lamented the billion dollars squandered annually on futile federal and state enforcement efforts. Claiming "[r]epeal is the one thing that will restore prosperity," Senator Hiram Bingham of Connecticut spoke of hundreds of thousands of jobs and a market for a hundred million bushels of grain, seven million tons of coal, and hundreds of locomotives and trucks. Industrialist Pierre du Pont took these arguments to the people in a 1932 radio address, motivated perhaps by du Pont's desire to shrink his personal tax load. With prohibition's repeal, he said, "[t]he income tax would not be necessary in the future and half of the revenue applied to the budget . . . would be furnished by the tax on liquor alone." Looking back at these debates shortly after repeal, Leonard Harrison and Elizabeth Laine traced prohibition's downfall as much to "the need for revenue as [to] the desire to eradicate the evils that grew out of that social experiment. . . . 'Turn the bootlegger's profits into public revenues,' became a watchword."[156]

Yet the allure of jobs and tax revenues likely could not have toppled prohibition had the nation stood committed to the morality of the drink ban. Alcohol prohibition fell not simply because it sacrificed massive tax revenues, but because it did so on the false altar of total abstinence. That is, prohibition died because it set a moral standard outside the social mainstream.

Over and over in the last three centuries, in a rash of temperance fever, legislatures have overreached public morality on the alcohol question. In every case, the result has been repeal or judicial negation. For in the struggle between moderation and total abstinence, the only stable stopping point is moderation.

---

[155] McGirr, *War on Alcohol*, pp. 53–60 (discussing poisonings, corruption, and gangland violence); ibid., pp. 233–37 (reviewing the forces behind repeal); Musto, *American Disease*, p. 131 (supplying tax revenues); *Statistics Concerning Intoxicating Liquors* (Washington: United States Government Printing Office, Jan. 1930), p. 3 (supplying alcohol revenue figures); "Prohibition and Prosperity," *New York Times*, Aug. 30, 1931, § 3, p. E1; Okrent, *Last Call*, p. 331 (noting income tax receipts).

[156] *Congressional Record*, vol. 75 (72d Cong., 1st Sess.), pt. 5, p. 5847 (Mar. 11, 1932) (remarks of Mr. Lamneck); ibid., pt. 14, p. 15655 (July 16, 1932) (remarks of Mr. Bingham); Pierre S. du Pont, "Prohibition Plainly Put" (CBS Radio, June 9, 1932), *in Drugs in America: A Documentary History* (David F. Musto ed., New York: New York University Press, 2002), pp. 147, 150; Leonard V. Harrison & Elizabeth Laine, *After Repeal: A Study of Liquor Control Administration* (New York: Harper & Brothers, 1936), p. 173.

That is true in part because there is no clear moral case for total abstinence. As the *Indianapolis Star* explained in 1913, when Congress was contemplating a federal mechanism to enforce state prohibition laws, "The impossibility of enforcing laws which penalize the decent use of liquors grows out of the inherent repugnance of man to a statute which brands him as a lawbreaker when he has done no wrong." Thirteen years later, with prohibition the law of the land, the *New York Times* agreed: "The preposterous Volstead act [dictating prohibition's terms] . . . is not and can not be enforced in great reaches of the country because it has no hold on the reason or the moral sense of the majority."[157]

In the eyes of traditional Western moralists, the sin always has lain in the excess—in the abandonment of reason and the escape into mindless pleasure. A broad consensus on the moral failing of drunkenness never has translated into consensus on the wrongfulness of drink. "I hope, no man will say," Lord Carteret argued in 1743, advocating repeal of England's gin ban, "there is any vice in drinking a single dram even of gin itself . . . . The vice consists in the immoderate use of it . . . ."[158] A half-millennium earlier, Aquinas had explored the twilight zone between the sin of excess and the safety of abstinence and hinted hesitantly at a moral sanction for moderate drinking in between. On this question little has changed. Claims that all drink sinfully tempts drinkers toward drunkenness never have won the public's accord.

Add to this reality a second—that a moderationist regime permits abstainers to abstain, while total abstinence enforced by law condemns moderation and ensures continuing conflict. We now can posit a historical theorem: within the traditional Western moral framework, alcohol prohibition cannot stand widely or for long. In this sense the lesson of national prohibition is not that it happened, but that it ended. After less than fourteen years national prohibition fell by acclamation. The Twenty-First Amendment bolted through state ratification debates in less than ten months—three months faster than the already-quick Eighteenth Amendment and faster than any constitutional amendment since 1804. The amendment's proponents had called for ratification conventions to evade state legislatures with their spotty sessions and entrenched rural majorities. Though this stratagem sped the process, the result was foreordained, as the public long since had lost its stomach for prohibition.[159]

In one sense the nation's turnabout from adoption of prohibition to repeal should shock us. The Constitution's framers made the document resilient to

---

[157] "A National Status for Prohibition," *Indianapolis Star*, Feb. 9, 1913, p. 16; Editorial, "Prohibition, as Usual," *New York Times*, Dec. 2, 1926, at 26. I thank Robert Post for the latter reference.

[158] *Hansard's Parliamentary Debates* (Lords), vol. 12, p. 1226 (1743) (remarks of Lord Carteret).

[159] Kyvig, *Repealing National Prohibition*, pp. 171–82. Ratification of the Twenty-first Amendment was the fastest of any since the Twelfth Amendment in 1803–1804, which required the approval of only twelve states. Ibid., p. 242 n.84.

change, amendable only by overwhelming national consensus. Two-thirds of each house of Congress must assent, together with three-fourths of the states. A reversal of such dominant sentiments in the span of fourteen years amounts to constitutional whiplash. Approaching the midpoint of that span in 1926, New York Congressman Hamilton Fish Jr. declared the feat unattainable. As "it takes only thirteen dry States to block or prevent any repeal of the Eighteenth Amendment," repeal "is as far off as the moon."[160]

In another sense, though, the path from prohibition to repeal should rouse no wonder. For we have seen this pattern before—and often enough to make it predictable. The English gin ban rose and fell in seven years. Georgia's rum ban rose and fell as fast. Maine laws swept fifteen states and territories between 1851 and 1855—but by 1858 seven states had repealed or retreated from these laws, and by 1875 only three state bans were standing. Seen in this light, the wonder is not that national prohibition fell but that it did not fall faster.

It would have fallen faster had a simple majority vote sufficed to bring prohibition down. For the public opinion polls of the day, flawed as they were, showed a fast falling-out between the people and their law. In the summer of 1922, less than three years into prohibition's reign, the editors of *Literary Digest* conducted the first major national opinion survey assessing public support of prohibition. They mailed ten million ballots to telephone subscribers and received 922,383 in return. The respondents were neither randomized nor representative of the broader electorate, for not everyone owned a phone, and not all who did felt moved to respond. Still, it's striking that prohibition already had lost its majority. Only 38.6 percent of respondents favored the existing laws, while 61.4 percent preferred either repealing the Eighteenth Amendment (20.6 percent) or changing the Volstead Act to permit light wines and beer (40.8 percent). Three years later, when *Collier's* magazine interviewed 263,583 adults across the country, prohibition's ranks had thinned further: only 32 percent favored the existing regime, and 68 percent stood opposed. *Collier's* proclaimed, "Booze is the Victor." Within another two years, twenty-seven of the forty-eight states had cut all funds for enforcing prohibition.[161]

It's true Al Smith's 1928 Democratic presidential run, in some ways a referendum on the prohibition amendment Smith despised, met crushing defeat at Herbert Hoover's hands. But Smith, a Catholic, was the grandson of immigrants and half-Irish to boot, challenging an incumbent party at a time of exuberant prosperity. Freed of his freight and propelled by economic collapse, the forces for

[160] "Fish Assails Wadsworth," *New York Times*, Aug. 14, 1926, p. 4.
[161] "Final Returns in 'The Digest's' Prohibition Poll," *Literary Digest* (Sept. 9, 1922), pp. 11–12; "Booze Is the Victor," *Collier's* (Oct. 10, 1925), pp. 8–9; Phillips, *Alcohol*, p. 262 (noting states' defunding enforcement). I thank Jordan Orosz for scouting out and assembling the widely scattered measures of public opinion during the prohibition years.

repeal rebounded fast. Midterm elections in 1930 almost doubled the ranks of anti-prohibition congressmen and sent wet Democrats to the Senate from such Republican strongholds as Ohio, Illinois, and even Kansas, a dry state since 1880. In two more years, Franklin D. Roosevelt rode the fervor for repeal to the White House.[162]

Prohibition's Aftermath

When prohibition ended, it ended as the English gin ban ended: with a renewed commitment to moderation and greater wisdom about how to achieve it. Parliament finally quelled England's gin craze when it put in place an effective moderationist regime. Lawmakers levied high duties directly on distillers, required registration of every cask to prevent evasion, doubled retail license fees, permitted licenses only for substantial taverns and other propertied sellers, and authorized searches and other enforcement tools to give its new rules bite. Within six years of this scheme's enactment, annual gin consumption fell by half, and the gin crisis began to recede into history.

As American states emerged from prohibition in 1933, they likewise built breakwaters against any return of the heavy-drinking saloon culture. Beginning even before repeal bells tolled, all but two of the forty-eight states erected new regulatory schemes. Only Kansas and Alabama tried to stay bone dry for more than a year or two, though neither succeeded for long. Most states retained such old-school features as mandatory closing hours. Many imposed state or local control on the number of sellers. Almost all forbade sales to minors. Somewhat fewer than half banned sales of distilled liquor by the glass—and most of these banned even ordinary wine by capping the potency of lawful beverages at 5 percent alcohol or less. The most stringent schemes allowed nothing stronger than 3.2-percent beer.[163]

---

[162] Okrent, *Last Call*, pp. 308–09 (assessing Smith's baggage); ibid., p. 338 (reviewing 1930 election results).

[163] Kansas law banned all "intoxicating liquors." In 1933 the Kansas Supreme Court ruled a defendant charged with sale of 3.2% beer must be allowed to present evidence that 3.2% beer is not "intoxicating as a matter of fact." *Kansas General Statutes* (1935), art. 21, § 21-2101, pp. 638–39; *State ex rel. Wyman v. Owston*, 138 Kan. 173, 183–84 (1933). The ruling "resulted in a wide-scale and relatively open sale of that beverage throughout the state." Harrison & Laine, *After Repeal*, p. 44 & n.2. Though bone dry to start, Alabama in 1937 authorized counties to permit sales of beer and wine in hotels, restaurants, and clubs and sales of spirits in state liquor stores. *See* Harrison & Laine, *After Repeal*, p. 231; Alabama Beverage Control Act, 1936–1937 *Alabama Laws*, Spec. Sess., no. 66 (Act of Feb. 2, 1937), p. 40.

Every other state had reauthorized sales of at least some alcoholic drinks by the end of 1935—that is, within two years of prohibition's end. My thanks to research assistants Matt Buckley, Brett Diehl, and Tyler Jones, who exhaustively researched the nation's post-prohibition laws. I also consulted Harrison & Laine's useful summaries of each state's post-prohibition regime. *See After Repeal*, app. IV, pp. 231–48.

The striking precision of the last figure oddly linked these latter-day moderationists with their eighteenth-century forebears. Congress had settled on 3.2-percent beer in March 1933, in prohibition's waning days, when it sought to relegalize alcohol without openly flouting the Eighteenth Amendment's ban on "intoxicating liquors." Yale physiologist Yandell Henderson later claimed to have played "consulting toxicologist" to Congress in recommending the 3.2 standard. Henderson said a key senator, Bingham of Connecticut, accepted Henderson's conclusion that the volume of 3.2 beer "that must be taken to induce even the lowest slightly intoxicating concentration of alcohol . . . is at the limit of the capacity of the human stomach." Here we have the same argument in defense of beer that Bishop Thomas Secker made during Gin Act debates in 1743, contending "a man must put a sort of force upon himself, before he can swallow down so much" beer as to become drunk—and Benjamin Rush made in 1805, claiming beer could "seldom be drunken in sufficient quantities to produce intoxication . . . without . . . distending the stomach."[164]

In delivering America from prohibition, state legislators of the early and mid-1930s went beyond such direct assaults on the means of intoxication and sought to reshape the culture of public drinking. Here their first step was to eliminate the stand-up saloon. Proclaiming an end to prohibition in December 1933, President Roosevelt asked "especially that no State shall by law or otherwise authorize the return of the saloon either in its old form or in some modern guise." Taking the president quite at his word, a dozen states banned the word *saloon*—and sometimes also *bar* and *barroom*—from the lexicon of drink. An Illinois law of 1934 was typical in announcing, "No person licensed to sell alcoholic liquors shall use the words 'saloon' or 'bar' in any sign or advertisement."[165] In 1945, in the wake of this spate of lawmaking, H. L. Mencken wrote, "So far as I know there is not a single undisguised *saloon* in the United States today. They are all *taverns*, *cocktail-lounges*, *taprooms*, *beer-stubes* or the like." Or as Harry S. Warner put it, "The saloon [was] re-named 'tavern.' "[166]

---

[164] *See* Cullen Beer Act, Act of Mar. 22, 1933, § 3, 48 Stat. 16, 17 (legalizing 3.2% beer); Yandell Henderson, "Public Service as an Element in the Life of the American Scientist," *Science*, vol. 77 (June 16, 1933), p. 584; Yandell Henderson, *A New Deal in Liquor: A Plea for Dilution* (New York: Doubleday, Doran & Company, Inc. 1934), pp. 63–64, 155–58; *Hansard's Parliamentary Debates* (Lords), vol. 12, p. 1205 (Feb. 15, 1743) (remarks of the Bishop of Oxford); Rush, *Inquiry* (1805 ed.), p. 3.

[165] Franklin D. Roosevelt, *The Public Papers and Addresses of Franklin D. Roosevelt*, vol. 2 (New York: Random House, 1938), pp. 511–12; "An Act Relating to Alcoholic Liquors," 1933 *Illinois Laws*, 1st Spec. Sess., § 22 (Act of Jan. 31, 1934), pp. 57, 74. The eleven other states were Alabama, California, Iowa, Massachusetts, Missouri, Montana, New Hampshire, Texas, Vermont, West Virginia, and Wisconsin. Six more states—Colorado, Georgia, Indiana, Pennsylvania, Virginia, and Washington—specifically banned "saloon[s]," but did not target use of the word.

[166] H.L. Mencken, *The American Language: Supplement I* (New York: Alfred. A. Knopf, 1988 (1945)), p. 268; Harry S. Warner, *An Evolution in Understanding of the Problem of Alcohol: A History of College Idealism* (Boston: Christopher Publishing House, 1966), p. 95; F. Lauriston Bullard, "Bay State Taverns 'Modified' Saloons," *New York Times*, Dec. 10, 1933, p. E7 ("The saloon, yclept a tavern, is coming back in Massachusetts.").

But change came not in name only. Banishment of the *saloon* so-called reflected a determination that drinking places would be genuinely social—that people would stop and stay awhile. *Taverns, lounges, grills,* and the like stood for the post-prohibition consensus that the only legitimate sort of drinking was social drinking. And social drinking emphatically did *not* mean social drunkenness. Harvard psychologist Hugo Münsterberg foretold America's post-prohibition accommodation with drink when he declared in 1910, "The saloon must disappear . . . . And with it must disappear the bar and the habit of drinking standing and of mutual treating." In place of the old stand-up saloons, "[t]he restaurant alone, with the hotel and the club, is the fit public place where guests sitting at tables may have beer and wine with their meals or after meals . . . ." And the law should "absolutely forbid" sale of intoxicants to inebriates. Münsterberg predicted hopefully that if the old saloons "disappear and customs grow which spread the spirit of geniality and friendly social intercourse over the foaming cup, the spell will be broken."[167]

Assessing fidelity to Roosevelt's 1933 request that states not reauthorize old-style saloons, the *New York Times* defined the saloon's "distinguishing feature [as] the bar at which customers can drink standing." Indeed in the years shortly after prohibition's repeal, only ten states reauthorized spirit sales by the glass over bars.[168] Nineteen states banned spirit sales by the glass altogether. Seventeen others allowed spirit sales but only in hotels, restaurants, or private clubs. Wary of evasion by latter-day saloons masquerading as restaurants, over half the states demanded that drinking places serve "meals"—or at least "food." Lawmakers in California took pains to define *meal* as a "quantity of food . . . ordinarily consumed" at dining tables "for the purpose of sustenance." In defining *restaurant*, Michigan and New York were especially finicky, requiring "suitable kitchen facilities" with "conveniences for cooking an assortment of foods, which may be required for ordinary meals" served "to guests for compensation." By "meals," lawmakers insisted, they did not mean "sandwiches or salads," which "shall not be deemed a compliance with this requirement."[169]

---

[167] Hugo Münsterberg, *American Problems from the Point of View of a Psychologist* (New York: Moffat, Yard and Company, 1910), p. 90.

[168] R.L. Duffus, "Ten Questions Left Unsettled by Repeal," *New York Times,* Dec. 10, 1933, p. XX1. The ten states that reauthorized sales of spirits by the glass over bars were Illinois, Louisiana, Maryland, Missouri, Nebraska, Nevada, New Jersey, Rhode Island, South Dakota, and Wyoming. I included a state in this category if, by the end of 1935 (that is, within two years of prohibition's repeal), the state had reauthorized sales of distilled liquor by the glass over bars.

[169] For examples of laws requiring that drinks be served only with meals, *see* "An Act to . . . Regulate the Manufacture, Distribution and Sale of Certain Beverages . . . ," 1933 *California Statutes,* ch. 178, § 19 (Act of Apr. 27, 1933), pp. 625, 633–34; "An Act Concerning the Manufacture and Sale of Alcoholic Liquors . . . ," 1935 *Colorado Laws,* ch. 142, § 20 (Act of Apr. 12, 1935), pp. 597, 624; Oregon Liquor Control Act, 1933 *Oregon Laws,* 2d Spec. Sess., ch. 17, § 20(6–7) (Act of Dec. 15, 1933), pp. 38, 50. For California's definition of *meal, see* "An Act to Control, License, and Regulate . . . Wine, Beer, and Intoxicating Liquor . . . ," 1933 *California Statutes,* ch. 658, § 4(l) (Act of June 3, 1933), pp. 1697, 1699.

And many states aimed to outlaw the saloon by forbidding its physical features. Missouri banned the barroom's trappings—its swinging doors and "mirror, or other fixtures having the appearance of a saloon"—as well as the bar itself. Eleven states targeted only the bar, defined in Indiana as a "counter or similar arrangement . . . at which patrons or customers are permitted to stand and be served and/or consume such [alcoholic] drinks."[170] *Twenty-one* states made the bar moot by banning the custom of drinking while standing. Here the forms of law varied. Colorado demanded that alcohol typically "not be served at any place, excepting tables and lunch counters with stools securely fastened to the floor." Delaware held a stricter line, compelling proprietors to forbid drinking by patrons "standing or sitting at a bar or counter." Oregon required not only that drinkers be "seated at tables" but that drinks be served "with bona fide meals only." Arizona and a few other states did not specify a patron's posture, but banned drink unless "served and consumed only with meals furnished in good faith." And Missouri, again more punctilious than the rest, banned drinking "while standing at or near any bar or counter" and pointedly permitted drinking "at tables or counters upon which food is served to customers while seated . . . ."[171]

Almost three-quarters of the states, finally, demanded that proprietors stop serving patrons who had crossed the broad line dividing conviviality from drunkenness. Several fortified this decree by making sellers and sometimes their landlords liable in some circumstances for injuries or lost support caused by a customer served till drunk.[172]

For examples of laws defining *restaurant* narrowly, *see* "An Act to Create a Liquor Control Commission . . . ," 1933–1934 *Michigan Acts*, Extra Sess., no. 8, § 2 (Act of Dec. 15, 1933), pp. 18–19; Alcoholic Beverage Control Law, 1934 *New York Laws*, vol. 1, ch. 478, § 3(27) (Act of May 10, 1934), pp. 1074, 1077; Pennsylvania Liquor Control Act, 1933 *Pennsylvania Laws*, Extra. Sess., no. 4, § 2 (Act of Nov. 29, 1933), pp. 15, 16.

[170] "An Act to Amend Chapter 93 . . . Relating to the Manufacture, Transportation, [and] Sale . . . of Non-Intoxicating Beer . . . ," 1933 *Missouri Laws*, § 1 (§ 13139z8) (Act of Mar. 15, 1933), pp. 256, 266 ("mirror, or other . . ."); Liquor Control Act, 1933–1934 *Missouri Laws*, Extra Sess., § 21a (Act of Jan. 13, 1934), pp. 77, 85 (banning swinging doors); "An Act Concerning Alcohol and Alcoholic Beverages . . . ," 1935 *Indiana Laws*, c. 226, §§ 10, 18 (Act of Mar. 11, 1935), pp. 1056, 1101, 1126. Alabama, California, Colorado, Delaware, Illinois, Iowa, Nebraska, New Hampshire, Pennsylvania, and Vermont also banned drink sales over bars.

[171] 1935 *Colorado Laws*, ch. 142, §§ 3(e), 4(n), pp. 597, 599, 605; 1932–1933 *Delaware Laws*, Spec. Sess., ch. 18, § 34(4), pp. 91, 130; 1933 *Oregon Laws*, 2d Spec. Sess., ch. 17, § 20(6–7), pp. 38, 50; "An Act Relating to the Manufacture and Sale of Spirituous Liquors . . . ," 1933 *Arizona Acts*, ch. 76, §§ 8–9 (Act of Mar. 18, 1933), pp. 304, 309–10; 1933 *Missouri Laws*, § 1 (§ 13139z7), pp. 256, 266. California's law required that drinks be "consumed only with meals furnished in good faith at regular public tables, or at eating counters at which . . . guests and patrons are seated . . . ." 1933 *California Statutes*, ch. 178, § 19, pp. 625, 633–34. *See also* Kyvig, *Repealing National Prohibition*, p. 188 (reviewing various post-prohibition alcohol regulations).

[172] Laws barring service to intoxicated persons: *see, e.g.*, 1935 *Colorado Laws*, ch. 142, § 3(b), pp. 597, 598; 1932–1933 *Delaware Laws*, Spec. Sess., ch. 18, § 17(4), pp. 91, 111; Dram Shops, 1933 *Illinois Laws*, 1st Spec. Sess., § 12, pp. 57, 71; Intoxicating Liquors, 1933–1934 *Missouri Laws*, Extra Sess., § 9, pp. 77, 81.

It's true many of these measures against the saloon's revival proved cosmetic, requiring tables at which no one sat and menus from which no one dared order. As Congressman John Wright Patman said in opposing a 1934 act regulating the newly legal drink trade in the District of Columbia, "the only difference between the saloon under this bill and the saloon under the old system is that in order to be served a drink in one of the new saloons you must sit down at a table[.]"[173] Many other measures did not outlive the passionate anti-saloon culture of the early post-prohibition years. Yet the old stand-up saloon largely *has* disappeared. Yes, many patrons today drink standing, and even in states still requiring food service, there are bars where only strangers order food. But the nineteenth-century image of men marching to the bar, quaffing their whiskey, and quitting the place "like an ignited sky-rocket" seems quaintly Old West today. For the culture of drink has changed. And while the reasons are varied, a chief cause was the pointed effort by prohibition's opponents to ensure that a culture of moderation rose to replace it.

The Culture of Social Drinking

Just as national prohibition was drawing to a close, John D. Rockefeller Jr. commissioned a book-length study of the best statutory mechanisms for reopening the alcohol trade. The first objective of any such regulatory regime, Rockefeller wrote in the foreword, was to end the lawlessness that prevailed under prohibition. The second was to focus "all the forces of society upon the development of self-control and temperance as regards the use of alcoholic beverages."[174]

So we return to Howard Crosby's ideology of moderation and his 1881 injunction that "[w]e are to develop self-control as much as possible."[175] Self-control typically was conceived as a moral virtue—what older theologians called *continence* and what Augustine, in the sexual context, called *continentia*. Now, as the United States emerged from prohibition, self-control gained ascendance as a social virtue.

Laws creating causes of action: *see, e.g.,* Dram Shops, 1933 *Illinois Laws,* 1st Spec. Sess., § 14, pp. 57, 72–73; 1935 *General Statutes of Kansas,* ch. 21, art. 21-2150–2155, pp. 649–50; "An Act to Create a Liquor Control Commission," 1933–1934 *Michigan Acts,* Extra Sess., no. 8, § 22 (Act of Dec. 15, 1933), pp. 16, 25.

[173] *Congressional Record,* vol. 78, pt. 1 (73d Cong., 2d Sess.), p. 265 (Jan. 9, 1934) (remarks of Mr. Patman).
[174] John D. Rockefeller Jr., "Foreword," *in* Fosdick & Scott, *Toward Liquor Control,* pp. vii, viii–ix.
[175] Crosby, "A Calm View," p. 10.

Hence journalist Alma Whitaker pitched *Bacchus Behave!*—her 1933 manifesto of the new culture of moderation—not to the nation's preachers or even its lawmakers but to its "hostesses." Aiming to reintroduce "the lost art of polite drinking" to a nation just emerging from prohibition, Whitaker called on the "hostesses of the United States" to enforce the new norms of drink. Only social drinking, she reminded them, and never social drunkenness, was acceptable: "Wines and spirits should be strictly a social lubricant."

Whitaker invested alcohol with all the qualities one could wish of a conversational drug. "Taken judiciously," wines and spirits "are a tonic to our sluggish brains, exert a mellowing influence on our dispositions, quicken our sympathetic perceptions, soften our more hypercritical faculties, and generally bring the nicer qualities of our characters to the fore. But," she warned, "there is a delicate point beyond which they expose all the less desirable qualities of our natures." So "in polite circles, the drunk cannot be tolerated." Whitaker drew this critical line between social drinking and drunkenness in terms of self-control: "One's inhibitions should be happily relaxed but should remain under control at all times." And lest anyone overrate his capacity for liquor, she set strict guidelines: "Two cocktails is the absolute limit. Positively"—unless the drink be gin, in which case the limit was one. Moreover, "[n]o portion of whisky at any time should ever exceed two fingers"—or one finger for the lady.[176]

In short, alcohol won moral sanction because, in Whitaker's words, "the cup that cheers . . . positively should not inebriate." And if alcohol's claim of need was its role as social lubricant, one had to drink only in society. Whitaker advised plainly, "Never drink alone." She saw what Lyman Beecher had seen a century before—the danger of the drinker who slipped "the eye of friendship" and "launche[d] out alone with his boat and bottle." Or as Hugo Münsterberg wrote in 1910, no drink "is more ruinous than the solitary drink, as soon as the feeling of repugnance has been overcome; there is no limit and no inhibition."[177]

Trailing Whitaker's book by two years, the New York–based "Council for Moderation" ran an eye-catching display ad in the *New York Times* of October 15, 1935. Though the ad did not disclose the Council's mission, the group's name perhaps spoke for itself. "There are only a few unpardonable social errors, and these are easily avoided," the Council declared. "Drinking to excess heads the list." Like Whitaker, the Council exalted self-control as a social virtue: "[T]here's always a tell-tale flaw in [a drunken man's] bearing, speech or deportment that shouts to the world that

---

[176] Alma Whitaker, *Bacchus Behave! The Lost Art of Polite Drinking* (New York: Frederick A. Stokes Company, 1933), p. 4 ("Wines and spirits . . ." and "Taken judiciously, . . ." and "in polite circles . . ."); ibid., p. 17 ("Two cocktails is . . ."); ibid., p., 21 ("One's inhibitions should . . ."); ibid., p. 27 ("No portion of whisky . . ."); ibid., p. 32 (one finger "for the lady"); ibid., p. 37 (just one serving of gin).

[177] Whitaker, *Bacchus Behave!*, p. 3 ("the cup that cheers . . ."); ibid., p. 8 ("Never drink alone."); Münsterberg, *American Problems*, p. 76.

some measure of his self-control is lost. Drunkenness," therefore, "or any approach to drunkenness—is always bad taste. . . . [M]oderation is the polite way of life . . . ."[178]

The ideal of moderation was not a passing flavor in the mores of American drink. A generation later, in his pioneering 1963 study of the American temperance movement, Joseph Gusfield observed that "[t]he contemporary American is less likely than his nineteenth-century ancestor to be either a total abstainer or a hard drinker. Moderation is his drinking watchword." By Gusfield's day, the concept of social drinking had become so culturally ingrained that he could label it a social necessity: "One must get along with others," he wrote, "and liquor has proven to be a necessary and effective facilitator to sociability."[179]

Alcohol Monogamy

As we turn now from alcohol regulation to the rise of antidrug laws, one question naturally arises: Why has the moral formula that rescued alcohol from prohibition not excused lawful use of other recreational intoxicants? The formula is simple enough, requiring but two elements. First is the excuse of necessity, satisfied in the case of alcohol by the concept of social drinking. Second is the rule of moderation, which shuns intoxication and exalts self-control. If other recreational drugs have failed to find the moral favor of social drinking, it's because in one way or another they've failed to fit this formula.

It's a hard formula to fit. Professor John Kaplan argued it was "impossible to draw any moral distinction" between alcohol and marijuana, as both "are intoxicants that are used recreationally for pleasure."[180] But in the nature of that pleasure lies great potential for "moral distinction." Mutual, sober, communicative drinking stands in the minds of mainstream moralists and average folks on a moral plane entirely different from drunkenness. Kaplan is right, therefore, only if a "social high" is the moral equivalent of "social drinking." The chatty garrulousness of an alcohol "buzz," falling well short of drunkenness, is achievable because drinkers can titrate the impact of alcohol by drinking slowly and stopping short. "Two cocktails is the absolute limit," Alma Whitaker warned. Rightly or not, the public long believed one can't achieve this measured state of subintoxication with any other recreational drug.

Let us now trace the consequences of this belief as we encounter opium—America's first new recreational drug.

---

[178] "Let's Talk Frankly about Men Who Drink Too Much!" *New York Times*, Oct. 15, 1935, p. 24 (advertisement).

[179] Gusfield, *Symbolic Crusade*, p. 9.

[180] John Kaplan, *Marijuana—The New Prohibition* (Cleveland: The World Publishing Company, 1970), p. 292.

4

Medical Drug Use versus Recreational Abuse

Dr. John Jones was not the first to tell the Western world of opium's medical wonders. Long before Jones's *Mysteries of Opium Reveal'd* appeared in London in 1700 as the first English text devoted to the drug, medical authors both ancient and modern had hailed this Eastern import's curative force. Like them, Jones spun long lists of symptoms and sicknesses that called for the opium cure. But in boosting opium's medical magic, Jones proved savvier than others before him. An Oxford-trained lawyer-turned-doctor, he promoted medical opium as a lawyer might—as an advocate for the cause, anticipating and guarding against a legal backlash that loomed distantly in the future.[1]

Jones knew opium's therapeutic prowess came at psychic, physical, and societal costs. Dependency was one grave risk—overdose and death another—abiding indolence a third. On the matter of addiction Jones was especially blunt: "[A]fter a long, and lavish Use," sudden deprivation could cause "*[g]reat, and even intolerable Distresses, Anxieties, and Depressions of Spirits*, which in few *days* commonly end in a most miserable *Death* . . . ."[2] Like any wise lawyer, Jones perhaps foresaw how opium's evils could lead one day to bans.

In defending the drug despite its risks, he proved at once brilliantly prescient and thuddingly dense. Shrewdly, he saw that opium's best defense was by analogy to alcohol. Over and over, in admitting opium's flaws, Jones said it did no worse than wine. Sure, taking a lot of opium causes "very considerable *Indolence*"— "much after the same manner as Wine." True, liberal use over time produces a "*dull, moapish, and heavy Disposition*"—just "as in old *Drunkards*." Both opium

---

[1] John Jones, *The Mysteries of Opium Reveal'd* (London: Richard Smith, 1700); Virginia Berridge, *Opium and the People: Opiate Use and Drug Control Policy in Nineteenth and Early Twentieth Century England* (New York: Free Association Books, 1999), pp. xxii–xxiii (sketching the earliest records of opium therapy, some dating to hundreds or thousands of years BCE); Stuart Handley, "John Jones," in *Oxford Dictionary of National Biography* (H.C.G. Matthew & Brian Harrison eds., Oxford: Oxford University Press, 2004), p. 548. Though Jones's appears to have been the earliest volume on opium written in English, a small Dutch text had appeared in English translation as early as 1618. *See* Angelus Sala, *Opiologia: or, A Treatise Concerning the Nature, Properties, True Preparation and Safe Use and Administration of Opium* (Tho. Bretnor trans., London: Nicholas Okes, 2d ed. 1618). My thanks to Katie Siler of Stanford's Crown Law Library, whose painstaking research helped confirm that Jones's was the first English text devoted to opium.

[2] Jones, *Mysteries of Opium Reveal'd*, p. 32.

Beware Euphoria. George Fisher, Oxford University Press. © Oxford University Press 2024.
DOI: 10.1093/oso/9780197688489.003.0005

and wine, used excessively, cause first mirth "and afterward a kind of Drunken *Sopor*"—the sleepy silence of Frederick Masters's San Francisco opium dens.[3]

But opium, Jones insisted, was no more stupefying than wine. He rejected an earlier author's "great *Mistake*" in saying opium gave users equanimity "by stupifying the *Senses, Brain, &c.*" Instead it worked by raising the spirits, "as *generous Wine* does before Men are fuddled, or overcome with it." And as for addiction, a long and liberal use of both wine and opium leads to "*Difficulty and Danger in suddenly leaving them off.*" Triumphantly, Jones concluded, "The short is this; *Wine* and *Opium* agree in all their *Effects*, saving such as are Consequences of their *different Accidents*, as the Quantity of *Wine* that must be used to cause the same *Effects* with a little *Opium* ...."[4]

Jones's next turn in defending opium was slyer still: he undertook to squeeze opium into the moral mold that shaped society's accommodation with alcohol. Yes, he said, opium poses risks—of stupor and addiction, indolence and death—but only when used in excess. *Used in moderation*, it was as inoffensive as moderate use of wine. "The Mischief[] of excessive Doses and lavish *Use* of either [wine or opium] is no *Argument* against their inspiriting *Nature*; if it were, then *Wine* is no *Cordial*, tho' made to *glad the Heart of Man* ...." After all, "[t]here is nothing so good, whereof an *intemperate Use* is not *mischievous*, God having so ordered it to deter from, and punish *Intemperance*, and the *Abuse* of his *Creatures* ...." Used *moderately*, opium was appealingly wholesome and even productive, fostering such admirable qualities as "*Promptitude, Serenity, Alacrity, and Expediteness in Dispatching and Managing of Business.*" When under the influence of the drug, users "are mostly enabled to *Work*, or *Labour*, tho' tired before."[5]

But if Jones's moderationist defense of opium displayed his keen sense of society's moral accommodation with alcohol, his raptures about opium's sexual powers proved him deaf to those same moral strains. Rather than distance his drug from wine's unflattering association with sex, Jones fixated on the topic, rehearsing it in ever plainer terms. There was first opium's aphrodisiac force. Applied externally, it "excites Venery"; taken internally in a moderate dose, it "*causes a great promptitude to Venery.*" Beyond increasing desire, it enhances erections "*especially if the dose be larger than ordinary.*" And if opium use is "long and lavish," those erections won't go away. Like a modern Cialis ad warning ominously yet alluringly of "erections lasting more than four hours," Jones insisted he "would have Men believe without experimenting . . . lest any should injure

---

[3] Ibid., p. 31 ("dull, moapish . . ." and "as in old"); ibid., p. 52 ("very considerable Indolence" and "much after the same . . ."); ibid., p. 88 ("and afterward . . .").

[4] Ibid., p. 22 ("great *Mistake*" and "by stupifying . . ." and "as *generous Wine* . . ."); ibid., p. 89 ("*Difficulty and Danger* . . ."); ibid., p. 90 ("The short is this . . . .").

[5] Ibid., p. 21 ("*Promptitude, Serenity, Alacrity* . . . ."); ibid., p. 84 ("are mostly enabled . . ."); ibid., p. 89 ("The Mischiefs . . ."); ibid., p. 245 ("There is nothing . . .").

themselves by too great a *Dose*." One needn't accept Jones's say-so, however, for he listed a brace of supporting authorities "whose Words I do not repeat, partly for *Modesty*'s, partly for *Brevity*'s sake."[6]

Modesty, however, did not keep Jones from recurring to the theme, over and over. Opium, he said, increased both seed and milk, both penis length and breast size. And for those whose sexuality was only of the mind, opium was an organic, premodern orgasmatron, causing "*Venereal Dreams*" and "*Nocturnal Pollutions*." The effect of even a moderate dose "has been compar'd (not without good cause) to a permanent gentle *Degree* of that Pleasure which Modesty forbids the naming of . . . ."[7]

Yet there was more—and stranger. Jones dwelt for pages on the similarity of opium and semen. Chemically and physiologically, he said, they are quite alike—from opium's "*rank* and vehement *Smell*," which is "most like" that of semen, to its capacity, like semen, to excite "*Venereal Fury*," to the sleepiness that follows the pleasure of both. Nor were these similarities happenstance. Rather they proved that semen itself "is an *Opiate*" and "would have much the same *Effects* with *Opium*, if it were fit to use it after the same manner." So "we need not wonder at [opium's] titillating to *Venery*, nor indeed its causing a *high* sense of *Pleasure* upon any *Membrane* . . . ." Among few differences between these substances was their duration of action, for opium delivers "a Sense of Pleasure more perma-nent, *viz.* for many *Hours*, . . . [while] the *Pleasure* of the other is *Momentary*."[8]

Jones surely did not mistake opium's aphrodisiac and orgasmic powers. On the contrary, a bevy of both older and modern authorities corroborate his claims of *Promptitude to Venery*. With long use, it's true, opium's magic fades, inducing instead persistent impotence among many men, failed menstruation and barren-ness among women, and decreased libido among both.[9] But Jones's error lay not

---

[6] Ibid., p. 18 ("excites Venery"); ibid., p. 24 ("*causes a great* . . . ," "*especially if the dose* . . . ," "would have Men . . . ," and "whose Words I do not repeat . . ."); ibid., pp. 304–05 ("long and lavish"). Cialis made news with its 2004 Super Bowl ads that warned, "Erections lasting more than four hours, while rare, require immediate medical help." One reporter replied, "Do they ever." Tim Goodman, "Super Bowl Ads Strain for Cheap Laughs," *San Francisco Chronicle*, Feb. 2, 2004, p. A2.

[7] Jones, *Mysteries of Opium Reveal'd*, p. 20 ("has been compar'd . . ."); ibid., p. 24 (increased seed); ibid., p. 25 ("*Venereal Dreams*," and "*Nocturnal Pollutions*"); ibid., p. 335 (increased milk, enlarged breasts and penis).

[8] Ibid., pp. 173 ("we need not wonder . . ."); ibid., p. 175 ("*rank* and vehement *Smell*" and "most like"); ibid., p. 189 ("*Venereal Fury*"); 190 (sleepiness); ibid., p. 191 ("a Sense of Pleasure more perma-nent . . ."); ibid., p. 192 (semen itself "is an *Opiate*" and "would have much . . .").

[9] Ibid., p. 38 ("*Promptitude to Venery*"); Edward M. Brecher, *Licit and Illicit Drugs* (Boston: Little, Brown and Company, 1972), pp. 28–29 (reporting evidence that opiates reduce sexual desire, delay ejaculation, delay or interrupt menstruation, and reduce the likelihood of pregnancy); H.H. Kane, *Drugs That Enslave: The Opium, Morphine, Chloral and Hashisch Habits* (Philadelphia: Presley Blakiston, 1881), pp. 41–42, 45 (reporting reduced breast size and sterility among women and increased short-term desire giving way to long-term partial or total impotence among men). Not all men report impotence with long-term use. See Brecher, *Licit and Illicit Drugs*, p. 28; Kane, *Drugs That Enslave*, p. 45.

in ignoring these darker shadows of opium's sexual lightshow but in showcasing opium's sexual side at all. While he aimed plainly to extol the drug's virtues and promote its use, his obsession with its status as sexual wonder drug doomed his mission. For he put the mainstream on guard of the moral threat in its midst.

Realizing his mistake too late, Jones flailed in his closing pages to cast opium's sexual powers in a moral glow. In a chapter addressing the proper uses of opium, he said he trusted doctors to prescribe the drug only "where there is a *just Cause* for its *Use*, which I will not expose to every lustful *Goat*." He insisted that while opium was "*of great use to excite to Venery, cause Erections*, [and] to actuate a dull *Semen*," all this was "for the sake of lawful *Propagation*." He even invoked biblical sanction for opium's sexual utility. "It is observable how desirous Rachel, being Barren, was of the *Opiate* call'd *Mandrake*, so that she parted with her *Beloved Husband* to her Sister Leah for a Night to purchase it . . . ."[10]

But these few lines, tacked at the end of a massive volume, could not save the situation. Taken as a whole, Jones's work celebrated and advertised opium as recreational sex aid. Yet the sexual wonders of opium, together with its other stupefying pleasures, eventually would spur its ban. True, Jones was not alone responsible for the ban, as a great many authorities wrote of opium's sexual side effects. Nor could Jones have hoped to succeed in his quixotic quest to bill opium as no worse than wine. Though he played down the drug's stupefying force, many others told of it plainly.[11] Still, whatever he hoped to gain in casting opium as the moral equivalent of wine he squandered in fetishizing the drug's sexual moxie. On balance he sped the day when the moral mainstream would turn its censorious eye on opium.

That day nonetheless lay far in the future. Opium did not face formal legal regulation in England till 1868, nor was it banned anywhere in America before 1875. Whatever its other qualities, opium was a medicine and an indispensable one. For a century and a half after Jones wrote, therefore, it survived unbound by law, sustained by its evident necessity.

Opium's Medical Wonders

Though Jones's homage to opium was on some fronts extreme, his paeans to the drug's medical merits were entirely conventional. True, no modern doctor would

---

[10] Jones, *Mysteries of Opium Reveal'd*, p. 357 ("*of great use to . . .*" and "for the sake . . ."); ibid., p. 357 (recounting the story of Rachel from Gen. 30:14–16, 22–23); ibid., p. 358 ("where there is a . . .").

[11] Irish physician Samuel Crumpe reported opium "occasions an increased disposition to venery" in many persons, but the drug's "more obvious effects" include "insensibility, sleep, stupor, &c." Samuel Crumpe, *An Inquiry into the Nature and Properties of Opium* (London: G.G. and J. Robinson, 1793), pp. 44, 94.

follow him in counseling opium for colds, hemorrhages, or shivering ague fits. But many would second his endorsement of the drug against dysentery and diarrhea, hacking coughs, and the tormenting pains of surgery, cancer, labor, and stones.[12]

Jones's ardor for opium as medicine aligned him with others of his era. A generation earlier, in 1681, physician Thomas Willis recommended opium where modern doctors wouldn't—for heart irregularities, asthma, and fevers. More soundly, he said "opiates "are necessarily and most properly used in case of Wakefulness," and "[d]ysenterical Maladies . . . can scarce be cured without Opium . . . ." As for pain, opium "is a remedy really divine. And truly we cannot sufficiently admire, how, when any bowel or member is under any signal and intolerable torture or pain, this Medicin, like a Charm, gives the Party immediate relief and ease . . . ." Around the same time English physician Thomas Sydenham declared "medicine would be a cripple without [opium]; and whoever understands it well, will do more with it alone than he could well hope to do from any single medicine."[13]

For another two hundred fifty years, doctors on both sides of the Atlantic turned to opium for a host of ills. In 1793 Irish physician Samuel Crumpe endorsed the drug in the usual cases of diarrhea, sleeplessness, and pain, as well as the doubtful cases of fevers, hemorrhages, and asthma—and added a collection of maladies from rheumatism, smallpox, and tetanus to pneumonia, sciatica, and hysteria. Crumpe's American contemporary Benjamin Rush so feared addicting his patients with medicinal alcohol that he often turned instead to opium, which he deemed "a thousand times more safe and innocent." Rush fondly recalled a patient who hailed his visit to her deathbed, crying, "here comes my physician, my friend, my opium."[14]

By 1834, American physicians reportedly prescribed opium "more frequently . . . than perhaps any other article of the Materia Medica." From there, a

---

[12] Jones, *Mysteries of Opium Reveal'd*, p. 23 (pain, colds, and ague); ibid., p. 25 (coughs, labor, and stones); ibid., p. 26 (hemorrhages); ibid., p. 369 (dysentery).

[13] [Thomas Willis,] *Dr Willis's Practice of Physick* (London: T. Dring, C. Harper, & J. Leigh, 1684 (1681)), bk. 9, ch. 1, pp. 128–32; Thomas Sydenham, *Medical Observations Concerning the History and the Cure of Acute Diseases (1676), reprinted in The Works of Thomas Sydenham* (London: Sydenham Society, 1848), vol. I, p. 173.

[14] Crumpe, *Inquiry into the Nature and Properties of Opium*, p. 220 (fevers); ibid., p. 248 (rheumatism); ibid., p. 252 (pneumonia); ibid., p. 264 (sciatica); ibid., p. 279 (hemorrhages); ibid., p. 234 (diarrhea, sleeplessness); ibid., p.l269 (smallpox); 288 (tetanus); 290 (asthma); 296 (hysteria); Benjamin Rush, *An Enquiry into the Effects of Spirituous Liquors* . . . (Philadelphia: Thomas Bradford, 1784), pp. 247–48 ("a thousand times . . ."); Benjamin Rush, *The Autobiography of Benjamin Rush* (Princeton: Princeton University Press, 1948), p. 292 ("here comes my physician . . ."). Rush applied opium to ailments ranging from toothache, diarrhea, and whooping cough to dengue fever, scarlet fever, and cholera. *See* David Freeman Hawke, *Benjamin Rush: Revolutionary Gadfly* (Indianapolis: The Bobbs-Merrill Company, 1971), pp. 242 (dengue fever); 252 (cholera); 269 (scarlet fever); 297 (toothache); 298 (whooping cough).

trail of testimonials stretched forward. One American observer of 1862 deemed no other solace "so trustworthy, and so sure, in the average of constitutions, to produce sleep, soothe pain, relax painful spasm, and support the vitality under the most terrible strains of severe injury, or the slow drainage of chronic disease." A second wrote in 1877, "[I]f there is but one medicine to be used, that medicine is opium." And a third, in 1921, pronounced it "our most useful and most important drug."[15]

So sure were doctors that they could exploit opium's therapeutic marvels without risking abuse or addiction that they didn't hesitate, at least in the early years, to advise the drug for children. The otherwise sober George Young endorsed opium in 1753 for the diarrhea suffered by weaning and teething infants. For rickets and scrofula, he recommended a prophylactic course of opium to ward off symptoms before they strike. "[I]f I had children that were threatened with either of these diseases, I would begin early the use of *liquid laudanum*"—a solution of opium in alcohol—"tho' they had neither pains or looseness."[16]

Opium's Medical Necessity

Like alcohol, then, opium readily claimed the excuse of medical need. In those days before modern dentistry, when dysentery ran rampant and cancer lacked any cure but excision, when surgery was wakeful, amputations common, and childbirth often fatal, when even aspirin lay undiscovered and only whiskey warded off everyday pains, life without opium was too brutish to bear. But slowly times changed. And as with alcohol, evolving notions of need shaped and altered the moral and legal regimes governing opium use.

We may begin with Dr. Samuel Johnson—not a physician, but a moralist and man of letters. One morning in 1783, an elderly, ailing Johnson told his friend and biographer Boswell of his peaceful night. Boswell wrote that Johnson "seemed much relieved, having taken opium the night before. He however protested against it, as a remedy that should be given with the utmost reluctance, *and only in extreme necessity*." It seems unlikely Johnson chose these words by

---

[15] George B. Wood & Franklin Bache, *The Dispensatory of the United States of America* (Philadelphia: Grigg and Elliot, 2d ed. 1834), p. 486; [Anon.,] "Narcotics," *North American Review*, vol. 95 (1862), pp. 374, 399; S.F. McFarland, "Opium Inebriety and the Hypodermic Syringe," *Transactions of the Medical Society of the State of New York, for the Year 1877* (Albany: Van Benthuysen Printing House, 1877), pp. 289, 293 (quoting a Dr. Kendall); Edward Huntington Williams, "Some Observations on the Narcotic Situation," *Medical Record*, vol. 100 (July 23, 1921), pp. 140, 142.

[16] George Young, *A Treatise on Opium* (London: A. Millar, 1753), p. 40 (recommending laudanum if weaning an infant causes diarrhea); ibid., p. 43 (and if teething leads to diarrhea); ibid., p. 45 (endorsing laudanum for scrofula); ibid., pp. 117–18 ("[I]f I had children . . . .").

chance. They were the formula by which Methodist founder John Wesley meas-ured the moral use of distilled drink. In 1743 Wesley had enjoined followers to avoid "buying or selling spirituous liquors, or drinking them, *unless in cases of extreme necessity.*" As an acquaintance of Wesley and a reader of all, Johnson al-most surely knew of Wesley's dictum. Even if not, Boswell's account confirms that Johnson saw overuse of opium in the same evil light as drunkenness. To Boswell's remark that the Turks' common use of opium suggested the drug was less pernicious than Johnson thought, Johnson replied with some pique "that it is as disgraceful in Turkey to take too much opium, as it is with us to get drunk."[17]

For Johnson, even the final extremity could not excuse opium intoxication. Told on his deathbed in December 1784 that he could not recover without a mir-acle, Johnson replied, "Then, I will take no more physick, not even my opiates; for I have prayed that I may render up my soul to God unclouded." Despite Johnson's stoicism, claims that opium served absolute needs predated and long outlived him. In his 1724 general medical treatise, Dr. George Cheyne named *"four Cases* in which [opium is] absolutely and eminently necessary; the *Cholick*; the *Stone*; the hard *Labours* . . . ; and in the *Gout* and *Rheumatism.*" Two centuries later Dr. Edward Huntington Williams wrote of those "suffering from painful afflictions, such as tuberculosis and cancer, whose condition made the continued use of an opiate an absolute necessity . . . ."[18]

Despite broad agreement that dire need often excused opium use, spe-cific claims of need sometimes met a skeptical audience. Those observers most inclined to see opium indulgence as a moral failing were least prepared to find claims of medical need persuasive. In his 1856 pharmacology treatise, Philadelphia physician George Wood listed the symptoms of "excessive abuse" by "slaves of opium." Subtly he shifted the focus from largely physical effects—impaired appetite, constipation, depressed liver function—to a "loss of interest in the usual concerns of life, and social relations." He then lapsed into unblended moral argot, deploying the language of degradation, indulgence, satiety, vice, and evil. "The lowest stage of degradation has been attained," he began, "when the indulgence ends in . . . indifference to the opinions of the community; and everything is sacrificed to the insatiable demands of the vice." Pointedly, Wood rejected the moral excuse of need—"the supposed necessity of obtaining relief from painful affections, such as cancer, and certain incurable cases of neuralgia." He allowed that opium offered "some palliation, [but] this is no satisfactory

---

[17] *Boswell's Life of Johnson* (R.W. Chapman ed., New York: Oxford University Press, 1953), p. 900 (Mar. 31, 1778) (on Johnson's acquaintance with Wesley); ibid., p. 951 (Apr. 15, 1778) (same); ibid., p. 1026 (May 3, 1779) (same); ibid., p. 1199 (Mar. 23, 1783) ("seemed much relieved . . ." and "that it is as disgraceful . . .") (emphasis added); Henry Wheeler, *Methodism and the Temperance Reformation* (Cincinnati: Walden and Stowe, 1882), pp. 16–17 (quoting Wesley's rule) (emphasis added).

[18] *Boswell's Life of Johnson*, p. 1390 (Dec. 1784); George Cheyne, *An Essay of Health and Long Life* (London: George Strahan, 1724), p. 218; Williams, "Some Observations," p. 142.

excuse; for, by proper management, considerable relief of pain can generally be obtained, without an excess sufficient to degrade the mind . . . ; and it is rather a weak yielding to the seductive pleasures of opium, than any necessity for its anodyne influence, that leads to the lowest depths of the evil."[19]

Even in rejecting the purported excuse of necessity, Wood implicitly yielded on the larger point—that in cases of true need for opium's palliation, there was no moral fault in its use. From this principle few dissented. Those lawmakers who might have been tempted to ban recreational opium abuse therefore confronted a stubborn reality: opium's undeniable utility in dulling pain obscured the distinction between medically necessary—and therefore moral—opium use and immoral indulgence in escapist, mindless pleasure. Indeed, it was harder to draw this distinction for opium than alcohol. The reasons—at least four—stem from the pharmacology of the two drugs and the customs of their use.

First and most plainly, opium played a more critical medical role than alcohol. Though George Wood trivialized such "painful affections" as cancer and counseled "proper management" of pain over opium use, most physicians saw opium and its promised reprieve from agony as an indispensable treatment option. For sheer pain relief, opium had no rival, nor could whiskey or anything else halt diarrhea as fast. Because a claimed need for "Alcoholic Therapeutics"— the title of one nineteenth-century article on the topic—never seemed as substantial, observers were quicker to suspect drinking was pure indulgence than they were to fault opium use.[20]

The converse also was true. Just as opium was a likelier medicine than alcohol, so alcohol was a likelier intoxicant. Here the difference was less pharmacological than customary. While recreational drunkenness had a history of biblical length, there was no timeworn Western tradition of opium indulgence. As late as 1868 an observer could claim that "[o]pium drunkenness is almost unknown to us in England. We may hear it rumoured of this or that individual, alive or dead; but it does not obtrude itself, we are not accustomed to it." Even on the American West Coast, where the first Chinese opium dens appeared by the 1860s, a federal judge wrote in 1886 of recreational opium abuse as something new: "In the East [opium] has been used for centuries, by smoking and mastication, to produce a kind of intoxication; but, until lately, such use has been unknown in the United States, and is now chiefly confined to the Chinese."[21] Because recreational opium

---

[19] George B. Wood, *A Treatise on Therapeutics and Pharmacology or Materia Medica* (Philadelphia: J.B. Lippincott & Co., 1856), vol. 1, pp. 733–34.

[20] "Alcoholic Therapeutics," *The Lancet*, vol. 80, no. 2045 (Nov. 8, 1862), p. 510.

[21] "The Alcoholic Controversy," *Fraser's Magazine for Town and Country*, vol. 78, no. 465 (Sept. 1868), pp. 277, 282; *Ex parte Yung Jon*, 28 F. 308, 311 (D. Ore. 1886). Chinese opium dens appeared in the *San Francisco Chronicle* as early as 1869. *See, e.g.*, "Horrors of a Great City," *San Francisco Chronicle*, Nov. 27, 1869, p. 5. Kane wrote in 1882 that "there were not over ten white smokers in the United States ten years ago." H.H. Kane, "Opium Smoking: A New Form of the Opium Habit Amongst Americans," *Gaillard's Medical Journal*, vol. 33, no. 2 (Feb. 1882), pp. 101, 103.

use was less common than drunkenness, those who claimed to take opium medicinally suffered less suspicion than those who said they drank for health.

Then there was the subtlety of the opium high. The same federal judge quoted the *American Cyclopedia*, which observed that opium is a vice "less easy of detection than alcoholic intoxication." There was nothing demonstrative about an opium binge. Opium "allows a man to be a gentleman," the Reverend Walter Colton said in 1836. "[H]is visions create no noise, no riots; they deal no blows, blacken no one's eyes, and frighten no one's peace." Just a few years earlier, an article in the *Boston Medical and Surgical Journal* told of a wife and mother whose medical use of opium had led to addiction: "No one had ever suspected this lady of using opium or any other stimulus, for she had *never*, in any one instance, been in the least degree *over-excited* by it. . . . Her husband even knew it not." An observer in the *Catholic World* added later that an addicted gentleman could "guard[] his secret from his nearest friend." Drunkenness, in contrast, with its slurring and staggering and stench, was hard to miss.[22]

Observers found it difficult to distinguish medicinal opium use from recreational abuse for a fourth reason: even when taken in a modest medicinal dose, opium could intoxicate. The sheer fact of opium intoxication, even if detected, was therefore no sure sign of abuse. Alcohol was very different. The typical medicinal dose of distilled liquor was a *dram*, defined by the *Oxford English Dictionary* as a "small draught of . . . spirituous liquor." The word came from the Greek *drachma*, later adopted as an apothecaries' weight for medicinal liquor. So *dram* had a peculiarly medical connotation, and while the size of a dram of spirits was unspecified, it meant no more than a drink—even a generous one could not intoxicate. On encountering a drunk, authorities could be pretty certain he had exceeded his medicinal dose. On encountering someone high on opium, they could not.

These four factors conspired to allow most recreational opium abusers to pass as medical users. The upshot was this: though social authorities of the eighteenth and nineteenth centuries in both Britain and America saw opium abuse and addiction as real or potential social evils, legislating against those evils remained impractical deep into the nineteenth century.

And one more factor put practical opium legislation past reach. A long tradition of self-medication made it still harder to discern medical use from recreational abuse—and created other obstacles to anti-opium lawmaking.

---

[22] *Ex parte Yung Jon*, 28 F. at 311; Walter Colton, "Turkish Sketches," *Knickerbocker*, vol. 7 (1836), p. 421; "Opium Eating," *Boston Medical and Surgical Journal*, vol. 9 (1833), pp. 66, 67; "The Opium Habit," *Catholic World*, vol. 33 (Sept. 1881), p. 828.

Self-Medication with Opium

There perhaps never was a time when doctors held a monopoly on opium therapy in the West. Physicians long lamented that quacks and lay folk presumed to practice with the drug. Dr. Thomas Willis quoted the memorable complaint his Parisian counterpart, Renodæus, uttered some four centuries ago—"that there is . . . no dull Piss-Doctor, no nor any pitiful Barber but professeth himself a *Laudanist*, or an Admirer of *Laudanum*." The same problem persisted in the late seventeenth century, Willis said, when there were "yet among us . . . a Swarm of Pretenders to Physick; whereof each one brags of his peculiar Laudanum, which they give in every Distemper . . . ; and if perchance it happen that the Patient sleeps and wakes again, immediately they triumph . . . when oftentimes they deserve a Gallows more than any thing else . . . ." Nearly eighty years later, Dr. George Young extended the complaint from lay persons and quack doctors to midwives and nurses: "[O]pium has already got into the hands of every pretender to practice, and is prescribed every day, not only by many charitable and well-meaning ladies, but even by the too officious and ignorant nurses; so that we must either assist the unskilful by our experience, or they will proceed boldly without us."[23]

At least by the mid-nineteenth century, Young's "pretenders" had grown to include most anyone with a laudanum bottle and eyedropper. In both Britain and America laudanum effectively became an over-the-counter drug. "Everyone had laudanum at home," Virginia Berridge writes of nineteenth-century Britain, and "[s]elf-medication was the most common reason for opiate use." Working-class people in particular looked after their own health, for regular doctors' visits were rare. And by the dose, opium was cheap. A penny could buy twenty or twenty-five drops of laudanum, containing about a grain of solid opium—the ordinary medicinal adult dose.[24]

Britain's broad tradition of self-medication obscured any stark outward distinction between legitimate medical use and recreational abuse. Opium "could originally have been taken for what can be called a 'medical' need—sleeplessness, headache, depression," Berridge writes, "but as it was often and quite normally self-prescribed, the use continued perhaps after the strict 'medical' condition

---

[23] [Willis,] *Dr Willis's Practice of Physick*, bk. 9, ch. 3, p. 139; Young, *A Treatise on Opium*, p. iv. Willis supplied no source for his quote from Renodæus, or Jean de Renou, who lived between 1568 and 1620 and first printed his famous *Dispensatorium* in Latin in, it seems, 1608. I thank Kevin Rothenberg for tracking down these biographical details.

[24] Berridge, *Opium and the People*, p. 25 (elaborating on opium's easy availability at drug stores and general stores across Britain); ibid., p. 28 (discussing self-medication and working-class medical care); ibid., p. 29 ("Everyone had laudanum . . ." and stating the cost of opium sold over the counter); ibid., p. 49 ("Self-medication was . . ."); "Narcotics," p. 386 (noting the standard dose and drops per grain).

had gone. In reality the medical uses of opium shaded imperceptibly into 'non-medical'" uses. And because it was rarely possible to peg a person's opium use as non-medical, "'recreational' use of opium . . . [was] rarely spoken of."[25] The tradition of self-medication therefore added another obstacle to anti-opium law-making, for it made recreational abuse very hard to detect.

Crossing the Atlantic to America, we find the same vexing obstacle to anti-opium legislation. A New York doctor put the problem plainly in 1877: "One of the worst features of opium drunkenness is that the drug is in everybody's hands and it cannot be reached. . . . [T]he number of persons who constantly keep opium in the house is astonishing . . . ."[26] An outright ban on home use was unthinkable. Perhaps in dense urban areas the law could require the sick to see doctors or druggists for an opium cure. But in the sprawling expanses of America's remote rural regions, any such law would have put an essential drug out of reach for millions. So politicians representing those regions rose to defend self-medication against bids to regulate sales.

Take for example North Dakota Senator James McCumber. During 1914 debates on the Harrison Narcotic Act, which effectively banned opium and co-caine sales except by doctor's prescription, McCumber pled the virtues of self-medication. He warned of a "greater danger and greater hardship . . . if we should prevent those people from getting at the ordinary drug stand what they want for the little ordinary ills of life and compel them to go to a physician in every instance." Ohio Senator Atlee Pomerene agreed, reminding his colleagues of "the difficulty which surrounds the country practitioner, whose patients may be 5, 10, 15, or 20 miles away from his office and away from a drug store." A year earlier, an Indiana legislator aimed a similar argument at a proposed statewide ban on opium sales without a doctor's prescription: "[T]he worried father seeking soothing medicine for a yelling infant . . . would be forced to go to a pharmacist in order to buy the stuff. They could not run to the corner grocery or general store as they now can do . . . ."[27]

Bygone Tolerance of Drug Abuse?

So there were many reasons neither Congress nor any state legislature banned recreational opium intoxication before the last few decades of the nineteenth century. Recreational abuse was comparatively rare and hard to detect. When

[25] Berridge, Opium and the People, p. 49.
[26] McFarland, "Opium Inebriety," p. 293 (quoting a Dr. Kendall).
[27] Congressional Record, vol. 51, pt. 14 (63d Cong., 2d Sess.), pp. 13761–62 (Aug 15, 1914) (remarks of Sen. McCumber); ibid., p. 13759 (remarks of Sen. Pomerene); "Sees Druggists' 'Joker' in Bill," Indianapolis Sunday Star, Feb. 2, 1913, p. 3 (quoting state representative George Sands).

detected, it was hard to distinguish from legitimate medical use. That was true both because outward symptoms were similar and because the tradition of self-medication meant there was no obvious marker—such as a doctor's prescription or its absence—that labeled some uses "medical" and others "recreational." And it was true because a great deal of opium use, even if not prescribed by a doctor, was *genuinely* medical, effective against diarrhea and insomnia and all manner of pain. Moreover, even when legislators sought to restrict opium sales, the tradition of self-medication resisted making physicians gatekeepers of legitimate, medicinal drug use.

The lack of anti-opium laws does *not*, though, suggest nineteenth-century society approved of recreational opium intoxication or even viewed it with indifference. With temperance fever raging, moral leaders and lawmakers hardly looked benignly on recreational drugs. On the contrary, as an 1881 passage in *Catholic World* makes clear, the same moral and social stigma attached to drunkenness and opiate addiction, at least when the latter claimed no medical excuse: "The gentleman who would not be seen in a bar-room, however respectable, or who would not purchase liquor and use it at home, lest the odor might be detected upon his person, procures his supply of morphia [derived from opium] and has it in his pocket ready for instantaneous use." Yet the same gentleman "zealously guards his secret from his nearest friend—for popular wisdom has branded as a disgrace that which he regards as a misfortune...."[28]

Modern advocates of more liberal drug laws nonetheless have sought to bend history to their cause. They make claims, technically true, about the absence of drug laws till the late nineteenth century and spy in this statutory silence complacency toward recreational use. Consider a passage from a 1993 challenge to the war on drugs titled *America's Longest War*. After noting that illicit drugs "provide ... pleasures to many" and "this has been true for centuries," the authors continue: "In fact, use of both opiates and cocaine was common among upright citizens in America and elsewhere in the latter half of the nineteenth century." Though each of these phrases is accurate, the impression that Americans deemed "upright" use of opiates as pleasure drugs is not. Likewise, in his important 1972 study, *Licit and Illicit Drugs*, Edward Brecher alleges, "The United States of America during the nineteenth century could quite properly be described as a 'dope fiend's paradise.'"[29] As a reference to the ready availability of over-the-counter and even mail-order opiates, this claim is quite true. But as a suggestion of widespread tolerance of recreational abuse, it is deeply misleading.

[28] [D.W. Nolan,] "The Opium Habit," *Catholic World*, vol. 33, no. 198 (Sept. 1881), pp. 827, 828.
[29] Steven B. Duke & Albert C. Gross, *America's Longest War: Rethinking Our Tragic Crusade Against Drugs* (New York: G.P. Putnam's Sons, 1993), p. 5; Brecher, *Licit and Illicit Drugs*, p. 3.

Such claims are troubling not merely because they mislead. They leave the impression that our modern drug laws have repressed a long-forgotten cultural libertinism, one that embraced the mindless pleasures of opium and its chemical cohort. Like arguments that point to the alcoholized rituals of the early Republic—barn-raisings, fence-railings, musters, and the like—and cast them as typical of daily life, claims of an openly narcotized nineteenth-century America appeal to a fondness for the sottish devils of our nature. This cultural romanticism would be harmless enough if policy prescriptions, together with predictions of success, did not come trailing. But these historical hobbyhorses come saddled with a proposed return to days of untethered recreational drug use. David Courtwright has written that modern calls for drug legalization "would reset the policy clock by more than a hundred years."[30] They would do much more than that. Modern-day legalizers advocate open abuse of recreational drugs—something without precedent in our national history.

Even Edward Brecher followed his claim that old America was a "dope fiend's paradise" with the admission that "nonmedicinal use of opiates, while legal in both the United States and England, was not considered respectable. Indeed," he wrote, citing the *Catholic World* article I mentioned earlier, "it was as disreputable as drinking alcoholic beverages." Drug use likely was deemed far worse. Between 1875 and 1905, the roster of states and future states banning alcoholic drinks grew from three to eight, then retreated again to three. Over the same three decades, the number banning either opium or opium dens or cocaine grew from one to forty-one.[31] By 1913, antidrug lawmaking had reached every state except Vermont. And whereas alcohol prohibition proved temporary in every state that embraced it, no state, having once banned either opium or cocaine, ever undid its ban.

Something changed in the last quarter of the nineteenth century to trigger this trend of antidrug lawmaking. That change did not concern mainstream attitudes toward recreational intoxication, which had been and remained negative. Instead, lawmakers came face to face with undeniable recreational drug abuse. Hence they had to devise a means to ban recreational abuse while sparing necessary medical use. From there illegalization followed almost as a matter of course.

[30] Courtwright, *Forces of Habit*, p. 201.
[31] Brecher, *Licit and Illicit Drugs*, p. 6. Between 1875 and 1905, twenty-four states or future states outlawed opium dens, ten partially overlapping states outlawed opium sales, and thirty partially overlapping states outlawed cocaine sales. These three groups included forty different states or future states. *See* Tables 4A 4C, and 6A at pages 180, 190, and 269.

Emergence of the Dens

Undeniable recreational abuse arrived undisguised. The change was not simply of style or attitude, but of the very form of the drug. All the opium mentioned in the works of Jones, Willis, Young, and Crumpe was *edible*—eaten or drunk in solutions such as laudanum. Opium smoking remained all but unknown in the West centuries after eaten opium had arrived along Eastern trading routes and become part of the medical mainstream. Neither Jones nor Willis nor Young nor Crumpe so much as mentioned an opium pipe.

In both England and America, opium dens arrived rather suddenly with the laboring Chinese of the last half of the nineteenth century. After the first wave of Chinese immigrants reached the American West Coast around 1850, the newcomers dispersed in search of work up and down the coast and throughout the intermountain states of Nevada, Idaho, Montana, and Wyoming. Where they went, they brought their imported narcotic pastime with them. A roving Western actor of the era wrote that wherever he lighted, even in little frontier towns, he found a smoking place with a pipe. If there was no formal den, the backroom of a Chinese laundry filled the need.[32] In time, dens dotted cityscapes and mining towns throughout the West. And as Chinese workers spread East and South, dens appeared in New York by 1873, Chicago, St. Louis, and New Orleans by 1876, Philadelphia by 1882, and Boston by 1884.[33]

Much like the sudden popularity of gin in early eighteenth-century England, the rather sudden appearance of opium dens in England and America introduced an old drug in a new administration. As with gin, contemporaries regarded opium's new guise as insidiously different. The simple presence of an opium pipe, unlike a pill bottle or laudanum vial, was usually unanswerable proof of recreational drug abuse.

The drug was undeniably intoxicating. No one doubted smoked opium delivered the mind-numbing pleasure of eaten opium to all but the most hardened addicts. Descriptions of the pleasure followed a standard formula, conjuring

---

[32] Kane, "Opium Smoking: A New Form," p. 103 (noting Chinese newcomers introduced opium smoking to the United States); David T. Courtwright, *Dark Paradise: Opiate Addiction in America before 1940* (Cambridge: Harvard University Press, 1982), pp. 63–64 (describing the early period of Chinese settlement of the West Coast from 1850 to 1880); Diana Lynn Ahmad, "'Caves of Oblivion': Opium Dens and Exclusion Laws, 1850–1882" (Ph.D. Dissertation, Univ. of Missouri-Columbia, 1997), pp. 5, 22 (reporting that the first Chinese immigrants arrived in California in 1848); H.H. Kane, *Opium-Smoking in America and China* (New York: G.P. Putnam's Sons, 1882), pp. 66–67 (quoting the actor); ibid., pp. 70–71 (mentioning laundry backrooms).

[33] Kane, "Opium Smoking: A New Form," p. 103 ("[T]his vice . . . has gradually spread eastward, keeping pace with the advance of the [Chinese] in the same direction."); "Kane, *Opium-Smoking in America and China*, p. 5 (Chicago, St. Louis, and New Orleans); "Chinese in New-York," *New York Times*, Dec. 26, 1873, p. 3 (New York); "Philadelphia's Opium Parlor," *New York Times*, Aug. 29, 1882, p. 2 (Philadelphia); "A Terrible Revelation," *Boston Globe*, Aug. 10, 1884, p. 4 (Boston).

from the smoke a languid, lighter-than-air escape from life's surly bonds. Frederick Masters cast the smoker "float[ing] away into a state of revolting enjoyment"; Harry Hubbell Kane had him slipping into a "lazy insouciance," a "listless calm and contentment," a "pleasant bubble" that wafted over the "unpleasant crudities of daily life"; Stephen Crane drew him lapsing into "a fine languor, a complete mental rest."[34]

Then there was the sex. From the physicians we hear many of the same symptoms lovingly detailed by Dr. John Jones a century and a half earlier. Dr. Alonzo Calkins told of smokers "habitually tormented with a satyriasis as abortive as it is insatiable." Dr. Kane wrote of "considerable erethrism" among both men and women—and a sexual appetite that "sometimes approaches to frenzy, the woman losing all modesty." Compounding the drug's effects were the immoral influences of the den itself—its darkness, its bunks, the general air of degradation, and the company. "The surroundings, the low companionship, and the effect of the drug," Kane wrote, "combine to effect any thing other than a raising of the moral tone." Most female smokers were prostitutes, and those "not already lost in point of virtue, soon become so," Kane said. "The women who are to be found smoking at the joints manifest no bashfulness in smoking with strange men . . . . They usually remove the shoes, loosen the corsets, and remain for hours on the hard wooden bunks." Indeed, "the laws against opium-smoking that have been enacted and enforced in this country had their inception in a knowledge of the fact that male smokers (Americans) . . . were continually beguiling women and young girls to try the pipe, and effected their ruin when they were under its influence."[35]

But if smoked opium set off all the escapist, hedonistic moral alarms of eaten opium, it lacked eaten opium's moral saving grace. For smoked opium had no recognized medicinal value. Exactly why doctors snubbed the pipe as a means of delivering the drug is not clear. Perhaps it was the difficulty of precise calibration. The typical dose of eaten opium was a grain, or 0.065 gram. Dissolved in solution, it could be divided into twenty-five drops of laudanum. Opium smoking by its nature permitted no similar exactness. Whereas medicinal opium was dried and powdered, smoked opium was boiled into a thick syrup and later burned in a pipe, making dosage conversions elusive. Even if smoked opium had been

[34] See Frederick J. Masters, "The Opium Traffic in California," *The Chautauquan*, vol. 24 (n.s. 15) (1896–97), p. 56; Kane, *Opium-Smoking in America and China*, p. 61 ("listless calm . . . ," "pleasant bubble," and "unpleasant crudities . . ."); ibid., p. 84 ("lazy insouciance"); Stephen Crane, "'Dope' Smokers," *Los Angeles Times*, May 17, 1896, p. 23.

[35] Alonzo Calkins, *Opium and the Opium-Appetite* (Philadelphia: J.P. Lippincott & Co., 1871), p. 71 (citing other authorities); Kane, *Opium-Smoking in America and China*, p. 74 ("The women who are . . ."); ibid., p. 81 ("The surroundings . . ." and "not already lost . . ."); ibid., p. 90 ("most of the female smokers are prostitutes"); ibid., p. 93 ("considerable erethrism"); ibid., pp. 131–32 ("the laws against . . ."); Kane, "Opium-Smoking: A New Form," p. 112 ("sometimes approaches . . .").

suitable as medicine, the den itself was a distinctly nonmedical milieu. Doctors may have rejected medicinal smoking because of its dank, unhygienic setting—a "bare, squalid" cellar, in Stephen Crane's 1896 telling, "occupied only by an odor that will float wooden chips."[36]

It's clear in any event that doctors turned their backs on the drug. Various sources report this verdict, albeit without explanation. Dr. Kane wrote in 1882 that "not a single grain [of smoked opium] is used as medicine." An 1892 editorial in the *Journal of the American Medical Association* alleged that smoked opium was "never used for any legitimate purpose. We never knew a physician to prescribe it . . . ." The editors charged that the "sole uses" of smoked opium were "as an intoxicant or as an aid to the perpetration of illegal and vicious acts"—presumably a reference to the seductions described by Kane and others. That same year Frederick Masters wrote that "[w]hatever may be said for crude opium and the medicinal uses to which it may be applied," opium prepared for smoking "can have no earthly use but to ruin men morally and physically . . . ." Or as a Western news editor wrote in 1881 in old-fashioned moral strains, opium smokers were "engaged to court the haunts of filth—engaged to . . . sink beneath the level of the beasts of the field—engaged to grovel in the lowest pools of bestial inhumanity, engaged to sink lower and lower . . . ."[37]

Still, there were defenders of smoked opium as medicine. An 1884 article in the *American Journal of Medical Sciences* wrote of German physician Johann Thudichum's view of "Opium Smoking as a Therapeutic Means." Thudichum claimed smoked opium could cure violent coughs, hay fever, and migraines. His views drew an almost instant rebuke from the *Journal of the American Medical Association*, which declared the drug's addictive potential disqualified it for treatment of these ailments. Dr. Kane allowed that smoked opium had proved "an excellent sedative" against an "excited and irregular" heart and was effective as well against organic cardiac disease—but went on to say that "so great is the danger of forming the habit [and] so disgusting the surroundings" that patients should turn instead to one of "many equally efficacious remedies."[38]

It's also true that an 1881 San Francisco ordinance, which imposed a licensing requirement on sales of smoked opium, exempted opium sold or exchanged "for medicinal purposes on the prescription of a practicing physician." But

[36] George Parsons Lathrop, "The Sorcery of Madjoon," *Scribner's Monthly*, vol. 20 (1880), pp. 417–18 (discussing the differing opium preparations and the manner of smoking); Crane, "'Dope' Smokers," p. 23.

[37] Kane, *Opium-Smoking in America and China*, p. 17; "'Opiokapnism' or Opium Smoking," *Journal of the American Medical Association*, vol. 18 (June 4, 1892), p. 719; Frederick J. Masters, "Opium and It's [sic] Votaries," *California Illustrated Magazine*, vol. 1 (May 1892), p. 645; "Opium Smoking," *Idaho Avalanche*, Jan. 15, 1881, p. 4 (reprinting article from the *Tuscarora* (Nev.) *Times-Review*).

[38] "Opium Smoking as a Therapeutic Means," *Journal of the American Medical Association*, vol. 3 (July 26, 1884), pp. 100–01 (rebutting "Opium Smoking as a Therapeutic Means," *American Journal of the Medical Sciences*, vol. 88 (July 1884), pp. 271–72); Kane, "Opium Smoking: A New Form," p. 113.

other lawmaking bodies ignored or rejected any medicinal potential for smoked opium. When Congress regulated opium imports in 1909, it pointedly foreclosed any medicinal purpose for smoked opium. The law banned importation of "opium in any form or any preparation or derivative thereof: Provided, That opium and preparations and derivatives thereof, *other than smoking opium or opium prepared for smoking*, may be imported for medicinal purposes only . . . ."[39]

And if smoked opium lacked eaten opium's claim to medical necessity, it also lacked alcohol's claim to social necessity. Recall the silence—"the hush of the grave," the "wicked, ominous hush"—that for Frederick Masters and George Parsons Lathrop distinguished the dens from "the hilarious shouts" and "seductive air of social re-union" of the saloon. Or consider again the den pictured in this book's introduction in Figure I.2, captured by Masters with flashlight photography. The photo appears to show four bunks—three laid end to end and one above. Even if awake, the smokers could not readily face one another, and though they could speak, the arrangement resisted conversation. Indeed, the smokers in Masters's photograph appear quite asleep. Masters wrote that after inhaling the drug, the smoker "sinks back, the pipe slips from his hand, and oblivious of everything around him, he drops off to sleep." As a Nevada news editor wrote in 1875, opium "does not produce the same 'sociability' as intoxicating liquors. Each man is wrapped in his own dreamy sensations, and he cares for little else."[40]

Again there were dissenters. Sympathetic depictions of the dens sometimes cast them in a more social light. William Rosser Cobbe, a one-time doctor, journalist, and (he claimed) addict, wrote in 1895 that "[i]n certain stages of the smoking the wretches are talkative and may be mirthful"—though "[n]ow and then one falls away into a stupor that has all the appearance of death." Another addict reported that smokers in New York dens joked, chatted, told stories, even sang. And Dr. Kane insisted the effect of smoking opium was "to *awaken* rather than to cause repose."[41] These accounts, however, stood apart from the norm. Even if they reflected some fragment of the smoking scene, they lay shadowed by more prominent images of deathly silence. In the minds of readers who never set

[39] "Providing for Imposing a License upon Dealers in Opium in the City and County of San Francisco," in *General Orders of the Board of Supervisors* (San Francisco: P.J. Thomas, 1888), no. 1615, § 1 (Ord. of Feb. 16, 1881), p. 179; "An Act to Prohibit the Importation and Use of Opium for Other Than Medicinal Purposes," Pub. L. 60-221, ch. 100, § 1, 35 Stat. 614 (Act of Feb. 9, 1909) (emphasis added).

[40] Masters, "Opium and It's Votaries," p. 636; "The Opium Dens," *Virginia Evening Chronicle*, June 8, 1875, p. 3.

[41] William Rosser Cobbe, *Doctor Judas: A Portrayal of the Opium Habit* (Chicago: S.C. Griggs and Company, 1895), p. 131; Thomas Byrnes, *Professional Criminals of America* (New York: Cassel & Company, 1886), pp. 381–83; Kane, "Opium Smoking: A New Form," p. 114. One of Cobbe's earliest reviewers, writing in the pages of the *American Journal of Psychology*, was agnostic about "whether [his book was] the work of a genuine victim of the habit." "*Doctor Judas*," *American Journal of Psychology*, vol. 7 (Jan. 1896), p. 294. On Cobbe, *see* "Who's Who among Doctors," *The Chicago Clinic Pure Water Journal*, vol. 20 (Feb. 1907), pp. 51–52..

foot in a den, the dominant image was of silence—and this silence denied dens the saloons' social saving grace.

Among those who deemed silence an emblem of opium's immorality was Immanuel Kant. Writing at the end of the eighteenth century, when the old moral argot still reigned, Kant condemned a drunkard as "simply like a beast"—or "even beneath the nature of an animal"—and "not to be treated as a human being." Such debasement could trace to alcohol or to "other stupefying agents such as opium." But wine, Kant said, "used almost to the point of intoxication," could be permitted "because it arouses a company to lively conversation and unites it in frankness." Wine drinkers could have "a moral end in view, namely to bring many people together for a long time in mutual communication." Neither opium nor distilled alcohol could claim this moral excuse of social drinking: "The use of opium and distilled spirits for enjoyment is closer to baseness than the use of wine because the former, with the dreamy euphoria they produce, make one taciturn, withdrawn, and uncommunicative."

Where the English translator writes "taciturn," Kant had said *stumm*—capturing both the stupefying force of opium and the end state of those who drug themselves dumb. And where the translator says "uncommunicative," Kant had written *unmitteilbar*—perhaps better rendered (as earlier translators had it) "unsocial." "Therefore," Kant continued, given the social uselessness of opium and distilled alcohol, "they are permitted only as medicines."[42] That is, lacking the moral excuse of social necessity, opium and distilled alcohol required the excuse of medical need. Smoked opium, which emerged in Europe after Kant wrote these words in 1797, could make neither claim, for doctors denied it a medical role.

Even William Rosser Cobbe, who claimed smokers sometimes were talkative and mirthful, denied them the moral excuse of opium eaters. While opium eaters could claim to have been addicted by their doctors or by "racking physical pain," opium smokers could blame only "wantonness of desire" and "moral depravity. The smoker . . . is a creature given over to his own lusts walking after the flesh . . . ."[43]

And if smoked opium could claim neither social nor medical necessity, it also lacked the broader moral safety zone of subintoxicating use, or use in

---

[42] Immanuel Kant, *The Metaphysical Principles of Virtue* (James Ellington trans., Indianapolis: Bobbs-Merrill, 1964 (1797)), pp. 88–89 (rendering Kant's *stumm, zurückhaltend und unmitteilbar* as "taciturn, withdrawn, and uncommunicative"). *Compare* Immanuel Kant, *The Metaphysical Elements of the Doctrine of Virtue* (J.W. Semple trans., Henry Calderwood ed., Edinburgh: T&T Clark, 3d ed. 1871 (1797)), p. 243 (rendering the same phrase as "mute, reserved, and unsocial"). For Kant's original, *see Die Metaphysik der Sitten: Der Streit der Fakultäten* (Benzion Cassirer ed., 1916), p. 239. My thanks to David Crandall for his assistance in gathering and comparing translations.

[43] Cobbe, *Doctor Judas*, pp. 124–25, 127.

moderation. That's because the drug was—or at least was seen to be—incapable of moderate use. A 1911 ruling of the California Supreme Court quoted a lower appellate court's comments on this front. The lower court had sought to explain why the legislature could ban possession of opium despite earlier rulings that it lacked power to penalize possession of alcohol. "[L]iquor is used daily in this and other countries as a beverage, moderately and without harm, by countless thousands," the lower court wrote. But "it appears there is no such thing as moderation in the use of opium. Once the habit is formed the desire for it is insatiable, and its use is invariably disastrous." The high court conceded it may be "unduly sweeping" to say opium must always be used in excess. Still, "[i]t is enough if the law-making body may rationally believe such facts to be established. If the belief that the use of opium, once begun, almost inevitably leads to excess may be entertained by reasonable men—and we do not doubt that it may—such belief affords a sufficient justification for applying to opium restrictions which might be unduly burdensome in the case of other substances, as, for example, intoxicating liquors . . . ."[44]

Some years later, as the nation emerged from prohibition, Alma Whitaker prescribed the proper regimen of pre-dinner cocktails. Alcohol "should be strictly a social lubricant," she said, and "the cup that cheers . . . positively should not inebriate." Hence "[t]wo cocktails is the absolute limit"—and a portion of whisky "should [n]ever exceed two fingers" or one finger for a lady. Smoked opium simply did not permit a two-cocktail, two-finger rule. In part that's because, as the California Supreme Court saw, opium was fiercely addictive: small doses led inexorably to larger. In part it's because the mechanics of smoking frustrated precise calibration. To load his pipe, the smoker dipped a needle into a tin and scooped out a gob of the drug, thick as molasses—whether a finger's worth or two couldn't be said.[45] Then he burned the gob and inhaled the smoke, in big gulps or small, but in no event with precision. And in part the problem was the drug's pharmacology, for even a little could intoxicate. *Smoking in moderation*, therefore, was an ideal past attainment.

---

[44] *In the Matter of Yun Quong, on Habeas Corpus*, 159 Cal. 508, 514–15 (1911) (quoting from lower appellate ruling).

[45] Whitaker, *Bacchus Behave! The Lost Art of Polite Drinking* (New York: Frederick A. Stokes Company, 1933), p. 3 ("the cup that cheers . . ."); ibid., p. 4 ("should be strictly . . ."); ibid., p. 17 ("Two cocktails . . ."); ibid., p. 27 ("should [n]ever exceed . . ."); ibid., p. 32 (one finger for the lady); "Female Opium Smokers," *San Francisco Chronicle*, Apr. 25, 1875, p. 5 (describing the process of smoking opium).

Banning the Dens

Opium dens confronted the Western world for the first time with a *recreational intoxicant*—a mind-numbing, pleasure-giving escape from reality that served no known nutritional or medicinal or social need and permitted no reliable subintoxicating use. Smoked opium was therefore our first *drug* in the sense meant by our *War on Drugs*.[46] Its legal fate was never much in doubt, as there was no tradition in either England or America of tolerating any intoxicant *as an intoxicant.*

Nor did the timing of the dens' arrival in America help their cause. For just at that moment, temperance battles flared across the nation. In California the Chinese dens rose in public consciousness soon after a "local-option" law of March 1874 had stirred anti-saloon passions throughout the state. The law empowered citizens to demand local elections to decide the saloon's fate in their communities. In succeeding months, even as the *San Francisco Chronicle* made little mention of opium smoking, it fixated on the saloon question. A series of articles from April through September reported on local-option elections in Oakland, San Jose, Santa Cruz, and cities and towns up and down the state.[47]

In September, before local option could reach the ballot in San Francisco, the state supreme court struck down the new law, agreeing with liquor makers and sellers that the law unconstitutionally delegated lawmaking powers to voters. Not waiting on the court's ruling, the San Francisco Board of Supervisors already had proposed to restrain the saloon traffic. In late summer or fall 1874, the board barred any "drinking cellar, saloon, or drinking place" from admitting women between 6 p.m. and 6 a.m. and forbade women to enter during those

---

[46] *See* U.S. Public Health Service, *State Laws Relating to the Control of Narcotic Drugs and the Treatment of Drug Addiction* (Washington: Government Printing Office, 1931), pp. 3–4 ("[T]he use of opium for smoking purposes constituted the first serious narcotic problem confronted by the States.").

[47] I have found only six *Chronicle* articles from 1872, 1873, and 1874 mentioning opium smoking or opium dens. One concerned a theater production of Mark Twain's *Roughing It* and said nothing of real-life dens. *See* "Dramatic and Musical," *San Francisco Chronicle*, Mar. 2, 1873, p. 6. Three were set in other places—New Jersey or London—and said nothing of opium smoking in San Francisco. *See* "Dens of a Great City," ibid., Mar. 24, 1872, p. 2; "The Jersey Celestials," ibid., June 30, 1873, p. 3; "Lascar Sal," ibid., Dec. 13, 1874, p. 6. A fifth dealt with a police raid on a suspected Chinatown gambling den. When the police discovered instead a Chinese man smoking opium, they left without stopping him. *See* "An Unsuccessful Raid through Chinatown," ibid., Dec. 9, 1874, p. 5. And a sixth mentioned in passing a Chinatown boarding house that contained an opium den and Chinese actors who smoked opium offstage. *See* "Roscius with a Pigtail," ibid., Aug. 30, 1874, p. 1. Meanwhile, articles focusing on local-option elections are too many to list. Among them: "Legislative Action," *San Francisco Chronicle*, Apr. 6, 1874, p. 3 (noting recent passage of the local option law); "Local Option," ibid., May 15, 1874, p. 2 (detailing the law's provisions and noting elections in Oakland, Santa Clara, Santa Cruz, and towns in Contra Costa, Nevada, Tulare, and Yolo Counties); "The Temperance Warfare," ibid., June 1, 1874, p. 3 (noting that in sixteen of twenty-two local-option elections held so far, the vote had been in favor of a drink ban).

hours. Violators—both proprietors and patrons—faced up to one hundred days' confinement.[48]

I've found no record revealing why supervisors closed saloons to women or why they did so then, in late 1874. Raging battles in nearby local-option elections likely heightened lawmakers' sensitivity to the moral threats saloons posed. They knew drunken women suffered worse moral and social stigma than drunken men—and knew saloon sojourns by night hinted at sexual depravity. They probably knew men-only rules had precedents elsewhere, in jurisdictions across the country.[49] But whatever roused supervisors to act, their new ordinance advertised vigilance in detecting and combating threats to feminine morals.

The Chronicle's reporting soon faced them with such a threat from a new quarter. Early in 1875, after several years of near silence on the matters of opium smoking and opium dens, the Chronicle turned to these topics in earnest. Opium dens were not yet illegal, either in San Francisco or anywhere in the United States. The Chronicle therefore covered their emergence not as a criminal menace, but as a slightly unpleasant artifact of the immigrant Chinese culture. Hence the first of several long articles from 1875 examining life in the dens ran under the slurring front-page headline, "John Chinaman: The Habits and Manners of the Mongolian."

In this account from late January and three others from February, April, and June, the Chronicle wrote of the city's Chinese district and the netherworld of the dens. Though never approving, never enchanted by the exoticism of these dungeons, the anonymous author at first avoided the shuddering revulsion that colored later notes from the underground. "The Chinese are the victims of two great vices," said the first article—gambling and smoking opium. Unable to shake his taste for the "cursed drug," the Chinese man "will smoke his pipe of opium every evening lying in his bunk and enjoying that pleasure that seems at first something almost divine . . . ." In time, the reporter warned, smokers fall victim to addiction, and the drug "exacts from its votaries such a fearful penalty." With that, his interest in the topic was spent.[50]

The second article cast opium smoking in even less alarmist tones. Here our reporter—still unnamed but likely the same—told of a night of upscale revelry at a "Celestial Banquet" thrown by Chinese cigar makers. After a posh dinner,

[48] Ex Parte Wall, 48 Cal. 279, 313–14 (1874); "The Plans and Prospects of the Liquor Dealers," San Francisco Chronicle, June 25, 1874, p. 2 (outlining the liquor interests' strategy for challenging the local-option law in court); "The Supervisors: A New Order to Exclude Women from Saloons at Night," San Francisco Chronicle, Sept. 1, 1874, p. 3 (printing the text of the proposed ordinance). I've not determined when the ordinance barring women from saloons at night passed or took effect. It surely became law, for six weeks after reporting the proposed ordinance, the Chronicle mentioned its enactment and reported an arrest under its power. See "Women in Saloons," ibid., Oct. 13, 1874, p. 3.
[49] See State v. Nelson, 10 Idaho 522, 524–26, 529 (1905) (quoting local ordinances from Boise, Denver, and Middlesboro, Kentucky, all forbidding saloons to admit women).
[50] "John Chinaman," San Francisco Chronicle, Jan. 31, 1875, p. 1.

he "lingered and was invited to try a pipe of opium." He followed his host to "an elegantly furnished alcove" where, he told readers without embarrassment, he inhaled "several blasts of strong-smelling smoke." Faint and qualmish, he despaired of the "delicious languor . . . one reads of," with its "succession of fairy realms" and its "sensation of being whirled through space."[51]

The reporter's next foray into the dens, in late April 1875, was decidedly more ominous. His title told his theme: "Female Opium Smokers: Midnight Meetings to Indulge in the Vice." On pretense of wanting a smoke, the reporter and an undercover police officer had stationed themselves inside a seedy den on that "battered and immoral thoroughfare," Dupont Street. There they saw two "young and pretty and very expensively attired" women, with "beaded silks, showy jewelry, and bright complexions." It was no time for respectable women to be out—after three on a Friday morning—and these two risked the twin moral dangers we have come to expect from opium smoking. First was the stupor—the narcosis of the smoke. The women were practiced smokers, the reporter judged, and lasted through seven pipes. But after the eighth, "the drug began to have its effect," and "they gave themselves up to THE INTOXICATION OF THE OPIUM." Soon they were "unconscious of the mean, grimy place and all its occupants."

Then there was the sex. The danger here was not the four Chinese patrons who slept in bunks at one end of the den. Nor was it the Chinese proprietor who lay alongside the pipe he was preparing for his lady patrons. True, the reporter found it "odd and painful" to see the younger of the two women sharing the proprietor's pillow, her "fair hair . . . arranged in a wild and coquettish tangle [that] fairly brushed the shaven crown of the unclean Chinaman." But the reporter need not have worried, for "the unappreciative heathen brushed [the woman's hair] away from his eyes."

The danger came instead from white men—"the brace of dissipated-looking bucks in shiny hats" who had squired the women into the den. As the women lay unconscious, their beaus tried to unnerve the reporter and undercover officer, "inquiring of one another why some people would stay where they weren't wanted." Taking the hint, reporter and cop slunk away, leaving the women prey to the "blasé scoundrels." It was just such scenes, one presumes, that led Harry Hubbell Kane to write six years later that the laws against opium smoking took rise from knowledge "that male smokers (Americans) . . . were continually beguiling women and young girls to try the pipe, and effected their ruin when they were under its influence."[52]

---

[51] "A Celestial Banquet," ibid., Feb. 22, 1875, p. 3.

[52] "Female Opium Smokers," *San Francisco Chronicle*, Apr. 25, 1875, p. 5; Kane, *Opium-Smoking in America and China*, pp. 131–32. A small blurb of similar ilk appeared in the *Chronicle* in late October 1875: "Detective Rogers and Mr. Cragin, the clerk of Mayor Otis, visited several of the opium dens in Chinatown on Friday night and drove a number of white women into the street, half-stupefied as they were with opium. There are about twenty of these dens in Chinatown, all of which are visited

Kane's parenthetical reference to "(Americans)" makes plain he had *white* scoundrels in mind. So did the reporter. The undercover officer disclosed that in surveilling the den, he had seen "women going in at all hours of the day and night"—fifteen women on the previous afternoon alone, together with "nearly as many young men. 'They go there to smoke opium,' said the officer, 'and what else I don't know. Most of the women are young, and the men are hoodlums and sports.'" *Hoodlums*, as we'll see in time, was a term assigned whites. Contemporaries rarely applied it to anyone else.

Both hoodlums and the women they squired turned up missing in the last of the *Chronicle*'s 1875 articles on the world of the dens. "The Orient in America" looked only at the Chinese and their ways. It bore a sadly typical subheading—"Habits of the Heathen Chinee"—yet offered a surprisingly tolerant account of Chinese culture, almost modern in its pained admission of the day's pervading racism: "To see the waves of Chinese humanity divide [on a San Francisco street] as the lordly American sweeps through them like an ironclad through a fleet of birch bark canoes, is to understand that the aristocracy of race did not end with Southern slavery." The reporter chided fellow whites for refusing to "see anything good, or curious, or wise, or interesting . . . under the brown guise of these strange Orientals, who have built our railroads, tilled our fields and otherwise brought their forty centuries of old-world aristocracy into meek submission to our despotic and semi-barbarous spirit of progress."

Despite so stout a defense of the maligned Chinese, the reporter could not abide their opium. Unmistakably, the dens revolted him—from the "steps slippery with accumulated filth" to the "slop and offal" outside the door to the "yellow clay-skinned" occupants within. Worse were the drug's effects on its devotees and the "somnolent inebriety" in which they lay: "By night or day anyone who enters here can see the same Chinamen at their pipes, or asleep, living from day to day a kind of life in death, with scarcely waking and lucent intervals long enough for successful theft or ordinary immorality. . . . It is only the novelty of a sight like this that prevents absolute disgust and sickness." This time the reporter thought better than to indulge. "[D]eclining an invitation to inhale the fumes of the sleepy drug," our scribe climbed back to "the glittering streets" of the city.[53]

Two more articles, appearing not in the *Chronicle* but in the rival *Alta California*, backdropped the San Francisco supervisors' assault on the dens. On September 30, 1875, less than two months before supervisors took action, police

---

by white females of bad reputation and their male associates." "Jottings About Town," *San Francisco Chronicle*, Oct. 31, 1875, p. 8.

[53] "The Orient in America," *San Francisco Chronicle*, June 13, 1875, p. 5. On the origins of the expression "heathen Chinee," *see* Ahmad, "Caves of Oblivion," pp. 25–26.

Detective James Rogers inspected a Chinatown den "frequented by a certain class of whites and Chinese, both male and female . . . ." Inside Rogers found "five young women from 18 to 23 years old, and some eight or nine young men, fumigating themselves in Oriental style amidst a pack of Chinese." Though the *Alta*'s account does not give the race of the "young women" and "young men," their placement "amidst a pack of Chinese" suggests they were white. Whether the women were in the company of the white men or their Chinese hosts also is unclear. But in the context of the *Chronicle*'s report of sporting white men leading young white women to the dens and of Kane's complaint "that male smokers (Americans) . . . were continually beguiling women and young girls to try the pipe," it seems likely the women were with the white men. At all events, they "were ordered to leave," presumably by Officer Rogers, "and informed that they would be prosecuted for vagrancy if found again in such degraded surroundings."[54]

On Detective Rogers's next reported descent into a den, almost a month later, he disturbed "[a] number of white women . . . at their favorite pastime of Oriental fumigation." This time the *Alta* said nothing of white men—indeed nothing of men at all. It is hard to know what contemporary readers would have made of this report. The paper's ten-line account said little more than that Rogers "ordered [the women] to depart, which they did, taking with them a warning not to be found in such places again . . . ."[55]

During these visits, Rogers made no arrests, for he lacked authority. Neither the women who smoked at the dens nor those who sold to them had broken the law. Barely a week later, however, on November 8, Mayor George Hewston called on city supervisors to ban the dens.[56]

The Drug War Begins

We cannot know whether the mayor and supervisors had this series of articles in mind when in November 1875 they adopted the nation's first ban of a nonalcoholic recreational drug. Dr. Kane perhaps spied a link between the articles and the lawmakers' action. His claim that the seductive wiles of young "Americans" gave rise to anti-den laws may have referred to the third of the *Chronicle* articles and its account of well-dressed women and their sporting young bucks. And Mayor Hewston's November 8 appeal to the supervisors seems to have

[54] "An Opium Den," *Daily Alta California*, Oct. 1, 1875, p. 1.
[55] "Raid on Opium Dens," *Daily Alta California*, Oct. 30, 1875, p. 1.
[56] "Board of Supervisors," *Daily Alta California*, Nov. 9, 1875, p. 1. I am grateful to Jim Baumohl for these citations to the *Alta* and the events reported in the last three paragraphs. Baumohl first retold Rogers's visits to the dens in "The 'Dope Fiend's Paradise,' Revisited: Notes from Research in Progress on Drug Law Enforcement in San Francisco, 1875–1915," *The Surveyor*, no. 24 (June 1992), pp. 3, 7.

built on the *Alta*'s reports of Detective Rogers's raids on the dens. Quoted by the San Francisco *Bulletin* under the heading, "The Opium Dens and Their White Frequenters," Hewston's brief address began with a pointed, one-sentence reference to whites in the dens. While he seemed most worried about white women, he was concerned for the men, too: "I would most respectfully call your attention," he said, "to the existence and increase of the opium smoking dens under Chinese supervision, and frequented by white males and females of various ages, from the school girl to the more mature."[57] He did not detail the danger he saw to those schoolgirls.

In answering the mayor a week later, the supervisors spoke with more clarity. Their new ordinance and statement of rationales responded to the twin moral dangers highlighted by the *Chronicle* and *Alta* articles: the drug's narcotizing stupor, which afflicted young white men and white women alike, and the drug's power to beguile respectable young women at the hands of unscrupulous men.

No official copy of the 1875 ordinance appears to have survived. Both the *Chronicle* and *Alta*, however, reprinted the text of the ordinance and a committee's report a day after the measure's approval. The ordinance itself is straightforward: it forbade anyone to "keep or . . . visit . . . any place, house or room where opium is smoked, or where persons assemble for the purpose of smoking opium . . . ." It made no mention of eaten opium or any other drug. Offenders faced between ten days' and six months' confinement or a fine of between $50 and $500 or both.[58]

The *Chronicle* also reprinted a legislative committee's report, which said much the law did not:

> At the meeting of the Board of Supervisors last night, the Health and Police Committee, to whom was referred the communication from the Mayor in relation to the opium-smoking dens kept by Chinese, reported that there are numbers of these places kept for Chinese only, and that there are now existing, within three blocks of the City Hall, eight opium-smoking establishments kept by Chinese, for the exclusive use of
>
> WHITE MEN AND WOMEN;

[57] Kane, *Opium-Smoking in America and China*, pp. 131–32; "Board of Supervisors," *San Francisco Daily Evening Bulletin*, Nov. 9, 1875, p. 1.

[58] "Board of Supervisors," *Daily Alta California*, Nov. 16, 1875, p. 1; "The Opium Dens," *San Francisco Chronicle*, Nov. 16, 1875, p. 3. The two papers' versions of the ordinance were virtually identical, though punctuation and formatting varied. *See also* "Board of Supervisors," *San Francisco Daily Evening Bulletin*, Nov. 16, 1875, p. 1 (reporting the same transactions). Final passage of the ordinance came a week later, on November 22. *See* "Board of Supervisors," *Daily Alta California*, Nov. 23, 1875, p. 1 (reporting on the previous evening's meeting and announcing, "The ordinance prohibiting the keeping of opium dens and opium smoking was finally passed"). I thank my research assistant Zehava Robbins for helping to confirm that no official copy of the ordinance survives.

That these places are patronized not only by the vicious and depraved, but are nightly resorted to by young men and women of respectable parentage and by young men engaged in respectable business avocations in the city; that the habitues of these infamous resorts inhale the fumes from the opium pipes until a state of stupefaction is produced . . . .

"[U]nless this most dangerous species of dissipation can be stopped in its inception," the committee concluded, "there is great danger that it will become one of the prevalent vices of the city . . . ."[59]

It is hard to miss the supervisors' pointed distinction between opium dens "kept for Chinese only" and those "kept . . . for the exclusive use of WHITE MEN AND WOMEN." The latter apparently touched a nerve. True, the distinctive typeface and setting of the words "WHITE MEN AND WOMEN" perhaps were the *Chronicle*'s whims and not the supervisors' message. But succeeding references to "young men and women of respectable parentage" and "young men engaged in respectable business avocations" suggest the board's dominant concern was the threat to the city's respectable white youth.

The nature of that threat took two now-familiar forms. First was the drug's narcotizing force: these young men and women "inhale the fumes from the opium pipes until a state of stupefaction is produced . . . ." That is, "stupefaction" was not a side effect of some other, more legitimate use of the drug, but rather the *reason* for smoking. As the *New York Times* reported two years earlier, that "death-like stupor . . . is the aim of all opium smoking."[60] Then there was sexual commingling. Twice the supervisors mentioned that both men and women haunted the dens. In stressing that those men and women were of respectable parentage, the supervisors warned that the threat to feminine virtue did not fall only on the fallen.

The Spread of Den Bans

San Francisco's 1875 ordinance was America's first true *antidrug* law in that it banned use of a recreational intoxicant other than alcohol. Despite its novelty,

---

[59] "The Opium Dens," *San Francisco Chronicle*, Nov. 16, 1875, p. 3. The *Alta*'s version of the committee's report differed in three ways. Where the *Chronicle* wrote "that there are numbers of these places kept for Chinese only," the *Alta* wrote "that there are numerous of these places kept by Chinese only." The *Alta* did not follow the *Chronicle* in centering and capping the reference to WHITE MEN AND WOMEN. And the *Alta* omitted the words "respectable parentage and by young men engaged in." The last omission was likely a typesetting error, as the omitted words appear in both the *Chronicle*'s and the *Bulletin*'s report of these events. *See* "Board of Supervisors," *San Francisco Daily Evening Bulletin*, Nov. 16, 1875, p. 1.

[60] "Chinese in New-York," *New York Times*, Dec. 26, 1873, p. 3.

neither the ordinance nor the supervisors' rationales in writing it should surprise us. Smoked opium had all the stupefying, reason-depriving, pleasure-inducing effects that had marked alcohol for attack. Yet it seemingly lacked alcohol's moral saving grace—the power to ease and enliven social interaction when taken in moderation. That opium surpassed alcohol as a sexual stimulant no doubt sped its doom. And the dens themselves were doubly bad, for their dim lighting and flat furnishings discouraged conversation even as they enabled sex.

Nor is it surprising that anti-den laws spread throughout the West, largely tracking the widening circles of Chinese settlement. Wherever the newcomers went, it seems, they brought their drug and its pipe and founded familiar haunts for its use. There is little reason to think the whites they encountered in each new community would react differently than those they had encountered before. On the contrary, the news and text of the last town's ban often arrived at the next outpost before the first den appeared.

Hence the nation's second anti-den law, adopted in September 1876 in Virginia City, Nevada, mimicked San Francisco's 1875 model virtually word for word. Lying two hundred miles to San Francisco's east, Virginia City rose from the dust of the Comstock region after the great silver lode discovery of 1859. Today known only to ghost town tourists, it once reigned as Nevada's leading city. The white and Chinese miners who flocked to the region attracted a stream of settlers to feed, clothe, and entertain them. Soon Virginia City hosted the largest Chinese community outside San Francisco.[61]

And soon the dens followed. In July 1874, a reporter entered a den in the city's Chinese quarter. Looking about, he noted all those features that marked the place for moral condemnation—the darkness ("[a]t first we can see nothing but the lamp" with its "dull red light that illuminates nothing"); the furnishings ("bunks, one above the other"); the silence ("[t]he cave of the Seven Sleepers was not more silent"); and the mindlessness ("[t]o a looker-on it is all vapid, vacuous stupefaction"). Those smokers who "have had enough," he wrote, "move no more than dead men." The den was dirty too—literally carved from the dirt slope of a hillside, with dirt floor and dirt ceiling and a smoke-blackened wooden door. All this the reporter told, yet he wrote without alarm, for there were no other whites present. "We feel that we have no business where we are."[62]

---

[61] For the Virginia City law's text, see "An Ordinance to Abolish Opium-Smoking Dens," in *Revised Ordinances of the City of Virginia* (Virginia, Nev.: Enterprise Steam Printing House, 1878), p. 116. Less than a year later a third community—Carson City, Nevada, which lay just twenty miles up the road—adopted an opium den ban. Carson City lifted its law's language largely from Virginia City's ordinance, itself copied almost verbatim from San Francisco's. "Ordinance No. 48," *Carson City Morning Appeal*, Mar. 1, 1879, p. 4 (reprinting verbatim ordinance of June 12, 1877). On Virginia City's early years, see Ahmad, "'Caves of Oblivion,'" pp. 33–34, 46.

[62] [Dan De Quille,] "A Cave of Oblivion," [Virginia City] *Daily Territorial Enterprise*, July 28, 1874, p. 3.

Within a year, however, the habit had spread to whites. In an article tellingly titled, "Our Opium-Smokers," the *Virginia Evening Chronicle* reported in March 1875 that the practice "is rapidly increasing among too many of the Caucasian residents of Virginia City . . . ." Had only the Chinese indulged, the paper added in June, the dens "would be scarcely worthy of notice," but their new white patrons, including "several citizens of respectability," compelled the paper to voice its concern. Still, as most of the city's white smokers were young men of the "sporting fraternity" and women of the "outcast classes," there was not yet cause for action.[63]

Another year later the vice had spread among respectable whites, touching especially the city's youth. The *Evening Chronicle* wrote in February 1876 that "large numbers of young white men and women," including school pupils, tarried at Chinatown's dens—news that "may well excite alarm among the parents of the city" and "should awaken the authorities to the importance of doing something to check the growth of this soul-and-body-killing habit." In March the Virginia City *Territorial Enterprise* warned in words worthy of Increase Mather that those "white men" who haunted the dens sank "to a level of degradation even lower than that of the pagan brutes with whom they daily and nightly herd." In April the editor shuddered at a tale of "YOUTHFUL DEPRAVITY": two white girls "of good and respectable parentage" almost lost their virtue after their "young gentlemen attendants" lured them to a Chinese opium den. "[T]here the whole party smoked the nefarious drug, till overcome by its power all tumbled on the couch together and remained for hours in the deep slumber induced thereby." By August the local press put the number who patronized Virginia City's Chinatown dens at "not less than one hundred and fifty white persons of both sexes—the majority of them being members of the respectable class of our citizens."[64]

The next month the Virginia City Board of Aldermen followed San Francisco's lead and language and adopted an almost identical anti-den law. The ordinance won notice in Harry Hubbell Kane's 1882 study, *Opium-Smoking in America and China*. Kane quoted a Dr. Harris of Virginia City, who traced a familiar story-line in explaining the forces that gave rise to the law. Opium smoking migrated from the Chinese to lower-class whites of the "*demi-monde*," Harris said, and from there to the "the younger class of boys and girls, many of the latter of the more respected class of families." Finally "it reached young women of more mature age . . . ." Then, with sexually vulnerable young women at risk, "the necessity

[63] "Our Opium-Smokers," *Virginia Evening Chronicle*, Mar. 31, 1875, p. 3; "The Opium Dens," ibid., June 8, 1875, p. 3.

[64] "Spread of the Opium Habit," ibid., Feb. 10, 1876, p. 2; "Opium Smokers," [Virginia City] *Territorial Enterprise*, Mar. 8, 1876, p. 2; "Youthful Depravity," ibid., Apr. 23, 1876, p. 2; "The Deadly Drug," *Virginia Evening Chronicle*, Aug. 4, 1876, p. 3.

for stringent measures became apparent, and was met by the passing of a city ordinance."[65]

Kane concluded from Dr. Harris's account and other evidence that Nevada's anti-den laws aimed chiefly to protect young white women's virtue from the designs of white "rascals." He reminded readers that opium can spur sexual "frenzy, the woman losing all modesty. Recognizing this fact," he said, "rascals have enticed young girls to these places to smoke and have then succeeded in ruining them. It was chiefly the recognition of this fact that led to the passage of stringent laws against the practice in California [and] Nevada . . . ."[66]

Looking across the country at life in Nevada in 1877, the New York Times drew a similar distinction between opium smoking by lower-class whites (readily ignorable) and that by middle-class youth (demanding attention). The den patrons of Eureka, Nevada, are those "considered outside the pale of society," the Times wrote, "men and women who have lost all self-respect and seek the comforting influences that steal over them after their indulgence . . . ." Of these smokers, mainly gamblers and "lewd women," the law need take little notice—"and if they were the only ones who gave themselves up to the drug it might be well enough not to interfere . . . ." But opium smoking in Eureka had "become fashionable among the boys" too, even boys who "have parents living in the town." During a recent visit the reporter saw "half a dozen youths, all the way from 16 to 20 years of age, lying curled up in the bunks . . . and smoking as vigorously as the most confirmed habitué." On these young men, the Times said a "heavy hand should be laid . . . and their dissolute course checked . . . ."[67]

There was no need for Eureka lawmakers to act, however, for almost six months earlier, in February 1877, the Nevada legislature had enacted the nation's first statewide ban on opium dens. The pattern of states that followed, shown in Table 4A and Figure 4.1, predictably tracked the pattern of Chinese migration, as shown in Table 4B and Figure 4.2. At the lead were those states of the Far West where the Chinese came ashore and went in search of work. Every state or territory with a Chinese population of 4 percent or more in the 1880 census banned opium dens. Several years behind were those Eastern states with major cities that had substantial Chinatowns—New York, Massachusetts, Pennsylvania, and Maryland—as well as those Midwestern states with major railroad hubs served by Chinese rail workers—Ohio, Missouri, Minnesota, Wisconsin and Iowa.[68]

---

[65] Kane, Opium-Smoking in America and China, p. 3 (quoting Dr. Harris).

[66] Kane, "Opium Smoking: A New Form," p. 112.

[67] "Opium Smoking in Nevada," New York Times, July 29, 1877, p. 10.

[68] See "An Act to Regulate the Sale or Disposal of Opium," 1877 Nevada Statutes, ch. 27, § 4 (Act of Feb. 9, 1877), pp. 69, 70. For the pattern of rail construction between 1885 and 1889, see Engineering News Series of Maps, No. 22 (Engineering News Publishing Co., 1888). For census figures, see Campbell Gibson & Kay Jung, Historical Census Statistics on Population Totals by Race, 1790 to 1990, and by Hispanic Origin, 1970 to 1990, for the United States, Regions, Divisions, and States (Washington: U.S. Census Bureau 2002), tbl. C-11("Asian Population for the United States, Regions, Divisions, and States: 1870 to 1890").

Table 4A Earliest State Bans of Opium Dens and Ranked Proportion of Chinese Persons in Population in 1880[a]

Nevada	1877	(2)*
Dakota Territory	1879	
Utah	1880	
Idaho	1881 (January 22)	(1)*
Montana	1881 (February 22)	(5)*
California	1881 (March 4)	(3)*
Washington	1881 (December 1)	(7)*
Wyoming	1882 (February 8)	(6)*
New York	1882 (May 15)	
Arizona	1883	(8)*
Ohio	1885 (February 6)	
Massachusetts	1885 (March 11)	
Pennsylvania	1885 (June 10)	
Oregon	1885 (November 25)	(4)*
Maryland	1886	
New Mexico	1887 (February 24)	
Missouri	1887 (March 22)	
Texas	1887 (March 29)	
Minnesota	1889	
Wisconsin	1891	
Georgia	1895	
Iowa	1896	
Florida	1905	
Connecticut	1907	

* Asterisks and boldface indicate that Chinese persons (as designated by the Census Bureau) made up more than 4 percent of the state's population in the 1880 census. Numerals in parentheses indicate relative rank in proportion of Chinese persons. No other state had a Chinese population exceeding one-half of one percent. Hawaii, not yet a state or included in census counts, presumably would have ranked first in proportion of Chinese persons.

[a] Only twenty-five states and territories—the twenty-four listed here and Alaska—enacted specific bans on opium dens. Alaska is not listed, though it banned opium dens in 1899. At that time Alaska copied its criminal code almost entirely from Oregon's. Alaska lawmakers apparently did not specifically choose to outlaw opium dens.

Those states absent from this list apparently never (till perhaps much later) acted to ban opium dens. Though my research assistants and I have checked this list against other sources and have selectively double-checked the laws of those states that seemed wrongly excluded, errors may remain. State law books from this era are often badly organized and badly indexed and hard to search with certainty. I am grateful to two of my research assistants, Duane Pozza and Zoe Scharff, who shouldered most of the task of digging out old state statutes. Their work undergirds this table and all similar tables of state laws.

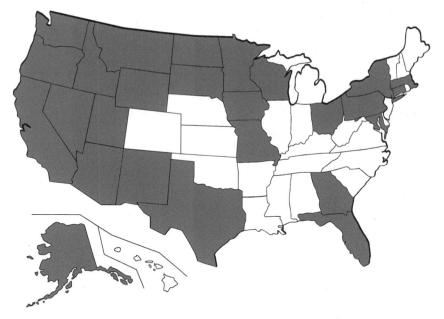

Figure 4.1: Those states or future states that specifically banned opium dens.

Only Florida by its presence and a few central states by their absence disturbed this pattern.

The link between Chinese migration and anti-den laws was direct and unsurprising: where the Chinese settled, they set up dens, and where dens cropped up, legislators moved to ban them. Whether white hatred of the Chinese, which infected Western states and much of the rest of the nation, spurred or sped anti-den laws is a formidable question; it consumes much of the next chapter. For now it's enough to see that attitudes toward the Chinese played no essential role. Even on the far-flung Eastern seaboard we find the same complacency toward Chinese opium smoking, alongside horror at opium smoking by respectable whites, that pervaded anti-den lawmaking in San Francisco and Virginia City. A quick glance eastward makes the point.

In August 1884, just seven months before Massachusetts became the second Eastern state to ban opium dens, the *Boston Globe* wrote of "A TERRIBLE REVELATION"—the appearance in town of a new den, "maintained by a civilized American" and "luxuriously fitted up and supported by a class of people several degrees higher in the social scale than the Chinamen and abandoned wretches" who haunted the city's older, grittier dens. Those dens, founded by newcoming

Table 4B States with Largest Chinese Populations in 1880 as a Proportion of Total Population[a]

STATE	% Chinese	# Chinese Persons
Idaho	10.36%	3,379
Nevada	8.70%	5,416
California	8.69%	75,132
Oregon	5.44%	9,510
Montana	4.51%	1,765
Wyoming	4.40%	914
Washington	4.24%	3,186
Arizona	4.03%	1,630
Utah	0.35%	501
Colorado	0.31%	612
New Mexico	0.30%	361
South Dakota	0.23%	230
Louisiana	0.05%	489
North Dakota	0.02%	8
Connecticut	0.02%	123

[a] Source: Campbell Gibson & Kay Jung, *Historical Census Statistics on Population Totals by Race, 1790 to 1990, and by Hispanic Origin, 1970 to 1990, for the United States, Regions, Divisions, and States* (Washington: U.S. Census Bureau, 2002), tbl. C-11 ("Asian Population for the United States, Regions, Divisions, and States: 1870 to 1890") (including separate category for "Chinese").

Had Hawaii, still an independent kingdom, been part of the United States in 1880, it likely would have ranked first on this table. In 1900, the first year in which the Census gathered data in Hawaii, its population was 16.7 percent Chinese.

I thank my research assistant Elena Saxonhouse for collecting the data for this and all other population tables.

Chinese, had posed no great concern. "If it had been possible to confine the habit among their own [Chinese] race," the *Globe* wrote, "the results of its introduction would not have been so deplorable." Even when the Chinese were joined by "the most degraded . . . of our own people, the case, although bad enough, was not so bad as now." So the police had "never made any decided attempt to wipe [the dens] out of existence." But this new den with its "claims to respectability" confronted Bostonians with a new danger—a place "where young fellows and girls can assemble and in private, if they wish, initiate themselves into the seductive charm of opium." Such dens, if allowed to spread, "will inevitably result most

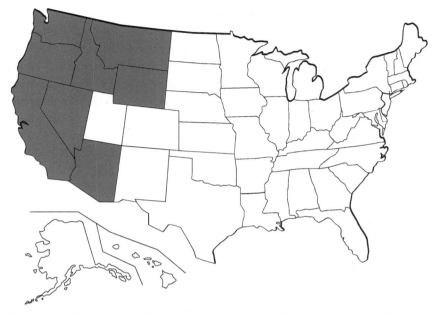

Figure 4.2: Those states or future states shown in the 1880 census to have a Chinese population of 4 percent or more.

disastrously." If no law empowers the police to close them, the *Globe* insisted, "then it is high time that a new law be added to our statute book."[69]

The Challenge of Banning Eaten Opium

The dens' ultimate demise was foreordained. In those days of anti-liquor agitation, houses of opium-induced intoxication—where patrons sucked a pleasure-inducing, passion-arousing, reason-depriving drug that stupefied consumers, silenced conversation, and promised neither warmth nor nourishment nor vigor nor cure—were doomed to fall under the legal ax. Such places could not survive in a day when even convivial liquor saloons hung on the edge of extinction. They hardly could survive today.

As if to punctuate the resolve with which lawmakers confronted this menace, the great majority of states that banned the dens did so outright, with no savings clause permitting medicinal use. Ever since the English Gin Act of 1736,

---

[69] "A Terrible Revelation," *Boston Daily Globe*, Aug. 10, 1884, p. 4; "An Act Forbidding the Sale and Use of Opium for Certain Purposes," 1885 *Massachusetts Acts*, ch. 73 (Act of Mar. 11, 1885), p. 549.

alcohol prohibition laws had taken pains to forbid only beverage use, not medicinal applications. Anti-den laws required no such proviso, for most doctors saw no therapeutic value in smoking opium, and dens offered no pretense of health-clinic hygiene. Hence San Francisco, Virginia City, and Carson City, Nevada, all banned opium dens without exception, as did seventeen of the twenty-four states and territories listed in Table 4A. Of the remaining seven states, three had medical savings clauses that applied to other provisions of the same law but *not* the ban on opium dens.[70] Only four states, therefore—Maryland, New Mexico, Pennsylvania, and Wyoming—recognized even a theoretical medical-necessity defense against a charge of visiting a den.

Eaten opium presented lawmakers with a harder case for a ban. Everyone knew of its euphoriant and aphrodisiac powers and its resulting recreational abuse. Everyone also knew of its curative wonders. Its recognized medicinal applications ranged so widely that almost any user could plausibly claim medical need. Any ban that allowed therapeutic use would have proved pointless without some way to distinguish legitimate medical users from malingering opium fiends. And any ban that forbade therapeutic use would have been cruel.

An apparent solution was to delegate such distinctions to medical professionals. Britain's Parliament had taken just this tack in crafting its 1736 gin ban. That law permitted "physicians, apothecaries, surgeons, or chymists [to use] . . . spirituous liquors . . . in the preparation or making up of medicines for sick, lame, or distempered persons only." But liquor dealers spied in this exception an escape, for Parliament had neglected to limit the class of "apothecaries." Hardly had the law taken effect when some distillers reportedly "commenced [as] Chymists [and] Apothecaries." Not to be outdone by distillers posing as druggists, some genuine druggists began to sell liquor as a beverage. "The Distillers are highly incensed against the Apothecaries," one paper reported, "for selling Gin publickly in their Shops . . . ."[71]

---

[70] Florida's law exempted "regular drugstores" from a provision that made presence of "drugs [or] preparations . . . commonly used in opium dens . . . prima facie evidence . . . that such building . . . is maintained as an opium den." "An Act to Define and Suppress Opium Dens," 1905 *Florida Acts*, ch. 5460 (no. 89), § 6 (Act of June [?] 26, 1905), pp. 154, 155. Nevada's law permitted opium sales by "druggists and apothecaries . . . on the prescription of legally practicing physicians," but offered no permission to keep "a place of resort by persons for the purpose of indulging in the use of opium . . . ." 1877 *Nevada Statutes*, ch. 27, §§ 1, 4 (Act of Feb. 9, 1877), p. 69 (emphasis added). Oregon's law took fundamentally the same form as Nevada's. "An Act in Relation to the Sale of Opium," 1885 *Oregon Laws* (Spec. Sess.) (Act of Nov. 25, 1885), p. 39.

[71] *An Act for Laying a Duty upon the Retailers of Spirituous Liquors, and for Licensing the Retailers Thereof*, 9 Geo. 2, ch. 23, § 12 (1736); "Domestick Occurrences," *Northampton Mercury*, Oct. 4, 1736, p. 98 ("commenced [as] Chymists [and] Apothecaries"); "Domestick Occurrences," ibid., Oct. 11, 1736, p. 103 ("The Distillers are highly incensed . . ."). One such apothecary, Robert Kirkpatrick, was quickly caught and convicted of "retailing Spirituous Liquors without Licence." *See* "Domestick Occurrences," ibid., Oct. 25, 1736, p. 111.

A century after the Gin Act, when the Massachusetts legislature launched its own experiment with liquor prohibition, it sought to close the loophole through which dram sellers had slipped as druggists. The state's fifteen-gallon law of 1838 empowered county commissioners to license "as many apothecaries or practising physicians as they deem necessary, to be retailers of spirituous liquors . . . for medicinal purposes . . . *provided*, that the number of persons so licensed shall not exceed one for every two thousand inhabitants . . . ." Whether this approach proved more effective than Parliament's is hard to say, as the Massachusetts law fell for other reasons within two years. Wry legislative critics charged that during the law's brief tenure, "it was shown, that the license to apothecaries, would tend greatly to increase the sort of sickness which requires this medicine."[72]

Perhaps wiser for this experience, when Massachusetts legislators embraced full-scale alcohol prohibition in 1852, they adopted a different, more centralized means to meet medical needs. The new law called on every city and town to appoint "some suitable person or persons as agent or agents of such city or town, to sell . . . spirits, wines, or other intoxicating liquors, to be used for medicinal . . . purposes, and no other . . . ." After just three years lawmakers soured on this system, which they had copied almost exactly from Maine's original prohibition law of 1851. Possibly they saw again an "increase [in] the sort of sickness which requires this medicine," for a new act of 1855 sought to stem illegitimate medical sales. The law obliged the agent who oversaw medical sales to "keep a book, in which he shall enter the date of every sale of spirituous liquor made by him, the person to whom sold, the kind, quantity, and price of the liquor sold, and the purpose for which it was sold . . . ." The law required that the book "shall at all times be open to the inspection of . . . sheriffs" and other officials and criminalized lies to the agent about the reason for purchase.[73]

Hard as it was for lawmakers in Massachusetts and other states to distinguish recreational from medical alcohol use, they found it far harder to draw that same distinction for eaten opium. Those features of eaten opium that let recreational abusers pass as medical users frustrated legislative attempts to criminalize one while exempting the other. First was the matter of quantity. Because those who used alcohol medicinally drank far less than drunks, an honest druggist or other agent could supply one while refusing the other—especially when

[72] "An Act to Regulate the Sale of Spirituous Liquors," 1838 *Massachusetts Laws*, ch. 157, § 2 (Act of Apr. 19, 1838), p. 442; "An Act to Repeal 'An Act to Regulate the Sale of Spirituous Liquors,'" 1840 *Massachusetts Laws*, ch. 1 (Act of Feb. 11, 1840), p. 179; William C. Churchill, "Minority Report Relating to the Sale of Spiritous Liquors," 1839 *Massachusetts Legislative Documents*, House No. 37 (Mar. 6, 1839), p. 42.
[73] "An Act Concerning the Manufacture and Sale of Spirituous or Intoxicating Liquors," 1852 *Massachusetts Laws*, ch. 322, § 2 (Act of May 22, 1852), pp. 257–58; "An Act for the Suppression of Drinking Houses and Tippling Shops," 1851 *Maine Acts*, ch. 211, § 2 (Act of June 2, 1851), pp. 210–11; "An Act Concerning the Manufacture and Sale of Spirituous and Intoxicating Liquors," 1855 *Massachusetts Laws*, ch. 215, §§ 6, 7 (Act of Apr. 20, 1855), pp. 623, 625–26.

required, as in the 1855 Massachusetts law, to record the amount sold each purchaser. That same druggist might struggle to distinguish opium abusers from medical users because an abuser, especially if inexperienced, could get high on a standard medicinal dose. Conversely, cancer patients and other chronic medical users grew tolerant to opium and demanded ever greater doses. Judged only by their consumption, they would seem as hopelessly abandoned as any confirmed dope fiend.

A second difficulty was the comparative subtlety of the opium high. Both pharmacists and law officers could tell a slurring, stinking, stumbling drunk from someone taking whiskey for insomnia or toothaches. An opium fiend made no similar spectacle of abuse.

It was, finally, easier to ban alcohol than eaten opium because when it came to alcohol, legislators could afford more mistakes. By the mid-nineteenth century, when American states first experimented with alcohol bans, wine and spirits played a far less central therapeutic role than before. Benjamin Rush and other medical leaders long since had debunked misconceived medicinal applications. When banning recreational drinking, states could risk drawing overly broad lines that barred some genuine patients from lawful liquor, for medical drinkers denied their drug would live. Opium, in contrast, was an indispensable medicine. For the wasting diarrhea of dysentery or the profound pain of cancer or stones, only opium could sustain life and make it bearable.

Regulating eaten opium therefore demanded a level of precision that the law of the mid-nineteenth century hadn't achieved. A law that simply mimicked the alcohol bans of Massachusetts and other states would have forbidden both too little opium and too much—too little because opium fiends might pass easily as chronic medical users and too much because druggists, faced with so difficult a distinction, might have erred on the side of refusal. Laws banning recreational abuse of eaten opium lagged till the last quarter of the nineteenth century, therefore, not because legislators did not recognize the problem or because they did not care, but because they lacked the lawmaking technology to solve it.

The Prescription Solution

Though every state and future state eventually banned eaten opium, it appears no state did so entirely. Every state preserved the possibility of medical use—and with one exception all employed the same basic mechanism. The outlier was Hawaii. Its 1874 opium ban would have been the nation's first had Hawaii, still an independent kingdom, been part of the Union. That law made it a crime punishable by up to two years' hard labor for anyone to distribute opium except a "Physician or Surgeon having a Diploma or Certificate from some

Medical college or University and who has a License to Practice Medicine in this Kingdom." Users who possessed opium from any other source hazarded a year's confinement. And physicians who gave opium "to any person in the habit of smoking, or otherwise using the same, or to any other person except as a remedy in case of sickness," faced a fine and, on second offense, loss of the privilege to distribute.[74]

Like the alcohol prohibition laws of Massachusetts and other jurisdictions, Hawaii's opium law aimed to ban recreational abuse while preserving access in cases of genuine medical need. By permitting only direct dispensing from doctor to patient, lawmakers achieved a tighter regulatory seal than those liquor bans that had let any doctor *or druggist* dispense. Still not content, lawmakers forbade doctors to give opium to *habitual users* of the drug, demanding instead medical need in the form of treatment for disease—an approach many states soon would mimic. But the resulting regulatory scheme fell short, for by permitting only direct distribution from doctor to patient, the law risked both underregulation and overregulation. By entrusting doctors with both prescriptions and sales, the law tempted them to over-prescribe for profit. And by requiring every patient who needed opium to visit a doctor, it put legitimate therapy past some patients' reach.

The risk that by mandating doctors' visits, lawmakers would deny essential drugs to poor or far-flung patients expanded with the size of the jurisdiction and the sparseness of its population. Hence when Nevada enacted the first fully American opium ban in 1877, it took a different approach: it limited legal opium distribution to druggists and provided that "druggists . . . shall sell it only on the prescription of legally practicing physicians." This seemingly simple innovation, which ultimately swept the remaining states, addressed both shortcomings of the Hawaii law. By separating prescriptions and profits, it guarded against greedy doctors pushing needless sales. And by widening distribution to drugstores, it expanded access without sacrificing a doctor's judgment that every sale was medically necessary. As the Nevada Supreme Court wrote in 1880, the state's new law restricted sale of opium as far as possible "consistent with its proper use as a remedial agent, in order to prevent its improper use as a means of intoxication."[75]

Legislators across the country apparently agreed, for in time every state would adopt Nevada's basic approach, though many broadened distribution further by

---

[74] "An Act to Restrict the Importation and Sale of Opium," 1874 *Hawaii Laws*, ch. 56, §§ 2, 3, 4 (Act of Aug. 8, 1874), pp. 60–61.

[75] "An Act to Regulate the Sale or Disposal of Opium," 1877 *Nevada Statutes*, ch. 27, § 1 (Act of Feb. 9, 1877), p. 69; *State v. Ah Sam*, 15 Nev. 27, 31 (1880). A West Virginia law of 1883 reflected the legislature's conscious intent to separate the discretion to prescribe from the profits to be made. After declaring that druggists could sell liquors only on a doctor's prescription, the law added: "[B]ut no druggist or registered pharmacist, who is a practicing physician, shall himself . . . sell any such liquors . . . upon his own prescription." "An Act to Amend . . . Chapter Fifty-Two of the Acts of One Thousand Eight Hundred and Eighty-One . . . ," 1883 *West Virginia Acts*, ch. 82, § 1 (Act of Feb. 22, 1883), pp. 123, 125.

permitting both doctors and druggists to dispense. Congress saw the wisdom in these regimes. The Harrison Narcotic Act of 1914 allowed sales of opium and cocaine only by prescription, but also allowed doctors to dispense directly to patients. The Volstead Act of 1919, which implemented national alcohol prohibition, permitted sales of alcohol by prescription, but generally barred physician dispensing.[76]

If conditioning druggists' sales on a doctor's prescription was so simple and effective, why didn't this statutory device emerge earlier? Why didn't Massachusetts, for example, take this tack in 1852, when it restricted alcohol sales to medicinal purposes? A full century earlier Henry Fielding had recommended reliance on physicians' prescriptions in calling for a renewed gin ban in England. Fielding knew what Massachusetts legislators discovered in 1838—that if the law simply banned liquor while permitting drugstores to dispense, "the Chemist . . . would soon probably become a common Distiller, and his Shop no better than a Gin-shop . . . ." Suppose instead, Fielding suggested, that "all spirituous Liquors were, together with other Poison, to be locked up in the Chemists or Apothecaries Shops, thence never to be drawn, till some excellent Physician calls them forth for the Cure of nervous Distempers!"[77]

Several American states ultimately adopted this approach to govern alcohol sales. Massachusetts took a first step with its 1875 liquor license law, which banned overnight and Sunday sales except by druggists "upon the prescription of a physician." A Mississippi law of 1878 broadened the principle, declaring that "no druggist shall sell vinous or spirituous liquors in any case unless on the prescription of a physician." A Missouri law of 1879 was similar. And in enacting its unusually durable liquor prohibition scheme in 1881, Kansas limited sales to druggists, who could sell only on doctors' prescriptions—and forbade doctors to prescribe except in cases "of actual sickness, and when in the judgment of such physician the use of intoxicating liquor is necessary as a remedy."[78]

The confluence of dates is striking. Five states adopted similar mechanisms in fast succession: Massachusetts in 1875, Nevada in 1877, Mississippi in 1878, Missouri in 1879, Kansas in 1881. I've seen no earlier law conditioning

[76] "An Act to . . . Impose a Special Tax upon All Persons Who . . . Deal in . . . Opium or Coca Leaves . . . ," Pub. L. 63-223, ch. 1, § 2(a) & (b), 38 Stat. L. 785, 786 (Act of Dec. 17, 1914) (Harrison Narcotic Act); National Prohibition Act, Pub. L. 66-66, ch. 85, §§ 6, 7, 41 Stat. 305, 310–11 (Act of Oct. 28, 1919).

[77] Henry Fielding, *An Enquiry into the Causes of the Late Increase of Robbers* . . . (London: A. Millar, 1751), pp. 32–33.

[78] "An Act to Regulate the Sale of Intoxicating Liquors," 1875 *Massachusetts Acts*, ch. 99, §§ 2, 6 (Act of Apr. 5, 1875), pp. 664–65; "An Act to Regulate the Tax on Privileges . . . ," 1878 *Mississippi Laws*, ch. 2, § 1 (Act of Mar. 5, 1878), p. 16; "An Act to Regulate the Sale of Intoxicating Liquors . . . ," 1879 *Missouri Laws*, § 3 (Act of May 19, 1879), pp. 165, 166; "An Act to Prohibit the Manufacture and Sale of Intoxicating Liquors . . . ," 1881 *Kansas Laws*, ch. 128, §§ 3, 4 (Act of Feb. 20, 1881), pp. 233, 235–36.

a pharmacist's sale of drugs or alcohol on a doctor's prescription in quite this way. The nearest appears to be Pennsylvania's 1860 poisons act, which provided that "[n]o apothecary . . . shall sell . . . any morphia, strychnia, arsenic [or other poison] except upon the prescription of a physician, or on the personal application of some respectable inhabitant of full age . . . ."[79] But this law seems different. By demanding that either a doctor or "respectable" adult endorse a poison sale, the law seems to have appealed to the doctor's personal rather than professional judgment, perhaps on the theory that doctors know their patients better than druggists know their patrons. The Pennsylvania law therefore avoided the delicate professional dynamic put in place by Nevada's 1877 opium ban and its imitators. Nevada's law unmistakably elevated doctors over druggists in the hierarchy of medical professionals by stilling the druggist's dispensing hand without the doctor's say-so.

Today this arrangement seems natural, for we have come to understand physicians as more highly trained than pharmacists and better able to judge a patient's needs. But till the 1870s druggists could dispense even dangerous agents on their own, and while lawmakers had begun to impose on druggists labeling and recordkeeping requirements, it seems the law had refrained from raising one professional guild over the other. Why lawmakers did so now, in the 1870s, is not clear. Whatever the triggering mechanism, the new regulatory technique proved attractive to lawmakers everywhere. Within two generations almost every state had adopted prescription-only sales as a means to ban nonmedical opium use.

Preserving Self-Medication

Yet most states did not do so right away. In the dozen years after Nevada enacted the nation's first prescription-only opium law, just three states or territories followed its lead. By the end of 1905, when Nevada's law had been standing twenty-eight years, only ten states and territories had opium bans—all but two in the West or Southwest. Table 4C reflects this halting, regional start in anti-opium lawmaking.

Suddenly, beginning in 1906, anti-opium laws swept the states. Between 1906 and 1915 thirty-one states or territories banned unprescribed opium sales. So we face two questions: Why were Western states the first to embrace prescription-only opium laws, and why did other states join in a clamor beginning in 1906? The latter question proves easier to answer, for in 1906 the structure of these opium bans abruptly changed.

---

[79] "An Act to Consolidate, Revise and Amend the Penal Laws of this Commonwealth," 1860 *Pennsylvania Laws*, no. 374, § 70 (Act of Mar. 31, 1860), p. 401.

Table 4C Earliest State Bans of Unprescribed Opium Sales[a]

Hawaii[b]	1874	Massachusetts	1910 (March 22)
Nevada	1877	Louisiana	1911 (?)
Dakota Terr.	1885 (March 13)	Utah	1911 (March 20)
Oregon	1885 (November 25)	Kentucky	1912
Montana	1889	Delaware	1913 (March 17)
Arizona	1899	Maine	1913 (April 12)
Wyoming	1903 (February 23)	Ohio	1913 (May 2)
Texas	1903 (April 6)	Connecticut	1913 (June 6)
Virginia	1904	Tennessee	1913 (September 25)
North Carolina	1905	New York	1914
Maryland	1906 (April 5)	Vermont	1915 (March 12)
Rhode Island	1906 (April 20)	Missouri	1915 (March 24)
West Virginia	1907 (March 1)	Nebraska	1915 (March 24)
California	1907 (March 6)	Colorado	1915 (April 9)
Indiana	1907 (March 9)	Minnesota	1915 (April 23)
Wisconsin	1907 (July 16)	Michigan	1915 (April 29)
Georgia	1907 (August 22)	Illinois	1915 (June 23)
New Jersey	1908	New Hampshire	1917 (April 19)
Idaho	1909 (March 13)	Pennsylvania	1917 (July 11)
New Mexico	1909 (March 18)	Kansas	1921
Washington	1909 (March 22)	Arkansas	1923 (February 27)
Florida	1909 (June 9)	Iowa	1923 (April 10)
Alabama	1909 (August 26)	Mississippi	1924
Oklahoma	1910 (March 15)	South Carolina	1934

[a] This table lists each state's earliest law criminalizing opium distribution without a doctor's prescription. Lesser restrictions on distribution—for example, requiring labels bearing opium content and the word "poison"—do not qualify as "bans." Though some states' first opium bans criminalized possession, most penalized only distribution, with possession bans following later.

Alaska is not listed on this table, though it banned unprescribed opium sales in 1899. Because Alaska copied almost its entire criminal code from Oregon's, Alaska lawmakers perhaps made no specific choice to ban opium. As I noted with regard to Table 4A, it is hard to be certain that my research assistants and I have succeeded in finding the earliest opium ban in every state. This table is the product of multiple cross-checking and is, I hope, error-free or nearly so.

[b] Hawaii remained in 1874 an independent kingdom and did not become a U.S. territory till 1900.

Let's begin by examining exactly what Nevada's 1877 opium law barred. Section 1 criminalized sale or distribution of "any opium" except by "druggists . . . on the prescription of legally practicing physicians." Like Hawaii's 1874 ban, which permitted only doctors to dispense the drug, Nevada's law made no accommodation for such common household remedies as paregoric, which contained a grain or two of opium per ounce of medicine, or the far more potent laudanum, with twenty to forty grains per ounce.[80] Also common but now forbidden was Dover's powder, a mixture of opium and ipecac, a plant-based expectorant. Nor did the law exempt "patent" or "proprietary" medicines—those all-purpose opiate-laced nostrums hawked under such homey tags as Children's Comfort, Ayer's Cherry Pectoral, and Dr. James' Soothing Syrup Cordial.[81]

Doctors, lawmakers, and journalists denounced patent remedies for concealing their opium content and addiction risk. Children's potions with treacly names—Dr. Moffett's Teethina (with opium) and Mrs. Winslow's Soothing Syrup (with morphine sulfate), among others—roused special outrage, as did addiction "cures" that calmed opium cravings by covertly feeding them. Of the former, Michigan doctor Orville Marshall cited claims in 1878 that each year American parents bought over 750,000 bottles of Mrs. Winslow's syrup spiked with enough morphine to kill half a million infants. Of the latter, Dr. S. F. McFarland wrote in 1877 that "[o]pium antidotes are probably all composed of opium in some form—at least those which are acceptable to the patient . . . ." Analyses of several of those "dangerous swindles" proved them all to contain either opium or morphine.[82]

Reformers and health officials alleged that fraudulent labels gulled addiction-averse consumers into believing their balms opium free. Perhaps the public knew better. After all, the tradition of self-medication with opium was old and widespread. Most consumers likely knew Ayer's Cherry Pectoral did not draw strength from the cherry; and some patent remedies, such as McMunn's Elixir of Opium, unabashedly headlined their active ingredient. Many householders perhaps shared the view voiced by Senator McCumber during 1914 debates

---

[80] In 1881 Dr. Harry Hubbell Kane supplied two laudanum formulas, which called for either one grain of opium per 25 drops of solution or one grain per 13 drops. As an ounce contained 480 drops by volume (or 480 grains by weight), these recipes supplied either 19.2 or 36.9 grains per ounce. *See* Kane, *Drugs That Enslave*, p. 27.

[81] Dr. Kane's recipe for Dover's powder called for one part opium, one part ipecac, and eight parts inert powder. *See* Kane, *Drugs That Enslave*, p. 27. The so-called "patent" remedies typically were trademarked but lacked true patents. Their formulas were undisclosed and closely guarded.

[82] *See* Orville Marshall, "The Opium Habit in Michigan," *in Sixth Annual Report of the Secretary of the State Board of Health of the State of Michigan* (Lansing: W.S. George & Co., 1878), pp. 61, 71; McFarland, "Opium Inebriety," pp. 290–91. On Dr. Moffett's and other children's products, *see* L.F. Kebler, "Habit-Forming Agents: Their Indiscriminate Sale and Use a Menace to the Public Welfare," *Farmer's Bulletin*, no. 393 (Washington: Government Printing Office, 1910), pp. 4–6; "Narcotics," pp. 401–02 ("[T]hese remedies are openly employed in the nursery, and perhaps clandestinely by indolent or sleepy nurses . . . .").

on the federal Harrison Act: proprietary remedies avoided repeated doctors' visits for "the little ordinary ills of life" and contained so little opium "that one could scarcely gain the habit unless he were to take a glassful of the medicine at one time." At all events professional condemnation failed to keep proprietary medicines and laudanum and other generics out of home medicine chests. "Few families are to be found," Dr. Marshall wrote in 1878, that "are without their stock of remedies . . . nearly all containing opium."[83]

All but a handful of state legislatures therefore shrank from a Nevada-style ban of all unprescribed opium sales. Those states and territories that hewed to Nevada's hard line, starred in Table 4D, lay largely in the West. Seeking to un-ravel the forces that gave rise to this pattern of lawmaking, we should focus on two dates: 1903 and 1906. Table 4D makes the significance of 1903 plain. Rather few states or territories acted to ban opium before 1903; all those that did lay in the West; and none made any accommodation for proprietary medicines or other low-concentration opium remedies. Indeed, some of these jurisdictions made it pointedly clear that in banning "opium," they also meant to ban mixtures containing opium. The Dakota Territory's 1885 act outlawed both opium and "any other commodity of which opium is an ingredient"; Oregon's law of the same year forbade both opium and "any preparation of which opium is the principal medicinal agent"; and Arizona's 1899 ban reached "any preparation . . . known to contain" opium.[84]

The diverging designs of the Wyoming and Texas laws of 1903 marked a wa-tershed: Wyoming joined the Western states in banning all unprescribed opium sales, while Texas haltingly launched a new trend that reached east and north and eventually swept the nation. The laws of these two states prove to be perfect counterpoints. Wyoming's act explicitly condemned both opium and "any patent or proprietary medicines, known to contain" opium. The Texas law, in contrast, first banned sale or distribution of opium except by prescription and then "pro-vided, that this Act shall *not* apply to proprietary medicines sold by druggists or others," even if those medicines contained opium.[85]

<hr>

[83] "Patent Medicine Bill to Curb Drug Users," *New York Times*, Mar. 15, 1906, p. 6 (quoting in-vestigative journalist Samuel Hopkins Adams, who alleged "[t]he poor and the ignorant . . . don't know what they are getting" in patent medicines); *Congressional Record*, vol. 51, pt. 14 (63d Cong., 2d Sess.), pp. 13761–62 (Aug 15, 1914) (remarks of Sen. McCumber); Marshall, "Opium Habit in Michigan," pp. 70–71.

[84] "An Act in Regard to the Selling and Smoking of Opium," 1885 *Dakota Territory Laws*, ch. 121, § 1 (Act of Mar. 13, 1885), p. 179; "An Act to Regulate the Sale of Opium, and to Suppress Opium Dens," 1885 *Oregon Laws* (Spec. Sess.), § 1 (Act of Nov. 25, 1885), p. 39; "An Act to Restrict the Sale of Morphine and Kindred Drugs," 1899 *Arizona Territory Acts*, no. 52, § 1 (Act of Mar. 16, 1899), p. 63.

[85] "An Act Regulating and Restricting the Sale and Use of Delirifacient Drugs . . . ," 1903 *Wyoming Laws*, ch. 98, § 1 (Act of Feb. 23, 1903), p. 129; "An Act to Regulate the Sale of Cocaine and Other Drugs . . . ," 1903 *Texas Laws*, ch. 115, § 3 (Act of Apr. 6, 1903), p. 181.

Table 4D Earliest State Bans of Unprescribed Opium Sales (Noting
Accommodation for Proprietary Medicines)

(Boldfaced and Starred States Are Those That Made No Accommodation
for Proprietary Medicines in Banning Unprescribed Opium Sales)

Hawaii	**1874***	Massachusetts	1910 (March 22)
Nevada	**1877***	Louisiana	1911 (?)
Dakota Terr.	**1885* (March 13)**	Utah	1911 (March 20)
Oregon	**1885* (November 25)**	Kentucky	1912
Montana	**1889***	Delaware	1913 (March 17)
Arizona	**1899***	Maine	1913 (April 12)
Wyoming	**1903* (February 23)**	Ohio	1913 (May 2)
Texas	1903 (April 6)	Connecticut	1913 (June 6)
Virginia	1904	Tennessee	1913 (September 25)
North Carolina	1905	New York	1914
Maryland	1906 (April 5)	Vermont	1915 (March 12)
Rhode Island	1906 (April 20)	Missouri	1915 (March 24)
West Virginia	1907 (March 1)	Nebraska	1915 (March 24)
California	1907 (March 6)	Colorado	1915 (April 9)
Indiana	**1907* (March 9)**	Minnesota	1915 (April 23)
Wisconsin	1907 (July 16)	Michigan	1915 (April 29)
Georgia	1907 (August 22)	Illinois	1915 (June 23)
New Jersey	**1908***	New Hampshire	1917 (April 19)
Idaho	1909 (March 13)	Pennsylvania	1917 (July 11)
New Mexico	1909 (March 18)	Kansas	1921
Washington	1909 (March 22)	Arkansas	1923 (February 27)
Florida	**1909* (June 9)**	Iowa	1923 (April 10)
Alabama	1909 (August 26)	Mississippi	1924
Oklahoma	1910 (March 15)	South Carolina	1934

Texas turned the tide of state lawmaking. Virtually every remaining state followed Texas in exempting certain opium-based medicines from its ban on unprescribed opium sales. Not one, however, adopted that state's general exemption for all "proprietary medicines." It's true Texas qualified this exemption by requiring that proprietary medicines not be "sold for the purpose of the evasion of this Act." But lawmakers in other states likely wondered how cops or courts could tell whether sales of Ayer's Cherry Pectoral were "evasion[s]" of the general ban.

So when Virginia banned opium a year later, it capped the concentration of permitted proprietaries, albeit clumsily. Its 1904 law applied only to "opium and its preparations, containing a higher percentum of opium than laudanum prepared in accordance with formula provided by the pharmacopœia of the United States . . . ." The 1905 edition of the *Pharmacopœia* detailed the cumbersome process of making laudanum from opium, alcohol, and water. The apothecary had to boil, pour, weigh, stir, pour again, shake, percolate, and pour a third time. When ready, the *Pharmacopœia* said, the laudanum "should contain in *one hundred cubic centimeters* not less than 1.2 nor more than 1.25 Gm. of crystallizable morphine."[86]

For perhaps obvious reasons, when North Carolina became the next state to ban unprescribed opium sales in 1905, it did not embrace Virginia's recipe. Rather it exempted "sales of laudanum and paregoric, or other preparation containing not more than thirty per cent. of . . . morphine or opium." Though the general approach of this exemption seems sound, the specific formula was hopelessly flawed. A 30-percent opium solution was heady stuff. Even the most potent laudanum contained only about forty grains of opium per ounce—a concentration of something less than 10 percent. Moreover morphine, which is an alkaloid of opium and its chief active ingredient, is hardly opium's equivalent. Dr. Kane rated it at six times opium's strength.[87] A 30-percent morphine solution was therefore a dramatic drug to exempt from any would-be ban.

Hence we arrive at 1906, when both Maryland and Rhode Island acted to ban unprescribed opium sales. Like Texas, Virginia, and North Carolina, these two states sought to permit many proprietary medicines. Now, however, legislators hit on a formula that won over most remaining states. Maryland's law, enacted in April 1906, exempted "paregoric and laudanum [and] *bona fide* proprietary medicines containing . . . not more than two grains of opium, or not more than two-fifths grain of morphine . . . in one fluid ounce . . . ." Rhode Island's

---

[86] "An Act to Amend and Re-enact Section 1764 . . . Relating to the Practice of Pharmacy," 1904 *Virginia Acts*, ch. 175, § 1 (Act of Mar. 14, 1904), pp. 296–97; *The Pharmacopœia of the United States of America* (Philadelphia: P. Blakiston's Son & Company, 8th rev. 1905), pp. 474–75.

[87] "An Act to Regulate the Sale of Cocaine, Opium and Morphine," 1905 *North Carolina Laws*, ch. 85, § 1 (Act of Feb. 2, 1905), p. 104; Kane, *Drugs That Enslave*, p. 18.

law, passed later the same month, mimicked Maryland's method but adjusted the tolerances. It allowed "preparations containing not more than six grains of opium, or not more than one-quarter grain of morphine . . . in one fluid ounce . . . ." And both states likely borrowed this grains-per-ounce concept from the model anti-narcotics law drafted by Professor James H. Beal for the American Pharmaceutical Association in 1903, which permitted "preparations containing not more than two grains of opium, or not more than one-eighth grain of morphine . . . in one fluid ounce . . . ."[88]

All but eight of the remaining thirty-six states listed in Table 4D adopted this approach of specifying grains-per-ounce tolerances to spare mild proprietary remedies. Of the outliers, a few—Indiana, New Jersey, and Florida—banned all unprescribed opium sales without exception; the other five allowed a class of low-potency medicines defined by other criteria.[89] And of the twenty-eight states that followed Maryland and Rhode Island in stating grains-per-ounce tolerances, all but two took Professor Beal's lead in setting the opium limit at two grains per fluid ounce. (Georgia permitted four grains per fluid ounce and Massachusetts 2.5 grains.) When the federal government moved to ban unprescribed opium sales in the 1914 Harrison Act, it too embraced Beal's two-grains-per-ounce exemption.[90]

---

[88] "An Act to Repeal Chapter 607 of the Acts of 1904 . . . ," 1906 *Maryland Laws*, ch. 523, § 1 (Act of Apr. 5, 1906), p. 1004; "An Act to Regulate the Sale of Certain Narcotics," 1906 *Rhode Island Acts*, ch. 1365, § 1 (Act of Apr. 20, 1906), pp. 111, 112; James H. Beal, "Draft of An Anti-Narcotic Law," *Proceedings of the American Pharmaceutical Association*, vol. 51 (1903), § 1, p. 485.

[89] Connecticut's law of 1913 banned opium, morphine, and heroin, as well as other substances. Its exemption clause reached low-concentration solutions of both morphine and heroin, but said nothing about crude opium. "An Act Concerning the Sale of Narcotic Drugs," 1913 *Connecticut Acts*, ch. 191, § 1 (Act of June 6, 1913), pp. 1814–15. Delaware's law of the same year avoided the grains-per-ounce formula and exempted "paregoric or any other mild compound of" opium as well as any other drug for "persons who are sick and in actual need of any of such drugs as a medicine." "An Act Regulating the Sale of Certain Drugs and Poisons," 1913 *Delaware Laws*, ch. 182, § 1 (Act of Mar. 17, 1913), p. 459. Oklahoma's rather wide-open law generally exempted "preparations containing opium . . . and recommended and sold in good faith . . . ." "An Act to Regulate the Sale of Cocaine and Certain Drugs . . . ," 1910 *Oklahoma Laws* (Extra. Sess.), ch. 52, § 1 (Act of Mar. 15, 1910), pp. 85, 86. Utah's law of 1911 said it "shall not apply to such preparations as are recognized by the United States Pharmacopeia, or to standard proprietary remedies." "An Act . . . Relating to the Sale of Cocaine, Morphine, Heroin, or Opium . . . ," 1911 *Utah Laws*, ch. 117, § 1 (Act of Mar. 20, 1911), pp. 193, 194. The 1909 Washington statute measured its exemption in terms of opium per dose rather than opium per ounce: "[N]othing herein contained shall . . . prohibit the sale of patent or proprietary medicines containing opium . . . wherein the dose of opium is less than one quarter grain . . . ." "An Act Relating to Crimes and Punishments . . . ," 1909 *Washington Laws*, ch. 249, § 257 (Act of Mar. 22, 1909), pp. 890, 970.

[90] *See* "An Act to Provide Against the . . . Traffic in Certain Narcotic Drugs . . . ," 1907 *Georgia Acts*, no. 220, § 1 (Act of Aug. 22, 1907), pp. 121, 122; "An Act to Regulate the Sale of Morphine and Other Narcotic Drugs," 1910 *Massachusetts Acts*, ch. 271, § 1 (Act of Mar. 22, 1910), pp. 207, 208. Section 6 of the Harrison Act states "[t]hat the provisions of this Act shall not . . . apply to . . . preparations and remedies which do not contain more than two grains of opium, or more than one-fourth of a grain of morphine . . . in one fluid ounce . . . ." Pub. L. 63-223, ch. 1, § 6, 38 Stat. L. 785, 789.

It seems states had been waiting for the Maryland solution. In the next four years, the number of state opium bans jumped from twelve to twenty-six. In four more years the total stood at thirty-five. Passage of the Harrison Act in December 1914 probably spurred the remaining states to act, for by 1918, all but five states had banned unprescribed opium sales.

We are left then with the two questions I posed earlier: Why were Western states the first to embrace prescription-only opium laws, and why did other states join in an onslaught beginning in 1906? The latter question now takes a new form: Why did Maryland and Rhode Island and the twenty-eight states that borrowed Maryland's grains-per-ounce exemption not find this formula sooner?

The timing of the Maryland and Rhode Island laws offers a clue, for both gained passage in April 1906, when Congress was considering what ultimately became the Pure Food and Drug Act of 1906. That law made it a crime to sell any drug in interstate commerce "if the package fail to bear a statement on the label of the quantity or proportion of any alcohol, morphine, opium . . . or any derivative or preparation of any such substances contained therein." The Food and Drug Act became law on June 30, 1906, but had been proposed in December 1905. And though the bill at first lacked the critical language requiring disclosure of a drug's opium concentration, Maryland and Rhode Island lawmakers may have anticipated that language's addition before the bill's final passage.[91]

It is hard to escape the conclusion that these two states took advantage of the new federal labeling rule. After all, the three previous state opium bans—those of Texas in 1903, Virginia in 1904, and North Carolina in 1905—had strived awkwardly to carve an exemption for certain proprietary medicines. The Maryland and Rhode Island grains-per-ounce formulas took a far better tack, but one that demanded disclosure by drug makers of the opium content of their products—something the Food and Drug Act ensured. A decade earlier William Rosser Cobbe had complained that "[i]f test were made of, say, laudanum, bought at six drug stores, no two of the samples would show corresponding strength."[92] The 1906 act demanded a precision that had been wanting. It enabled states to make the most highly intoxicating opium preparations available only by prescription while preserving for convenient home use low-concentration remedies that cured a host of common ills, yet posed (many thought) little risk of intoxication or addiction. That is, states now could outlaw recreational opium abuse while sparing what they deemed legitimate medical use. Having found this long-sought statutory mechanism, states embraced it with dispatch.

---

[91] "An Act for Preventing the Manufacture, Sale, or Transportation of Adulterated or Misbranded . . . Foods, [or] Drugs . . . ," Pub. L. 59-384, ch. 3915, §§ 2, 8, 34 Stat. L. 768, 770 (Act of June 30, 1906); "A Bill for Preventing the Manufacture, Sale, or Transportation of Adulterated or Misbranded . . . Foods, [or] Drugs," S. 88 (59th Cong., 1st Sess.) (Dec. 6, 1905).

[92] Cobbe, *Doctor Judas*, pp. 166.

Opium Bans in the West

We are left with the seven Western jurisdictions that forbade unprescribed opium sales without exempting proprietary medicines: Hawaii in 1874, Nevada in 1877, the Dakota Territory and Oregon in 1885, the Territories of Montana and Arizona in 1889 and 1899, and Wyoming in 1903. Unlike almost every other state, these seven subjected even traditional home remedies to the requirement of a doctor's prescription. Harry Hubbell Kane hinted at one plausible explanation in suggesting Westerners had cause to loathe proprietary medicines and those who flogged them. In *Drugs That Enslave* of 1881, he complained of "the lying pretensions of a few charlatans, *notably in the West*, who, by specious advertisements and deceitful lies, induce the victims to these [narcotic] habits to buy their medicines . . . ."[93]

David Courtwright has offered a second explanation, one rooted in demographics, for the readiness of Western lawmakers to outlaw all over-the-counter opium preparations. Chronic medicinal opium use was particularly common among two groups—middle- and upper-class women, who took laudanum and other preparations to relieve both menstrual pain and the nonspecific nerve pain known as neuralgia, and Civil War veterans hobbled by battlefield injuries and amputations. Courtwright reports Union doctors alone doled out almost 10,000,000 opium pills and over 2,841,000 ounces of other opium products to throngs of soldiers injured in battle or stricken with malaria or dysentery, who then became addicts for life. He cites a series of surveys dated 1878 to 1885 showing that between 61 and 72 percent of opium and morphine addicts were women and many of the rest veterans.[94] These chronic users would have suffered most from any anti-opium law making low-concentration remedies available only by prescription, especially as most such laws made opium prescriptions nonrefillable.

And these two groups—women and Civil War veterans—were scarce precisely in those Western frontier states that first banned eaten opium. Of the seven states and future states that failed to spare over-the-counter sales, two did not appear in the census tallies of 1890—Hawaii and Arizona. The other five—Nevada, the Dakota Territory (by 1890, North and South Dakota), Oregon, Montana, and

---

[93] Kane, *Drugs That Enslave*, p. 220 (first emphasis added); *see also* Kane, *Opium-Smoking in America and China*, pp. 104–05 (similar).

[94] Courtwright, *Dark Paradise*, pp. 36–37 (noting dominance of women among opium and morphine addicts); ibid., p. 48 (pointing to the role of neuralgia, dysmenorrhea, and uterine and ovarian complications); ibid., pp. 54–56 (describing the Civil War's role); ibid., pp. 170–71 n.101 (noting the contemporary meaning of *neuralgia*); Marshall, "Opium Habit in Michigan," p. 71 (tracing the predominance of female opium addicts to the frequency of painful menstruation and "diseases of the female organs of generation"); [Horace B. Day,] *The Opium Habit* (New York: Harper & Brothers, 1868), p. 7 (lamenting the "[m]aimed and shattered survivors from a hundred battle-fields," who "added greatly" to addicts' ranks).

Wyoming—all stood among the ten states and territories with the smallest pro-portion of female residents:

STATES OR FUTURE STATES WITH THE

SMALLEST PROPORTION OF FEMALE RESIDENTS

IN THE 1890 CENSUS

Montana	33.5%
Wyoming	35.2%
Nevada	36.2%
Washington	37.7%
Idaho	39.2%
Colorado	40.5%
Oregon	42.0%
California	42.1%
North Dakota	44.4%
South Dakota	45.2%

The same states were among those with the fewest Civil War veterans:

STATES OR FUTURE STATES WITH THE

FEWEST CIVIL WAR VETERANS

IN THE 1890 CENSUS[95]

Nevada	645
Utah	989
Wyoming	1265
Arizona	1458
Idaho	1852
North Dakota	2112
New Mexico	2388
Montana	2949
Oklahoma	3089
Delaware	3603
Oregon	6280
Rhode Island	6354
South Dakota	7251

[95] Source: "General Tables: Soldiers and Widows," *Report of the Population of the United States at the Eleventh Census: 1890*, pt. 2, tbls. 123–124 (Washington: Government Printing Office, 1897), pp. 803–04.

A third possible explanation for the readiness of Western states to ban all unprescribed opium sales emerges from a comparison of Tables 4A and 4C. Of the seven states and territories that acted to end unprescribed opium sales in 1903 or earlier, all but one either had banned opium dens already or enacted such a ban within the same law that criminalized all unprescribed sales. Perhaps legislators in those states believed their den bans would do little good if addicted smokers simply ate opium instead. When a man "change[s] from an opium smoker to an opium eater," Frederick Masters wrote in the mid-1890s, "he has simply jumped out of the frying pan into the fire."[96]

Plausible as these explanations seem, we can't know for sure why seven Western states and territories proved less concerned than their Eastern and Southern counterparts to preserve over-the-counter sales of low-concentration opium cures. So we can't know for sure why these states and territories led the nation in adopting prescription-only opium laws. But our ignorance on this score is tolerable, for the more important lesson is that in time *every* state sought to regulate opium sales by making the drug generally available only by prescription. That is, every state attacked the recreational abuse of eaten opium while striving to preserve the drug's legitimate use in cases of medical need.

The Consequences of Prescription-Only Laws

Once established, the requirement of a doctor's prescription to buy all but the smallest quantities of opium had several far-reaching results. Most centrally, the rule framed in law the moral principle that medical need could excuse otherwise immoral indulgence in a euphoric drug. In this sense, medical necessity operated at both the front and back ends of many states' laws. At the front end, every state followed Nevada in exempting prescription-based opium sales from the law's general ban—a rule that effectively suspended the state's opium ban if a doctor signed what amounted to an affidavit of medical need.

At the back end, over half the states followed Hawaii in forbidding doctors to prescribe for patients who used opium habitually. Then virtually all these states empowered doctors to trump this restriction with a finding of medical need. The form of the trump was the work of Professor James Beal, the lawyer and pharmacist who drafted a model state narcotics law for the American Pharmaceutical Association in 1903. Beal's model law generally forbade prescribing opium and other drugs for addicts, but specifically permitted a doctor to "prescrib[e] in good faith for the use of any habitual user of narcotic drugs such substances as

---

[96] Masters, "The Opium Traffic in California," p. 56.

[the doctor] may deem *necessary* for the treatment of such habit." At least twenty-four states adopted identical or similar language.[97]

It appears very few states or future states forbade doctors to prescribe opium for habitual users without also empowering doctors to overcome this bar in cases of need. Hawaii's original opium ban of 1874 and Rhode Island's law of 1906 are the only examples I've seen. A U.S. Surgeon General's report of 1931 condemned the laxity of back-end, necessity-based releases from the rules against prescribing for addicts: "The effect of such qualifying provisions is practically to nullify the intent of law" in banning prescriptions for habitual users.[98] The Surgeon General did not appreciate, however, that what these laws lost to laxity, they gained in consistency. For at both front and back ends, they hewed rigidly to the moral line dividing medically necessary drug use from the forbidden recreational realm.

Laws making opium available only by doctor's prescription had a second consequence: they gave law-enforcement agencies a means to distinguish medical users of eaten opium from recreational abusers. In the earlier era of opium self-medication and liberal administration by doctors, the law had no ready way to isolate and criminalize recreational abuse because its effects so nearly resembled those of medical use. Under the new laws, a doctor's prescription functioned as a certificate of medical need. Police now could assume anyone who possessed opium or showed signs of its use yet lacked a prescription was an abuser.

In a similar way, prescription-only laws enabled authorities to distinguish *medical addicts*, whose drug addiction traced to earlier medical treatment, from *recreational addicts*, whose addiction arose from pleasure seeking and dissipation. The plight of the former roused sympathy, for many had fallen prey to their doctors' profligacy with prescriptions. Various authors of the nineteenth and

---

[97] James H. Beal, "Draft of An Anti-Narcotic Law," *Proceedings of the American Pharmaceutical Association*, vol. 51 (1903), pp. 485–86 (emphasis added). On Beal and his work, *see* Musto, *American Disease*, pp. 15, 17–18; Dennis B. Worthen, "James Hartley Beal (1861–1945): Educator–Statesman," *Journal of the American Pharmacists Association*, vol. 45, no. 5 (Sept.–Oct. 2005), p. 629. For example, Georgia's 1907 opium ban barred prescriptions for habitual users, but then provided that a doctor may prescribe "in good faith for the use of any habitual user of narcotic drugs who is under his professional care such substances as he may deem necessary for [the patient's] treatment . . . ." "An Act to Provide Against the Evils Resulting from . . . Certain Narcotic Drugs," 1907 *Georgia Acts*, No. 220 (Act of Aug. 22, 1907), pp. 122–23. Thirteen states included similar or identical provisions in their original opium bans: Maryland (1906), West Virginia (1907), Wisconsin (1907), Alabama (1909), Idaho (1909), Massachusetts (1910), Oklahoma (1910), Louisiana (1911), Utah (1911), Maine (1913), Illinois (1915), Minnesota (1915), and Nebraska (1915). At least nine others later amended their opium bans to include such language: Texas (1905), North Carolina (1907), Virginia (1908), California (1909), Nevada (1913), Wyoming (1913), New York (1917), North Dakota (1917), and Michigan (1929). Tennessee's 1913 anti-opium law had no such provisions, but under a regulation adopted to enforce the act, a doctor who prescribed for an addict had to aver that "the opium compound called for by this prescription is absolutely necessary to said [addict] for the maintenance of life and reason . . . ." Lucius P. Brown, "Enforcement of the Tennessee Anti-Narcotics Law," *American Journal of Public Health*, vol. 5, no. 4 (Apr. 1915), pp. 323, 324–25 (quoting from "Physician's Certificate" provided in the governing regulation).

[98] U.S. Public Health Service, *State Laws Relating to the Control of Narcotic Drugs*, p. 22.

early twentieth centuries saw medical opium addicts as "good citizens, who have become addicted to the use of the drug innocently and who are, in every sense of the word 'victims' " using the drug "from necessity." Most had "never experienced pleasure from narcotic drug[s]" and therefore were "proper subject[s], not for *reproof*, but for *medical treatment.*" Recreational addicts in contrast prompted contempt: they were "dope fiends" whom contemporaries branded with the usual old-style moral epithets—"pleasure users," "moral degenerates," creatures of "pure self-indulgence."[99]

Once prescription-only opium laws had been in operation for a stretch of years, medical addicts stood out as those with a history of purchases by prescription or of physician administration of the drug. Because virtually every state's anti-opium law made prescriptions nonrefillable, a patient could become an addict lawfully only through a doctor's indulgence in writing repeated prescriptions. Legal authorities therefore could presume that addicts lacking a medical track record gained the habit through criminal abuse.

This presumption of criminal abuse grew stronger over the last quarter of the nineteenth and first decades of the twentieth centuries as cases of true medical addiction grew scarcer. Medical addiction diminished in part because prescription-only drug laws discouraged self-medication and perhaps made doctors more cautious in prescribing opiates. Many states required doctors or pharmacists to keep detailed records of opiate prescriptions and sales. Some states went further, decertifying doctors or even deeming them criminals for prescribing opium except in cases of true medical need. Hence Wyoming's 1903 opium law revoked the license of any doctor who prescribed the drug "except in cases where its [use] is necessitated and required by the then existing physic[a]l or mental condition of the" patient. New Jersey's opium ban of 1908 made it a misdemeanor for a doctor to prescribe "except for a legitimate and necessary purpose in the practice of his profession." Washington's law of 1909 and Nevada's of 1911, using identical language, made it a "gross misdemeanor" to prescribe

---

[99] George D. Swaine, "Regarding the Luminal-Treatment of Morphine-Addiction," *American Journal of Clinical Medicine*, vol. 25, no. 8 (Aug. 1918), pp. 610, 611 ("good citizens . . ."); "Opium Eating," p. 66 ("from necessity"); Ernest S. Bishop, *The Narcotic Drug Problem* (New York: The Macmillan Company, 1921), p. 3 ("never experienced pleasure . . ."); Fitz Hugh Ludlow, "What Shall They Do to Be Saved?" *Harper's New Monthly Magazine*, vol. 35 (1867), pp. 377, 379 ("proper subject[s] . . ."); S. Dana Hubbard, "Some Fallacies Regarding Narcotic Drug Addiction," *Journal of the American Medical Association*, vol. 74, no. 21 (May 22, 1920), p. 1439 ("dope fiends"); Charles E. Sceleth & Sydney Kuh, "Drug Addiction," *Journal of the American Medical Association*, vol. 82 (1924), p. 679 ("pleasure users"); G.P. Sprague, "Some Essential Points in the Etiology, Pathology and Treatment of Morphine Addiction," *Lancet-Clinic*, vol. 88, no. 24 (Dec. 14, 1907), p. 585 ("moral degenerates"); C.B. Burr, *A Handbook of Psychology and Mental Disease* (Philadelphia: F.A. Davis Company, 4th ed. 1916), p. 92 ("pure self-indulgence").

opium or other banned drugs "except to a patient believed in good faith to require the same for medicinal use, and in quantities proportioned to the needs of
such patient . . . ."[100]

Medical addiction diminished as well because doctors raised the alarm.
Medical writings of the last quarter of the nineteenth century warned insistently of the danger. As older physicians made way for younger, the therapeutic
traditions of the nineteenth century, with their reliance on opium for a range of
afflictions, gave way to a near aversion to the drug unless the patient was past
hope or cure. "The present generation has been so thoroughly warned," a New
Hampshire doctor wrote in 1902, "that now they are in many instances so very
afraid to give it, even for the worst pain, that the patient suffers agonies worse
than any hell for want of one-eighth of a grain of morphine."[101]

Then, too, medical addiction receded as doctors and health planners
found new ways to suppress ailments once treated primarily by opium. David
Courtwright cites improved sanitation in reducing dysentery and the development of a typhus vaccine as two among several important advances. The
emergence of therapeutic alternatives to opium for many other maladies—and
particularly aspirin and kindred medications for pain—likewise shrank the rolls
of opium-using patients. Already in 1889 a contributor to the *Boston Medical and
Surgical Journal* heralded an era of "Substitutes for Opium in Chronic Disease"
and decreasing reliance on opiates against pain, diarrhea, and insomnia.[102]

Despite all such advances, however, doctors often made addicts of their
patients, sometimes negligently, sometimes unavoidably while treating chronic
pain, and sometimes—it was said—greedily, in hopes of profiting from repeat
business. Courtwright points to the carelessness of those late-nineteenth-century
doctors who left their patients with morphine and syringe and instructions to

---

[100] "An Act Regulating and Restricting the Sale and Use of Delirifacient Drugs . . . ," 1903 *Wyoming
Laws*, ch. 98, § 3 (Act of Feb. 23, 1903), pp. 129–30; "A Supplement to an Act Entitled, 'An Act for the
Punishment of Crimes,' . . ." 1908 *New Jersey Acts*, ch. 197, § 4 (Act of Apr. 13, 1908), pp. 399, 400;
1909 *Washington Laws*, ch. 249, § 258 (Act of Mar. 22, 1909), p. 970; "An Act Concerning Crimes and
Punishments . . . ," 1912 *Nevada Revised Laws.*, vol. 2, § 279 (codified as § 6544) (Act of Mar. 17, 1911),
p. 1866.

[101] Charles Warrington Earle, "The Opium Habit," *Chicago Medical Review*, vol. 2, no. 7 (Oct. 5,
1880), pp. 442, 444 ("[T]he greater number of men and women who are now completely enslaved to
the different preparations of opium, received their first dose from members of our profession"); J.M.
Hull, "The Opium Habit," in *Third Biennial Report of the State Board of Health of the State of Iowa* (Des
Moines: Geo. E. Roberts, 1885), pp. 535, 537 ("The habit in a vast majority of cases is first formed
by the unpardonable carelessness of physicians, who are often too fond of using the little syringe
. . . ."); Oscar C. Young, "On the Use of Opiates, Especially Morphine," *Medical News*, vol. 80 (1902),
p. 154, *quoted in* Courtwright, *Dark Paradise*, p. 54 ("The present generation . . ."); Courtwright, *Dark
Paradise*, p. 50 (noting warnings about medical addiction in professional writings of the last quarter
of the nineteenth century); ibid., pp. 113–14 (discussing doctors' increasing reluctance to prescribe
opiates).

[102] Courtwright, *Dark Paradise*, p. 52; J.F.A. Adams, "Substitutes for Opium in Chronic Disease,"
Boston Medical and Surgical Journal, vol. 121 (1889), pp. 351–56.

use as needed. Complaints of physician-induced addiction continued well into the next century. In 1910 Lyman F. Kebler, Chief of the Division of Drugs of the federal Department of Agriculture, charged that "some doctors will write a large number of [narcotics prescriptions] for 25 cents each." Dr. Charles Terry said many physicians handed out doses of opiates "to office patients with apparently as little concern as a dose of calomel." Tennessee's State Food and Drug Commissioner, Lucius Brown, reported that "well over 50 per cent. of existing cases of narcotic addiction are due to the indiscreet administration of drugs by physicians." Lawmakers took notice of such complaints. In urging passage of the Harrison Act in 1914, Senator Atlee Pomerene called on colleagues to "protect the country from the physician or druggist who is encouraging the drug habit for purely commercial purposes."[103]

While doctor-induced addiction did not disappear, prescription-only laws, together with doctors' growing awareness of the problem and the development of new drug therapies, made medical addiction rarer. Meanwhile, the passing years thinned the ranks of Civil War veterans, among the largest contingents of medical addicts. As medical addicts grew scarce, recreational addicts grew proportionately more common. By 1928, former Surgeon General Rupert Blue could tell Congress that medical addicts were "few in number" and easily addressed under the Harrison Act, which allowed sales by prescription. The "real addicts," he said, were the "dissipators, or persons who habitually use narcotics for other than medical reasons." A few years earlier, Drs. Charles Sceleth and Sydney Kuh reached a similar conclusion: "Fifteen or twenty years ago, most addicts acquired the habit through physical disease or discomfort. Today the number of new addictions through physicians' prescriptions is small. The great majority of cases now result from association with addicts . . . and searching for new sensations."[104]

As medical addiction diminished, the addict population changed. It grew younger, poorer, more male, more urban. And with time, as prescription-only drug laws sank roots, lawmakers more readily assumed most or all addicts came by their habits recreationally. In days when most addicts' habits traced to earlier medical crises, when most were women and often of the "better" sort, lawmakers hesitated to punish with severity. Now they turned predictably more punitive. As Richard Bonnie and Charles Whitebread have written, once the likelihood of "accidental addiction" was minimized, "the image of the 'dope fiend'—the

[103] Courtwright, *Dark Paradise*, pp. 48, 50; Kebler, "Habit-Forming Agents," p. 12; C.E. Terry, "Drug Addictions, a Public Health Problem," *American Journal of Public Health*, vol. 4 (1914), pp. 28, 33; Brown, "Enforcement of the Tennessee Anti-Narcotics Law," p. 329; *Congressional Record*, vol. 51, pt. 14 (63d Cong., 2d Sess.), p. 13759 (Aug. 15, 1914), p. 13759 (remarks of Sen. Pomerene).
[104] Courtwright, *Dark Paradise*, pp. 56, 61 (discussing the generational shift as Civil War veterans passed on); U.S. House, *Establishment of Two Federal Narcotic Farms: Hearings Before the Committee on the Judiciary* (70th Cong., 1st Sess.) (1928), p. 102 (statement of former Surgeon General Rupert Blue); Sceleth & Kuh, "Drug Addiction," p. 679.

immoral 'street user' "—became the focus of policymaking. "What had been formerly viewed as an unfortunate sickness with organic causes now was viewed as yet another immoral behavior of the criminal class."[105]

Yet even as policymaking evolved in response to the changing face of addiction, basic moral attitudes remained largely constant. The greater severity of American drug laws over the first half of the twentieth century therefore reflects not something new, but a new application of old beliefs about the wrongfulness of pleasure-seeking intoxication. Prescription-only drug laws and other changes denied most opium addicts a claim of medical need and therefore exposed them to moral condemnation as recreational abusers—as dissipators, hedonists, and degenerates.

The Role of Race

Any law that lets only those with doctors have drugs will skew the class of legal users toward the moneyed, largely white elite and the class of illegal abusers toward the more non-white poor. Prescription-only drug laws therefore helped divide the drug-using population into race-coded legal and illegal camps. And what proved true of opium and its narcotic kin proved true as well of cocaine and cannabis, which soon fell within the only-by-prescription drug law regime.

As time passed and perceptions of drug-using populations took grip, it grew harder to discern cause and effect and easier to argue the race of the users gave rise to the laws banning use. Such arguments have proved especially tempting concerning those drugs that arrived on scene already linked with racial or ethnic groups. Among these were smoked opium, brought by Chinese laborers, and marijuana, which grew wild across the United States but took a Spanish name when popularly tied to Mexican migrants. Even cocaine, an Austro-German medical import, was linked with Southern African Americans, whose wide use of the drug, real or imagined, sparked frenzied reporting and public anxiety.

Yet a long look backward makes it hard to see a causal role for race in the passage of early prescription-only drug laws. Events explored in the last several chapters suggest instead that these laws sprang from old moral notions that emerged in the context of sex and later regulated alcohol in England and America, long before racial divisions infected our marketplaces in illegal drugs. Familiar moral forces—an aversion to mind-numbing euphoria and deference

---

[105] Courtwright, *Dark Paradise*, pp. 113–14, 143 (describing the changing nature of the addict population); Richard J. Bonnie & Charles H. Whitebread II, *The Marihuana Conviction: A History of Marihuana Prohibition in the United States* (Charlottesville: University Press of Virginia, 1974), p. 21.

to medical need—are perhaps enough, standing alone, to explain the course of early antidrug lawmaking.

But that case remains unfinished. In tracing early laws against opium dens and eaten opium, we have seen racial images flickering across the page: repeated references to "John Chinaman"; allusions to the "unclean" and "unappreciative heathen"; snide wordplay on the "Manners of the Mongolians" and the "Habits of the Heathen Chinee." When the *Oakland Tribune* wrote in 1875 that "Ah Dong has been arrested on suspicion of being a Chinaman," the paper anticipated modern references to "Driving While Black," the crime of being non-white.[106]

So there remains much to be said. We can learn more about race's role in prompting early anti-den laws by studying those laws' enforcement. And to judge whether the story of anti-opium laws is typical of all antidrug laws, we can explore other early laws, especially those governing cocaine and cannabis. On close examination, claims that early laws against opium dens, cocaine, and cannabis took rise from racial hatred prove to be myths, albeit myths with very long pedigrees.

These investigations will lead us across the country and back again. For now, however, we return to San Francisco to witness the nation's first antidrug law in force.

---

[106] "Police Court," *Oakland Tribune*, Jan. 5, 1875, p. 3.

PART II
RACIAL MYTHS

5

Race in the Dens and Miscegenation Myths

In late December 1876, thirteen months after the San Francisco Board of Supervisors adopted the nation's first true antidrug law, the *New York Times* got the story wrong. The paper reprinted an item from the San Francisco *Bulletin* telling of the law's passage. "A little over a year ago a great many white people of both sexes patronized the opium dens," the *Bulletin* wrote. "The Board of Supervisors deemed it best to put a check upon the growing evil . . . ." This much was true. The supervisors had voiced concerns that young "WHITE MEN AND WOMEN" of respectable parentage indulged in the stupefying smoke. The *Bulletin*'s account then veered from fact: "[A] stringent law was passed, making it a penalty of not less than $50 nor more than $500 for the keeper of any opium den to allow a white person to smoke in the place."[1] Here there were two errors. The less important concerns the law's penalty scheme, which also provided for a jail term of between ten days and six months.

The critical error concerns that word *white*. "White" appeared nowhere in the supervisors' ordinance: "*No person*," the law began, shall "keep . . . or visit . . . any place, house or room where opium is smoked." And "*[a]ny person* who shall violate" this law will be guilty of a misdemeanor. Apparently, the *Bulletin*'s error was no random typo, for a sentence later it repeated the wayward reference to race: "It was also made a criminal act for any *white* person to be found in an opium den . . . ." The *Bulletin* then noted this racial restriction's racial consequence: "Since the passage of this law the dens drive a less lucrative business. Their customers are all Chinese . . . ."[2]

Nor may we dismiss the *Bulletin*'s story as stray sloppy reporting, for it had authoritative precedent. In early December 1875, just three weeks after the supervisors approved their pioneering ban on opium dens, the *Alta California* reported "[t]he first raid under the new ordinance against *white* persons who frequent opium dens . . . ." All the alleged smokers nabbed by Detective James Rogers and a police posse on that raid had distinctly non-Chinese names: Fannie Whitmore, Cora Martinez, James Dennison, Charles Anderson. Nor was the

---

[1] "San Francisco Opium Den," *New York Times*, Dec. 23, 1876, p. 7 (quoting account from the San Francisco *Bulletin*).
[2] "Board of Supervisors," *Daily Alta California*, Nov. 16, 1875, p. 1 (reprinting the proposed ordinance) (emphasis added); "San Francisco Opium Den" (quoting account from the San Francisco *Bulletin*) (emphasis added).

Beware Euphoria. George Fisher, Oxford University Press. © Oxford University Press 2024.
DOI: 10.1093/oso/9780197688489.003.0006

New York Times the only distant paper to spread the *Bulletin's* false lead. Dailies in Chicago, St. Louis, Lowell, Massachusetts, and likely elsewhere repeated the news that San Francisco had made it a crime to sell to white smokers and for whites to smoke in dens.[3]

The accounts in the *Times* and *Alta* also found later corroboration. In May 1883, the *San Francisco Chronicle* reported that police court judges had resolved "to give opium smokers the full benefit of the law in imprisonment." Leaflets flooded Chinatown "warning the keepers of opium dens against renting pipes and bunks to whites, or allowing them in the dens." The leaflets added that "all inmates of a den where whites are admitted will be sent to the House of Correction for three months without the alternative of a fine." The proposed penalty stemmed from a San Francisco general order of 1880, which had displaced earlier ordinances and imposed a three-month sentence for keeping or visiting an opium den. But that law retained word for word the race-neutral language of the 1875 original: "*No person* shall . . . keep . . . or visit . . . any place, house, or room where opium is smoked . . . ."[4]

Still, the leaflets apparently worked. On a police-guided tour of the dens, a *Chronicle* reporter found "that the order was being generally obeyed, several joints being entered where no traces of the presence of white patrons for days were discoverable." This news, too, traveled far. In his *Demon of the Orient*, published in New York later in 1883, journalist Allen S. Williams wrote that in "San Francisco the dens in the Chinese quarter, to which white men resorted formerly, have nearly all been closed up . . . in so far as the police know . . . ."[5]

Months later the *Bulletin* affirmed that "[t]he rule adopted seems to be to allow the Chinese to smoke opium all they wish without interference, but the line is drawn when white people smoke in the 'joints.'" This rule had staying power. In his 1892 description of San Francisco's opium dens, Frederick Masters observed, "A white person convicted of visiting such a place is now sentenced to three months' imprisonment without the option of a fine." And in an 1898 issue of *Scientific American*, C. F. Holder told of scores of opium dens "in the Chinese

---

[3] "Raid on Opium Dens," *Daily Alta California*, Dec. 6, 1875, p. 1 (emphasis added); "Celestial Smokers" (Chicago) *Daily Inter Ocean*, Apr 18, 1878, p. 3 (reporting that San Francisco's law made it a misdemeanor to "allow a white person" in a den and "for any white person to be found in an opium den"); "San Francisco Opium Den," *St. Louis Globe–Democrat*, Jan. 4, 1877, p. 2 (directly quoting the *Bulletin's* mistaken report); [Untitled], *Lowell Daily Citizen*, Jan. 3, 1877, p. 1 ("heavy penalties have been imposed on both the keepers and the white habitues, should the latter be found there"). I thank my research assistant Justin Barnard for locating the reference in the *Alta*.

[4] "The Opium Smokers," *San Francisco Chronicle*, May 19, 1883, p. 2. Frederick Masters supplied the citation of the 1880 general order, the penalty scheme, and the date of passage. Frederick J. Masters, "Opium and It's [*sic*] Votaries," *California Illustrated Magazine*, vol. 1 (May 1892), pp. 631, 641, 644. For the law's language, *see General Orders of the Board of Supervisors*, 61 (San Francisco: P.J. Thomas, Printer, 1889), p. 39 (emphasis added).

[5] "The Opium Smokers"; Allen S. Williams, *The Demon of the Orient and His Satellite Fiends of the Joints* (New York: By the Author, 1883), p. 132.

quarter of every large city. There the Chinaman can buy his pipe and smoke in peace. In San Francisco," however, despite the indulgence granted Chinese smokers, "white people are forbidden to visit these dens . . . ."[6]

As renditions of the law in print, all these reports were wrong. It appears no San Francisco ordinance or California statute ever forbade only whites to keep or visit opium dens or to smoke opium. But all these authors can be forgiven their failure to read the law, for their statements of the law *in force* were right. Police and courts applied the city's anti-den ordinance mainly against whites who patronized opium dens and denkeepers who sold to them. On this score, the evidence is abundant and far ranging.

Enforcement with an Unequal Hand

Six years after San Francisco's anti-den ordinance took hold, a *Chronicle* reporter accompanied Officer James Mahoney on a tour of some of the city's most notorious dens. Mahoney began the 1881 outing with an upbeat assessment of police efforts to suppress the dens. "We have . . . closed up the opium dens," he said. "I mean by that the places formerly kept by Chinese in Chinatown, where anyone could go and smoke opium by paying for the privilege. These places were supported principally by the patronage of white men and women. The likely chance of having to pay $20 in the Police Court for the privilege has made the white smokers find other means of hitting the pipe."[7] Here the officer disclosed two things: The police had targeted those dens that catered principally to whites, apparently ignoring those with an all-Chinese clientele. And mainly white smokers, it seems, faced police court discipline and its $20 fines.

At the first den toured, in Chinatown's Bartlett Alley, the reporter saw the consequences of whites-focused policing. Six Chinese patrons lay by their pipes. "[M]ost of the shelves in the den whereon white smokers erstwhile sought dreamy oblivion showed evidences of not having been used for weeks. . . . All of the dens, whose white patrons the vigilant officers have driven away, are now occupied by the lowest class of Chinese sneak thieves."

The tour led next to Jackson Street, where Officer Mahoney pointed out a den cleverly disguised behind several hidden doors. "The den is still patronized late at night, the officers think, by white men and women" who managed to elude police with an elaborate signaling mechanism. In yet a third establishment, abutting Pacific Street, Mahoney told how police had searched in vain for a

---

[6] "Opium Joints," *San Francisco Daily Evening Bulletin*, Feb. 16, 1884, p. 1; Masters, "Opium and It's Votaries," pp. 641, 644; C.F. Holder, "The Opium Industry in America," *Scientific American*, vol. 78, no. 10 (Mar. 5, 1898), p. 147.

[7] "A Growing Evil," *San Francisco Chronicle*, July 25, 1881, p. 3.

certain visitor. "[O]ne night some officers were informed that a white man was smoking in that den." They promptly broke down the door and sent in a trained dog with the simple command, "Seek them out, Scotchy." Even the dog knew the quarry in question was white. For Scotchy ignored the "one lone . . . Chinaman" in the den, "snuffed all about the place, and came back to its master with tail dragging." The reporter's tour of the dens complete, he expressed his "conviction that Chinatown had indeed been cleared of white opium smokers. . . . The anti-opium-smoking ordinance," though race-blind in print, "drove the white smokers out of Chinatown . . . ."[8]

The department's race-targeted enforcement of a facially race-neutral law persisted long after the reporter's 1881 tour. In 1892 Frederick Masters congratulated police on their continued vigilance against white—and only white—smokers. "It should be mentioned to the credit of our police that the visits of white men and girls to opium hells in Chinatown, so often described a few years ago, have now been stopped. . . . If done at all," Masters continued, "it must be very secretly. The movements of white people about Chinatown are so carefully watched, and the different hells under almost half-hourly surveillance, that it would be impossible for them to frequent these places without soon attracting the attention of the police." Masters marveled at the officers' success: "During the last six years . . . I have failed to discover a single Caucasian in one of these dens, or even suspiciously near one."[9]

The officers' focus on whites flowed from official policy. Longtime San Francisco Police Chief Patrick Crowley publicly endorsed Officer Mahoney's view that the city's anti-den ordinance outlawed mainly those places "supported principally by the patronage of white men and women." The law's *point*, Crowley insisted in 1895, was to target those dens that drew a white clientele. "Of course the Chinese smoke," he said. "All we can do is to keep them from opening places where whites might resort to smoke." This task Crowley thought his men had discharged "pretty thoroughly."[10]

[8] Ibid.

[9] Masters, "Opium and It's Votaries," p. 641.

[10] "A Growing Evil"; "Chief Crowley on Opium," *San Francisco Call*, Aug. 3, 1895, p. 14; Jim Baumohl, "The 'Dope Fiend's Paradise' Revisited: Notes from Research in Progress on Drug Law Enforcement in San Francisco, 1875–1915," *The Surveyor* (June 1992), pp. 3, 6. I thank Jim Baumohl for alerting me to the Crowley quote and Zehava Robbins for discovering its source in the *San Francisco Call*. On Chief Crowley's tenure, *see* "Chief Crowley Has Resigned," *San Francisco Chronicle*, Mar. 1, 1896, p. 25 (noting his twenty-three years as chief).

Unequal Enforcement Elsewhere

Police enforcement looked much the same down the coast in Los Angeles. Like San Francisco's 1875 anti-den ordinance, California's statewide ban of 1881 applied to "[e]very person who opens or maintains" an opium den "and every person who visits . . . any such place . . . ." Yet a string of articles in the *Los Angeles Times* reveals officers' almost single-minded focus on white smokers. Hence when a *Times* reporter followed a police captain on a tour through L.A.'s Chinatown in April 1882, the reporter noted no action against the Chinese smokers whose cadaverous forms the tour group spied in the dens. But "[a] few white men, with some shame left, were occasionally noticed to be hurriedly getting out of sight on the officer's approach."[11]

Six years later, when officers suspected "that an opium joint on Marchessault alley, kept by Ah Wen, was frequented by depraved white men and women," they raided the place, "capturing the proprietor and two white women, who were caught in the act of 'hitting the pipe.'" The next month a *Times* reporter made personal use of his knowledge of police priorities. Annoyed at a Chinese den owner he found presiding over a "nest of Chinese opium smokers," the reporter "didn't kill the impudent heathen, but . . . had the whole gang arrested soon after for selling opium to white friends"—presumably a typo for "white fiends."[12]

Most striking was an account of "A Successful Raid" on a "notorious opium joint" made by one Officer Phelan in October 1888. The *Times* hailed the officer's capture of "a white man and two women, as well as the Chinaman who had been in the habit of selling the habitues of the place their 'dope.'" Phelan had waited for whites before striking. "The officer has been watching the [den] for some time," the paper reported, "as he was certain of its character, but heretofore has been unable to get sufficient evidence on which to convict. Yesterday afternoon, however, he saw a white man go into Ah Yek's place and purchase some opium, which he carried to the joint." Having seen his white prey, Phelan raided the den and arrested the white man, William Scott, and two women found with him, Katie Boyd and Nellie Wilson. The seller, Ah Yek, was charged not with selling opium, but "with selling opium *to a white man*." As historian David Courtwright has noted, "In Los Angeles the police left Chinese smokers alone; only white smokers were occasionally prosecuted."[13]

---

[11] 1881 *California Statutes*, ch. 40, § 1 (Act of Mar. 4, 1881), p. 34; "Hell's Half Acre," *Los Angeles Times*, Apr. 14, 1882, p. 3.

[12] "The City in Brief," *Los Angeles Times*, July 23, 1888, p. 8; "In Demand: People Who Send for a Reporter and Get Him," ibid., Aug. 20, 1888, p. 2.

[13] "Opium Den: A Successful Raid by Officer Phelan Yesterday," *Los Angeles Times*, Oct. 25, 1888, p. 2 (emphasis added); David T. Courtwright, "Drug Laws and Drug Use in Nineteenth-Century America," in *The Constitution, Law, and American Life: Critical Aspects of the Nineteenth-Century Experience* (Donald G. Nieman ed., Athens: The University of Georgia Press, 1992), pp. 123, 131 n.3.

With anti-den laws spreading east from California, so too did the fixation on white smokers and the dens that served them. I noted in the last chapter that authorities in Virginia City, Nevada, enacted the nation's second anti-den law in September 1876 only after they saw whites—and especially young whites "of the more respected class of families"—visiting the dens. Troubled by the youths' conduct, an editor of the *Virginia Evening Chronicle* alleged that "[t]he San Francisco Supervisors recently passed an ordinance ordering the arrest of any *white* person found in an opium house, and our Board should at once follow the example."[14]

It's true the very first arrest under the Virginia City ordinance was of a Chinese smoker. But in reporting this arrest on September 14, 1876, the Virginia City *Territorial Enterprise* noted "[t]here has been some talk as to whether the Chinese were included in the ordinance." The editor dismissed such reservations, for "the reading [of the ordinance] is plain, and any one frequenting, keeping, or patronizing a smoking-den is liable to arrest." Indeed, the Virginia City ordinance tracked almost word for word the race-neutral language of San Francisco's 1875 original.[15]

The remarkable thing, then, is that townsfolk doubted "whether the Chinese were included in the ordinance." A day after insisting the race-neutral language of the ordinance "is plain," the *Territorial Enterprise* recanted and reasserted the law's proper focus on *white* smokers: the law was "designed to put a stop to the practice of *white* men and women going down to opium dens in Chinatown and steeping their brains with the insidious drug. Never mind John," the editor continued, uttering a common epithet for Chinese males. "*Let him smoke his brains out if he likes it*, but stop young men from forming a habit which is worse than death, especially stop young girls from acquiring a taste for something which is sure to end in unfitting them from filling any place that nature designed them for in life." The evidence is plain—and supports Courtwright's finding that in Virginia City as in San Francisco and Los Angeles, enforcement of anti-den ordinances "was selective; dens patronized by whites were the most likely to be raided."[16]

---

[14] H.H. Kane, *Opium-Smoking in America and China* (New York: G.P. Putnam's Sons, 1882), p. 3 (quoting Dr. Harris) ("of the more respected class . . ."); "Spread of the Opium Habit," *Virginia Evening Chronicle*, Feb. 10, 1876, p. 2 ("The San Francisco Supervisors . . .") (emphasis added). Likewise see "The Deadly Drug," ibid., Aug. 4, 1876, p. 3: "[N]ot less than one hundred and fifty white persons of both sexes—the majority of them being members of the respectable class of our citizens—were under the influence of the deadly drug.").

[15] "First Blood for Curby," [Virginia City] *Territorial Enterprise*, Sept. 14, 1876, p. 3; "An Ordinance to Abolish Opium-Smoking Dens," in *Revised Ordinances of the City of Virginia* (Virginia, Nev.: Enterprise Steam Printing House, 1878), p. 116.

[16] "Opium-Smoking," [Virginia City] *Territorial Enterprise*, Sept. 15, 1876, p. 2 (emphasis added); David T. Courtwright, *Dark Paradise: Opiate Addiction in America before 1940* (Cambridge: Harvard University Press, 1982), p. 78.

Likewise in Carson City, Nevada's capital, authorities apparently enforced race-neutral laws mainly against those dens that served whites. In April 1879, the Carson City *Morning Appeal* sent a reporter to the local Chinatown "to ascertain to what extent opium smoking has been practiced by white men and women." One Chinese businessman recalled "that before the law prohibiting the Chinese from selling the drug *to white people* was passed, the traffic carried on here was astounding." As in San Francisco, then, locals read *white* into the law, though neither the original Nevada anti-den law of February 1877 nor the Carson City ordinance of June 1877 nor the amended state law of March 1879 applied only to white smokers or sales to whites. All applied instead to any "person" who kept an opium den regardless of the race of the smokers. And except for the state law of 1877, which punished only sellers and denkeepers but not users, these laws punished any "person" who visited a den to smoke. Yet the Chinese businessman told the *Morning Appeal* that since the passage of these laws, "the respectable Chinese merchants refuse to sell the drug even to their countrymen who are suspected of encouraging *the smoking of it among the whites.*" Satisfied with this result, the paper declared "[i]t was high time that a stringent law was passed to forbid the opium traffic *among our own kind.*"[17]

In succeeding weeks, the *Morning Appeal* complained the law permitted arrest only of those den patrons caught while smoking. The editor told of a police officer who had found two young men, one from "a highly respectable family in this city," reclined in a local den, but could make no arrest because they were "not caught in the act of whiffing." The law was "defective," the editor declared. "[I]t should have provided for the arrest and conviction of every *white* person found in one of these infamous hells, unless such *white* person could prove beyond any question of doubt that he or she had business of a respectable nature there."[18]

Far from Carson City in the northeastern Nevada town of Elko, observers again suggested the state's race-neutral opium-dens statute applied peculiarly to whites. In November 1877, some nine months after the state first outlawed opium dens, the *Elko Post* grumbled, "There are several dens in Chinatown in full operation, and at one or two of them whites, as well as Chinese, are served with the stupefying drug." The paper then exhorted authorities: "Laws have been enacted for the suppression of this traffic, yet we seldom hear of an arrest being

[17] "The Opium Vice," *Carson City Morning Appeal*, Apr. 12, 1879, p. 3 (emphasis added); "An Act to Regulate the Sale or Disposal of Opium, and to Prohibit the Keeping of Places of Resort for Smoking . . . That Drug," 1877 *Nevada Statutes*, ch. 27 (Act of Feb. 9, 1877), pp. 69–70; "Ordinance No. 48," *Carson City Morning Appeal*, Mar. 1, 1879, p. 4 (quoting text of Carson City ordinance of June 1877); "An Act Amendatory . . . of . . . 'An Act to Regulate the Sale or Disposal of Opium . . . ,'" 1879 *Nevada Statutes*, ch. 116 (Act of Mar. 8, 1879), pp. 121–22.
[18] "Opium Smokers," *Carson City Morning Appeal*, May 20, 1879, p. 3 (emphasis added). Diana Lynn Ahmad's excellent dissertation, "'Caves of Oblivion': Opium Dens and Exclusion Laws, 1850–1882" (Ph.D. Dissertation, Univ. of Missouri-Columbia, 1997), steered me to many of the sources I have cited in this segment.

made. It may be that our officers are not aware that *whites* frequent these dens, yet the fact stares us in the face and cannot be denied."[19]

Two states away in Colorado a similar story played out. On a "Midnight Prowl through Denver's Opium Joints" in March 1880, a *Rocky Mountain News* reporter visited a few of the seventeen dens that served Denver's community of only one hundred fifty Chinese. There "[t]he man who wants to make a hog of himself" pays for his pipes, lies down "like a hog," and "smokes himself into dreamy forgetfulness and stupidity." If this Chinese vice "was confined to themselves and they were the only sufferers," the reporter mused, echoing other Western writers, "it would not matter so much. But the majority of the patrons of these filthy 'joints' are white people and the contagion is spreading."[20]

Within three weeks the Denver city council, by a vote of eight to two, made it a misdemeanor for any person to keep an opium den or be found in one. Press accounts over the next several months said little of police enforcement. Then the death in October of eighteen-year-old William McClellan aroused public passion and spurred police action. Though it seemed the young man died of a perforated intestine, his family and friends blamed his frequent visits to Chinese dens. The *Rocky Mountain News* declared that when opium dens are "traps for mere children, leading them to sacrifice their health and lives, it is high time some measures were taken to wipe [them] out . . . ." Days later the coroner's jury deemed "the excessive use of opium" smoked at the dens of Fong Lee and Ah Joe to have been a "remote cause" of young McClellan's death. Within hours police squads descended on Denver's Chinese dens.[21]

That night the police arrested every opium smoker they found, all apparently Chinese. But in less fraught circumstances, it seems the Denver police focused on white smokers and those who sold to them. On a raid two months later, they encountered a Chinese smoker who reported that the Chinese "did not sell opium any more to Melicans [Americans] since they had been arrested for doing so." A *Rocky Mountain News* writer who had tagged along for the raid concluded "that no opium is now being sold there to Americans, but that the Chinamen themselves are using it as much as ever . . . ."[22]

[19] "Opium Smoking at Elko, Nevada," *San Francisco Daily Evening Bulletin*, Nov. 20, 1877, p. 4 (reprinting item from the *Elko Post*) (emphasis added). *See also* "Opium Smoking," *Tybo (Nevada) Weekly Sun*, Nov. 24, 1877, p. 3 (paraphrasing the same *Elko Post* report).

[20] "Fumes from the Orient," *Rocky Mountain News*, Mar. 28, 1880, p. 8.

[21] *The Charter and Ordinances of the City of Denver* (John L. Jerome ed., Denver: Tribune Publishing Company, 1881), ord. 15, ch. 6, art. 4, pp. 113–14 ("Opium Joints"); "The City Solons," *Rocky Mountain News*, Apr. 16, 1880, p. 8 (reporting passage of the anti-den ordinance); "Deadly Opium," ibid., Oct. 9, 1880, p. 8 (reporting McClellan's death; "traps for mere children . . ."); "The Opium Case," ibid., Oct. 12, 1880, p. 8 (reporting the verdict of the coroner's jury); "Celestials Corraled," ibid., Oct. 12, 1880, p. 1.

[22] "Deadly Drugs," *Rocky Mountain News*, Dec. 12, 1880, p. 2. For an excellent account of many of these events, *see* Henry O. Whiteside, "The Drug Habit in Nineteenth-Century Colorado," *Colorado Magazine*, vol. 55 (1978), pp. 47, 50–54.

Meanwhile in Helena, Montana, a newsman set out in 1880 to test rumors "that opium dens existed in Chinatown which were frequented by white men." When the scribe tried to buy opium from local Chinese dealers, however, he met with suspicion. "Me no sell opium to white man," said one denkeeper in the pidgin English the press assigned the Chinese. "Me don't know you," said another—"*policeman telle me finee me one hundred dollar if me give white man opium*."[23]

Arresting Those Who Sold to Whites and Those Who Smoked with Them

In several Western jurisdictions where authorities focused on white smokers, Chinese *sellers* who catered to whites also found themselves in the law's grip. Hence Detective Rogers's raid under the new San Francisco ordinance in December 1875 netted several white smokers "and two Chinamen who kept the place." Likewise, the Elko, Nevada, editor who was distressed to find whites visiting the dens urged "punishment of the heathen who are engaged in the fearful traffic." The *Reno Evening Gazette* deemed it "passing strange that the officers do not take some steps to enforce the law against the Pagan dealers in this living death. . . . That white men and women daily and nightly visit these loathsome resorts of degradation is an open and notorious fact." The *Gazette* later added that while "[p]apers from nearly all the towns in the state contain accounts of the arrest and conviction of Chinamen for keeping opium dens," the Chinese keepers of Reno have escaped punishment. "There are opium dens in Reno and they are frequented by whites. Why this traffic is not suppressed is a mystery." Indeed, the Nevada law apparently fell harder on Chinese sellers than on white buyers. Diana Lynn Ahmad reports that in 1879 and 1880 a dozen Chinese offenders—but not one white—served time in state prison for violation of Nevada's opium statute.[24]

Then, too, Chinese *smokers* were not immune from prosecution if they shared a den with white smokers. Harry Hubbell Kane reprinted two California news items from 1881, one bylined Stockton and one Oakdale, reporting raids on dens and arrests of both white and Chinese patrons. The Stockton raid snagged three whites and a single Chinese smoker; the Oakdale outing nabbed just two whites

---

[23] "Opium Dens in Helena," *Helena Weekly Herald*, Jan. 15, 1880, p. 2 (emphasis added).
[24] "Raid on Opium Dens," *Daily Alta California*, Dec. 6, 1875, p. 1; "Opium Smoking at Elko, Nevada," *San Francisco Daily Evening Bulletin*, Nov. 20, 1877, p. 4 (quoting item from the *Elko Post*); "Opium Smoking," *Reno Evening Gazette*, Feb. 21, 1879, p. 3; "Opium Smoking," *Reno Evening Gazette*, Apr. 4, 1879, p. 3; Diana L. Ahmad, *The Opium Debate and Chinese Exclusion Laws in the Nineteenth-Century American West* (Las Vegas: University of Nevada Press, 2007), p. 64. Ahmad similarly reported that in Oregon in 1886 and 1887 at least four Chinese men but no whites served time in the state penitentiary for opium crimes. *See* ibid., p. 64.

against eighteen Chinese patrons. Even the same *San Francisco Chronicle* article that detailed Officer James Mahoney's whites-focused enforcement practices noted a den raid under the city's ordinance that swept up "thirteen Chinamen and three white boys."[25]

Still, a careful survey of the *San Francisco Chronicle*, apparently the most thorough surviving record of the early practices of the San Francisco Police Department, reveals an almost single-minded emphasis on those dens that served whites. In the first five years after passage of the city's November 1875 anti-den law, the *Chronicle* reported forty arrests of smokers in opium dens. No doubt the *Chronicle*'s coverage was incomplete—and may have emphasized cases involving whites. The numbers nonetheless are striking. In twenty-five of the forty cases, every alleged smoker was white. Twelve cases concerned both white and Chinese smokers. In *only three* cases, or 7.5 percent of the total, were all the alleged smokers Chinese.[26] Yet all sources suggest the city's opium smokers were overwhelmingly Chinese.

Hence the *Chronicle*'s reporting supports what so many other sources of this era disclose: authorities largely tolerated opium smoking among the Chinese while anxiously combating it among whites. And if still more proof were needed, there is the curious case of Idaho.

The Idaho Ban

All the anti-den laws I've mentioned so far took race-neutral forms. Yet it seems none was race neutral as applied. By a principle broadly understood, colorblind laws gave rise to color-coded, whites-focused law enforcement.

Idaho's original den ban of 1881 followed the standard colorblind formula: "Any person or persons who shall set up . . . any house or place as a resort for the purpose of smoking opium . . . shall be guilty of a misdemeanor." Likewise, "[a]ny person" who bought opium for smoking in a den faced punishment, as did "any person" found in a den without lawful business.[27]

Six years later, however, Idaho's territorial lawmakers dropped the dodge of race neutrality and rashly spoke the truth: "Every *white* person," an 1887 law declared, "who opens, maintains or keeps" an opium den "shall be guilty of a misdemeanor" and face a fine of up to $300 or up to six months in jail or both. "Every *white person* who bargains for, buys, takes or accepts any opium" in any

[25] *See* Kane, *Opium-Smoking in America and China*, pp. 9–10; "A Growing Evil," *San Francisco Chronicle*, July 25, 1881, p. 3.

[26] I detail the technique of my online search of the *Chronicle* in note 66.

[27] "An Act to Prohibit the Keeping of Places of Resort for Smoking Opium or Frequenting the Same," 1881 *Idaho General Laws*, §§ 1–3 (Act of Jan. 22, 1881), p. 276–77.

such place faced a similar fate. And "[e]very *white person* who is found" in any opium-smoking establishment "without any lawful business" risked a smaller fine or up to three months in jail.[28] The new act displaced the earlier, race-neutral language and left Idaho without any territorial anti-den law that applied to Chinese smokers or den keepers. Though the new act's clear aim was to keep whites from the dens—and legislators could have advanced that goal by barring *any* denkeeper from catering to whites—the act punished only those keepers who happened to be white.

Idaho's lawmakers surely did not act thoughtlessly in a matter touching white–Chinese relations. In 1880 the territory had the largest Chinese contingent of any state or territory as a proportion of the population (see Table 4B, in Chapter 4).[29] Yet if lawmakers recorded their reasons for writing this color-coded law, they hid their records well. No committee report or sponsor's statement or floor debate seems to have survived. Nor, it seems, did local newspapers so much as comment on the new law's racial focus, much less offer a rationale.[30] But whatever explains the 1887 law's focus on white smokers and denkeepers, the statute supplies a critical link in our understanding of the racial dynamics underlying anti-den lawmaking throughout the West. For it forecloses any claim that the whites-focused enforcement seen in San Francisco, Los Angeles, and cities and towns throughout the West was either a local fluke or a false scent left by scattered sources. Idaho legislators differed from those in neighboring states only in putting in print what others intended but dared not draft.

Lawmakers elsewhere had reason to shun their Boise brethren's' candor. The Idaho law's racial restriction flatly affronted the Fourteenth Amendment's guarantee of equal protection of the laws. The San Francisco supervisors who wrote the nation's first anti-den law in 1875 had learned this lesson from recent local history. In 1874 California lawmakers had taken up a bill to remove the word "white" from a law granting all "white children" a free public education. In

[28] "Opium Smoking," 1887 *Idaho Revised Statutes*, tit. 8, ch. 7, §§ 6830–6832 (Act of Feb. 10, 1887), pp. 736–37 (emphasis added).

[29] Census figures from 1880 show that Chinese residents made up 10.4 percent of the population of Idaho Territory. Nevada's Chinese contingent ranked second with 8.7 percent.

[30] Two of my research assistants, Helen Kim and Micah Myers, tried in vain to find contemporary sources or secondary studies casting light on the law's background. Ms. Kim examined legislative and executive papers as well as microfilmed issues of three important newspapers: the *Idaho Weekly Statesman* (searched from January 1, 1886, to March 12, 1887); the *Idaho Triweekly Statesman* (January 4, 1887, to February 28, 1887); and the *Idaho World* (early August 1886 to the end of April 1887). Research assistant Jason Despain found a simple *mention* of the law's passage: in February 1887 the *Idaho Tri-Weekly Statesman* reported that the governor had approved a long series of new laws, including "[a]n act . . . [p]unishing keeping or frequenting opium dens by white persons." "Enactments of the Legislature," *Idaho Tri-Weekly Statesman*, Feb. 15, 1887, p. 1. Assisted by librarian Sonia Moss, I've examined the surviving legislative documents, which show the 1887 act gained unanimous passage in both legislative chambers, but disclose no rationale for or debate about its racial restriction. *See* 1887 *Idaho House Journal*, p. 193; 1887 *Idaho Council Journal*, p. 169.

truth, lawmakers disliked the notion of integrated public schools. But Governor Newton Booth had won office on a pledge to delete *white* wherever it appeared in the statute books and insisted that "'white' and 'colored' should be stricken from our school law. They are a badge of the past." Ultimately, the measure to strip *white* from the school law failed, but not before the *San Francisco Chronicle* had announced its support, urging that "[o]ur State laws must conform to the supreme law of the land . . . ." And when schooling was not in issue, California lawmakers proved truer to their race-blind principles. In February 1874, just weeks after legislators abandoned school integration, they amended an old law "for the suppression of Chinese Houses of ill fame" by striking the word "Chinese."[31]

It's true an anti-den law *penalizing* whites would have differed from a school law privileging them. Still, cautious lawmakers were wise to worry a whites-only crime law would fail constitutional scrutiny. Hence when San Francisco supervisors banned the dens in 1875, they did not ban only those that served whites or bar only whites from smoking. Nor did lawmakers in Virginia City or Carson City or, it seems, any other place but Idaho. Only in Boise were lawmakers so bold—and even they retreated soon enough. In 1893, six years after their whites-focused den ban hit the books, Idaho legislators reverted to a law like all the others, punishing "[e]very person" who kept or visited an opium den. Again they left no record of their reasons. The press too largely ignored the law change, though one paper reported that a senate "bill to make the law concerning opium smoking apply to all persons instead of white persons only" had advanced toward passage.[32]

The whites-only version of Idaho's anti-den law drew back the curtain on other states' lawmakers, whose rules were neutral on their face but enforced as Idaho's was written. Of all these lawmakers we may ask why they were so intent on stopping mainly whites from smoking—and so content to let the Chinese continue.

---

[31] "Colored Children in the Public Schools," *San Francisco Chronicle*, Jan. 7, 1874, p. 2 (quoting existing law and insisting on the supremacy of federal law); "White," ibid., Jan. 28, 1874, p. 2 (reporting on a bill that would have amended the school law "to admit colored children into the public schools but to exclude the Chinese children"); "The Word 'White,'" ibid., Jan. 31, 1874, p. 1 (supplying more detail on the pending bill, recounting the governor's campaign statement "in favor of striking out the word 'white' everywhere . . . ," and noting the bill's failure); "The New Laws," *San Francisco Chronicle*, Feb. 11, 1874, p. 1. Governor Booth called for public school integration in his 1871 inaugural address: "The doors of our schools should be open to all, with no prejudice of caste without, and no sectarian teaching within, which will prevent any child from freely entering." Newton Booth, "Inaugural Address" (Dec. 8, 1871), *online at* http://governors.library.ca.gov/addresses/11-Booth.html.

[32] "An Act to Amend . . . ," 1893 *Idaho General Laws*, §§ 1–3 (Act of Feb. 16, 1893), pp. 22–23; "The Wagon Road Bill," *Idaho Daily Statesman*, Feb. 2, 1893, p. 5. Like the 1887 act, the 1893 amendment passed through both legislative houses without dissent. *See* 1893 *Idaho House Journal*, p. 162 (Feb. 14, 1893); 1893 *Idaho Senate Journal*, p. 111. David Crandall, one of my research assistants, searched without success for further legislative history and newspaper commentary concerning the 1893 law change.

Why Whites-Focused Policing?

Fondness for the Chinese

Let us dismiss any answer that supposes warmhearted indulgence toward the immigrant Chinese. While some few Western whites expressed grudging tolerance of the immigrants' presence and even admiration of their quiet and steady work habits, the wider white community said the Chinese must go. Consider the climate in Idaho in the run-up to its whites-focused den ban of February 1887. After party conventions in September 1886, Idaho Republicans declared themselves "unalterably opposed to placing our workingmen in competition with . . . Chinese contract labor" and pledged to fight Chinese immigration. Democrats declared themselves "unalterably opposed to Chinese immigration" and pronounced Chinese labor "an unmixed evil." They called for "the deportation of the Chinese from this country, and their exclusion forever." And in proclaiming it "the right and duty of the people of Idaho Territory to withhold their patronage from the Chinese," Democrats seemed to endorse an ongoing Boise-area boycott against Chinese laborers and their white employers.[33]

As politicians vied for the anti-Chinese vote, some Idahoans took matters into their own, more brutal hands. After a white merchant's murder in Pierce City in September 1885, a masked band lynched five Chinese suspects. Months later, with tensions roused, an anti-Chinese convention concluded with a resolution to "get rid of" the Chinese "in a peaceful and lawful manner." Another such convention, held in February 1886 in Weiser, ended with a call "to rid our yet unsullied community of the few lecherous, uncivilized heathens who now infest it, and to prevent their further encroachment upon us." Then in June someone set a charge under a Chinese laundry in Broadford, wrecking the building and wounding an employee. At Clark Fork in northern Idaho, a white contingent tossed bombs into Chinese shelters. And in May 1887, three months after passage of Idaho's whites-only dens law, thirty-one Chinese miners were murdered on the Snake River, apparently by white marauders. That month also saw a weeklong riot in Salmon, about 160 miles northeast of Boise, as whites rode wild through the Chinese district, breaking windows and shooting into homes.[34]

[33] "Republican Platform of Idaho," *Idaho Semi-Weekly World*, Sept. 28, 1886, p. 2; "Democratic Platform," ibid., Sept. 17, 1886, p. 2; "How to Get Rid of the Chinese," *Idaho Tri-Weekly Statesman*, Dec. 31, 1885, p. 2 (describing the boycott); "The Chinese, or Pinto Party," ibid., July 22, 1886, p. 2 (assessing the boycott's success).

[34] "Investigating an Outrage: The Governor of Idaho at Pierce City, Idaho, Investigating the Lynching of Five Chinese," *Idaho Tri-Weekly Statesman*, July 22, 1886, p. 3; Li-hua Yu, "*Chinese Immigrants in Idaho*" (Ph.D. Dissertation, Graduate College of Bowling Green State University, 1991), p. 255 (describing the Pierce City affair); ibid., pp. 256–58 (recounting the Snake River massacre); ibid., p. 259 (recounting the Weiser convention); ibid., p. 262 (discussing the Clark Fork

Amid such violent anti-Chinese feeling, Idaho's lawmakers hardly intended their 1887 law to supply generous safe haven for Chinese opium smokers. Yet their law *did* shield Chinese smokers from prosecution, as did policing practices in San Francisco and Los Angeles and those Western towns where police generally left Chinese smokers unmolested while arresting and charging whites. Though precise reasons for this apparent tolerance of Chinese opium smoking are past knowing, several forces may have been at work.

Supposed Resistance to Addiction

Some whites simply thought the Chinese immune to opium's power to addict and stupefy. Exactly when this view took hold is unclear. It appeared as early as Dr. Alonzo Calkins's foundational 1871 treatise, *Opium and the Opium-Appetite*. "The peoples of the Orient generally," Calkins said, "are able to bear with more certain impunity than Europeans, not stimuli only but narcotics as well, be these alcoholic liquors or opium or tobacco." A San Francisco–based writer for the *St. Louis Globe-Democrat* added in 1885 that among Americans "no one can escape the regularity of the indulgence who comes once under the influence of [opium]. The Chinese, on the other hand, seems to have his appetites under better control. He seldom allows himself to be ruled by the habit . . . ." While "Chinamen seem able to thrive" on opium, the *San Francisco Examiner* wrote in 1889, "[t]here is no vice so dangerous to a white community as the use of opium. . . . [T]o a white man it means moral, mental and physical ruin. It saps the vigor of our race . . . ." New York journalist Jacob Riis popularized the principle in his celebrated 1890 account of New York's nether realms, *How the Other Half Lives*: "The Chinaman smokes opium as Caucasians smoke tobacco, and apparently with little worse effect upon himself. But woe unto the white victim upon which his pitiless drug gets its grip!"[35]

Though similar statements appeared in the 1890s, not all authorities agreed. The *New York Times* quoted one doctor's 1895 denial that "such great differences exist between the various branches of the human race."[36] And many visitors to

incident and the Salmon riot); "Chinese Meeting," *Idaho Tri-Weekly Statesman*, Dec. 31, 1885, p. 3 ("get rid of" and "in a peaceful and lawful manner"); "A Chinese Laundry Blown Up with Giant Powder—One Chinaman a Little Hurt," *Idaho Tri-Weekly Statesman*, June 29, 1886, p. 3.

[35] Alonzo Calkins, *Opium and the Opium-Appetite* (Philadelphia: J.P. Lippincott & Co., 1871), p. 132; G.H.F., "The Opium Habit," *St. Louis Globe-Democrat*, May 25, 1885, p. 4; "The Opium Bill," *San Francisco Examiner*, Mar. 3, 1889, p. 4; Jacob A. Riis, *How the Other Half Lives: Studies Among the Tenements of New York* (New York: Charles Scribner's Sons, 1890), p. 65. I am grateful to Jim Baumohl for sharing with me the *Examiner* article cited here.

[36] William Rosser Cobbe, *Doctor Judas: A Portrayal of the Opium Habit* (Chicago: S.C. Griggs and Company 1895), pp. 125–26 ("Dark races, as the African and Asiatic, are not so easily affected by the pipe as the white peoples. While it is impossible for one of the latter to leave off smoking, once the

the dens wrote of Chinese smokers lying stupefied alongside spent pipes. In the 1870s and 1880s, however, when the nation's first anti-den laws took hold, it seems many whites saw opium as a threat to themselves alone.

Opium Wars' Legacy

Whites' indulgence of Chinese smokers also may trace to the belief, widely held, that because whites had enslaved the Chinese to opium, whites were at fault for Chinese addicts. "England forced opium upon the Chinese at the point of the bayonet," Dr. Kane charged in 1882, and did so with no higher motive than to enrich the British East India Company, which counted on China to consume India's massive opium crop. The Chinese government had sought to halt opium importation in 1779 and reinforced the ban in 1799, lamenting "that our Countrymen should blindly pursue this destructive and ensnaring vice." In 1838 the Daoguang Emperor again tried to abolish the trade. Yet Britain waged war to reclaim the Chinese market, first from 1839 to 1842 and again from 1856 to 1858. Victorious in both Opium Wars, the British demanded and won free access to China's massive population of addicts and potential addicts—and so, Kane wrote, must bear "direct responsibility for having fostered and forced a vice that numbers fifteen millions among its victims."[37]

Here Kane shared common ground with commentators across the country. Between 1865 and 1885, the *San Francisco Chronicle* or *Daily Evening Bulletin* printed at least eleven similar denunciations of Britain's China policy; the *New York Times* or *Tribune* printed at least thirteen. Each alleged in substance that "to compel the Chinese to receive opium," English cannon had pounded crowded streets, "and the gutters ran with the blood of women and children." George Parsons Lathrop joined in denouncing Britain's "barbarous destruction"

---

habit is formed, it is by no means uncommon for members of the former class to quit of their own volition . . . ."); "The Effects of Opium: What New-York Doctors Say of British Commission's Report," *New York Times*, Apr. 29, 1895, p. 8 (quoting Dr. Allan McLane Hamilton) ("Asiatics have a tolerance for opium which is absent in Europeans. Our Chinese smoke opium all their lives and it never seems to hurt them."); ibid. (quoting Dr. T.S. Robertson) ("such great differences . . .").

[37] H.H. Kane, "Opium Smoking: A New Form of the Opium Habit Amongst Americans," *Gaillard's Medical Journal*, vol. 33, no. 2 (Feb. 1882), pp. 101, 103 ("England forced opium . . ."); Thomas Dormandy, *Opium: Reality's Dark Dream* (New Haven: Yale University Press, 2012), pp. 127, 136 (noting the Chinese government's 1779 edict and 1799 reinforcement); Hosea Ballou Morse, *The Chronicles of the East India Company Trading to China, 1635-1834*, vol. 2 (Oxford: Clarendon Press, 1926), app. M, pp. 344–46 (quoting the 1799 edict); Virginia Berridge, *Opium and the People: Opiate Use and Drug Control Policy in Nineteenth and Early Twentieth Century England* (New York: Free Association Books, 1999), p. 174 (reviewing the history of the Opium Wars); Ahmad, *The Opium Debate*, pp. 20–22 (same); Kane, *Opium-Smoking in America and China*, p. 117 ("direct responsibility . . .").

in forcing on China a "pestilent practice" that "the Imperial government has striven most earnestly to exclude." Frederick Masters, too, charged that Britain had compelled China "to legalize a traffic that her rulers saw would entail misery and ruin upon her people."[38]

In letting the Chinese have their opium, then, local lawmakers and law officers perhaps chose to forgive Chinese addicts for feeding a hunger imposed by conquest.

Chinese Flight

A fourth possible motivation for whites-focused law enforcement demanded no such tolerant understanding. Even unsympathetic whites could see their Chinese neighbors fleeing in the face of endless assaults on their dignity and safety. Whites knew, as one Idaho paper wrote in November 1886, that "by their voluntary deportation and mortality they will soon disappear." To many whites, Chinese immigrants had seemed bent from the start on returning home. The newcomers, overwhelmingly male, had left their families behind and ostentatiously resisted assimilation. "Perhaps no other foreign emigrant to the shores of America clings so tenaciously to his national habits as does the Chinese," the New York Times said in 1873. "John [is] a man with us, but not of us," the Chronicle added. "John leaves us and our laws, customs and institutions severely alone." The settlers aimed simply to gain their fortunes and "go home as fast as they could."[39]

Far from forcing these stay-apart strangers to assimilate, most whites preferred their speedy and permanent departure. After the Chinese Exclusion Act of 1882 barred immigration of Chinese laborers and miners, those who left for home largely weren't replaced. Idaho's Chinese contingent therefore dwindled fast—from 4,274 in 1870 to 3,379 in 1880, then to 2,007 in 1890. As a proportion of the territory's booming population, the drop was even steeper—from 28.6 percent in 1870 to 10.4 percent in 1880 to a mere 2.4 percent in 1890. The Idaho legislators of 1887 who forbade only whites to visit opium dens had seen the Chinese leaving. And by the time Idaho lawmakers replaced their whites-only

---

[38] "A Plea for Protection," New York Tribune, Feb. 15, 1884, p. 8 ("to compel the Chinese . . ." and "and the gutters ran . . ."); George Parsons Lathrop, "The Sorcery of Madjoon," Scribner's Monthly, vol. 20 (1880), pp. 416, 420; Masters, "Opium and It's Votaries," p. 632.

[39] [Untitled], Idaho Semi-Weekly World, Nov. 30, 1886, p. 2; "Chinese in New-York," New York Times, Dec. 26, 1873, p. 3 (claiming that among 500 Chinese residents of New York, there was not one woman); "John Chinaman," San Francisco Chronicle, Jan. 31, 1875, p. 1. Across the nation the population of Chinese men increased from 33,000 in 1860 to over 100,000 in 1880, while the population of Chinese women grew from only 1,800 to 4,800. Ronald Hamowy, "Introduction: Illicit Drugs and Government Control," in Dealing with Drugs: Consequences of Government Control (Lexington, Mass.: Lexington Books, 1987), p. 12 & n.25.

ban with one punishing "[e]very person" who kept or patronized a den in 1893, very few Chinese smokers remained. In California and Nevada, the Chinese population likewise shrank over the last two decades of the century both in absolute numbers and as a proportion of each state's population: from 8.9 percent in California and 9.1 percent in Nevada in 1880 to 3.1 percent and 3.6 percent in 1900.[40] As their Chinese neighbors scattered or fled or died off, many whites must have looked with unconcern on threats to Chinese morals.

Prison Costs

That was especially true when mending those morals cost money. Western whites had discovered an annoying and expensive habit of their Chinese guests. When convicted of a crime and assessed a fine or jail time, Chinese defendants often chose time and put the county to the cost of their keep. San Francisco supervisors sought to fight this trend with an 1876 ordinance directing jailers to clip convicts' hair "to an uniform length of one inch from the scalp." The consequence for a Chinese convict was the loss of his queue, a mark of shame and a bad harbinger for the life to come.[41]

Forced in federal court to justify this rule, the supervisors explained "that only the dread of the loss of his queue will induce a Chinaman to pay his fine. . . . [A]nd the state or county will [then] be saved the expense of keeping him during the imprisonment." Or as the *Chronicle* put it, these were "men for whom imprisonment with food is no punishment, to whom incarceration is no shame, and for whom the only penalty that can be found is to cut their hair." The mayor likewise deemed it "no punishment for a vagabond Chinaman to be put upon a bread, meat and coffee diet with nothing to do but eat and sleep"—and others echoed the theme. But the court voided the hair-cropping rule as a violation of Chinese inmates' equal protection rights and left the city paying their board.[42] Rather

[40] "An Act to Execute Certain Treaty Stipulations Relating to Chinese," Pub. L. 47-126, ch. 126, 22 Stat. 58 (Act of May 6, 1882) (repealed 1943); U.S. Census of Population and Housing, "Historical Census Browser" (University of Virginia Library). My population percentages consider only Idaho's non-Indian residents because the census tallies of 1870 and 1880 seem to undercount Native Americans by a wide margin.

[41] *Ho Ah Kow v. Nunan*, 12. F. Cas. 252, 253 (C.C. D. Calif. 1879) (Field, J.); Edwin R. Meade, "The Chinese Question," in *California State Senate, Special Committee on Chinese Immigration, Chinese Immigration, Its Social, Moral and Political Effects* (Sacramento: State Publishing Office, 1878), pp. 291, 299 (noting the loss of one's queue "is regarded [among the Chinese] as a personal disgrace").

[42] *Ho Ah Kow*, 12. F. Cas. at 255–56; "Sacred to the Memory of Forbes, Story and Taylor," *San Francisco Chronicle*, June 5, 1873, p. 2 ("men for whom . . ."); "What Shall We Do with Our Vagabonds," ibid., Dec. 8, 1875, p. 2 ("no punishment for . . ."); "The Case Against John," ibid., June 16, 1876, p. 3 (quoting members of a commission on Chinese immigration: The Chinese "accept imprisonment in our County Jail as a relief, and regard it as a home of luxury;"); "Chinatown," ibid., July 22, 1885, p. 2 (similar).

than foot this cost to enforce its anti-den law, the city perhaps chose to leave the law alone as long as the Chinese kept their opium to themselves.

Across the state line in Nevada, authorities chafed at the same choice. The *New York Times* reported in 1881 that Nevadans resented the cost of jailing Chinese denkeepers when the denkeepers seemed so fond of jail: "Chinamen are often convicted of keeping opium dens, and sentenced to pay a fine, with the alternative of imprisonment. They almost invariably accept the alternative," the *Times* wrote, "as they do not mind being imprisoned. The fine is served out at the rate of $2 per day in a comfortable jail, where the prisoners get plenty to eat and are not obliged to work. Two dollars a day and board is more than the average Chinaman can earn."[43]

Idaho's original anti-den law of the same year provided for up to six months' confinement or a fine of up to $100 or both—and specified that a convict who failed to pay could work off both fine and court costs at hard labor in the sheriff's charge "at the rate of one dollar per day." Perhaps a Chinese propensity to exercise this option moved Idaho lawmakers to replace this 1881 law, which applied to "[a]ny person," with their whites-focused den ban of 1887.[44] Faced with an itinerant population impervious to punishment, Western lawmen may have wondered why they should squander public funds to lift the morals of these unrooted strangers.

Legal Obstacles

Lastly, it's possible court rulings complicated enforcement of anti-den laws against the Chinese. Though the San Francisco supervisors' 1875 ordinance forbade anyone to "keep or . . . visit . . . any place, house or room where opium is smoked, or where persons assemble for the purpose of smoking opium," a *Chronicle* reporter hinted in 1881 that courts had read the law more narrowly: unless smokers "were paying for the privilege . . . smoking opium does not constitute an offense against the law . . . ." Hence a "limited number of Chinamen may be smoking in a den . . . , for the excuse is available that the place is the keeper's domicile and the smokers his friends."[45]

[43] "Topics in the Sagebrush," *New York Times*, Feb. 21, 1881, p. 1.

[44] 1881 *Idaho General Laws*, § 1, p. 276. The 1887 law also provided that a convict who failed to pay his fine could be confined and repaid for his prison labor at the rate of a dollar a day. 1887 *Idaho Revised Statutes*, tit. 8, ch. 7, § 6830, pp. 736, 737. But this law of course applied only to whites.

[45] "The Force of Silence," *San Francisco Chronicle*, Jan. 9, 1881, p. 1. A year later the *Chronicle* again mentioned "a technicality which makes it no offense to loan one's [smoking] layout to a friend," with the result that only "the large dens have been shut up." "Literature: Dr. Kane's 'Opium-Smoking in America and China,'" ibid., Feb. 5, 1882, p. 6.

Indeed, on visiting several dens, the reporter found no more than five Chinese smokers in each—few enough for a private party. And the reporter, a white man, couldn't buy a smoke anywhere. Though admitted to the dens, he found that "[t]he privilege of smoking is a much more difficult thing to obtain."[46] He saw no need to explain what his would-be Chinese hosts so clearly understood—that no court would believe a Chinese denkeeper who claimed his white guest was a friend.

If the reporter had in mind particular court rulings, I have not found them. Six years later, however, the California Supreme Court implied without holding that certain private vices were past the public's power to ban. On reviewing Stockton's anti-den ordinance, the court balked at section three, which made it a crime for "two or more persons to assemble, be, or remain in any room or place for the purpose of smoking opium." Stripped of a public or commercial context, the justices suggested, simple smoking was no crime. "To prohibit vice is not ordinarily considered within the police power of the state. . . . The object of the police power is to protect rights from the assaults of others, not to banish sin from the world or to make men moral." Or as Justice Paterson wrote in a concurring opinion, "Every man has the right to eat, drink, and smoke what he pleases in his own house without police interference . . . ."[47] Because the court decided the case on other grounds, the justices' words lacked the force of law. But such sentiments, if prevailing generally in California courtrooms, could explain how Chinese smokers in Chinese dens slipped beneath the legal radar. For Chinese smokers could claim they were sharing a friendly pipe among countrymen.

Lessons of Whites-Focused Policing

We need not discern with certainty why Western whites so often tolerated dens kept by and for their Chinese neighbors. For the critical question is not why early Western lawmakers opened a window of tolerance for opium smoking by the Chinese. It is instead why they enforced those laws so stringently *against whites*.

That is, *these were laws about whites*. Several modern historians have suggested early anti-den laws arose as defenses against the Chinese community. Dean Latimer and Jeff Goldberg claimed San Francisco's first-in-the-nation den ban aimed to neuter the threat Chinese laborers posed to working whites. The city suppressed opium smoking, they said, "because it was believed that the drug

---

[46] "The Force of Silence," p. 1.

[47] *In the Matter of Sic, on Habeas Corpus*, 73 Cal. 142, 145 (1887); ibid. at 150 (Paterson, J., concurring). *See also* "Chief Crowley on Opium," *San Francisco Call*, Aug. 3, 1895, p. 14(quoting San Francisco Police Chief Phillip Crowley: "A man has as much right to smoke opium in his home as tobacco.").

stimulated coolies into working harder than non-smoking whites." Taking a slightly different tack, John Kaplan wrote that in banning opium dens, authorities aimed to "deprive the Chinese of this drug in the United States and so cause their return to China."[48]

Both these claims founder in the face of whites-focused enforcement. Far from denying "coolie" laborers their power drug or Chinese addicts their fix, police in San Francisco and other Western cities winked at those dens that served only Chinese smokers and cracked down mainly when whites indulged. Idaho's whites-only anti-den law was wholly powerless to act as Latimer and Goldberg and Kaplan alleged.

It's true some advocates of opium bans believed denying the Chinese their drug would drive them away. One California congressman expressed this view in promoting a ban on opium imports in 1884. But in commenting favorably on what was known as the Miller bill, the *Chronicle* stressed the ban's likely impact on whites. "The bill has two objects in view: First, to put a stop, or at least a severe check, to the use of opium by our own people, which has of late become a crying evil in many American cities, where opium dens are multiplying as fashionable resorts of males and females; and second, to cut off the supplies of the Chinese residents to whom nearly all such shipments are consigned . . . ." Only then did the *Chronicle* add that with opium imports banned, Chinese "consumers will be forced to quit the use of the drug or to quit the country, and most of them will prefer the alternative. At least that is the theory of the Miller bill." Yet the Miller bill never passed. And even after the federal government first constrained opium imports in 1887, opium did not disappear from the dens of San Francisco and other Western jurisdictions.[49]

Commenting in the same spirit as Latimer and Goldberg and Kaplan, Markus Dubber has charged that Oregon's 1887 law banning opium dens and personal

---

[48]   Dean Latimer & Jeff Goldberg, *Flowers in the Blood: The Story of Opium* (New York: F. Watts, 1981), p. 208; John Kaplan, "A Primer on Heroin," *Stanford Law Review*, vol. 27 (1975), pp. 801, 804. Kaplan also anticipated the point made by Latimer and Goldberg: "A parallel hope was that insofar as opium provided the Chinese with their energy and ability to tolerate hardship . . . its prohibition would deprive the aliens of an unfair advantage over American workmen." Ibid. Steven Duke and Albert Gross more recently repeated the claim. *See* Steven B. Duke & Albert C. Gross, *America's Longest War: Rethinking Our Tragic Crusade Against Drugs* (New York: G.P. Putnam's Sons, 1993), p. 59.

[49]   "National Topics," *San Francisco Chronicle*, Mar. 18, 1884, p. 5 (paraphrasing Representative Budd: "[T]he cessation of the importation of the drug would cause a large exodus of" the Chinese); "National Topics," ibid., Mar. 27, 1884, p. 3 (noting Senator Miller's role in promoting the bill to ban opium imports by Chinese nationals); "Miller's Opium Bill," ibid., Mar. 28, 1884, p. 2; "An Act to Provide for the Execution of the Provisions of . . . the Treaty Concluded between the United States . . . and . . . China . . . ," 24 Stat. 409, ch. 210, §§ 1, 3 (Act of Feb. 23, 1887), pp. 409–10 (forbidding Chinese citizens to import opium into the United States and barring U.S. citizens from importing opium into China or trading in opium there). *See also* C.W. Stoddard, "New China," *San Francisco Chronicle*, Mar. 30, 1879, p. 1 ("Cut off the opium supplies and the Chinese will either go of necessity or they will rise against us with the ferocity of famishing beasts . . . .").

opium possession "amounted to an all out war on the Chinese and opium." The aim, he says, was to "extinguish[] them as potential sources of threats . . . by subjecting them to intensive police control . . . ." Dubber points to a notably frank allegation by U.S. District Judge Matthew P. Deady, who reviewed (and ultimately upheld) a conviction under Oregon's original anti-den law of November 1885. Writing less than a year into the law's tenure, Judge Deady noted that "until lately" opium-based intoxication "has been unknown in the United States, and is now chiefly confined to the Chinese." Because "[s]moking opium is not *our* vice," he reasoned, "it may be that this legislation proceeds more from a desire to vex and annoy the 'Heathen Chinee' in this respect, than to protect the people from the evil habit."[50]

But the very case in which Deady sat belied his reasoning. For though the defendant, Yung Jon, was Chinese, he stood accused of selling opium to one B. F. Caldwell. The case report tells us nothing about Caldwell, but the name hardly sounds Chinese. And as Yung Jon was prosecuted in Baker County, where the 1880 Census counted only eight African American residents in a county numbering 4,616, the odds are strong Caldwell was white.[51] So it seems plausible Oregon's legislators, like lawmakers in San Francisco, Virginia City, and cities and states across the West, banned opium dens because they saw *whites* resorting to them.

An 1877 editorial comment in the *Portland Standard* suggests as much. The paper complained that Portland's five or six opium dens were "patronized almost exclusively by young men and boys between the ages of fifteen and twenty-five years. Why the authorities do not take some means to arrest this evil is a query that we are unable to answer." The nature of the evil was long familiar: The dens "are filled with those who have acquired an uncontrollable appetite for this narcotic. Last evening two boys were borne home by their friends in a state of complete stupefaction . . . . This morning they were unable to attend to business . . . ." Though the *Standard* said nothing about the race of the "boys," the tone of the report, lacking the usual anti-Chinese slurs, suggests they were white.[52]

Whatever the reasons for Deady's accusation, policing practices seen across the West hardly suggest vexing the hated Chinese was a motive in banning the dens. Whites-focused policing sapped whatever power anti-den laws might

---

[50] Markus Dirk Dubber, "Policing Possession: The War on Crime and the End of Criminal Law," *Journal of Criminal Law and Criminology*, vol. 91 (2001), pp. 829, 951; *Ex Parte Yung Jon*, 28 F. 308, 311, 312 (1886) (emphasis added); "An Act to Regulate the Sale of Opium, and to Suppress Opium Dens," 1885 *Oregon Laws* (Spec. Sess.) (Act of Nov. 25, 1885), pp. 39–40.

[51] In Oregon as a whole, African Americans made up 0.28 percent of the population in 1880 and 0.37 percent in 1890. *See* U.S. Census of Population and Housing, "Historical Census Browser" (University of Virginia Library). I thank Sara Mayeux, who pointed me to the Baker County population figures.

[52] "Opium Smoking in Portland," *St. Louis Globe-Democrat*, Feb. 8, 1877, p. 10 (repeating a *Portland Standard* account).

have had in harassing Chinese immigrants or driving them away. Still, one form of racism undeniably infused whites-focused policing and its narrow concern for white morals: tolerance of Chinese-only dens revealed white indifference to Chinese morals. "Never mind John," wrote the editor of the Virginia City *Territorial Enterprise. "Let him smoke his brains out if he likes it . . . ."*[53] Perhaps such indifference stemmed from the expected departure of the visiting Chinese or an unwillingness to bear the cost of jailing them. More likely it grew from something more deeply fundamental—a tendency of groups to guard most closely the morals of their own kind and to disregard the morals of others.

Over and over, from parts near and far, came similar reports—wherever whites and especially respectable whites and especially white women and youth were found in opium dens, local authorities sprang to action. Hence in Salt Lake City in 1878, "a prominent citizen found his son and forty other boys in a Chinese opium den, and . . . complained of the nuisance to the City Council, which appointed a Committee to investigate and suppress such dens." After residents of Bodie, Nevada, learned in 1879 that they could "at last boast of several opium dens, which have become resorts for many of our young people," the *Bodie News* declared "some law should be enacted to check the evil if possible." In June 1880, a New Orleans grand jury "visited the Chinese dens . . . where white persons, male and female, assemble to smoke opium. A special report will be made directing the attention of the city authorities to this evil." That month the *Idaho City World* warned of a new "Chinese den in this city where men and women congregate to smoke opium." The patrons were mainly newcomers to town, "but there is danger at all times of our youth being enticed into the vile practice and ruined. In all the towns of the coast where these dens are opened, the authorities immediately break them up." And in 1881 in Alameda, California, a speaker appearing "before the Board of Alameda said he knew of at least twenty young men of that town addicted to the habit of opium smoking. An ordinance," we are told, "is to be drafted on the subject."[54]

Here is racism, but *not* the racism of spiting groups we despise by banning their drugs. This was the racism of protecting one's own while malignly neglecting others. Still, modern historians mount two *other* charges of racism rooted in racial hatred and arguably supported by whites-focused enforcement. These allegations—miscegenation panic and fear of racial contagion—prove largely unfounded but demand scrutiny.

[53] "Opium-Smoking," [Virginia City] *Territorial Enterprise*, Sept. 15, 1876, p. 2 (emphasis added).

[54] "Not Guilty," *San Francisco Chronicle*, Oct. 17, 1878, p. 3; "Opium Dens in Bodie," *San Francisco Chronicle*, Mar. 24, 1879, p. 3; "Opium Smoking," *San Francisco Chronicle*, June 1, 1879, p. 3 (reprinting item from the *Bodie Standard*); "Opium Smoking in New-Orleans," *New York Tribune*, June 20, 1880, p. 7; "Opium-Smoking in Idaho," *San Francisco Chronicle*, June 28, 1880, p. 4 (reprinting item from the *Idaho City World*); "Coast Notes," *San Francisco Chronicle*, Jan. 17, 1881, p. 1.

The Specter of Miscegenation

It's easy to cobble a case that miscegenation panic drove whites to ban the dens. Visions of opium dens haunted readers with the risk of racial mixing. A San Francisco policeman told in 1876 of finding "white women and Chinamen side by side under the effects of this drug—a humiliating sight to any one with anything left of manhood." In Carson City, Nevada, a den visitor reported in 1881 that "[a]ll pretense to decency is thrown aside; often [the smoker] lies in his sensual stupor side by side with Chinamen and creatures, male and female . . . ." And across the country, a *New York Times* reporter came upon a "squalidly dressed young white girl" when touring a Chinese clubhouse in 1873. She was "lying upon a bed, apparently stupid from the opium fumes that filled the room." Asked about the girl, the Chinese tour guide "replied with a horrible leer, 'Oh, hard time in New-York; young girl hungry. . . . Chinamen always [have] something to eat, and he like young white girl! He! he!' "[55]

That creepy "He! he!" no doubt revolted "any one with anything left of manhood"—and understandably might have spurred lawmakers to cast corrective legislation. And this 1873 *Times* article followed another, of 1871. On an earlier excursion to the dens, the author found two or three white women, longtime opium addicts, who had taken to life and even motherhood below ground. "Everywhere a mixed throng of men and women—the women, nearly always white—the men Chinese."[56]

Embracing such evidence, several drug-war historians have traced early anti-den laws to fear of miscegenation. For David Musto, the concern that opium "facilitated sexual contact between Chinese and white Americans" advanced his general thesis that "[t]he most passionate support for legal prohibition of narcotics has been associated with fear of a given drug's effect on a specific minority." James Morone links early anti-den laws to the worry that "Chinese men used the drug to enslave 'white girls, hardly grown to womanhood.' A whole genre of lurid exposés," he says, "touted the Chinese danger to our innocent white daughters." And David Courtwright points to common reports "that some shameless smokers persuaded 'innocent girls to smoke in order to excite their passions and effect their ruin.' Fear of miscegenation made such a spectacle all the more shocking." Hence one of the "real motives" behind occasional police crackdowns on whites' use of Chinese dens, Courtwright says, was "revulsion

---

[55] California State Senate, *Chinese Immigration*, p. 217 (quoting 1876 report of San Francisco Police Officer James R. Rogers); "Topics in the Sagebrush," *New York Times*, Feb. 21, 1881, p. 1 (printing correspondence from Carson City); "Chinese in New-York," ibid., Dec. 26, 1873, p. 3.

[56] "Isaac Idler's Rambles, No. III: Round about Donovan's Lane," *New York Times*, Jan. 22, 1871, p. 5. Despite the expert assistance of Sonia Moss, I've not discovered Isaac Idler's identity. The *Times* apparently never disclosed the author's true name.

against miscegenation—the racial stereotype was of a fiendish, long-fingernailed Chinese man preying upon a wayward, narcotized young beauty . . . ."[57]

Yet fear of racial mixing seemingly played little or no role in the rise of early anti-den laws. Fear of *sex*, it's true, particularly sex among youth, helped fuel passage of these laws. But we shouldn't mix sex with racial mixing.

Consider first David Courtwright's claim: "It was commonly reported that . . . some shameless smokers persuaded 'innocent girls to smoke in order to excite their passions and effect their ruin.' " Courtwright drew the quote from Harry Hubbell Kane's 1882 landmark, *Opium-Smoking in America and China*. Read alone, Kane's reference to seduction in the dens permits Courtwright's comment that "[f]ear of miscegenation made such a spectacle all the more shocking." But some forty pages later, Kane returned to the matter of seduction long enough to clarify the villains he had in mind. As we've seen, he attributed newly enacted laws against opium-smoking to "the fact that male smokers (Americans) . . . were continually beguiling women and young girls to try the pipe, and effected their ruin . . . ." Though Kane's was perhaps the most cited drug text of the day, neither Courtwright nor it seems any other modern author quotes his reference to "(Americans)."[58]

Kane's reference wasn't thoughtless. In another 1882 publication, Kane noted that smoking opium produced "a marked increase in the sexual appetite and power; most marked in women. This sometimes approaches to frenzy, the woman losing all modesty." Again he linked the drug's aphrodisiac power with its ban: "Recognizing this fact, rascals have enticed young girls to these places to smoke and have then succeeded in ruining them. It was chiefly the recognition of this fact that led to the passage of stringent laws against the practice in California [and] Nevada . . . ." *Rascals* was not code for Chinese. It was in this era a term that disapproving elders often applied to delinquent young men, almost always of their own race. Hence within days of the publisher's announcement of Kane's book, the *New York Times* printed an account of a white sixteen-year-old,

---

[57] David F. Musto, *American Disease: Origins of Narcotic Control* (New York: Oxford University Press, 3d ed. 1999), pp. 294–95; James A. Morone, *Hellfire Nation: The Politics of Sin in American History* (New Haven: Yale University Press, 2003), p. 465; Courtwright, *Dark Paradise*, p. 78 (quoting Kane, *Opium-Smoking in America and China*, p. 93) ("innocent girls to smoke . . ."); Courtwright, "Drug Laws and Drug Use," pp. 123–24 ("real motives" and "revulsion against miscegenation . . ."). *See also* Michael M. Cohen, "Race, Coca Cola, and the Southern Origins of Drug Prohibition," *Southern Cultures*, vol. 12, no. 3 (2006), pp. 55, 56 ("The nation's first drug laws had appeared in San Francisco in the 1870s, unsuccessfully prohibiting whites from patronizing opium dens in Chinatown lest some white woman should fall into the hands of the yellow peril").

[58] Courtwright, *Dark Paradise*, p. 78; Kane, *Opium-Smoking in America and China*, pp. 93, 131–32. My thanks to Shay Elbaum of the Crown Law Library, who helped me confirm the absence of modern references to Kane's "(Americans)."

John McEntee, who had confessed to killing his uncle. McEntee said his uncle "clapped his hands to his chest and cried: 'You little rascal, you have shot me.' "[59]

As Kane suggested, wariness of rascals bent on ruining young white women may have moved the San Francisco Board of Supervisors in November 1875 to write the nation's first anti-den law. Recall the *Chronicle*'s April 1875 article, "Female Opium Smokers: Midnight Meetings to Indulge in the Vice." Several well-to-do women faced no apparent danger from their Chinese den host, an "unappreciative heathen." Instead, their peril lay in the "brace of dissipated-looking bucks in shiny hats" who hovered menacingly as the women smoked themselves senseless. These men were white, it appears, for they conversed in English. An officer who stood watch outside "had counted fifteen female visitors and nearly as many young men. 'They go there to smoke opium,' said the officer, 'and what else I don't know. Most of the women are young, and the men are hoodlums and sports.' " Like *rascals*, the terms *bucks*, *hoodlums*, and *sports* typically applied to wayward young whites, whose elders reserved other epithets for the Chinese. As one California minister called white delinquents in 1877, "European-American hoodlums, 'poor white trash.' "[60]

Recall, too, that the San Francisco supervisors who enacted the nation's first anti-den law voted after hearing a report that concerned not racial mixing, but *racially segregated* dens—those set aside "for the exclusive use of WHITE MEN AND WOMEN." If city supervisors said anything of racial mixing, the *Chronicle* and its cross-town rivals did not report it.[61]

[59] Kane, "Opium Smoking: A New Form of the Opium Habit," p. 112 ("a marked increase . . ."); "A Boy Sentenced for Life," *New York Times*, Jan. 13, 1882, p. 3 (reprinting account from the *Buffalo Express*, which quoted McEntee's confession); "A Noble Woman," *New York Times*, June 5, 1881, p. 12 (branding a man of "highly respectable" family connections "a Rascal"); "A Plausible Rascal," ibid., Apr. 16, 1882, p. 5 (calling an English army colonel a "Rascal"); "An Ungrateful Young Rascal," ibid., Aug. 15, 1882, p. 2 (deeming a thievish "German lad" a "Rascal"). The Kane article was read to (and presumably prepared for) an 1881 meeting of the New York County Medical Society before its 1882 publication in *Gaillard's Medical Journal*. See Kane, "Opium Smoking: A New Form of the Opium Habit," p. 101.

[60] "Female Opium Smokers," *San Francisco Chronicle*, Apr. 25, 1875, p. 5; "Address of Rev. S.V. Blakeslee," in California State Senate, *Chinese Immigration*, pp. 241, 249. A California legislative report of 1875 and several other contemporary authorities applied the term *hoodlums* to shiftless young whites. See California State Senate, *Chinese Immigration*, p. 53; ibid., p. 117 (testimony of Abram Altemeyer); ibid., p. 196 (testimony of Matthew Karcher); Willard B. Farwell, *The Chinese at Home and Abroad* (San Francisco: A.L. Bancroft & Co., 1885), p. 83 (using *hoodlums* to refer to young white men "who have grown up in idleness, without occupation of any kind, and who, in various ways, prey upon society"); "A New Charge," *New York Times*, May 13, 1883, p. 8 (applying "hoodlums" to a rowdy white crowd) "Frisco's Hoodlum," *Boston Sunday Globe*, Dec. 7, 1890, p. 13 (describing in detail the phenotype of a San Francisco hoodlum, whose "greatest delight is to see the Chinamen dodge quickly out of sight"). In one instance, however, a police witness before the California legislative committee used *hoodlums* to refer to Chinese criminals. See California State Senate, *Chinese Immigration*, p. 182 (testimony of Charles P. O'Neil). And I have come across a reference to "a Chinese hoodlum" in a Sacramento newspaper. "Opium and the Lottery," *Sacramento Daily Record-Union*, Feb. 23, 1876, p. 1.

[61] "The Opium Dens," *San Francisco Chronicle*, Nov. 16, 1875, p. 3.

Miscegenation Silence

Beyond such stark evidence that early lawmakers banned the dens to protect young white women from other *whites*, there seems to be almost no evidence they acted to protect young women from the *Chinese*. Even in trolling broadly among newspapers, tracts, and other documents of the day and in scouring the most likely sources, I have found exactly two clear references before 1883 to seduction of white women or girls by Chinese men in opium dens. I have mentioned both already. The first was the 1871 *New York Times* account of a reporter's visit to a Chinese den in Manhattan where women bore and raised children underground: "Everywhere a mixed throng of men and women—the women, nearly always white—the men Chinese." The second was the 1873 *Times* article, maybe by the same author, telling of the "squalidly dressed young white girl" and her host's chilling boast, "Chinamen always [have] something to eat, and he like young white girl. He! he!" That article also reported "what is far more terrible, a large number of young white girls" living in Chinatown who were "rapidly becoming addicted" to opium smoking. "They live with the Chinese when they can find no other home, for although people of their own race close their doors against them, they are always welcome at the firesides of those to whom they sell their souls for the sustenance of their bodies."[62]

Harrowing as these accounts were, they made no apparent mark on the nation or even New York. Even in a day when newspapers borrowed freely, I have found no mention of either account in other nineteenth-century sources. A broad search of many local and national newspapers and a scouring search of several have turned up no reference to these articles. Even the *New York Times* never mentioned them again. Nor did *any* source I have seen make *any other* clear reference to miscegenation in the dens before 1883, a year after passage of New York State's den ban and more than seven years after San Francisco's anti-den ordinance.[63] That is, these *Times* accounts of 1871 and 1873, perhaps a single author's work, stand alone. They are not the tip of massive miscegenation panic, but islands in a sea of silence. Yet modern historians have cited and recited them for two generations.[64]

---

[62] "Isaac Idler's Rambles, No. III," p. 5; "Chinese in New-York," p. 3.

[63] Both Katie Siler of the Crown Law Library and I searched intensively for references to the *New York Times* accounts of 1871 and 1873 discussed in the text—and found none. In conducting this search—and in hunting generally for references to miscegenation in opium dens—I've read broadly among contemporary and modern studies of early opium dens and scoured reams of microfilmed copies and online reproductions of old newspapers from towns big and small. Together my research assistant Yonatan Arbel and I read over 3,000 news articles printed in papers around the country between 1865 and 1890 that touched on opium dens or miscegenation or mentioned both white women or girls and Chinese persons or used various synonyms of these search terms. I would be happy to supply more details of our search.

[64] "An Act in Relation to the Sale and Use of Opium," 1882 *New York Laws*, ch. 165 (Act of May 15, 1882), p. 205; Ahmad, *The Opium Debate*, p. 33 (quoting the 1873 article); Courtwright, *Dark*

In only one other article before 1883 did the *Times* even approach the topic of miscegenation in the dens—and that article dismissed the very notion that respectable women patronized opium joints. In an 1877 April Fools' Day account mockingly headlined "Wicked Manhattan," the author marveled at the New York bunk bought by distant rubes. "There are very few of us born and bred in the Metropolis who, in our travels East, West, or South, have not been told of things here that we had never heard of." A Kansas innkeeper shared his "extraordinary," "peculiar," and "exceedingly queer" notions of New York City about which "the most observant New-Yorker is profoundly ignorant." Among these were "dens down town where women repair[ed] to smoke opium until they are stupefied with its fumes." The reporter wondered, "How do such absurd stories get into circulation?" The problem was that many correspondents of the out-of-town press were "reckless and deliberately false" and made up "for poverty of style by affluence of fabrication."[65] Yet the delusional innkeeper had suggested only that women smoked opium in New York dens, and surely they did. He never hinted of anything more wicked.

Miscegenation panic never struck New York or it seems any other American town before May 1883. Not till then did the New York press explode with the story that Chinese men were ravishing young white women and girls in opium dens. That tale electrified the city's tabloid press and bolted across the nation. Alarming as it was, however, this episode came too late to help explain passage of many anti-den laws. As Table 4A in Chapter 4 reports, by May 1883 ten states and territories had adopted such laws, as had many cities and towns. What's more, as we'll see, the shocking claims of May 1883 proved as flimsy as they were fleeting, dismissed as fabrications after a weeklong flare.

Between the Chinese denkeeper's leering "He! he!" of December 1873 and the venomous claims of May 1883 lay a decade of silence about miscegenation in the dens. I hope now to document this silence. As proof of silence is never certain, I will proceed methodically and cautiously, dividing the decade into stages. Despite this deliberate method, evidence of miscegenation panic may have eluded me. There is never *affirmative* evidence of silence, and contrary evidence may lurk in corners I failed to explore. Yet several laborious and far-reaching searches of newspapers East and West and of other sources elsewhere have uncovered in the years before 1883 exactly two clear references to cross-racial sex in opium dens—the *Times* articles of 1871 and 1873.

Paradise, p. 78 & n.63 (citing the 1873 article); Constance Backhouse, "The White Women's Labor Laws: Anti-Chinese Racism in Early Twentieth-Century Canada," *Law & History Review*, vol. 14 (1996), pp. 315, 338 n.81 (quoting the 1873 article).

[65] "Wicked Manhattan," Apr. 1, 1877, p. 1.

Had there been fear of miscegenation in the dens, the people and press of San Francisco and other areas of Chinese migration surely would have said so, for whites rarely censored their slander of the Chinese. Still, to assure those who are skeptical that silence has meaning, let me delay documenting that silence long enough to mention louder evidence that miscegenation panic did *not* drive early lawmaking against opium. Here the police and judges of San Francisco spoke loudest, for they enforced the nation's first anti-den law. And they proved eager to arrest and punish both white *men* who visited opium dens and *white men and women* who visited those dens together, though neither circumstance posed a real risk of miscegenation.

Consider the numbers. I mentioned earlier that in the first five years of the den ban, the *San Francisco Chronicle* reported forty arrests of smokers in opium dens.[66] In thirty-four of these cases *all* of the alleged smokers were male—either all white (twenty cases),[67] white and Chinese (eleven cases), or all Chinese (three cases). In five cases, the smokers included both white men and white women.[68] A final case involved four white men together with a white woman and a Chinese man. In *not one case*, then, was a white woman or a group of white women alone in a Chinese den.

Though the *Chronicle* seemed to report police raids big or small, the paper may have highlighted the most sensational cases. Yet any bias toward sensation would have sharpened the focus on cases hinting at miscegenation, and such

---

[66] To isolate these reports, I performed a series of searches for any article containing, for example, the word *opium* or *opium-smoking* together with *den(s)*, *joint(s)*, *place(s)*, *celestial(s)*, *coolie(s)*, *Asiatic(s)*, or any word beginning *Chin*. My classification of these cases as involving whites or Chinese depended largely on names, though many articles identified participants by racial group. The overall case count also depended somewhat on my judgment calls. If an article reported the arrest, say, of an unnamed Chinese denkeeper and if another article, two or three days later, reported the trial or sentencing of an unnamed Chinese denkeeper, I generally concluded the two articles referred to the same case rather than two different cases. Varying circumstances sometimes called for different results. I have retained and would be happy to share my record of these cases and of the searches that uncovered them.

[67] The *Chronicle*'s rushed report of one of these twenty cases allowed initial uncertainty. The article said "Mary Brown, visiting an opium den, and seven Chinamen, for visiting a gambling place, were found guilty." "The Police Court," *San Francisco Chronicle*, May 6, 1880, p. 2. The juxtaposition of Mary Brown with the Chinese gamblers made it seem Mary Brown might have been smoking with the Chinese gamblers. The *Alta California*'s report of the same case, however, altered the facts a bit and made clear no Chinese were involved in Mary Brown's arrest: two officers "raided an opium den, kept on California street by Mary Brown, and arrested the proprietress, John T. O'Brien, James Kelly, William J. Harrison and Matthew Sullivan." "Police News," *Daily Alta California*, May 5, 1880, p. 1.

[68] Again, the *Chronicle*'s report of one of these five cases allowed initial uncertainty. In early December 1875 the paper printed a report of a police raid: "[A] posse of officers raided on several opium dens. At a place on Dupont street, near California, two white women—Fanny Whitmore and Cora Martinez—two men and the two Chinese proprietors were found and arrested." Though the *Chronicle* never said whether the "two men" arrested with the white women and the Chinese proprietors were white or Chinese, the *Alta California*'s report of the same arrest was clear: "[A] posse of police . . . made a descent on the [den] . . . and arrested Fannie Whitmore, Cora Martinez, James Dennison, Charles Anderson, and two Chinamen who kept the place." "Police Matters," *San Francisco Chronicle*, Dec. 7, 1875, p. 1; "Raid on Opium Dens," *Daily Alta California*, Dec. 6, 1875, p. 1.

cases never appeared. Not one reported case presented a real risk of cross-racial sex. These forty cases therefore supply a useful backdrop to a decade of miscegenation silence, which I now aim to trace.

Miscegenation Silence: 1873 to 1877

We begin in San Francisco in the first several years of this silent decade. Here I draw from a search of the *San Francisco Chronicle* that swept in over a thousand possibly relevant articles between 1865 and 1885, uncovering *no* mention of cross-racial sex in the dens before 1883.[69] Less complete searches of other area newspapers likewise turned up no such reference. I gave special scrutiny to three broad indictments of the Chinese in California that appeared in the years surrounding San Francisco's 1875 anti-den law. These, too, while itemizing long lists of grievances against the Chinese, said nothing of cross-racial sex in the dens.

The first such indictment appeared in September 1873. In an article titled "The Chinese in California," *Chronicle* editors aired their grievances with the city's unwanted guests. First was the guests' stubborn refusal to assimilate with whites. Chinese immigrants lived apart and played apart, ate their own foods, and worshipped their own gods. Second was their assault on white labor. Crowded together in downtown warrens, they could subsist on lower wages, stranding unskilled whites without work. In their morals, too, the Chinese were deemed a nasty lot. They were "more treacherous and artful" than other peoples and had noisier and more barbarous amusements. "In the indulgence of their grosser appetites they are indescribably bestial." Little wonder they loaded prisons with criminals and asylums with the demented and insane.

Yet none of these alleged indiscretions—and the list went on—hinted at miscegenation in opium dens or elsewhere. "Their vices corrupt our youth," the *Chronicle* charged, but said nothing of which vices—gambling or opium or sex— or which youth—boys or girls. The *Chronicle* complained that Chinese skill at laundering and housekeeping robbed white women of honest work and drove them to whoredom. But even here, when speaking of Chinese morals and white women's vulnerability, the editors said not a word of opium, opium dens, or Chinese sex with whites.[70]

The next multicount indictment of the Chinese, dated April 1876, appeared in the *Chronicle* less than five months after San Francisco's anti-den law took force. It bore a promising title: "The Moral Side of the Chinese Question." The editors focused on those evils that threatened "the entire system of morals held by the

---

[69] I describe the broader search of which this search is a part in note 63.
[70] "The Chinese in California," *San Francisco Chronicle*, Sept. 18, 1873, p. 2.

Anglo-Saxon race." Here, if anywhere, we would expect to see complaints of sexual mixing in opium dens. Instead we learn that "[n]ineteen-twentieths of the Chinese women in this city are prostitutes," and "[g]ambling is a universal passion." We learn the Chinese "have no religion," "no belief in future punishment or accountability beyond the grave," and "no system of morality that forbids lying, theft, murder or any of those other offenses which we call crimes." Yet amid all this "pollution and demoralization," this "pagan rottenness and uncleanness," the editors made but the barest mention of opium dens and one vague reference to the "vilest forms of moral debasement." They suggested no link between the dens and these "forms of moral debasement" and offered no detail about den patrons, whether men or women, young or old, white or Chinese, or about the forms of "moral debasement." Beyond alleging Chinese women were mainly prostitutes, they said nothing of sex.[71]

The last of the three indictments, styled "The Case Against John" and printed in June 1876, took the form of a memo to the Senate Foreign Relations Committee from three San Francisco commissioners. It explained why "all classes of society unite in the opinion that Chinese emigration" threatens "danger to our material interests and destruction to our civilization." Beyond familiar charges of isolation in low-cost housing and of low-cost labor that denied white boys their trades and left white women no way to "lead lives of virtuous independence," the commissioners added a raft of sanitary and security and moral complaints. Chinatown was a "cesspool of . . . poverty, misery, squalor, filth and disease," where "ten thousand criminals hide and plot" and "two thousand prostitutes ply their vocation." Their "syphilitic diseases are horrible," and "leprosy, the most terrible of all contagions, is not unknown among them." Reaching for rougher rhetoric than earlier broadsides, the memo charged that "a seething mass" of Chinese "rats . . . ply their games of tan and lotteries" and "stupefy themselves upon opium" and "practice their unnatural debaucheries in defiance of all laws of morality and decency. . . . Young [Chinese] girls are purchased from their parents, imported to our coast and indentured to a life of infamy." Yet amid all this crime and filth, "in[n]oculating our population with the perfected vices of four thousand years of paganism," not a word appears of sex in the dens or of sex with whites.[72]

Time and again the people and press of San Francisco delivered a bill of grievances against their Chinese guests, yet never in the broad scope of my search did they complain of cross-racial sex in the dens. Nor were they too demure to speak of sex when sex was on their minds. For in the next general indictment of

[71] "The Moral Side of the Chinese Question," *San Francisco Chronicle*, Apr. 3, 1876, p. 2.

[72] "The Case against John," *San Francisco Chronicle*, June 16, 1876, p. 3. In an editorial printed the same day, the *Chronicle* endorsed the commissioners' memo. See "The Case Fairly Stated," *San Francisco Chronicle*, June 16, 1876, p. 2.

the visiting Chinese, by far the longest and most detailed, cross-racial sex came up frankly and often, but in an entirely different context with a very different import.

Miscegenation Silence: The 1877 California Senate Report

An 1877 report by the California Senate's Special Committee on Chinese Immigration was noisy with racism yet strangely silent about miscegenation. Appointed early in 1876, the committee aimed to persuade Congress and the American people of the need "to turn back this tide [of Chinese immigration] and to free the land from what is a monstrous evil."[73] To its fifty-page "Address to the People of the United States upon the Evils of Chinese Immigration" the committee appended 160 pages of testimony collected at hearings in Sacramento and San Francisco in the spring of 1876, when San Francisco's den ban was just months old, and 100 pages of statistics, speeches, papers, and comments on "the Chinese question."

At the 1876 hearings a train of witnesses detailed the alleged faults of the unwelcome Chinese: their filthy and hive-like living quarters; their lying and thievish ways; their willingness to work for a pittance, which stranded white boys in idleness, spawning "a class commonly known as 'hoodlums,'" and drove jobless white women "to the last resort."[74] And for every young white woman forced by cheap Chinese labor to sell her body there were many Chinese women imported for precisely that purpose. These women prompted the only clear references to miscegenation in the committee's entire book-length report.

Such references concerned not white women and Chinese men but Chinese women and white boys—and not opium dens but brothels. Witness upon witness complained of Chinese prostitutes eager to service American boys, scarring them with syphilitic tokens of their sins. Prompted by rapt questions from committee members, a dozen or more witnesses bid down the ages at which white boys succumbed to the charms and cheap sex of Chinese brothels. One witness

---

[73] California State Senate, *Chinese Immigration*, p. 4.

[74] On Chinatown's filth, *see, e.g.,* ibid., p. 178 (testimony of Chief Ellis); ibid., p. 207 (Officer Jackson). On the crowded living quarters of the Chinese, *see, e.g.,* ibid., pp. 258–59 (Mr. Boalt); ibid., p. 296 (Mr. Meade). On the alleged mendacity of the Chinese, *see, e.g.,* ibid., p. 183 (Deputy O'Neil); ibid., p. 189 (District Attorney Jones). On their alleged thievishness, *see, e.g.,*: ibid., p. 113 (Officer Duffield); ibid., p. 147 (District Attorney Murphy). On their frugality and low wage demands, *see, e.g.,* ibid., p. 142 (Captain Joy); ibid., pp. 190–91 (expressman Duffy). On the impact of joblessness on white boys, *see* ibid., p. 53 (Special Committee on Chinese Immigration, "An Address to the People of the United States upon the Evils of Chinese Immigration") ("a class commonly known as 'hoodlums'"); ibid., p. 117 (shoe manufacturer Altemeyer). On the impact of joblessness on young white women, *see, e.g.,* ibid., p. 195 (testimony of ex-Chief Karcher); ibid., p. 216 (Officer Rogers) ("to the last resort").

put them at "fifteen, sixteen, seventeen, and eighteen years of age"—another "as young as thirteen, with gonorrhœa" and "all sorts of venereal diseases." A police officer reported lads aged twelve or fourteen "fairly crippled" from disease, "hardly able to put one foot before the other." An expressman "saw a woman entice a boy of about eleven years of age into her house." A doctor reported "boys eight and ten years old with diseases they told me they contracted on Jackson Street. It is astonishing," he said, "how soon they commence indulging in that passion." Astonishing, perhaps, but not enough to win this perverse bidding war. That honor went to Presbyterian minister S. V. Blakeslee, who said Sacramento police had told him they'd "taken boys under eight years of age, and of respectable, wealthy families, from the occupied couches of Chinese creatures."[75]

All this concern for the health and morals of young white boys stood apart from the matter of opium dens. Neither the committee nor its witnesses suggested a link between the dens and liaisons of white boys with Chinese prostitutes. The prostitutes did not use opium to tempt the boys but more practical allurements, for unlike white prostitutes, they offered sex at prices the boys could afford. "Chinese women charge only two and four bits," one witness reported, "and as a rule these boys have not much money." And unlike white women, who balked at preteen patrons, the Chinese prostitutes "do not care how old the boys are, whether five years old or more, as long as they have money."[76]

Having spoken so bitterly and often of the Chinese threat to white boys' virtue, the committee and its witnesses surely would have condemned miscegenation in the dens had any such thing caught their eye. They surely denounced *the dens*, particularly those patronized by whites. "In almost every house is found a room devoted to opium smoking," the committee complained, "and these places are visited by white boys and women, so that the deadly habit is being introduced among our people."[77]

But in this entire volume of some 330 pages, printed within three years of the San Francisco supervisors' 1875 den ban and presenting testimony collected within months of the supervisors' action, there is at most a single, uncertain reference to cross-racial sex in the dens. We have seen it already. Deep in the volume, the committee reprinted an 1876 report by San Francisco Police Detective James Rogers. It was Rogers whose visits to San Francisco's dens in autumn 1875, as

---

[75] Ibid., p. 146 (Officer Supple) ("fairly crippled . . ." and "hardly able . . ."); ibid., p. 168 (Dr. Toland) ("boys eight and ten . . ."); ibid., p. 174 (testimony of jailkeeper Bovee) ("fifteen, sixteen . . ."); ibid., p. 178 (industrial school superintendent Woods) ("as young as thirteen . . ." and "all sorts of . . ."); ibid., p. 190 (expressman Duffy) ("saw a woman . . ."); ibid., p. 245 (Rev. Blakeslee) ("taken boys under eight . . .").

[76] Ibid., p. 169 (testimony of Dr. Toland) ("do not care . . ."); ibid., p. 174 (testimony of jailkeeper Bovee) ("and as a rule . . .").

[77] Ibid., p. 35 (committee report). *See also* ibid., p. 114 (Officer Duffield) (mentioning two Chinese dens frequented by whites); ibid., p. 183 (Deputy O'Neil) ("There are three or four places w[h]ere white women went to smoke . . . .").

reported in the *Alta California*, perhaps helped spur the supervisors' decision weeks later to ban the dens. Now again Rogers wrote of young white men and women visiting the dens. Toward the end of his two-page report to the senate committee, he devoted a single paragraph to the topic of "OPIUM SMOKING." There were places, he said, "where parties smoke until insensible, then sleep off the deadly effects. While this was practiced among the Chinese alone, no particular attention was given the subject, but very recently not less than eight places have been started" that are "conducted by Chinamen, and patronized by both white men and women, who visited these dens at all hours of the day and night . . . ." Because of these eight dens, "the habit and its deadly results [became] so extensive as to call for action on the part of the authorities, and an ordinance was passed" to break them up.[78]

These probably were the same dens that had prompted the San Francisco supervisors to pass their 1875 ban. The supervisors had cited "eight opium-smoking establishments kept by Chinese, for the exclusive use of WHITE MEN AND WOMEN." To the familiar account of these dens, Rogers's 1876 report now added a single sentence: "The Department of Police, in enforcing the [1875] law with regard to this matter, have found white women and Chinamen side by side under the effects of this drug—a humiliating sight to any one who has anything left of manhood."[79] Then Rogers moved on to "THE PRACTICE OF GAMBLING" and said nothing more of the dens.

"*[A] humiliating sight to any one who has anything left of manhood.*" Those twelve words, seen in isolation, surely seem to hint at cross-racial sex in the dens, and several modern scholars have read them that way.[80] Seen in context, however, right after Rogers complained of dens "patronized by both white men and women," they carry murkier meaning. Sadly, Rogers offered no clarification. His treatment of the topic ended there, after a single paragraph. Neither elsewhere in his 1876 report nor in his two appearances before the committee did he mention either opium dens or cross-racial sex with white girls or women. Nor did the committee or any other witness mention Rogers's "manhood" remark or racial mixing in the dens. Nor did the *San Francisco Chronicle*, which I have scoured for any sign of this remark, nor did any other newspaper or popular contemporary source I have seen. It seems Rogers's words appear in only one other

---

[78] California State Senate, *Chinese Immigration*, p. 217 (report of Officer Rogers); "An Opium Den," *Daily Alta California*, Oct. 1, 1875, p. 1 (recounting Officer Rogers's visit to the dens); "Raid on Opium Dens," ibid., Oct. 30, 1875, p. 1 (similar).

[79] "The Opium Dens," *San Francisco Chronicle*, Nov. 16, 1875, p. 3; California State Senate, *Chinese Immigration*, p. 217 (report of Officer Rogers).

[80] *See, e.g.*, Duke & Gross, *America's Longest War*, p. 83; Robert M. Hardaway: *No Price Too High: Victimless Crimes and the Ninth Amendment* (Westport, Conn.: Praeger, 2003), p. 89; Catherine Lee, *Fictive Kinship: Family Reunification and the Meaning of Race and Nation in American Immigration*, pp. 55–56 (New York: Russell Sage Foundation, 2013); Erik Grant Luna, "Our Vietnam: The Prohibition Apocalypse," *DePaul Law Review*, vol. 46 (1997), pp. 483, 493.

nineteenth-century source: a five-volume set of U.S. Senate committee reports that reprinted his report as an appendix toward the back of volume three.[81]

Around this time another tale of miscegenation, but not miscegenation in the dens, emerged farther east. Published in Buffalo in 1880, Mary Mathews's memoir of life in the West, *Ten Years in Nevada*, went seemingly unnoticed in her time—I have searched broadly but in vain for even the briefest reference to the book in the day's press. Yet Mathews has won the eye of modern historians with her vitriolic attacks on the Chinese. Like the California Senate's report, Mathews's account of Chinese depravity focused on the very young. Memorably, she warned white parents, "Our little daughters are not safe under the same roof with them, as Virginia City, Gold Hill, Carson City, San Francisco, Sacramento, and other places on the Coast can testify to." Mathews presumably meant this warning for those whites who employed Chinese men as household servants, for the victims she had in mind were "little children, all the way from four to twelve years of age—mere babes ruined for life."[82]

Despite a fertile imagination uncensored by truth and a zest for slandering the Chinese, Mathews never dared suggest that girls aged four to twelve somehow strayed into Chinese opium dens. She condemned the dens, but aimed her concern at older girls and at the white boys who went with them. "Not only men and women visit the opium dens," she wrote, "but I am informed, by good authority, that girls and boys visit them, and often have to be helped home by their companions. Girls and boys, from twelve to twenty, are daily being ruined by this opium smoking." What worried Mathews was not miscegenation in the dens, therefore, but what young whites did there—"they lie on bunks around the table and smoke till they become unconscious."[83] That is, she worried about the same stupefaction and perhaps white-on-white seduction we have seen before.

[81] *Reports of Committees of the Senate of the United States* (44th Cong., 2d Sess.) (Washington: Government Printing Office, 1877), vol. 3, p. 1169 (app. E). My thanks to Katie Siler, who searched for other appearances of Rogers's words and uncovered this Senate publication.

[82] M[ary] M[cNair] Mathews, *Ten Years in Nevada: Or, Life on the Pacific Coast* (Buffalo: Baker, Jones & Co., 1880) (reprint University of Nebraska Press, 1985), p. 257. Again I thank Katie Siler, who searched in vain for evidence anyone read or spoke of Mathews's book in her time. Ms. Siler found but one trace of the book: its listing amid the vast holdings of the California State Library. *See* Talbot H. Wallis, *Catalogue of the California State Library (General Dept.)* (Sacramento: State Office, 1889), p. 685.

[83] Mathews, *Ten Years in Nevada*, p. 259. On Mathews's loose regard for the truth, the authors of the foreword to a reprinted edition of her book write that "factual accuracy is not always [the book's] strong point. Its author includes much that is hearsay and unsubstantiated." Mary Lee Spence & Clark C. Spence, "Foreword," *in* ibid., p. 4.

Miscegenation Silence: 1882 Rallies against the Chinese

One last episode of miscegenation silence rounds out our study of this silent decade. In early March 1882, in cities and towns throughout California, crowds gathered to shout their support of what would become the Chinese Exclusion Act of 1882. In force in slightly altering forms till 1943, the act closed the country to incoming Chinese laborers and miners and barred unnaturalized Chinese residents from citizenship. A day after the March 4 rallies boosting the act's passage, the *San Francisco Chronicle* pronounced the assembled throngs "OF ONE MIND." The subheadings were blunt: "No Coolie Laborers Wanted"; "The People Say So, and Mean It."[84]

Two full pages of newsprint repeated the words of some three dozen speakers, each aiming to persuade Eastern senators of the grave threat Chinese labor posed in the West to white workers, white peace, and white morals. To swell the crowds, the governor had declared the day a legal holiday, freeing workers to turn out. Armies of fervent believers eager for a crusade stood massed before the speakers' platforms.

Though the threat to white labor was the official theme of the day, some speakers veered from script to denounce Chinese prostitution. Others threatened violence, arguing "[t]here was but one attorney for us to consult, and that was [Judge] Lynch." Still others turned to opium. To the Chinese, they said—that "opium-smoking, pestilence-breeding, famine-stricken race"—we owe "opium and gambling dens, the epidemic of smallpox and all sorts of horrors in our midst." And their opium had reached our youth: "Hundreds of our young men, aye, and of our young women, are being ruined by opium-smoking, the facilities for which are furnished by these loathsome barbarians." Imported "to stupefy the senses and to stimulate debauchery," the drug has littered our streets with "great numbers of the juvenile classes . . . , whose pallid cheeks and sunken eyes proclaim they are the victims of the subtle poison."

To these themes Colonel Philip A. Roach added a few words ambiguous to modern ears: "And what is the result of this vice—the commingling of races? Better to have no commerce with China than maintain it with plague spots in our cities . . . ." Though "commingling of races" sounds sexual today, Roach's nineteenth-century audience most likely heard his words in a social sense. A bit later a different speaker used a similar expression with decidedly nonsexual intent. Colonel George Flourney praised judges and laborers alike for suspending their work to join the March 4 crowds: "I hail it, then, . . . as a pleasure in the

---

[84] "An Act to Execute Certain Treaty Stipulations Relating to Chinese," Pub. L. 47-126, ch. 126, 22 Stat. 58 (Act of May 6, 1882) (repealed 1943); "OF ONE MIND," *San Francisco Chronicle*, Mar. 5, 1882, p. 8.

commingling of all parties and of all creeds . . . ." Yet Roach's reference was the closest any speaker came to hinting of miscegenation in the dens.

The single likely reference in the day's events to cross-racial sex had nothing to do with opium or opium dens. John T. Cutting, chair of the San Francisco Republican committee, complained "that to-day in this city there are factories in which white girls work side by side with these Chinese barbarians . . . . White girls can be found in the cigar factories every day in the week, working

UNDER A CHINESE MASTER,

Forced into association with these people. We, who know something of the habits of the Chinese," Cutting concluded ominously, "know what it means." Yet as oblique as Cutting's words were, it seems no other local speaker came even this close to suggesting Chinese men preyed on young white women.

The lesson of these 1882 rallies extends more broadly. No source I've seen hints that San Franciscans worried about cross-racial sex in opium dens before 1883. Nor has any such complaint turned up in other Western states in the late 1870s and early 1880s, when the first anti-den laws took form. Save for the two *New York Times* accounts of 1871 and 1873, apparently not reprinted elsewhere, the whole matter of miscegenation in the dens went missing till 1883. Even where complaints of threats posed by opium dens to white women's virtue should have been most prominent, they were lacking. Press, public, and politicians repeatedly cataloged Chinese misdeeds without claiming cross-racial seduction in the dens. Not till the startling events of May 1883 did the *Times* and papers across the country sound that alarm.

Origins of New York's 1882 Anti-Den Act

The opium dens scandal that rocked New York City in May 1883 arose in part from the state's 1882 law against opium dens and that law's spotty enforcement. The story of the law's enactment offers one final case of miscegenation silence in the silent decade that ended with the scandal.

A hunt for the law's origins leads us to the appearance in September and October 1881 of two *Harper's Weekly* articles by Dr. Harry Hubbell Kane.[85] The title of both articles, "American Opium-Smokers," declared their theme, repeated in the first article's opening paragraph: "At a low estimate there are in this country, to-day, from three to five thousand Americans, male and female,

---

[85] H.H. Kane, "American Opium-Smokers," *Harper's Weekly* (Sept. 24, 1881), pp. 646–47; H.H. Kane, "American Opium-Smokers" (Part II), ibid. (Oct. 8, 1881), pp. 682–83.

smoking opium once or twice daily, having formed a habit from which they find it impossible to free themselves."

Kane meant this information to shock. Not long before, he said, anyone who had "predicted that in a few years' time the number of white men indulging in this Eastern vice would be counted by the thousands would have been pronounced insane." Not only were whites in great numbers smoking opium, they were doing so all over. "[A]ctors and travelling salesmen . . . have never found a city yet, East or West, where smoking places were not to be found, and where from one to twenty whites, male and female, were smoking." A New Yorker himself, Kane listed "the principal places in this city where opium is smoked," including "one in Twenty-Third Street, which is presided over by a white woman and her two daughters."

Only twice in these articles did Kane refer to sex—once in noting impotence among opium's side effects, once in highlighting the drug's spread among whites: "In San Francisco so great did the evil become, so many women and young girls were led to these opium-houses and taught smoking and other evil practices, that in 1876 [*sic*] it was found necessary to pass a city ordinance . . . ." Though Kane did not specify who "led" white women and girls to San Francisco's dens, all other references in these articles to the dens' female patrons put them in the company of white men. And Kane's *Opium-Smoking in America and China*, which hit bookshelves just three months later, would make clear the male malfeasors were "(Americans)." Most telling, however, was the illustrated "Interior of a New York Opium Den," which *Harper's* ran together with Kane's second article in October 1881 (see Figure 5.1). Eight smokers appear in the engraving together with one Chinese server. A white woman sleeps unmolested alongside several white men, while another, reclining prominently in the foreground with pipe in mouth, lies in the white-armed clutches of her beau.[86]

As his articles hit newsstands, Kane was not yet thirty. A quarter-century later he would die of tuberculosis, disgraced by a fraud conviction and prison sentence after bilking a kidney patient for a "radium cure." But in these heady days of late 1881, riding the success of an earlier book on addictive drugs and his newly published *Harper's* articles, Kane stood among the nation's premier authorities on the opium habit. His disclosure in *Harper's* that whites by the thousand were addicted to smoking opium sparked fretful news accounts nationwide.[87]

---

[86] My thanks to Lisa Goodman, who pointed me to this engraving.

[87] "Radium Cure Swindle Charged to Physicians," *New York Times*, Jan. 24, 1905, p. 1 (noting Kane's age as fifty-one and reporting his arrest on fraud charges); "Dr. H.H. Kane Dead," *New York Times*, July 1, 1906, p. 9; "Opium Smoking," *The Congregationalist* (Boston), Oct. 5, 1881, p. 7 (reprinting an item from the Springfield *Republican*); "An Eastern View of Chinamen," *San Francisco Bulletin*, Oct. 7, 1881, p. 3 (crediting the *Springfield Republican*). Kane's 1881 book appeared under the title *Drugs That Enslave: The Opium, Morphine, Chloral and Hashisch Habits* (Philadelphia: Presley Blakiston, 1881).

Figure 5.1: "Interior of a New York Opium Den" (1881).

In the midst of the hubbub, the *New York Tribune* interviewed Kane. The paper had trained its eye on opium smoking four months before, when a reporter told of a late-night tour of a San Francisco den under the headline, "Slaves to Opium." The reporter warned of the "Spread of the Vice Among Americans": "There are many squalid opium 'dens' in the Chinese quarters, and these have their regular white customers." Worse was the vice's spread among white youth: "The bane of opium-smoking in California is seen in the younger generation. California children are very precocious" and easily lured into Chinese laundries doubling as opium dens. "Young boys learn there to smoke opium and contract the habit which ruins them body and soul." Only boys prompted the reporter's unease. "The Chinese receive boys with great favor, and are always ready to initiate them into any vice." Of girls, the *Tribune* reporter said nothing.[88]

The spread of opium smoking among whites and especially among "respectable and educated people" remained the *Tribune*'s central concern in interviewing Kane, for now it was clear the plague had struck New York. "Have you been investigating at all the extent of opium smoking among white people?" the reporter asked. Kane said he had—and estimated "between four and five

---

[88] "Slaves to Opium," *New York Tribune*, June 19, 1881, p. 7; "The Use of Narcotics," *New York Tribune*, Oct. 16, 1881, p. 2 (presenting Kane interview).

thousand white opium smokers in the United States, and three or four hundred in this city." He said nothing of cross-racial sex. Instead he hinted that the white women who smoked in the dens could take care of themselves: "Among women the habit is almost entirely confined to prostitutes and actresses. There are a few 'society' women who smoke in the better class of opium dens."

Kane perhaps intended this October 1881 interview and his *Harper's* articles to plug his hugely influential *Opium-Smoking in America and China*. Putnam's announced the book's appearance in early January 1882. Within three weeks it had been reviewed in St. Louis and San Francisco and had drawn notice in Chicago. Reviews spotlighted Kane's revelation of widespread white opium addiction and the moral threat to women. Hence the *St. Louis Globe–Democrat* repeated his assessment of "at least 6,000 American smokers," including "many women and young girls, as also young men of respectable family." The *San Francisco Bulletin* worried, "What is worse still, women are taking to the habit. Men and women may be found smoking in the vilest of Chinese dens." Likewise the *New York Times*: "Particularly are women destroyed in mind and morals as well as body by the use of the pipe."[89] Though "the pipe" and respectable "young men" may have threatened women's morals, no review I've seen warned of miscegenation in the dens.

Kane's *Harper's* articles and *Tribune* interview perhaps moved the *New York Sun* to print a November 1881 account of two white women smoking in a Chinese den. The article hinted at sex before disclosing a very different threat to white morals. "A Chinaman and an Irish woman lay in bunks smoking opium in a basement of the rear building at 39 Mott street yesterday," the story began. Later the reporter added, "She was a buxom, merry-eyed, amiable creature, with a row of good teeth . . . ." But she could more than hold her own in a den. She smoked two or three times daily and had at home a "man" and a daughter, for whose benefit she smoked at the den. "When I used to smoke at home my little girl used to know the pipe when I brought it out. She would smack her lips and cry 'Mamma—'moke.'" To the reporter's inquiry if she let her child smoke opium, the woman replied less than firmly, "Oh, God, no; only for a little . . . .'" Another Irish woman at the same den had at home a son. "[W]hen I see the pipe I must smoke," she said. "Even my little boy soon got to like it . . . ."[90]

---

[89] [Classified Advertisement], *The Congregationalist* (Boston), Jan. 11, 1882, p. 5 (Putnam's announcement); "Opium-Smoking," *St. Louis Globe–Democrat*, Jan. 31, 1882, p. 11; "Opium Smoking," *San Francisco Bulletin*, Jan. 24, 1882, p. 2; "Books Received," *The Daily Inter Ocean* (Chicago), Jan. 21, 1882, p. 10; "New Publications: Recent Books," *New York Times*, Mar. 7, 1882, p. 7.

[90] "In a Chinese Opium Den," *New York Sun*, Nov. 21, 1881, p. 3.

The 1882 Act's Passage and Early Enforcement

On February 8, 1882, less than three months after this *Sun* article and a month after Kane's book hit store shelves, New York state senator Joseph Koch introduced the state's first ban on opium dens. An almost word-for-word copy of California's 1881 anti-den law, Koch's bill made it a misdemeanor punishable by up to three months in prison and a fine of $500 to keep an opium den, dispense from one, or visit one to smoke. Though we can't know for sure if Koch acted in response to revelations by Kane and others of white opium smokers in New York City, circumstances point that way. Koch hardly could have missed the ruckus kicked up by Kane's articles and book and the resulting public handwringing. Kane's was a familiar name, and educated New Yorkers of Koch's ilk took note of *Harper's* articles and Putnam's books. Moreover Koch and Kane traveled in the same orbit. Koch's district, a broad swath south of Midtown, stretched within a mile's walk of Kane's West 14th Street clinic. And Koch, a Columbia-educated lawyer and former judge enrolled in the city's best clubs, likely mixed socially with those of Dr. Kane's set.[91]

What is more, Koch acted just two days after the *New York Times* printed some confirmation of Kane's claim of widening white opium use. "A Row in an Opium Den," the *Times* announced on February 6. There followed the tale of "fashionably dressed" Delia Maguire and her weekend arrest for disorderly conduct. Police alleged Maguire had destroyed property in the First Street house of Chin Tin and his white wife after arriving to claim her husband, Barney. He was an opium addict, his wife told the police court judge, and she had gone to Chin Tin's place to take Barney home after hearing he was there smoking. The judge dismissed the case and pronounced Mrs. Maguire justified in her course. "In his opinion," the *Times* wrote, "the opium dens in this City were evils which called loudly for suppression." Elsewhere it's told that "Delia, who is almost as much of a fiend as Barney himself, laughed till she cried when safely beyond the ken of the court . . . ."[92] But Senator Koch perhaps took the judge's comments more gravely.

---

[91]   1882 *New York Senate Journal*, p. 92 (noting Koch's introduction of the bill on February 8, 1882); "An Act in Relation to the Sale and Use of Opium," 1882 *New York Laws*, vol. I, ch. 165 (Act of May 15, 1882), p. 205; "An Act to Amend . . . ," 1881 *California Statutes*, ch. 40 (Act of Mar. 4, 1881), p. 34; Williams, *Demon of the Orient*, p. 130 (telling of Koch's role in sponsoring the New York law); *Manual for the Use of the Legislature of the State of New York* (Albany: Weed, Parsons and Company, 1882), p. 278 (putting Koch's tenth senatorial district between 30th and 40th Streets and between Third and Eighth Avenues); *Frank Leslie's Illustrated Newspaper*, June 9, 1883, p. 258 (printing classified ad for Dr. Kane's treatment of opium and alcohol addiction and stating his address as 46 West 14th Street). On Koch's life, *see Representative Men of New York: A Record of Their Achievements*, vol. 3 (Jay Henry Mowbray ed., New York: The New York Press, 1898), pp. 106–08. I thank Stanford law librarians Sonia Moss, Kate Wilko, and George Wilson for their help in assembling these materials on Koch.
[92]   "A Row in an Opium Den," *New York Times*, Feb. 6, 1882, p. 8; Williams, *Demon of the Orient*, pp. 27–29.

Koch's anti-den bill cakewalked through the legislature, clearing the Senate by a vote of twenty-two to one and the Assembly eighty-eight to one. The act took effect with the governor's signature on May 15, 1882. Some evidence suggests New York authorities at first enforced the ban just as Western authorities had enforced theirs—against dens that sold to whites. In May 1883, the *New York Sun* observed, "So long as it was believed that Chinamen themselves were the only patrons of such dens, the public were little concerned about them." And at least one Chinese denkeeper believed the courts would not molest him if he served only his own countrymen. Hauled into Manhattan police court after an August 1882 arrest, Wing Lee insisted he would go free. Though police had closed his den the night before, he "boasted . . . that it would be kept open 'alle samee,' as it was carried on exclusively for the delectation of Chinese, and no Anglo-Saxons were admitted." By so publicly proclaiming his impunity, however, Wing Lee perhaps assured the law's retribution. A few days later, when one Ah Sing was running the same den, police raided the place, though it seems only Chinese patrons were smoking there.[93]

The New York Affair of 1883

Though many New Yorkers tolerated Chinese dens that catered only to Chinese smokers, the Irish parishioners of the city's Church of the Transfiguration did not. By 1883, the city had absorbed a Chinese population of about a thousand, a fragment of San Francisco's 22,000 Chinese residents, with comparative ease. But New York's Chinatown had encroached on the Catholic Church of the Transfiguration, which rose above Mott and Park Streets amid what the *Times* called "the filth and festering humanity of . . . a few acres of Pekin[g]." Their Chinese neighbors had chafed at the church's parishioners at least since 1880, when churchgoers complained "they had to cut their way through an army of 'haythen'" on their way to Sunday services. Defending their territory, a corporation acting for the parishioners secured the leases on several tenements surrounding the church and sent several hundred Chinese tenants packing. The tenants left, but not for long, scattering to nearby buildings held by slumlords hungry for the higher rents paid by the homeless Chinese.[94]

[93] 1882 *New York Senate Journal*, p. 315 (noting a vote of 22 to 1); 1882 *New York Assembly Journal*, vol. 2, p. 1001 (noting a vote of 88 to 1); "The Opium Joints," *New York Sun*, May 12, 1883, p. 2; "An Opium Den Closed," *New York Times*, Aug. 18, 1882, p. 2; "An Opium Den Reopened and Closed," *New York Times*, Aug. 21, 1882, p. 1.

[94] *See* Campbell Gibson & Kay Jung, *U.S. Census Bureau, Historical Census Statistics on Population Totals by Race, 1790 to 1990 . . .* (Washington: U.S. Census Bureau (2005)), tbls. 5, 33; "Driving Out the Chinese," *New York Times*, May 6, 1880, p. 8 ("the filth and festering . . ." and "they had to cut . . ."). I'm assuming most of those represented in the cited census tables as "Asian and Pacific Islander" were Chinese, though surely some had Japanese or other origins. Other counts diverged. *See* J.E.R.,

Smoldering tensions flared in May 1883. Incensed that Chinatown's opium dens still thrived a year after the state banned them, the "hearty and decent young Irish workingmen" of the church's Catholic Young Men's Association spied "evil hemming them in" and resolved to act. Chillingly journalist Allen S. Williams wrote, "Young blood will tell."[95]

Choosing words as weapons, the young men alleged on May 7 "one of the most revolting evils that has existed in the city of New York." Their honorary president, Father James T. Barry, the church's assistant pastor, acted as "instigator of the movement." Barry had collected signatures a year before in support of the state's 1882 den ban and now complained the evil "has greatly increased." He detailed the group's harrowing allegations: "[M]any girls who live in this neighborhood have been ruined by these Chinamen. Children as young as 11 and 12 years have been led astray. Women entice them into the opium dens, where they are induced to stupefy themselves with opium." Darkly he added, "Revolting incidents occur daily in Mott street."[96]

As heated headlines swept the land, the city's newspapers fed the sensation. "War on the Chinese Dens" proclaimed the *Sun*, adding in boldface, "The Abominations of the Sixth Ward Colony Provoke a Citizens' Movement." A day later, at the top of page one, the paper announced a battle between "the Christian and the Pagan Camps." The *Herald* told of "very young girls who had been lured into the opium dens and ruined." The *Brooklyn Eagle* wrote that "Chinamen have been selling candy with opium mixed in it with such fiendish ingenuity that the children of the neighborhood have been given an insatiable longing for the drug. . . . Girls as young as 11 years, and from that up to 17, were found in great numbers."[97]

Now the "wicked Chinamen" discovered that "the hell fires of immorality they had kindled suddenly burst forth in retribution upon themselves." The *Times* warned of "an outburst of mob violence against them on the part of the ignorant Irish." Days later the paper added, "Crowds of young 'hoodlums' gather in Mott-street and support the cause of morality and Christianity by throwing stones through the windows of the houses occupied by Chinamen." That "a mob has not

"Chinese in New York," *San Francisco Chronicle*, May 27, 1883, p. 1 (numbering New York's Chinese residents at 3,500).

[95] J.E.R., "Chinese in New York" ("hearty and decent . . ."); Williams, *Demon of the Orient*, p. 32 ("evil hemming them in" and "Young blood will tell").

[96] Williams, *Demon of the Orient*, p. 33 ("one of the most . . ." (quoting the young men's resolution)); "War on the Chinese Dens," *New York Sun*, May 9, 1883, p. 3 ("instigator of the movement" and Barry quotes).

[97] "War on the Chinese Dens"; "War Begun in Mott Street," *New York Sun*, May 10, 1883, p. 1; "The Mott Street Revelations," *New York Herald* (quoted without date in Williams, *Demon of the Orient*, pp. 36–37); Williams, *Demon of the Orient*, p. 44 (quoting the *Brooklyn Eagle* without title or date).

risen and swept the Chinamen into the river" was a wonder, said the *Brooklyn Eagle*. "Their only protection lies in flight just now."[98]

With media klieg lights trained on Mott Street, police acted with fresh vigor, raiding dens and nabbing owners. The Chinese sagely took cover. Mott Street was "more dead than alive and as quiet as a closed church." Its "haunts . . . were apparently hermetically sealed." On Sunday the Church of the Transfiguration celebrated Mass, but nearby "opium joints . . . were shut up tight," and "Chinamen were scarce in the street . . . ." On Monday "[t]he opium joints were so well guarded . . . that it was impossible for any but the initiated who knew the proper signal to enter." A "remarkable change has been apparent in Chinatown," one observer wrote. "[T]here is a general air of decency and order, both night and day . . . ." Even Father Barry had to credit the neighborhood with "a semblance of respectability it has not had for fifteen years."[99]

Doubts Emerge

As the Chinese battened hatches against the storm, questions stirred. The *Times* and *Tribune*, less virulent than their rivals, first cast doubt. "Curiously," the *Times* wrote on May 10, three days after the Young Men's Association first mounted charges, "no one appears to have discovered the Mott-street infamies except certain philanthropists of Irish nationality"—and only within the last few days. No one else had noticed "that the Chinamen of Mott-street give candy impregnated with opium to little girls, and, having thus made them slaves to the drug, promptly plunge them into the most horrible immoralities . . . ." Somehow "the parents of the 'one hundred or more' little girls who have been made moral and physical wrecks by means of opium do not seem to have suspected that anything was the matter with their children." And though "scenes of infamy in Mott street are perpetrated openly and in broad daylight, the police have apparently been ignorant of them." A few days later, the *Times* spoke more bluntly of the "monstrous charges brought against the Chinamen by the Irish residents of the

<hr>

[98] Williams, *Demon of the Orient*, pp. 32–33 ("wicked Chinamen" and "the hell fires . . ."); 44 (quoting the *Brooklyn Eagle* without title or date); "The 'Leprous Heathen,'" *New York Times*, May 10, 1883, p. 4; "A New Charge," *New York Times*, May 13, 1883, p. 8.

[99] J.E.R., "Chinese in New York" ("more dead than alive . . ."); "Chinese In[i]quities," *Truth* (New York), May 11, 1883, p. 1 ("haunts . . . were apparently . . ."); "Mott Street Picketed," *New York Sun*, May 11, 1883, p. 1 ("opium joints . . . were shut . . ." and "Chinamen were scarce . . ."); "Arrested Over Their Opium," *New York Sun*, May 12, 1883, p. 1 ("The opium joints were so . . ."); "Purifying Chinatown," *San Francisco Chronicle*, May 18, 1883, p. 3 (quoting the *New York Herald*, which quoted Father Barry) ("remarkable change . . ." and "there is a general air . . ." and "a semblance of respectability . . .").

neighborhood.... [T]hat the charges are preposterous there is hardly any reason to doubt."[100]

The *Tribune's* May 12 headline, "Exaggerated Tales of Dissipation," set the paper's tone. "The sensational efforts of Father Barry," the paper reported, had found no favor with Barry's superior, parish rector Thomas F. Lynch. Charges "that the Chinese have been debauching large numbers of young girls," Lynch said, were "grossly exaggerated." In Lynch's eighteen months as parish priest "not a single instance of the ruin of a young girl by a Chinaman has come under his notice." As far as he could tell, "the Chinese in the parish are no more immoral than the Christians.... [T]he story is sensational in the highest degree" and risks "stirring up a race prejudice." Father Lynch did not speak from inordinate fondness for the Chinese. Only months before he had told the *New York Sun* that unless they took Catholic wives, Chinese men were beyond Christian conversion. "These people, who are chiefly the very scum of their nation, care, as a rule, nothing whatever about religion."[101]

The police, too, rejected the Irishmen's charges. They "pooh pooh[ed] the efforts of the young Catholics" and "said they had never seen anything of this corruption of young girls." But the cops lacked credit, for they hardly could admit such lechery had seethed beneath their gaze. Indeed, the *Herald* floated charges that officers took bribes to blinker their eyes. And the New York *Truth* congratulated Father Barry for "put[ting] to shame . . . several lazy or willfully blind officers of the law." As Dr. DeWitt Talmage alleged in a Brooklyn speech, the police showed "their usual determination not to see iniquity, if they are paid to let it alone . . . ."[102]

Most startling were the doubts of E. Fellows Jenkins, superintendent of the Society for the Prevention of Cruelty to Children. "Mr. Jenkins . . . investigated one or two of the cases thoroughly," Allen Williams wrote in *Demon of the Orient*, "and then made the rather broad declaration that there was little or nothing in the whole of the sweeping charges against the Chinamen." Quoted in the *Sun*, Jenkins dismissed the allegations wholesale. "I don't believe these charges are true as concerns the decoying of girls of tender years into the joints," he said. "I will give $50 to any one who can show me any evidence that will convict any Chinaman or joint keeper of the practices laid to them by Father Barry or the

---

[100] "The 'Leprous Heathen' "; "A New Charge."

[101] "Exaggerated Tales of Dissipation," *New York Tribune*, May 12, 1883, p. 5; Williams, *Demon of the Orient*, p. 35 (also reporting Lynch's doubts); "Religion Among the Chinese," *New York Sun*, Feb. 18, 1883, p. 2.

[102] J.E.R., "Chinese in New York" ("pooh-pooh[ed] the efforts . . ." and "said they had never . . ."); "The Mott Street Revelations," *New York Herald* (quoted without date in Williams, *Demon of the Orient*, p. 37); "Advice to Clergymen," *Truth* (New York) (quoted without date in Williams, *Demon of the Orient*, p. 43); Williams, *Demon of the Orient*, pp. 44–45 (quoting without date or title the *Brooklyn Eagle's* report of Talmage's remarks).

members of the Young Men's Association of his church. . . . I have said once to-day that this was all buncombe," Jenkins concluded, "and I say so still."[103]

But those New York readers who wished to believe allegations deemed "pre-posterous" by the *Times* and "pure fictions" by the *Tribune* could take heart, for police raids spurred by the Irishmen's charges had uncovered in a Chinatown den at least one white girl—Katie Crowley, "a little thing, just out from an in-stitution." Several weeks later, three other girls alleged "they were subjected to fiendish treatment by the Mongolians . . . ." These were not, however, the little girls Father Barry had in view. "Little" Katie Crowley was either fifteen or nine-teen, depending on the source, and the other three girls were all either thirteen or fourteen.[104] Broader support of the Irishmen's charges apparently went wanting.

The Chronicle's *Frenzied Reporting—And Sheepish Retraction*

Despite substantial grounds for doubt, the *San Francisco Chronicle* rehearsed the New York allegations without qualm. They were just "the old story with which we are familiar in San Francisco—the inveigling of young girls into the dens of vice and the spreading of all kinds of vicious practices . . . ." But this smug told-you-so had scant prologue. It seems the *Chronicle* never told such stories be-fore 1883 and came close only once, in March 1882, when it printed a claim that New York's Chinese launderers had lured young white girls "by presents of small coin and candy"—girls later "found by the police living in the room behind some laundry." That allegation, made fourteen months before the Irishmen's charges, said nothing of opium.[105]

Only one other story of note had appeared in the *Chronicle* before the New York affair of May 1883. In March 1883, the paper ran a one-paragraph tale of "A Precocious Girl," aged sixteen, who was "about as hardened a young miss as it would be possible to find in the city." San Francisco police had found her amid "nearly a score" of Chinese men in an opium den. "[A]ppearances indi-cate that the Chinamen were endeavoring to stupefy her with the pipe fumes in order to get her into their power." Beyond the two *New York Times* accounts of

---

[103] Williams, *Demon of the Orient*, p. 34; "Mott Street Picketed."

[104] "A New Charge" ("preposterous"); "San Francisco," *New York Tribune*, June 3, 1883, p. 5 ("pure fictions"); "City and Suburban News," *New York Times*, May 11, 1883, p. 8 (reporting discovery of Katie Crowley in a Mott Street den); J.E.R., "Chinese in New York" ("a little thing . . ."); "Charged with Atrocious Assault," *New York Tribune*, June 23, 1883, p. 8 ("they were subjected . . ."); "War Begun in Mott Street" (stating Katie Crowley's age as fifteen); "Results of the Raids," *Truth* (New York), May 13, 1883, p. 1 (attributing to Superintendent Jenkins the information that Katie Crowley was nineteen).

[105] "A Rude Awakening," *San Francisco Chronicle*, May 10, 1883, p. 2; J.E.R., "A Cosmopolitan City," *San Francisco Chronicle*, Mar. 12, 1882, p. 1.

1871 and 1873, this story marks the earliest clear reference to miscegenation in the dens I have seen anywhere. Yet the *Chronicle*'s brief account drew little notice, perhaps because its moral lessons were tangled in the history of the "hardened . . . young miss," underscored by a closing note that she was "sent to the Magdalen Asylum for safekeeping."[106] The story hardly foretold the much more explosive events two months later in New York, for those charges involved "innocent" girls "lured" and "enticed" into the dens.

Even if the *Chronicle* never predicted those events, it flogged the breaking news with gusto. Its opening salvo on May 8 heralded the New York *Truth*'s claim that "Chinese demons have been setting their traps successfully for little girls of respectable parentage, who are on the average not more than 11 or 13 years old . . . ." The paper quoted a member of the Young Men's Association: "This is something frightful. . . . Why, the orgies that those Chinese have been guilty of could hardly be described in print!" There followed a weeklong wildfire of headlines and subheads: "Chinese Immorality," on May 8, and then "Exposure of Mongolian Immorality in New York," "Crime and Disaster," "Debauching Young Girls," and a half-dozen more, sometimes two a day. Unquestioningly, the *Chronicle* repeated Father Barry's claims that he had "seen girls fill and light pipes for Chinamen" and even had "attended the death-beds of many of these poor ruined creatures, who have been killed by the opium habit."[107]

Then suddenly the storyline swiveled. On May 15, a week after the *Chronicle* first reported the young men's charges, the paper reprinted from the previous day's *San Francisco Bulletin* three brief sentences:

NEW YORK, May 14.—A former editor of the *Truth*, [Allen] S. Williams, has just completed a book, entitled "The Demon of the Orient." It is prospectused and advertised as the "best view of Chinatown in New York ever given." As the recent sensational opium-joint stories appeared originally in the *Truth*, it is now generally believed that they were merely advertising harbingers of this new work.[108]

---

[106] "A Precocious Girl," *San Francisco Chronicle*, Mar. 5, 1883, p. 3.

[107] "Chinese Immorality," *San Francisco Chronicle*, May 8, 1883, p. 3 (reprinting an item from *Truth* of May 7, 1883, which quoted the association member); "Beyond the Rockies," ibid., May 10, 1883, p. 3 ("Exposure of Mongolian . . ." and "seen girls fill . . ." and "attended the death-beds . . ."); "Crime and Disaster," ibid., May 12, 1883, p. 3; "Chinese in New York," ibid., May 27, 1883, p. 1 ("Debauching Young Girls").

[108] "The Chinese Curse," *San Francisco Chronicle*, May 15, 1883, p. 3. It appears the *Chronicle* lifted this red-faced admission word for word from the previous day's issue of the *Bulletin*, its cross-town rival. *See* "A Supposed Advertising Dodge," *San Francisco Bulletin*, May 14, 1883, p. 3.

That is, the whole hullabaloo was a hoax—a marketing scheme concocted to pump up interest in Williams's *Demon of the Orient*, a forthcoming exposé of New York's opium-smoking subculture.

Indeed, New York's *Truth* had been the first to trumpet the Irishmen's charges, leading with an explosive May 7 account. Under front-page headlines alleging "Chinese Moral Leprosy" and "Mongolians Who Systematically Entice Girls of Tender Years," *Truth* left little doubt one of its staff had broken the story: "From investigations which TRUTH has recently made, *he* can say," the story began. The author, presumably Williams, explained "HOW THE PREY IS CAPTURED": "The effect of opium upon females is understood. The girls not only become 'fiends' "— or addicts—"but recruits of that vast army of degraded femininity that pander to men's vices in New York." Insisting the affair "was first exposed in TRUTH," the paper said Father Barry was "very thankful to TRUTH for the publicity it has given this matter."[109]

Having boasted so boldly, *Truth* buried its later about-face even more abashedly than the *Chronicle*. Whereas the *Chronicle* fessed up on May 15, just a week after the scandal erupted, *Truth* loitered till June 3, weeks after Williams's unexplained departure. Even then *Truth* spoke indirectly, running its tiny, three-sentence retraction under the lackluster headline, "A Western Opinion," and beneath an even blander attribution to the Booneville *News*:

A Western Opinion.
From the Booneville (Mo.) News.
The queerest twist to the story about opium dens and the ruin of young girls in New York is the report that the whole thing is a clever arranged scheme, not so much for the purpose of righting an evil as for promoting private interests. A gentleman formerly on the paper that first gave publicity to the sensation has written a book on opium smoking in New York and elsewhere, and took this means of advertising it. Before its publication, the New York press, not knowing this, gave publicity to the subject that could not have been otherwise obtained
. . . .

Then, in a closing clause likewise credited to the Booneville paper, *Truth* allowed that "the author is quietly laughing at their gullibility."[110]

---

[109] "Chinese Moral Leprosy," *Truth* (New York), May 7, 1883, p. 1 (emphasis added); "Chinese In[i]quities" ("was first exposed in TRUTH" and "very thankful . . ."). My discussion of *Truth*'s role in inciting the scandal and of the paper's later retraction relies heavily on my research assistant Luke Weiger's sharp-eyed culling of relevant items from hundreds of microfilmed pages of *Truth*.

[110] "A Western Opinion," *Truth* (New York), June 3, 1883, p. 5 (reprinting item from the Booneville, Mo., *News*).

When his *Demon of the Orient* appeared in July 1883, Williams said the scandal had exploded when his manuscript was "in the hands of my printers." Presumably, he snatched the pages from the presses and made hasty revisions, for the book rehashed at length the events of May 1883. Having claimed he would make "but a brief mention of a horrible truth," Williams devoted sixteen of the book's 140 pages to the young Irishmen's allegations.[111] Stripped of this material, his little book hardly would have merited hard covers, for the balance mostly retold or reprinted faded journalistic forays into the dens. Williams likely knew his volume wanted heft and foresaw uncertain future sales. Perhaps he spied in scandal a means to spark popular interest. At only twenty-five, he maybe was ambitious and rash enough to risk discovery. And he had motives beyond pride, for he published the volume himself—no publisher's marketing machinery would pitch the book to public or press. All this the *Chronicle* and Booneville *News* saw clearly and branded the whole affair fake news.

Ducking such charges of chicanery, Williams closed his account of the scandal before its denouement: "As I write these closing lines this young men's citizens' movement is still progressing hotly. I cannot foretell the outcome of it . . . ." He pronounced himself "glad that the general public is awakening to the hitherto horrible secrets of the new social evil." Never did he hint these hidden horrors were fiction.[112]

The *Chronicle*, having confessed the contrivance, promptly airbrushed the affair from its pages. After a week of breathless headlines, it uttered not another word of the matter—except for one final account of May 27 that broke almost two weeks of silence. Consuming a column and a half of front-page newsprint, this last retelling of the Irishmen's charges added the lurid claim that in one Pell Street establishment "there were often as many as thirty little girls at a time, absolutely without clothing as long as they remained in the house."[113] The *Chronicle* offered no excuse for this dramatic rerun of a debunked scandal and no reminder of its earlier retraction.

Persistence of Miscegenation Myths

Disclosure of Williams's fraud by the *Chronicle* and other papers silenced for a while the responsible press, which said no more of the May 1883 affair. But the pod had burst and spread its spores, sowing copycat claims of conniving Chinese who lured young girls with opium.[114] Eventually even *Demon of the Orient*, with

---

[111] Williams, *Demon of the Orient*, pp. 30–46.

[112] Ibid., p. 46.

[113] J.E.R., "Chinese in New York."

[114] As noted earlier, the *Chronicle* copied its confession of Williams's likely contrivance from the previous day's *Bulletin. See* "A Supposed Advertising Dodge." For copycat claims that Chinese men

its sixteen-page recap of the 1883 sensation, emerged as an authoritative account. But the tale found its greatest champion in Jacob A. Riis, whose 1890 master-work, *How the Other Half Lives*, won an immense and influential readership.[115] With his chatty tableaus of city life, Riis opened readers' uptown eyes to lower Manhattan's ethnic enclaves and tenement slums. Photos of sallow-chested men and sooty urchins on open-guttered streets appealed mutely for sanitation and safety regulation. Progressives hailed Riis a reformer and proclaimed his book a manifesto for renewal of crime-ravaged ghettoes.

Yet *How the Other Half Lives* merits no Progressive mantle. Rank stereotypes sully Riis's cityscapes. His portraits of the ethnic poor range from wry to mocking to cruel. Among the cruelest depicts the Chinese, marked in Riis's rendering by greed, cunning, lack of Christian charity, and lust. Shamelessly, Riis reprised the 1883 allegations absent reference to Williams's contrivance. In "the conventional households of the Chinese quarter" the men are all Chinese, he wrote, and "the women [are] all white, girls hardly yet grown to womanhood, worshipping nothing save the pipe that has enslaved them . . . ." Horrid as it was, the girls' fate was utterly routine: "There are houses, dozens of them, in Mott and Pell Streets, that are literally jammed, from the 'joint' in the cellar to the attic, with these hapless victims of a passion which, once acquired, demands the sacrifice of every instinct of decency to its insatiate desire." Thankfully, though, "[t]here is a church in Mott Street, at the entrance to Chinatown, that stands as a barrier between it and the tenements beyond. Its young men have waged unceasing war upon the monstrous wickedness for years, but with very little real result."[116] Here was Williams's tale retold, without credit or qualification.

In his eagerness to roust these allegations from retirement, Riis joined Williams in larding the historical record with evidence of miscegenation panic. When modern historians look back for the forces that spurred early antidrug laws, Riis's 1890 book and Williams's 1883 *Demon of the Orient* loom large in their view, obscuring the earlier era of miscegenation silence. Hence Courtwright, Musto, Morone, and others cite Williams or Riis or both to support claims that

---

lured white girls with opium, *see, e.g.*, "Hop Wah's Laundry," *New York Times*, Aug. 26, 1883, p. 2 ("[I]t was suspected that an opium joint was in full blast there, and that young girls were enticed into the place and initiated into the habit of smoking by Chinamen."); "Making War on Opium Dens," *Weekly Los Angeles Mirror*, Dec. 13, 1884, p. 4 ("Newspapers [in Chicago] are beginning to make attacks upon the Chinese laundrymen in the city, on the ground that they are engaged in systematically enticing young girls and women who have already acquired the opium habit into their dens.").

[115] Jacob A. Riis, *How the Other Half Lives: Studies Among the Tenements of New York* (Cambridge: Belknap Press of Harvard University Press, 1970) (1890). Riis was a police reporter for the *New York Tribune* from about 1878 to 1890. Sam Bass Warner Jr., "Editor's Introduction," *in How the Other Half Lives*, pp. xi–xiv.

[116] Riis, *How the Other Half Lives*, pp. 65–66.

early anti-den laws took root in miscegenation fears.[117] But it seems no modern historian has mentioned the many observers who immediately voiced doubts about the Irishmen's 1883 claims or the quick retraction of the whole storyline by the *Chronicle*, *Truth* itself, and other papers.

Absent Williams's and Riis's later distortions, the evidence shows lawmakers first banned opium dens when whites and especially respectable white youth took to visiting them in numbers. When young white men went to the dens with innocent girls and sex on their minds, lawmakers acted with dispatch. The police saw all this and enforced the new laws largely against white smokers and those who sold to them. *After* the New York affair of 1883, miscegenation panic may have driven some anti-den lawmaking. That affair, however fraudulent, lingered in the public imagination and proved resilient to facts. But before the scandal erupted in May 1883, ten states and territories and dozens of cities and towns already had banned the dens.

Even *Truth*'s Allen Williams, writing as the scandal flared hot, admitted existing bans owed much to the fear of *white* men's debauchery of young white women. True, he made this admission backhandedly, as he sought to highlight his recent exposure of Chinese predation. First he distinguished older concerns of white-on-white corruption: "TRUTH thought the extreme horror of the terrible practice [of opium smoking] had been reached when respectable young women were traced to the doors of the rooms kept by white men." After this admission of past ignorance, he continued, "But the revelations of the past few days are even yet more shocking. The enticing of young girls by the Chinamen into their filthy dens for ulterior purposes . . . has added a new horror to the story."[118] Even as Williams hyped his miscegenation claims, then, he undermined modern myths that miscegenation panic lay behind early anti-den laws. For till "the past few days," he said, those laws may have responded to a decidedly different concern.

Why then have historians clung so doggedly to the miscegenation thesis? One reason is an inherent ambiguity that has led modern observers to spy hints of miscegenation where contemporaries might have seen none. Opium dens by their nature involved both sex and racial mixing. The Chinese ran most dens, whites of both sexes went there, and the drug they smoked sometimes fueled sexual appetite. As den patrons reclined in darkness while smoking and shed jackets and shoes or loosened corsets, descriptions of the dens seem sexual. And as many or most whites disliked both the Chinese and the immoral influence of the dens, the common rhetoric of the day condemned the dens and their keepers in one breath.

---

[117] Courtwright, *Dark Paradise*, p. 186, n.63 (citing Riis and Williams); Musto, *American Disease*, p. 319 n.82 (citing Riis); Morone, *Hellfire Nation*, pp. 465, 557 n.31 (citing Riis); Ahmad, "Caves of Oblivion," p. 88 (citing Riis).

[118] "The Illegal Opium Dens," *Truth* (New York), May 11, 1883, p. 2.

Hence what seem today expressions of miscegenation panic often prove on closer view to be frets about *whites in the dens*. Consider an 1881 Carson City report quoted earlier: "All pretense to decency is thrown aside," an observer wrote of the city's opium dens. "Often [the smoker] lies in his sensual stupor side by side with Chinamen and creatures, male and female . . . ." At first this mixed-race scene seems sexual. But the bracketed "smoker" replaces the pronoun *he*. And the next sentence focuses on males: "The worst of it is that the victims are mostly young men or boys verging on manhood." The writer attributed the same concern to the leaders of many Western towns: "In San Francisco, Virginia City, Portland, Oregon, Salt Lake City, and, in fact, in every town on the coast where there is a Chinaman . . . the habit of opium smoking is practiced by white men and boys." Finally, he turned his attention to sex *among whites*: "In all the interior towns every Chinese wash-house, store, and house of prostitution is an opium den, frequented night and day by boys, men, and white prostitutes."[119] Nowhere did he mention miscegenation.

Many other oft-quoted exhibits of miscegenation panic appeared *after* the New York affair of 1883, when observers were readier than before to see miscegenation in their midst. San Francisco physician Winslow Anderson's 1887 report finds frequent repetition today: "The writer has witnessed the sickening sight of young white girls from sixteen to twenty years of age lying half-undressed on the floor or couches smoking with their 'lovers.' Men and women, Chinese and white people, mix indiscriminately in Chinatown smoking houses." Though Dr. Anderson's observations were wholly consistent with the white-on-white seduction risk seen in San Francisco since the mid-1870s, they took on a more sinister, mixed-race hue after the events of 1883. Like Williams's and Riis's rehearsals of the scandal, Anderson's remarks tempt modern historians to see miscegenation fear in earlier years, when so much evidence says it was lacking.[120]

A Theory of Racial Contagion

Even if early anti-den laws owed nothing to miscegenation panic, some modern historians say we can trace those laws to *another* form of anti-Chinese bigotry. Hence Ronald Hamowy deemed "racist in origin" laws intended to keep whites away from Chinese dens, for such laws sought "to protect whites from what was

[119] "Topics in the Sagebrush," *New York Times*, Feb. 21, 1881, p. 1 (printing correspondence from Carson City).
[120] "Morphio-Mania," *Medical Record*, vol. 32 (Nov. 5, 1887), p. 595 (quoting San Francisco doctor Winslow Anderson); "The Opium Habit in San Francisco," *Medical and Surgical Reporter*, vol. 57 (Dec. 10, 1887), p. 784 (same). Thomas Dormandy misquoted Anderson by adding the word *Oriental* before "*lovers*," creating the specter of miscegenation where it was lacking. Dormandy, *Opium*, p. 159.

commonly regarded as a loathsome Oriental vice." Likewise, David Courtwright argues anti-den lawmaking stemmed in part from "the desire to protect whites from acquiring an alien vice."[121]

This theory of *racial contagion* turns not on the sexual immorality of the dens but on the perceived contamination of whites by something Chinese. The theory finds support in writings warning of contagion both figurative and literal. Figuratively, an 1879 Nevada news item, typical of many across the West, called opium smoking "a hideous, loathsome moral leprosy." Literally, white and Chinese den patrons shared the same air, bunks, pillows, and notably pipes. Another Nevada paper told in 1876 of an Elko den where whites, "in common with Chinamen, quietly recline on a filthy bunk and drink in the smoke of the fatal drug." Visiting this den, the author "saw a white woman, a white man and two Chinamen, in close proximity—about a foot apart." Three years later, a third Nevada editor "wonder[ed] how anybody not utterly debased can . . . indulge in a smoke from pipes which have undoubtedly been used by leprous Chinese . . . ." Even Dr. Kane warned of the "danger of contracting that loathsome disease, syphilis, from the pipe-stem that has passed from mouth to mouth" and cited cases of such transmission among his own patients. Worse still, some whites believed the opium served by Chinese denkeepers was the ashy remains of the premium article, smoked before by Chinese patrons. A *Chronicle* editor shuddered in 1877 to think of the "festering compound . . . put to the lips of Christian" smokers, already "smoked in the vilest dens of Mongol depravity [and] breathed upon by the fetid breath of hideous leprosy-stricken wretches . . . ."[122]

Whites-focused enforcement of early anti-den laws does nothing to disprove this theory of racial contagion. Driving whites from Chinese dens was one way to stop such contagion. Somehow we must distinguish this racially tinged fear from a very different distress for the morals of white opium smokers, who stupefied their minds in search of unreasoning, escapist pleasure. So let's return to San Francisco in the early years of anti-den laws. By focusing on *white-owned* dens and police treatment of them, we may begin to discern whether fear of racial contagion drove enactment of these new laws.

---

[121] Hamowy, "Introduction," pp. 12–13; Courtwright, "Drug Laws and Drug Use," p. 124. Diana Ahmad also noted that whites worried most when other whites smoked opium, but she did not venture an explanation. *See* Ahmad, *The Opium Debate*, p. 31 ("Generally, Americans were not concerned when the Chinese used the narcotic, but when Anglo-American men and women smoked it, the issue took on a greater significance.").

[122] "Opium Smoking," *Reno Evening Gazette*, Feb. 21, 1879, p. 3; "Opium Smoking," *Weekly Elko Independent*, Sept. 10, 1876, p. 3; "The Opium Smokers' Outfit," *Winnemucca (Nev.) Daily Silver State*, Oct. 2, 1879, p. 3; Kane, *Opium-Smoking in America and China*, p. 78; "Death in the Pipe," *San Francisco Chronicle*, Feb. 23, 1877, p. 3. For a more balanced assessment of the risk of leprosy transmission posed by the Chinese, *see* "Leprosy in New York," *New York Sun*, Apr. 24, 1883, p. 3.

White-Owned Dens and the Police

In the aftermath of the supervisors' 1875 ban, as San Francisco police struggled to close Chinatown's dens to whites, white smokers drifted south across Market Street and patronized instead a cottage industry of white-run dens. All evidence suggests the police and courts dealt as sternly with these dens as with their Chinese kin. Consider a *Chronicle* article of March 1882 headlined simply, "White Opium Den." Officers had raided Henry Smith's Market Street den just before midnight and arrested half a dozen smokers. "[A]ll the captives were convicted" in police court the next morning. The *Chronicle* offered telling commentary: "The prisoners, who all gave assumed names, are socially above the average of 'pipe-hitters,' and fear of arrest in Chinatown evidently led to the establishment and patronage of the more aristocratic Market-street den."[123] That is, even upscale folks who patronized "aristocratic" dens faced arrest and conviction. Their pointed desertion of Chinatown and escape from the risk of cross-racial sex or contagion did not spare them.

Even white women did not escape arrest for keeping or patronizing dens populated only by whites. As early as October 1877, less than two years into the den ban's tenure, San Francisco police conducted a midnight raid on what the *Bulletin* deemed the "Fashionable Opium Den" of Mrs. Jennie Perkins. The officers arrested Perkins and, in a rooftop room equipped for smoking, snagged John Lynch, George Nichols, Edward Wilson, and "a young girl named Maud Clifford."[124]

Despite her 1877 arrest and public shaming, Perkins proved obstinate. In January 1885, San Francisco police discovered a Mission Street den run by "the notorious Jennie Perkins," who "has been arrested time and again" for her "Vile Work." Police promptly arrested Perkins and six of her patrons, three of them women. The women "were young and evidently intelligent and well brought up." The men were "of the lowest scum of the city's population," though nothing suggests they were Chinese. A neighbor told the *Chronicle* "that he had seen young girls, some of them not possibly over 12 years of age, standing in front of [Perkins's] place sick and staggering from the effects of opium." Indeed, the *Chronicle*'s headline branded Perkins "A Corrupter of Youth," a concern even absent the lecherous Chinese. Several months later, police raided the same den,

---

[123] "White Opium Den," *San Francisco Chronicle*, Mar. 15, 1882, p. 4.

[124] "A Fashionable Opium Den," *San Francisco Daily Evening Bulletin*, Oct. 22, 1877, p. 3; "A Bush-street Opium Room," *San Francisco Chronicle*, Oct. 22, 1877, p. 3 (naming Clifford and the male arrestees).

still run by Perkins, and arrested her and her three guests—James Tools, George Smith, and George Edwards.[125]

Not every press report about a white-owned den was so detailed, but none suggested tolerance of such dens or their white guests. Time after time, the *Chronicle* or *Bulletin* told of a San Francisco police raid that unearthed a white denkeeper and white patrons, and each time officers arrested the light-skinned offenders.[126] In other California communities the same practice seemingly prevailed—white operators and their white patrons, when found by police, faced arrest and conviction.[127] And scattered reports from the mid-1880s in Philadelphia, Boston, and Chicago show no greater tolerance of white denkeepers or their white patrons. It's true a *New York Times* reporter wrote with apparent admiration of Mrs. Kate Chisom's lavish Philadelphia den, "over whose threshold only wealthy women [could] step." But the wariness with which Chisom admitted the visiting reporter and kept her blinds tightly drawn suggests her business enjoyed no refuge from the law.[128]

In an interview with a *Chronicle* reporter days after Jennie Perkins's arrest in January 1885, a San Francisco police officer explained the concerns raised by white-owned dens. "There are no less than 3000 white opium smokers in San Francisco to-day," he said. His proposed solution took the reporter by surprise: "The terrible vice is on the increase, and it never will be checked until a law is enacted making it a *felony* to sell opium to white persons for smoking purposes." The reporter protested that punishing den-keeping as a misdemeanor rather than a felony was "generally supposed" to have had the "desired effect." Here the officer drew a critical distinction: that penalty "had the effect of stopping those people from smoking in Chinatown, and a good many of the opium joints were closed up. But the fiends began to get their own pipes . . . ." The officer was referring to *white* fiends, and to prove his point, he led the reporter to

---

[125] "Bogus Coin and Opium," *San Francisco Chronicle*, Jan. 18, 1885, p. 8 ("**the notorious** . . ."); "A Corrupter of Youth," ibid., Jan. 19, 1885, p. 3 (all other quotes); "An Opium Den Raided," ibid., May 1, 1885, p. 3.

[126] *See, e.g.*, "Criminal Courts," *San Francisco Chronicle*, July 24, 1880, p. 1 (reporting the arrest of two white smokers and a white denkeeper, all male); "Opium Smokers Arrested," *San Francisco Daily Evening Bulletin*, Mar. 25, 1882, p. 3 (arrest of a white male denkeeper and his eight white patrons, including at least two women); "Opium Joints Raided," ibid., Sept. 24, 1884, p. 2 (arrest of the white keeper of a Fifth Street opium spot and his two patrons, a white couple); "Jottings About Town," *San Francisco Chronicle*, Jan. 29, 1885, p. 3 (arrest of Fourth Street denkeeper Harry Page and his three patrons, George Thompson, Henry Goldsmith, and William Phillips).

[127] *See, e.g.*, "An Opium Den Raided," *San Francisco Chronicle*, Mar. 27, 1883, p. 3 (reporting the arrest of Vallejo den owner Conrad Miller, together with three patrons of unstated race); "Coast Notes," ibid., July 8, 1885, p. 4 (arrest of two white men, presumably smokers, found in a Salinas opium den kept by a white man); "Opium Fiends," *Oakland Tribune*, Sept. 21, 1885, p. 3 (arrest of the white keeper of an Oakland opium den, his white patron, and his white landlord).

[128] "Raid on an Opium Joint," *North American* (Philadelphia), Mar. 18, 1884, p. 1; "An Opium Joint Raided," *Boston Daily Advertiser*, Sept. 26, 1885, p. 8; "Police Court Jottings," (Chicago) *Daily Inter Ocean*, Dec. 25, 1886, p. 8; "Philadelphia's Opium Parlor," *New York Times*, Aug. 29, 1882, p. 2.

the haunts of some opium fiends. Behind one after another rooming-house door they found "White Slaves to the Vice" sucking on their pipes.[129]

Other observers agreed that stopping sales by whites to whites warranted stronger measures. Allen Williams, albeit a doubtful authority, wrote in *Demon of the Orient* of a white-owned Midtown opium den. "The fact of an American ... in the business of propagating a body-killing, soul-destroying vice like this one of opium smoking is sufficient to evoke a feeling of disgust," he wrote, "and should call down the strongest condemnation"—even if the denkeeper was a "devoted yachtsman" with a den boasting "a rich and gorgeous interior."[130]

Nor was Williams the only New Yorker who felt this way. In March 1885, as Jennie Perkins faced yet another prosecution in San Francisco, New York denkeeper Charles White came before the Court of Special Sessions. "[I]t was bad enough," the prosecutor told the court, "for a Chinaman to be charged with this offense, but it was crime of more importance when one of our own race is caught in the act of selling this cursed drug . . . ." Not only were patrons of White's den white, but at least one was well off, sporting a Prince Albert coat and silver-headed cane. Far from excusing the crime, the race of all involved aggravated it. The prosecutor "implored the court to show no leniency to the accused," and the court obliged, fining White $500 and packing him off to the penitentiary for three months. "This is the highest penalty of the law," the *Times* wrote, "and the *only time* it has ever been imposed on an 'opium joint' keeper in this city." In Gotham, it seems, the worst of all opium sellers was White.[131]

Miscegenation, Racial Contagion, and Other Drugs

We need not search far for more proof that authorities pursued white drug users even absent any whiff of racial mixing. For lawmakers proved ready to ban any recreational intoxicant save alcohol whatever its racial cast and without the intimacy of a shared bunk and pipe.

Take first opium. Eaten opium was a staple of Western medicine long before Dr. John Jones hailed its virtues in 1700. Though Chinese druggists sold eaten opium in nineteenth-century America, white druggists sold it, too, and had

---

[129] "Smoking of Opium," *San Francisco Chronicle*, May 10, 1885, p. 8 (emphasis added).

[130] Williams, *Demon of the Orient*, pp. 46–47.

[131] "The Dude Smoked Opium," *New York Times*, Mar. 7, 1885, p. 8 (emphasis added). Decades later another New York judge said flatly that the worst opium dealers were white. "My investigation of opium smoking," said Judge Charles M. Hough in sentencing a former army civil engineer to six months on Blackwell's Island for running a Manhattan opium den, "leads me to believe that it is the selling of the drug by white men to white persons that spreads this horrible vice. Maybe the Chinam[a]n has to have his opium, but there is no excuse for the white man engaging in this traffic." "Opium Smoking Alarming," *St. Albans* [Vt.] *Messenger*, Sept. 27, 1912, p. 2.

been the standard source long before Chinese miners settled Western shores. Laudanum and paregoric retained in America their European popularity as oral opium preparations, as did patent medicines with such consoling monikers as Kopp's Baby's Friend. Yet laws banning opium dens gave way in fairly short order to laws banning unprescribed sales of eaten opium, which swept thirty-five states and territories before the Harrison Narcotic Act of 1914 effectively nationalized the ban (see Table 4C in Chapter 4).

Dread of miscegenation or contagion surely had nothing to do with this trend, for that dread allegedly attended the *dens*—their darkness, their bunks, their mixed clientele, and their drug with its shared pipes and famed aphrodisiac force. And though eaten opium "excites Venery," as Jones reported, there's no reason to think it fostered racial mixing. On the contrary, while anti-den laws drove white addicts out of dens and into druggists' shops, where they bought eaten opium to quiet their craving, newer laws banning eaten opium might have driven them back to the dens and to the risks of miscegenation and contagion.

Nor was eaten opium the only "white" drug readily banned. For years after cocaine's American debut in 1884, most reported cocaine addicts were doctors and pharmacists and their wives and girlfriends. Yet as we'll see, several states banned cocaine before the first reports of underclass use emerged. Chloral hydrate, a synthetic sedative widely banned in the late nineteenth and early twentieth centuries, claimed no special racial identity. And several drugs of later vintage—LSD, Ecstasy, various barbiturates, and others—faced matter-of-course bans despite their favor among the white middle class. Even the history of early cannabis bans, traced in Chapter 7, proves surprisingly free of anti-Mexican motives.

Rhetorical Confusion

Still, it's no surprise the rhetoric of the American West condemned the Chinese and their drug in a single scattershot assault. "Opium Smoking," ran a headline in the *Reno Evening Gazette* in 1879, "The Hideous Heathen Vice in Our Midst." The text raged about "the Chinese, those soulless human reptiles, [who] are directly responsible for this blighting vice. They imported and introduced the curse, and at their door must it be laid with a thousand other moral sins."[132]

But which way did the bad association run? Was the vice bad because of its heathen sponsors, or was their blighting vice just one more reason to loathe them? Perhaps, as so many historians have said, whites condemned opium

---

[132] "Opium Smoking," *Reno Evening Gazette*, Feb. 21, 1879, p. 3.

smoking because it came with "those soulless human reptiles." But reviews of Chinese tea suggest otherwise. For both journalists and celebrities praised the Chinese newcomers for their "exquisite," "splendid," and "superb" tea, their "nectar fit for the gods," a "finer tea . . . than any we have on the Eastern coast."[133] Opium, in contrast, *was* a blighting vice, leading many to dissipation, degradation, and ruin. It offered one more count in the indictment against the despised intruders.

Consider, too, the view of opium smoking in China. In 1729, almost one hundred fifty years before San Francisco supervisors approved the nation's first anti-den law, the Yongzhang Emperor forbade sale of smoked opium in China. An edict of 1813 forbade opium entirely. A series of laws adopted between 1830 and 1870 broadened and refined the original bans—all without a racial motive to fuel them.[134]

Race in the Dens

The lesson of early anti-den lawmaking is not that racism played no role. Racism's role simply was not the one expected, not the one historians have claimed. The new anti-opium laws did not target the Chinese. On the contrary, Chinese smokers and those who sold to them often enjoyed immunity from the laws' enforcement. Early lawmakers therefore could not have hoped that banning opium dens would drive Chinese addicts back to China for their fix or sap Chinese sellers of their livelihoods or reduce Chinese laborers, steeled by opium, to the level of their weaker white foes. Racism's role was subtler than these theories suggest and teaches broader lessons about why we ban drugs. For just as Chinese emperors forbade opium smoking to save their people from a demoralizing addiction, American lawmakers sought to save *their* people and the morals of their community and their children—hence the horror and rapid response when lawmakers discovered dens peopled by whites and especially by respectable women and youth. Lawmakers often overlooked opium smoking and

---

[133] "Chinatown by Night," *San Francisco Chronicle*, Aug. 8, 1885, p. 2 ("the tea was exquisite"); "Nilsson in Chinatown," ibid., Dec. 17, 1882, p. 8 (quoting a famed Swedish singer in a Chinatown restaurant: "The tea is splendid!"); "An Opium Joint," *St. Louis Globe-Democrat*, July 9, 1884, p. 5 (quoting a New Yorker's comment that the tea served in a Chinese opium den was "superb"); "Scenes in Chinatown," *San Francisco Bulletin*, Dec. 14, 1876, p. 1 ("nectar fit for . . ."); "The Chinese in California," *New York Times*, Oct 18, 1867, p. 2 ("finer tea . . . than any . . .").

[134] Jonathan Spence, "Opium Smoking in Ch'ing China," *in Conflict and Control in Late Imperial China* (Frederic Wakeman Jr. & Carolyn Grant eds., Berkeley: University of California Press, 1975), pp. 143, 148, 156–61; Ahmad, *The Opium Debate*, p. 19.

sales among the Chinese at least in part because they thought little and cared less about the morals of their Chinese guests.

This seeming disregard of Western lawmakers for Chinese morals was assuredly racist. But this racism, far from driving early laws against opium dens, instead limited those laws' reach. Overwhelmingly, the evidence shows that even in an all-white world, white lawmakers would have banned opium dens, for they acted to protect their own.

6

Crazed Racial Coke Fiends

"Negro Cocaine 'Fiends' Are a New Southern Menace."

So warned a page-wide headline in the *New York Times Magazine* of February 8, 1914, perhaps the most quoted artifact in the history of America's war on drugs. "Nine men killed in Mississippi . . . by crazed cocaine takers, five in North Carolina, three in Tennessee—these are the facts that need no imaginative coloring."[1]

More than any single exhibit, this article by Dr. Edward Huntington Williams shoulders the claim that American lawmakers banned drugs to combat the racial group that used them. It is the source most memorably of "the cocaine-sniffing negro" who proved invulnerable to bullets. Running amok in a coke-fueled rage, the man drew a knife and slashed a lawman's shoulder. The lawman responded with a short-range shot to the heart that "did not even stagger the man," who kept charging even after a second shot ripped through his arm and into his chest. Cops across the South learned from this episode and rushed to switch their suddenly puny pistols for "guns of greater shocking power."

Dr. Williams more than anyone has convinced modern readers that drug *fiends* denoted devilish and mostly non-white drug users. Yet in all the years before, a *cocaine fiend* was just an *addict*, no more or less, whether white or non-white, male or female, fierce or friendly. As a New York pharmacist explained to a reporter in 1889, "[W]hen I say *fiends*, I do not mean any thing peculiarly demon[i]c or suggestive of that sulphurous realm . . . . I am only using an old term in the pharmaceutical trade for people who get into the habit of using some pernicious drug." The word still lacked demonic or racial meaning in 1913, when the

---

[1] Edward Huntington Williams, "Negro Cocaine 'Fiends' Are a New Southern Menace," *New York Times Sunday Magazine*, Feb. 8, 1914, p. 12. Williams presumably based the Mississippi account on a *New York Times* report of September 29, 1913, datelined Harriston, Mississippi, and captioned, "Drug-Crazed Negroes Start a Reign of Terror." The story varied somewhat from Williams's retelling. The *Times* counted ten dead, including the two suspected attackers. "10 Dead, 20 Hurt in a Race Riot," *New York Times*, Sept. 29, 1913, p. 1. Or Williams may have read the *Herald*'s account of the same crime. "10 Die in Orgy of Drug-Mad Negroes," *New York Tribune*, Sept. 29, 1913, p. 1.

Beware Euphoria. George Fisher, Oxford University Press. © Oxford University Press 2024.
DOI: 10.1093/oso/9780197688489.003.0007

New York Tribune headlined an account of medical cocaine addiction, "Doctors Make Drug Fiends . . . ."[2]

Dr. Williams was not the first to feed fear of African American cocaine abuse. Claims of cocaine-charged violence committed by African Americans had appeared as early as 1897. But Williams gave what had been a largely Southern theme its most prominent Northern expression. And he proved canny in his timing. He purveyed his Southern theme in the Northern press in February 1914, just ten months before the federal Harrison Act effectively banned retail sales of cocaine and opium except by doctor's prescription. Moreover, Williams gave historians their weightiest reason to write that drug bans grew from such racist panic. When historian David Musto wrote that "cocaine was supposed to enable blacks to withstand bullets which would kill normal persons" and that such "fear of a given drug's effect on a specific minority" generated the "most passionate support for legal prohibition of narcotics," he had Williams's account in view. Those historians who have echoed Musto's claim almost always mention Williams too.[3]

Hence Dr. Williams has distorted the study of cocaine just as Allen Williams, who wrote a generation earlier, distorted that of opium dens. The specter of non-white fiends crazed by cocaine looms as large on the historical landscape as that of white girls lured by opium-soaked candy. Though Dr. Williams, unlike Allen Williams before him, did not fashion from smoke his tales of drug-driven cross-racial crimes—for such tales had been told before—he mimicked in a different way his earlier namesake: Both men spoke too late in the day to have influenced many early drug bans. Allen Williams's New York scandal erupted only after ten states and territories and many cities and towns had banned opium dens.

----

[2] "Opium and Antipyrin," *Livingston* (Mont.) *Enterprise*, July 6, 1889, p. 4 (quoting statement made to a New York correspondent of the *St. Louis Globe Democrat*) (emphasis added); "Doctors Make Drug Fiends, He Charges," *New York Tribune*, Jan. 30, 1913, p. 6. *See also* "Is Jupiter among the Other Drugs," *Chicago Tribune*, May 20, 1894, p. 34 ("The educated eye discovers the cocaine 'fiend' in all the upper walks of life . . . ."); "Boy Cocaine Snuffers Hunted by the Police," *New York Times*, Jan. 8, 1907, p. 6 ("The cocaine habit had spread so rapidly . . . that thousands of New Yorkers—boys, girls, and men and women—were now in the cocaine fiend class.").

[3] "An Act to . . . Impose a Special Tax upon All Persons Who . . . Deal in . . . Opium or Coca Leaves . . . ," Pub. L. No. 63-223, ch. 1, § 2(b), 38 Stat. L. 785, 786 (Act of Dec. 17, 1914) (Harrison Narcotic Act); David F. Musto, *The American Disease: Origins of Narcotic Control* (New York: Oxford University Press, 3d ed. 1999), p. 294. Professor Musto assembled a long roster of articles recounting crimes by African American cocaine users in the medical and popular press between 1898 and 1914, when Williams's article appeared. Ibid., pp. 304–05 n.15. As Musto noted, Williams elaborated on his claims in the *Medical Record* in 1914. Edward Huntington Williams, "The Drug-Habit Menace in the South," *Medical Record*, vol. 85 (Feb. 7, 1914), pp. 247–49. Modern historians citing Williams include David T. Courtwright, *Dark Paradise: Opiate Addiction in America before 1940* (Cambridge: Harvard University Press, 1982), p. 97 & n.79; H. Wayne Morgan, *Drugs in America: A Social History, 1800–1980* (Syracuse: Syracuse University Press, 1981), p. 93 & n.24; James A. Morone, *Hellfire Nation: The Politics of Sin in American History* (New Haven: Yale University Press, 2003), p. 465; Kathleen Auerhahn, "The Split Labor Market and the Origins of Antidrug Legislation in the United States," *Law & Social Inquiry*, vol. 24 (1999), pp. 411, 427.

Dr. Williams's account of crazed African American coke fiends appeared only after *forty-six* states had banned cocaine (see Table 6A).

Both Williamses, moreover, spoke after long silences. Allen Williams's scandal helped break a decade of miscegenation silence. And long before Dr. Williams warned so loudly of bullet-resistant African American coke fiends, there had been years of silence on the theme of cocainized violence. After cocaine's arrival

Table 6A Earliest State Bans of Unprescribed Cocaine Sales

Oregon	1887	Missouri	1905 (March 9)
Montana	1889	Minnesota	1905 (March 15)
Colorado	1897 (March 31)	Nebraska	1905 (March 28)
Illinois	1897 (June 11)	Connecticut	1905 (June 5)
Massachusetts	1898 (March 17)	Michigan	1905 (June 20)
Louisiana	1898 (July 12)	Rhode Island	1906
Arizona	1899 (March 16)	South Carolina	1907 (February 20)
Maine	1899 (March 16)	California	1907 (March 6)
Arkansas	1899 (May 8)	West Virginia	1907 (March 6)
Mississippi	1900	Indiana	1907 (March 9)
Tennessee	1901 (February 7)	Utah	1907 (March 25)
Kansas	1901 (February 22)	New York	1907 (June 5)
Kentucky	1902 (March 20)	Wisconsin	1907 (July 16)
Iowa	1902 (March 22)	Alabama	1907 (August 6)
Ohio	1902 (April 28)	Idaho	1909 (March 13)
Georgia	1902 (December 5)	New Mexico	1909 (March 18)
Wyoming	1903 (February 23)	Washington	1909 (March 22)
Texas	1903 (April 6)	New Hampshire	1909 (April 9)
Pennsylvania	1903 (April 22)	Oklahoma	1910
Florida	1903 (May 14)	Nevada	1911
Virginia	1904 (March 14)	Delaware	1913
New Jersey	1904 (March 28)	South Dakota	1915 (March 9)
Maryland	1904 (April 12)	Vermont	1915 (March 12)
North Carolina	1905 (February 2)	Alaska	1921
North Dakota	1905 (February 28)	Hawaii	1931

on American shores in October 1884, it seems nobody wrote of *any* crime by cocaine-fired African Americans for thirteen years, and nobody wrote of African American *use* of cocaine, except during surgery or dentistry, for a decade. Yet during these overlapping silences, the first statewide cocaine bans took form.

These silences, like miscegenation silence, are hard to hear today. Just as the New York opium affair of 1883, rising on the historical horizon, blocks our view of what came before, we must strain to see past stories of race-coded cocaine criminals when we look back to find the roots of America's first anti-cocaine laws. Better, then, to begin at the beginning and travel forward from there. Viewed this way, the evidence shows that most early anti-cocaine laws, like early laws against opium dens, were *laws about whites.* They aimed to protect whites and especially respectable whites and especially women and youth against this new recreational intoxicant and its demoralizing force.

Enter Cocaine

When Göttingen Chemist Albert Niemann announced in 1860 he had isolated and analyzed the active ingredient of the coca leaf, it seems no one in America took notice. No American wrote of *cocaine* before 1870, when Vassar professor James Orton passingly referred to Niemann's discovery (wrongly crediting Niemann's mentor, Friedrich Wöhler) in his anthropological travelogue, *The Andes and the Amazon.* Orton's reference, too, escaped public notice. Hence when the *New York Tribune* and *New York Times* printed back-to-back reports on cocaine in October 1884, they could proclaim discovery of a "New Anæsthetic." In their histories the drug traced back only a year to its use in Viennese throat clinics. And the real moment of revelation was even more recent: the Heidelberg Congress of Ophthalmologists in September 1884, when Sigmund Freud's colleague Carl Koller amazed the world with his discovery of cocaine's capacity to numb the eye in surgery.[4]

A New York doctor visiting Heidelberg relayed Koller's news home. Weeks later a fifty-three-year-old cataract patient at New York's Mount Sinai Hospital

---

[4] H. Richard Friman, "Germany and the Transformations of Cocaine, 1860–1920," *in Cocaine: Global Histories* (Paul Gootenberg ed., New York: Routledge, 1999), pp. 83–84 (relating Niemann's discovery); James Orton, *The Andes and the Amazon* (London: Sampson Low, Son, & Marston, 1870), p. 292; "Operating with a New Anæsthetic," *New York Tribune*, Oct. 22, 1884, p. 1; "The New Anæsthetic," *New York Times*, Oct. 29, 1884, p. 2 (reprinting a story from the *Albany Argus* of October 25); Carl Koller, "Cocaine's Finder," ibid., May 24, 1936, p. E9; Joseph F. Spillane, *Cocaine: From Medical Marvel to Modern Menace in the United States, 1884–1920* (Baltimore: The John Hopkins University Press, 2000), p. 7 (reviewing discovery of cocaine's anesthetic powers). In 1885 the *Times* traced Koller's announcement to an 1883 medical conference in Copenhagen instead. "A Remedy for Many Ills," *New York Times*, Sept. 2, 1885, p. 8. My thanks to Kevin Rothenberg of the Crown Law Library, who guided me through the sources on Niemann's early work.

became perhaps the first American to undergo cocaine anesthesia in surgery. As the *Tribune* told it, the patient lay awake and serene as doctors held her eyeballs in place with serrated forceps, sliced through her corneas, cut out her irises, and extracted her lenses. She then counted fingers held before her eyes and was bandaged up and taken to her ward. A week later the *Times* reported three similar demonstrations at Albany Medical College—one successful and two others in which "entire insensibility of the parts" was not achieved.[5]

These *Tribune* and *Times* articles document cocaine's true coming out in America, eclipsing Orton's forgotten 1870 reference. Hence cocaine arrived stateside in October 1884 as an Austro-German medical import. Just over a year passed before the *New York Times* mentioned the drug in a nonmedical context. Meanwhile the *Times*, *Tribune*, and other newspapers joined the medical press in heralding a savior, a wonder drug that made drilling teeth "almost a pleasure" and combated hay fever, insomnia, asthma, coughs, and maybe even seasickness. "Cocaine as a Cure-All," the *Tribune* proclaimed.[6]

True, cocaine didn't cure Ulysses S. Grant's throat cancer. For months the *Times* and other papers chronicled the old general's decline and demise despite repeated doses of cocaine. Yet even in dying in July 1885, Grant gave this upstart drug respectability. Weeks later the *Times* hailed cocaine as a children's cure, predicting that "if a child has the earache cotton and laudanum will be forgotten as its mother asks for the cocaine jar." What's more, many doctors found during self-experimentation that cocaine sped and sharpened their thinking, broadening the drug's appeal. The *Times* warned, however, where medical overuse might lead: "Poisoned by Cocaine," a headline announced in November 1885. A Kansas City woman had taken cocaine for a toothache and dosed herself to death.[7]

Even when cocaine first appeared in the *Times* in a nonmedicinal guise, the context remained medical. In November 1885, the paper told of America's first known cocaine abuser, Charles Bradley, a prominent physician of Chicago's North Side, "who ha[d] become crazed from excessive indulgence in cocaine" and now was "a slave to its use." Two months later, accounts surfaced of

---

[5] "Operating with a New Anæsthetic"; "The New Anæsthetic."

[6] "Surgery Without Pain," *New York Daily Tribune*, Mar. 8, 1885, p. 10 ("almost a pleasure . . ." and treatment for insomnia and asthma); "The Cocaine Remedy: Experimenting with a New Cure for Hay Fever," *New York Times*, Aug. 29, 1885, p. 8; "A Remedy for Many Ills," ibid., Sept. 2, 1885, p. 8 (seasickness cure); "Cocaine as a Cure-All," *New York Daily Tribune*, Sept. 14, 1885, p. 4 (cough drops).

[7] "His Fatal Illness," *New York Times*, July 24, 1885, p. 5 ("Muriate of cocaine was applied to relieve the General from the intense pain in the angle of the mouth . . . ."); "A Remedy for Many Ills," ibid., Sept. 2, 1885, p. 8; Spillane, *Cocaine*, p. 18 (reviewing doctors' self-experimentation); "Poisoned by Cocaine," *New York Times*, Nov. 19, 1885, p. 5.

New York's first reported cocaine abuser, a Civil War surgeon who "had been treating himself for nervousness with hypodermic injections of cocaine . . . ."[8]

Finally, in May 1886, the *Times* wrote of a cocaine abuser who was not a doctor. She was a doctor's daughter. She and her father were guests at an Elmira, New York, hotel when proprietors told police they "were acting like a pair of maniacs. They had torn the beds to pieces . . . ." Officers arrived to find A. S. Hazen, a well-educated Evansville physician, together with his daughter. "[I]t was soon established that the pair . . . were addicted to the habit of hypodermically injecting cocaine."[9]

Somewhat later, of course, it emerged that Dr. Hazen's nineteen-year-old traveling companion was no "daughter." As his brother told the Elmira police, the doctor had "left a wife and a nice family of three sons and one daughter for . . . that girl." Hence we have our first known case of recreational cocaine abuse tinged with illicit sex. As the *Times* wrote, Dr. Hazen "would thrust the hypodermic syringe containing the drug promiscuously into his and her flesh . . . ."[10]

The paper's next report on cocaine abuse, in July 1886, revealed "Another Physician a Victim to the Baneful Drug"—another "Slave to Cocaine." This time the doctor was J. W. Underhill, "one of the most prominent physicians" of Cincinnati and now "the third authenticated case on record in the United States." In August the paper mentioned another cocaine abuser—and in January 1887 another. These, too, were doctors, one from New York, one from Pennsylvania. Later in January, the paper reported that Dr. Bradley, the original cocaine fiend, had been arrested in Chicago after trying and failing to score a fix. Bradley had "been practicing every form of deception to procure the drug . . . ."[11]

Just as doctors first introduced recreational cocaine use, so doctors first debated its morality. In defense of nonmedical use stood one-time Surgeon General William A. Hammond, who wrote in 1886 of self-experiments with increasing injections of cocaine. Not only did these trials leave him "with no sign of habit," they convinced him of the moral case for cocaine. Though very high doses left him "intensely exhilarated and finally oblivious," a "*moderate* quantity taken in wine will stimulate the imagination, and enable one to write more brilliantly and with less effort than he otherwise could." After a moderate dose, Hammond "was in a very happy frame of mind—a sociable mood—and no doubt would have been quite agreeable company." The effect was "similar to that produced by two or three glasses of champagne." Hence, like Dr. John Jones, who

---

[8] "Cocaine's Terrible Effect," *New York Times*, Nov. 30, 1885, p. 1; "Dr. Farley Becomes Insane," ibid., Feb. 6, 1886, p. 8.

[9] "Victims of Cocaine," ibid., May 25, 1886, p. 2.

[10] "Victims of Cocaine," ibid., May 30, 1886, p. 7.

[11] "A Slave to Cocaine," ibid., July 4, 1886, p. 1; "Charged against Cocaine," ibid., Aug. 23, 1886, p. 1; "A Physician's Sad Plight," ibid., Jan. 17, 1887, p. 1; "Cocaine's Destructive Work," ibid., Jan. 25, 1887, p. 2.

defended moderate opium use almost two centuries before by comparing it with wine, Dr. Hammond sought to cast a suspect drug in alcohol's moral mold.[12]

Minneapolis doctor and sometime addiction-cure huckster Robert D'Unger met Hammond on his moral turf. The cases of Drs. Bradley and Hazen, he argued, proved cocaine was addictive, a view soon shared by the medical mainstream. And Dr. Hazen's sexual odyssey with a woman he "claimed as his sister [*sic*]" displayed the drug's moral dangers. D'Unger framed his indictment in old-fashioned moral argot: "There are four very bad drug demoralizers in the world—opium, alcohol, chloral, and cocaine." Of the four, the most benign is alcohol, "for a man may occasionally indulge in a teaspoonful of [alcohol] and preserve a little self-respect," but the same was not true of the other drugs. "[W]hen either opium, chloral, or cocaine is used as a brain stimulant or intoxicant all the finer qualities of manhood or womanhood fly away, as it were, and in their place is to be found the most brutish and lewdest of passions. In many instances there is a development of passions lower than that of the hog." Far from sparking the intellect, as Dr. Hammond claimed, cocaine "first stimulates, then paralyzes, or vice versa, and its use can only result in either partially or totally paralyzing the nerve cells of the brain."[13]

In Boston in the 1890s another hawker of addiction cures struck similar moral chords. The German Remedy Company urged its cure for the morphine, opium, alcohol, and cocaine habits, imploring the addict to "throw off his bondage before he loses all control of self" and becomes an "object[] of disgust" to himself. Once freed, he can "become once more a man [and] repossess himself of those faculties with which God endowed him . . . ." Here we have pure Augustinian tones, complete with indulgence of life's necessities. In an ad titled, "Man Cannot Be Blamed," the company absolved from fault those addicts hooked during medical treatment: "With morphine, opium and cocaine, the habit is often acquired it by first taking it to allay pain, and in a short time it becomes *absolutely necessary to existence*."[14]

Still, there was one distinction between the moral indictments of opium and cocaine: few observers spoke of cocaine *stupor*. Cocaine committed other moral offenses: it roused unreasoning pleasure and fueled sexual passion, and in addicting users, it robbed them of their self-control, rendering them slaves to pleasure. These sins assured the drug's moral and legal condemnation even when the opium smoker's deathlike silence was lacking.

[12] "The Effect of Cocaine," *Chicago Tribune*, Dec. 28, 1886, p. 9 (emphasis added).
[13] R. D'Unger, "Doctors Will Disagree," ibid., Jan. 1, 1887, p. 5; Spillane, *Cocaine*, pp. 32–33 (noting that mainstream doctors of the day accepted cocaine's addictive potential).
[14] "Morphine, Opium, Cocaine, and Liquor Habitue," *Boston Daily Globe*, Apr. 25, 1894, p. 4 ("throw off his bondage . . ." and "become once more . . ."); "Morphine, Opium, Cocaine and Chloral Habits Cured," ibid., Sept. 6, 1893, p. 3 ("object[] of disgust"); "Man Cannot Be Blamed," *Boston Sunday Globe*, Sept. 10, 1893, p. 9 (emphasis added).

Emergence of State Cocaine Bans

By late February 1887, when the first statewide cocaine ban took form, the *New York Times* had reported seven cases of cocaine abuse involving six doctors and a doctor's mistress. There was no sign those doctors—or Dr. Hazen's "daughter"—were anything but white. Crazed African American cocaine fiends were very far from view. Moreover, the first state to ban the drug was Oregon, host to one of the nation's smaller contingents of African Americans. In 1890 just 1,186 Oregonians—or 0.37 percent—were African American. Table 6A and the maps in Figures 6.1 through 6.3 suggest that in the pattern of early state law-making against cocaine, very little correlation appears between a state's proportion of African American residents and the timing of its first anti-cocaine law.[15]

Of course, the scarcity of African Americans does not mean they did not scare Oregon's whites. Not till 1926 did Oregon repeal a constitutional clause banning "free negro[es]" from migrating to, contracting in, or even visiting the state.[16] Still there's little reason to suspect fear of coke-addled African Americans prompted the state's 1887 cocaine ban. The surest guides to legislative intent, recorded floor debates and committee reports, either never existed or haven't survived. But an examination of two leading Oregon newspapers—the *Morning Oregonian* and *Oregon Statesman*—yields no evidence of racial bias in the law's enactment. In the six months before passage of the ban in February 1887 and in the month after, neither paper whispered a concern about racially tinged cocaine use. The word *cocaine* turned up in only eight items: five ads, two articles mentioning cocaine's use as a medical anesthetic, and one account of an opium and coca exhibit at the local fairgrounds. None bore reference to race.[17]

Despite a few slighting references to African Americans and one instance of outright mockery about vote selling by Black citizens, the papers' general attitude

---

[15] For census figures, *see* Campbell Gibson & Kay Jung, *Historical Census Statistics on Population Totals by Race, 1790 to 1990, and by Hispanic Origin, 1970 to 1990, for the United States, Regions, Divisions, and States* (Washington: U.S. Census Bureau 2002), tbl. A-16 ("Race for the United States, Regions, Divisions, and States: 1890 (General Enumeration)").

[16] Article XVIII, § 4, of Oregon's original 1857 constitution provided for a popular vote on the status of "free negroes." *Original Constitution of the State of Oregon* (n.p., 1857), p. 68. The resulting ban was later incorporated as art. I, § 35, of the constitution.

[17] In hawking a cure for cocaine addiction, two of the five advertisements featured Cincinnati's Dr. Underhill—"[t]hat leading physician who became a victim of the cocaine habit." "The Cocaine Habit," *Morning Oregonian*, Oct. 28, 1886, p. 2; "The Cocaine Habit," *Oregon Daily Statesman*, Dec. 23, 1886, p. 4. Cocaine appeared as a medical anesthetic in "Local and General," *Morning Oregonian*, Oct. 28, 1886, p. 5, and "Local and General," ibid., Dec. 29, 1886, p. 3. And cocaine came up in an account of a trade fair in "The Mechanics' Fair," ibid., Oct. 22, 1886, p. 3. Manish Kumar, one of my research assistants, scoured the pages of the *Morning Oregonian* and the *Oregon Statesman* hunting for relevant references. A broader online search of the *Morning Oregonian* and other papers added detail and color, but didn't alter the basic story line. I am grateful to Todd Shaffer of the Oregon State Archives, who confirmed that beyond brief entries in the Oregon House and Senate Journals, no legislative documents bearing on the state's 1887 antidrug law remain.

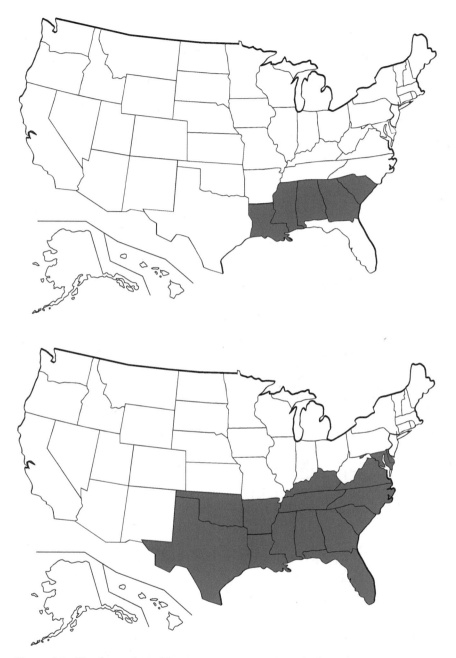

Figure 6.1: Top five and top fifteen states in proportion of African American population in 1890.

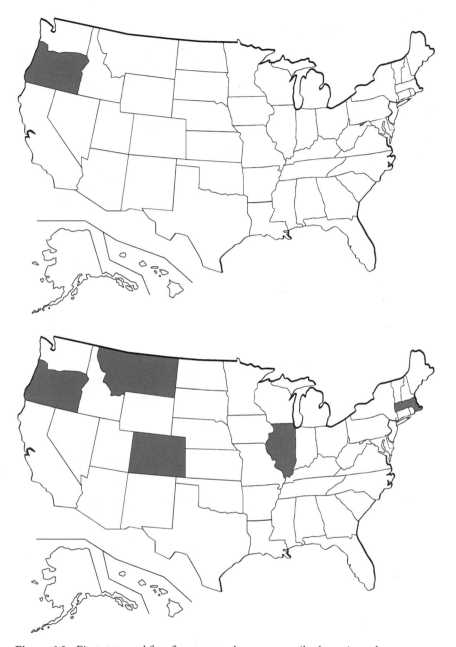

Figure 6.2: First state and first five states to ban unprescribed cocaine sales.

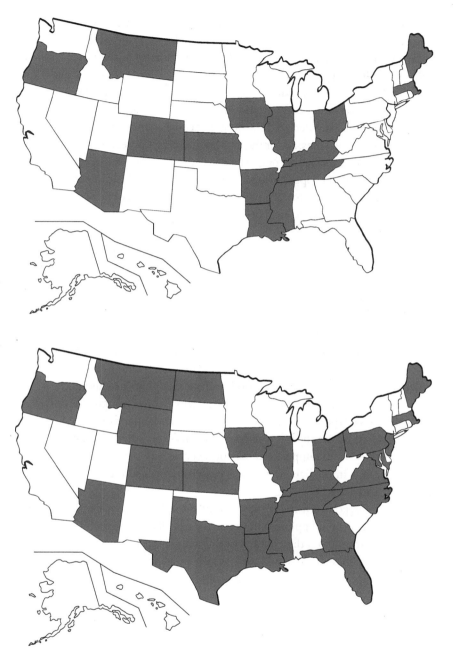

Figure 6.3: First fifteen and first twenty-five states and future states to ban unprescribed cocaine sales.

toward African Americans was studiously benevolent. Hence a *Statesman* head-line in September 1886 announced, "The Colored Race Progressing," and offered as two proofs the success of African American farmers in the South—"the re-sult of their industry"—and "the good use" Black children were making of their schools. And when South Carolina voters turned out of office the last remaining African American congressman, the *Statesman* scoffed at "the recent ceremony called an election" and declared the outgoing congressman the winner by fifteen or twenty thousand votes. As for the new law banning unprescribed cocaine sales that was wending its way through the legislature, these newspapers were silent but for its occasional appearance as House Bill 115, listed without commentary among bills proceeding toward passage. Each time it bore the shorthand title, "Regulating sale of opium, etc.," or "Prohibiting the sale of opium, etc.," with no reference to cocaine.[18]

The papers' failure to mention that Oregon's 1887 opium law also banned cocaine—and that it was the nation's first such ban—is perhaps evidence of the motives behind the legislature's action. The legislature first banned opium dens and unprescribed sales of eaten opium in November 1885. When it returned to the drafting table less than fifteen months later, it widened the original law to criminalize possession as well as sale—and broadened the banned drugs from opium alone to "opium, morphine, eng-she or cooked opium, hydrate of chloral or cocaine." If neither the press nor legislature fussed about extending the old opium ban to cover morphine, chloral, and cocaine, that's because doing so may have seemed the obvious next step. At least lawmakers seemingly saw it that way. After the bill's introduction in the Oregon House on January 18, 1887, less than a month elapsed before the bill won approval, fifty-four votes to none. And when the bill arrived in the upper chamber on February 17, senators suspended the rules to permit immediate action and passed the measure that same morning thirty votes to none.[19]

In short, Oregon's lawmakers apparently did not target cocaine. They simply enlarged their original opium ban to reach *all similar substances*. In later years, state legislatures across the country prohibited a class of "narcotic" substances defined to include most commonly regulated drugs. Here the Oregon law listed almost every well-known nonalcoholic intoxicant. The first three were

---

[18] "A Pathetic Incident," *Oregon Daily Statesman*, Dec. 3, 1886, p. 1 (depicting "Colored Citizens" as selling their vote and speaking an exaggerated urban argot); "The Colored Race Progressing," *Oregon Daily Statesman*, Sept. 23, 1886, p. 2; *Oregon Daily Statesman*, Jan. 13, 1887, p. 2 (commenting in a brief, untitled editorial about the South Carolina election). For examples of passing references to the pending legislation, *see* "The Legislature," *Morning Oregonian*, Jan. 19, 1887, p. 4; "The New Laws," *Oregon Statesman*, Feb. 20, 1887, p. 1; "The New Laws," *Oregon Daily Statesman*, Feb. 23, 1887, p. 3.
[19] "An Act to Regulate the Sale of Opium, and to Suppress Opium Dens," 1885 *Oregon Laws* (Act of Nov. 25, 1885), p. 39; "An Act to Regulate the Sale or Gift of Opium, Morphine, Eng-she or Cooked Opium, Hydrate of Chloral or Cocaine," 1887 *Oregon Laws* (Act of Feb. 21, 1887), p. 87; 1887 *Oregon House Journal*, pp. 60–61, 599, 606; 1887 *Oregon Senate Journal*, pp. 583, 597–98.

opiates—opium itself, its alkaloid morphine, and the ashy residue of the smoking process called eng-she. Chloral hydrate was a widely used synthetic sedative, chemically unrelated to opium. And cocaine was a stimulant made from a different plant grown on a different continent. What they all had in common was a capacity to intoxicate that made them subject to abuse and a power to addict that made such abuse abiding. By banning their sale or possession except by prescription, the legislature aimed to preserve their legitimate medical *use* while criminalizing their recreational and addiction-driven *abuse*.

So it's no surprise that fear of crazed African American coke fiends played no role in this first-in-the-nation cocaine ban. Such fear had no more to do with Oregon's cocaine ban than with the state's prohibition of chloral hydrate. Having established with Oregon's original anti-den law the principle of barring nonalcoholic intoxicants that served no recognized nonmedical need, lawmakers simply widened that prohibition to include any similar substance that crossed their view.

On to Montana

Two years later, when Montana enacted the nation's second cocaine ban, the new law again swept up cocaine within a broader list of forbidden drugs. Montana's territorial legislature had outlawed opium dens in 1881, but had not banned sales of eaten opium or any other drug. When lawmakers returned to the topic in 1889, they titled their new statute, "An Act to Prevent the Sale of Certain Noxious Drugs," and forbade unprescribed sales of opium, morphine, chloral hydrate, and cocaine.[20] As in Oregon, the course of lawmaking reveals no targeting of cocaine, much less of coke-crazed African Americans. The legislature seemingly corralled all prominent nonalcoholic intoxicants, deemed them worthless save as medicine, branded them "Noxious Drugs," and banned the whole lot unless prescribed.

As in Oregon, the state's demographic and political dynamics suggest Montana's drugs ban owed nothing to anti-Black bias. The territory's contingent of African Americans was larger than Oregon's but still tiny, amounting in 1890 to just 1.04 percent of the total, or 1,490 persons out of nearly 143,000. Close examination of the *Helena Independent* in the twelve months before passage of the 1889 law and the six weeks afterward reveals little hint of Black–white racial tension. True, the *Independent*'s attitude toward African Americans was decidedly less sympathetic than that of the Oregon press. "The masses of the race

---

[20] "An Act to Prohibit the Keeping of Opium Dens," 1881 *Montana Laws* (Act of Feb. 22, 1881), p. 65; "An Act to Prevent the Sale of Certain Noxious Drugs," 1889 *Montana Laws* (Act of Mar. 14, 1889), p. 123.

are still ignorant, improvident, shiftless, lazy," the editors intoned. Grudgingly, they allowed that though "a vast majority of them are unfitted for the privileges they possess as free citizens of the republic," they are advancing "as fast as circumstances will permit." On the matter of cocaine, however, there was no hint of bias. Not one article mentioned use of cocaine or any other drug by African Americans.[21]

Sweeping the day's press more broadly does not disturb this silence. A computer-assisted search of a dozen newspapers scattered across Montana turns up 103 articles or advertisements mentioning cocaine between late October 1884, when cocaine entered the American scene, and mid-March 1889, when Montana banned the drug. *Not one*, it seems, concerned cocaine use by non-whites. Yet the problem of cocaine abuse was very much in view: nine articles told of the familiar cortege of doctors and their dependents and concubines addicted to the drug; four more mentioned the general problem of cocaine abuse; and eighteen ads flogged one or another cure for the cocaine habit. Only four articles addressed nonmedical cocaine use by nonmedical folks: in one case a bank cashier, in another Frenchwomen "of morbid habits," and in two cases persons called only by name—May Preston and J. A. Fisk. Though the reporters never mentioned these addicts' race, the silence was telling, for the protocols of the day demanded no reticence around race. Montana articles reporting *other* offenses freely labeled the wrongdoer "Chinaman" or "Mongolian" or "heathen" or "colored" or "Sioux." Yet only once did a news story suggest a cocaine user's race. In June 1886, the *Butte Semi-Weekly Miner* told of a Butte laundress, forsaken in love, who attempted suicide with cocaine. The paper never named "the jilted maiden," but its reference to her as "[o]ne of the *fair* ones who manipulates linen in the Butte Steam Laundry" hinted she was white.[22]

[21] U.S. Census of Population and Housing, "Historical Census Browser" (University of Virginia Library); "Negro Progress," *Helena Independent*, Dec. 1, 1888, p. 4 (quoting—and deeming true—the words of T. T. Fortune, past editor of the *New York Freeman*). One of my research assistants, Blair Hornstine, tackled the labor-intensive task of examining each page of each issue of the *Helena Independent* across a thirteen-month period. She has a sharp eye and caught many well-hidden references to race, but some may have missed detection.

[22] [Untitled], *Butte Daily Miner*, Apr. 16, 1886, p. 2 (telling of the cocaine addiction of a Detroit "bank cashier named McDonald and one J.A. Fisk"); [Untitled], *Butte Semi-Weekly Miner*, Apr. 17, 1886, p. 2 (same); "An Explanation," ibid., Mar. 14, 1888, p. 3 (noting that May Preston, a boarder who recently died in a Butte home, was "a victim to morphine and cocaine and . . . invariably under the influence of stimulants"); "Women of the Day," *Helena Daily Independent*, Jan. 13, 1889, p. 6 (reporting that Parisian "women of morbid habits" were "no longer content with chloral, opium, [or] cocaine"); "Killed by a Chinaman," *Helena Independent*, Dec. 11, 1888, p. 1; "Braden's Supposed Slayer," ibid., Dec. 12, 1888, p. 1 (calling the suspect "the murderous Mongolian" and "the heathen"); "Tortured to Death," ibid., Dec. 18, 1888, p. 1 ("Fanny Jones (colored) is under arrest . . . ."); "Crazed with Liquor," ibid., Dec. 18, 1888, p. 1 ("a Yankton Sioux, while intoxicated, made a murderous attack . . ."); "Almost a Suicide," *Butte Semi-Weekly Miner*, June 12, 1886, p. 2 ("the jilted maiden" and "[o]ne of the fair ones"). The 103 articles mentioned in the text appeared in the *Billings Herald*, the *Butte Daily Miner*, the *Butte Semi-Weekly Miner*, the *Dillon Tribune*, the *Great Falls Tribune*, the *Helena Independent*, the *Livingston Enterprise*, the *Mineral Argus* (Maiden), the *New North-West* (Deer Lodge), the *Philipsburg*

Though race played no discernible part in shaping Montana's 1889 anti-narcotics act, the *youth* of one particular victim of a deadly drug, though not co-caine, seems to have touched a legislative nerve and helped spur action. The story unfolded in Montana's distant southwest. On January 12, 1889, five days before the legislative session opened in Helena, the *Helena Independent* announced the death in Butte of a "girl named Ruby Gr[a]y." Ruby was beautiful, the story said, but had been downhearted. "Goodbye; I can stand this life no longer," she wrote before overdosing with morphine. On the next page of the same issue, the *Independent* promptly appealed for new legislation. "In view of the prevalence of the use of narcotics, such as morphine and coc[a]ine, in this city, a statute more strictly regulating the sale of poisonous narcotics should be enacted." The editors complained that "[u]nder the existing laws, . . . any man, woman or child may purchase freely so long as they have money to pay for it. The ignorant use of these drugs is working the ruin of hundreds in this territory every year."[23]

As the Ruby Gray story spread from paper to paper, so did calls for a restrictive new drug law. On January 16, the very eve of the new legislative session, the *Butte Semi-Weekly Miner* ran a long and melancholy account of Ruby's last days. She was about twenty and had left her Philadelphia family for a new life in the West. A "separation from her 'lover' . . . drove her to sprees to drown her sorrows." On the afternoon of January 11, while recovering from one such spree, she rang for a messenger boy and asked him to fetch a bottle of morphine. Though only six-teen, the lad had no difficulty securing the drug and delivered it to Ruby in her bed, where she died hours later. "Send my body to my father," said a note under her pillow.[24]

As the *Miner* took pains to note, the coroner's jury "strongly condemned the laxity that prevails here in allowing the sale of deadly drugs to any and every person who presents the price of the same—even children—without the war-rant of a physician's prescription." The practice was "criminal in the extreme," the jurors said, and they "recommended that the sale in future be surrounded with safeguards against the indiscriminate vending of poisons." Immediately, the *Miner* endorsed the jurors' proposal. On the same page bearing the jurors' verdict, the editors spoke directly to lawmakers: "If there is one single subject that calls for immediate correction at the hands of the coming session of the Legislature more than another, it is the sale of opium and all its compounds . . . . That it should be possible for mere children to be able to go to a drug store an-ywhere in this Territory and by paying the price asked receive in return enough

Mail, the *River Press* (Fort Benton), and the *Daily Yellowstone Journal* (Miles City). I ran these online searches in September and October 2015.

[23] "I Cannot Stand This Life," *Helena Independent*, Jan. 12, 1889, p. 1; [Untitled Editorial], ibid., p. 2.
[24] "One More Unfortunate," *Butte Semi-Weekly Miner*, Jan. 16, 1889, p. 3.

of a deadly poison to kill a hundred grown people . . . is worse than criminal." Noting "the sale of a bottle of morphine to a District Messenger boy in this city, Friday last," the editors proposed it "be made . . . a crime to sell poison without proper medical prescription." Despite repeated references to *poisons* the editors did not mean merely drugs that could kill. "[T]he opportunities for the procurement of such drugs," they said, "whether to be used as poisons *or as means of self-indulgence*, should be reduced by every means possible to the smallest margin . . . ."[25]

Other press outlets in southwest Montana joined the *Miner*'s demand for legislation. On January 18, just a week after Ruby Gray's death, the *New North-West* of Deer Lodge County insisted that the legislature "prohibit the sale of morphine, unless prescribed by a physician. The instance of a girl suiciding at Butte last week with morphine, for which she had sent a 16-year-old messenger boy, illustrates the fact that there are no safeguards against any one obtaining this deadly poison in Montana." And six days later, the *Philipsburg Mail* reminded readers that morphine was not the only problem drug: "The recent suicides from morphine, cocaine, etc., show the imperative necessity of regulating the sale of such dangerous drugs, which fact our legislature appears to understand."[26]

As the *Mail*'s closing words suggest, the legislature—or at least one legislator— already had responded to the press's calls for action. On January 20, nine days after Ruby Gray's death and only three days into the legislative session, newly seated Representative Clinton H. Moore announced his intention to "introduce a bill for an act to restrict the sale of opium, morphine, cocaine and other poisons." Moore hailed from Deer Lodge County, which sits not far from Butte and Philipsburg. Having won election for the first time two months before, he seemed an unlikely figure to pioneer narcotics legislation. Nothing in his peripatetic resume—he was cow herder, school principal, college president, schoolteacher, census supervisor, stationer, school superintendent, postmaster, and goldmine superintendent—hinted of an interest in medicine or drug policy. Perhaps, though, his stints in education betray an interest in the welfare of youth.[27]

At all events, the *Miner* saw nothing odd about Moore's sponsorship of this pathbreaking legislation, for he simply was doing as the editors had urged. "The

[25] "One More Unfortunate," *Butte Semi-Weekly Miner*, Jan. 16, 1889, p. 3 ("be made . . . a crime . . ." and reporting on the coroner's jury); "The Sale of Poisons," ibid., Jan. 16, 1889, p. 3 ("If there is one . . ."; "the sale of a bottle . . ."; and "[T]he opportunities for the procurement . . .") (emphasis added).

[26] [Untitled], *The New North-West*, Jan. 18, 1889, p. 2; [Untitled], *Philipsburg Mail*, Jan. 24, 1889, p. 2.

[27] "The House," *Helena Independent*, Jan. 20, 1889, p. 5. For Moore's biographical details, *see* "Montana's Solons," *New North-West*, Jan. 18, 1889, p. 6, and "C.H. Moore, Pioneer of State, Dies," *Montana Standard*, June 27, 1932, p. 1. My thanks to Sonia Moss of the Crown Law Library, who tracked down Moore's obituary.

suggestion of THE MINER that the legislature enact a measure to prevent the present loose and indiscriminate sale of poisons, seems likely to be carried out," they wrote. "The Hon. Clinton H. Moore, of Deer Lodge, introduced into the Council, Saturday, a bill to restrict the sale of opium, morphine, cocaine, etc. It ought to pass." Indeed Moore's antidrug bill coursed through the legislature with hardly a hint of dissent, sweeping the House by a vote of twenty-two to zero and the Territorial Council nine to one.[28]

Though Montana's second-in-the-nation anti-cocaine law seems to have taken rise unlinked to the exhilaration and dissipation that had sounded moral alarms in Eastern accounts of cocaine abuse, those concerns soon enough touched home. On March 15, 1889, a day after the new law's final passage, the *Independent* told of the arrest of two "opium, morphine, and coc[a]ine fiends," Carrie and John Nesbitt. "To look at them is sickening," the paper said. Clad in rags and living in squalor, they took their morphine and cocaine "by use of a small glass injector, which is placed in an opening in the left arm or leg" and left those limbs "covered with scabs." The Nesbitts faced no charge under Montana's new law, for it punished only unprescribed *sale* of cocaine and morphine, not purchase or possession. Instead they faced trial for "lunacy"—and were acquitted.[29]

Ten days later, when the *Butte Semi-Weekly Miner* printed the text of the territory's new law, the editors appended a form of preamble explaining the legislature's motives. In part lawmakers had acted "to suppress the fatal facility with which poison enough to kill a regiment can be procured by a child at any drug store without a word of question." In part they sought "to diminish[] the curse of opium-smoking, morphine-eating and the indiscriminate use of drugs generally." Then, perhaps with a nod to the Nesbitts, the *Miner* faulted the new law for failing to punish physicians who prescribed drugs "other than medicinally. The law is practically nullified," the editors complained, "if any physician gives his prescription for a bottle of morphine to a morphine 'fiend' to pamper his diseased appetite, as it is alleged has already been done since the law was passed."[30] In Montana, therefore, if the *Miner's* account is sound, the legislature hoped to protect youth, to forestall suicide, and to bar fiends from pampering their diseased appetites.

Meanwhile, in the two years that separated Oregon's first-in-the-nation cocaine ban from Montana's second, the *New York Times* had extended its streak of stories on physician cocaine addicts. Six more articles told tales of cocaine

[28] [Untitled], *Butte Semi-Weekly Miner*, Jan. 23, 1889, p. 4; 1889 *Montana House Journal*, p. 262 (Mar. 13, 1889); 1889 *Montana Council Journal*, p. 309 (Mar. 14, 1889).
[29] "Repertorial Notes," *Helena Independent*, Mar. 15, 1889, p. 4 ("opium, morphine, and . . ."); "Objects of Pity," ibid., Mar. 16, 1889, p. 4 ("To look at them . . ."; "by use of a small . . ."; and "covered with scabs"); "Victims of the Drug," ibid., Mar. 17, 1889, p. 4 (noting that the Nesbitts—here spelled "Nesbit"—were tried for and acquitted of "lunacy").
[30] "The Sale of Drugs," *Butte Semi-Weekly Miner*, Mar. 27, 1889, p. 2.

abuse, and all concerned doctors. One offered an update on the sad plight of Dr. Bradley, the Chicago physician reduced to knocking on random doctors' doors to feed his habit. Five others told of "a prominent physician" of Auburn, "a well-known . . . physician" of Pittsburgh, a doctor who "a few years ago had a large practice" in Chicago, a Brooklyn doctor, and one of Jersey City.[31] In sum, by the time Montana enacted the nation's second cocaine ban in March 1889, the *Times* had told of thirteen cocaine abusers—eleven doctors, one doctor's wife and one "daughter." All were likely white.

Early Cocaine Regulation in New York

Though New York did not ban cocaine till 1907, proposals and half-measures surfaced much earlier. In December 1885, only fourteen months after the new drug's American debut, it faced what may have been its first proposed ban. The New York Medical Society reportedly was drafting a bill to outlaw cocaine sales except by prescription. Explaining the Medical Society's motives, the *Chicago Tribune* said cocaine's enormous success as a local anesthetic had "led to a promiscuous and very hurtful use as a swallowed exhilarant. So great has the demand for it become that, in the form of chewing-pastes, it is on sale in most of the drug-stores." The paper predicted that drug makers, eager to preserve a potentially lucrative market, would "interpose at Albany against the passage of any law on the subject."[32] Perhaps such lobbying explains the bill's fate, for it seemingly died with little trace.

Yet the *Tribune's* account reveals a lot. After barely a year on American shores cocaine had slipped the confines of medical use into the wider world of recreational "exhilarant[s]." An 1895 *Webster's* said *exhilarate* meant "[t]o make merry or jolly; to enliven; to cheer." This new exhilarant now came in a convenient and likely tasty form. Cocaine chewing gum must have seemed especially alluring given the alternative. Doctor and concubine alike had suffered a hypodermic cocaine regimen that first addicted, then disfigured. Septic needles left users scabbed with abscesses. "[T]heir looks were ghastly," wrote the *New York Times* of Dr. Hazen and the traveling companion who was not his daughter—their arms

---

[31] "Work of an Awful Habit," *New York Times*, Nov. 30, 1887, p. 3 (updating the condition of Dr. Bradley of Chicago); "Crazed by Drugs," ibid., Mar. 8, 1887, p. 8 (telling of Dr. Le Grand Schaffer of Brooklyn); "All Caused by Morphine," ibid., May 4, 1887, p. 8 (Dr. Francis M. Deems, who had a practice in Jersey City Heights and apparently abused both morphine and cocaine); "Used Morphine and Cocaine," ibid., Mar. 24, 1888, p. 3 (Dr. F.M. Hamlin of Auburn); "A Victim to Cocaine," ibid., Aug. 29, 1888, p. 1 (Dr. N.H. Borland of Pittsburg); "Victim of Cocaine and Morphine," ibid., Sept. 17, 1888, p. 1 (Dr. Edward L. Tons of Chicago).

[32] "Curbing the Coca Habit," *Chicago Daily Tribune*, Dec. 6, 1885, p. 26. The *New York Times* apparently made no mention of this proposal. Joseph Spillane writes of a chewing paste called Coca-Bola that delivered 710 milligrams of cocaine in each ounce of the product. Spillane, *Cocaine*, pp. 83–84.

"covered with wounds and scars."[33] Against this potent disincentive to cocaine abuse, drugstore sales of cocaine chewing pastes perhaps seemed an irresistibly easy entrée into a world peopled by a medical elite.

Though the Medical Society's early alarm went unheeded, New York ultimately passed one of the nation's first anti-cocaine laws. In 1893, six years after Oregon banned unprescribed cocaine sales and four years after Montana followed course, the New York legislature decreed, "No pharmacist . . . or other person shall refill more than once, prescriptions containing opium or morphine or . . . cocaine or chloral . . . except upon the written order of a physician" or unless the dose fell below specified very low amounts. This law added cocaine and chloral to a similar New York act of 1887 that banned refills of opium and morphine prescriptions. As in Oregon and Montana, New York's first anti-cocaine law treated cocaine on much the same terms as eaten opium.[34]

Unlike the Oregon and Montana laws, however, New York's 1893 act did not ban all unprescribed sales of the listed drugs. Because New York still permitted over-the-counter sales *without prescriptions* of all these drugs, it's a puzzle what the legislatures of 1887 and 1893 accomplished by banning prescription refills. In 1891 the *Chicago Tribune* reported that New York *did* ban unprescribed sales, and the *New York Times* said so too as late as January 1907. But the law books prove otherwise. Not till June 1907 did a New Yorker need a doctor's say-so to buy cocaine—and not till 1914 did the ban reach opium and morphine.[35]

Deciphering the New York legislature's intent in framing the 1893 law is both impossible and easy—impossible because the legislature left no enduring record of its aims, easy because lawmakers obviously *meant* their ban on prescription

---

[33] *Webster's Academic Dictionary* (Chicago: American Book Company, 1895), p. 208; "Victims of Cocaine," *New York Times*, May 30, 1886, p. 7 (reporting Dr. Hazen's case). *See also* "Work of an Awful Habit," *New York Times*, Nov. 30, 1887, p. 3 (reporting that a police officer "saw that the arms of [Dr. Bradley and his wife] were one mass of wholly or partially healed sores and small, freshly-made wounds"); J.B. Mattison, "Cocainism," *Medical Record*, vol. 43 (Jan. 14, 1893), pp. 34, 35 (documenting scarring among patients who used cocaine hypodermically). A Helena, Montana, drug clerk advised a reporter: "Very few women use morphine hypodermically, for the reason, I suppose, that the punctures necessary mar the beauty of their arms, where it is principally used." "Victims of Opiates," *Helena Independent* (Nov. 17, 1888), p. 4.

[34] "An Act in Relation to the Public Health," 1893 *New York Laws*, vol. 2, ch. 661, § 208 (Act of May 9, 1893), p. 1561; "An Act to Regulate the Sale of Morphine by Druggists and Apothecaries in this State," 1887 *New York Laws*, ch. 636, §§ 1–3 (Act of June 21, 1887), p. 848.

[35] "Death's Door Wide Open," *Chicago Daily Tribune*, May 31, 1891, p. 35; "Boy Cocaine Snuffers Hunted by the Police," *New York Times*, Jan. 8, 1907, p. 6; "An Act to Amend the Penal Code, in Relation to the Sale of Certain Drugs," 1907 *New York Laws*, ch. 424, § 1 (Act of June 5, 1907), p. 879 (banning unprescribed cocaine sales); "An Act to Amend the Public Health Law, in Relation to the Sale of Habit-Forming Drugs," 1914 *New York Laws*, ch. 363, § 1 (Act of April 14, 1914), p. 1120 (banning unprescribed opium and morphine sales). A New York City ordinance requiring a doctor's prescription to buy cocaine also dates to 1907. Sanitary Code § 182 (Jan. 28, 1907), *in Code of Ordinances of the City of New York* (Arthur F. Cosby ed., New York: The Banks Law Publishing Co., 1908), p. 385. My thanks to David Crandall, who scoured many volumes of New York statutes and session laws to establish the absence of any earlier ban on unprescribed cocaine sales.

refills to combat recreational cocaine abuse. Though legislators apparently goofed in banning refills without banning over-the-counter sales, it's worth asking what moved them in 1893 to *try* to ban nonmedical cocaine use. Two things seem clear. As in Oregon in 1887 and Montana in 1889, legislators in New York addressed a growing problem of recreational cocaine abuse by subjecting cocaine to the same restrictions that governed eaten opium and morphine. And nothing on the face of these laws betrays concern about cocaine abuse by non-whites. Indeed it seems the 1893 law took hold before a *single* prominent press report disclosed cocaine abuse by non-white New Yorkers.

Out there somewhere may lurk a report of non-white cocaine abuse. Claiming a negative always hazards disproof. But this much is sure: neither the *New York Times* nor the *Chicago Tribune* nor even the *Atlanta Constitution* hinted at non-white cocaine abuse in the United States as early as 1893. All three papers eagerly identified African Americans as perpetrators of *other* offenses. All three printed many reports of recreational cocaine abuse—a collective eighty-one such accounts during the drug's first decade in America, ending in October 1894. Fifty-three of these reports concerned medical professionals or pharmacists or their friends and family members, all apparently white. Twenty dealt with lawyers or others of wealth or distinction. Another eight addressed middle- or working-class abusers or addicts of no specified race or station. Three *other* reports—one in each newspaper—mentioned South American natives or whites who sometimes chewed coca leaves for pleasure. *Not one* account concerned a North American cocaine abuser who was obviously or likely non-white. Reports in medical journals looked much the same. Joseph Spillane counted twenty-eight cases of cocaine addiction reported in the medical press in the 1880s and 1890s. Seventeen accounts concerned doctors, eight concerned professionals of other stripes, and three listed no occupation. From all that appears, not one involved non-whites.[36]

The Colorado Cocaine Ban

Little had changed by 1897, when Colorado (in March) and Illinois (in June) followed Oregon and Montana (and New York's partial ban) to become the

---

[36] On the readiness of these papers to use racial markers, *see* "Joe Mayo's Mail Robbery," *Atlanta Constitution*, Dec. 12, 1885, p. 2 ("[T]he colored office boy, took some $30 out of the drawer."); "The Northwest," *Chicago Daily Tribune*, July 2, 1885, p. 6 ("Villa[i]nous Assault upon a Little Girl by a Burly Negro at Rockford, Ill."); "City and Suburban News," *New York Times*, May 2, 1885, p. 8 ("Pauline Shackler and her negro husband, Charles Bond, were committed for trial yesterday by Justice Smith for robb[ery] . . . ."). The three South American reports are: [Untitled], *Atlanta Constitution*, Oct. 27, 1885, p. 4; "Cocaine," *Chicago Daily Tribune*, Aug. 3, 1885, p. 5; "Coca," *New York Times*, Dec. 27, 1885, p. 10. Spillane reports that even "[a]s late as 1898, physicians were thought to constitute 30 percent of those with the [cocaine] habit." Spillane, *Cocaine*, p. 39.

third and fourth states to forbid unprescribed cocaine sales.[37] Whatever principle drove Colorado to join the ranks of the first states to ban cocaine, race is not a suspect. Surviving Colorado sources permit little detailed storytelling, but display no concern about non-white cocaine fiends. On the contrary, in Colorado as in other states, most early press accounts of cocaine abuse dealt with doctors, druggists, and their patients and hangers-on.[38] A search of Colorado newspapers, legislative documents, and historical studies uncovers but a single report of non-white cocaine abuse predating the state's cocaine ban. That report, which I'll address shortly, hailed from Missouri and appeared *after* Colorado's proposed ban already was marching through the legislature.

Though Colorado lawmakers, like those in Oregon and Montana, left no surviving record of their motives, widely scattered evidence suggests recreational cocaine abuse among miners helped prompt action. Mining camp commissaries sold cocaine presumably to enhance energy, but encountered concerns it sparked violence or insanity. An 1894 report in the *Cleveland Medical Gazette* noted that "in some portions of the West, especially in the mining regions, the use of cocaine . . . as a stimulant is becoming very common." Closer to home, a brief *Denver Post* article of May 1896 told of a Cripple Creek miner who overdosed on cocaine. And legislative records reveal that Andrew R. Lewis of Durango, a miner who represented the mining region of La Plata County, introduced the 1897 anti-cocaine law in the Colorado House.[39]

Not all miners were white, of course, and Colorado mining communities, like many across the West, often erupted in racial strife. But the rival races typically

[37] "An Act to Prohibit Druggists . . . from Selling Cocaine without a Prescription . . . ," 1897 *Colorado Laws*, ch. 38 (Act of Mar. 31, 1897), p. 138; "An Act for the Regulation [of] the Sale of Cocaine . . . ," 1897 *Illinois Laws* (Act of June 11, 1897), p. 138. Unlike the Illinois law, which prohibited "any druggist or other person to retail or sell or give away cocaine," the Colorado act of 1897 operated only against pharmacists and their clerks. But the effect was the same, as a Colorado law of 1893 had barred cocaine sales by non-druggists. "An Act in Relation to the Practice of Pharmacy . . . ," 1893 *Colorado Laws*, ch. 131 (Act of Apr. 17, 1893), p. 365.

[38] *See, e.g.*, "Ruined by Cocaine," *Rocky Mountain News*, May 23, 1886, p. 1 (telling the story of Dr. Hazen); "Took an Overdose," ibid., June 20, 1896, p. 3 (concerning Dr. John K. Carver, a morphine and cocaine addict); "Expired in the City Jail," ibid., Jan. 2, 1897, p. 2 (relating the death of Denver doctor McLeod Smith, who had an "inordinate appetite for cocoaine and morphine").

[39] *See* Henry O. Whiteside, *Menace in the West: Colorado and the American Experience with Drugs, 1873–1963* (Denver: Colorado Historical Society, 1997), pp. 13–14 (reporting cocaine sales by mining camp commissaries and the drug's "reputation for causing violence and insanity"); C.P. Ambler, "Cocaine: Its Uses and Abuses," *Cleveland Medical Gazette*, vol. 10 (1894–1895), pp. 54–62 (quoted in Spillane, *Cocaine*, p. 92); "Cocaine or Epilepsy—Cripple Creek Miner Causes a Scare in a Lodging House," *Denver Evening Post*, May 12, 1896, p. 5; "Little Opposition to Mr. Teller," *Denver Evening Post*, Jan 19, 1897, p. 2 (reporting A. R. Lewis's introduction of an anti-cocaine bill in the Colorado House); 1897 *Colorado House Journal*, p. 181 (Jan. 19, 1897) (same). I thank Aly Jabrocki of the Colorado State Archives for providing what remains of the legislative records of Lewis's bill. My thanks as well to Sara Mayeux, one of my research assistants, who meticulously assembled the available sources on the Colorado cocaine ban.

were whites and Chinese, not whites and African Americans. The economic rivalry between immigrant Chinese miners and their white counterparts was often bitter and sometimes violent.[40] Yet I've seen no report of cocaine use or abuse among Chinese immigrants in Colorado and no evidence the state's 1897 cocaine ban targeted Chinese miners in particular or the Chinese community in general. As for tension between white miners and their African American counterparts, historian Jesse Moore suggests whites may have seen African Americans not as a threat but as a hedge against the hated Chinese. Nor is there evidence of stark Black–white tension outside mining communities. That an African American joined the ranks of the Arapahoe County Sheriff's Office as early as 1865, of the Denver Police Department as early as 1880, and of the state legislature as early as 1892 suggests a measure of harmony, even if segregation survived in other realms of life.[41]

If worries of cocaine abuse among Colorado miners sped passage of the state's 1897 ban, those worries likely focused on *white* miners, who probably accounted for most of this abuse. But it seems such concerns arose too sporadically to have moved lawmakers to act. Instead Colorado lawmakers likely acted for about the same reasons as lawmakers in Oregon and Montana: they saw cocaine breaking out of its medical mold and into the realm of recreational abuse. As long as cocaine addiction remained an unfortunate but largely unavoidable consequence of legitimate medical use, cocaine won grudging deference from lawmakers. But once the lay public, including perhaps miners, began to indulge in the drug for sport, lawmakers took action.

---

[40] *See* Carl Abbott et al., *Colorado: A History of the Centennial State* (Boulder: University Press of Colorado, 4th ed. 2005), pp. 207–208 (noting that by 1890 the Chinese had been driven out of most of the mining towns); James Edward Wright, *The Politics of Populism: Dissent in Colorado* (New Haven: Yale University Press, 1974), pp. 26–27 (describing attacks on the Chinese by militant labor organizers and mining-town mobs).

[41] Historians differ somewhat in their assessment of Black–white relations in Colorado in this era. Jesse Moore and James Wright have delivered more positive assessments. *See* Jesse T. Moore Jr., "Seeking a New Life: Blacks in Post–Civil War Colorado," *Journal of Negro History*, vol. 78 (Summer 1993), pp. 166, 170–71 (reporting that "black migration to Colorado was encouraged because untold numbers of whites believed that blacks 'would help to keep out the Chinese, who were then regarded as a threat to American labor'"); Wright, *Politics of Populism*, p. 26 (describing white Coloradans' attitudes toward African Americans as "paternalistic—if condescending"—with little evidence of conflict). Quintard Taylor and William King, in contrast, emphasize evidence in Denver of persistent segregation in housing, education, hotels, restaurants, and theaters. *See* Quintard Taylor, *In Search of the Racial Frontier: African Americans in the American West, 1528–1990* (New York: W.W. Norton & Co., 1998), p. 204; William M. King, "The End of an Era: Denver's Last Legal Public Execution, July 27, 1886," *Journal of Negro History*, vol. 68 (Winter 1983), p. 38.

Henry O. Wagoner served as Arapahoe County's first African American deputy sheriff between 1865 and 1875; Isaac Brown and John Bell joined the Denver police force in 1880 and 1881; and Joseph H. Stuart won a seat in the state legislature in 1892. *See* Taylor, *In Search of the Racial Frontier*, p. 204; Kareem Maddox, "Denver's Long History of African American Police Officers Showcased in Exhibit," Colorado Public Radio (June 23, 2015).

Evidence of recreational abuse surfaced about a year and a half before Representative Lewis placed his anti-cocaine bill before the Colorado House. Scary headlines grabbed the public's eye: "The Cocaine Habit—A Swift Road to Mental and Physical Destruction" and "Cocaine—The Demand Steadily Increasing and Its Evil Effect Grows."[42] These articles made no mention of cocaine use among non-whites, miners, or the underclass. They warned instead of the spread of cocaine outside the medical fold.

One article stands out. Printed in the *Colorado Springs Gazette* just two weeks before Representative Lewis took action, it proclaimed "The Latest New Intoxicant": "Now comes news from a Connecticut town that cocaine snuff has become the rage with its inhabitants, and that they are wasting their substance and ruining their health by its use." It seems an unnamed doctor had devised this cocaine snuff as "a remedy for catarrh." A *catarrh*, as *Webster's* explained in 1895, was "a cold in the head or lungs." A *catarrh snuff*, therefore, was a cold remedy—and a remarkably alluring one when laced with cocaine.[43]

The particular catarrh snuff described in the *Colorado Springs Gazette* contained not merely cocaine, but milk sugar and either menthol or peppermint. Cocaine cut with sweetener and flavorings must have proved doubly delicious to youth and others who could claim a cold. The mixture was "applied to the nostrils like tobacco snuff," a mode of use that, like the chewing pastes of New York, must have appealed to those who shrank from the pain and scabs of hypodermic injection. And because the powder had "been found to possess also exhilarating qualities," its use "has spread to all classes of the population," including "children of tender years, and hundreds of factory work people." Those abusing the new "cure" as an exhilarant were not thugs or toughs, therefore, and wore no particular racial identity. Yet an "appeal to the legislature [was] talked of to pass a law to suppress the evil . . . ."[44]

That article appeared in the *Colorado Springs Gazette* on January 4, 1897. Though it told of events in a Connecticut town, it concerned a drug readily available in Colorado. Writing of the same Connecticut town and also of cocaine's widening use in Colorado, the *Pueblo Opinion* declared "that a law should be passed by the legislature restricting the sale of this deadly drug only on physician's prescriptions"—an appeal reprinted on January 8 by the *Telluride*

---

[42] "The Cocaine Habit—A Swift Road to Mental and Physical Destruction," *Denver Evening Post*, June 19, 1895, p. 7; "Cocaine—The Demand Steadily Increasing and Its Evil Effect Grows," ibid., Dec. 11, 1895, p. 2.

[43] "The Latest New Intoxicant," *Colorado Springs Gazette*, Jan. 4, 1897, p. 4; *Webster's Academic Dictionary* (Chicago: American Book Company, 1895), p. 96.

[44] "The Latest New Intoxicant," *Colorado Springs Gazette*, Jan. 4, 1897, p. 4.

Daily Journal. Eleven days later Representative Lewis introduced his proposal to forbid unprescribed cocaine sales.[45]

As that bill wound through the legislature, the press blared new warnings of the powders menacing Connecticut. "A Connecticut Town Goes Crazy over Cocaine Snuff," announced the *Leadville Herald Democrat* on January 24. "Cocaine Crazed—An Entire Town Goes Mad from the Use of the Drug," echoed Denver's *Rocky Mountain News* on January 31. The catarrh snuff had been "passed around, and now hundreds of persons have become slaves to the stuff," said the latter report. "The cases of the boys are specially pitiful," wrote the former. The victims included not only youth and factory workers, but also the "well-known men and women" who went night and day to a local druggist's home, pleading for a fix.[46]

Two weeks later the Colorado House unanimously approved Lewis's cocaine bill, first proposed less than a month before. The House attached to the measure an emergency clause deeming the law so urgent it must take effect immediately on passage. On March 9, as the Senate weighed the bill, the *Colorado Springs Gazette* explained that the proposed legislation "will be directed toward patent medicines. It appears the cocaine habit is increasing to an alarming extent and this increase is attributed in measure to the sale of snuffs and balms for catarrh filled with the dreaded narcotic." Within two weeks, the bill secured Senate approval without debate or dissent, and at month's end, the governor signed it into law.[47]

Throughout this lawmaking season and in the many months before, hardly a hint of non-white cocaine abuse stirred the airwaves. While newspapers in Denver, Leadville, Pueblo, Telluride, and Colorado Springs wrote of the catarrh snuffs snorted by the presumably white residents of a coke-crazed Connecticut town, a single Colorado paper told instead of African American cocaine abuse in Missouri. On February 5, 1897, and again on March 3, the *Grand Junction Daily Sentinel* reprinted a single story from the *St. Louis Republic*. Headlined "The Cocaine Habit," the article led with a lesson relevant to all Coloradans: "Don't use catarrh snuffs unless you want to become a cocaine fiend." The allure of cocaine—"the most exhilarating of the drugs used for anaesthetic purposes"—has made "[t]he habit of taking catarrh snuff . . . one of the insidious growing evils of

[45] "A Social Evil," *Telluride Daily Journal*, Jan. 8, 1897, p. 2 (reprinting item from the *Pueblo Opinion*); 1897 *Colorado House Journal*, p. 181 (Jan. 19, 1897).

[46] "The Queer Side of Life," *Leadville Herald Democrat*, Jan. 24, 1897, p. 6; "Cocaine Crazed," *Rocky Mountain News*, Jan. 31, 1897, p. 19.

[47] 1897 *Colorado House Journal*, p. 516 (Feb. 16, 1897) (noting the bill's House passage, 54 votes to 0); "Scared by the Scorcher," *Rocky Mountain News*, Feb. 17, 1897, p. 9 (noting the bill's passage in the House with an emergency clause attached); [Untitled], *Colorado Springs Gazette*, Mar. 9, 1897, p. 4; "With Many Amendments," *Rocky Mountain News.*, Mar. 23, 1897, p. 5 (reporting unanimous Senate passage); 1897 *Colorado Senate Journal*, p. 829 (Mar. 22, 1897) (recording the bill's Senate passage 29 votes to 0); "Sale of Cocaine," *Rocky Mountain News*, Apr. 1, 1897, p. 10 (noting the governor's signature and reprinting the text of the new law).

the day." Only after this prelude did the author add, "Negroes especially take to it for some reason. There is hardly a 'coon' in the Bad Lands that isn't addicted to it...."[48]

Vile as this slur is, I've seen no evidence it caught the eye of lawmakers or of anyone outside Grand Junction, which lies far west of Denver, a spit from the Utah border. The article hardly could have moved Representative Lewis to act, for he had proposed his cocaine ban in the Colorado House weeks earlier. Instead the article's significance is the proof it offers of the fast spread of catarrh snuffs and of consequent public alarm. These snuffs and the trouble they brewed follow us as we move now from Colorado, the third state to ban cocaine, to Illinois, which soon became the fourth.

The Illinois Ban

The *Chicago Tribune*'s accounts of cocaine's first years on American shores looked much like those in the Eastern press. Early reports of the drug's miraculous anesthetic powers soon gave way to overeager claims of a medical cure-all.[49] Then came tales of addiction and falls from grace. First among the fallen was Chicago's own Dr. Charles Bradley, who plummeted from his North Side practice to a Bellevue psych ward. Bradley first drew hometown headlines in late November 1885, barely a year after cocaine's American landfall, when he was "sent to the asylum a physical and mental wreck from the free use of cocaine." Reports he conscripted his wife and children as experimental subjects, injecting them with cocaine to see its effects and addicting them in the bargain, deepened his moral stain.[50]

[48] "The Cocaine Habit," *Grand Junction Daily Sentinel*, Feb. 5, 1897, p. 2; "The Cocaine Habit," ibid., Mar. 3, 1897, p. 3.

[49] On cocaine's value as a local anesthetic *see, e.g.*, "Hydro-chlorate of Cocaine," *Chicago Daily Tribune*, Feb. 9, 1885, p. 8. Claims of broader curative powers appear in "Cure for Drunkenness or Morphinism," ibid., Jan. 12, 1885, p. 9; "For the Throat and Nerves," ibid., Nov. 25, 1885, p. 11 (ad for Allen's cocaine tablets, which "[c]ure sore throat, neuralgia, nervo[u]sness, headache, and sleeplessness"); "The New Remedy," ibid., Dec. 2, 1885, p. 1 (another ad for Allen's tablets, this time promising "A POSITIVE CURE FOR CATARRH, Asthma, Hay Fever, COLD IN THE HEAD").

[50] On Bradley, *see, e.g.*, "The Cocaine Habit: Its Blighting Influence on a North-Side Doctor," *Chicago Daily Tribune*, Nov. 30, 1885, p. 8 (referring to Bradley's North Side practice, his experiments on his wife and children, and his addiction, descent into insanity, and initial commitment); "Dr. Bradley Again in Trouble," ibid., Jan. 24, 1887, p. 5 (reporting that Bradley, now "known through his utter abandonment to the opium and cocaine habit," was arrested after being found "in a helpless state" on a Chicago street); "The City," ibid., Jan. 28, 1887, p. 8 (noting he was adjudged insane and committed); "In General," ibid., Dec. 1, 1887, p. 3 (discovering him in Bellevue Hospital, having been committed "for an attempt to swindle for the purpose of obtaining cocaine"). In a long interview with the *New York Herald* reprinted in the Chicago *Daily Inter Ocean*, Bradley denied reports he experimented with his wife and children. "His Own Story," *Daily Inter Ocean*, Dec. 31, 1887, p. 24 (reprinted from the *New York Herald*).

In Bradley's wake followed a familiar flock of doctors and druggists, together with the occasional congressman, law student, or other cardholder of the privileged class. That *every* cocaine abuser so far mentioned in the *Tribune* was seemingly white and usually respectable did not bar introduction in March 1895 of an Illinois House bill forbidding the drug's manufacture and sale.[51] Though that measure came to naught, a series of events beginning late in 1894 reshaped the landscape of cocaine abuse in the run-up to the state's 1897 adoption of a ban on unprescribed sales.

Those events dealt with cocaine abuse by young whites and with a new way to administer the drug, themes that emerged in a long *Tribune* article of December 1894. Under the warning, "CURE IS THE WORST," the editor wrote of a frightening new phenomenon: "Users of Catarrh Powder Contract the Cocaine Habit." Users applied the "fine white powder . . . directly to the membrane lining the nose by means of a small tube and blowpipe."[52] Abuse was inescapable, and among the earliest initiates were youths.

Two such youths appeared in the same article. At a drugstore on Chicago's Fifth Avenue, the manager explained why he no longer sold catarrh powders containing cocaine: "I have seen too many instances . . . where a patient begins to take these powders for a cold in the head, and eventually becomes a confirmed and almost incurable cocaine fiend." The manager spoke of "[o]ne young fellow, somewhat on the tough order," who first bought the drug for a slight cold, but soon found himself consuming a bottle a night. Then it seemed he had lost his job, for he began asking the druggist to accept partial payment. At last he resorted to threats and theft. More telling, though, was the story of a boy in the druggist's own employ. This seemingly respectable lad "got thin and white, and did not attend to his work." Eventually, the druggist learned he was "taking the stuff on the sly" and reported the boy to his parents. Yet "even after his parents had taken him in hand he used to gather up his pennies and slip out to buy the powder at other drug stores."

It was just such a lad whose plight gripped Chicagoans in October 1896, months before the state's first anti-cocaine law took form. Unlike the "thin and

---

[51] "Crazed by Cocaine," *Chicago Daily Tribune*, July 4, 1886, p. 1 (Dr. Underhill of Cincinnati); "A Maniac from Cocaine," ibid., Oct. 3, 1886, p. 17 (Columbia law student Albert Durer); "A Victim of the Cocaine Habit," ibid., Dec. 25, 1886, p. 6 (druggist David Jones of Columbus); "News of the Northwest: Crazed by Cocaine," ibid., Jan. 24, 1887, p. 3 (Dr. G. Paterson of Beloit, Wis.); "Cocaine and a Woman," ibid., Dec. 9, 1887, p. 6 (Dr. Frank Sanders of Morristown, N.J., who abandoned a high-born wife and ran off with a seamstress); "A Victim of Cocaine," ibid., July 3, 1888, p. 1 (Chicago Congressman John R. Thomas from Illinois' 20th congressional district); "Street Car Passengers Scared," ibid., July 28, 1894, p. 6 (E. Meyers, employee of a Chinese medicine firm); "To Amend Three Articles at a Clip," ibid., Mar. 23, 1895, p. 9 (reporting that Representative Simon Shaffer of Chicago had proposed a bill "[t]o prohibit the manufacture and sale of chloral hydrate, opium, cocaine, cigarets, or any other article containing opium").

[52] "Cure Is the Worst," ibid., Dec. 16, 1894, p. 38.

THE CHICAGO TRIBUNE: WEDNESDAY, OCTOBER 21, 1896.

BEFORE TAKING.   AFTER TAKING.

MAX OHLE.

Figure 6.4: "Max Ohle: Before Taking and After Taking" (1896).

white" but nameless boy just mentioned, this lad had a trusty Chicago moniker, Max Ohle, and respectable working-class roots as a North Side barber's son. He had a face, too, depicted by a *Tribune* sketch artist in "before taking" and "after taking" forms. Both before and after cocaine, Max was handsome, wide-eyed, and white. But after cocaine he appeared haggard and unkempt (see Figure 6.4). He was, the *Tribune* lamented, "NOT YET 15 YEARS OLD."[53]

His story commanded the October 20 page-one headline, "BOY SLAVE TO COCAINE." Max had worked as a shop and errand boy at the Kinzie pharmacy and had proved so reliable his boss trusted him with the firm's books. Then Max found cocaine. "He learned to like the drug while using a catarrh cure and soon became a slave to it," the *Tribune* explained. To feed his addiction, he forged

[53] "Boy Slave to Cocaine," ibid., Oct. 20, 1896, p. 1; "Max Ohle," ibid., Oct. 21, 1896, p. 7 (presenting "before taking" and "after taking" sketches of Max Ohle). Though the *Tribune* declared Max was "NOT YET 15 YEARS OLD," census records say he was born in March 1881 and therefore would have been going on sixteen. *See* 1900 United States Census, Enumeration District No. 802 (Precinct 25: Lake View, Chicago, city Ward 26), p. 4, line 23. My thanks to Stephanie Alessi, who assembled a rich trove of materials on Max Ohle and the passage of county and state anti-cocaine laws.

orders for a "particular cocaine catarrhal remedy" that had "a dangerous proportion of cocaine." When his boss caught him and cut him off, Max turned to other North Side drugstores, where he bought the cure using his boss's cards. He had squandered perhaps ten weeks' wages before his boss, suspecting theft from the cash drawer, discharged Max and sent him home. Now he was "a prisoner in the family apartments back of his father's barber shop," not to be released till cured.[54]

The next day the *Tribune* announced that the makers of Birney's Catarrh Cure, compounded in Chicago since 1893 and among the nation's most popular brands, had "Admit[ted] Cocaine Is in It." Here was no news, for every bottle of Birney's powder declared its contents to be 2 percent cocaine. The news was that Birney's proved on analysis to contain nearly 4 percent cocaine, the same strength "usually used to produce local anæsthesia." Though a former health commissioner had deemed this concentration "sufficient to develop the cocaine habit," Birney's makers apparently broke no law. Max Ohle's father "bewail[ed] the fate that prevent[ed] those who sold the stuff from being punished for it." Meanwhile young Max remained "a physical and moral wreck," the *Tribune* said, "Still in a Somnolent Condition."[55]

Two days later the *Tribune* devoted more front-page turf to "the latest victim to be added to the list of those who have become slaves to cocaine through the use of patent medicines." Like young Max, wood finisher William Thompson had fallen victim to Birney's Catarrhal Powders. Addicted at twenty-three, he lost his job and no longer could support his mother or his habit. So he stole the powder from a Chicago druggist who had him arrested. Freed pending trial, Thompson was back in court a week later having lifted more catarrh cure from a different drugstore.[56]

Yet another young man fell to the catarrh cure before the law finally came down on powdered cocaine sold over drugstore counters. Patrolman John J. Mooney, aged thirty-three, a nine-year veteran of the Chicago Police Department, had been deemed "[o]ne of the best policemen" on the force before he "narrowly escaped destruction by the use of the catarrh cure." His addiction and fall prompted a detailed case history in the *Tribunes* of March 7 and 9, 1897. "A year ago [Officer Mooney] began to use a catarrh cure that contained a large percentage of cocaine. Then he was one of the strongest and most robust men on the force. Now he has become, through the catarrh cure, a physical and mental

[54] "Boy Slave to Cocaine."
[55] "Admit Cocaine Is in It," *Chicago Daily Tribune*, Oct. 21, 1896, p. 7. The Birney Catarrhal Powder Company was incorporated in Chicago in January 1893. *See* "New Incorporations," ibid., Jan. 12, 1893; "Boston Store," ibid., Feb. 26, 1893, p. 11 (advertising for sale Birney's Catarrhal Powder). Joseph Spillane reports that a 4 percent cocaine content was typical of 1890s catarrh snuffs. Some were weaker, while few were stronger than five percent cocaine. Spillane, *Cocaine*, pp. 85–86.
[56] "William Thompson a Cocaine Slave," *Chicago Daily Tribune*, Oct. 23, 1896, p. 1; "Hypnotic Cure Failure," *Chicago Daily Tribune*, Nov. 1, 1896, p. 18.

wreck." Recently, Mooney failed to report for roll call. Unseen for several days, he turned up miles away in Evanston, where it seems he'd wandered in a cocaine haze. Nursed to health by his sister, he stayed several days in bed, "prostrated from the use of the drug."[57]

Two days before the *Tribune* first reported these unfolding events, Democratic Alderman Frank Gazzolo acted with brilliant timing. He alerted the paper that Chicago's corporation counsel was preparing at his request a "Sweeping Ordinance" that would outlaw sale of "Preparations Containing Cocaine" except by prescription. "It is well known," he said with some exaggeration, "that the sale of a certain catarrh cure containing 10 per cent of cocaine has resulted in the ruin of many lives." Users of this powder "snuff it up the nostrils to relieve colds in the head. It gives them a feeling of exhilaration, and they soon get in the habit of using it for its pleasing effects, whether in need of it or not." Then, assuring himself prominent coverage, Gazzolo nodded to poor Max Ohle: "The TRIBUNE several months ago called attention to the harmful effects from the use of this powder, and I believe did much to put a stop to it." The next day, the *Tribune* heralded a "WAR ON VILE NOSTRUMS.—Ald. Gazzolo to Start a Crusade Against Harmful Drugs."[58]

When Officer Mooney's unfolding story sparked a new headline the next day, Gazzolo's timing proved perfect. "HE IS A COCAINE VICTIM," the *Tribune* declared of the young officer. Then, linking Mooney's affliction with Gazzolo's announcement, the paper began: "One of the best policemen in the Chicago department has narrowly escaped destruction by the use of the catarrh cure at which Ald. Gazzolo's nostrum ordinance is aimed." The reporter sketched out Mooney's dazed rovings only to return to the alderman's plan: "Gazzolo's ordinance prohibiting the sale of these nostrums is to be presented to the Council tomorrow night."[59]

Whether the alderman's good timing was happenstance or strategy is hard to say. Gazzolo was a pharmacist by trade and no doubt knew how Birney's users craved for more, so his measure may have grown from long deliberation. Or he may have acted only after learning of Mooney's plight. Mooney's prolonged absence left Gazzolo time for planning—and Mooney's saga proved Gazzolo's proposal both prophetic and wise. Days after Gazzolo first put forward his

[57] "He Is a Cocaine Victim," *Chicago Daily Tribune*, Mar. 7, 1897, p. 4 ("One of the best . . ."; "narrowly escaped . . ."; failure to appear for roll call; appearance in Evanston; and "prostrated from the use . . ."); "Police Care for 'Cure' Victims," ibid., Mar. 9, 1897, p. 8 ("A year ago . . ." and nine-year veteran). On Mooney's age, *see* 1900 United States Census, Enumeration District No. 623 (North Town, Chicago, city Ward 20), p. 9, line 33. *See also* "Mooney," *Chicago Tribune*, July 4, 1921, p. 21 (printing Mooney's obituary and giving his middle initial as J). I am grateful to Alisa Philo for tracking down Mooney's elusive personal data.

[58] "War on Vile Nostrums," *Chicago Daily Tribune*, Mar. 6, 1897, p. 6.

[59] "He Is a Cocaine Victim," *Chicago Daily Tribune*, Mar. 7, 1897, p. 4.

anti-cocaine ordinance, the *Tribune* reported the measure would "prohibit[] druggists from handling at all Birney's catarrh powder," the drug that likely laid Mooney low.[60]

Whether luck or craft, Gazzolo's method prompted mimicry. On March 10, four days after the *Tribune* reported the alderman's plan and three days after it first told of Officer Mooney's ordeal, Assemblyman Henry D. Nichols (often Nicholls) of Chicago introduced a copycat bill in Springfield. Nichols proposed to bar retail sales of cocaine or of preparations containing cocaine except on a doctor's unrefillable prescription. First offenders would face fines of $10 to $50; second offenders risked $200 and thirty days' jail time.[61] So similar were the two men's measures that the state law's passage in June perhaps mooted Gazzolo's proposed ordinance, which seemingly fell from sight.

Like Gazzolo, Nichols may have acted suddenly or with forethought. The Chicago police force had on its rolls an Officer Henry Nichols. Perhaps—though evidence eludes me—they were the same man. If so, Nichols may have acted in sympathy with fellow Officer Mooney by banning the drug that brought him down. Weeks later, though, a *Tribune* report hinted Nichols had planned his bill long before Mooney's case surfaced. Noting House passage of the assemblyman's bill in late May, the paper called it his "pet measure, the one in whose interests he came to Springfield."[62]

---

[60] Gazzolo claimed he had been a pharmacist for fifteen years. *See* "War on Vile Nostrums," *Chicago Daily Tribune*, Mar. 6, 1897, p. 6. I found his name among Chicago's druggists as early as 1892, but not earlier. [Classified Advertisements], Chicago *Daily Inter Ocean*, Dec. 26, 1892, p. 7. Gazzolo listed himself as a druggist in the 1900 census. The 1890 census return apparently has not survived. For the impact of Gazzolo's proposed ordinance on Birney's Catarrh Cure, *see* "Proceedings of Council," *Chicago Daily Tribune*, Mar. 9, 1897, p. 2.

[61] "An Act for the Regulation for the Sale of Cocaine and of Preparations Containing Cocaine," Illinois General Assembly, H.B. No. 448 (introduced March 10, 1897), *enacted as* "An Act for the Regulation for the Sale of Cocaine . . . ," 1897 *Illinois Laws*, p. 138 (Act of June 11, 1897).

[62] Henry D. Nichols (or Nicholls) was elected to the Illinois Assembly in 1896 and declined to run for a second term in 1898. The *Tribune* referred to an "Officer Nicholls of the Twelfth Street Station" in 1887; a "Policeman Henry Nichols" in 1893; "Policeman Nichols of the Stanton Avenue Station" in 1898; and "Detective Henry Nichols" or "Detective Nichols" or something similar several times in January 1900. Because Assemblyman Nichols lived on West Twelfth Street, an assignment to the Twelfth Street Station seems plausible. On the other hand, census forms show Nichols's occupations to have been a carpenter in 1870, a "Manager" apparently of a "Saw works" in 1880, and a "Manager Merchant" in 1900. The relevant census form for 1890 apparently hasn't survived. He sometimes was called Captain Nichols, but I don't know why.

See "City Intelligence," *Chicago Daily Tribune*, Dec. 23, 1887, p. 6 ("Officer Nicholls . . ."); "Guard and Inspector in a Fight," ibid., Dec. 13, 1893, p. 8 ("Policeman Henry Nichols"); "Cocaine Bill Goes Through," ibid., May 29, 1897, p. 9 ("pet measure . . ." and "Captain Nichols"); "Broomstick for an Intruder," ibid., Jan. 19, 1898, p. 5 ("Policeman Nichols . . ."); "Renominate John J. Morrison," ibid., June 12, 1898, p. 4 (reporting that H. D. Nichols "declined the nomination"); "Sugar Casks May Hold Beer," ibid., Jan. 7, 1900, p. 8 ("Detective[] Harry Nichols"); "Druggists Pay Federal Tax," ibid., Jan. 28, 1900, p. 3 ("Detective[] . . . Henry Nichols"); "City vs. Federal License System," ibid., Jan. 31, 1900, p. 6 ("Detective Henry Nichols" and "Officer Nichols"). I thank Stephanie Alessi for her creative and diligent collection of sources on Nichols.

Whatever moved Nichols to act, he readily won others to his cause. His bill churned through the Assembly, clearing the House by a vote of ninety to six and the Senate without dissent. In an official interpretation of the new law, the Illinois attorney general declared in January 1898 that "a druggist has no right to sell 'Berney's Catarrh Remedy,' if that remedy contains cocaine . . . ."[63]

Lessons of the Illinois Law

The first lesson of the new Illinois law recalls our earliest laws banning opium dens: lawmakers aimed chiefly to snuff out a threat to white youth. Feverish coverage of Max Ohle and Patrolman Mooney, together with prominent treatment of William Thompson and the proximity of all three stories to passage of the 1897 act, suggest cocaine abuse among working- and middle-class young men roused special concern. That lawmakers acted in fear of non-white cokeheads finds no support. As in Oregon, Montana, and Colorado, I've seen in Illinois no evidence lawmakers witnessed *any* non-white cocaine abuse before the state banned unprescribed sales. Even out-of-state stories of non-white cocaine abusers went wanting in the Illinois press. It seems no such report appeared before January 1898, almost nine months after Nichols's anti-cocaine law gained final approval.[64]

Other lessons of the Illinois cocaine ban trace to the rise of catarrh cures. Lawmakers saw that cocaine powders threatened broader abuse than hypodermic injection, till then the chief source of cocaine addiction. Syringes and needles were scarce and pricey, easily available only to doctors and the well to do. Addicts reused costly equipment, and germy needles left a trail of painful scars and ulcers. "His body was found to be covered from neck to heel with small sores and scabs," the *New York Times* wrote of an addicted pharmacy clerk in 1899. Beyond hazarding health and beauty, the scabs risked reputation too, for they exposed hidden habits. The expense of syringes, together with the pain and immodesty of the scabs, likely suppressed cocaine abuse. As late as July 1894, a druggist in Chicago's levee district told a reporter that among the drug addicts of the neighborhood, "[c]ocaine is used by few. It has about the same effect as opium, but it is usually hypodermically injected."[65]

---

[63] 1897 *Illinois House Journal*, p. 994; 1897 *Illinois Senate Journal*, p. 1066; Edward C. Akin, *Biennial Report of the Attorney General of the State of Illinois* (Springfield: Phillips Brs., 1899), p. 378 (letter of Jan. 29, 1898).

[64] That 1898 story hailed from Paducah, Kentucky, and appeared not in Chicago's flagship *Tribune* but in the city's lower-profile *Inter Ocean*. Or so it seems. I have failed to find the Paducah story in the pages of the *Daily Inter Ocean*. But the *New York Tribune*, in reprinting the account, identified it as "Paducah (Ky.) correspondence of the Chicago Inter Ocean." "Cocaine Victims Organize," *New York Tribune*, Jan. 10, 1898, p. 2. In any event the story said nothing of coke-fueled violence.

[65] "A Drug Fiend Extraordinary," *New York Times*, Mar. 14, 1899, p. 4; "Chicago Morphine Fiends," *New Orleans Daily Picayune*, July 4, 1894, p. 2 (quoting from report in the *Chicago Herald*).

Seeking to sate their habits by means other than syringes, cocaine addicts at first found few alternatives. "Nasal tabloids" offered an early option, but not an appealing one. "These Tabloids are in the form of suppositories," the maker of one product boasted, "and are applied direct to the nasal passages." The appearance of commercial catarrh powders in the early 1890s liberated users from dirty needles and nasal suppositories. "In the powder form the drug had as much effect" as when injected, the *Atlanta Constitution* wrote in 1900, "and at the same time left no evidence by an abrasion of the skin."[66]

Though a temptation to all, catarrh powders perhaps proved especially attractive to youth. In this as in every era, youth were vain and surely shrank from the scabs of hypodermic injection. And youth, with shallower pockets, could less afford hypodermic kits. Catarrh powders cost just fifty cents and a straw. Then there was the ease of use. A Birney's trademark from 1892, reproduced in Figures 6.5 and 6.6, shows a woman blowing the powder up her nostrils with an effortless puff on a straw. As the *New York Tribune* wrote almost two decades later, "the simplicity of its use" has propelled cocaine's sale: it "is now generally snuffed in the form of a powder or of fine crystals, so that no expensive or inconvenient apparatus is required for its use."[67]

Beyond widening the risk of abuse, catarrh powders undermined whatever moral excuse cocaine addicts might have claimed as victims of medical treatment gone awry. Accounts of patients addicted by injected cocaine were legion. Harried doctors on hurried house calls too often left patients with injection kits and cocaine solution and instructions for future doses. Other doctors condemned the practice and advised their peers to give each shot themselves and conceal from patients the agent of their solace, frustrating requests for more of the same.[68] Physicians who ignored this advice and abetted new addictions opened themselves to moral condemnation, but absolved their patients of blame. For even after treatment ended and medical need expired, the persisting addiction had a medical genesis and therefore a moral excuse.

This medical excuse proved elusive to those addicted by catarrh cures. Even in an era when household medicines commonly stood in for the professional sort, few buyers likely fell for Birney's claims to cure. The cocaine doctors

[66] "The New Remedy," *Chicago Tribune*, Dec. 2, 1885, p. 1 (advertising Allen's Cocaine Nasal Tabloids); "Use of Cocaine Alarms Police," *Atlanta Constitution*, Dec. 3, 1900, p. 7.

[67] "Cocaine on the Streets," *New York Tribune*, Dec. 2, 1912, p. 8; Spillane, *Cocaine*, p. 86 ("Most of the leading brands [of catarrh snuff] sold at retail for 50¢, although some brands offered a range of product sizes as cheap as 25¢ and as expensive as $1.").

[68] Lewis H. Adler Jr., "The Status of the Hydrochlorate of Cocaine in Minor Surgery . . . ," *Therapeutic Gazette*, vol. 15, no. 8 (Aug. 15, 1891), pp. 518, 522, 532 (reprinting survey responses in which some doctors advised reducing the risk of addiction by administering cocaine themselves and not disclosing to patients the nature of the drug); Louis H. Adler Jr., "The Status of the Uses of Cocaine in General Medicine . . . ," *International Medical Magazine*, vol. 2, no. 3 (Apr. 1893), pp. 246, 252–53, 259, 313 (same).

Figure 6.5: Dr. Birney's Catarrhal Powder (Product Box).

injected when cutting flesh or pulling teeth served an obvious medical need; cocaine-laced catarrh snuffs did not. Cold sufferers maybe suffered less if they used Birney's, but they suffered just as long. The appearance in the late 1890s of advertisements for a "Catarrh Cure that *Cures Catarrh!*" suggests cocaine snuffs fooled few. Absent power to cure, they lacked medical excuse and stood revealed as recreational drugs. As Joseph Spillane writes, "cocaine sniffing (like opium smoking) became a vice, rather than a necessity, earning only condemnation."[69]

Indeed the distinctions between injected and inhaled cocaine closely tracked those between eaten and smoked opium and had similar moral consequences: they separated often legitimate medical *use* from recreational, mind-altering *abuse*. Eaten opium, though often abused, won moral sanction as medicine, for it killed all manner of pain. Smoked opium killed pain too, but

[69] "Free Treatment!" *Boston Daily Globe*, May 14, 1899, p. 9; Spillane, *Cocaine*, p. 104. Spillane condemns the doctors of the day for prescribing cocaine for asthma and hay fever "while frankly acknowledging that its effect was only temporary and palliative." Spillane, *Cocaine*, p. 24.

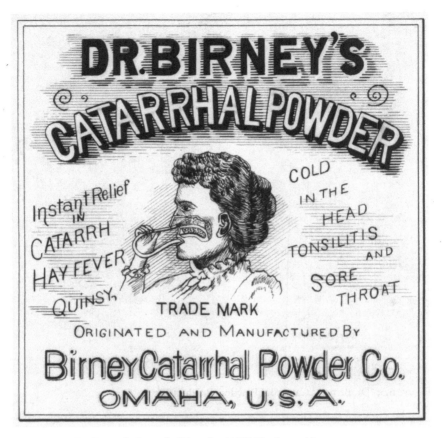

Figure 6.6: Dr. Birney's Catarrhal Powder (1892 Trademark).

in a decidedly nonmedical way. Unlike finely gauged vials of opium in solution, smoked opium came in uncalibrated clouds inhaled in sooty subsurface dens. So too with cocaine: the steely precision of needles and syringes secured a medical imprimatur that snorted snuff couldn't claim.[70] Septic as needles were, they were sterile to the eye.

As sibling medical mockeries, smoked opium and snorted cocaine met similar fates. Authorities banned both after learning of recreational abuse, especially if that abuse ensnared white youth. The San Francisco supervisors who launched

---

[70] Stressing precision, Dr. M. Krogius of Helsinki recommended that to anesthetize a finger, a surgeon should inject at its base a cubic centimeter of a 2 percent solution of hydrochlorate of cocaine. *See* "Impure Drinking Water," *New Orleans Daily Picayune*, Aug. 19, 1894, p. 2; "Cocaine Analgesia," *St. Louis Medical Journal*, vol. 68 (Jan.–June 1895), p. 123 (repeating Krogius's recommendation, though in less detail).

the nation's war on drugs with their 1875 opium den ban explained their action in precisely these terms, fretting about dens reserved for the exclusive use of whites and "nightly resorted to by young men and women of respectable parentage." Young Max Ohle and others like him roused similar concerns in the context of cocaine.

Discovery of recreational cocaine abuse followed soon after cocaine snuffs and similar products hit the market. First there were the chewing pastes of New York, "on sale in most of the drug-stores." They "led to a promiscuous and very hurtful use as a swallowed exhilarant" and prompted the New York Medical Society in December 1885 to propose what would have been, if passed, the nation's first statewide cocaine ban. Cocaine snuffs soon followed. The *Fort Worth Gazette* reported in September 1887 that Chicago's Dr. Seth Bishop had proposed a cocaine-based catarrh snuff in an essay honored by the U.S. Hay Fever Association. That a Fort Worth paper announced an honor bestowed on a Chicago doctor by an organization based in New Hampshire is some evidence druggists nationwide noted this snuff recipe. Some five months later, the *Chicago Tribune* printed the first account I've seen of a cocaine addict felled by a catarrh cure. Chicago lawyer George C. Buell had tried to kill himself with an overdose of cocaine, which he had been taking "as a medicine." Later the Chicago *Inter Ocean* added that Buell "was crazed by the use of cocaine as a snuff to cure catarrh." Meanwhile, in 1887 and 1889, Oregon and Montana had passed the nation's earliest statewide cocaine bans.[71]

By the early 1890s, Birney's Catarrh Cure and other commercial cocaine powders crowded druggists' shelves.[72] Evidence that abuse of snorted cocaine weighed on lawmakers' minds when they adopted the next two cocaine bans in 1897 proves suggestive in Colorado, far stronger in Illinois. In search of more conclusive evidence, let's press ahead to 1898, which saw passage of anti-cocaine laws spanning North and South. If these widely scattered measures likewise trace to abuse of catarrh cures, something like proof of this connection emerges.

---

[71] "Curing the Coca Habit," *Chicago Daily Tribune*, Dec. 6, 1885, p. 26 (reporting events in New York); [Untitled], *Ft. Worth Gazette*, Sept. 6, 1887, p. 3; "United States Hay Fever Association," in *The World Almanac and Encyclopedia, 1895* (New York: The Press Publishing Co., 1895), p. 231 (identifying the Hay Fever Association's base as Bethlehem, N.H.); Musto, *American Disease*, p. 7 (noting the U.S. Hay Fever Association's embrace of cocaine as its official remedy); "A Story with Little Foundation," *Chicago Tribune*, Feb. 18, 1888, p. 3; "Mentally Unbalanced," *Daily Inter Ocean* (Chicago), Aug. 16, 1889, p. 7. Elsewhere Dr. Bishop discussed his cocaine-based catarrh cure in more detail. *See* Seth S. Bishop, "Cocaine in Hay Fever," *Journal of the American Medical Association*, vol. 6, no. 6 (Feb. 6, 1886), pp. 141, 143–44.

[72] Spillane reports that popular cocaine snuffs first hit drugstore shelves in the early 1890s. Spillane, *Cocaine*, p. 85.

The Massachusetts Cocaine Ban

Trailing Illinois by some nine months, Massachusetts became the nation's fifth anti-cocaine state in March 1898. These five states appear in the lower map in Figure 6.2 as spots spattered almost randomly across the continent. If they followed any pattern, it was *not* one tied to fear of African American coke fiends. None of the five had an African American population in the 1890s greater than 2 percent of the whole.

News sources examined in Massachusetts reveal not one report of a non-white cocaine abuser before the state banned cocaine.[73] High-status abusers seemingly drew even more attention than elsewhere. The *Boston Globe* and other papers recited the familiar litany of medical luminaries: Drs. Bradley of Illinois, Hazen of Indiana, Underhill of Ohio, Borcheim of Georgia, Saunders of New Jersey, Sanford of Massachusetts, Manaton of New York and the usual coterie of druggists, patients, and paramours. If nonmedical members of the middle and lower classes abused cocaine in Massachusetts in the years before the drug's ban, the state's newspapers allotted them very little type. In 1888, as if to underscore this emphasis on high-born addicts, the *Globe* called Representative John R. Thomas of Illinois, a survivor of throat surgery and cocaine anesthesia, the "latest distinguished victim of the cocaine habit."[74]

All told, thirty-six reports of cocaine addiction focusing on twenty-two different addicts emerged in my search of various Boston newspapers in the years before passage of the state's 1898 ban. Doctors and druggists and their ilk accounted for twelve of those addicts.[75] The others included Representative Thomas, a former "Mining King," a "Noted Mind-Reader," a "member of a prominent and highly respectable family," the son of "a rich contractor," the wife of a former assemblyman, the husband of actor Sarah Bernhardt, an agent for the

---

[73] I read every news story mentioning cocaine before April 1898 in several Massachusetts newspapers available in an online text-searchable form, including the *Boston Globe*, the *Boston Daily Advertiser*, the *Boston Investigator*, and the *Congregationalist*. I searched over a shorter time frame the *Lowell Sun* and other, more minor papers. And with the aid of Jake Gardener, who spent long hours scrolling through microfilm reels, I read selected accounts in the *Daily Evening Transcript*. All told, I reviewed over a thousand Massachusetts news accounts or advertisements.

[74] "A Crank on Cocoaine," *Boston Daily Globe*, Nov. 29, 1885, p. 2 (Dr. Bradley); "Intoxicated by Cocaine," *Boston Daily Advertiser*, May 25, 1886, p. 6 (Dr. Hazen); "Crazed by Cocaine," *Boston Daily Globe*, July 4, 1886, p. 2 (Dr. Underhill); "Dr. Borcheim's Suicide," ibid., Sept. 12, 1887, p. 2; "Dr. Frank Saunders Runs Away with Mrs. Merritt," ibid., Dec. 9, 1887, p. 1; "Tragic Climax," ibid., July 13, 1893, p. 1 (Dr. Abbott Sanford of Everett, Mass.); "They Fetched a Policeman," ibid., Jan. 7, 1894, p. 1 (Dr. W. P. Manaton of Greenport, Long Island); "Cocaine Habit," *ibid.*, July 7, 1888, p. 5 (Rep. Thomas).

[75] Beyond sources listed in the last footnote, *see* "A Victim of Cocaine," *Boston Daily Globe*, Nov. 2, 1886, p. 6 (Dr. J. H. Borland of Pittsburg); "Cocaine Slavery Ended," ibid., Dec. 23, 1889, p. 8 (Elton A. Fay, "Once [a] Well-to-Do Pharmacist"); "Cocaine Prescriptions," ibid., Aug 18, 1894, p. 1 (chemist Fred Olert); "Crazed by Drugs," ibid., Sept. 27, 1895, p. 7 (Dr. S. R. L. Benenga, apparently of Boston); "Granite State Notes," *Boston Daily Advertiser*, Mar. 16, 1896, p. 2 (W. C. Sheffield, a former New Hampshire druggist).

Mutual Life Insurance Company, and two men of unspecified job and station.[76] All were likely white.

News accounts in Massachusetts suggest the principal concern impelling passage of the state's 1898 cocaine ban was not race, but the same misgiving that motivated cocaine bans in Illinois and perhaps Colorado in 1897: the temptation posed by newcoming catarrh snuffs. My evidence on this score is hardly voluminous, consisting of just a few news items, most of them brief, and a series of classified ads. Nor did the legislature record its reasons. But surviving evidence, considered alongside events in Illinois months before, speaks plainly.

We may begin in late December 1896, about thirteen months before the Massachusetts cocaine ban appeared on the legislative docket. The *Boston Globe* told of the same Connecticut town that had made a news splash two time zones away in Colorado. Reporting on page one that "many of the residents have become addicted to the habitual use of cocaine in combination with other drugs," the *Globe* never mentioned the catarrh snuff that apparently gave rise to the rash of addiction. Instead the paper cast doubt on the whole affair and on its relevance to Massachusetts. Asked if he knew of "any such excessive use of cocaine in any city or hamlet of the commonwealth," Dr. Samuel W. Abbott, secretary of the Massachusetts Board of Health, "replied that he had heard of nothing of the kind." Three days later the *Globe* printed a two-sentence "Editorial Point[]" that made light of the Connecticut town's woes: "A new intoxicant known as 'cocaine snuff' is said to have been invented in Connecticut. The land of steady habits should exile the deviser."[77] The editors' evident unconcern with the encroaching epidemic apparently infected the legislature. Unlike lawmakers in Colorado, who set to work on a statewide cocaine ban within weeks of the first news from Connecticut, lawmakers in Massachusetts seemingly sat out the season, taking no action on this front.

Yet danger signs mounted, if slowly. In January 1896—and again in March and December 1897—a classified ad for Dr. Agnew's Catarrhal Powder, a cocaine-laced snuff made in New York, appeared in the *Globe*. As the 1898 legislative season opened, it seems the threat posed by cocaine powder weighed on the minds of two critical players. One was Secretary Abbott of the Board of Health, who had undergone a conversion on the cocaine question. On January 31, the

[76] "Was a Mining King," *Boston Daily Advertiser*, Oct. 18, 1895, p. 4; "Victim of Cocaine," *Boston Daily Globe*, May 13, 1889, p. 1 (Washington Irving Bishop, "The Noted Mind-Reader"); "Victim of Drugs," ibid., July 15, 1892, p. 4 ("a member of a . . ."); "Insane and at Large," ibid., Nov. 2, 1893, p. 2 (Frank L. Kimball, son of "a rich contractor in Baltimore"); "Wife Addicted to Use of Drugs," ibid., Oct. 3, 1896, p. 2 (the wife of former Assemblyman Hiram Howard); "Personal," *Boston Daily Advertiser*, Sept. 3, 1889, p. 4 (husband of Sarah Bernhardt); "Suicide of A. L. Davis," *Boston Daily Globe*, Nov. 16, 1897, p. 12 (life insurance agent); "Editorial Points," ibid., Jan. 11, 1894, p. 4 ("[a] New York victim of the cocaine habit"); "Sentenced for Forgery," *Boston Daily Advertiser*, Jan. 23, 1895, p. 6 (A. A. Balch of New Hampshire).
[77] "Man with a Cocaine 'Jag,'" *Boston Daily Globe*, Dec. 28, 1896, p. 1; "Editorial Points," ibid., Dec. 31, 1896, p. 4.

Massachusetts Senate revived a petition Abbott had filed the year before "calling for protection for the public against poisonous patent medicines." Though no source I've found discusses the petition in detail, Abbott soon hinted at some particulars. On February 9, the *Boston Evening Transcript* reported he had appeared before the senate committee on public health and "urged the adoption of legislation for a stricter inspection of foods and drugs." The *Transcript* added: "Certain catarrh recipes containing cocaine he also mentioned, saying that they were likely to fix the cocaine habit for life on users, and that these articles were labelled harmless" by their makers. Dr. Abbott offered only a modest fix—"that these articles should be labelled so that purchasers should know exactly what they are getting."[78]

As the "Poisons Bill" of 1898 first took form, it apparently would have added cocaine to "the list of poisons of which a record of sales must be made by persons dealing in these articles . . . ." That is, druggists still could have sold cocaine powders and other cocaine products as long as they recorded these transactions. Our second critical player, Senator Charles E. Folsom of Boston's Dorchester district, chairman of the public health committee, championed the bill. In what seems the sole surviving record of Senator Folsom's motives, the *Boston Daily Advertiser* offered telling evidence: in urging his colleagues to advance the legislation, Folsom "cited the case of a young man who became a victim of the cocaine habit by the use of a catarrh remedy."[79]

Reasoning that "the young man would have become a victim just the same if a record of the sale had been made," Senator William H. Cook "objected to such drastic legislation." Exactly what Cook deemed drastic about requiring druggists to keep records of cocaine sales is not clear. But he can't have been pleased by the next turn of events. Sometime between his remarks on February 21, 1898, and final passage of the new law on March 17, someone penned an amendment ultimately enacted along with the rest of the poisons bill. The amendment, scribbled on a draft of the bill, addressed Senator Cook's objection that a simple recording requirement would not have saved the "young man" from his addiction to cocaine-spiked cold medicine. To the senator's likely chagrin, however, the handwritten amendment made the legislation *more* drastic, declaring flatly that "no sale of cocaine or its salts shall be made except on the prescription of a physician" (see Figure 6.7).[80]

---

[78] "Catarrh and Colds Relieved in 10 to 60 Minutes," *Boston Daily Globe,* Jan. 29, 1896, p. 2; "Is Your Ailment Catarrh?" ibid., Mar. 20, 1897, p. 3; "Painless and Delightful Catarrh Remedy," ibid., Dec. 4, 1897, p. 3; "Is Your Ailment Catarrh?" ibid., Dec. 11, 1897, p. 3; Spillane, *Cocaine,* p. 87 (stating Agnew's source and content); "Clerks Overwhelmed," ibid., Feb. 1, 1898, p. 5 (noting action on Dr. Abbott's petition); "Restricting Poison Sales," *Boston Evening Transcript,* Feb. 9, 1898, p. 8.

[79] "The Legislature: List of Poisons," *Boston Daily Advertiser,* Feb. 22, 1898, p. 5 (reporting debate on the poisons bill); "The Committee on Public Health," *Boston Daily Advertiser,* Jan. 28, 1898, p. 5 (identifying Folsom as health committee chair).

[80] "The Legislature: List of Poisons"; "An Act Relative to the Sale of Poisons," 1898 *Massachusetts Acts,* ch. 192, § 1 (Act of Mar. 17, 1898) p. 127. My thanks to Alethea Sargent for securing the record reproduced in Figure 6.7 from the Massachusetts Archives.

Commonwealth of Massachusetts.

IN THE YEAR ONE THOUSAND EIGHT HUNDRED AND NINETY-*eight*

AN ACT

Relative to the Sale of Poisons.

Be it enacted by the Senate and House of Representatives in General Court assembled, and by the authority of the same, as follows :—

SECTION 1. Section twenty of chapter three hundred and ninety-seven of the acts of the year eighteen hundred and ninety-six is hereby amended by striking out the whole of said section and inserting in place thereof the following :—

Section 20. Whoever sells arsenic (arsenious acid), atropia or any of its salts, chloral hydrate, chloroform, cotton root and its fluid extract, corrosive sublimate, cyanide of potassium, Donovan's solution, ergot and its fluid extract, Fowler's solution, laudanum, McMunn's elixir, morphia or any of its salts, oil of pennyroyal, oil of ...oil of tansy ...Paris green, Parsons' vermin exterminator, phos... ...s, prussic acid, "rough on rats," strychnia or any of its salts, tartar emetic, tincture of aconite, tincture of belladonna, tincture of digitalis, tincture of nux vomica, tincture of veratrum viride, *or carbolic acid* without the written prescription of a physician, shall keep a record of such sale, the name and *quantity* of the article sold, and the name and residence of the person or persons to whom it was delivered, which record shall be made before the article is delivered, and shall at all times be open to inspection by the officers of the district police and by the police authorities and officers of cities and towns, and by any member of the Massachusetts board of registration in pharmacy, or by its agents;

[A]

but no sale of Cocaine *or its salts shall be made except on the Prescription of a physician*

Figure 6.7: Handwritten Anti-cocaine Amendment to Massachusetts Poisons Legislation of 1898.

In Massachusetts as in Illinois and perhaps Colorado, therefore, a clear link emerges between the danger posed to youth by cocainized catarrh snuffs and the state's earliest cocaine ban.

Looking South for Race-Based Cocaine Bans

Evidence that *race* drove the first five statewide cocaine bans—those of Oregon in 1887, Montana in 1889, Colorado and Illinois in 1897, and Massachusetts in 1898, as well as New York's near ban of 1893—is wholly lacking. Race hardly could have been a driving force when press reports in these states said virtually nothing of cocaine abuse by non-whites before the new laws took force. Instead it seems concern for the health and morals of whites—and especially of white youth—powered this legislative trend, just as such concerns had impelled anti-den lawmaking a decade or two before.

When statewide cocaine bans first turned south in 1898, prominent reports at last emerged of non-white abuse. Indeed a few Southern reports appeared sooner. The earliest I've seen, dated 1894, perhaps escaped broad notice. It turned up not in the day's press but in the *American Druggist and Pharmaceutical Record*. Dallas pharmacist Richard Schweickhardt warned readers, "The cocaine habit is incomparably more dangerous than the liquor habit." Amazingly, Schweickhardt knew of at most two habitual drunks in Dallas but between five hundred and six hundred cocaine addicts. To that stunning newsbyte he added two more: "A representative of chemists who manufacture cocaine . . . informs me that the consumption of cocaine in Texas has increased fully tenfold within the past two years, and that negresses are giving up snuff-dipping and taking to the cocaine habit." Less prone to worry, the *Record*'s editors declared their faith that "Mr. Schweickhardt has over estimated the magnitude to which this evil has grown."[81]

Some two years passed, it seems, before non-white cocaine abuse again hit the news. This time the forum was a mainline paper, the *New Orleans Daily Picayune*. As late as December 1895, the *Picayune* had written of cocaine indulgence as something peculiarly white: "The 'cocaine habit' is a recognized fact in America, where our Teutonic race, subjected to an intenser climate and an intenser life than in Europe, developed a quicker sensibility and more irritable nerves." That claim appeared in a *Picayune* editorial titled "Drugs and Drink: Stimulants That Cause More Harm Than Alcohol." The editor said respectable folks, especially women, had fallen into the grip of opium, morphine, or cocaine because victims

[81] Richard Schweickhardt, "Cocaine in Texas," *American Druggist and Pharmaceutical Record*, vol. 24 (1894), pp. 301–02.

of these drugs "do not regard themselves as drunkards." They fail to see the likeness between the relief they feel after a dose of their drug and "the stupor of vulgar drunkenness." Opium and other drugs "are for us Anglo-Saxons, except in rare instances, subtle and pernicious foes."[82]

Within four months of this pronouncement, the *Picayune* told of a "young negro woman, Ada Williams," who died after taking a suicidal dose of cocaine, to which she'd grown addicted. Whether Williams's addiction had medical or recreational roots the *Picayune* did not say. Soon enough, however, the *Picayune* ran a report of undeniable recreational abuse among African Americans. Though buried on page sixteen in the dog days of August 1896, the *Picayune*'s warning of the "COCAINE HABIT'S ALARMING GROWTH" surely grabbed notice. One line down, the editors added, "Especially Among the Colored Population of the City." Betraying no alarm, the reporter's tone was mocking: neighbors "say the vim with which the colored folk who gather in the dance halls in the neighborhood of Customhouse and Liberty streets, passeth understanding. It is frequently to be noticed that a young woman mingling in these dances continues the physical exertion for a time, and with a vigor that are almost incredible."[83]

Soon reprinted elsewhere, this story bears scrutiny on several fronts. The alarming trend that sparked it, first of all, surprised even well-informed observers: "It is perfectly amazing," a local druggist declared, "the proportions to which the cocaine trade has grown in this city, and it is still more remarkable how, with the exception of a few abandoned white women, its use is confined almost exclusively to the colored folk." And this trend was new: "[T]he passion for its use by the colored folks seems to have been of a recent date." This amazing and rather sudden trend, moreover, did not involve cocaine-driven criminality. Instead the *Picayune* highlighted the sort of sexual debauchery and moral degradation we've seen before—the "vim," "vigor," "exertion," and "endurance" of the young women, together with "the wild expression of the eye, the muscular jerking of the limbs and other portions of the body, . . . the abnormal, strange pleasure and exhilaration." The druggist spoke even of the "constant danger of a dethronement of the reason," calling to mind Augustine's injunction that "reason, which presides in the mind, ought like a king in control to restrain the impulses of the

---

[82] "Drugs and Drink," *New Orleans Daily Picayune*, Dec. 20, 1895, p. 6.

[83] "Suicide Succeeds," *New Orleans Daily Picayune*, Apr. 12, 1896, p. 15; "Cocaine Habit's Alarming Growth," *New Orleans Daily Picayune*, Aug. 23, 1896, p. 16. Two other references to cocaine use by African Americans appeared in contexts that allow no clear conclusion of recreational abuse. One ran under the heading, "Two Accidental Suicides." The abbreviated report said only that "Edna Edwards, colored, died suddenly to-day, it is believed, from the effects of an overose [sic] of cocaine, administered by herself." "Shreveport," *New Orleans Daily Picayune*, Dec. 27, 1893, p. 8. The second alleged without detail that a "negro haridan named Maggie Williams, in a fit of despondency, attempted suicide at 10 o'clock last night by taking a dose of cocaine . . . ." "The Cocaine Cure," *New Orleans Daily Picayune*, May 30, 1895, p. 12.

lower flesh . . . ."[84] Here, though, "dethronement of the reason" perhaps suggested insanity, not lust. The *Picayune's* reporter drew a clearer sexual link in telling of three women recently charged with lewd conduct, all either addicted or once addicted to cocaine.

The *Picayune's* account of cocainized dancing women taught another lesson we've learned before. Asked how its devotees used the drug, the local druggist explained that cocaine came as "little crystals" sold by irresponsible druggists in five-cent packages. "The user takes a crystal and places it in his or her nostril. The effect soon begins." Or as a reformed cocaine addict later tried for lewdness told the court, "You sniff it up." Worried that cocaine in powdered form, then "much in vogue," was "working enormous damage to the colored race in this city," the *Picayune's* reporter called "for an exacting enforcement" of an existing law requiring unprescribed cocaine to be labeled "Poison."[85]

Four months later, in early January 1897, the *Picayune* warned again of the menace of cocaine snuffs. In a short item relaying the news of the Connecticut cocaine epidemic we've encountered in the *Boston Globe* and several Colorado papers, the *Picayune* printed, "The evil had its inception about a year ago, when a local druggist compounded a preparation of the drug and menthol, which could be used as a snuff. . . . [T]he prescription was passed round and now it is stated that hundreds have become slaves to the habit."[86]

Within another two months a New Orleans city councilman had proposed an ordinance to ban cocaine—the first significant Southern law barring unprescribed sales.[87]

The New Orleans Anti-Cocaine Ordinance

As 1897 opened, it seems the press had said nothing of cocaine-driven crime among African Americans (or among others) and had said rather little of African American cocaine abusers. The sole substantial report of Black addicts in New Orleans, which told of the frenzied dancers, had said nothing of crime or violence. Instead it had warned of sexualized self-indulgence spurred by the easy availability of cheap, ready-to-use cocaine that had slipped free of the medical mold and morphed into a recreational drug.

---

[84] St. Augustine, Sermon 8, "On the Plagues of Egypt and the Ten Commandments of the Law," in *The Works of Saint Augustine: A Translation for the 21st Century*, vol. III/1 (Edmund Hill trans., Brooklyn: New City Press, 1990), ¶ 8, pp. 244–45.

[85] "Cocaine Habit's Alarming Growth."

[86] "Personal and General Notes," *New Orleans Daily Picayune*, Jan. 2, 1897, p. 4.

[87] "Algiers Viaduct Wins by a Nose," *New Orleans Daily Picayune*, Feb 24, 1897, p. 7; "The City Council," *New Orleans Times-Democrat*, Feb. 24, 1897, p. 6.

The new year was not two months old when a New Orleans City Council member proposed "[a]n ordinance prohibiting the sale of cocaine or its salts, unless on a doctor's prescription."[88] Made law on March 30, the ordinance may have imposed the first cocaine ban in the South. The remarkable lawmaker who sponsored it, Dr. Quitman Kohnke, like the *Picayune* story that went before, seemingly said nothing of racialized crime and spoke instead in long-familiar moral strains.

Kohnke's name first appeared in the political press of New Orleans early in 1896 under the page-one headline, "THIS IS A REAL CLEAN TICKET." The *Picayune* congratulated the Citizens' League on the slate of candidates it had placed before the city's "Independent Voters," presumably those not in liege to party chieftains. "Not a Ward Boss or a Man with a Master Has a Place in This List," the *Picayune* declared, deeming the ticket the "embodiment of honesty, integrity and ability." Named as the First Ward's councilmanic nominee, Kohnke was making his first run for public office. A follow-up article two days later pictured him bearded and balding, youthful but sage, with wire-framed spectacles and a discerning gaze. Then in his late thirties, Kohnke had practiced medicine in a surgical ear, nose, and throat department since 1891. On the side, he served the poor through the Society of St. Vincent de Paul and other charitable groups.[89]

Two weeks later Kohnke claimed victory, took his council seat, and promptly assumed leadership of the health committee. Donning the cape of a public-health crusader, he tackled issues more gritty than glamorous, ranging from garbage to smallpox to sewage. With "detective camera" in hand, he exposed heaps of rotting refuse dumped amid residential housing by the city's private trash collector. His outrage moved fellow councilmen to terminate the collector's contract by unanimous vote. Next he unmasked the incompetent and heartless management of the city's smallpox hospital, so swollen with patients that some lived in tents. Later he trained his unsparing eye on the spotty service of the city's stunted sewer system. He left the *Picayune* struggling to find new ways to praise this "indefatigable and patriotic" council member, "so vigilant and fearless" in protecting the public. "No member of the councilmanic body has been held in higher esteem than he."[90]

---

[88] "Algiers Viaduct Wins by a Nose." The ordinance as adopted and printed is available on microfilm held by the New Orleans Public Library. New Orleans City Ordinance 13,194, Council Series (Mar. 30, 1897), *in Biennial Report of the Louisiana State Board of Health to the General Assembly of the State of Louisiana, 1906–1907* (Baton Rouge: The Daily State Press, 1908), p. 133: "That it shall be unlawful for any person in the City of New Orleans to sell cocaine or its salts to any person, except to the bearer of a prescription . . . or to a regular practicing physician." I thank my research assistant Rani Gupta, who secured a copy of the ordinance.

[89] "This Is a Real Clean Ticket," *New Orleans Daily Picayune*, Apr. 15, 1896, p. 1; "Clean Council without a Master," ibid., Apr. 17, 1896, p. 9.

[90] "New Council's First Night," ibid., Apr. 29, 1896, p. 1 (noting Kohnke's chairmanship of the health committee). On the garbage issue, *see*: "An Outrage against the City's Health," ibid., June 17, 1896,

Between smallpox and sewage, Kohnke turned to cocaine. Here he presumably spoke with expertise. As an ear, nose, and throat surgeon, he likely used cocaine as a local anesthetic and knew its habit-forming risk. His fellow surgeon and hospital colleague, Dr. William Scheppegrell, wrote in the *Medical News* of October 1898 that the cocaine "habit follows more frequently from its application in the nose and throat than in any other branch of medicine . . . ."[91] Yet Kohnke himself does not appear to have written on the topic.

Surviving sources disclose a single statement of his motives in battling cocaine. Addressing the city council's health committee four days before the council voted on his proposed ordinance, Kohnke complained of the easy availability of cocaine powders. "[C]ertain druggists," he said in words summarized by the *Picayune*, were "selling the stuff in 5 and 10-cent packages . . . . The application of it was through the nostrils; the cocaine was . . . so seductive that the more used the more required." That is, New Orleans druggists were making the same over-the-counter sales of cheap packets of cocaine snuff that figured in early cocaine bans in Colorado, Illinois, and Massachusetts. Moreover, neither sellers nor buyers could claim the moral license of medical need. "There was no excuse for the use of it," Kohnke said of cocaine. "It did not alleviate pain, and was only taken for the pleasant effect it produced for the time." He assured his fellow council members that "[b]y passage of the ordinance there would be no interference with its medicinal use," as patients with true medical needs still could get the drug by prescription. Instead the law "would have the moral effect of restraining the sale of the insidious drug . . . to irresponsible people," presumably those who sought the drug only for its "seductive" and "pleasant effect."[92]

---

p. 9 (presenting engravings copied from Kohnke's snapshots of dump sites); "More of the Garbage Outrage," ibid., June 28, 1896, p. 4 ("indefatigable . . ." and "so vigilant . . ."); "Garbage Dumped in Open Squares," ibid., June 28, 1896, p. 10 (mentioning Kohnke's "detective camera" and noting council's unanimous vote). On the smallpox hospital, *see*: "Council Continues Its Indictments," ibid., June 20, 1896, p. 7 (presenting Kohnke's report describing the layout of the smallpox hospital and the conditions of care); "The Pesthouse to Be Reformed," ibid., July 23, 1896, p. 9; "Stamping Out the Smallpox," ibid., Aug. 8, 1896, p. 3 (reporting that Kohnke chaired an interagency planning meeting to address the hospital's deficiencies). On the inadequate sewer system, *see*: "Nine Councilmen to Study Sewerage," ibid., Apr. 21, 1897, p. 7; "A Public Debate about Sewerage," ibid., Aug. 6, 1897, p. 9 (identifying Kohnke as "chairman of the city council special committee on sewerage"). *See also* "A Health Board for the Parish," ibid., Aug. 10, 1898, p. 7 ("No member . . . .").

[91] W. Scheppegrell, "The Abuse and Dangers of Cocaine," *Medical News*, vol. 73 (Oct. 1, 1898), pp. 417, 420–21. Scheppegrell and Kohnke both practiced surgery at the Senses Hospital of New Orleans. *See* "The Senses Hospital," *New Orleans Daily Picayune*, Aug. 3, 1893, p. 8 (reporting Scheppegrell's position as assistant surgeon at the hospital); "Clean Council without a Master," ibid., Apr. 17, 1896, p. 9 ("Dr. Kohnke was elected assistant surgeon in the ear, nose and throat department of the senses hospital in 1891, under Dr. De Roaldes."). *See also* William Oliver Moore, "The Physiological and Therapeutical Effects of the Coca-Leaf and Its Alkaloid," *New York Medical Journal*, vol. 41 (Jan. 3, 1885), pp. 19, 22 ("In the surgery of the pharynx and larynx, [cocaine] was an agent surpassing any hitherto known . . . .").

[92] "Mr. Cucullu's Tax on Telegraph Poles," *New Orleans Daily Picayune*, Mar. 27, 1897, p. 6.

Four days later, without reported debate, the full council approved Kohnke's proposal to ban sales of cocaine or its salts "to any person, except to the bearer of a prescription of a regular practicing physician." The law's preamble rehearsed Kohnke's stated concern that the drug's use "as a deliriant and intoxicant . . . has assumed large and dangerous proportions and is daily increasing to such an extent as to threaten . . . public health and morality." The law targeted not only pure cocaine but also catarrh powders and other "combinations of drugs which may be now or hereafter made wherein the ingredient cocaine is in such proportions as to make its deliriant or intoxicant effect the main reason for their use." With an eye to the grasping druggists who sold the stuff to anyone with a nickel or dime to spare, the preamble condemned those who "aided and encouraged the cocaine habit by the indiscriminate sale of the drug . . . ." The law therefore punished druggists, not their hapless patrons, with a fine of $25 or thirty days' imprisonment.[93]

An article in the *New Orleans Times-Democrat* two weeks before the law's passage may have sharpened concerns about catarrh cures. Bearing the headline "DEADLY COCAINE" and filling a page-long column, the item yet again reminded readers of the Connecticut townsfolk who ran amok on cocaine-laced catarrh snuff: "[C]ocaine made its entrance to South Manchester," we're told, "under seductive labels as a remedy for catarrh." Cold sufferers found "[t]he stuff works like a charm. All the pain and distress of the mucous membranes of the throat and nose vanish[ed] . . . ." Having been charmed by the drug's remedial powers, patients were seduced by its euphoriant force, delivering "perfect peace, ecstasy, superlative joy, love of all mankind and womankind. The patient sees only a beatific vision." Then come the shackles of addiction, together with the "bodily wasting, mental decay and moral perversion of cocaine."[94] Little wonder Kohnke and his fellow councilmen attacked the drug with resolve.

Racism's Role in Kohnke's Anti-Cocaine Ordinance

That Kohnke sought to target cocaine snuffs seems clear. The dancing women whose vim and vigor sparked the August 1896 report of the "Cocaine Habit's Alarming Growth" took their drug by "sniff[ing] it up." The cocaine epidemic that ravaged the Connecticut town "had its inception," the *Picayune* reported, "when a local druggist compounded a preparation of the drug and menthol, which could be used as a snuff." The *Times-Democrat*'s March 16 account of

[93] "Corruption in City Contracts," *New Orleans Daily Picayune*, Mar. 31, 1897, p. 11; New Orleans City Ordinance 13,194, Council Series.
[94] "Deadly Cocaine," *New Orleans Times-Democrat*, Mar. 16, 1897, p. 10.

"Deadly Cocaine" reminded readers that cocaine entered the Connecticut town "under seductive labels as a remedy for catarrh." And Kohnke himself declared the drug he sought to ban was taken "through the nostrils."[95]

Though his pharmacological foe seems plain, the question of Kohnke's motives remains. Did racism incite his cocaine ban? Some evidence surely permits that verdict. In the statement just quoted, advising the city council's health committee of his purpose in banning cocaine, Kohnke said the habit "had taken a strong hold upon an ignorant class of people, and they were making physical wrecks of themselves."[96] Kohnke never said here or apparently anywhere who composed this "ignorant class of people." Nor did any member of the city council in any recorded statement hint that the addicts who prompted the ban weren't white.

Still there are grounds to suspect Kohnke's "ignorant class" was code for African Americans. Under the headline of the *Picayune's* striking account of the "Cocaine Habit's Alarming Growth," printed six months before Kohnke introduced his ordinance, the editors added, "Especially Among the Colored Population of the City." The report quoted a local druggist who said it was "remarkable how, with the exception of a few abandoned white women, [cocaine's] use is confined almost exclusively to the colored folks." Using the same term Kohnke later used to describe the targets of his proposed ordinance, the druggist added, "How on earth these *ignorant* people ever learned the effects of this powerful and dangerous drug, I am at a loss to say . . . ." Later he clarified, "I do not allude, of course, to the most self-respecting of the race, though even some of them indulge the vice, but to the shiftless and *ignorant* contingent."[97]

Kohnke's colleague, Dr. William Scheppegrell, likewise suggested cocaine abuse in New Orleans centered among African Americans. A year and a half after passage of Kohnke's ordinance, Scheppegrell wrote in *Medical News* that a "pecul[i]ar phase of the cocain[e] habit" that had "developed in New Orleans and in a number of other cities in the South is the contraction of this habit by the negroes." Among most white cocaine addicts "a prescription of the physician is responsible for the evils which result," but the African American addicts took up the drug "on account of its exhilarating effects."[98]

That Kohnke acted with African American addicts prominently in view therefore seems likely. Hence his cocaine ban, conceived to guard the health and morals of an "irresponsible" and "ignorant class of people," was perhaps more condescending than kind. Even if patronizing, however, the law wasn't punitive. Far from targeting addicts, Kohnke's ordinance sought to "deter many *druggists*

---

[95] "Cocaine Habit's Alarming Growth"; "Personal and General Notes"; "Deadly Cocaine"; "Mr. Cucullu's Tax on Telegraph Poles."

[96] "Mr. Cucullu's Tax on Telegraph Poles."

[97] "Cocaine Habit's Alarming Growth" (emphasis added).

[98] Scheppegrell, "The Abuse and Dangers of Cocaine," p. 421.

from making sales to irresponsible people" and therefore punished only sellers. The *Picayune* correctly called the proposal "Dr. Kohnke's ordinance to prohibit *the sale by druggists* of cocaine."[99] And the druggists likely were white.

Whether Kohnke's motives were racist turns largely on whether he would have taken the same patronizing tack had the recreational addicts he sought to protect been white. The evidence suggests his course would have been no different. His ordinance after all targeted white pharmacists, not their African American buyers, and it seems unlikely he would have treated more forgivingly druggists who victimized whites. And Kohnke's motives toward African Americans appear from this distance genuinely sympathetic. The offenses that fueled his program of reforms—rotting refuse, scanty sewers, a shabby smallpox hospital—fell hardest on the poor and working class. Kohnke objected to proposals that would tread on the disempowered and to measures he deemed "class legislation" favoring the privileged. In scores of articles covering his political activities and his later leadership of the city's health commission, the *Picayune* never quoted him speaking disrespectfully of African Americans. Yet the paper readily reprinted others' use of "darkies" and harsher racial epithets.[100]

Moreover, evidence of Kohnke's open sympathy with African Americans emerged in the weeks and months leading up to his anti-cocaine ordinance. In hearings he conducted in September and October 1896 on conditions and treatment at the smallpox hospital, Kohnke repeatedly sponsored testimony by Black patients and family members. He "stated that the object . . . was to prove by witnesses the character of the service rendered by Dr. [Joseph C.] Beard," who had contracted with the city to care for the smallpox patients. Kohnke confronted the white Dr. Beard with African Americans' accusations that he never attended a sick five-year-old who lost his eye to smallpox and tried to bribe Black patients to swear falsely to their good treatment. And in November 1896, less than four months before he put his proposed cocaine ban before the city council, Kohnke recommended that the city help fund a training center and sanitarium for poor Black residents.[101]

---

[99] "Mr. Cucullu's Tax on Telegraph Poles," *New Orleans Daily Picayune* (emphasis added).

[100] "Algiers Viaduct Wins by a Nose" (reporting Kohnke's argument concerning a proposed ordinance that in his view, "the city should not impose the obligation of going to court upon the poor gardeners"); "That Three Hundred Asked by Wheelmen," *New Orleans Daily Picayune*, May 12, 1897, p. 3 (reporting Kohnke's complaint that a proposed appropriation of $350 to pave bicycle lanes would amount to "class legislation" and his regret that he voted to repair the fans in the council chamber though that too amounted to class legislation); "Women Will Work for City Sanitation," ibid., Mar. 30, 1898, p. 3 (quoting Kohnke's view that "[r]eal, true sanitation must benefit all classes alike"); "Cocaine Habit's Alarming Growth" (reprinting a druggist's reference to "darkies"); "A Star Witness for Doctor Beard," *New Orleans Daily Picayune*, Sept. 25, 1896, p. 8 (reprinting a witness's use of "n__ __r").

[101] "Smallpox Hospital under Investigation," ibid., Sept. 15, 1896, p. 8 ("stated that the object . . ." and presenting testimony by at least five African Americans about their poor treatment when patients in the smallpox hospital); "Smallpox Hospital Being Investigated," ibid., Sept. 22, 1896, p. 3 (relating an African American mother's testimony that Dr. Beard never attended her five-year-old son, who

Racism's Role in Other Southern Cocaine Bans

Yet in Louisiana as a whole and elsewhere in the South, racism's role in driving anti-cocaine legislation proves plainer. Evidence of blatant bigotry scarred the historical record. Whites romanticized their guardianship of an inferior race and demanded in return abject submission.

Hence it matters that the sponsor of Louisiana's first statewide cocaine ban was Democratic state senator Thomas Charles Barret (often Barrett). Evidence of Barret's views on race flows freely. A lawyer by training, he married the daughter of a Confederate colonel deemed by the *Picayune* "the foremost man" in the Shreveport region. He took his senate seat in April 1896 and promptly broadcast his stance on perhaps the most highly charged race-related issue of the day: the rules governing who could vote. At a Democratic caucus in June, Barret offered a resolution declaring in the *Picayune'*s words "that it is the first and foremost obligation of the party . . . to eliminate the irresponsible voters from the right of franchise."[102] Here was thinly veiled code for exclusive white suffrage.

Lest any doubt linger, Barret made plain his views of Black suffrage late in 1899, about eighteen months after Louisiana had embraced a slate of blatantly biased voting rules. Those rules granted suffrage only to literate or propertied males and to those who could vote—or whose fathers or grandfathers could vote—in 1867, before African Americans and former slaves had gained that right. The Democrats' platform produced under Barret's leadership trumpeted the party's endorsement of the new rules: "We congratulate the people that the organic laws of the state have . . . been so amended as to insure the supremacy of the white race and the salvation of Caucasian civilization in Louisiana . . . ."[103]

In May 1898, less than two weeks after the state adopted these new voting rules, Barret introduced a bill to "regulate the sale of cocaine, morphine and opium" throughout Louisiana. His proposal swept through the legislature, winning in the Senate twenty-eight to three and in the House sixty to two. Stripped along the way of references to morphine and opium, the act banned retail sales of cocaine except on prescription. When signed into law July 12, some fifteen

---

lost his eye to smallpox, and a former patient's testimony that Dr. Beard offered to pay him to lie about his treatment). On Kohnke's recommendation of assistance for poor African Americans, *see* "A Proposition to the Light Plant," ibid., Oct. 13, 1896, p. 3; "Wharf Lessees Still Stubborn," ibid., Nov. 3, 1896, p. 3.

[102] "Colonel J.M. Hollingsworth Dead," ibid., Jan. 9, 1894, p. 12; "These Figures Look Better," ibid., Apr. 23, 1896, p. 2 (listing Barret as the newly elected senator for the Twentieth District); "The Caucus Has Spoken," ibid., June 10, 1896, p. 1.

[103] *Constitution of the State of Louisiana* (New Orleans: H.J. Hearsey, 1898), art. 197, §§ 3–5, pp. 77–78 (adopted May 12, 1898); "The Ticket Completed," *New Orleans Daily Picayune*, Dec. 22, 1899, p. 6.

months after Kohnke's New Orleans ordinance, it became the first statewide co-caine ban in the South.[104]

Of Senator Barret's motives in presenting the bill, the state's official publications and commercial press disclose little. We can say only one thing with certainty: despite clear evidence of Barret's bigotry, his anti-cocaine law did not target African Americans. Like Kohnke's New Orleans ordinance, Barret's statute punished only unlawful sellers, not buyers or users or mere possessors. All evidence suggests sellers most commonly were pharmacists and presumably white. So while Barret's views on race likely deepened his anxiety about African American cocaine abuse and helped drive Louisiana's 1898 cocaine ban, the law gave police and prosecutors no new power to harass or imprison African Americans.

Pattern of State Cocaine Bans

Reports of cocaine-driven crime among African Americans emerged at the very end of the nineteenth and beginning of the twentieth centuries. By then four states had outlawed unprescribed cocaine sales—Oregon, Montana, Colorado, and Illinois—and at least one more, New York, had passed a partial ban. Massachusetts and Louisiana were crafting their bans just as tales of such crime took rise. Only in Louisiana does the record raise suspicion of racial motives. And even in Louisiana, Dr. Kohnke's dominant role in shaping the earlier New Orleans ban complicates conclusions. Racial animus may have driven Senator Barret to act, but Kohnke and presumably others throughout the South hoped to stanch cocaine abuse for reasons rooted in public health and morals.

Still, Table 6A and the maps in Figure 6.3 chart a surge of Southern anti-cocaine laws trailing in Louisiana's wake. This sudden swell perhaps had racial tailwinds. Mounting reports of crimes by African American cocaine "fiends" harden suspicion of race-driven lawmaking. The first I've seen, dated October 1897, concerned a Dallas ice-factory worker "wild with cocaine or some other drug, or else insane," who "assaulted every man he came in reach of . . . ." A second followed months later in New Orleans, where a domestic dispute between "two negro cocaine fiends" ended with a woman's bloodied face. Then, after a long lull, the *Atlanta Constitution* reported in July 1900 that "Robert Charles, the negro

---

[104] "Governor's Message to Go in To-day," *New Orleans Daily Picayune*, May 24, 1898, p. 1 (noting 1898 bill's introduction); 1898 *Louisiana Senate Journal*, p. 111 (June 15, 1898) (recording vote on Senate passage); *Calendar of the House of Representatives of the State of Louisiana* (1898) (recording House vote); 1898 *Louisiana House Journal*, p. 289 (June 22, 1898) (noting amendment to strike out references to opium and morphine); "An Act to Regulate the Sale, Gift or Exchange at Retail of Cocaine . . . ," 1898 *Louisiana Acts*, no. 85 (Act of July 12, 1898), pp. 110–11.

murderer who was killed in New Orleans yesterday afternoon, was a victim of the cocaine habit." Again, in December 1900, the *Constitution* reported a "Bloody Fight in Cocaine Dive." After a "difficulty" between two African American women, one had stabbed the other in the back.[105] None of these reports had the prominence of Dr. Williams's 1914 sensation in the *New York Times*, but their combined force may have been great.

As years ticked by, the stories grew more strident. In 1901 the *Constitution* warned of the "Growing Evil" of child life insurance. A local lawyer charged that "hundreds of negroes in the state . . . would put their children to death to secure money with which to purchase cocaine or other drugs." In 1903 the *New York Tribune* printed a long interview with Colonel J. W. Watson of Georgia, who pronounced himself "satisfied that many of the horrible crimes committed in the Southern States by the colored people can be traced directly to the cocaine habit." Two years later, a Memphis police captain fretted about the city's African American cocaine abusers. When "sniffed up the nostrils" in the form of a white powder, the captain said, cocaine produces an effect "much more violent than that of whisky. . . . [T]here is nothing too awful for [a cocaine user] to attempt when thoroughly under its influence."[106]

As stories of African American cocaine abuse percolated through the South, lawmakers elsewhere perhaps took heed. Table 6A and the maps in Figure 6.3 show that after 1898, cocaine bans appeared up and down the Mississippi River. Between 1899 and 1905, Arkansas, Mississippi, Tennessee, Kentucky, Iowa, Missouri, and Minnesota outlawed unprescribed sales. These states may have witnessed heavy cocaine use among Black roustabouts from New Orleans, "who found that the drug enabled them to perform more easily the extraordinarily severe work of loading and unloading steamboats . . . ." A 1902 account in the *Medical News* said the cocaine habit had spread from such roustabouts to "levee camps along the Mississippi, where the work is hard . . . ."[107]

Flying over the country and looking down, then, we can't rule out racism's role in prompting the Northern and Western anti-cocaine laws of the very late nineteenth and early twentieth centuries. Only through close, on-the-ground

---

[105] "Texas," *New Orleans Daily Picayune*, Oct. 1, 1897, p. 12; "A Cocaine Duel," ibid., Dec. 16, 1897, p. 2; "The Passing Throng," *Atlanta Constitution*, July 28, 1900, p. 11; "One Woman Stabs Another," ibid., Dec. 15, 1900, p. 7 (noting that both women appeared in court a day and a half later).

[106] "Child Life Insurance Seems a Growing Evil," *Atlanta Constitution*, Mar. 16, 1901, p. 6; "Cocaine Sniffers," *New York Tribune*, June 21, 1903, pt. II, p. 11; "Negro Cocaine Evil," *New York Times*, Mar. 20, 1905, p. 14.

[107] "Negro Cocaine Fiends," *Medical News*, vol. 81, no. 19 (Nov. 8, 1902), p. 895. In 1896 and 1901, the *Chicago Tribune* mentioned illicit cocaine use in the levee district, but without reference to race. See "Hypnotic Cure Failure," *Chicago Daily Tribune*, Nov. 1, 1896, p. 18 (quoting a Chicago judge's reference to "all of the cocaine fiends who visit the levee"); "Sale of Cocaine and Morphine Increases," ibid., June 27, 1901, p. 8 (alleging that "the drug stores on the levee sell cocaine to . . . any one who is willing to buy").

scrutiny can we tell what goaded lawmakers to act. Such scrutiny uncovered no evidence of racial motives in the first five anti-cocaine states. But as the last of those states, Massachusetts, banned cocaine in 1898, just as reports of drug-driven violence penetrated public consciousness in the South, we can't assess the sway such tales later held in the North. With this goal in mind, let's return to the biggest Northern state, one where a large population of African Americans might have influenced legislation. If any state affords a test case for the North, that state is New York.

New York's 1907 Smith Act

New York first sought to quash cocaine abuse in 1893, when the legislature forbade pharmacists to "refill more than once, prescriptions containing . . . cocaine" unless in very weak doses. The state failed, however, to ban cocaine sales without a prescription, mooting the matter of refills. Halfhearted though the measure was, it must have satisfied its makers. Over and over, New York legislators passed up thoughtful proposals for change. Assemblyman John F. Maher's failed 1899 bid to ban any "headache, catarrh or hay fever remedy, in powdered form, having in it or containing cocaine" alerts us that the catarrh-cure problem had arrived in New York, yet didn't rouse Maher's colleagues to act.[108]

Nor did they stir a year later when Senator Timothy D. Sullivan proposed to penalize sales of "any proprietary or patent medicine or tonics, snuff, tobacco, or headache, catarrh, or hay fever remedy containing cocaine." And even as the Assembly approved a 1906 bill that would become New York's counterpart to the federal Pure Food and Drug Act of the same year, it rejected an amendment that would have made it a felony to sell opium or cocaine without a physician's prescription or for a doctor to prescribe either drug except for medical use.[109]

By 1907, New York lawmakers had let fourteen years lapse since their first, largely feckless measure forbidding cocaine prescription refills. Yet that year they acted with command, declaring it a felony punishable by up to a year in prison and a fine of up to $1,000 to sell or dispense any product containing cocaine without a doctor's prescription.[110] The forces that triggered decisive action after long delay are both complex and familiar. They are complex because by 1907 reports of cocaine abuse among African Americans and others were

---

[108] "An Act in Relation to the Public Health," 1893 *New York Laws*, vol. 2, ch. 661, § 208 (Act of May 9, 1893), p. 1561; "Legislative Notes," *New York Times*, Mar. 30, 1899, p. 5.

[109] "Other Bills in the Senate," *New York Times*, Feb. 1, 1900, p. 8; "Patent Medicine Bill to Curb Drug Users," ibid., Mar. 15, 1906, p. 6.

[110] "An Act to Amend the Penal Code in Relation to the Sale of Certain Drugs," 1907 *New York Laws*, vol. 1, ch. 424 (Act of June 5, 1907), p. 879.

too commonplace to document. Though such reports could sustain the claim that racialized fear fed legislative fires, a closer view, focused on forces nearest home, leads to a different but familiar conclusion: the 1907 act traces instead to a worry that fast-acting cocaine in a kid-friendly form had proved too tempting to white youth.

The Case for Racial Causation

As the Assembly dithered, accounts of African American cocaine abuse drifted North. In what seems the first such report in the local press, the *New York Tribune* reprinted the *Daily Picayune*'s 1896 story of strangely vigorous dancing among cocaine-sniffing African American women in New Orleans. A year later the *Tribune* cited a Memphis medical journal's conclusion that "it is the working people, and the negroes especially, who seem to find an especial solace in this narcotic." And in 1898 the *Tribune* repeated reports from Paducah, Kentucky, of a "Colored Cocaine Club" where African Americans gather "at 'coke parties' to enjoy the drug. The negroes . . . sniff cocaine, diluted with water, up their nostrils."[111]

These early accounts had little impact in New York, where the press deemed them doubtful or beneath mention. The *New York Times*, like the *Chicago Tribune*, denied them a single line of type. Even the *New York Tribune*, having at first headlined these stories, later had qualms. In December 1900, it scoffed at reports of New Orleans druggists who sold cocaine to "poor negroes. . . . [H]ow is it that cocaine is so cheap in Louisiana that it can be sold at a profit to colored men of small means, while in the North it is so expensive as to be out of the reach of any one who draws the wages of unskilled labor?" Three months later, the *Tribune* balked at "[s]ingular reports . . . from Alabama of the ravages caused among negroes by the prevalence of the cocaine habit." Cocaine is costly, the editors repeated. "Where do poor negroes in Alabama get money with which to buy cocaine?" Even as the story spread across the South, the *Tribune* cast doubt. "Strange tales get into print now and then," the editors wrote in 1903. "Absurd myths of a widespread craze for cocaine among the plantation hands of the South" were a case in point. "Cocaine is not cheap. In what way could poor negroes obtain a great deal of it?"[112]

Yet as Southern reports of African American cocaine abuse persisted, they gained currency. No longer silent, the *Times* warned in 1902 of "the alarming

---

[111] "Increase of the Cocaine Habit," *New York Tribune*, Sept. 6, 1896, p. A5; [Untitled Editorial], ibid., Mar. 2, 1897, p. 6; "Cocaine Victims Organize," ibid., Jan. 10, 1898, p. 2.

[112] [Untitled Editorial], ibid., Dec. 12, 1900, p. 6; [Untitled Editorial], ibid., Mar. 19, 1901, p. 6; [Untitled Editorial], ibid., Feb. 26, 1903, p. 8.

growth of the use of cocaine among the negroes of Mississippi." In 1903 the paper reported a study presented to the Hampton, Virginia, Negro Conference estimating that more than two hundred thousand African Americans were addicted to cocaine and other drugs. Across town the *Tribune* was quoting Colonel J. W. Watson's claims of "the horrible crimes committed in the Southern States by the colored people" hooked on cocaine. And the *Times* wrote in 1905 of a Mississippi judge who urged a grand jury to "show no mercy in dealing with druggists" who plied "cocaine promiscuously to negroes." The *Times* buried the item on page fourteen, but gave it the compelling headline, "Negro Cocaine Evil."[113]

Though all these reports appeared in New York newspapers, all told Southern stories. Some New Yorkers may have spied in them a gathering storm creeping north; others likely shared the *Tribune*'s skepticism and mistrusted any Southern smear of African Americans. At any rate, these were distant crimes. By mid-January 1907, when Assemblyman Alfred E. Smith introduced what became New York's first true cocaine ban, neither the *Times* nor the *Tribune* had reported a single act of cocaine-fueled violence by an African American in New York. Nor had either paper written of a single Black cocaine addict in New York. Though surely such addicts existed, they weren't the talk of the town. And Dr. Williams's incendiary tale of bullet-resistant Southern fiends still lay seven years down the road.

Yet two references to cocaine-linked crimes by African Americans in New York perhaps caught careful readers' eyes. Both were fleeting and third-hand and buried in a larger text. Still they may have betrayed a broader social understanding.

The first remark appeared in the *Tribune* in March 1906. The paper reviewed testimony before a state senate committee about a bill that later became New York's version of the federal Pure Food and Drug Act. William Jay Schieffelin, head of a leading pharmaceutical firm claimed to be the nation's largest cocaine importer, broke ranks with competitors in supporting the law's demand that drug makers disclose all dangerous and habit-forming ingredients, including cocaine. In listing the drug trade's predations, Schieffelin turned briefly to one group of sellers: "I am told there are negroes in the Tenderloin district who peddle the drug around." That remark likely prompted the second such reference in December. Rebutting complaints that the State Board of Pharmacy had acted too aggressively against druggists who sold improperly labeled cocaine, board president C. O. Bigelow said, "[I]t is a startling fact that cocaine is sold on

[113] "Cocaine Evil Among Negroes," *New York Times*, Nov. 3, 1902, p. 5; "Hampton Negro Conference," ibid., July 16, 1903. p. 2; "Cocaine Sniffers," *New York Tribune*, June 21, 1903, pt. 2, p. 11; "Negro Cocaine Evil," *New York Times*, Mar. 20, 1905, p. 14.

the street in the Tenderloin, and other parts of the city, by Negroes, who carry powders in their pockets."[114]

The discourse of the day, however, focused not on African American middlemen, but on unscrupulous druggists who typically sold directly to users. The discourse focused, too, on the product sold, for many such "powders" often came packaged as a claimed catarrh cure. And the discourse focused finally on the buyers, who far too often were youth—sometimes homeless waifs, sometimes scions of the middle class, always seemingly white.

Catarrh Cures Reach New York

The problem of cocaine-laced catarrh cures came late to New York. These cures appeared in Chicago in 1893, when the Birney Catarrhal Powder Company took form there. They appeared in New Orleans by 1896, in time to explain the startling vim and vigor of the cocainized dancing women. Because river stevedores endured long days, high heat, and heavy labor, they may have carried cocaine north from New Orleans along the Mississippi, while miners who endured similar heat and long labors perhaps carried it west to Colorado and other mining states and territories. So the late appearance of catarrh powders in New York is a puzzle. The city had masses of stevedores and a catarrh cure company of its own, the Anglo-American Medicine Company, which made Dr. Agnew's Catarrhal Powder. Dr. Agnew's cocaine-spiked formula had reached Boston by 1896. Yet New York somehow evaded all such cures—or at least their arrival evaded mention in New York's press—for another three years.[115]

The *Times* first nodded to the problem in 1899 in reporting Assemblyman Maher's failed attempt to ban any "headache, catarrh or hay fever remedy, in powdered form, having in it or containing cocaine." Again the problem emerged early in 1904, when Assemblyman Charles J. Hewitt offered a bill "[p]rohibiting the use of cocaine in manufacturing patent medicines, wines, liquors, or snuffs." Two weeks later, the *Times* told of Beatrice Mallerau, a postal employee of unstated age, arrested for thieving cash from the mails. "[H]er mother, who lives on Staten Island, said she believed her to be irresponsible because of her addiction

---

[114] "Alarming Increase of Indulgence by New Yorkers in Powerful Narcotics," *New York Tribune*, Mar. 25, 1906, p. C1; "Hits Pharmacy Board," ibid., Dec. 7, 1906, p. 7; "Drug Habit Increasing," ibid., Mar. 10, 1906, p. 8 (reporting Schieffelin's claim that his firm was the largest cocaine importer).

[115] "New Incorporations," *Chicago Tribune*, Jan. 12, 1893, p. 10; "Negro Cocaine Fiends," *Medical News*, vol. 81, no. 19 (Nov. 8, 1902), p. 895 (explaining stevedores' use of cocaine); "Catarrh and Colds Relieved in 10 to 60 Minutes," *Boston Daily Globe*, Jan. 29, 1896, p. 14; Spillane, *Cocaine*, p. 87 (telling of Agnew's source and contents).

to the use of cocaine taken as a snuff." The legislature nonetheless failed to act, and Hewitt's bill came to naught. Mallerau meanwhile slipped from view.[116]

Little by little the press trained its gaze on the topic. In October 1904, the *Times* told of a meeting of the New York County Medical Society. Dr. C. H. Richardson warned of "the fondness for catarrh cures and for preparations that are known to contain large quantities of cocaine." Soon the craze had a catchy name. Under the headline, "Blowing the Burners," the *Times* reported the March 1905 robbery trial of Austin Phillips, who invoked his snuffing habit "as an excuse" for holding up a cashier and swiping $10 from the till. "Blowing the Burners," we're told, was Tenderloin slang for "inhal[ing] a powder composed largely of cocaine . . . , which has gained a large sale as a patent catarrh cure." The *Times* didn't explain the theory of Phillips's defense. Perhaps his counsel claimed his addiction impelled his theft or left him briefly insane. At all events unimpressed, the judge sentenced Phillips, of unstated race and age, to nine and a half years. In what seemed a confession of past ignorance, the police commissioner announced he would "institute an investigation in regard to the vice as practiced by men and women in dives about the city."[117]

Six weeks later, catarrh cures were back in the news. A correspondent to the *Times* wrote of "a poor, broken-hearted woman" whose husband's habit wrecked their marriage and impoverished their family. "[O]ne of the numerous cocaine, catarrh snuffs that are freely advertised over the country" had brought him down. "In the South," the letter continued, "some of the worst crimes committed by the negroes result from the use of cocaine." At the same time, the author sounded the theme of white youth at risk, warning that these cocainized snuffs were destroying "[s]ome of the finest of our young men and women." A *Tribune* report of January 1906 likewise focused on upper-class users, if not youth. The Medical Society's counsel charged that "[m]any cocaine fiends have been made by use of catarrhal snuffs, whose formulæ were unknown to the users." He told of a lawyer who treated a cold with a free sample of catarrh snuff. It offered so much relief that the lawyer bought bottle after bottle until, fifteen bottles later, he was a "cocaine fiend." The state health superintendent added that catarrh snuffs had claimed many doctors, among whom "[t]he proportion [of addicts] is greater than in other walks of life."[118]

Early in 1906, as complaints of cocaine-powered catarrh cures mounted, the focus turned again toward women and youth. In March the *Tribune* proclaimed,

[116] "Legislative Notes," *New York Times*, Mar. 30, 1899, p. 5; "Bills in the Legislature," ibid., Feb. 12, 1904, p. 6; "Girl Held for Postal Theft," ibid., Feb. 26, 1904, p. 1.

[117] "Medical Society's Year," ibid., Oct. 25, 1904, p. 7; "Blowing the Burners," ibid., Mar. 14, 1905, p. 5; "The Growing Menace of the Use of Cocaine," *New York Times Magazine*, Aug. 2, 1908, pt. 5, p. 1 ("'Blowing the Birney's' is the colloquial term for the vice among its city victims and the police.").

[118] D.B., "Cocaine Habit's Horrors," *New York Times*, Apr. 30, 1905, p. 6; "Put Not Your Faith in Drug Stores," *New York Tribune*, Jan. 28, 1906, p. C1.

"Some Brands Make Women Drug Fiends." A speaker before the Woman's Municipal League had warned that "[m]any catarrh cures contain cocaine" and "women were the chief victims of injurious proprietary medicines . . . ." Later that month, when boosting a bill to ban unprescribed cocaine sales, William Jay Schieffelin alleged, "[T]here are three or four of the two thousand druggists in the city who make a practice of giving away samples of cocaine to young men and girls for the purpose of building up the habit that destroys moral as well as mental responsibility."[119]

Calling up images of New York's 1883 opium dens scandal, Schieffelin charged that "of the 250 white girls, some no more than 14 years old, now living in Chinatown, New York, 60 per cent. were cocaine and opium fiends." This time the alleged purveyors were not Chinese den owners but the neighborhood's white pharmacists. Under the heading, "FEMALE 'DOPE FIENDS,'" a Tribune reporter seeking to confirm Schieffelin's claim told of a fact-finding mission to Chinatown. The reporter surveilled a "procession of the 'dope fiends'"—"the thin but incessant stream of fallen humanity that sets in toward various 'shady' drug stores . . . ." A neighborhood rescue worker pointed to the culprit: "The form in which the women seem to take cocaine around here is that of powder. . . . They take it into the nostrils much in the same way as they would snuff." The reporter concluded of the drug: "Age, sex and condition of life seem to set no barrier to its blighting ravages."[120]

Despite this drumbeat of bad press early in 1906, a bill before the New York Assembly that would have banned unprescribed cocaine sales failed. A year later, however, a similar bill slid through both houses without drawing a single negative vote. If any single factor steeled public support and unified the legislature in the intervening twelve months, it was the appearance of a white poster child hooked on cocaine. The wayward and fallen white girls of Chinatown did not

---

[119] "Menace of Medicines," New York Tribune, Mar. 9, 1906, p. 10 ("Some Brands Make . . ."); "Drug Habit Increasing," ibid., Mar. 10, 1906, p. 8 ("there are three or four . . ."). See also "Publicity for Nostrums," ibid., Mar. 25, 1906, p. 6 (The "manufacturers of so-called catarrh cures which contained this drug [cocaine] were in the habit of distributing free samples of their wares on the sidewalks" with the end of addicting passers-by); "Lack Food Inspectors," ibid., Jan. 12, 1907, p. 7 ("Professor Coblentz . . . referred to the reprehensible habit of certain druggists who distribute free samples of catarrh snuff.").

[120] "Patent Medicine Bill to Curb Drug Users," New York Times, Mar. 15, 1906, p. 6 ("of the 250 white girls . . ."); "Alarming Increase of Indulgence by New Yorkers in Powerful Narcotics," New York Tribune, Mar. 25, 1906, p. C1 ("FEMALE 'DOPE FIENDS,'" "procession of the 'dope fiends,'" and succeeding quotes). Though I've found no demographic breakdown of New York pharmacists in this era, a 1907 roll of the New York City members of the American Pharmaceutical Association suggests they were mostly and perhaps overwhelmingly white. Only two of the 127 listed names appear to be Asian: Jokichi Takamine and Keizo Woyenaka. Though many apparently Anglo names could be those of African Americans, the near absence of Asian names makes it likely the profession was predominantly white. See Proceedings of the American Pharmaceutical Association (Baltimore: American Pharmaceutical Association, 1907), pp. 1006–07. My thanks to Alex Zhang of the Crown Law Library for locating this list.

qualify. On order was a youth of the respectable middle class with champions to speak for him.

White Youth and the Smith Act

One such champion stepped forward in August. Aiming to defend those he called "my boys," the young men of his congregation, Father James B. Curry of St. James Roman Catholic Church took up the anti-cocaine cudgel. Rooted in New York's Cherry Hill district just three blocks south of Chinatown's Church of the Transfiguration, Father Curry played in some ways the anti-cocaine counterpart of Father James Barry, the opium dens warrior of 1883. But whereas Father Barry slandered Chinese denkeepers with wild claims they debauched white schoolgirls, Curry targeted the neighborhood's druggists, all or most presumably white.

Curry first appeared in this role in the *Times* of August 25, 1906, tucked at the bottom of page fourteen under the small-type header, "Priest Wants Cocaine Sales Stopped." He had urged Acting Mayor P. F. McGowan to "proceed against druggists in the vicinity of his church who sold cocaine in ten-cent quantities to various persons." Three days later, the *Tribune* boosted Curry to page four, enlarged his name in bold type, and declared that "the vigorous rector" had "started a crusade against the sale of cocaine within the limits of his parish." Curry had told McGowan "he did not want such traffic so close to his boys' club." He complained that just the day before, "four young women and two grown up boys staggered up to the rectory and told him they could not stop 'eating that stuff.'" Though Curry said cocaine use "is very general among the negroes, who seem to have been the originators of the practice" in his district, he consistently attacked the neighborhood's white druggists as the source of the cocaine. "A cocaine fiend . . . is so lost to shame," he explained, "that we . . . cannot reform him, but I think we can reform the people who sell the vile stuff." Some years later he added that the abuse traced to a product sold over the counter by druggists: "I believe the use of so-called snuff for catarrh created in the beginning much of the liking for the drug."[121]

Soon Father Curry had a comrade in his anti-cocaine cause. The *Times* hailed her arrival in January 1907 under the arresting header, "Boy Cocaine Snuffers

[121] "Priest Wants Cocaine Sales Stopped," *New York Times*, Aug. 25, 1906, p. 14; "Health Board Against Cocaine," *New York Tribune*, Aug. 28, 1906, p. 4 ("four young women . . ."); "Checks Cocaine Sale," ibid., Sept. 1, 1907, p. 10 ("is very general among . . ." and "A cocaine fiend . . ."); "The Growing Menace of the Use of Cocaine," *New York Times Magazine*, Aug. 2, 1908, pt. 5, p. 1 ("When [the cocaine habit] commenced to reach out toward 'his boys,' as the Father calls the young men of his parish, he rose to combat it."); "Urges a Federal Law against Cocaine Evil," *New York Tribune*, Dec. 3, 1912, p. 4 ("I believe the use of so-called snuff . . .").

Hunted by the Police." Then, in smaller type: "Mother Has Her Son Arrested, Saying He Is a 'Fiend.' " The mother in question was Mrs. Annie Fromme of Hell's Kitchen. If Father Curry played counterpart to Chinatown's Father Barry, Mrs. Fromme, the white wife of a white truck driver, stood in for barber Julius Ohle, father of Chicago's Max Ohle, the "Boy Slave to Cocaine." But even the elder Ohle, who had vowed to imprison his son at home till cured of his cocaine habit, did not go to Annie Fromme's lengths. Her sixteen-year-old George, the *Times* said, was "now in the Tombs, awaiting examination on a charge made by his mother." He "had become a cocaine fiend," she charged, in league with "other boys who bought cocaine in catarrh powders from west side druggists." She alleged she had "found her boy engaged in snuffing the co[ca]ine."[122]

Mrs. Fromme did not rest with jailing her son, for she had learned on "further examination . . . that many boys living on the west side of town had become addicted to the cocaine habit." The true targets of her wrath were the druggists who sold to them, and already she had goaded authorities to act against the profiteers. Captain Russell of the West Thirty-Seventh Street Station, the *Times* said, would investigate "certain druggists who, it was alleged, had been selling cocaine to boys of tender age." Some of the druggists interviewed by the *Times* readily admitted "it was customary to sell catarrh powders containing cocaine. The cocaine habit had spread so rapidly, some of them said, that thousands of New Yorkers—boys, girls, and men and women—were now in the cocaine fiend class." This perverse boast received confirmation from Bellevue Hospital's chief psychopathologist, who warned "that unless something was done to put a stop to the manner in which some druggists sold cocaine, the hospitals would soon be filled with cocaine users." The *Times* wrongly declared "it was a criminal offense for a druggist to sell cocaine to any one who did not have a physician's prescription . . . ." There was as yet no such law—nor is it clear on what charge young George lay festering in the Tombs—but Mrs. Fromme's dramatic press debut would prove a powerful legislative catalyst.[123]

On January 9, 1907, a day after Mrs. Fromme's story ran in the *Times*, the State Board of Pharmacy announced it had "enlisted itself in the war on the indiscriminate sale and use of cocaine . . . . [T]he board took steps toward securing

---

[122] "Boy Cocaine Snuffers Hunted by the Police," *New York Times*, Jan. 8, 1907, p. 6; "Boy Slave to Cocaine," *Chicago Daily Tribune*, Oct. 20, 1896, p. 1. For the elder Ohle's first name, see 1900 United States Census, Enumeration District no. 802 (Precinct 25: Lake View, Chicago, city Ward 26), p. 4, line 23. For the elder Mr. Fromme's occupation and for his and his wife's and children's race, see 1905 United States Census, 5th Election District, block A, 13th Assembly District (Manhattan), pp. 11–12. *See also* Spillane, *Cocaine*, pp. 108, 111–12 (discussing the Fromme case). Though the *Times* put George Fromme's age at sixteen, *see* "Boy Cocaine Snuffers Hunted by the Police," the census pages cited here suggest he would have been seventeen or eighteen in January 1907. My thanks to Sonia Moss and Alex Zhang of the Crown Law Library for tracking down the Ohle and Fromme families' census data.

[123] "Boy Cocaine Snuffers Hunted by the Police," *New York Times*, Jan. 8, 1907, p. 6.

legislation at this session to prohibit the sale of the drug in any form except on a physician's prescription." The measure would be "drastic enough," the *Tribune* reported, "to reach many so-called catarrh remedies and other concoctions known to contain cocaine."[124]

Five days later Assemblyman Alfred E. Smith introduced just such a bill. Later, as a four-term New York governor, Smith would become the first Roman Catholic to run for president under a major party's banner. Now he represented the Second Assembly District, which encompassed Father Curry's St. James Parish. Having served as an altar boy at St. James, Smith received what little formal education he had at St. James School and matured to manhood under Father Curry's watchful eye. Curry in turn was "the chief advocate of the Smith legislation," the *Times* said. What became known as the A.E. Smith Anti-Cocaine Act made unprescribed cocaine sales felonies punishable by up to a year's imprisonment and a $1,000 fine.[125] The law punished only sellers—it did not criminalize purchase, possession, or use.

Months before the Smith Act gained final approval, New York City's Board of Health achieved much the same end within city limits. On January 28, not quite three weeks after Annie Fromme's war on youth-preying coke vendors captivated the press, the board amended the Sanitary Code to decree, "No cocaine or salt of cocaine, either alone or in combination with other substances, shall be sold at retail by any person in The City of New York except upon the prescription of a physician." Though violations were mere misdemeanors, the code's bite could sting, as druggist Charles Hitsch discovered. Hitsch's store stood at Mott and Worth Streets, just south of Father Barry's Transfiguration Church and just north of Father Curry's St. James. In April 1907, after one of his clerks sold fifteen cents' worth of cocaine to an undercover agent from the Board of Health, Hitsch was hauled to court and fined a hefty $250 (roughly $5,000 today). His was a test case—"the first conviction of the kind secured by the Health Department," the *Tribune* said. Slow to learn, Hitsch was back before the court in early August, arrested again under the same city ordinance. No longer a lonely test subject, he

[124] "To Wage War on Cocaine," *New York Tribune*, Jan. 10, 1907, p. 2.

[125] "Board of Elections of the City of New York," *New York Tribune*, Nov. 2, 1903, p. 11 (stating the addresses of polling places in the Second Assembly District); "Assemblyman Smith to Act," *New York Times*, Jan. 26, 1904, p. 5 (identifying Smith as representing the Second Assembly District); "Oliver Puts in Bills," *New York Tribune*, Jan. 15, 1907, p. 2; "Anti-Cocaine Bill Passed," *New York Times*, Mar. 29, 1907, p. 5 ("the chief advocate . . ."); "Board of Elections of the City of New York," ibid., Oct. 8, 1907, p. 14 (stating the addresses of polling places in the Second Assembly District); "Alfred E. Smith Dies Here at 70; 4 Times Governor," ibid., Oct. 4, 1944, p. 1 (stating Smith received his only formal education at St. James Parochial School); Henry F. Pringle, *Alfred E. Smith: A Critical Study* (New York: Macy-Masius 1927), pp. 107–08 (describing Father Curry's role in Smith's youth); American Guild of Organists, "Church of St. James," *online at* https://www.nycago.org/Organs/NYC/html/StJamesRC.html (noting Smith served as an altar boy at St. James); "An Act to Amend the Penal Code, in Relation to the Sale of Certain Drugs," 1907 *New York Laws*, ch. 424 (Act of June 5, 1907), p. 879.

now numbered among more than twenty druggists and several officers of retail drug corporations facing charges under the ordinance.[126]

Meanwhile the Smith Act advanced with the determined backing and supportive testimony of Father Curry and Assemblyman Smith, who steamrolled the bill over the "drug interests" and patent remedy purveyors. When the final Assembly vote arrived on March 28, 1907, the act triumphed by acclamation, drawing not one opposing vote. In early May, the Senate likewise embraced the bill unanimously, disposing entirely with debate. The only hint of hesitation surfaced in the Senate Codes Committee, which reduced violations of the act from felonies to misdemeanors. But the full Senate rejected the switch and restored the original penalty scheme by a vote of forty-two to two.[127]

The new act won the governor's signature on June 5 and took effect September 1. The *Tribune* declared it "the direct result of the agitation started nearly a year ago by the Rev. Father James B. Curry, rector of St. James's Catholic Church . . . ." Father Curry predicted the law would "put an effectual check on the operations of certain druggists and their agents," who sometimes were "out in the streets selling the 'dope.'" Agreeing that the law targeted sellers, Assemblyman Smith later said it was "impossible to punish users of the drug. If a man wishes to become a drug fiend there is no law on earth to prevent his becoming one . . . ." In truth, police had such tricks as vagrancy laws for scooping haggard addicts off streets and dropping them in jail. But in Father Curry's mind, users had "no conscience, no honor" and were past reform, while "we can reform the people who sell the vile stuff."[128]

---

[126] N.Y.C. Sanitary Code § 182 (Jan. 28, 1907); "An Act to Amend the Greater New York Charter Relative to the Code of Ordinances," 1904 *New York Laws*, vol. 2, ch. 628, § 3 (Act of May 6, 1904), p. 1492 ("Any violation of said sanitary code shall be treated and punished as a misdemeanor."); "New Cocaine Ordinance," *New York Times*, Jan. 31, 1907, p. 5; "Fined for Selling Cocaine," *New York Tribune*, Apr. 23, 1907, p. 5; "Darlington Gets Hot," ibid., July 26, 1907, p. 7 (reporting other prosecutions under the anti-cocaine ordinance); "Arrested for Selling Cocaine," ibid., Aug. 1, 1907, p. 8; "Checks Cocaine Sale," ibid., Sept. 1, 1907, p. 10. The *Tribune* and *Times* differed on the spelling of Hitsch's name. Census records and records of the College of Pharmacy of the City of New York suggest the *Tribune* had it right: the pharmacist's name was Hitsch, not Hitch. *See* Twelfth Census of the United States, Schedule no. 1—Population (Manhattan, Enumeration District no. 662) (June 9, 1900), p. 17 (listing Charles Hitsch, druggist, born June 1873); "New York," *American Druggist*, vol. 21 (Jan. 1, 1892), pp. 175–76 (including Charles Hitsch of New York among recent graduates of the College of Pharmacy). I am grateful to Leizel Ching and Sonia Moss of the Crown Law Library for tracking down these records.

[127] "New Cocaine Ordinance," *New York Times*, Jan. 31, 1907, p. 5; "Fight Anti-Cocaine Bill," ibid. Feb. 21, 1907, p. 4 (mentioning Smith's and Father Curry's testimony before the Assembly Codes Committee); "Anti-Cocaine Bill Passed," ibid., Mar. 29, 1907, p. 5 (noting the Assembly vote); "To Restrict Sale of Cocaine," *New York Tribune*, May 1, 1907, p. 2 (reporting the Senate's reversal of the Codes Committee change); "Two Anti-Cocaine Bills Passed," ibid., May 8, 1907, p. 2 (reporting the Senate's final approval).

[128] "Checks Cocaine Sale," *New York Tribune*, Sept. 1, 1907, p. 10 ("the direct result . . ." and "put an effectual . . ." and "no conscience, no honor . . ."); "Urges a Federal Law against Cocaine Evil," ibid., Dec. 3, 1912, p. 4 (quoting Smith).

As some evidence police had other ways to arrest cocaine users, the *Times* reported in early September 1907 the courtroom appearance of "[t]wo youths, victims of the cocaine habit." Thomas

By the time druggist Charles Hitsch returned to court in mid-October, now to face trial on the illegal-sale charge that had led to his arrest in late July, a new penal regime was in force. The Smith Act's felony provision overshadowed the mere misdemeanor status of city ordinance violations. Yet even the city ordinance dealt harshly with Hitsch. Inspector Hugh Masterson of the Board of Health testified he had visited Hitsch's pharmacy, presumably under cover and without a prescription, and bought twenty-five cents' worth of cocaine. But "[o]ne of the strongest witnesses against Hit[s]ch," the *Times* said, "was the Rev. Father J. B. Curry. . . . Curry testified that a score of boys and young men of his parish had been ruined by the cocaine habit" and "that the young men obtained the drug at Hit[s]ch's store." Curry, too, had investigated, sending "several reliable young men to the drug store, and they had no difficulty in getting cocaine without a prescription." Later, having helped secure Hitsch's conviction, Curry "pleaded with the Justices to send the offender to jail. He said a fine would do no good." Hitsch reaped six months in the penitentiary.[129]

New York's Lessons

The same forces that conspired in producing several of our earliest anti-cocaine laws came together again in forging the 1907 Smith Act. New York lawmakers saw that a new and newly convenient way to consume cocaine had loosed the risk of abuse and addiction on the community at large. When that plague infected respectable white youth, lawmakers banned the drug's sale except when prescribed. As was true of whites-focused enforcement of early laws banning opium dens, racism was at work, but not racism of the expected sort. Authors of early anti-cocaine laws largely did not aim to oppress African Americans, just as authors of early anti-den laws generally did not aim to oppress the Chinese. They acted instead to protect *their kids.*

Like early anti-den laws, early anti-cocaine laws did not target non-whites. New York City's 1907 anti-cocaine ordinance and Assemblyman Smith's 1907 act both prompted prosecution of pharmacists and their clerks, almost all white, and

Healey, "a mere boy of 16," reprised the role of young George Fromme. His mother, Mrs. Catherine Healey, had brought him to court, and he was "anxious to have his mother send him away where he couldn't get" cocaine. After Healey explained that an older boy at school had hooked him on "a catarrh snuff," the magistrate met his request for confinement with two days in lockup. The other man, aged twenty-three, was in court against his will, having been arrested after an officer found him at the North River "warming his hands at a small fire he had built." He was sentenced to six months on Rikers Island on unnamed charges. "Young Victims of Cocaine," *New York Times*, Sept. 3, 1907, p. 3.

[129] "6 Months for Cocaine Sale," *New York Times*, Oct. 15, 1907, p. 16; *People v. Hawker*, 152 N.Y. 234, 240 (1897) (deeming it an *ex post facto* violation to prosecute under "an act that aggravates a crime or inflicts a greater punishment than the law annexed to it when committed").

left buyers unscathed. The twice-tagged Hitsch was not a lonely white poster boy of colorblind justice; he represented instead the targeted class.

Rather quickly, however, the dynamics of the cocaine market evolved in ways that shifted defendants' demographics. The druggists who once dominated the market were the first to transgress the new bans and the first to bear the brunt of those bans in court. In fairly short order they mostly abandoned the criminal trade. Druggists, after all, proved simple to find, simple to surveil, and simple to catch when they sold contrary to law. And they proved simple to deter with even short stints in prison. Charles Hitsch, the *Times* reported, on hearing the court's pronouncement of a six-month sentence, "turned pale and staggered."[130] His social status and business success stood at risk, and he knew his next offense would be as easily spotted. Moreover, he had sold cocaine out of greed, not hunger, and had no need to resume the illicit trade to survive.

Yet demand did not evaporate once Hitsch and other druggists dropped the criminal trade. A new class of economic entrepreneurs therefore took to the streets. As the *Tribune* wrote in 1912, "The strict regulations regarding the sale of cocaine by druggists are probably responsible for its sale on the streets." Unlike druggists, street dealers had "no business to be ruined by their imprisonment" and faced little financial risk in daring detection and capture. Less rooted by nature, they proved harder to find, harder to catch in the act, and harder to deter, for their hopes of evasion so often proved sound. Less moneyed and less educated than the druggists they displaced, they also were less likely white. Even before the Smith Act took force, signs of this evolutionary dynamic had surfaced. Schieffelin's remark in March 1906 that he had heard "there are negroes in the Tenderloin district who peddle the drug around" presaged a racial dynamic that would dominate after druggists largely left the illegal trade.[131]

This racial dynamic turned toxic as another element emerged. The *users* of cocaine, white from the start because doctors commanded supplies, remained largely white. In a mainly white society that is a natural result, reinforced by cocaine's high cost. And though users did not for long remain wholly exempt from prosecution, as they were under the Smith Act and the 1907 New York City ordinance and many other early anti-cocaine laws, penalties for simple use rarely approached the severity of penalties for sales. Sellers seemed the worse criminals. They had economic motives, they traded in volume, and they victimized the vulnerable, very often youth. The druggists who hawked free samples to breed future clients roused the bitterest contempt. "Would you believe," Schieffelin asked in horror, "there are a few men in this city. . . so utterly lost to all moral sense as

---

[130] "6 Months for Cocaine Sale."
[131] "Alarming Increase of Indulgence by New Yorkers in Powerful Narcotics," *New York Tribune*, Mar. 25, 1906, p. C1; "Cocaine on the Streets," ibid., Dec. 2, 1912, p. 8 ("The strict regulations . . ."); "Crime of Cocaine Selling," ibid., Dec. 3, 1912, p. 8 ("no business to be . . .").

not only to dispense these drugs in an illegal manner, but actually to give away sample doses in order to create a craving and demand for them?" Cocaine users, said New York Judge Joseph Mulqueen in 1912, "are sinned against rather than sinning."[132]

This toxic evolutionary dynamic had three elements: increasing street sales by often non-white peddlers, comparative leniency toward largely white users, and increasing severity toward hard-to-deter sellers. By 1912, when the Smith Act marked its fifth year in force, the first two elements were solidly in place. Late that year, Father Curry and Assemblyman Smith again linked arms, this time to toughen the Smith Act's penalty scheme and put in place element three.

New York's 1913 Anti-Cocaine Law

Joining Curry and Smith in the fight was Judge Edward Swann. From Swann's seat on the Court of General Sessions, the trial forum for street-level drug crimes, he could see firsthand a problem the *Tribune* reported: "[I]t is virtually impossible under the law to obtain a conviction for selling cocaine." Conviction required proof of actual sale, but police rarely caught sales in progress. Proving *attempted* sale was a bit easier, as lawmakers had amended the Smith Act in 1910 to make simple possession of cocaine "presumptive evidence of an attempt to sell." That presumption stood subject to the defendant's rebuttal, however, and was so easily rebutted that convictions remained scarce. "[A]ll the prisoner had to do to evade the penalty," the *Tribune* complained, "was to show that he was a user of cocaine and that he intended the drug in his possession for his own use." Moreover, those convicted of attempted sale faced at most six months' confinement and a $500 fine. Even the rare conviction for selling cocaine won the defendant no worse than the year's confinement and $1,000 fine that Assemblyman Smith had provided in the original act five years before.[133]

Judge Swann deemed the solution harsher penalties for sales. Declaring "[y]ou can't make the punishment too severe for that crime," he recommended hiking the current one-year maximum at least fivefold. Father Curry agreed and conveyed his view to Assemblyman Smith, who resolved to amend his original

---

[132] "Alarming Increase of Indulgence by New Yorkers"; "Stricter Cocaine Law Favored by Judges," ibid., Dec. 3, 1912, p. 4.

[133] "New Laws Needed to Kill Cocaine Traffic," ibid., Nov. 11, 1912, p. 14 ("it is virtually . . ."); "Stricter Cocaine Law Favored by Judges," ibid., Dec. 3, 1912, p. 4; "Judges Join War on Cocaine Trade," ibid., Dec. 3, 1912, p. 1; "Urges a Federal Law Against Cocaine Evil," ibid., Dec. 3, 1912, p. 4 (presenting Smith's analysis of the 1910 amendment to the anti-cocaine law); "Crime of Cocaine Selling," ibid., Dec. 3, 1912, p. 8 (commenting on the difficulty of proving actual sales); "Cocaine Bill Passes Assembly," ibid., Apr. 9, 1913, p. 4 ("all the prisoner . . ."); "An Act to Amend the Penal Law, in Relation to the Sale of Cocaine or Eucaine," 1910 *New York Laws*, ch. 131, § 1, p. 233 (Act of Apr. 21, 1910).

act in the 1913 legislative session to raise the possible maximum "to something like five years." Others endorsed change. "The punishment of the trafficker in cocaine," said a health department doctor, "should be as drastic as that meted out to the man who menaces society with a revolver or a stiletto . . . . 'In that way the traffic could be effectually curtailed.' "[134]

All this the *Tribune* related without racial reference or comment. Yet in the midst of sober analysis, buried toward the bottom of a long column of print, the tone shifted. The words remained the reporter's, but they seemed to paraphrase Judge Swann's off-the-record concerns, offered to support the proposed five-year maximum for selling cocaine. "One case which was particularly revolting was that of 'Professor' John Coey, a big negro . . . ." Coey's drug trade apparently thrived, for his "cocaine establishment was fitted up with flashy but expensive furnishings . . . said to cost at least $5,000." And he had mounds of cocaine— "[b]ottles and cans of the stuff sufficient to fill a peck measure." Worse than his ostentation was the company Coey kept. Under the boldfaced heading, "Negroes and Whites Together," the *Tribune* revealed something more shocking: "One of the white women [present when the police entered], hardly more than a girl, . . . [was] the daughter of a reputable physician of this city."[135]

Neither Curry nor Smith lowered himself to such race baiting. Instead it seems Judge Swann showcased Coey's operation. He had spoken with the young woman's father, who was "well-nigh prostrated when he learned the conditions under which his daughter had been arrested." Moreover, Swann had investigated Coey's case and presided at his trial. And he went out of his way several months later, as the legislature neared final debate on what became New York's 1913 anti-cocaine law, to dredge up the Coey affair in a statement to lawmakers: "Judge Swann called attention to the negro known as Professor Coey who conducted a cocaine den where white women consorted with negroes," the *Tribune* recounted. "In illustrating the breaking down of all sense of decency caused by cocaine he told of a daughter of a prominent New York physician who had been found in this den." No doubt it chagrined Swann that no one saw Coey sell coke. Convicted apparently of an attempt to sell, he got from Swann "the maximum penalty under the law—six months in the penitentiary and a fine of $500."[136]

Having eagerly amplified Swann's race-hued tale, the *Tribune* added an incongruous proviso: "The records at the District Attorney's office seem to show

---

[134] "New Laws Needed to Kill Cocaine Traffic" (quoting Swann and noting Curry's views); "Stricter Cocaine Law Favored by Judges" (discussing Smith's planned amendment of his anti-cocaine act); "Druggists Denounce Cocaine Law Laxity," *New York Tribune*, Dec. 4, 1912, p. 3. (paraphrasing and quoting Dr. William H. Guilfoy, register of the Department of Health); "New Cocaine Law, Leaders Promise," ibid., Dec. 5, 1912, p. 1 (offering specifics on Smith's planned amendment, including the five-year maximum).

[135] "New Laws Needed to Kill Cocaine Traffic," ibid., Nov. 11, 1912, p. 14.

[136] Ibid.; "Amended Cocaine Bill Finds Favor in Senate," *New York Tribune*, Apr. 24, 1913, p. 1.

that the majority of the users of cocaine are American by birth, and, contrary to general belief, are white, not negroes." Even those convicted of attempted sales were overwhelmingly white. Of forty-two such defendants in the first ten months of 1912, only six were African American, the *Tribune* said, and all but five American born. Three weeks later, when the *Tribune* pictured several "Types of Cocaine Sellers and Victims," every type pictured was either white or too smudgy to tell (see Figure 6.8). And the seller featured in the adjoining article was not merely white but female and elegantly appointed. Within two weeks, another white woman's cocaine sales hit the news—and her *buyers* were African American. Catherine De Lorenzo, a mother of eight, served among "the chief sources of supply for the negro victims of the drug in the San Juan Hill section."[137]

Despite the handwringing over John Coey, press accounts in the months leading to the 1913 law change fretted most about cocaine's abuse by young whites. During a single two-week stretch in December 1912, the *Tribune* printed at least six reports of the drug's depredations among white girls and boys. One of the first, dated December 6, relayed chilling news from Boston: "[t]he revelation that young girls, some not yet out of school, are being made 'drug fiends' through cheap dance halls and men who haunt them selling cocaine . . . ." Police investigators surveilling the dance halls saw ill-willed men of no specified race selling "the dancers a 'dash,' the slang for an injection, for prices ranging from 15 to 25 cents." Girls who dared dabble "before long became confirmed users of morphine or 'coke.'"[138]

Casting the theme of victimized girls in harsher hues, the *Tribune* headlined a page-one account, "Horrors of Traffic in Girls Revealed." Social savior Rose Livingston, a "freelance missionary of Chinatown," told of her struggle to rescue "350 young American girls . . . living lives of sin in the neighborhood of Mott, Doyers and Pell streets." These streets are familiar, for Father Barry's Church of the Transfiguration stands at the intersection of Mott and Pell and not far from Doyers. "[P]ractically all the girls eventually learn to use opium, cocaine, morphine and cigarettes," we're told, and some "take several bottles of cocaine a day." Though the neighborhood remained Chinatown by name, the girls were "slaves of Italian and Jewish masters, mostly." Only very rarely were their victimizers Chinese.[139]

---

[137] "New Laws Needed to Kill Cocaine Traffic"; "Poodle Dog a 'Coke' Sign Used by Woman Dealer," *New York Tribune*, Dec. 2, 1912, p. 2; "Court Frees Woman Who Sold Cocaine," ibid., Dec. 13, 1912, p. 6. My thanks to Lisa Goodman for discovering the images reproduced in Figure 6.8.

[138] "Boston in Cocaine War," ibid., Dec. 6, 1912, p. 2.

[139] "Horrors of Traffic in Girls Revealed," ibid., Dec. 19, 1912, p. 1.

TYPES OF COCAINE SELLERS AND VICTIMS.
Sketches made by a Tribune artist in the haunts of the users of the drug.

THE HEROIN SALE

THE OHIO KID

THE WOMAN MESSENGER

SLEEPING OFF THE 'COKE'

Figure 6.8: "Types of Cocaine Sellers and Victims" (1912).

Two other accounts stand out, for the troubled youth had by their sides the worthy Fathers Flynn and Farrell, who filled in this period the role Father Curry played in 1907, when the original Smith Act took form. Father Flynn appeared first. On December 6, 1912, the *Tribune*'s page-one roundup of Kings County court business included the case of James Randolph, arrested in Brooklyn with a mass of cocaine concealed on his person. Sources said Randolph had "been heard of as a seller." Worse, "his activities in that line concerned themselves with young boys and girls of the Brownsville section of Brooklyn."[140]

On cue, the parish priest stepped in to rescue his flock's youth. Father James Flynn, pastor of the Church of Our Lady of the Presentation in the heart of Brownsville, had been "an ardent worker against the insidious growth of the cocaine traffic in his parish." He drew strength from his indignation at cocaine dealers who "have not scrupled to create a demand for it among children." In a claim scarcely credible but for its source, Father Flynn said he knew "at least 150 children between thirteen and seventeen years old . . . who have been habitual cocaine or heroin users. They even carry it into their schoolrooms, concealed in hollow pencils . . . ." And the vilest dealers, those for whom "hanging is too good," Flynn added, were those who sold cocaine to young girls, for they "were in league with agents of the 'white slave' traffic. . . . 'I know that young girls have been stupefied with the drug and then taken to disorderly houses . . . .' "[141]

Two days later the *Tribune* returned to this theme under the block-faced headline, "COCAINE AN ALLY OF 'WHITE SLAVERS.' " Now the children's protector was Father William B. Farrell of the Church of St. Peter and St. Paul in the Williamsburg section of Brooklyn. Farrell had found to his horror that the children of his district "had been taught to sniff the 'white stuff' and that they were buying it in quantities" from street peddlers. If these peddlers "confined their degrading activities to selling cocaine," he said, "they would be bad enough, but after grafting the habit on innocent girls of thirteen and fourteen years of age they use it to lure them away to worse degradation and crime."[142]

When the first press accounts of the proposed 1913 anti-cocaine bill appeared several weeks later, both the *Times* and *Tribune* featured Father Curry's approval of the proposed law's toughened terms. Curry's old partner in anti-cocaine lawmaking, Assemblyman and now Speaker Al Smith, had solicited a veteran anti-cocaine prosecutor and Judge Swann to draft the new measure. Boosted by Curry and Swann, the bill breezed through both houses of the legislature, clearing the Senate forty-one votes to six and the Assembly unanimously. Governor William Sulzer made the bill law on May 9 or 10. The act exposed persons who sold unprescribed cocaine to seven-year terms, far surpassing the one-year maximum then in place. Though the *Tribune*, which had flogged the evils of the cocaine trade for months, insistently claimed credit for the law's passage,

[140] "Cocaine Victim Begs for Prison," ibid., Dec. 6, 1912, p. 1.
[141] Ibid.
[142] "Cocaine an Ally of 'White Slavers,' " ibid., Dec. 8, 1912, p. 3.

Governor Sulzer instead paid tribute to Father Curry. The bill "is now a law," Sulzer telegrammed Curry, "largely through your instrumentality."[143]

Looking Back at Early Cocaine Bans

In the mainstream view of modern historians, early antidrug laws took root in racially poisoned soil. Lawmakers, they say, expressed hatred of certain groups by banning their drugs of choice. A close-up look at early anti-cocaine laws has told a far more complex tale. Having arrived in 1884 as an Austro-German medical import, cocaine first cast its euphoric spell on doctors and druggists and their wives, girlfriends, and hangers-on. For years the drug's expense and hypodermic administration largely confined its ravages to these groups. Yet in 1887, within three years of cocaine's arrival on our shores, Oregon banned its unprescribed sale. Montana, Colorado, Illinois, and Massachusetts all followed by century's end. New York outlawed cocaine prescription refills in 1893, hinting lawmakers aimed to permit the drug's use only as prescribed.

The poster children of all these laws were white doctors and their cohort, scattered white derelicts, and—increasingly—white youth. Chicago's Max Ohle proved the prototype of all the white working-class youth who came later. His before-coke and after-coke portraits in the *Chicago Tribune*, together with parental anxiety about a debasing and demoralizing drug, did more to prompt Illinois' 1897 cocaine ban than any worry of non-white abuse, about which the *Tribune* had uttered not a word.

---

[143] Ibid. (noting Smith's solicitation of Swann and Assistant District Attorney James A. Delahanty); "New Cocaine Bill Adds to Penalties," *New York Times*, Jan. 17, 1913, p. 7; "Rigid Cocaine Bill Drafted," *New York Tribune*, Jan. 17, 1913, p. 1 (reporting Judge Swann also claimed credit for prompting Delahanty to draft the new law); "Rigid Cocaine Bill Drafted" (noting the proposed bill would make unprescribed cocaine sales "a felony, punishable by seven years' imprisonment instead of by not more than one year"); "Drug Slaves Fight Bill," *New York Tribune*, May 1, 1913, p. 3 (reporting Father Curry's support); "Judge Swann Working for Anti-cocaine Bill," ibid., May 1, 1913, p. 3; "Cocaine Bill Sweeps Senate," ibid., May 3, 1913, p. 1; "Tribune Wins in Cocaine Crusade," ibid., May 4, 1913, p. 1 (noting unanimous Assembly passage); "Governor Signs Anti-cocaine Bill," ibid., May 11, 1913, p. 1 (reporting the governor signed the legislation on May 10); "An Act to Amend the Penal Law, in Relation to the Sale or Possession of Cocaine or Eucaine," 1913 *New York Laws*, ch. 470, § 2(g) (Act of May 9, 1913), p. 988 (deeming unprescribed sales a felony); "An Act to Establish a Penal Code," 1881 *New York Laws*, vol. 3, ch. 676, § 14 (Act of July 20, 1881), p. 3 (making felonies, when no penalty is specified, punishable by not more than seven years' imprisonment or a fine of not more than $1000 or both); "An Act to Amend the Penal Law, in Relation to the Sale or Possession of Cocaine or Eucaine," 1910 *New York Laws*, ch. 131, § 1, pp. 231, 233 (Act of Apr. 21, 1910) (deeming unprescribed sales a felony punishable by up to one year's confinement); "Signing of Walker Bill Causes Rejoicing Here," *New York Tribune*, May 11, 1913, p. 2 (quoting Assemblyman James J. Walker, who introduced the bill in the legislature and who assigned the *Tribune* "most of the credit" for the new law); "Tribune Praised for Battle on Cocaine," ibid., May 12, 1913, p. 4 (quoting several commendations of the *Tribune*); "Cocaine Bill Signed?" ibid., May 10, 1913, p. 1 (quoting the governor's telegram to Father Curry).

Later, it is true, the perceived fondness for cocaine among African Americans perhaps spurred some lawmakers to ban the drug. Louisiana's anti-cocaine law of 1898, the first statewide ban in the South, possibly reflected the unconcealed bigotry of its sponsor. But racism's role emerged much later in the North. Hence New York's anti-cocaine law of 1907, like Illinois' ban a decade earlier, responded not to tales of non-white drug use but to high-profile abuse and addiction among white working-class youth—Father Curry's flock at St. James Church and George Fromme and his midtown set. Not till 1912, when New York's toughened anti-cocaine law of 1913 took form, did racism infect the public debate. Even then Judge Swann's obsession with the drug-trafficking, white-womanizing "big negro" John Coey competed with a resurgent Father Curry, now joined by Fathers Flynn and Farrell and their lamblike parish youth.

Yet within fifteen months Edward Huntington Williams had printed "Negro Cocaine 'Fiends' Are a New Southern Menace," the screed that opened this chapter. Passage of the federal Harrison Act effectively banning unprescribed cocaine and opium followed just over ten months later. Modern observers looking back understandably find it hard to see past Williams's supercharged rhetoric and racist imagery to the years of anti-cocaine lawmaking and unracialized rhetoric that went before.

Once before we've encountered a historical curtain blotting from view all that came earlier. Allen Williams's 1883 libel of New York's Chinese community, accusing Chinese den owners of luring white girls with opium-laced candy, shadowed later anti-den lawmaking with the specter of miscegenation. But the anti-den laws and city ordinances that dotted the American West in the years before the New York scandal seemingly owed nothing to such race-infused fears. Instead both lawmakers and law enforcers focused not on Chinese smokers and their Chinese suppliers, but on whites—and especially young whites—trapped in opium's thrall.

Again, in the next chapter, we find a story often told in racial terms that in truth had far more to do with youth, typically white. The earliest anti-cannabis laws, like the earliest laws banning opium dens and cocaine, tell an old-fashioned morality tale about a societal aversion to escapist, euphoric pleasure that blots out reason—and about a desperate concern for the morals of youth. Yet we begin with a name almost every modern drug-war chronicle has linked with the most vile sort of racialized fear mongering.

7

Marijuana: Assassin of Youth

"THE sprawled body of a young girl lay crushed on the sidewalk . . . ."

With this frightful image Harry J. Anslinger opened his 1937 anti-cannabis screed, "Marijuana: Assassin of Youth." The overheated essay appeared in *The American Magazine*'s summertime issue, featuring on its cover a gap-toothed lad in cap and pinstripes, his bat poised for the next pitch.

Having commenced with a corpse, Anslinger fingered the killer. The girl had fallen from the fifth floor of a Chicago apartment house. "Everyone called it suicide," he wrote, "but actually it was murder. The killer was a narcotic known to America as marijuana, and to history as hashish." Used in the form of cigarettes, it's "dangerous as a coiled rattlesnake."[1]

And having led with suicide, Anslinger followed with murder—and then murder after murder, a total of ten homicides in a four-page article. "In Chicago, two marijuana-smoking boys murdered a policeman." In Los Angeles "a boy of seventeen killed a policeman." Asked why, he replied, "I don't know . . . . He was good to me. I was high on reefers." And to murder Anslinger added sexual assaults, for "peddlers preached also of the weed's capabilities as a 'love potion.'" He wrote of "a young male addict . . . hanged in Baltimore for criminal assault on a ten-year-old girl. His defense was that he was temporarily insane from smoking marijuana. In Alamosa, Colo., a degenerate brutally attacked a young girl while under the influence of the drug."[2]

Such tales of rape and slaughter by marijuana-crazed rogues were the stuff of this master anti-pot propagandist and justly maligned commissioner of the Federal Bureau of Narcotics. Having steered the Bureau from its founding in 1930 till John F. Kennedy ushered him from power in 1962, Anslinger earned the scorn of modern drug-war historians, who tag him with inciting anti-pot panic. His round head plopped neckless atop a fireplug torso, Anslinger seemed

---

[1] H.J. Anslinger with Courtney Ryley Cooper, "Marijuana: Assassin of Youth," *American Magazine*, vol. 124, no. 1 (July 1937), p. 18. Excerpts from this chapter appeared earlier in George Fisher, "Racial Myths of the Cannabis War," *Boston University Law Review*, vol. 101 (2021), pp. 933–77.
[2] Anslinger & Cooper, "Assassin of Youth," pp. 18, 19, 150.

Beware Euphoria. George Fisher, Oxford University Press. © Oxford University Press 2024.
DOI: 10.1093/oso/9780197688489.003.0008

die-cast to play the villain—and earned the part. His sneering prose brewed racial code words with armchair moralisms vilifying society's castaways. As an architect and vocal promoter of the Marihuana Tax Act of 1937 and its attempt
to squelch nonmedical sales of the drug, he deployed tales of deranged addicts
to stoke public fear and whip up support. "Assassin of Youth" appeared just
as Congress neared final consideration of the Tax Act and supplied a strident
weapon in this campaign. Lest readers miss the point, Anslinger alerted them
that "[a]s this is written a bill to give the federal government control over marijuana has been introduced in Congress . . . ."[3]

His punning title, "Assassin of Youth," nodded not merely to pot's purported
power to spur suicides and killing sprees but also to the asserted etymology of
the word *assassin*. "Marihuana is the same as Indian hemp, hashish," Anslinger
told a congressional committee during hearings on the Tax Act in April 1937.
And in Persia, "a thousand years before Christ, there was a religious and military
order founded which was called the Assassins, and they derived their name from
the drug called hashish . . . ." Here Anslinger botched the oft-told tale of a medieval band of Islamic killers whose name, the *Haschischin* (variously spelled),
supposedly derived from the drug that emboldened their acts and gave rise to the
English *assassin*.[4]

Of all the rogues in Anslinger's assassins' gallery, the one who claimed and
retains the tightest hold on the public imagination was Victor Licata, one of at
least four siblings in a Tampa home of no known distinction. Anslinger told of
Licata elsewhere, but nowhere as fully as in "Assassin of Youth":

[3] Richard J. Bonnie & Charles H. Whitebread II, *The Marihuana Conviction: A History of
Marihuana Prohibition in the United States* (Charlottesville: University Press of Virginia, 1974), pp.
65–67 (noting Anslinger became acting commissioner of the Federal Bureau of Narcotics on July
15, 1930, and was confirmed to the post by the Senate on December 18, 1930); David F. Musto, *The
American Disease: Origins of Narcotic Control* (New York: Oxford University Press, 3d. ed. 1999),
pp. 235, 238 (noting Anslinger's 1962 retirement); John C. McWilliams, "Unsung Partner against
Crime: Harry J. Anslinger and the Federal Bureau of Narcotics, 1930–1962," *Pennsylvania Magazine
of History and Biography*, vol. 113, no. 2 (Apr. 1, 1989), pp. 207, 231–33 (describing the circumstances
of his retirement); Anslinger & Cooper, "Assassin of Youth," p. 153; Marihuana Tax Act of 1937, ch.
553, 50 Stat. 551 (75th Cong., 1st Sess.) (Act of Aug. 2, 1937).

[4] *Hearings Before the Committee on Ways & Means, House of Representatives . . . on H.R. 6385* (75th
Cong., 1st Sess.) (Apr. 27, 1937), pp. 18–19, 153 (statement of H. J. Anslinger) ("Anslinger House
Testimony on H.R. 6385"). On the apparent etymological link between *assassin* and *hashish*, *see*
"Assassin," *Oxford English Dictionary Online* (3d ed. 2014). For a few of the many American retellings
of this etymological tale (or a similar one), *see* "Narcotics," *North American Review*, vol. 95, no. 197
(Oct. 1862), pp. 374, 379–81; "Do You Smoke Hemp?" *Boston Daily Globe*, June 24, 1893, p. 12;
"Greek Hashish Drug," *Springfield Daily Republican*, Jan. 28, 1908, p. 13. For a generally skeptical
account, *see* Jerry Mandel, "Hashish, Assassins, and the Love of God," *Issues in Criminology*, vol. 2,
no. 2 (Fall 1966), pp. 149–56. And for a fuller account of the assassins story and its origins, see Adam
Rathge's excellent dissertation. Adam R. Rathge, "Cannabis Cures: American Medicine, Mexican
Marijuana, and the Origins of the War on Weed, 1840–1937" (Ph.D. Dissertation, Boston College,
2017), pp. 289–95.

It was an unprovoked crime . . . . An entire family was murdered by a youthful addict in Florida. When officers arrived at the home they found the youth staggering about in a human slaughterhouse. With an ax he had killed his father, his mother, two brothers, and a sister.

Asked why he did it, "[t]he boy said he had been in the habit of smoking something which youthful friends called 'muggles,' a childish name for marijuana."[5]

For these and other tales of cannabis carnage Anslinger has suffered the contempt of modern historians, who allege he ignored prominent studies refuting the notion cannabis stokes violence. Professors Richard Bonnie and Charles Whitebread point to the Indian Hemp Drugs Commission of 1893 to 1894, which concluded after close study that "for all practical purposes it may be laid down that there is little or no connection between the use of hemp drugs and crime." And the Panama Canal Zone study of 1925 revealed that despite American troops' rampant use of locally grown marijuana, the judge advocate had attributed only seven cases of insubordination or violence in three years to cannabis use.[6]

Faulting Anslinger on a different score, Professor John Kaplan exhumed the facts about young Mr. Licata and questioned the connection between his crimes and marijuana. Yes, there was evidence he used the drug: Tampa's chief detective reported after the killings that Licata had been under investigation for his "addict[ion] to smoking marijuana cigarettes"—and a state narcotics inspector said he was poised to file charges against Licata when word of the murders came down. Still, Kaplan wrote, it was far from clear the drug impelled the crime. Police disclosed they had filed a lunacy petition to commit Licata the year before the killings, but his family's protests kept the boy free. A psychiatric exam after the murders yielded a diagnosis of criminal insanity, likely inherited. Committed to a state hospital, Licata hanged himself in 1950. "It is obviously difficult," Kaplan concluded, "to show whether Licata was under the influence of marijuana at the time of the killings or . . . whether it was the drug, rather than any underlying schizophrenia, that could be said to have caused the killings."[7]

[5] Anslinger & Cooper, "Assassin of Youth," pp. 19, 150; Anslinger House Testimony on H.R. 6385, p. 23 (briefly reporting Licata's killing spree); *Taxation of Marihuana: Hearing before a Subcommittee of the Committee on Finance, United States Senate . . . on H.R. 6906* (75th Cong., 1st Sess.) (July 12, 1937), p. 12 (statement of H. J. Anslinger) ("Anslinger Senate Testimony on H.R. 6906") (same). Bonnie and Whitebread quote from Anslinger's 1934 report to the Cannabis Subcommittee of the League of Nations Advisory Committee on Traffic in Opium and Other Dangerous Drugs, in which Anslinger briefly related the Licata murders. *See* Bonnie & Whitebread, *Marihuana Conviction*, p. 148.

[6] Bonnie & Whitebread, *Marihuana Conviction*, pp. 130–35 (reviewing the Indian Hemp Drugs Commission Report and the Panama Canal Zone Report). Professor Rebecca Carroll found the Panama Canal report and excerpts of the Indian Hemp Drugs report among Anslinger's papers. *See* Rebecca Carroll, "A Rhetorical Biography of Harry J. Anslinger, Commissioner of the Federal Bureau of Narcotics" (Ph.D. Dissertation, University of Pittsburgh, 1991), pp. 28–33.

[7] John Kaplan, *Marijuana—The New Prohibition* (Cleveland: World Publishing Co., 1970), pp. 94–96. There has been some confusion about Kaplan's sources, but it appears he drew the facts

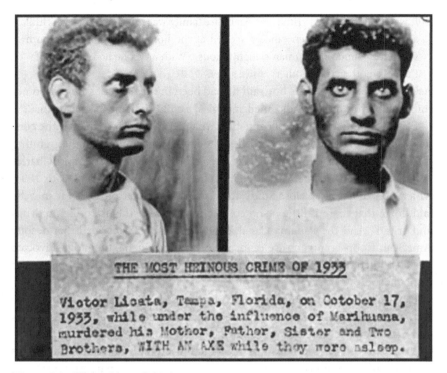

THE MOST HEINOUS CRIME OF 1933

Victor Licata, Tampa, Florida, on October 17, 1933, while under the influence of Marihuana, murdered his Mother, Father, Sister and Two Brothers, WITH AN AXE while they were asleep.

Figure 7.1: Victor Licata (1933).

If Anslinger's retellings of the Licata murders spurned medical evidence and ignored inconvenient facts, they abstained from another sin often laid to the commissioner: race-baiting. Anslinger had in his files a mugshot of Victor Licata depicting a rather dark-skinned young man (see Figure 7.1). Though apparently of Italian descent, Victor Fiorito Licata bore a name many might mistake as Mexican.[8] Yet Anslinger apparently never called Licata by name or displayed

noted in the text from "Crazed Youth Kills Five of Family with Ax in Tampa Home," *Tampa Morning Tribune*, Oct. 18, 1933, p. 1; "Report Shows Ax Slayer of Family Insane," ibid., Oct. 31, 1933, p. 1; "Son Held in Tampa Slayings," *St. Petersburg Evening Independent*, Oct. 18, 1933, p. 1; "Alienist Says Licata Insane," *Tampa Daily Times*, Nov. 2, 1933, p. 5; Letter to John Kaplan from Dr. C. A. Rich, Clinical Director of Florida State Hospital, Dec. 30, 1968. Though sources differ on Licata's age, the most accurate source is likely his family's household record from the 1930 census, which lists his age as sixteen, but supplies no date of birth. *1930 United States Census*, Licata (Tampa, Hillsborough County, Florida, ED 74), film no. 320, pp. 12B, 13A, family 255, image 216. As his crime took place on October 16 or 17, 1933, he could not have aged more than twenty. I thank Uncle Mike for his very valuable website and source citations on the Licata case, which sadly no longer seem accessible online.

[8] *1930 United States Census*, Licata (noting Licata's mother and all four grandparents were born in Italy). At L'Unione Italiana Cemetery in Tampa, site of the Licata family mausoleum, the registry includes Michele, Rosalia, Providence, Philip, and Joseph Licata, all with a death date of October

his mugshot. In various renditions of the affair, Licata was merely "a youthful addict," "the youth," a "young man," "[t]he boy," "a young boy," "a 20-year-old boy," or "a 21-year-old [*sic*] boy." Nor was Licata unusual on this score. Of the eighteen pot-smoking assailants and thieves Anslinger marshaled to his cause in "Assassin of Youth," not one carried a racial or ethnic label or even a name or physical description. Yet all but one, called simply "a degenerate," bore some marker of youth: "boy," "young," "youth," or "nineteen-year-old."[9]

Of course, in an article titled "Assassin of Youth" in a magazine picturing the gap-toothed lad, readers would expect a focus on the dread drug's youthful victims. But even the featured pot *purveyors* largely lacked ethnic badges. Of more than two dozen marijuana peddlers mentioned in the essay, only two—"a hot tamale vendor" and "a hot-tamale salesman"—wore any ethnic cast. Two other passing mentions of marijuana as having been "introduced into the United States from Mexico" and of "the Mexican border" as an area rich in marijuana-smoking musicians round out Anslinger's references to Mexico or Mexicans in "Assassin of Youth." His sole other ethnic label fell on the father of "an Italian family" who grew carloads of marijuana on his Louisiana farm and allowed his children to smoke it.[10]

Rather than vilify sellers for their race, Anslinger scorned them for selling to youth. He wrote of an Ohio garage owner arrested for supplying "school kids." He wrote of a fifteen-year-old runaway found in a Detroit den run by a married couple: "How many children had smoked there will never be known." Again, in St. Louis an investigation uncovered "marijuana 'dens,' all frequented by children of high-school age." And again in Louisiana, Ohio, Colorado—"in fact, from coast to coast."[11]

17, 1933. *Online at* https://www.findagrave.com/cgi-bin/fg.cgi?page=gsr&GSiman=1&GScid=1979 335&GSfn=&GSln=licata. The mugshot of Licata reproduced in Figure 7.1, apparently taken after his arrest on suspicion of murdering his family, lies among Anslinger's papers housed in the Eberly Family Special Collections Library, Penn State University Libraries, collection 1875, series 9, box 14, folder 3. My thanks to Alex Bainbridge of the Penn State Libraries for supplying a copy of the image. Victor Licata's middle name, Fiorito, appears in the lunacy decree issued by a Hillsborough County judge after the murders.

[9] Anslinger & Cooper, "Assassin of Youth," pp. 18–19, 150–53; Bonnie & Whitebread, *Marihuana Conviction*, p. 148 (quoting Anslinger's 1934 report to the Cannabis Subcommittee of the League of Nations Advisory Committee on Traffic in Opium and Other Dangerous Drugs); Anslinger Senate Testimony on H.R. 6906, p. 12; Anslinger House Testimony on H.R. 6385, p. 23. Anslinger did call one "young" man, the alleged murderer of a Michigan lawman, a "desperado" and a "bandit." But as the accused, "Alcide (Frenchy) Benoit," was apparently of French descent, it's doubtful Anslinger meant those terms as ethnic markers. Anslinger & Cooper, "Assassin of Youth," p. 150; "Trail of Ex-Convict in Michigan Police Killing," *Chicago Daily Tribune*, Jan. 21, 1937, p. 3 (supplying the suspect's name and nickname). For perceptive discussions of Anslinger's focus on marijuana's threat to youth, *see* Jerome L. Himmelstein, *The Strange Career of Marihuana: Politics and Ideology of Drug Control in America* (Westport, Conn.: Greenwood Press, 1983), pp. 59–60, 65–67, 93, 141; Rathge, "Cannabis Cures," pp. 302–07.

[10] Anslinger & Cooper, "Assassin of Youth," pp. 18–19, 150–53.

[11] Ibid., pp. 150–51.

Testifying before the House and Senate Committees that vetted the Marihuana Tax Act, Anslinger followed the same playbook. He refrained almost pristinely from ethnic coding of addled criminals while slathering the record with references to youth. He told the House Ways and Means Committee of at least thirteen marijuana-smoking assailants and thieves and told a Senate Finance subcommittee of at least seven, with overlap between the two groups. To all but one of these smokers Anslinger applied some label of youth, either "boy" or "young man." In general, he told the House committee, "the marihuana smoker is quite young," and the drug "is low enough in price for school children to buy it." Whereas "[t]he opium user is around 35 to 40 years old," he said in the Senate, "[t]hese [marijuana] users are 20 years old . . . ." Only once did he apply to any of these young miscreants a racial or ethnic stamp. Even then Anslinger did not speak in his own voice, but instead read into the record a letter sent him by a New Jersey prosecutor. "[L]ast January," his correspondent wrote, "I tried a murder case for several days, of a particularly brutal character in which one colored young man killed another, literally smashing his face and head to a pulp . . . ."[12]

Anslinger's private writings, it's true, betrayed no such reticence around race. Popular drug-war historians have unearthed his "gore file," where Anslinger apparently kept stories of pot-hued crimes and sex acts worthy of government propaganda campaigns. It's a tawdry collection laced with lurid, race-tinged plotlines, as two snippets suggest:

> Two Negroes took a girl fourteen years old and kept her for two days in a hut under the influence of marihuana. Upon recovery she was found to be "suffering from" syphilis. . . .[13]

> Colored students at the Univ. of Minn. partying with female students (white) smoking and getting their sympathy with stories of racial persecution. Result pregnancy.[14]

[12] Anslinger House Testimony on H.R. 6385, pp. 22–24, 28; Anslinger Senate Testimony on H.R. 6906, pp. 11–12, 15 (quoting letter of Ric[h]ard Hartshorne). Though Anslinger identified his source, "Ricard Hartshorne" [sic], as a "prosecutor at a place in New Jersey," other sources suggest Richard Hartshorne was a judge of the Essex County Court of Common Pleas. See "Guide to the Hartshorne Family Papers, 1840–1979 (Bulk 1950–1967)," New Jersey Historical Society (2005) (no. MG 1312), online at https://jerseyhistory.org/guide-to-the-hartshorne-family-papers-1840-1979bulk-1950-1967/.

[13] John C. McWilliams, The Protectors: Harry J. Anslinger and the Federal Bureau of Narcotics, 1930–1962 (Newark, Del.: University of Delaware Press, 1990), p. 53 (quoting Anslinger).

[14] "Reports of Insanity Due to Marijuana, circa 1930–1940," H. J. Anslinger Papers, 1835–1975 (01875). Historical Collections and Labor Archives, Eberly Family Special Collection Library, Penn State University Libraries. My thanks to Alex Bainbridge of the Penn State Libraries for supplying a copy of this document and its citation.

Even in public forums Anslinger sometimes slurred race with drug policy, but in a low-profile way. Though his 1937 congressional testimony made almost no reference to race or ethnicity, it seems he placed in the House committee's record two statements by local observers who trucked in ethnic shout-outs. A Colorado newspaper editor told Anslinger's office of "a sex-mad degenerate, named Lee Fernandez, [who] brutally attacked a young Alamosa girl. . . . I wish I could show you what a small marihuana cigaret can do to one of our degenerate Spanish-speaking residents." And two New Orleans officials cited reports from Colorado that "the Mexican population there cultivates on an average of 2 to 3 tons of the weed annually. This the Mexicans make into cigarettes, which they sell at two for 25 cents, mostly to white school students."[15]

These statements, if popularized at the time, could justify allegations that Anslinger conjured racial imagery to win passage of the Marihuana Tax Act. But the words of the Colorado editor and New Orleans officials lay buried within vast congressional records, and no evidence I've seen suggests either legislators or citizens or journalists took much note of them at the time.[16] The same is true of three other statements traced by modern historians to Anslinger. Professors Bonnie and Whitebread point to a 1934 report submitted by the United States to the League of Nations Advisory Committee on Traffic in Opium and Other Dangerous Drugs. They attribute to Anslinger, an American representative to the Cannabis Subcommittee, the report's claim that American narcotics officers estimated that "fifty per cent of the violent crimes committed in districts occupied by Mexicans, Turks, Filipinos, Greeks, Spaniards, Latin-Americans and Negroes, may be traced to the abuse of marihuana." Though this statement sadly was made in the name of the United States, I've found no evidence the mainline press reported it to the American people.[17]

[15] *Hearings before the House Committee on Ways & Means on H.R. 6385* (75th Cong., 1st Sess.) (Apr. 27, 1937), p. 32 (quoting letter from Floyd K. Baskette to the Bureau of Narcotics, Sept. 4, 1936); ibid., pp. 32–33 (quoting Frank R. Gomila & Madeline C. Gomila, *Marihuana: A More Alarming Menace to Society Than All Other Habit-Forming Drugs* (n.d.)). Toward the conclusion of his House testimony Anslinger said he "would like to put in the record the statement of the district attorney that I referred to. I also have a statement showing the seizures of marihuana . . . ." Anslinger made no mention of the items I've quoted in the text. At the conclusion of his transcribed testimony, however, the clerk wrote, "The following statements were submitted by Mr. Anslinger," and then printed the quoted statements. Anslinger House Testimony on H.R. 6385, pp. 28–29, 32.

[16] The only other contemporary reference I've seen to the Colorado account appeared more than nineteen months later in the *San Antonio Light.* In a general broadside against marijuana, the paper reported that "a sex-mad degenerate brutally attacked a young Alamosa girl." The article identified the attacker as "Fernandez," but made no other reference to ethnicity. Mrs. William Dick Sporborg, "Marihuana War Urged throughout the United States to Save Youth from Dope," *San Antonio Light,* Dec. 11, 1938, p. 63. I thank my research assistant Abbee Cox for locating this item. Anslinger referred to the Colorado incident in "Assassin of Youth," but did not name the attacker or suggest his ethnicity. Anslinger & Cooper, "Assassin of Youth," p. 150. I've seen no contemporary reference to the statement by New Orleans officials placed in the Congressional Record.

[17] Bonnie & Whitebread, *Marihuana Conviction,* pp. 136, 145–46 (quoting League of Nations, Advisory Committee on Traffic in Opium and Other Dangerous Drugs, *The Abuse of Cannabis in the*

Bonnie and Whitebread point as well to a 1936 letter from Anslinger to two former Wisconsin prosecutors relating a Baltimore case in which "a twenty-five-year-old Puerto Rican charged with criminally assaulting a ten-year-old girl, entered a plea on grounds of temporary insanity caused by smoking marihuana cigarettes." Far from exposing Anslinger as a race-baiter, these words show how reluctant he was to deploy race when stumping for the Marihuana Tax Act. Testifying in support of the act before the House Ways and Means Committee, Anslinger called the Baltimore assailant simply "a young man." Before a Senate Finance subcommittee he spoke again of "a young man." And again before the public in "Assassin of Youth," Anslinger ignored ethnicity and labeled the Baltimore rapist "a young male addict." I've seen no evidence Anslinger called him a Puerto Rican in public.[18]

A third statement threatened to cost Anslinger his job. On December 4, 1934, he issued to all his district supervisors a memo warning them an informant named Edward Jones wasn't trustworthy. Describing his complexion, Anslinger said Jones "might be termed a 'ginger colored n____r.'" Somehow the memo went public. Within two weeks Robert L. Vann, a Black special assistant to Attorney General Homer Cummings, warned President Franklin D. Roosevelt's secretary that "an avalanche of protest against Mr. Anslinger is headed toward the White House." The *Baltimore Afro-American* reported Treasury Secretary Henry Morgenthau Jr. had been "bombarded with numerous protests and demands for Anslinger's dismissal." Yet the reaction of the mainline press was silence. The *New York Times* and *Washington Post* and *Chicago Tribune* all lavished glowing coverage on Anslinger's nationwide crackdown on drug offenders, staged less than a week after he issued the offending memo, but neither paper said a word of the Edward Jones affair.[19] Still, the blowback from this episode perhaps prompted Anslinger's reticence around race when hawking the Marihuana Tax Act.

United States (Addendum) (O.C. 1542 (L), Nov. 10, 1934)). Bonnie and Whitebread say this "fifty per cent" claim was reprinted in the *Union Signal*, a publication of the Woman's Christian Temperance Union. They offer two different dates for this publication—April 1935 and February 1936. Bonnie & Whitebread, *Marihuana Conviction*, pp. 106, 320 n.41. My own search of the *Union Signal* of April 1935 and February 1936, assisted by Hai Jin Park and Kevin Rothenberg, did not turn up the "fifty per cent" claim or anything similar.

[18] Bonnie & Whitebread, *Marihuana Conviction*, p. 149 (quoting letter from Anslinger to Otto and R[udolph] Schlabach, Apr. 14, 1936); Anslinger House Testimony on H.R. 6385, p. 23; Anslinger Senate Testimony on H.R. 6906, p. 12; Anslinger & Cooper, "Assassin of Youth," p. 150. Otto M. Schlabach was identified as district attorney of La Crosse County in *State ex rel. Johnson v. County Boards*, 165 Wis. 164 (1917), and as a former district attorney in "From Factory and Salesroom," *Telephony*, vol. 78, no. 1 (Mar. 20, 1920), p. 40. On Rudolph Schlabach, who served as La Crosse district attorney from 1928 to 1932, see his listing on PoliticalGraveyard.com, *online at* http://politicalgraveyard.com/bio/schlacter-schmies.html.

[19] Memorandum from H.J. Anslinger to District Supervisors and Others Concerned (Dec. 4, 1934); Letter from Robert L. Vann to Louis McH. Howe (Dec. 17, 1934). My thanks to Kirsten Strigel Carter of the FDR Presidential Library in Hyde Park, who kindly supplied copies of these documents. They are housed in Official File 21x—Department of the Treasury—Narcotic Bureau (1933–1937

Though Anslinger's private racial attitudes may have fed the ferocity of his assault on marijuana, it seems the commissioner never played voters or lawmakers as racist chumps. Instead he appealed to people's intense concern for the morals and well-being of youth. "That youth has been selected by the peddlers of this poison," he wrote in "Assassin of Youth," "makes it a problem of serious concern to every man and woman in America." Early in 1937 he urged in a different forum that "[t]he time to stamp out this lethal marihuana habit is NOW—before it places an indelible stamp upon the easily molded mentality of increasing numbers of our youth, who seem to be its chief victims." Or as Anslinger told a magazine reporter when the fight for the Marihuana Tax Act was long behind him, "People get a bit hysterical about reports of narcotics sales around school children."[20]

A discerning view of the history of early anti-cannabis lawmaking in the states would have taught Anslinger this lesson, for what was true of opium and cocaine proved true as well of cannabis: it was not the race of the drug's source or even fear of crime in the community that moved the earliest lawmakers to act. Perhaps in later times and other places the belief that "Chicanos in the Southwest were . . . incited to violence by smoking marihuana" gave rise to anti-cannabis laws.[21] But this theorem of David Musto finds almost no support in the histories of the earliest state laws against cannabis. Rather, what drove most intensely early lawmaking in the states was the desire to keep cannabis from the hands of white youth.

The Pattern of State Anti-Cannabis Lawmaking

It's in the states we must begin, for anti-cannabis legislation arose there two decades before Harry Anslinger conceived his campaign to incite public panic around pot. By the time Anslinger took the helm of the newly launched Federal Bureau of Narcotics late in 1930, twenty-six states and territories already had

---

correspondence). For evidence of African-Americans' anger about Anslinger's memo, see "Treasury Recalls Snooty Letter," Baltimore Afro-American, Jan. 26, 1935. For examples of favorable coverage of Anslinger's nationwide crackdown, see "Narcotic Seizures Go On, Reach 765," New York Times, Dec. 10, 1934, p. 2; "765 Jailed, U.S. Plans New Drive on Drug Traffic," Washington Post, Dec. 10, 1934, p. 1; "U.S. Launches Nation-Wide War on Dope Traffic," Chicago Daily Tribune, Dec. 9, 1934, p. 9.

[20] Anslinger & Cooper, "Assassin of Youth," p. 18; H.J. Anslinger, "Marihuana" (speech delivered before the Women's National Exposition of Arts and Industry (New York: Mar. 30, 1937), H.J. Anslinger Papers (Box 1, File 07)); "Teen-Age Dope Addicts: New Problem?" U.S. News & World Report, June 29, 1951, pp. 18, 19. My thanks to Kevin Rothenberg of the Crown Law Library for hunting tirelessly for evidence of Anslinger's deployment of race in advocating for the Marihuana Tax Act.

[21] Musto, American Disease, p. 295.

criminalized sales of cannabis absent a doctor's prescription. By the time he helped secure passage of the Marihuana Tax Act in 1937, *all fifty* states and future states had forbidden unprescribed sales (see Table 7A). Like the federal Harrison Act of 1914, which effectively outlawed opium and cocaine only after thirty-five states and territories had banned opium and forty-six had banned cocaine, the

Table 7A   Earliest State Bans of Unprescribed Cannabis Sales

Massachusetts	1911	Michigan	1929
Wyoming	1913 (February 26)	Alabama	1931 (February 11)
Indiana	1913 (March 6)	South Dakota	1931 (March 6)
Maine	1913 (April 12)	Arizona	1931 (March 25)
California	1913 (June 11)	Hawaii	1931 (April 27)
Vermont	1915 (March 12)	Illinois	1931 (July 3)
Utah	1915 (March 17)	North Dakota	1933 (March 6)
Nevada	1917 (February 20)	Delaware	1933 (April 11)
Colorado	1917 (April 17)	Oklahoma	1933 (April 12)
Rhode Island	1918	Pennsylvania	1933 (May 22)
Texas	1919	Florida	1933 (May 24)
Iowa	1921	New Jersey	1933 (June 5)
Oregon	1923 (February 8)	Mississippi	1934 (February 26)
Arkansas	1923 (February 27)	Kentucky	1934 (June 14)
Washington	1923 (March 3)	Missouri	1935 (February 27)
New Mexico	1923 (March 7)	West Virginia	1935 (March 8)
Alaska	1923 (April 30)	Georgia	1935 (March 24)
Louisiana	1924	Maryland	1935 (March 29)
Idaho	1927 (March 1)	Minnesota	1935 (April 29)
Montana	1927 (March 8)	North Carolina	1935 (May 11)
Kansas	1927 (March 12)	Connecticut	1935 (June 13)
New York	1927 (April 5)	New Hampshire	1935 (June 21)
Nebraska	1927 (April 13)	Virginia	1936
Ohio	1927 (May 2)	Tennessee	1937 (February 11)
Wisconsin	1927 (July 13)	South Carolina	1937 (March 26)

Marihuana Tax Act claimed center stage far too late to explain why lawmakers sought to drive the drug from the nonmedical marketplace.

Again states lined up against the new drug threat in no predicted order. Defying expectations that those states nearest the supposed source of the offending drug would act first, Southwestern states largely trailed a Northern and Western anti-cannabis crusade. Table 7A and the maps in Figures 7.2 through 7.4 reveal a lawmaking course almost random but for the unexpected leadership of several New England states. Massachusetts acted first in 1911, two years ahead of Wyoming, Indiana, Maine, and California. Vermont edged out Utah in 1915, Colorado joined Nevada in 1917, and Rhode Island trailed closely in 1918. In seven years, ten states had joined the fray—and three of the first six lay in New England. Together with Indiana, these three New England states must lead our analysis, for by taking action without a brown-skinned threat to fuel them, they expose a different force driving these new laws.[22]

The Northern Vanguard

A notable omission marked the pathbreaking laws of the three New England states that, together with Indiana, caught the early anti-cannabis wave: these laws said not a word about *marijuana* or *pot* or *Mary Jane* or any other slang for that drug. Instead they banned *cannabis indica* and sometimes also *cannabis sativa*.[23] Both terms applied to the hemp plant. Though meanings have drifted over time and remained unsettled even as these laws took shape, it seems *cannabis sativa* denoted at the time a broader botanical category that embraced *cannabis*

---

[22] For census figures, *see* Campbell Gibson & Kay Jung, U.S. Census Bureau, *Historical Census Statistics on Population Totals by Race, 1790 to 1990, and by Hispanic Origin, 1970 to 1990, for the United States, Regions, Division, and States* (Washington: U.S. Census Bureau, 2002), tbl. E-7 ("White Population of Mexican Origin, for the United States, Regions, Divisions, and States: 1910 to 1930"). Gibson and Jung explain that persons of Mexican ancestry were separately tabulated only in the 1930 census. The 1930 census reports estimated the Mexican population in 1910 and 1920 based largely on places of birth.

[23] "An Act Relative to the Issuance of Search Warrants for Hypnotic Drugs . . . ," 1911 *Massachusetts Acts*, ch. 372, §§ 1, 3 (Act of Apr. 29, 1911), pp. 359–60 (criminalizing possession of *cannabis indica* or *cannabis sativa* without a doctor's prescription); "An Act to Regulate the Sale of Morphine and Other Hypnotic or Narcotic Drugs," 1913 *Maine Acts*, ch. 211, §§ 3, 6 (Act of Apr. 12, 1913), pp. 300–03 (criminalizing unprescribed sales or possession of *cannabis indica* or *cannabis sativa* or of their salts, compounds, or preparations); "An Act to Regulate the Sale of Opium, Morphine and Other Narcotic Drugs," 1915 *Vermont Acts and Resolves*, no. 197, § 1 (Act of Mar. 12, 1915), pp. 336–37 (banning unprescribed sales of *cannabis indica* or *cannabis sativa* or their salts, compounds, or preparations); "An Act to Amend . . . 'An Act Pertaining to Sale of Drugs and Prescribing Penalties for Violation Thereof,'" 1913 *Indiana Laws*, ch. 118, § 1 (Act of Mar. 6, 1913), pp. 306–08 (banning unprescribed possession and sales of *cannabis indica* and its salts, compounds, derivatives, and preparations).

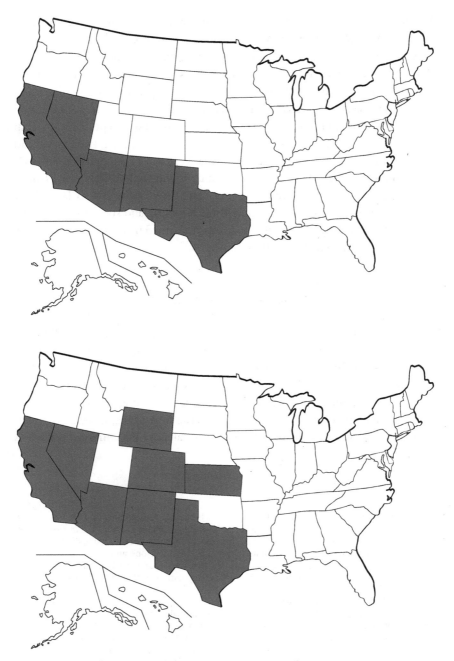

Figure 7.2: Top five and top eight states in proportion of Mexican American population in 1920.

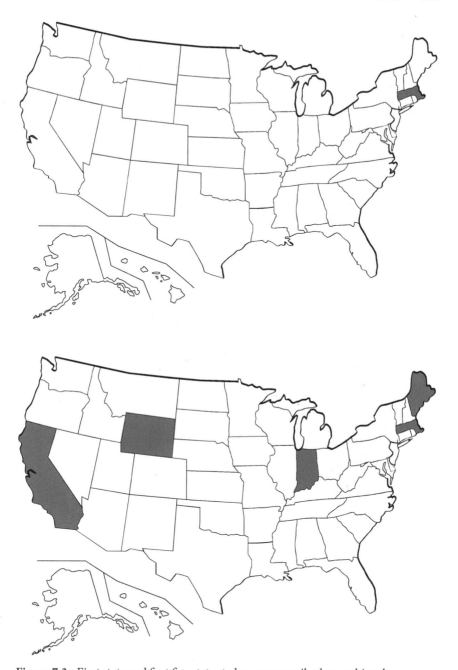

Figure 7.3: First state and first five states to ban unprescribed cannabis sales.

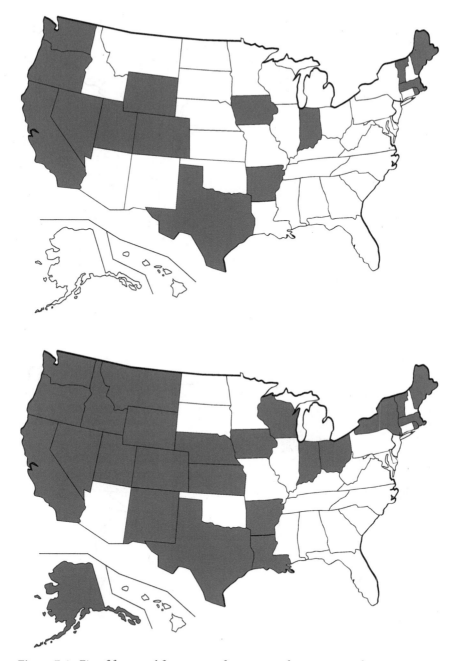

Figure 7.4: First fifteen and first twenty-five states or future states to ban unprescribed cannabis sales.

indica—or Indian hemp—as one variety and native *cannabis Americana* as another.[24]

Cannabis indica commonly took the form of hashish, a product not of Mexico but of India, Turkey, Egypt, and parts east. Made from resin pressed from the plant's flowering top, hashish was a denser, more potent cannabis preparation than marijuana. Then as now, marijuana consisted of the dried leaves and flowering tops of the cannabis plant. At times it took the specific name *cannabis Americana*, and authorities commonly traced its origins to Mexico. Hashish and marijuana are biological twins, differing in their preparation and sometimes their potency, but not greatly in their euphoric effects. Hence observers and lawmakers sometimes used *cannabis indica* or even *Indian hemp* to embrace marijuana.[25] Still, the failure of these New England and Indiana laws to mention *marijuana* or *cannabis americana* or any other term clearly distinguishing marijuana from hashish is some evidence lawmakers did not have marijuana or Mexicans on their minds when enacting them.

Nor did news accounts hint that lawmakers in these states feared marijuana or the Mexican "desperados" who sometimes smoked it. Broad searches spanning years or decades have turned up no sign of *any* local use of marijuana before each state's ban, at least none local papers thought worthy of mention. It's true these states had among them hundreds of newspapers, and much may have slipped my gaze. Yet nothing in the sometimes rich, sometimes spare journalistic and legislative histories of these four anti-cannabis laws betrays wariness of Mexican newcomers or of the marijuana some Mexicans favored.

Of course tales of marijuana use in Mexico or Arizona or Texas or California sometimes filtered east. Several reports printed in New England and Indiana claimed pot-crazed Mexicans in the distant Southwest had ravaged or killed. Still it seems no such concern prompted these Eastern states to ban cannabis. In Maine and Vermont I've found not one news account even mentioning marijuana

[24] In his 1912 *Essay on Hasheesh*, Victor Robinson, a Columbia University pharmaceutical chemist, explained: "[T]he intoxicating hemp-plant [is] scientifically known as *Cannabis sativa* and popularly famed as Hasheesh . . . . [I]ts botanical name is *Cannabis sativa*, with *Cannabis indica* as one variety, just as *Cannabis americana* is another variety." Dr. Charles E. Terry and Mildred Pellens agreed: "[T]he genus of *cannabis sativa* . . . includes the two species *cannabis indica* and *cannabis americana*." Harry Anslinger collapsed the categories of *cannabis indica* and *cannabis sativa*, casting the difference one of local custom: "Marijuana is a weed of the Indian hemp family, known in Asia as *Cannabis Indica* and in America as *Cannabis Sativa*." Victor Robinson, *An Essay on Hasheesh, Including Observations and Experiments* (New York: Medical Review of Reviews, 1912), pp. 12, 14; Charles E. Terry & Mildred Pellens, *The Opium Problem* (New York: The Bureau of Social Hygiene, 1928), p. 809; Anslinger & Cooper, "Assassin of Youth," pp. 18, 19.
[25] *See, e.g.,* "Stamping Out New Drug: Hemp Now Replaces Expensive Opium in California," *St. Albans Messenger*, Sept. 16, 1915, p. 1 ("The new 'dope' is Marihuana, or Indian hemp, and it is secured from a plant common to northern Mexico."); "An Act to Prohibit the Sale . . . [of] Cigarettes, Cigars, or Tobacco . . . in Which There Is a Mixture of the Drug Cannabis Indica . . . ," 1930 *Mississippi Laws*, ch. 13, § 1 (Act of Feb. 27 1930), p. 13 (banning smoked products containing "Cannabis Indica, commonly known as Mari Juana").

before each state banned cannabis. I found only a handful in Massachusetts (the latest dated 1905) and Indiana (the latest dated 1908). As Massachusetts did not ban cannabis till 1911 and Indiana not till 1913, none of these stories likely triggered legislators to act. And all these accounts told of faraway events. Of all the pre-1920 news reports I found in these states mentioning marijuana, not one spoke of a Mexican encroaching closer to home than Texas or, in one outlying case, Kansas.[26] *Any* mention of nearby Mexicans was rare, and if anyone feared a future influx of Mexican migrants, the press didn't say so. The legislative histories of these states' laws likewise betray no fear of lurking Mexican pot smokers or of a gathering wave of Mexican newcomers.

That is not to say Mexicans went missing from the day's press. Coverage of the unending Mexican Revolution pockmarked and sometimes blanketed newspapers throughout most of the 1910s. Many accounts told of violence by Mexican rebel armies. Mexican bandits sometimes targeted rich American expatriates, reportedly seizing them for ransom or sexually assaulting the women. These stories might have prompted some readers to fear all Mexicans, including those far from the fighting and living nearby. But *very* few Mexicans lived nearby. Of the three New England states that enacted early anti-cannabis laws, only Massachusetts had enough Mexican American residents to mention— a grand total of 29 by 1910 census figures, or 0.001 percent of the state's population. Though that number almost doubled to an estimated 57 residents by 1920, the average rate of increase was fewer than three newcomers per year. Maine and Vermont *together* had precisely four Mexican American residents according to 1910 census figures and only three in 1920.[27] Even if census counters missed some immigrants, their presence likely did not spur these states' anti-cannabis laws.

Even in Indiana, which like Maine banned *cannabis indica* in 1913, the number of Mexican immigrants was modest. The Census reported only 85 Mexican Americans in 1910, accounting for 0.003 percent of the state's population, and 725 residents or 0.025 percent of the whole in 1920. Mexican movement into Southwestern states of course was larger and growing faster. In August 1912, the *Indianapolis Commercial* reprinted a report from the *Financial Chronicle* on the "Movement of Aliens." The "most striking" phenomenon, the *Chronicle* noted,

---

[26] "Dangerous Mexican Plants," (Greenfield, Mass.) *Gazette and Courier*, Jan. 28, 1905, p. 9; "Use for Deadly Weed," *Kokomo (Ind.) Daily Tribune*, Oct. 8, 1908, p. 6; "Using New Narcotics," *Logansport (Ind.) Daily Tribune*, July 18, 1916, p. 9 ("A new problem in habit-forming drug sales is confronting Kansas health officials. . . .").

[27] For examples of stories of Mexican banditry, *see* "Rebels Rob and Burn Train," *Logansport Pharos*, Dec. 5, 1912, p. 7; "Trouble in Juarez Feared," *New York Times*, Aug. 10, 1913, p. 2. On the Mexican Revolution, *see* Kelly Lytle Hernández, *Bad Mexicans: Race, Empire, and Revolution in the Borderlands* (New York: W.W. Norton & Company, 2022), pp. 7, 279–302. For census figures, *see* Gibson & Jung, *Historical Census Statistics*, tbl. E-7.

was "the remarkable increase in the number crossing the border from Mexico." Though only 715 Mexicans immigrated to the United States in 1901–1902, that figure surged to 5,682 in 1907–1908 and 25,702 in 1911–1912. Still the *Chronicle* expressed no worry. The theme of the article, disclosed in the opening sentence, was the overall *decrease* of immigration: there was "[i]ndisputable evidence that the movement of aliens to this country during the late fiscal year was less than in either 1910–11 or 1909–10 and not materially greater than in 1908–09 . . . ." Meanwhile, immigrants were leaving so quickly that "the addition to the foreign-born population of the United States in 1911–12 was materially less than in any year since 1903–04, only excepting 1907–08, when d[ep]ression existed here." And set against Italian immigrants, who numbered as many as 167,492 in 1909–1910, the new Mexican tide perhaps merited no more notice than the one sentence, already quoted, the *Chronicle* gave it.[28]

When the *Indianapolis Commercial* addressed the same newly released census figures in July 1912, it said not a word about Mexicans, though the report consumed a full column and a half of newsprint. The paper said simply that all "foreign-born whites," presumably including many Mexicans among other immigrant groups, made up 5.9 percent of Indiana's population. When the *Commercial* broke down this cohort, it mentioned newcomers from Germany, Hungary, Austria, Ireland, England, Russia, Italy, Canada, Sweden, Scotland, and "other countries," but said nothing of Mexicans. It seems no racial or ethnic group roused the *Commercial*'s concern. On the contrary, the paper noted that between 1910 and 1912, "native whites of native parentage" had shown "a slight increase in . . . relative importance," rising from 77.6 percent of the whole to 78.9 percent.[29]

More evidence that Mexican marijuana fiends did not fuel passage of these Northern anti-cannabis laws emerges from news accounts of crazed pot smokers printed shortly *after* lawmakers acted. Maine presents the most striking case. The state's anti-cannabis law was just twelve days old when the *Kennebec Journal* of April 24, 1913, ran the eye-catching story, "Plants Cause Madness." The recent "degradation of the social conditions of [Mexican] soldiers," the article said, traced to "the habit of smoking marihuana, a deadly native plant of Mexico" that "makes the smoker wilder than a wild beast." Sometimes prompting "wild orgies," sometimes stilling "all control of . . . mental faculties," marijuana charges users with bravado and "superhuman strength" and drives them finally to murder. Yet even while warning that Americans living in Mexico had smoked the drug with violent results, the *Journal* never thought to reassure readers that Maine had

---

[28] Gibson & Jung, *Historical Census Statistics*, tbl. E-7; "Movement of Aliens," *Indianapolis Commercial*, Aug. 10, 1912, p. 4 (reprinted from the *Financial Chronicle*).

[29] "Indiana's Population," *Indianapolis Commercial*, July 5, 1912, p. 2.

banned the substance less than two weeks before. It appears the editors didn't link the law's passage with tales of violence from Mexico.[30]

So, too, in Indiana, where the anti-cannabis law won passage in March 1913 and an alarmist account of a marijuana-crazed Mexican followed eight months later. The *Logansport Pharos* reported that the former governor of a Mexican district, "while under the influence of Marihuana cigarettes," had ordered the execution of political prisoners. Later the governor was "declared insane from excessive smoking" of marijuana. Yet the *Pharos* never told readers this dread drug was now banned at home.[31]

Likewise in Vermont. There I saw no press account of marijuana before mid-September 1915, six months after the state banned *cannabis indica* and *cannabis sativa*. Datelined San Francisco, a report in the *St. Albans Daily Messenger* warned that a "new drug to replace opium . . . has gained an alarming foothold" in California. "The new 'dope' is Marihuana, or Indian hemp," the author continued, "and it is secured from a plant common to northern Mexico."[32] Nowhere did the *Messenger* say this exotic Mexican varietal then stood banned in Vermont.

So for all that appears, neither Mexican newcomers nor fear of their smoked leaves triggered anti-cannabis lawmaking in these three New England states and Indiana. What then drove these bans?

The New England Watch and Ward Society

Let us return to Boston, for Massachusetts was the first state to act. *Banned in Boston* seems today a cliché for every puritanical crusade against life's small pleasures. But the phrase referred first of all to the book-banning efforts of Anthony Comstock and the New England Watch and Ward Society. That story took rise on May 28, 1878, when the famed Comstock, founder of New York's Society for the Suppression of Vice, addressed Bostonians gathered at their city's storied Park Street Church. Though billed as a public meeting and attended by four to five hundred men, the event was closed to women, for organizers deemed the topic too coarse for feminine ears.[33]

As godfather of an 1873 law that criminalized mailing or delivering "obscene, lewd, or lascivious" material as well as contraceptives or information about them, Comstock turned on the Boston stage to a favorite topic: pornographers.

---

[30] "Plants Cause Madness," *Kennebec Journal*, Apr. 24, 1913, p. 5.

[31] "Expect General Huerta to Quit Place Saturday," *Logansport Pharos*, Nov. 14, 1913, p. 1.

[32] "Stamping Out New Drug: Indian Hemp Now Replaces Expensive Opium in California," *St. Albans Daily Messenger*, Sept. 16, 1915, p. 1.

[33] "The Society for the Suppression of Vice," *Boston Daily Globe*, May 25, 1878, p. 1 (announcing the formative Park Street Church meeting on May 28); "Anniversary Week," *Boston Daily Advertiser*, May 29, 1878, p. 1 (describing Comstock's address and its reception).

They were, he said, at work in Boston. "One method of conducting the business was to secure the names of the pupils in the schools, private and public, and then to send them the advertisements of the infamous matter . . . ." Such practices in Boston and its environs had led to the arrests of sixteen persons and convictions of thirteen.[34]

The meeting concluded with a series of resolutions. One "declar[ed] the circulation of sensational and demoralizing literature among the young a national evil calling for . . . suppression . . . ." Another "recommend[ed] the formation of a New England society for the suppression of vice." Such a group promptly took form, first as a branch of Comstock's New York society and four years later as a separate organization. Claiming among its officers the presidents of Yale, Dartmouth, Amherst, and Brown and boasting patrons named Eliot, Cabot, Lodge, and Lowell, the New England Society for the Suppression of Vice marched forth with all the cachet and moral gravitas Boston's starched-collared Brahmins could give it.[35]

Later renamed the New England Watch and Ward Society, a nod to the old Watch and Ward constabulary, the group turned for day-in, day-out guidance not to the listed luminaries but to two men of a less exalted family named Chase. Serving for twenty-five years as the society's first agent and administrator, Henry Chase advanced the Watch and Ward's moralizing mission, which he defined as "the removal, by both moral and legal means, of those agencies which corrupt the morals of youth." On his watch, the society launched prosecutions against pornographers, brothel keepers, and bookmakers. Aiding Chase in that fight were laws of his own design, banning not only what was obscene but also what "manifestly tend[ed] to the corruption of the morals of youth." By the end of his tenure he could claim credit for extending the society's work to all six New England states.[36]

[34] "Anniversary Week," *Boston Daily Advertiser*, May 29, 1878, p. 1; "An Act for the Suppression of Trade in, and Circulation of, Obscene Literature and Articles of Immoral Use," ch. 258, § 2, 17 Stat. 598 (42d Cong., 3d Sess.) (Act of Mar. 3, 1873).
[35] "Anniversary Week," *Boston Daily Advertiser*, May 29, 1878, p. 1 ("declar[ed] the circulation . . ." and "recommend[ed] the formation . . ."); Neil Miller, *Banned in Boston: The Watch and Ward Society's Crusade against Books, Burlesque, and the Social Evil* (Boston: Beacon Press, 2010), pp. 3, 11–13, 47; Allan Carlson, "Pure Visionary: The Life & Times of Anthony Comstock, Moral Crusader," *Touchstone*, vol. 22, no. 5 (June 2009), p. 20 (identifying the society's prominent officers and contributors); Paul S. Boyer, *Purity in Print: Book Censorship in America from the Gilded Age to the Computer Age* (Madison: University of Wisconsin Press, 2d ed. 2002), pp. 7–8 (same).
[36] Miller, *Banned in Boston*, pp. 7, 10, 15, 41; Henry Chase, "America," in *The White Slave Trade: Transactions of the International Congress on the White Slave Trade* (London: Office of the National Vigilance Association, 1899), pp. 154–56 ("the removal . . ." at p. 154); "An Act to Amend [an Act] Concerning Offences against Chastity, Morality and Decency," 1880 *Massachusetts Acts*, ch. 97 (Act of Mar. 13, 1880), p. 64 ("manifestly tend[ed] to . . ."). For evidence of the family connection between the two Chases, *see* "Our Mid-Year Reunion," in *The Chase Chronicle*, vol. 4, no. 2 (Boston: The Executive Committee, Apr. 1913), pp. 18–19.

After Henry Chase passed from the scene in 1907, his distant kinsman Jason Franklin Chase, a Methodist minister turned moral vigilante, shepherded the Watch and Ward for nearly two decades more. Young and hale, with a "wellknit body" and "bull-dog jaw," Frank Chase cut a commanding figure on the Boston streetscape. Though nominally the Watch and Ward's secretary, he swapped inkwells for gumshoes and stood shoulder to shoulder with cops and sheriffs, busting brothels and drug dens, shuttering lottery shops, and haunting hotel lounges to spy out women for hire.

His lust for the trenches perhaps traced to his working-class roots. "[B]orn with a clinched fist" in the factory town of Chelsea north of Boston, Chase fought for sport. "There was a time," he later reminisced, "when I had licked every red-headed man in Chelsea." Even after bettering himself and entering Wesleyan with the help of a church loan, he quit his college gridiron only after breaking two ribs and fracturing a collarbone. His vaunted pugnacity—"I've got plenty of red blood and I like to fight"—belied his calling to the ministry, which he abandoned on joining the Watch and Ward. He never lost his thirst for combat. "Nowadays when I go into a raid," he told a reporter in 1916, "I always take my glasses off and fight with my fists first."

Though sometimes mocked for his righteous fervor, Chase drew admiring support from Boston's clergy and found respect on the national stage. Four times President Woodrow Wilson named him a delegate to the International Congress of the World's Purity Federation, a group dedicated to "the annihilation of the white-slave traffic [and] the suppression of public vice." Yet his enduring fame traces not to like-minded admirers but to contemptuous adversaries and most notably H. L. Mencken, who branded Chase a "Pecksniff" who savored the smut he suppressed. Mencken goaded Chase into banning a Mencken publication, then beat him in court, humiliating Chase and scarring his legacy only months before his death in 1926 at just fifty-four.[37]

[37] Details of Chase's life appear in Professor Neil Miller's study of the Watch and Ward Society and various Chase profiles and obituaries. Miller, *Banned in Boston*, pp. ix–xi, 40–45, 56–57, 63–64, 87–96; John W. Hawkins, "J. Frank Chase, The Clean-Up Specialist," *New Bedford Sunday Standard*, July 16, 1916, p. 21 ("wellknit body," "bull-dog jaw," "[B]orn with a . . . ," "There was a time . . . ," "I've got plenty . . . ," and "Nowadays when I . . . " and offering a sketched portrait of Chase); A. L. S. Wood, "Keeping the Puritans Pure," *American Mercury* (Sept. 1925), p. 74 (mockingly profiling Chase); *The Editor, the Bluenose and the Prostitute: H.L. Mencken's History of the "Hatrack" Censorship Case* (Carl Bode ed., Boulder, Colo.: Roberts Rinehart, Inc., 1988), pp. 119, 150 (presenting a 1926 snapshot of Chase); "Hatrack," *Time*, Apr. 19, 1926, pp. 26–27 (noting Chase's appointments to the "International Purity Federation" and reviewing the Mencken episode); Senate Rept. No. 822, "Ninth International Congress of the World's Purity Federation" (Oct. 8, 1914), pp. 1–2, in *Senate Reports* (63d Cong., 2d Sess.) (Washington: Government Printing Office, 1914) ("the annihilation of . . ."); H. L. Mencken, "The 'Hatrack' Case: The American Mercury vs. The New England Watch and Ward Society, the Postmaster-General of the United States, et al.," in Bode, *supra*, pp. 37, 151 (deeming Chase a "Pecksniff"); *Twenty-Ninth Annual Report of the New England Watch and Ward Society for the Year 1906–1907* (Boston: Office of the Society, 1907), p. 5 (reporting J. Frank Chase's 1907 accession as secretary); "Milestones," *Time* (Nov. 15, 1926), p. 33; "Vice Crusader Dead," *Lowell Sun*, Nov. 4, 1926, p. 8; "Rev. Jason Frank Chase," The Chase Chronicles (Oct.–Dec. 1926).

Chase's Antidrug Campaign

Before Frank Chase took charge of the Watch and Ward Society in 1907, dirty books, betting, and brothels absorbed almost all its law-enforcing zeal. Drug-busting absorbed almost none. The group's annual report for 1908 to 1909 claimed Watch and Ward agents had secured convictions that year in twenty-two pornography cases, forty-eight gambling cases, and seven "miscellaneous" cases. Drug sales and abuse merited not one line of text.[38]

That soon changed. In the first paragraph of the next year's report, Chase announced the Watch and Ward had inaugurated a "new department" focused on "suppression of habit-producing drugs." It was, he said, "the notable work of the year." Second only to obscene pictures, "the vices of the habit-producing drugs seem to be the most demoralizing in their effects, stultifying both body and soul." Behind the society's newfound focus lay a familiar tale: "It originated in the complaint of a parent that her boy, still a minor, had contracted a habit that had become a curse to him. . . . [S]he begged us to co-operate in preventing him from securing the drug which had proven his downfall."[39]

Here we have yet another antidrug campaign sparked by an iconic young man's fall under a drug's evil spell. As was true of Max Ohle, the pharmacy boy whose ordeal perhaps sped passage of the 1897 Illinois anti-cocaine law, and young George Fromme, whose arrest on his mother's complaint figured in New York's 1907 cocaine ban, Chase's unnamed young man was hooked on cocaine, which Chase deemed "probably the leading active-narcotic vice of our city." Like Ohle and Fromme, this boy had a parent desperate to wean him of his habit. And though Chase tells us nothing else about the boy, it seems likely from Chase's silence that this boy, like Ohle and Fromme, was white.

Spurred perhaps by the boy's plight, the Watch and Ward launched its new antidrug assault with vigor. An accounting of narcotics cases brought by the society shows a stunning year-over-year change. Having commenced not a single such case in 1908 to 1909, Watch and Ward agents lodged forty-one drug prosecutions the next year, most involving cocaine. And the society's antidrug unit achieved a crucial legislative milestone. Though Massachusetts had banned opium dens in 1885 and became the first Northeastern state to ban unprescribed cocaine sales in 1898, it proved a slacker in the fight against eaten opium and related drugs. Only in March 1910, after twenty-four states and territories had

[38] *Thirty-First Annual Report of the New England Watch and Ward Society for the Year 1908–1909* (Boston: Office of the Society, 1909), p. 18.

[39] *Thirty-Second Annual Report of the New England Watch and Ward Society for the Year 1909–1910* (Boston: Office of the Society, 1910), p. 5 ("new department . . ." and "suppression of . . ."); ibid., p. 15 ("the vices of . . ."); ibid., pp. 26–27 ("the notable work . . ." and "it originated in . . .").

outlawed sales of opium and related drugs, did Massachusetts finally tag along, banning unprescribed sales of opium, morphine, heroin, and codeine.[40]

Legislative records reveal Frank Chase's unmistakable hand in crafting this new law. In January 1910, Chase and Delcevare King, treasurer of the Watch and Ward Society, petitioned the legislature for the new act and supplied a complete proposed text. As Chase recalled several years later, "In 1910 the Secretary of this Society [Chase] introduced a law against opium and its products which was as thoroughgoing and drastic as the present Federal law" against unprescribed sales of opiates and cocaine. Chase's proposal lost some bite, however, in its course through the legislature. Wiser voices counseled him that his "drastic . . . ideal could be reached only by slow steps"—and a "compromise bill" instead prevailed. As enacted, the 1910 law banned unprescribed sales of several opiates, but made no mention of "cannibis indica," which Chase and King's original draft had consigned to the list of banned substances.[41]

Another year would pass before Massachusetts adopted the nation's first anti-cannabis law, perhaps Chase's most notable legacy. Again legislative records expose the new law as his handiwork in whole or greater part. On January 14, 1911, Representative John J. Conway of West Roxbury, Chase's home district, presented a petition signed by Chase and the Reverend Frederick Baylies Allen, president of the Watch and Ward Society. Calling for antidrug legislation "substantially as per annexed bill," Chase and Allen appended another fully drafted anti-narcotics law. Their text proposed to ban unprescribed possession of a range of drugs including "cannabis indica" and "cannabis sativa" and threatened violators with six months' confinement or a fine of up to $100. The bill survived legislative vetting largely unchanged. On March 28, the Committee on Public Health considered "the petition of J. Frank Chase and another" and amended their proposal by adding registered nurses to a list of persons permitted to possess the banned drugs. The proposal underwent other changes, but these too were small. Six weeks after its passage, the *Lowell Sun* declared simply, "The law was framed by the Watch and Ward society."[42]

[40] *Thirty-Second Annual Report*, pp. 17–20; "An Act Forbidding the Sale and Use of Opium for Certain Purposes," 1885 *Massachusetts Acts*, ch. 73 (Act of Mar. 11, 1885), p. 549; "An Act Relative to the Sale of Poisons," 1898 *Massachusetts Acts*, ch. 192, § 1 (Act of Mar. 17, 1898), p. 127; "An Act to Regulate the Sale of Morphine and Other Narcotic Drugs," 1910 *Massachusetts Acts*, ch. 271 (Act of Mar. 22, 1910), pp. 207–08.

[41] 1910 *Massachusetts House Journal* (Jan. 20, 1910), p. 116 (noting Chase's petition for the 1910 legislation banning opium, morphine, and related drugs); 1910 *Massachusetts Senate Journal* (Jan. 21, 1910), p. 113 (same); Massachusetts House Bill No. 416 (Jan. 20, 1910) (presenting Chase and King's proposed text of the 1910 act); *Thirty-Second Annual Report*, p. 3 (identifying Delcevare King as treasurer); *Thirty-Seventh Annual Report of the New England Watch and Ward Society for the Year 1914–1915* (Boston: Office of the Secretary, 1915), p. 12 (presenting Chase's memories of the 1910 legislative process). I thank my research assistant Gabriel Schlabach, who tracked down the legislative records of the 1910 act and of several other law changes mentioned in this chapter.

[42] "An Act Relative to the Issuance of Search Warrants for Hypnotic Drugs and the Arrest of Those Present," 1911 *Massachusetts Acts*, ch. 372 (Act of Apr. 29, 1911), p. 359; Massachusetts Legislative

With a two-year head start on the anti-cannabis law of any other state, the Massachusetts act of 1911 set the national standard. In March 1915, the founder of New York's Big Brother movement, Ernest Coulter, "congratulate[d] the New England Watch and Ward Society on the splendid campaign which it has conducted in the past five years." Even before passage of the federal Harrison Act of 1914, Coulter noted, Massachusetts had adopted an antidrug law that "was in almost every respect as high as the National ideal." Indeed, the Massachusetts law outstripped the Harrison Act, which effectively outlawed opium and cocaine but failed to ban cannabis. And Chase persisted in refining the Massachusetts ban. He returned to the legislature in 1912, 1914, and 1915 with more pre-scripted proposals that won fast passage, sometimes in barely altered form, strengthening his original act and easing its enforcement. In 1916 he told a news reporter that he "regard[ed] the dope clean-up as the greatest constructive work of his career."[43]

Among Chase's backers in his antidrug campaign was Dr. William F. Boos, a Massachusetts General Hospital toxicologist and for years a member of the Watch and Ward's board of directors. Dr. Boos addressed the society in Boston on March 5, 1911, as Chase's bill was wending its way through the legislature. Notably, Boos spoke of hashish, a preparation of *cannabis indica* targeted by Chase's bill together with *cannabis sativa*. "Hasheesh is being introduced lately, by foreigners," Boos warned, "and its use is growing. It is 1000 times more harmful than either morphine or opium and is the favorite drug of murderers in India." As quoted in the *Lowell Sun*'s brief account, Boos never said which "foreigners" he feared, though his reference to India is some hint. And he never

---

Record of House Bill No. 1321 (1911), including a March 28, 1911, report by the Committee on Public Health; "An Opium Raid," *Lowell Sun*, June 14, 1911, p. 12. I am grateful to Alethea Sargent for her admirable resourcefulness in assembling the legislative record. Adam Rathge addresses Frank Chase's role in crafting the Massachusetts anti-cannabis law of 1911 as well as 1914 substitute legislation in Rathge, "Cannabis Cures," pp. 157–61.

[43] "Advocates Segregation," *Boston Daily Globe*, Mar. 29, 1915, p. 10 (quoting Coulter); *Thirty-Seventh Annual Report*, p. 40 (same); "An Act Relative to Certain Hypnotic Drugs," 1912 *Massachusetts Acts*, ch. 283 (Act of Mar. 21, 1912), p. 191 (providing that possession of cannabis or other banned narcotics "shall be presumptive evidence that such possession was in violation of law" and requiring trial judges to order forfeiture and destruction of illegally possessed drugs); Massachusetts Legislative Record of House Bill 1852 (1912) (showing Chase led a list of four petitioners who presented a fully scripted act to the legislature with a petition seeking its adoption); "An Act to Regulate the Sale of Opium, Morphine and Other Narcotic Drugs," 1914 *Massachusetts Acts*, ch. 694 (Act of June 22, 1914), p. 704 (forbidding drugstores to refill prescriptions of opium, morphine, heroin, *cannabis indica*, and *cannabis sativa* except on the written or in-person order of the prescriber); Massachusetts Legislative Record of Senate Bill 372 (1914) (showing Chase among three petitioners who presented a fully scripted act to the legislature with a petition seeking its adoption); "An Act Relative to Search Warrants under the Law Relating to Certain Drugs," 1915 *Massachusetts Acts*, ch. 159 (Act of Apr. 12, 1915), p. 146 (consolidating provisions governing warrants to search for illegally held narcotics); Massachusetts Legislative Record of Senate Bill 326 (1915) (showing Chase presented prescribed act); Hawkins, "The Clean-Up Specialist," p. 21. The "[s]egregation" mentioned in the *Globe* article's headline referred to Chase's recommendation that drug-using inmates at Boston's Deer Island prison be separated from other inmates for medical treatment.

expanded on his mention of murderers, likely a reference to the derivation of *assassin* from *Haschischin* cited by Harry Anslinger decades later when testifying in support of the Marihuana Tax Act.[44]

So if we may judge from Boos's remarks, the nation's first cannabis ban had nothing to do with marijuana. It was instead *hashish*, the newly insurgent cannabis preparation of the Orient, that roused warnings from Dr. Boos and action by J. Frank Chase and the Watch and Ward Society. Hence the cannabis they feared had not slipped northward from Mexico and did not carry in tow a despised immigrant population. Even if hashish too hailed from abroad, I've seen no evidence those who brought it here prompted loathing in the Bay State in the early 1910s.

Nor did Chase and Boos soon drop hashish from their sights. In December 1915, more than four years after Chase's anti-cannabis bill became law, Bostonian Charles Costis faced charges after having passed hashish to an agent of the Watch and Ward Society. Dr. Boos's testimony that the seized substance proved on chemical analysis to be "Indian hemp or hasheesh" figured critically in Costis's conviction.[45]

The Watch and Ward's Mission

Why then did the Watch and Ward and its leaders launch their drug-fighting crusade, striking at hashish along with opium and morphine and cocaine? Chase's tale of the young addict's distressed mother supplies a clue. Even if more fictive than real, the mother's plea offered a parable of the Watch and Ward's mission. Statements of that mission varied in their precision. At one extreme was Chase's request, godlike in breadth, printed on the flyleaf of almost every annual report between 1907 and at least 1920: "We ask any person aware of evils that require correction to notify the Secretary, MR. J. FRANK CHASE." With more refinement, longtime president and co-founder Frederick Allen portrayed the society's mission as fighting "those who are coining money out of the weaknesses of humanity." Time and again Allen and Chase insisted their targets were not vice's "weak and wretched victims," as Allen put it, but its purveyors—"those who for money carry on an organized system of exploitation." Pointing to his record,

---

[44] "Smoking Opium," *Lowell Sun*, Mar. 6, 1911, p. 3 (quoting Dr. Boos). Boos's name first appeared among the Watch and Ward's directors in the annual report for 1910–1911 and remained there every year until at least 1920. *See Thirty-Third Annual Report of the New England Watch and Ward Society for the Year 1910–1911* (Boston: Office of the Society, 1911), p. 3; *Forty-Second Annual Report of the New England Watch and Ward Society for the Year 1919–1920* (Boston: Office of the Society, 1920), p. 3.

[45] "Dr Boos Found It Was Hasheesh," *Boston Daily Globe*, Dec. 16, 1915, p. 9.

Chase assured a reporter in 1916, "We have never arrested any of the victims unless they were engaged in the traffic."[46]

The victims the society most sought to protect were youth. Early in 1909, on the eve of the Watch and Ward's entry in the drug war, Allen looked backward: "For nearly a third of a century our little Society has stood like a sentinel between our boys and girls, our young people, the weak, the foolish, the unwary, and those who for money would tempt and corrupt them." The next year, with the Watch and Ward's antidrug campaign in gear, Chase compared the society to a father struggling to save his sons from twin serpents, vice and crime: "We might have [chosen] . . . as a Society motto the words written upon the father's agonizing face:—'For God's sake, save the boys.'" That same year the Reverend Francis H. Rowley congratulated the Watch and Ward on its success in this mission. The society's efforts, Rowley said, had helped make Boston "a better city in which one's children might grow up, a safer city—safer from many of the temptations that lure so often the best of childhood and of youth into evil."[47]

Chase was less sure of success. Two years after Rowley's hopeful words, Chase fretted that "[d]uring the past year we have seen boys from respectable homes in the suburbs made victims of these dread [drug] habits in the space of a few months by nightly visits to the city." He therefore recommitted himself to the struggle. In 1916, with the Watch and Ward's drug war at full tilt, Chase assured the press the society's resolve had not wavered: "The one thing we are trying to do is to make the environment of the community such that boys and girls can grow up decent if they want to: so they will not be forced to see on every side the guideposts to the road of iniquity."[48]

Alongside repeated vows to guard the morals of victimized youth stands a notable silence: neither the society's records nor its leaders said much about the race or ethnicity of vice's purveyors or victims. Though Protestant through and through—the Watch and Ward's board of directors included only an occasional Catholic or Jew—the society mostly abstained from the anti-immigrant invective common among moral enterprises of the day. It's true Chase often alleged pornography had an "Italian" or "French" or "South America[n]" source. And

[46] Twenty-Ninth Annual Report (flyleaf) ("We ask any . . ."); Forty-Second Annual Report (flyleaf) (same); Thirty-Sixth Annual Report of the New England Watch and Ward Society for the Year 1913–1914 (Boston: Office of the Society, 1914), p. 20 ("those who are coining..."); Fortieth Annual Report of the New England Watch and Ward Society for the Year 1917–1918 (Boston: Office of the Society, 1918), p. 19 ("weak and wretched . . ." and "those who for money . . ."); Hawkins, "The Clean-Up Specialist," p. 21 ("We have never arrested . . .").
[47] Thirty-First Annual Report, p. 23 ("For nearly a third . . ."); Thirty-Second Annual Report, p. 29 ("We might have . . ."); ibid., p. 22 ("a better city . . .").
[48] J. Frank Chase et al., The Dope Evil (Boston: New England Watch and Ward Society, 1912), reprinted in American Perceptions of Drug Addiction: Five Studies, 1872–1912 (Gerald N. Grob ed., New York: Arno Press, 1981), p. [5] ("During the past..."); Hawkins, "The Clean-Up Specialist," p. 21 ("The one thing . . .").

he linked opium with the Chinese. "All the opium illegally sold in Boston this year, concerning which we were able to secure any evidence," he wrote in 1910, "was sold by Chinese." Moreover, the Watch and Ward's annual report for 1914 to 1915 printed an essay by Ernest Coulter decrying the "fearful havoc" wrought by cocaine in the South, "especially among the negroes." Generally, however, the Watch and Ward's records and Chase's other writings lacked racial or ethnic coding—and never linked cannabis with any specific group.[49]

Instead, over and over, the drug purveyors Chase called out were doctors. He wrote in his annual report for 1915 to 1916 of "The Problem of the Corrupt Physician." The danger was in those "unscrupulous physicians" who perpetuate addicts' habits, "profiting by their misfortune." Again the next year he wrote, "The great task of the year . . . has been the struggle to curb the practice on the part of certain physicians of issuing prescriptions for large amounts of narcotic drugs, when not medically or morally justified." With some satisfaction, he reported the Watch and Ward had prosecuted four doctors that year. "The first prosecution of a physician under our State law was initiated by this Society," Chase boasted, adding that public officials brought such cases only after the Watch and Ward had marked the way. Another year later, he remained on theme, condemning the "fraudulent prescribing of large quantities of drugs under the pretext of a medical treatment by some unscrupulous physicians" and relating with pride the society's prosecution of several such offenders.[50]

I've seen no evidence the doctors Chase hauled to court trafficked in cannabis-laced cures. The Watch and Ward's focus on corrupt physicians matters for a different reason: in vilifying doctors, the society underscored its general indifference to the ethnicity of a drug's purveyor and its readiness to regard users as victims. And though sources shed little light on the demographics of cannabis

---

[49] Miller, *Banned in Boston*, pp. 11–12 (noting the Watch and Ward's Protestant makeup and absence of anti-immigrant rhetoric); *Thirty-Eighth Annual Report of the New England Watch and Ward Society for the Year 1915–1916* (Boston: Office of the Society, 1916), p. 43 (quoting President Allen boasting of a Catholic director of many years' standing); *Thirty-Second Annual Report*, pp. 6–7 ("The most common source of [obscene literature] during the past year has seemed to be the steamers from foreign ports, especially from Buenos Ayres, South America."); ibid., p. 25 (noting "the sale of books in both the French and Italian language which were as degenerate as language could become"); *Thirty-Second Annual Report*, p. 17 ("All the opium . . ."); *Thirty-Seventh Annual Report*, pp. 30, 35–36 (reprinting Coulter essay); *see also Thirty-Third Annual Report*, p. 13 ("[Opium] is sold almost exclusively by the Chinese in the Chinese quarters of the city."). Catholic layman Bernard J. Rothwell served as one of the Watch and Ward's many vice presidents from 1915 to at least 1920. Social reformer Meyer Bloomfield served on the board from 1906 to 1908, as did Rabbi Harry Levi of Boston's Temple Israel from 1918 to at least 1920. *See Twenty-Eighth Annual Report of the New England Watch and Ward Society for the Year 1905–1906* (Boston: Office of the Society, 1906), p. 4; *Fortieth Annual Report*, p. 3.

[50] *Thirty-Eighth Annual Report*, pp. 9–10 ("The Problem of the Corrupt Physician" and "unscrupulous physicians"); *Thirty-Ninth Annual Report of the New England Watch and Ward Society for the Year 1916–1917* (Boston: Office of the Society, 1917), pp. 8–9 ("The great task . . ."); ibid., pp. 21–22 ("The first prosecution . . ."); ibid., p. 24 (presenting a tally of the society's prosecutions); *Fortieth Annual Report*, pp. 12–13 ("fraudulent prescribing . . .").

users in Massachusetts, we've seen already in Harry Anslinger's writings and testimony—and we'll see again—that the perceived victims of the cannabis trade commonly were youth.

Frank Chase and Maine's Anti-Cannabis Law

Two years after Massachusetts launched the American war against cannabis, four more states took up arms. In the legislative season of 1913, Maine, Indiana, Wyoming, and California all banned unprescribed cannabis. Though scattered across the American landscape with nothing clear to unite them, these four states acted almost in concert. Lawmakers introduced the relevant measures on three successive Tuesdays—January 28 in California, February 4 in Maine and Indiana, February 11 in Wyoming.[51] As timing does not distinguish these laws, let us examine them instead geographically, moving north and then west from our natural starting point, first-in-the-nation Massachusetts.

This plan follows Frank Chase's declared strategy. In 1912, still tasting his legislative triumph in Massachusetts the year before, Chase proclaimed he would seek to convert other New England states to his antidrug cause. In a pamphlet memorably titled *The Dope Evil*, he announced the "earnest hope" of a "group of earnest people in Boston . . . that their experience may be fruitful in placing upon the statute books of all states of New England at least laws which shall be effective in properly regulating the sale of these [habit-forming] drugs and in suppressing their illegal sale."[52] Indeed, Chase succeeded in putting anti-cannabis laws on the books in Maine in 1913 and Vermont in 1915, though a 1913 campaign in New Hampshire fell short. His labors therefore explain in greater part why New England contributed three of the first six anti-cannabis states.

Hence we go first to Maine. Having been part of Massachusetts till 1820, Maine often looked to its southern parent for legislative guidance—and the parent state sometimes looked north. Their filial bond proved especially tight in the realm of recreational intoxicants. In banning alcohol the younger state proved precocious: Maine pioneered statewide prohibition in 1851, while Massachusetts trailed in 1852. But the elder acted first against other drugs. After Massachusetts led the East in forbidding unprescribed cocaine sales in 1898, Maine followed with almost identical language in 1899. And after Massachusetts banned opium,

---

[51] 1913 *California Assembly Journal* (Jan. 28, 1913), pp. 285, 288 (reporting Assemblyman Sutherland's introduction of A.B. 907); 1913 *Maine Legislative Record—House* (Feb. 4, 1913), p. 270 (reporting Representative Clark's introduction of Maine's anti-cannabis bill); 1913 *Indiana House Journal* (Feb. 4, 1913), pp. 667–70 (recording introduction and House passage of Representative Sands's amendment to H.B. 277, adding the words "cannabis indica"); 1913 *Wyoming House Journal* (Feb. 11, 1913), pp. 261, 265 (recording Representative Hopkins's introduction of H.B. 243).

[52] Chase et al., *The Dope Evil*, p. [1].

morphine, heroin, and codeine in 1910 and cannabis in 1911, Maine banned all five drugs in 1913.[53]

Behind Maine's 1913 narcotics act lay the heavy hand of Frank Chase and the New England Watch and Ward Society. Though the state's laconic legislative documents divulge no secrets of the law's passage, clear evidence of Chase's role lies squirreled in several corners of the historical record. The local press offers the first clue. Tucked at the bottom of page ten of the *Kennebec Journal* of March 5, 1913, just after an update on "the bill regulating hatpins and other decorative utilities," the *Journal* reported in tiny type what appears to have been the only testimony taken by the Maine legislature on the 1913 anti-narcotics bill. On March 4, the House Committee on Public Health heard from a sole witness in favor and a sole witness opposed. The state's chemist, Henry Evans, stood opposed—not to the wisdom of banning the named drugs, but to his being sacked with the task of testing for them. Evans offered "[t]he only opposition," the *Journal* reported: he complained "the State laboratories were not at present equipped for the work."

As for supporters of the bill, the *Journal* mentioned only one: "J. Frank Chase, secretary of the New England Watch and Ward Society, appeared in favor . . . ." What Chase said we never learn. But his 150-mile trek to a wintry northern capital suggests the bill held claim to his passions. And his view prevailed. In deference to chemist Evans's concerns, the committee apparently altered the original bill and reassigned the task of drug testing to the Maine Agricultural Experiment Station. Then, three days after Chase's visit, the Committee reported the bill "ought to pass."[54]

A second exhibit linking Chase to Maine's anti-cannabis law appears not in the legislative record or local press, but in the Watch and Ward's papers. At the

---

[53] "An Act for the Suppression of Drinking Houses and Tippling Shops," 1851 *Maine Acts*, ch. 211 (Act of June 2, 1851), p. 210; "An Act Concerning the Manufacture and Sale of Spirituous or Intoxicating Liquors," 1852 *Massachusetts Acts*, ch. 322 (Act of May 22, 1852), p. 257; "An Act Relative to the Sale of Poisons," 1898 *Massachusetts Acts*, ch. 192, § 1 (Act of Mar. 17, 1898), p. 127; "An Act to Prevent Incompetent Persons from Conducting the Business of an Apothecary," 1899 *Maine Acts*, ch. 96, § 17 (Act of Mar. 16, 1899), pp. 103, 107; "An Act to Regulate the Sale of Morphine and Other Narcotic Drugs," 1910 *Massachusetts Acts*, ch. 271 (Act of Mar. 22, 1910), pp. 207–08; "An Act Relative to the Issuance of Search Warrants for Hypnotic Drugs and the Arrest of Those Present," 1911 *Massachusetts Acts*, ch. 372, §§ 1, 3 (Act of Apr. 29, 1911), pp. 359–60; "An Act to Regulate the Sale of Morphine and Other Hypnotic or Narcotic Drugs," 1913 *Maine Acts*, ch. 211 (Act of April 12, 1913), pp. 300–03.

[54] "Appoints Frank J. Ham," *Kennebec Journal*, Mar. 5, 1913, pp. 1, 10 (reporting testimony before House Committee on Public Health); 1913 *Maine Legislative Record—House*, p. 698 (Mar. 7, 1913) (noting the Committee on Public Health had concluded the new bill "ought to pass"). On the change made in response to chemist Evans's concerns, compare the bill as first proposed on February 4, 1913, with the version reported out of the Committee on Public Health on March 7. "An Act to Regulate the Sale of Morphine and Other Hypnotic or Narcotic Drugs," House Doc. No. 134, § 9 (Feb. 4, 1913), p. 7 (calling for testing by "[t]he state board of health"); "An Act to Regulate the Sale of Morphine and Other Hypnotic or Narcotic Drugs," House Doc. No. 449, § 9 (Mar. 7, 1913), p. 7 (calling for testing by "[t]he director of the Maine Agricultural Experiment Station"). I thank Micah Myers and Alethea Sargent for their careful and detailed reconstruction of the legislative record.

outset of the society's annual report for 1912 to 1913, Chase offered a detailed roundup of the year's activities. The group's work in Massachusetts consumed fifteen pages. Then followed two sentences about Maine's new law: "We have introduced laws uniform with that of Massachusetts on the regulation of habit-forming drugs, into the Legislatures of Maine, New Hampshire and Vermont. We have thus far obtained success in Maine only."[55]

Here Chase magnified his role, for neither he nor the Watch and Ward Society had "introduced" the Maine legislation. That step was the work of Representative Seth Clark of Portland, who offered the relevant bill on February 4, 1913. Perhaps Clark, a traveling salesman, knew Chase, but no connection has emerged. Nor was Chase's claim of "success" quite accurate, at least not yet. His annual report was dated March 1, 1913, three days *before* his testimony in Augusta and almost six weeks before Maine's new law won the governor's signature on April 12. Perhaps what Chase deemed "success" on March 1 was that Clark had introduced the bill and prospects for passage looked good.[56]

No doubt Chase was proud, for the Watch and Ward Society and its collaborators had written almost every word of Maine's act. Proof of the society's hidden handiwork lies in a largely forgotten 1912 tract bearing the society's imprint. I have mentioned this pamphlet already. Titled *The Dope Evil*, it largely rehashed and repackaged old material as a collection of views on the drug scourge. Its thirty-eight pages presented essays by Chase, Dr. Boos, and Dr. Lyman F. Kebler, chief of the Drug Division of the U.S. Department of Agriculture. Offering "a Reformer's Point of View," Chase reprinted almost word for word an address called "The Dope Vice" he had given at the Watch and Ward's annual meeting of February 25, 1912. Dr. Boos, who delivered "a Physician's Point of View," likewise recycled almost verbatim the address he gave before the society on March 5, 1911. Dr. Kebler's "Statistician's Point of View" excerpted the results of a physician survey Kebler first published in 1910.[57]

It's the fourth part of the 1912 pamphlet, unsigned and titled simply "Model Law," that most concerns us. A decade before the American Medical Association first debated a uniform state anti-narcotics act and almost two decades before Harry Anslinger committed the Federal Bureau of Narcotics to framing a uniform state act, Chase and his cohort embraced this approach, producing a

[55] *Thirty-Fifth Annual Report of the New England Watch and Ward Society for the Year 1912–1913* (Boston: Office of the Society, 1913), p. 20.

[56] 1913 *Maine House Legislative Record* (Feb. 4, 1913), p. 270 (reporting Rep. Clark's introduction of Maine's anti-cannabis bill); "The 76th Maine Legislature: Stenographic Reports of Yesterday's Sessions of the Senate and House of Representatives: House," *Kennebec Journal*, Feb. 5, 1913, p. 2 (same); "The Biographies: Sketches of the Men Who Form the 76th Legislature," *Kennebec Journal*, Jan. 1, 1913, pp. 11, 13.

[57] Chase et al., *The Dope Evil*. See also *Thirty-Fourth Annual Report of the New England Watch and Ward Society for the Year 1911–1912* (Boston: Office of the Society, 1912), pp. 19–26 (printing Chase's address, "The Dope Vice"); *Thirty-Third Annual Report*, pp. 27–33 (printing Dr. Boos's address).

polished and comprehensive model anti-narcotics act. In breadth and boldness it far outstripped James Beal's brief and comparatively modest uniform law of 1903. Beal's model act banned only distribution of opium, cocaine, and chloral hydrate and their analogs and derivatives. It said nothing of cannabis and left simple drug possession unpunished. And beyond threatening violators with a notably forgiving schedule of penalties, Beal's scheme offered nothing to guide its enforcement.[58]

Spanning almost nine pages, the Watch and Ward's model law had bigger ambitions. Crucially, it added *cannabis indica* and *cannabis sativa* to the roster of banned substances, and it punished possession along with distribution. Reflecting Chase's concern with "corrupt physicians," the law forbade doctors to dispense the named drugs "except in good faith as medicines for diseases indicated." Violators of these provisions, whether doctors, dealers, or users, and even on a first offense, faced up to a year's imprisonment or a $1,000 fine or both. Again reflecting Chase's interests, the model law empowered private persons—and therefore such groups as the Watch and Ward Society—to trigger police searches and arrests. On any person's sworn complaint supported by probable cause, the law compelled judges to command police officials to search premises and arrest any person found possessing narcotics unlawfully. Finally, there was the provision that prompted chemist Evans's objection in Maine, which required the state board of health to analyze suspected drugs at the request of any county prosecutor and made the chemist's certificate presumptive evidence of the substance's makeup.[59]

Within four months of its publication this model act, almost unaltered, became the law of Maine. Of the 1,644 words in Maine's 1913 antidrug law, 1,560 came straight from the Watch and Ward's model act. A single sentence added to Maine's law accounted for most of the rest.[60]

Who then wrote this model act? An unsigned preface says the act was "drafted from the laws now on the statute books of Massachusetts." Those laws, of course, were largely the work of Frank Chase and the Watch and Ward Society. Chase and Delcevare King, treasurer of the society, personally presented to the legislature

[58] Chase et al., *The Dope Evil*, pp. [29–38] (presenting model anti-narcotics act); James H. Beal, "Draft of An Anti-Narcotic Law," *Proceedings of the American Pharmaceutical Association*, vol. 51 (1903), pp. 485–86. On the development of a uniform state anti-narcotics act by the American Medical Association and Federal Bureau of Narcotics, *see* Bonnie & Whitebread, *Marihuana Conviction*, pp. 67, 76–91.

[59] Chase et al., *The Dope Evil*, pp. [29–38].

[60] *Catalogue of Copyright Entries*, New Series, vol. 10, no. 1 (Washington: Government Printing Office, 1913), p. 194 (showing Chase registered *The Dope Evil* with the Library of Congress Copyright Office in Washington on December 16, 1912); "An Act to Regulate the Sale of Morphine and Other Hypnotic or Narcotic Drugs," 1913 *Maine Acts*, ch. 211, pp. 300–03 (Act of April 12, 1913). My thanks to Leizel Ching and Sonia Moss of the Crown Law Library, who confirmed the date of *The Dope Evil*'s publication.

a draft of the 1910 Massachusetts law banning unprescribed sales of opium, morphine, and heroin. Chase and Frederick Allen, president of the society, sponsored and apparently drafted the 1911 act banning unprescribed possession of cannabis. And Chase led the list of four petitioners who in 1912 tendered a Massachusetts act strengthening certain enforcement provisions. Parts of all these laws, sometimes largely word for word, found their way into the 1912 model act. Moreover, Chase held the copyright to the 1912 pamphlet containing the model act, and his signed introduction opens the volume. So there's a weighty case to conclude Chase drafted or at least commissioned the 1912 model act and therefore Maine's nearly identical 1913 law.

But whatever its similarities to Massachusetts law, the model act presented a cleaner, more streamlined piece of lawmaking, perhaps surpassing Chase's legislative craft. In hunt of more practiced legislative hands behind the drafting, we find likely suspects on *The Dope Evil*'s title page. At the top are listed the three essayists whose work consumes most of this slim volume—Chase, Boos, and Kebler. At the bottom appears without explanation a three-person "Advisory Legislative Committee for the State of Vermont." It was a distinguished committee, composed of the presidents of the Vermont Board of Health and the University of Vermont as well as S. Hollister Jackson, a lawyer, former state representative, and future lieutenant governor. Their listing here is curious. The Boston-based Watch and Ward Society published *The Dope Evil*, and nothing in this small volume explains the Vermont connection. Yet it seems plain the Vermont Legislative Committee compiled the model act. The committee's designation as "Legislative" suggests its lawmaking function. And its listing on *The Dope Evil*'s title page after the names of the pamphlet's three essayists hints at the committee's hand in shaping Part IV of the pamphlet—the otherwise unsigned model anti-narcotics act.

The role of these three Vermonters in drafting what became Maine's 1913 anti-narcotics law turns our investigation slightly westward. For in 1915 Vermont became the third state in New England and the sixth in the nation to ban cannabis. It also became the third state to act at least in part under the sway of the New England Watch and Ward Society.

On to Vermont

Though Vermont enlisted early in the anti-cannabis campaign, it lagged every other state in the larger war on drugs. In banning cannabis in 1915, the legislature for the first time forbade opium and cocaine too. Only thirteen states waited longer to ban opium; only Alaska and Hawaii waited longer to ban cocaine. *No state waited longer to launch antidrug lawmaking.*

So it's striking that in 1912, after Vermont's long reign as a drug war laggard, lawmakers took up—and took seriously—what could have become the most far-reaching antidrug law in the nation. On November 11, Senator Herbert H. Blanchard, a Springfield lawyer, introduced "An act to regulate the sale of morphine and other hypnotic or narcotic drugs." The bill would have conditioned both sales and possession of most major mind-altering drugs, including *cannabis indica* and *cannabis sativa*, on a doctor's prescription, refillable only on the doctor's written order. Had the bill passed, it would have become the nation's second anti-cannabis act, trailing only the pathbreaking Massachusetts law of 1911. And unlike the Massachusetts law, which banned only unauthorized *possession* of cannabis, Blanchard's bill would have banned unprescribed sales too.[61]

Though sponsored by Senator Blanchard, the bill apparently was the work of the three-man "Advisory Legislative Committee for the State of Vermont," which joined with Frank Chase and Drs. Boos and Kebler in producing the 1912 pamphlet, *The Dope Evil*. That pamphlet appeared in print barely a month after Blanchard introduced his bill. The model anti-narcotics act that consumed the last quarter of the pamphlet must have circulated earlier, for it supplied the full text of Blanchard's bill.[62] Blanchard borrowed all but nine words of his seven-page bill directly from *The Dope Evil*'s script.

Coursing through the legislature, the bill at first won substantial support. On January 14, 1913, after adopting three minor amendments proposed by Blanchard, the Senate passed a substitute bill that still tracked *The Dope Evil*'s model act and sent it to the House. There it ran aground. Seemingly routine amendments failed passage and took the bill down with them. Ten days later a dejected Chase recorded this defeat in the Watch and Ward's annual report: "We have introduced laws uniform with that of Massachusetts on the regulation of habit-forming drugs, into the Legislatures of Maine, New Hampshire and Vermont," he wrote in language I quoted earlier. "We have thus far obtained success in Maine only."[63]

[61] 1912 *Vermont Senate Journal*, p. 151 (Nov. 11, 1912). For the text of Blanchard's bill, *see* "An Act to Regulate the Sale of Morphine and Other Hypnotic or Narcotic Drugs," S. 94, *reprinted in Vermont Senate Bills* (Oct. Sess. 1912), p. 260. I am grateful to the reference staff of the Vermont State Library, which kindly supplied a copy of the bill. On Blanchard, *see The American Bar: Contemporary Lawyers of the United States and Canada* (James Clark Fifield ed., Minneapolis: James C. Fifield Co., 1918), p. 674, and *New England Families, Genealogical and Memorial: A Record of the Achievements of Her People in the Making of Commonwealths and the Founding of a Nation* (William Richard Cutter ed., New York: Lewis Historical Publishing Co., 1915), vol. 2, p. 870.

[62] As I mentioned in the last paragraph and footnote 61, Blanchard introduced his bill on November 11, 1912. Chase registered *The Dope Evil* with the Library of Congress Copyright Office on December 16, 1912.

[63] For the text of the January substitute bill, *see* "An Act to Regulate the Sale of Morphine and Other Hypnotic or Narcotic Drugs," S. 194, *reprinted in Vermont Senate Bills* (Oct. Sess. 1912), p. 678. For the legislative history of Blanchard's original bill and its substitute, *see* the 1912 *Vermont Senate Journal*, p. 434 (Jan. 10, 1913), p. 455 (Jan. 13, 1913), p. 848 (Feb. 19, 1913); "Official Record

Indeed, the news in New Hampshire was no better. On January 15, 1913, just as Senator Blanchard's bill reached the Vermont House, New Hampshire Representative Levin J. Chase introduced "An act to regulate the sale of morphine and other hypnotic or narcotic drugs." Chase, a distant cousin of J. Frank Chase, acted under the Watch and Ward's unmistakable influence. His bill, like Blanchard's in Vermont, was a near carbon copy of *The Dope Evil*'s "Model Law." The New Hampshire bill added one sentence, dropped one section, and made smaller additions and deletions, but otherwise matched the Watch and Ward's model law word for word, comma for comma. Like the model law, the New Hampshire bill proposed to ban sales and possession of opium, cocaine, *cannabis indica, cannabis sativa*, and various related drugs.[64]

As in Vermont, the bill failed. New Hampshirites apparently had no humor for a full-throttle antidrug regime. Though their state had outlawed cocaine in 1909, it retained lawful opium sales till 1917 and banned cannabis only in 1935, lagging all but three other states. Against the state's live-free spirit, Levin Chase's sweeping anti-narcotics bill perhaps stood little chance. Or perhaps Chase, having introduced the bill as a favor to his Boston cousin, was content to watch it die of neglect. At all events, the bill died on March 12, when the House Public Health Committee declared it "inexpedient to legislate."[65]

Turning the Vermont Tide

Back in Vermont, it took two more years and three new laws in neighboring jurisdictions to overcome lawmakers' aversion to waging a drug war. In 1914 Vermont's southern and western neighbors and the federal government all enacted newly stringent anti-narcotics statutes. To the south, the Massachusetts legislature repaired a deficiency in the state's antidrug laws that long irked Chase. In petitioning the legislature for the law change, Chase and two other Watch and

of Day: House—Morning," *Burlington Free Press and Times*, Feb 20, 1913, p. 5 (reporting the bill's death). Chase's statement appears in the *Thirty-Fifth Annual Report*, p. 20.

[64] 1913 *New Hampshire House Journal* (Jan. 15, 1913), p. 105 (noting Chase's introduction of anti-narcotics act). My thanks to Gabriel Schlabach, who retrieved the legislative papers documenting Levin J. Chase's failed anti-narcotics bill, and Michael Morillo, who gathered news coverage of Chase and noted his family connection to J. Frank Chase. My thanks as well to Brett Diehl, who consulted various genealogical publications and websites, together with Chase family records, in confirming this family connection. Levin Chase's lineage traces to Aquila (I) Chase (ca. 1580-?) of Chesham, England, whose son Aquila (II) (1618–1670) died in Newbury, Massachusetts. J. Frank Chase's American lineage traces to William Chase (ca. 1605–1659), who first settled in Roxbury, Massachusetts. William and Aquila (II) were most likely either brothers or cousins, making Levin and J. Frank Chase either eighth or ninth cousins.
[65] *See* 1913 *New Hampshire House Journal* (Mar. 12, 1913), p. 592 (noting the Public Health Committee's verdict that Chase's bill was "inexpedient to legislate").

Ward leaders explained that "the use of habit forming drugs is still extensive" and that a leading cause was "the custom of the refilling of prescriptions on the part of certain drugstores." Elsewhere Chase condemned druggists who refilled prescriptions "as many as four times in one night." The legislature decreed that as of January 1, 1915, prescriptions of opium, morphine, heroin, *cannabis indica*, and *cannabis sativa* "shall not again be filled" except on the written or in-person order of the original prescriber.[66]

Likewise in New York, where the Smith Act of 1907 had outlawed cocaine, the Boylan Act of 1914 extended the ban to opium, morphine, and heroin. Effective July 1, 1914, sales of all these drugs required a doctor's prescription, to "be filled but once." And the federal Harrison Act, which secured passage in December 1914 and took effect the next March, followed the lead of Massachusetts and New York and thirty-one other states in effectively banning both cocaine and opium except by prescription.[67]

Even before the Harrison Act took effect, Vermonters felt the impact of toughened antidrug regimes in Massachusetts and New York. On January 14, 1915, Representative Arthur E. Hollister introduced the legislation that would become Vermont's first ban on unprescribed sales of opium, morphine, cannabis, and cocaine. Reporting the proposal a few days later, the *St. Albans Weekly Messenger* offered a rationale: "This measure is considered a timely one. With the state of New York enforcing a strict law against traffic in these drugs, it is claimed that a considerable trade in them has sprung up on the western side of the state, the customers being drug fiends of the Empire state who come over to Vermont to lay in a stock." The *Rutland News* agreed the problem was cross-border addicts from states with tougher statutes: "In Massachusetts and New York there are stringent laws concerning the sale of these habit-forming drugs. The enforcement of these laws in neighboring States has driven a great many 'dope fiends' to this State, and every Vermont druggist can attest to a large demand upon the part of non-residents for these deadly drugs." The solution, the *News* continued, was that "Vermont should have a law equally as stri[n]gent in its regulations. This

---

[66] "An Act to Regulate the Sale of Opium, Morphine and Other Narcotic Drugs," 1914 *Massachusetts Acts*, ch. 694, § 1 (Act of June 22, 1914), p. 704; Massachusetts Legislative Record of Senate Bill 372 (1914). On Chase's agitation about the failure of past laws to ban refills of drugs other than cocaine, *see Thirty-Fifth Annual Report*, p. 15; *Thirty-Sixth Annual Report*, pp. 9–10. Refills of cocaine prescriptions had been banned since 1906. *See* "An Act Relative to the Labelling of Certain Patent or Proprietary Drugs and Foods," 1906 *Massachusetts Acts*, ch. 386, § 4 (Act of May 11, 1906), pp. 362–63.

[67] "An Act to Amend the Public Health Law, in Relation to the Sale of Habit-Forming Drugs," 1914 *New York Laws*, vol. 2, ch. 363, § 1 (Act of Apr. 14, 1914), pp. 1120–21; "An Act to . . . Impose a Special Tax upon All Persons Who . . . Deal in . . . Opium or Coca Leaves . . . ," Pub. L. No. 63-223, ch. 1, § 2(b), 38 Stat. L. 785, 786 (Act of Dec. 17, 1914) (Harrison Narcotic Act).

State desires no unenviable notoriety as being the mecca for those addicted to the opium and morphine habits."[68]

We can't know for sure that the editors of the *Messenger* and *News* channeled Representative Hollister's motives in proposing his anti-narcotics act. I have found no record of his views. But Hollister hailed from Bennington in the southwest corner of the state, about five miles from the New York state line and about twelve from Massachusetts—a likely destination for cross-border addicts seeking a fix. If this was his worry, the news soon confirmed his fears. On March 4, days after the Harrison Act took effect and less than two weeks before Hollister's anti-narcotics bill became law, the *Burlington Free Press* ran a story datelined Bennington, March 1. Police had arrested William Cummings of North Adams, Massachusetts, and charged him with the brazen theft of cocaine and several hundred heroin tablets from a Bennington drugstore. "[A]s strict laws have been in effect in the neighboring States of Massachusetts and New York for some time," the *Free Press* explained, "the fiends have been haunting Bennington and purchasing supplies in expectation that it will be more difficult to secure the narcotics in the future."[69]

Even before New York banned opiates and Massachusetts toughened its law, the problem of cross-border drug traffic had infected Vermont. "Dope Bought Here?" asked the *St. Albans Daily Messenger* in August 1912, about ten weeks before Senator Blanchard introduced his failed antidrug bill. Montreal police had announced that after "several round-ups of 'fiends,'" officers at last had identified and arrested the source of their dope. Frank Bailey, nabbed in Montreal after his arrival from St. Albans in far-northern Vermont, was carrying "a quantity of morphine and opium" and a receipt reflecting purchase in St. Albans. Though Bailey's stateside drug buy was lawful, his Canadian sales were not, as Canada's Parliament had banned unprescribed sales of opium in 1908 and of morphine and cocaine in 1911. The Montreal police chief declared his belief that "most of the opium and morphine being peddled around [Montreal's] red light district was purchased across the line . . . ."[70]

With Vermont serving as duty-free drugstore for narcotic tourists from three abutting jurisdictions, the state's lawmakers at last felt compelled to act. On March 10, 1915, less than two months after Representative Hollister laid his

[68] 1915 *Vermont House Journal* (Jan. 14, 1915), p. 67; "House Kills Hedgehog Bill," *St. Albans Weekly Messenger*, Jan. 21, 1915, p. 8; "Vermont Should Have Stringent Drug Law," *Middlebury Register*, Jan. 22, 1915, p. 2 (reprinting item from the *Rutland News*).

[69] 1915 *Vermont House Journal* (Jan. 14, 1915), p. 67 (noting Hollister represented Bennington); "This Vermonter Hit Hard by the New Drug Law," *Burlington Free Press*, Mar. 4, 1915, p. 7.

[70] "Dope Bought Here?" *St. Albans Daily Messenger*, Aug. 29, 1912, p. 1; *see* "An Act to Prohibit the Importation, Manufacture and Sale of Opium for Other Than Medicinal Purposes," S.C. 1908, ch. 50 (Act of July 20, 1908) (Can.); "The Opium and Drug Act," S.C. 1911, ch. 17 (Act of May 19, 1911) (Can.). Months later a follow-up article suggested Bailey's Canadian cache also included cocaine. *See* "'Dope King' Is Insane," *St. Albans Weekly Messenger*, Nov. 7, 1912, p. 5.

proposal before the House, they embraced his act with no recorded opposition or debate.[71] That cross-border drug trafficking supplied the chief motive for the law seems likely. But three other lessons emerge from the history of the Vermont act: Frank Chase and the Watch and Ward Society had extended their considerable influence to Montpelier; the law's inclusion of *cannabis indica* and *cannabis sativa* as banned substances owed little or nothing to whatever racial or ethnic cast those substances may have had; and the welfare of white youth proved a weightier concern.

A brief investigation reveals the Watch and Ward's fingerprints on Hollister's original bill. Hollister cribbed the first five of his bill's seven sections directly from the Massachusetts anti-narcotics act of June 1914, which for the first time in that state had made prescriptions for opiates and cannabis nonrefillable. Frank Chase helped engineer that law with a trademark petition to the Massachusetts legislature attaching the text he wanted enacted. At the Watch and Ward's annual meeting that April, a speaker referred to the pending bill as "the outcome of the work of this Society for the last year or two." Indeed the 1914 Massachusetts law drew most of its substance and much of its language from the 1912 model act printed in Chase's jointly authored *Dope Evil*, published by the Watch and Ward Society. Hollister's 1915 bill tracked the Massachusetts law word for word in banning sales of all common opiates and *cannabis indica* and *cannabis sativa* absent a doctor's nonrefillable prescription. Other parts of his bill took their text straight from the Watch and Ward's 1912 model act. All told, Hollister contributed exactly eight words to his six-page bill, while the Watch and Ward wrote much of the rest.[72]

Set against clear signs of the Watch and Ward's influence, no evidence suggests that in banning cannabis in March 1915, Vermonters acted out of racial animus. I've seen no mention of non-whites selling or using cannabis and no evidence Vermonters linked the drug to any racial group before the new law's passage. Instead the evidence suggests that in pondering anti-narcotics legislation in 1912 and adopting it in 1915, Vermont lawmakers responded to the artful lobbying

[71] 1915 *Vermont Senate Journal* (Mar. 10, 1915), p. 366; "Woman Suffrage Killed in House: Vote Is 129 to 100," *Burlington Free Press*, Feb. 25, 1915, p. 1 ("The House ordered to a third reading the Hollister bill prohibiting the sale of narcotic drugs, without any discussion."); "Vail's Gift Favored," *St. Albans Weekly Messenger*, Mar. 4, 1915, p. 6 ("The law restricting the sale of narcotic drugs was passed [in the House] without opposition . . . ."); "Referendum Bill to Third Reading by Big Majority," *Burlington Free Press*, Mar. 11, 1915, p. 1 ("The Senate passed the narcotic drugs act without debate . . . .").

[72] *See* "An Act to Regulate the Sale of Opium, Morphine and Other Narcotic Drugs," H. 68, *reprinted in Vermont House Bills* (Jan. Sess. 1915), pp. 147–52; "An Act to Regulate the Sale of Opium, Morphine and Other Narcotic Drugs," *1914 Massachusetts Acts*, ch. 694, § 1 (Act of June 22, 1914), p. 704; Massachusetts Legislative Record of Senate Bill 372 (1914) (showing Chase among three petitioners who presented a fully scripted act to the legislature with a petition seeking its adoption); *Thirty-Sixth Annual Report*, p. 37 (quoting Rev. Alexander Mann). I am grateful to Paul Donovan of the Vermont State Library, who kindly supplied the original text of Hollister's 1915 bill.

of the Watch and Ward Society and the fear of cross-border traffic—*and* to the desire to guard their youth from euphoric drugs and the ravages they wrought.

Consider the evidence from October 1912, less than three weeks before Senator Blanchard introduced his failed anti-narcotics bill seeking to ban cannabis together with opiates and cocaine. Cautioning that parents addicted to cocaine and opiates were neglecting their offspring, the *Rutland News* urged passage of "legislation that shall make dope-producing less easy in Vermont[.] Nothing could carry more benefit to the children who need the state's care."[73]

Sixteen months later, after Blanchard's bill met defeat and as the next legislative session loomed, the *St. Albans Weekly Messenger* took up the antidrug banner and the theme of protecting youth. It "make[s] the blood boil," the editor lamented under the heading, "The Drug Evil," to hear accounts of "men and women who make their living selling cocaine and heroin to boys and girls and adults. . . . There is no crime that can compare with the deliberate starting of a boy or a girl in the practice of taking drugs, for to do so is to make criminals and murderers." The solution was to "bring down upon the heads of these spoilers of human life a quick and severe punishment." The editor said nothing of the race or ethnicity of sellers or users, but laid blame on one group in particular: prescribing physicians. "The doctor has a heavy responsibility resting on his shoulders. It is easy to quiet pain at the start by the use of drugs; it is almost impossible to stop the craving once the habit is formed."[74]

As Representative Hollister's anti-narcotics bill neared final passage in mid-March 1915, the Vermont press pointed more directly to *whites'* role in the drug trade. "One of the appalling facts in connection with the drug traffic," wrote the *Messenger*, "is that our immigrants are not drug users. The drug fiend is essentially American, as in China he is essentially Chinese." An *American* in the demographic jargon of 1915 was a native-born white. Not only were addicts white, they were largely respectable working people: "[S]ubstantially half the habitues who sought [doctors] for relief [from addiction] were persons who pursued professions or arts and one-eighth were housewives or women engaged in occupations that called for technical skill and long and careful training." And physicians, pharmacists, and nurses "are frequently trapped" by addiction.[75]

Three months later, reflecting on passage of the federal Harrison Act, the *Brattleboro Reformer* returned to the theme of guarding vulnerable youth. "The framers of the Harrison law aimed more than all else to save the next generation by putting beyond the reach of the boys and girls of to-day the drugs that will injure

[73] "Press Opinion," *St. Albans Weekly Messenger*, Oct. 24, 1912, p. 9 (reprinting item from the *Rutland News*).
[74] "The Drug Evil," *St. Albans Weekly Messenger*, Feb. 19, 1914, p. 1.
[75] "Uncle Sam after Drug Users," ibid., Mar. 4, 1915, p. 12.

them."[76] The Vermont anti-narcotics law, passed two weeks after the Harrison Act took effect, likely shared in this motive to save youth. The specter of marijuana-crazed Mexicans seems far more remote, for very little marijuana had caught the eye of the New England press, and very few Mexicans were in view.

The Path to Indiana's Cannabis Ban

Even Frank Chase's crusading zeal could not march his Watch and Ward warriors west to Indiana. Though Chase sometimes spoke far from home, I've found no evidence he or his writings touched down in Indiana. So when Indiana edged out Maine to become the nation's third anti-cannabis state in March 1913, the state's lawmakers possibly owed nothing to his guidance. Still, they shared with Chase a wariness of intoxicating pleasure and a fear for the morals of youth.[77]

Among perceived threats to those morals, cannabis at first didn't figure prominently. Lawmakers spied instead a different danger, one with a complicated relationship to cannabis—and one with potential to threaten every state. That danger was cigarettes, Turkish cigarettes in particular. Their spiking popularity in the years before the first cannabis bans may help explain the anti-cannabis laws of some states that lay beyond the reach of the Watch and Ward Society and largely beyond the immigrant crowds driven north by the Mexican Revolution.

Long before 1913, before cigarettes had claimed a notable chunk of the nation's tobacco trade, rumors about cigarette rolling papers ran rampant. As early as 1887 and as far off as Boise, the editor of the *Idaho Tri-Weekly Statesman* fretted about cigarettes' hold on "little boys, many of them school children." Bad enough was the habit of smoking among adults—it "is doubly injurious to young people . . . and ten times worse in the form of cigarettes than in the pipe." Yet it was "no uncommon thing in Boise City to see little boys . . . smoking cigarettes." Quoting the *Chicago Mail*, the editor declared that smoking stunts growth and fogs minds. Worse, growing children "inhale the poisonous odors of chemically prepared paper [and] opium . . . ." How else besides opium to explain cigarettes' insidious hold on our youth? "There is just stimulant enough in the cigarette to create a demand for something stronger, and . . . a confirmed appetite before

---

[76] "Press Opinion," ibid., June 3, 1915, p. 9 (reprinting item from the *Brattleboro Reformer*). I am grateful to my research assistant Alisa Philo, who painstakingly reconstructed the course of anti-cannabis lawmaking in Vermont.

[77] "'Problem Novel' Blamed for Vice," *Indianapolis Star*, Nov. 11, 1913, p. 2 (reporting an address Chase gave in Minneapolis); "An Act to Amend . . . 'An Act Pertaining to Sale of Drugs and Prescribing Penalties for Violation Thereof,'" *1913 Indiana Laws*, ch. 118, § 1 (Act of Mar. 6, 1913), p. 306.

they are very far advanced in years." And when cigarettes no longer satisfy child addicts, "it will either be whisky or morphine."[78]

Three months later the *New York Times* replayed the *Weekly Statesman's* concerns about cigarettes and rolling papers. Editors alleged that cigarette smoking, carried to excess, could kill. The chief villains were nicotine and the way cigarette smokers inhale (when cigar smokers don't) and smoke nonstop (when cigar smokers pause). Though wrapping papers typically posed no danger, "[t]he wrappers of some Turkish cigarettes are impregnated with opium, and these, of course, do harm . . . ." Prompting these comments was the untimely passing of Russell Hotchkiss Knevals, aged twenty-three, a medical student and son of President Chester A. Arthur's law partner. Found dead in his bed, Knevals had succumbed to natural causes, doctors said, either heart disease or apoplexy. But the coroner thought otherwise. "Cigarettes Killed Him," the *Times* announced, reporting the coroner's verdict. Sixty cigarettes a day had sacked Knevals with a "tobacco heart," both "flabby and fatty."[79]

Cigarettes and Boys

Two themes of these Boise and New York reports threaded through the early history of cigarettes in America. First was the favor cigarettes found among young men and boys. The theme dates at least to 1879, when the *New York Times* issued an alarum titled "Tobacco for Boys": "Lads at school acquire a taste for tobacco by surreptitiously smoking cigarettes—cigarettes which have done more to demoralize and vitiate youth than all the dram-shops of the land." A lad of eleven died of "tobacco narcossus" (and a related fall from stilts) in 1887; a boy of eight succumbed to a three-year habit in 1890. An Indiana news editor lamented in 1887 "the pernicious habit of cigarette smoking by boys." Even "the veriest mites," a New York doctor grumbled a decade later, "learn to smoke as soon as they do to swear." In 1905 the *Times* reported with earnest concern the unlikely findings that 90 percent of Providence schoolboys were smokers and that "schools elsewhere [were] about as bad." Still later, in 1909, the *Times* pictured four " 'East Side' Boys and Cigarettes." With oversized heads and stunted bodies, the boys struck poses by turn roguish, sullen, and checked out from the world (see Figure 7.5).[80]

[78] "Cigarette Smoking," *Idaho Tri-Weekly Statesman*, May 14, 1887, p. 2.

[79] "Cigarettes," *New York Times*, Aug. 14, 1887, p. 4; "From Joy to Mourning," ibid., Aug. 8, 1887, p. 5 (describing the discovery of Knevals's body); "Cigarettes Killed Him," ibid., Aug. 10, 1887, p. 2.

[80] "Tobacco for Boys," ibid., Jan. 11, 1879, p. 4; "Killed by Cigarette Smoking," ibid., Nov. 23, 1887, p. 9; "Cigarette Smoking Killed Him," ibid., Sept. 27, 1890, p. 3; [Untitled Item,] *Logansport Chronicle*, May 14, 1887, p. 4; "Women Using Narcotics," *New York Times*, Jan. 10, 1897, p. 13 (quoting Dr. Catherine G. Townsend) ("the veriest mites . . ."); "Schoolboys and Cigarettes," ibid., Oct. 27, 1905, p. 8; "The War on the Cigarette," ibid., Aug. 8, 1909, p. SM8. I thank Cassandra Tate for

Figure 7.5: "'East Side' Boys and Cigarettes" (1909).

The perception of cigarettes as a vice of youth persisted to the eve of World War I and beyond. Charles B. Towns, a purveyor of addiction cures, warned in 1912 that "virtually all boys who smoke start with cigarettes." James J. Jeffreys made "SAVE THE BOY" the motto of his 1912 anti-cigarette screed, *The Curse of the Nation*, which claimed most smokers began to use tobacco between ages six and sixteen. Two years later, automaker Henry Ford opened his *Case against the Little White Slaver* with the greeting, "To My Friend, the American Boy." Ford noted a New York magistrate's report "that 99% of the boys between the ages of 10 and 17, who come before him charged with crime have their fingers disfigured by cigarette stains." Carrying his concerns from boys to college men, Ford flogged widely cited findings that cigarette addicts "seldom if ever lead in their studies."[81]

Despite such dire warnings, the nation's youth took up smoking in hordes. Americans bought some 2.6 billion cigarettes in 1900, doubled that consumption in eight years, doubled it again in four more years and nearly again in another four years. In 1916 sales passed 21 billion. The nation's march toward war ensured this trend would not abate. The War Department, YMCA, Salvation Army, and Red Cross all sent billions of smokes to Europe, pushing sales by war's end to nearly 37 billion. These donors abandoned their earlier, sometimes strident antipathy to cigarettes in the face of the troops' apparent *need*. Cigarettes were a "necessary comfort," government officials claimed—"necessary to the comfort of the soldiers," the YMCA echoed.[82]

Authorities generally agreed cigarettes hurt youth more than adults. The *Chicago Mail*'s 1887 charge was typical of the era: cigarette smoking among youth was "stunting to their growth, enervating to their nerves, and blinding to their minds." Cigarette smoking strikes hardest at "immature bodies," William Rosser Cobbe alleged eight years later, "stunting the moral and intellectual as well as the physical growth." Such fears for children's well-being ripened with time and with widening awareness of cigarettes' health hazards and addictive grip. Meanwhile diffuse fears about cigarettes' moral danger to adults dissipated. State statute books reflect the results: though fifteen states and territories banned cigarettes outright, starting with Washington in 1893 and running through Utah in 1921, all these laws sooner or later fell to repeal or court rulings. By 1927, all were gone or defunct (see Table 7B). At least twenty-two other states and territories considered and rejected such laws, sometimes repeatedly, between 1892 and 1930.[83]

Yet in the same era and in state after state, lawmakers joined in an overwhelming and abiding national consensus to ban cigarette sales to minors,

pointing me to several of these sources. Cassandra Tate, *Cigarette Wars: The Triumph of "The Little White Slaver"* (New York: Oxford University Press, 1999), pp. 29, 167 n.63.

[81] Charles B. Towns, "The Injury of Tobacco and Its Relation to Other Drug Habits," *Century* (Mar. 1912), p. 768; James J. Jeffreys, *The Curse of the Nation: A Knock-out Blow for Tobacco in Six Rounds* (Marshall, Mich.: For the Author by Nashville Book Company, 1912), pp. 1, 3; Henry Ford, *The Case against the Little White Slaver* (Detroit: Henry Ford, 1914), pp. 3, 9; Jack Jacob Gottsegen, *Tobacco: A Study of Its Consumption in the United States* (Chicago: Pitman Publishing Corporation, 1940), pp. 100–102 (presenting findings of two studies, dated 1910 and 1912, that in every one of twelve colleges where comparisons were made, nonsmokers earned higher grades than smokers).
[82] Gottsegen, *Tobacco*, p. 27 tbl. X (noting yearly cigarette consumption); Tate, *Cigarette Wars*, pp. 72, 77–81 (reporting claims of necessity).
[83] "Cigarette Smoking," *Idaho Tri-Weekly Statesman*, May 14, 1887, p. 2 (quoting the *Chicago Mail*); William Rosser Cobbe, *Doctor Judas: A Portrayal of the Opium Habit* (Chicago: S.C. Griggs and Company, 1895), p. 153. Cassandra Tate's list of anti-cigarette laws and legislation is the clearest, most comprehensive I have seen. Tate, *Cigarette Wars*, pp. 159–60. Jack Jacob Gottsegen's list is similar but less complete. Gottsegen, *Tobacco*, p. 154 tbl. 44.

Table 7B   State Cigarette Bans

	Passage	Repeal (or Other Action)
	1893	1893 (declared unconstitutional) 1895 (repealed)
Washington	1907 (re-enacted)	1911
North Dakota	1895	1925
Iowa	1896	1921
Tennessee	1897	1921
Oklahoma	1901	1915
Indiana	1905	1909
Nebraska	1905	1919
Wisconsin	1905	1915
Arkansas	1907	1921
Illinois	1907	1907 (made ineffective by court ruling[a]) 1967 (repealed)
Kansas	1909	1927
Minnesota	1909	1913
South Dakota	1909	1917
Idaho	1921	1921
Utah	1921	1923

Sources: Jack Jacob Gottsegen, *Tobacco: A Study of Its Consumption in the United States* (Chicago: Pitman Publishing Corporation, 1940), pp. 154–55; Cassandra Tate, *Cigarette Wars: The Triumph of "The Little White Slaver"* (New York: Oxford University Press, 1999), pp. 46, 159–60; Lee J. Alston et al., "Social Reformers and Regulation: The Prohibition of Cigarettes in the United States and Canada," *Explorations in Economic History*, vol. 39 (2002), p. 432.
[a] In December 1907 the Illinois Supreme Court ruled that in banning "cigarette[s] containing any substance deleterious to health, including tobacco," the legislature did *not* intend to ban "cigarettes which contained only pure tobacco." Instead, the act's reference to tobacco included only "tobacco which was deleterious to health by reason of being impregnated with drugs or otherwise." *People ex rel. Berlizheimer v. Busse*, 231 Ill. 251, 255 (1907).

usually defined as those aged sixteen or younger. New Jersey and Washington started the trend in 1883, and within seven years at least twenty states and territories had joined them. When Virginia, the final holdout, followed course in 1922, bans on sales to youth blanketed the nation.[84]

---

[84] Tate said that as of 1920, Rhode Island and Virginia had failed to ban sales to youth; Gottsegen reported in 1940 that Texas had failed to do so. Tate, *Cigarette Wars*, pp. 4–5. 30; Gottsegen, *Tobacco*,

Dope-Spiked Cigarettes

Beyond warning of cigarettes' hold on boys, the 1887 editors of the *Idaho Weekly Statesman* and *New York Times* pursued a second common theme: cigarettes' unusual allure, they said, traced in part to dope-spiked tobacco and doctored rolling papers. The *Statesman* worried children "inhale the poisonous odors of chemically prepared paper [and] opium . . . ." The *Times* alleged "[t]he wrappers of some Turkish cigarettes are impregnated with opium . . . ." Such claims demanded proof, and in 1888 the *Evening News* set out to determine "What Science Finds Rolled Up in the Deadly 'Paper Pipe.'" Commissioned to analyze eleven popular brands, Chicago chemist Marc Delafontaine pronounced them all adulterated. In two well-known brands, Old Judge and Sweet Caporal, Delafontaine found opium or morphine, and he suspected three other brands concealed jimsonweed or belladonna, "both highly dangerous narcotics, producing stupefying effects upon the nerves."[85]

Suspected additives included also cannabis. *Something* gave cigarettes their peculiar aroma, the *Saturday Review* insisted in 1889. "The flavor and odour of the cigarette, at least the popular manufactured Turkish or Egyptian cigarette . . . , are, in great part, not those of tobacco at all, but of something quite distinct from, and added to, tobacco . . . ." A paragraph later the *Review* wrote with less evasion of "Turkish tobacco hemped, or opiated, or simply perfumed, or whatever it is." When the *Springfield Republican* of western Massachusetts addressed "How Cigarets Are Drugged" in 1892, the paper wrote with greater certitude. Reprinting an item from the *Boston Transcript*, the *Republican* expressed "no doubt that opium, valerian and cannabis indica are utilized to the largest extent." The choice of drug depended on the maker's target audience and desired effect. "Each manufacturer may be said to create a special drug-habit among those who smoke his brand, so that they are not satisfied with any other." Hence the "ingenious cigaret-maker" would add opium "to pleasantly soothe the nerves of the smoker." And *cannabis indica*, described as the product of the East Indian hemp plant and the basis of hashish, would deliver the "most pleasing exhilaration" in small doses or "drowsiness and stupor" in large.[86]

p. 155. But Rhode Island and Texas both had earlier bans. See *Rhode Island General Laws*, tit. 36, ch. 347, § 29 (1909), p. 1280 (banning cigarette sales to minors under age sixteen); "An Act to Prevent the Sale of Cigarettes and Tobacco to Persons under the Age of Sixteen . . . ," *1899 Texas Laws*, ch. 139 (Act of May 23, 1899), p. 237. It appears Virginia did not ban cigarette sales to minors till 1922. See "An Act to Amend and Re-enact Section 4695 of the Code of Virginia," *1922 Virginia Acts*, ch. 418 (Act of Mar. 24, 1922), p. 731. I thank my research assistant Abbee Cox for helping to confirm this count.

[85] "Cigarette Smoking," *Idaho Tri-Weekly Statesman*, May 14, 1887, p. 2 (quoting the *Chicago Mail*); "Cigarettes," *New York Times*, Aug. 14, 1887, p. 4; "Cigarettes Analyzed," *Chicago Tribune*, Nov. 16, 1888, p. 9 (reporting an investigation by the *Evening News*). Again I thank Cassandra Tate, who pointed me to the several sources linking cigarettes and narcotics. See Tate, *Cigarette Wars*, pp. 26–27, 166–67 nn.54–55.
[86] "Cigarettes," *Saturday Review*, May 4, 1889, p. 528; Rene Bache, "How Cigarets Are Drugged," *Springfield Republican*, Sept. 17, 1892, p. 3 (apparently reprinting an item from the *Boston Transcript*).

Apparently moved by such reports to weigh banning cigarettes statewide, a joint committee on public health of the Massachusetts legislature set out to assemble the evidence on cigarette adulteration. The fruits of that investigation, issued in 1892 as *The Cigarette: What It Contains and What It Does Not Contain*, included reports by half a dozen academic or government chemists and the live testimony of a seventh. Lead author Harvey Washington Wiley, chief chemist of the U.S. Department of Agriculture, set the tone for the collection. Dismissing with a pen stroke concerns of narcotic adulterants in cigarettes, Wiley declared, "I have examined samples of the following brands of cigarettes . . . and found them entirely free of any trace of arsenic or of opium or any of its active principles." Among the thirteen brands he analyzed and found opium-free were Old Judge and Sweet Caporal, the two deemed opiated by chemist Delafontaine four years before. Years later, as chief architect and enforcer of the Pure Food and Drug Act of 1906, Wiley would become a vigorous antidrug warrior. Still later, as director of *Good Housekeeping*'s Bureau of Foods, Sanitation, and Health, he would brand nicotine "the quickest and most deadly poison known," second only to prussic acid.[87] On the question of adulterants, however, he was no alarmist.

Nor were his coauthors. Georgia state chemist G. F. Payne examined three cigarette brands for both opium and "Indian hemp (hashish)" and found no trace. And Boston chemist James F. Babcock denied "any recognized authority state[s] that [cigarettes] contain cannabis Indica, or any poisonous drug." He too analyzed several brands and found them "all tobacco, nothing but tobacco." Even Monopol cigarettes, made from imported Turkish tobacco, were narcotic free despite "a popular prejudice that Turkish tobacco may contain or does contain opium." Very simply, Babcock said, "The trouble with tobacco is nicotine, that is the poison . . . ." There was no need to condemn cigarettes with talk of "hashish and opium and arsenic and white lead, and other absurdities."[88]

Despite their sterling credentials and confident verdicts, these authors did little to stanch stories of dope-spiked cigarettes. Their 1892 report lay buried in the archives of the Massachusetts legislature and remains unpublished today. Accusations of adulteration therefore continued unchecked till, by 1898, *Scientific American* apparently had seen enough. Writing in its pages under the title, "Cigarettes and Science," John Wallace condemned such rank speculation. He deployed the usual tools of "those accustomed to the methods

[87] W.H. [*sic*] Wiley et al., *The Cigarette: What It Contains and What It Does Not Contain* (Boston: Unpublished Reports to the Joint Committee on Public Health of the Massachusetts Legislature, 1892), pp. 2, 7–8; Harvey W. Wiley, "The Little White Slaver," *Good Housekeeping*, vol. 62, no. 1 (Jan 1916), p. 91. On Wiley, *see* Musto, *American Disease*, pp. 22–23, 34.

[88] Wiley et al., *The Cigarette: What It Contains*, pp. 12–13 (presenting Payne's findings); ibid., p. 16 ("any recognized authority . . ."); ibid., p. 17 ("all tobacco . . ." and "a popular prejudice . . ." and presenting Babcock's Monopol findings); ibid., p. 22 ("The trouble with . . ." and "hashish and opium . . ."); ibid., pp. 28–29 (and presenting further Monopol findings).

of science"—investigation and demonstration. These he unleashed on each of the lay press's allegations about cigarettes, chief among them the charge that cigarettes contain "either in the fillers or in the paper wrappers, opium, morphine . . . cannabis indica, cocaine and other 'appetite kindling drugs.'" If such grave accusations proved false, Wallace warned, their indulgence by "otherwise intelligent minds is evidence of appalling indolence and ignorance." Yet false they proved to be. With a weary "Here are the facts," Wallace laid out "unanimous and therefore conclusive" findings "that no trace of anything except pure tobacco and pure paper entered into the composition of American cigarettes." The *Boston Globe* apparently agreed. It quoted Wallace's conclusions at length even as anti-cigarette legislation lay pending in Massachusetts.[89]

Lucy Page Gaston's Indiana Crusade

Though Massachusetts never banned cigarettes, fifteen other states did, at least briefly. Urging passage of these laws were the Woman's Christian Temperance Union (WCTU) and especially the Anti-Cigarette League of America, a spin-off of the WCTU conceived in 1899 by Frances Willard's friend and protégé, Lucy Page Gaston. Born to a temperance family and rooted in the temperance town of Harvey, Illinois, Gaston was to cigarettes what Willard was to liquor—the opposition's spokesperson, strategist, charismatic leader, and moralizing scold. A 1904 photo depicts her as a drag queen's parody of a church lady—thin faced, thin lipped, high collared, with a grim stare that dared onlookers to comment on her improbably flowered hat. By 1901, her Anti-Cigarette League claimed three hundred thousand members with outposts spanning the United States and Canada. Confronting them across the legislative battlefield were James Duke and his American Tobacco Company, which dominated the cigarette industry till its 1911 breakup under the Sherman Antitrust Act. Duke and his trust deployed legislative and legal might to defeat anti-cigarette laws or repeal them or secure their rejection in the courts.[90]

In Indiana, which outlawed cigarettes in 1905, repealed the ban in 1909, and reopened the question in 1913, both Gaston and the tobacco industry held

---

[89] John Wallace, "Cigarettes and Science," *Scientific American*, vol. 78 (Mar. 12, 1898), p. 173, *quoted in* "On Cigarettes," *Boston Globe*, Mar. 26, 1898, p. 7.

[90] Lee J. Alston et al., "Social Reformers and Regulation: The Prohibition of Cigarettes in the United States and Canada," *Explorations in Economic History*, vol. 39 (2002), pp. 425, 431–32 (noting prevalence of cigarette prohibition nationwide); ibid., pp. 435–36 (describing the rise of the WCTU and Anti-Cigarette League); ibid., pp. 437–38 (reporting American Tobacco's lobbying efforts); Tate, *Cigarette Wars*, p. 39 (noting claimed membership of 300,000); ibid., pp. 39–43 (narrating Gaston's early life and describing her friendship with Willard); ibid., pp. 48–49 (discussing the early history of the Anti-Cigarette League); ibid., p. 92c (presenting a Gaston photo).

footholds. Gaston's anti-cigarette campaign had made her a familiar figure in the local press long before the 1905 ban. After the law's passage she stormed the state promoting the ban's strict enforcement. Both in print and on the ground she focused her reforming efforts on the group targeted by her monthly anti-cigarette magazine, *The Boy*. One among her many strategies fingered telegraph and messenger companies and other firms that hired young men and boys in droves. Gaston lobbied their leaders to forbid messenger boys and other young male staff to smoke, a rule some companies enforced against boys both on and off duty. She also appealed directly to boys, recruiting them to an anti-smoking pledge before their young habit claimed them for life. In a 1911 Chicago news photo, four young men, aged eleven to fourteen, raise their right hands in solemn obeisance to an unsmiling Miss Gaston. Grimly, they intone, "I will not smoke another cigaret" (see Figure 7.6).[91]

In 1906 Gaston appeared in Logansport, Indiana, to lend mettle to the state's year-old anti-cigarette law. The *Logansport Journal*'s seven-column front-page headline announced, "Arch Enemy of Cigaret Begins Campaign Here Today." Her law-enforcement methods proved strikingly modern. Troubled to see "dozens of small boys on the streets smoking the forbidden cigarettes," Gaston dispatched a young scout with instructions to procure papers, tobacco, and cigarettes from local dealers. The lad "returned in a half hour with his pockets bulging" and named six dealers as his sources. These purveyors had made no fuss of the law or of their clientele's youth, but instead were "selling the stuff right along." And the buyers were not the town's ruffians. "All these boys . . . [were] bright faced, well dressed and evidently belonging to well to do homes." Gaston vowed she would demand prompt prosecution and would stay in Logansport till she saw "the alleged offenders hauled before the bar of justice."[92]

Nor did Gaston shrink from tackling Big Tobacco, which she denounced in July 1906 for buying lawmakers' votes. "A Woman Uncovers Alleged Wholesale Bribery in Indiana Legislature," declared one local paper. "Woman Assails Tobacco Trust," headlined another. Yet neither Gaston's labors nor whiffs of

---

[91] "An Act to Regulate and in Certain Cases to Prohibit the Manufacture, Sale, Keeping, . . . Owning, or Giving Away of Cigarettes," 1905 *Indiana Laws*, ch. 52 (Act of Feb. 28, 1905), p. 82; "An Act to Amend . . . 'An Act to Regulate . . . Cigarettes . . . ,'" 1909 *Indiana Laws*, ch. 28 (Act of Feb. 27, 1909), p. 71; Alston et al., "Social Reformers," p. 436 (mentioning Gaston's magazine, *The Boy*); "Must Not Smoke," *Logansport Reporter*, Aug. 21, 1900, p. 3 (reporting Gaston's work with telegraph and messenger companies); "Prisoners of Cigaret War Swearing Fealty," *Chicago Daily Tribune*, Oct. 21, 1911, p. 3. Gaston's anti-cigarette pledge got press in Indiana too. *See* "Waging War on the Cigarette," (Fort Wayne) *Weekly Sentinel*, July 18, 1906, p. 1.

[92] "Arch Enemy of Cigaret Begins Campaign Here Today," *Logansport Journal*, July 8, 1906, p. 1; "Anti-Cigarette Crusade Begun," *Logansport Daily Reporter*, July 9, 1906, p. 1 ("dozens of small . . ." and "returned in a half hour . . ."); "Anti Cigarette Laws," *Logansport Pharos*, July 9, 1906, p. 8 ("selling the stuff . . ." and "All these boys . . ."); "Arrests Will Be Made Tomorrow," *Logansport Daily Reporter*, July 13, 1906, p. 1 ("the alleged offenders . . .").

Prisoners of Cigaret War Swearing Fealty.

[From a photograph taken for THE TRIBUNE]

LUCY PAGE GASTON

" *I WILL NOT SMOKE ANOTHER CIGARET* "

Figure 7.6: "Prisoners of Cigaret War Swearing Fealty" (1911).

scandal could spare Indiana's indifferently policed cigarette ban from repeal. It came down in 1909 after just four years in force and with few fans to mourn its passing. The legislature's passage of the repeal bill—by votes of forty to zero in the Senate and sixty-two to thirty in the House—stirred no perceptible dissent in the press. For all the public record reveals, the repeal bill sped from introduction to passage in barely a month without a fight waged to save the old ban. In its place was put a law against those sales that most troubled Gaston—sales to youth.[93]

[93] "Letters Tell of Crooked Work," *Fort Wayne Journal-Gazette*, July 10, 1906, p. 9 (bearing the subheadline, "A Woman Uncovers..."); "Woman Assails Tobacco Trust," *Fort Wayne Weekly Sentinel*, July 11, 1906, p. 16; "An Act to Amend ... 'An Act to Regulate ... Cigarettes ... ,'" 1909 *Indiana Laws*, ch. 28 (Act of Feb. 27, 1909), p. 71; 1909 *Indiana Senate Journal* (Feb. 17, 1909), pp. 1047–48 (reporting Senate repeal vote); 1909 *Indiana House Journal* (Feb. 25, 1909), pp. 1086–87 (reporting House repeal vote); "House Passes Bill to Repeal State Police Act," *Fort Wayne Sentinel*, Feb. 18, 1909,

The Cigarette–Cannabis Nexus

Even before Indiana jettisoned its cigarette ban in 1909, suspicions that cigarette makers doctored their papers with dope had resurfaced in the state. In 1908, a decade after *Scientific American's* slapdown of rolling-paper rumors, a Logansport paper ran a story headlined "Rice Paper." This French import, "with which cigarettes are made, has nothing to do with rice, but is made . . . more commonly of fine new trimmings of flax *and hemp.*" Months later the same story appeared in Maine's *Kennebec Journal.* Then, after a two-year lag, a rash of copycat accounts showed up in newspapers in Philadelphia, San Francisco, Los Angeles, and several small towns in between. Like most of these newspapers, the *Courier* of Kempton, Indiana, reprinted the 1908 Logansport text largely unchanged, but also assured readers that in the making of cigarette papers, "[o]nly new material—flax and hemp trimmings—is used, and these are thoroughly purified." In June 1911, the *Los Angeles Times* printed this longer version and named a surprising source: *Scientific American.* Indeed a month earlier *Scientific American* had reprinted the enhanced Logansport text almost word for word notwithstanding the magazine's earlier contempt for claims of doped papers.[94]

Catching her cue from one such source or another, Lucy Page Gaston appeared in October 1911 before the Chicago City Council on a mission to broaden an 1897 ordinance she had helped secure. Already the ordinance outlawed cigarettes containing opium and morphine and forbade cigarette sales within two hundred feet of a school. Gaston argued in 1911 that the measure also should ban cigarettes containing hemp and arsenic and a few other substances. "I have heard," she said, "that all these are used in the manufacture of cigarets." Gaston's proposed amendment, which apparently never ripened into law, also sought to end sales of cigarette papers to minors, supplementing an existing ban on cigarette sales to youth.[95]

Meanwhile an advertising motif had emerged in the *Logansport Reporter* and eventually in papers nationwide heralding a new era in cigarette salescraft.

p. 8 (reporting Senate's unanimous repeal vote); "Sunday Ball Vetoed," *Elkhart Daily Review,* Feb. 26, 1909, p. 1 (reporting passage of repeal in the House, but stating no vote); "Dealers Must Now Look Up New Law," *Richmond Morning News,* Mar. 3, 1909, p. 1 (reporting governor's signature).

[94] "Rice Paper," *Logansport Pharos,* Apr. 29, 1908, p. 1 (emphasis added); "Cigarette Paper," *Daily Kennebec Journal,* Sept. 23, 1908, p. 8; "France Makes Most Cigarette Paper," *San Francisco Chronicle,* Oct. 2, 1910, p. 31 (citing the *Philadelphia Record*); "Making Cigarette Paper," *Kempton Courier,* Oct. 21, 1910, p. 3; "Making Cigarette Paper," *Postville* (Ia.) *Review,* Oct. 21, 1910, p. 3; "Cigarette Paper," *Los Angeles Times,* June 24, 1911, p. I12 (reprinting from *Scientific American*); "Cigarette Paper," *Scientific American,* May 13, 1911, p. 491.
[95] "Would Amend Cigaret Law to Curtail Sale of Papers," *Chicago Daily Tribune,* Oct. 31, 1911, p. 2. On the Chicago ordinance of 1897, *see Proceedings of the City Council of the City of Chicago for the Municipal Year 1896–1897* (Chicago: John F. Higgins, 1897), pp. 1714–15 (Mar. 1, 1897); Tate, *Cigarette Wars,* pp. 34, 47, 168 n.80.

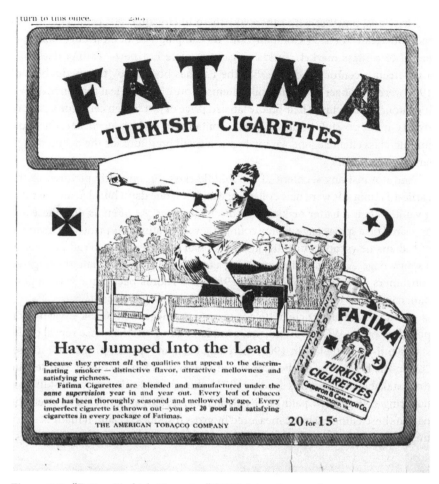

Figure 7.7: "Fatima Turkish Cigarettes" (1909 Advertisement).

On May 7 and May 11, 1909, the *Reporter* printed large display ads announcing "Fatima Turkish Cigarettes." Fatimas "Have Jumped into the Lead," claimed the first ad, which showed a hurdler in mid-flight before admiring spectators (see Figure 7.7). A Fatima box pictured in the ad featured a veiled woman, an Ottoman star and crescent, and the boldfaced words, "*TURKISH CIGARETTES*." "[S]ales have grown within five years from almost nothing to over *one hundred million* a year," claimed the May 11 item. Though a tiny fraction of the six billion cigarettes Americans bought in 1909, Fatima's booming sales seized attention.[96]

[96] "Fatima Turkish Cigarettes," *Logansport Daily Reporter*, May 7, 1909, p. 10; "Fatima Turkish Cigarettes," ibid., May 11, 1909, p. 6; Gottsegen, *Tobacco*, p. 27 tbl. 10 (supplying 1909 national cigarette sales). The Fatima ads that began to appear in Indiana in May 1909 were perhaps the earliest

These ads, together with others like them in city after city, came courtesy of the American Tobacco Company and its campaign to pitch a once-boutique brand to a mass market. Turkish cigarettes were not new—Fatima itself had a nineteenth-century pedigree. But the Fatimas boosted by the media blitz of 1909 were no longer the hand-rolled items of pure Turkish leaf that once drew a high-toned following. Their boldly labeled price of just fifteen cents for a pack of twenty, made possible because Fatimas contained a Turkish *blend*, beckoned to a middle-class clientele, one willing to pay a small premium for the distinction of smoking Turkish.[97]

And not just any segment of the middle class. Prominently pictured in the earliest Fatima ads were hale college-age athletes, one day a hurdler, another day a vaulter, then a batter or kicker or discus thrower. As often as not, these ads appeared on a sports page. By my count of seventy Fatima ads printed in a sample of Indiana newspapers in 1909, just shy of half occupied the top right corner of a sports page. A special offer appearing a few years later made plain the targeted consumers. In February and March 1912, each Fatima pack came with "a pennant coupon, 25 of which secure a handsome felt college pennant."[98]

Perhaps troubled by cigarette ads targeting college men, Culla J. Vayhinger, president of the WCTU of Indiana, complained in 1910 that since repeal of the state's anti-cigarette law in 1909, there had been an "appalling" increase in use. "Upon the boy in the public school and the young man in college, you see the unmistakable marks of this deadly evil." Vayhinger's objections notwithstanding, targeting college men paid off. By September 1909 Fatima declared itself the nation's bestselling cigarette measured by gross revenues, a claim it made at every turn for four years. "You know who started the popularity of Fatima Cigarettes,"

such ads in the nation. I have found none earlier. The second Fatima ad I found, printed four days after the first on May 11, 1909, claimed that "Fatima Cigarettes have never before been advertised . . . ." "Fatima Turkish Cigarettes," *Logansport Reporter*, May 11, 1909, p. 6. I saw no similar claim in any other Fatima ad.

[97] The Fatima brand was consigned to Liggett & Myers after the tobacco trust's breakup in late 1911. Richard B. Tennant, *The American Cigarette Industry: A Study in Economic Analysis and Public Policy* (New Haven: Yale University Press, 1950), pp. 60–61. Richard Tennant noted the heavily Turkish Fatimas were more expensive than some all-domestic brands or "pseudo-Turkish" blends of cheap Turkish and domestic tobacco, but were cheaper than all-Turkish cigarettes. Ibid., pp. 46, 50 & n.61, 157, 159. *Fortune* magazine reported in 1931 that Fatimas were 40% Turkish tobacco and 60% domestic. "Camels of Winston-Salem," *Fortune*, vol. 111, no. 1 (Jan. 1931), p. 45.

[98] "Fatima Turkish Cigarettes," *Logansport Reporter*, May 7, 1909, p. 10 (picturing a hurdler); "Fatima Turkish Cigarettes," ibid., May 11, 1909, p. 6 (pole vaulter); "Fatima Turkish Cigarettes," ibid., May 21, 1909, p. 10 (discus thrower); "Fatima Turkish Cigarettes," ibid., Sept. 6, 1909, p. 6 (football player); "Fatima Turkish Cigarettes," ibid., Oct. 15, 1909, p. 6 (batter); "Fatima Turkish Blend Cigarettes," *Fort Wayne Journal-Gazette*, Feb. 3, 1912, p. 6 (offering pennant coupon); "Fatima Turkish Blend Cigarettes," ibid., Mar. 29, 1912, p. 3 (same). Aided by electronic searching, I counted seventy Fatima ads in the smattering of Indiana newspapers published in 1909 and available online. Of seventy ads, thirty-four occupied the top right corner of a sports page.

began a surprisingly frank entry in the *Indianapolis Star* in August 1912. "It was the college man . . . ."[99]

Together with lesser rivals bearing such names as Omar, Helmar, Mecca, and Turkish Trophies, Fatima fueled a fad for Turkish cigarettes. Sold alongside them were Egyptian-themed varieties dubbed Mogul and Egyptian Deities and the like. "The Turkish or Egyptian cigarette was an unknown quantity in the United States in the early nineties," wrote an editor of the journal *Tobacco* in 1912. "Now the consumption in this country runs up to over five and three-quarter billion cigarettes," accounting for "much over 90 per cent." of total annual cigarette consumption. Other contemporary counts measured Turkish sales more modestly, but all showed a spiking rise from the late 1890s through the early 1910s.[100]

And the steepest ascent lay ahead, for Camel Turkish-blend cigarettes hovered just over the horizon. R.J. Reynolds introduced Camel in autumn 1913 and began advertising the brand in Indiana in July—too late to have shaped the Indiana cigarette and anti-cannabis laws adopted earlier that year, but capable of influencing the many states that acted later. Marketed to compete with Fatima, Camel left its rivals gasping. With a half-billion sold in 1914 and over twelve billion in 1917, the brand claimed at least 35 percent of the market just in time to ride the tidal wave of wartime demand. Camel proudly wore its banner, "Turkish & Domestic Blend," into battle even as war with the Germans and Turks meant its Turkish tobacco no longer grew in Turkey. The irony did not dampen sales. Camel did not doff its crown as America's leading brand till 1930.[101]

[99] "Madam President Vayhinger's Annual Address to Indiana W.C.T.U.," *Fort Wayne Weekly Sentinel*, Oct. 19, 1910, p. 14; "Fatima Turkish Cigarettes," *Fort Wayne Journal-Gazette*, Sept. 6, 1909, p. 6 ("Fatima Cigarettes have become the leading brand everywhere . . . ."); "Fatima," *Indianapolis Star*, Aug. 21, 1913, p. 5 ("Largest selling cigarette on the market."); "Fatima Turkish Blend Cigarettes," ibid., Aug. 20, 1912, p. 4 (referring to the college man). Richard Tennant noted that Fatima "did not attain the volume of Piedmont [a popular all-domestic brand] or of the pseudo-Turkish brands." Tennant, *American Cigarette Industry*, p. 46. Hence Fatima's claim of market leadership was carefully worded to emphasize gross revenues: "The sales tell—more money is spent for Fatima than for any other cigarette." "Fatima Turkish Blend Cigarettes," *Fort Wayne Journal-Gazette*, Nov. 12, 1912, p. 11.
[100] A.B. M'Attammany, "Romance in Cigarette Smoke," *Los Angeles Times*, Feb. 4, 1912, p. III-24 (authored by an associate editor of *Tobacco*); "'Turkish' Goes Up," ibid., June 23, 1910, p. II-13 (reporting the rise in Turkish cigarette sales from fewer than two million in 1904 to 7.2 billion in 1909); Tennant, *American Cigarette Industry*, p. 47 (showing the stunning rise of Turkish and Turkish-blend cigarettes between the late 1890s and early 1910s, but suggesting more modest sales than did M'Attammany); ibid., p. 70 (discussing the proliferation of Turkish and pseudo-Turkish brands after the breakup of the American Tobacco Company in 1911).
[101] Tennant, *American Cigarette Industry*, pp. 76–78 (noting the release of Camel in Cleveland and early success); ibid., p. 287 (noting Camel was introduced to compete with Fatima); Tate, *Cigarette Wars*, p. 107 (reporting Camel's 1917 market share of 35% and the cutoff of Turkish tobacco during the war); Gottsegen, *Tobacco*, p. 192 (putting Camel's market share in 1917 at about 40%). The first Camel ad I've found in Indiana appeared in the *Fort Wayne Journal-Gazette* on July 11, 1913 (p. 26). For an excellent retrospective on the brand and its impact on the industry, *see* "Camels of Winston-Salem," *Fortune*, vol. 111, no. 1 (Jan. 1931), pp. 45–55.

The Indiana Cannabis Ban

Almost from the first arrival of Turkish tobacco on American shores, occasional observers wondered what *else* an herbal Turkish import might contain or conceal. We've seen already the 1887 pronouncement of the *New York Times* that "[t]he wrappers of some Turkish cigarettes are impregnated with opium . . . ." And I've noted chemist James Babcock's 1892 reference to "a popular prejudice that Turkish tobacco may contain or does contain opium."[102] A telling anecdote tucked in a 1912 anti-tobacco tract shows such fears had come home to Indiana—and had shifted focus to cannabis—with ample time to influence events that concern us.

"State Senator Beardsley and wife, of Indiana, took a trip to Egypt." So wrote James J. Jeffreys, a field secretary of Gaston's Anti-Cigarette League, in his *Curse of the Nation* of 1912, a motley array of anti-tobacco salvos rooted in the drug's effects on health, morals, and personal finance. The state senator in question was likely Albert R. Beardsley, who served two terms in the Indiana Senate between 1905 and early 1909. During their travels in Egypt, Jeffreys wrote, Senator Beardsley and his wife noticed children "very carefully sweeping up the *droppings* from the *camels*, and taking the droppings away with them." When the Beardsleys asked what use was made of the droppings, "the guide told them that their sweepings were placed in an oven and dried, then crushed fine and sprinkled with a herb called 'hashish,' then rolled into Cigarettes and imported and sold in this country as Egyptian Cigarettes."[103]

Such alarmist accounts of the refuse of which cigarettes were made were the regular fare of anti-tobacco zealots. Yet the Beardsley story warrants closer scrutiny than others of its ilk. Consider first its source. Albert Beardsley was not just a Hoosier, but one of notoriety and influence. As a successful and prosperous businessman—his Elkhart mansion is now a museum—and the third in his family to hold a seat in the state senate, he claimed attention when he spoke. He spoke with particular credibility on health-related topics, as he had served since 1890 as general manager of the Miles Medical Company, later Miles Laboratories.

---

[102] "Cigarettes," *New York Times*, Aug. 14, 1887, p. 4; Wiley et al., *The Cigarette: What It Contains*, p. 17.

[103] Jeffreys, *Curse of the Nation*, pp. 12, 54. At least four members of the Beardsley family of Elkhart, Indiana, served in the state senate. Charles Beardsley (1827–1878) died long before the 1913 appearance of *Curse of the Nation* and seems unlikely to be the source of the Jeffreys anecdote. James Rufus Beardsley (1829–1902) is a more plausible candidate. But as he served in the state senate in 1875 to 1876 and later as mayor of Elkhart, Indiana, it's unlikely Jeffreys would have referred to him in 1912 as "State Senator Beardsley." Then, too, Andrew Hubble Beardsley (1864–1936) did not win election to the Indiana Senate till 1916 and therefore cannot be our man. So Albert Rapier Beardsley (1847–1924), having served rather recently in the state senate, stands as the likeliest candidate.

He was moreover in the Indiana Senate in 1905 and had voted for the state's hard-fought cigarette ban, deepening his interest in the topic.[104]

Consider as well the timing. Jeffreys' 1912 retelling of Beardsley's account followed closely on a nationwide resurgence of rumors that cigarette papers are composed of "flax and hemp trimmings." Just a year earlier *Scientific American* had reprinted this rumor, circulating in Indiana at least since 1908.[105]

Consider finally the substance of Senator Beardsley's report. The additive he specified was *hashish*, also known as *cannabis indica* or Indian hemp. *Scientific American* had spoken of hemp. So had the *Chicago Tribune*, when it told in January 1912 of Lucy Page Gaston's renewed efforts to persuade the Chicago City Council to amend the city code "concerning the adulteration of cigarets." "Hemp in Campaign Cigars?" the *Tribune* headlined the account. Explaining that "[h]asheesh, an extract of Indian hemp, is used by oriental addicts," the paper said Gaston had sought a ban on cigarettes containing hemp.[106]

Soon the Indiana legislature would inscribe *hemp oil* and *cannabis indica* into its statute books. The critical year was 1913, when Indiana became the nation's third anti-cannabis state and one of four states to join an anti-cannabis wave that spring. We begin on February 10 with State Senator Warren N. Hauck's seemingly unrelated proposal to reinstate Indiana's one-time ban of cigarette manufacture and sales, lifted only four years before. Seeing "little likelihood of this Legislature passing any such drastic regulation as an anti-cigarette bill," fellow senators promptly declared Hauck's proposal doomed. Hauck perhaps foresaw his measure's futility. As if to distance himself from likely defeat, he explained that "he presented the bill at the request of the members of an Indianapolis W.C.T.U. organization."[107]

Though Senator Hauck did not mention Lucy Page Gaston by name, his bill honored her long labors. And when his bid to reinstate Indiana's old cigarette ban predictably hit a legislative reef, the fallback bill likewise reflected Gaston's preaching. Lawmakers replaced Hauck's proposed ban on *all* cigarette sales with a law barring possession or use of cigarettes or rolling papers *by minors*, defined as persons under twenty-one.[108]

---

[104] For Albert Beardsley's personal data, *see* http://www.findagrave.com/cgi-bin/fg.cgi?page=gr&GRid=96472637. On his 1905 vote, *see* 1905 *Indiana Senate Journal* (Feb. 3, 1905), p. 674.

[105] For reprintings of the rolling-papers rumor, *see* note 94 and especially these sources: "Rice Paper," *Logansport Pharos*, Apr. 29, 1908, p. 1; "Cigarette Paper," *Daily Kennebec Journal*, Sept. 23, 1908, p. 8; "Making Cigarette Paper," *Kempton Courier*, Oct. 21, 1910, p. 3; "Cigarette Paper," *Scientific American*, May 13, 1911, p. 491.

[106] "Would Amend Cigaret Law to Curtail Sale of Papers," *Chicago Daily Tribune*, Oct. 31, 1911, p. 2.; "Hemp in Campaign Cigars?" *Chicago Daily Tribune*, Jan. 13, 1912, p. 18.

[107] "Anti-Cigarette Bill Presented in Senate," *Indianapolis Star*, Feb. 11, 1913, p. 8.

[108] "An Act to Prohibit the Selling, Buying, Receiving and Using of Cigarettes...by Minors...," 1913 *Indiana Laws*, ch. 223 (Act of Mar. 14, 1913), p. 643; "May Bar Cigarettes to Persons under Twenty-One," *Indianapolis Star*, Feb. 14, 1913, p. 6 (noting resistance to the cigarette ban and the W.C.T.U.'s acquiescence in an age limit instead).

Six years earlier Gaston had focused her reformist zeal on these young men. "Growing Boys Not Twenty-One," ran an Indiana headline in October 1907, when the state's old cigarette ban was in place. The underlying article told of Gaston's resolution to organize a group of anti-smoking Evansville boys. She urged all boys aged ten and up to "pledge not to use tobacco until they are twenty-one." Even college men were at risk, for "[t]he brightest students are invariably those who are free from the coffin-tack habit." And as for girls, "the cigarette has picked out the fairest and best," mere teens, and made them "cigarette fiends," their brains "stolen by the subtle thief of virtue." Cigarettes are "urging on the once good and pure girl to all the further orgies that follow the insidious poison of the weed . . . ."[109]

In banning cigarette possession by minors, Indiana's 1913 law hardly stood out. Well over half the states already outlawed sales to youth. Senator Hauck's defense of the age line—that cigarette "use in young persons stunts their growth as well as their minds"—likewise was entirely ordinary. More remarkable was the law's generous definition of youth: most states drew the line at age sixteen, as Indiana law had done in 1889. But the *most* noteworthy feature of the new law forbade those under twenty-one to possess "any paper or wrapper containing morphine, nicotine, oil of hemp, or any deleterious or poisonous ingredient." This ban on doped wrappers apparently was part of Hauck's original bill. Though no copy of his bill appears to have survived, a February 11 news account explained that Hauck's proposal "makes it unlawful to manufacture or sell cigarettes anywhere in Indiana [and] . . . states that where the wrappers of cigarettes contain morphine, nicotine or oil of hemp, their sale shall be prohibited." Hence it seems Hauck first conceived of his bill as banning all cigarettes *and* dope-spiked rolling papers, including those spiked with "oil of hemp."[110]

As Hauck's proposed cigarette ban tottered on defeat, Senator Otis L. Ballou stepped in to salvage the component Ballou deemed essential. Ballou represented LaGrange and Noble Counties, just east of Senator Beardsley's Elkhart County in northeastern Indiana, and he shared Beardsley's distress over drugged cigarettes. "Ballou Will Demand 'Dopeless' Cigarettes," the *Indianapolis Star* announced on February 16. The *Star* explained that if Ballou had his way, "[c]igarettes may be

---

[109] "Growing Boys Not Twenty-One," *Washington* (Ind.) *Democrat*, Oct. 29, 1907, p. 4; "Girls' Spirit Goes Up in Smoke," *Logansport Reporter*, Mar. 23, 1909, p. 3.

[110] "An Act to Prohibit the Selling, Buying, Receiving and Using of Cigarettes . . . by Minors . . . ," 1913 *Indiana Laws*, ch. 223 (Act of Mar. 14, 1913), p. 643; "An Act Making It Unlawful to Give, Barter or Sell Tobacco to Certain Children . . . ," 1889 *Indiana Laws*, ch. 131 (Act of Mar. 9, 1889), p. 271; Gottsegen, *Tobacco*, p. 155 (reporting that twenty-six states had banned sales of tobacco products to minors by 1890); "Anti-Cigarette Bill Presented in Senate," *Indianapolis Star*, Feb. 11, 1913, p. 8 (reporting Hauck's original bill); "Anti-Cigarette Bill," *Fort Wayne Daily News*, Feb. 28, 1913, p. 14 ("use in young persons stunts their growth . . ."). My thanks to Alan January of the Indiana State Archives, who supplied copies of the surviving papers associated with Hauck's legislation.

bought and sold as of yore," but "no more 'dope' laden 'smokes' will come into the state."[111]

Ballou deemed it "useless to expect any law to be observed that would prohibit the use of cigarettes entirely." Still, he insisted, two bans were critical. First, because "[a]ny kind of a stimulant is injurious to the young," lawmakers would "cooperate with the women of the W.C.T.U. in restricting [cigarettes'] sale" to youth. "But it seems to me," he said, "that the principal thing is to see to it that the 'dope' variety of cigarettes is kept out of the state," for there was talk "that some of the papers are soaked in drugs." Ballou therefore would seek to amend the bill to demand that all cigarettes and cigarette papers "shall hold a printed guarantee that such cigarettes or papers contain no opium, oil of hemp, or other substances injurious to health." At bottom, then, he aimed to ban all cigarettes for those under twenty-one and to forbid dope-laced cigarettes for everyone.[112]

The fate of Ballou's plan is hard to discern. His hope that all cigarettes and wrapping papers "shall . . . contain no opium, [or] oil of hemp" never found its way into law. As enacted, the cigarette law banned only doped wrappers, not doped cigarettes, and applied only to their possession or use by those under twenty-one. What then became of Ballou's insistence that "no more 'dope' laden 'smokes' will come into the state"?[113] The answer appears to lie in the business of the *other* legislative chamber. For even as Senator Hauck's original bill and Senator Ballou's proposed revision strived to remove cannabis and opiates from cigarettes and wrapping papers, two members of the House sought to rid Indiana entirely of those substances for nonmedical use.

That process began around January 27, 1913. Representative John J. Keegan of Indianapolis introduced a measure to add heroin to the state's list of forbidden narcotics and otherwise update Indiana's antidrug laws, which had banned unprescribed sales of opium, morphine, and cocaine since 1907. Keegan's measure said nothing about cannabis till Representative George S. Sands moved to amend the bill on February 4 to include "cann[a]bis indica" among the outlawed substances. Sands hailed from South Bend in St. Joseph County, which abuts Beardsley's Elkhart County on the west, and he too apparently shared Beardsley's concern about hashish. The House approved his amendment on February 4, but did not pass the whole bill and send it to the Senate till February 14. By then Senator Hauck already had proposed to ban cigarettes and drug-laced rolling papers, including papers infused with "oil of hemp." Both

[111] "Ballou Will Demand 'Dopeless' Cigarettes," *Indianapolis Star*, Feb. 16, 1913, p. 7. For Ballou's district, *see* 1913 *Indiana Senate Journal*, Senators' Index, p. 402.

[112] "Ballou Will Demand 'Dopeless' Cigarettes."

[113] Ibid.; "An Act to Prohibit the Selling, Buying, Receiving and Using of Cigarettes, Cigarette Papers, [or] Cigarette Wrappers . . . by Minors . . . , 1913 *Indiana Laws*, ch. 223, § 1 (Act of Mar. 14, 1913), p. 643.

Hauck's proposal and Ballou's announcement that he would seek to outlaw all dope-spiked cigarettes and wrappers, first reported on February 16, very possibly were made without knowledge of Sands's amendment or the House's action, which seemingly went unreported in the press.[114]

All four of these actors, then, working almost in unison but apparently not in concert, aimed to fortify Indiana's defenses against psychoactive drugs. Three of them—Hauck, Ballou, and Sands—specifically included "oil of hemp" or "cann[a]bis indica" among the drugs they would ban. And Hauck and Ballou shared a particular concern for drug-spiked cigarettes and smoking by youth. Sands's amendment, by adding *cannabis indica* to Keegan's general anti-narcotics bill, effectively mooted Ballou's proposal that all cigarettes be "Dopeless," for banning *all* unprescribed cannabis sales surely banned the drug in cigarettes.

In the end, Hauck's proposed cigarette ban, modified to apply only to smokers under age twenty-one, passed into law with no other apparent change. It forbade youth to buy or have "any cigarette, cigarette paper, cigarette wrapper or any paper or wrapper containing morphine, nicotine, oil of hemp, or any deleterious or poisonous ingredient." Meanwhile Keegan's bill, as modified by Sands's amendment, retained Indiana's existing bans on opium, morphine, and cocaine and added heroin and *cannabis indica* to the forbidden list. Both bills passed readily. Hauck's cigarette measure snagged only three negative votes on its victory march through the legislature. Keegan's anti-narcotics bill, as amended by Sands, drew only one.[115]

What prompted all these men to act at once? Perhaps their sensitivity to drug use and especially drug use among youth traced to the advocacy of Lucy Page Gaston and her unyielding campaign against smoking by boys. Her attempts in 1911 and 1912 to persuade the Chicago City Council to add hemp to the list of substances banned from cigarettes supplied a possible template for similar measures proposed by Senators Hauck and Ballou in 1913. Perhaps former Senator Beardsley's alarm on learning of hashish rolled in Egyptian cigarettes, publicized in Jeffreys' 1912 volume, caught the ear of legislators from abutting counties—Ballou and Sands. Or maybe all these lawmakers took their cue from the recent

---

[114] See "An Act to Amend . . . an Act to Regulate the Sale of Opium, Morphine or Cocaine . . . ," 1907 *Indiana Laws*, ch. 227 (Act of Mar. 9, 1907), p. 430; 1913 *Indiana House Journal*, pp. 487 (Jan. 27, 1913); ibid., pp. 667, 669–70 (Feb. 4, 1913); ibid., pp. 942–43 (Feb. 14, 1913); "Ballou Will Demand 'Dopeless' Cigarettes." My thanks once again to Alan January of the Indiana State Archives, who kindly sent me the entire record of Keegan's bill.

[115] "An Act to Prohibit the Selling, Buying, Receiving and Using of Cigarettes . . . by Minors . . . ," 1913 *Indiana Laws*, ch. 223, § 1 (Act of Mar. 14, 1913), p. 643; "Anti-Cigarette Bill Passed by Senate, 33 to 2," *Indianapolis Star*, Feb. 28, 1913, p. 1; "Anti-Cigarette Bill Goes to Governor for Approval," ibid., Mar. 7, 1913, p. 6 (noting passage in House with a sole dissent); 1913 *Indiana House Journal*, pp. 942–43 (Feb. 14, 1913) (noting passage in the House of Keegan's anti-narcotics bill, as amended by Sands, with a sole dissent); 1913 *Indiana Senate Journal*, pp. 1370–71 (Feb. 28, 1913) (noting unanimous passage in the Senate of the anti-narcotics bill).

spate of news reports about cigarette papers made of "fine new trimmings of flax and hemp."

What seems clear at least is that these lawmakers did *not* act from racial animus and did not relate cannabis or "oil of hemp" to any particular racial or ethnic group. Surviving records disclose not a word about race uttered by either the lawmakers or the press in reporting their work. The only motive that appears was the urgency to protect youth and particularly boys, long thought dangerously fond of cigarettes and therefore vulnerable to whatever drugs they might conceal.

Nor did these lawmakers act alone. Across the country at least nine states acted to outlaw cigarettes doctored with dope or generally "adulterated." Hence when Washington effectively repealed its first-in-the-nation cigarette ban of 1893, then just two years old, lawmakers took care to retain a ban on cigarettes "containing any injurious drug, narcotic or other deleterious matter." In 1930, four years before Mississippi finally forbade cannabis, lawmakers banned all smoked products "in which there is a mixture or compound of the drug Cannabis Indica, commonly known as Mari Juana." Likewise Virginia enacted no general cannabis ban till 1936, but in 1934 added marijuana to the list of substances forbidden in cigarettes and cigarette papers, a list that had included opium since 1910. And though Vermont banned all cannabis sales absent a doctor's prescription in 1915, lawmakers took care in 1935 to outlaw cigarettes or tobacco containing "a mixture or compound of the drug cannabis indica, otherwise known as Indian hemp."[116] As cigarette smoking transcended racial boundaries but skewed strongly toward youth, these laws and others like them seem designed to protect youth, not to spite one or another racial group.

---

[116] "An Act Making It Unlawful . . . to Buy, Sell, or Give Away . . . Cigarettes or Cigarette Paper," 1893 *Washington Laws*, ch. 51 (Act of Mar. 7, 1893), p. 82; "An Act to Provide for the Better Protection of the Public Health in Relation to . . . Cigarettes," 1895 *Washington Laws*, ch. 70, § 5 (Act of Mar. 15, 1895), pp. 125–26; "An Act to Prohibit the Sale . . . [of] Cigarettes, Cigars, or Tobacco . . . in Which There Is a Mixture of the Drug Cannabis Indica . . . ," 1930 *Mississippi Laws*, ch. 13 (Act of Feb. 27 1930), p. 13; "An Act Making It Unlawful to Have in Possession or to Sell . . . Cannabis Indica," 1934 *Mississippi Laws*, ch. 339, § 1 (Act of Feb. 26, 1934), p. 623; "An Act to Prohibit the Use of Opium in the Manufacture of Cigarettes," 1910 *Virginia Acts*, ch. 246 (Act of Mar. 16, 1910), p. 358; "An Act . . . Relating to the Use of Opium, Marihuana, Loco Weed, and Other . . . Hypnotic Drugs," 1934 *Virginia Acts*, ch. 268 (Act of Mar. 28, 1934), pp. 411–12; "An Act to Prohibit the Sale . . . of Drug Known as Derivatives of Plant Cannabis Sativa," 1936 *Virginia Acts*, ch. 212 (Act of Mar. 21, 1936), p. 361; "An Act to Prohibit . . . the Sale, Etc. of Cigarettes . . . Containing Cannabis Indica," 1935 *Vermont Acts and Resolves*, no. 204, § 1 (Act of Apr. 9, 1935), pp. 216–17. Several states banned adulterated cigarettes without specifically mentioning narcotics. *See, e.g.,* "An Act to Provide against the Evils Resulting from the Traffic in Cigarettes . . . ," 1894 *Ohio Acts*, § 6 (Act of May 18, 1894), pp. 311–13 (banning "cigarettes . . . containing any substance foreign to tobacco and deleterious to health"); "An Act to Prohibit the Manufacture, Sale or Use of Adulterated Cigarettes . . . ," 1907 *Minnesota General Laws*, ch. 386, § 1 (Act of Apr. 24, 1907), pp. 544–45 (banning sales of "any cigarette containing any substance foreign to tobacco"). I thank Cassandra Tate and Abbee Cox for directing me to several of these state laws.

The Wyoming Cannabis Ban

Our westward march through the first anti-cannabis states stops now in Wyoming. In late February 1913, two years after Massachusetts opened the anti-cannabis front in America's war on drugs, Wyoming adopted the nation's second statewide ban on unprescribed cannabis sales. Three other states trailed Wyoming in close succession—Indiana by nine days, Maine by seven weeks, and California by four months.

Wyoming hosted more Mexican residents than its Eastern anti-cannabis counterparts—and its Mexican contingent, modest at first, was mounting. In 1910 the state's 328 Mexicans made up a mere 0.23 percent of Wyoming's population of more than 140,000. By 1920, their numbers had swollen to 2,000 out of just over 190,000. Still accounting for barely 1 percent of the total, Mexican newcomers found cold welcome in Wyoming, at least in some quarters. Then as now, labor competition was a fertile source of tension. Hence the earliest evidence I've seen of possible anti-Mexican feeling dates to the big-time mining strikes. In February 1889, the Helena, Montana, *Independent* reported eight Mexican prospectors lay dead near a long-abandoned mine in northern Wyoming. Bearing the page-one headline, "Murdered for Gold," the story told of dead miners robbed of horses and tools.[117]

Clearer evidence of ethnic enmity emerged later, suspiciously close to passage of Wyoming's 1913 anti-cannabis law. The Mexican Revolution had sparked fury as one or another warring band reportedly tormented Americans living south of the border or lobbed assaults at opponents in the States. Mounting tension prompted a racist screed that ran atop the front page of the Pinedale, Wyoming, *Roundup* on April 11, 1912. An editor raged at the "gang of cut-throat robbing greasers," "that dirty gang of Mexicans," who had arrested Americans and confined them in "dirty prisons . . . on fictitious charges." Then followed a threat: "Give Mexico and her citizens collectively and individually 24 hours notice to quit it or wipe 'em off the face of the earth . . . ."[118]

Chilling as this editorial was, it hinted at no link between Mexican rebels or Mexican immigrants and marijuana use. Several broad searches of legislative histories, newspapers, and secondary materials likewise turned up no evidence anti-Mexican feeling prompted Wyoming's 1913 anti-cannabis law. The law's *text* supports no such link. Its sole reference to cannabis was the addition of "Indian hemp" to the state's list of banned intoxicants, which had included cocaine and opium and their derivatives since 1903. Though sometimes used to mean

---

[117] Gibson & Jung, *Historical Census Statistics*, tbl. E-7; "Murdered for Gold," *Helena Independent*, Feb. 10, 1889, p. 1.
[118] "British Flag Protects Americans," *Pinedale Roundup*, Apr. 11, 1912, p. 1.

marijuana, "Indian hemp" typically denoted *cannabis indica*, the plant source of hashish. The 1913 act said nothing of *marijuana, cannabis americana,* or any other term commonly used for the Mexican version of the drug.[119]

The clearest evidence Wyoming lawmakers did not aim their "Indian hemp" ban at marijuana appears in the first Wyoming statute that specifically outlawed the weed. A 1929 act expanded the state's list of forbidden intoxicants to include "Cannabis Americana, commonly known as Marihuana or any compound, derivative, or preparation thereof." To justify the new law's "emergency" status and its immediate effective date, legislators confessed their past oversight: "Whereas there is no adequate law relating to . . . Cannabis Americana and this law is necessary for the immediate preservation of the public peace, health and safety, an emergency is hereby declared to exist . . . ."[120]

Unlike the 1913 "Indian hemp" ban, the 1929 "Marihuana" law perhaps responded to long-simmering anti-Mexican feeling. Wyoming's experience with surging Mexican immigration was then two decades old. Having grown from 328 to 2,000 residents between 1910 and 1920, the state's Mexican American population swelled to 7,174 by 1930. And these figures likely missed the seasonal influx of migrant farmworkers. By the late 1920s, debate about Mexican immigration had taken modern form. Fearing displacement by low-wage labor, many whites looked on Mexican newcomers with resentment and mistrust. Observers more attuned to employers' needs urged the importance of a cheap foreign workforce.[121]

Evidence that ethnic fear and rivalry may have fueled enactment of the 1929 marijuana ban emerges most clearly from a *Wyoming Eagle* article printed January 25, 1929, just three weeks before the law's passage. Seemingly squeezed onto page twelve as the paper went to press, the story consumed but three sentences cast in rough staccato syntax:

---

[119] Wyoming's 1913 act amended sections 2907, 2908, and 2909 of the Wyoming Compiled Statutes of 1910. Those 1910 provisions in turn incorporated Wyoming's 1903 ban on opium, cocaine, and their derivatives. *See* "An Act to Amend and Re-enact Sections 2907, 2908 and 2909 . . . ," 1913 *Wyoming Laws,* ch. 93 (Act of Feb. 26, 1913), p. 101; 1910 *Wyoming Compiled Statutes, Annotated* §§ 2907–2909, p. 749; "An Act Regulating and Restricting the Sale and Use of Delirifacient Drugs . . . ," 1903 *Wyoming Laws,* ch. 98 (Act of Feb. 23, 1903), p. 129. My thanks to several excellent research assistants—Blair Hornstine, Alethea Sargent, and Kathryne Young—and to Karen Kitchens of the Wyoming State Library, all of whom helped me hunt for evidence of a racial motive behind the 1913 Wyoming law and a 1929 Wyoming law I will take up shortly. Our search spanned legislative records, secondary studies, and newspapers printed between 1875 and 1930.

[120] "An Act Relating to . . . Cannabis Americana . . . ," 1929 *Wyoming Laws,* ch. 57 (Act of Feb. 15, 1929), p. 67.

[121] Gibson & Jung, *Historical Census Statistics,* tbl. E-7; "'Kendrick of Wyoming' Gives Account of 12 Years of Service," *Wyoming Eagle,* Oct. 12, 1928, p. 3 (quoting U.S. Senator John B. Kendrick, who told Wyoming laborers he favored admission of Mexican field hands to harvest Western beet fields if they "return to their native country as soon as they have completed their work," for the beet crop fed the state's sugar factories).

Marihuana, "Indian Hemp"

Officials at State Penitentiary, Rawlins, say Marihuana, "Indian Hemp," put majority of Mexican prisoners there. Say Marih[ua]na ad[d]icts not unusual among prisoners from Mexico.

Reports are that Marihuana, weedlike in appearance, is being grown extensively in Colorado and attempts by officials there to stamp out traffic to drive both addicts and growers into Wyoming unless measures taken.

It seems a stretch to suggest so slight a story claimed lawmakers' attention, and I've seen no similar account in other press of the day. Yet the timing hints at a causal role. As first proposed, the 1929 act would have banned peyote and mescal but said nothing of marijuana. Within three weeks after this story ran, the Wyoming House broadened the bill to forbid "Can[n]abis Americana, commonly known as Marihuana." Fifty-four representatives supported the act as amended; none opposed.[122] If this little article did not prompt the change, another like it perhaps did.

In equating "Marihuana" with "Indian Hemp," the story's headline suggests courts may have been applying Wyoming's 1913 ban on "Indian hemp" against those who sold or possessed marijuana. But I've seen no sign of that practice in either the day's press or published appellate court records. Moreover, the legislature's 1929 confession that the state had "no adequate law relating to . . . Cannabis Americana" suggests lawmakers did not equate Indian hemp with marijuana. So if the article quoted is correct—and "Marihuana, 'Indian Hemp,' put majority of Mexican prisoners" in the Rawlins State Penitentiary—it's likely marijuana's causal role was indirect, sending to Rawlins those who thieved to feed their marijuana habit or who first fed their habit, then raged. Either way, this small item in the *Wyoming Eagle* gave lawmakers cause to tighten the old 1913 law. The 1929 act specifically banning "Cannabis Americana, commonly known as Marihuana," presumably was the sort of "measure[]" the *Eagle*'s editor urged in warning of an onslaught of marijuana addicts and growers.

The *Eagle*'s editor was *not* merely seeking tougher penalties for violators of the old 1913 law—or if that was the *Eagle*'s aim, lawmakers weren't listening. For the new act made marijuana sales and possession mere misdemeanors with penalties capped at six months in county jail and $500 fines. The 1913 law had punished

---

[122] "Marihuana, 'Indian Hemp,'" *Wyoming Eagle*, Jan. 25, 1929, p. 12 (reproduced in full and verbatim); 1929 *Wyoming Senate Journal*, p. 406 (Feb. 12, 1929) (reflecting the House's unanimous vote and the Senate's concurrence in the House amendment). My thanks to Karen Kitchens of the Wyoming State Library, who helped me track and interpret the legislative record.

THE WYOMING CANNABIS BAN 397

Indian hemp sales and possession as felonies carrying one to three years in state prison and fines of $500 to $1,000.[123]

So it seems the 1929 law established Wyoming's first marijuana ban. And that ban perhaps responded at least in part to worries that a Colorado crackdown could drive marijuana addicts and growers, many presumably Mexican, into Wyoming. Still it would be hasty to attribute Wyoming's 1929 law to ethnic hatred. If Mexican migrants and their fondness for marijuana brought the drug to Wyoming, they did no more than Chinese newcomers who brought opium smoking to California and its Western neighbors. Each group prompted a ban on its favored drug, but maybe did so only by spreading a substance lawmakers deemed undesirable. As we saw in the context of early bans on opium dens, legislators and law enforcers separated hatred of the Chinese from disgust at their drug and focused their punitive response on the latter.

If ethnic bias need not have spurred Wyoming's 1929 marijuana ban, there's even less reason to attribute the state's 1913 Indian hemp ban to racism. Like several states to its east, Wyoming saw fit in 1913 to ban *another* form of cannabis, one with no link to Mexican arrivals, many years before Mexican migrants prompted the state to ban marijuana. But if not racism, what moved Wyoming's lawmakers to strike out in 1913 against Indian hemp?

The likeliest explanation, familiar to observers of today's lawmaking machinery, is an impulse toward completeness. Having outlawed many recreational intoxicants already, today's legislators ban each newcoming drug almost as soon as they hear of its abuse. Hashish was an odd omission from Wyoming's antidrug scheme of 1903, which plainly intended to reach all recreational intoxicants except alcohol. Beyond banning opium, cocaine, and chloral hydrate by name, the act forbade all their derivatives *and* a catchall chemical category: "any other drug or combination of drugs, the natural effect of which is to induce delirium." Though the statute did not define *delirium*, the term appeared in an 1895 *Webster's Academic Dictionary* as "[a] state in which the thoughts and actions are wild and incoherent."[124]

The 1903 law's reference to drugs that "induce delirium" survived a 1909 amendment, but vanished without explanation from the 1913 act. Instead the 1913 act added by name not only Indian hemp, but several mimics and derivatives of cocaine and opium, including eucaine, morphine, and heroin. Though no reported Wyoming case had addressed the category of delirium-inducing drugs,

---

[123] "An Act to Amend and Re-enact Sections 2907, 2908 and 2909 . . . ," 1913 *Wyoming Laws*, ch. 93, § 2 (Act of Feb. 26, 1913), pp. 101–02; "An Act Relating to . . . Cannabis Americana . . . ," 1929 *Wyoming Laws*, ch. 57, § 2 (Act of Feb. 15, 1929), p. 67.

[124] "An Act Regulating the Sale and Use of Delirifacient Drugs . . . ," 1903 *Wyoming Laws*, ch. 98 (Act of Feb. 23, 1903), p. 129; "Delirium," *in Webster's Academic Dictionary* (New York: American Book Company, 1895), p. 156.

a fair inference from this legislative history is that lawmakers or law enforcers grew wary of defending an arguably vague or overbroad criminal ban based on a concept—*delirium inducing*—that seems absent from the early antidrug laws of every other state and territory. The simplest, clearest remedy was to replace that term with specific substances of concern. That the 1913 act passed by unanimous votes in both houses of the legislature suggests lawmakers may have regarded it as a mere clarification of an existing ban.[125]

Hence as we look west from Wyoming toward California, which in June 1913 became the fifth state to ban unprescribed cannabis, we have yet to spot sound evidence that lawmakers in the first anti-cannabis states acted out of fear of marauding Mexican marijuana fiends. California could prove a critical test case, as it shares a border with Mexico and had in 1910 the nation's third-largest population of Mexican Americans. California's cohort of 48,391 Mexican Americans swamped Wyoming's 328. It fell just shy of Arizona's count of 49,108 and lagged far behind the Texas crowd of 226,466. But as Arizona did not ban cannabis till 1931 and Texas not till 1919, California emerges as the state most likely to expose a link between early anti-cannabis laws and anti-Mexican passions.[126]

The California Cannabis Ban

Long before the public turned its ire on Mexicans and their marijuana, the California legislative record foretold the doom of cannabis-based drugs. As in Wyoming, which sought to ban all drugs that "induce[d] delirium," California's lawmakers set their sights on suppressing all recreational intoxicants. The list of such intoxicants took humble form in an 1872 act regulating pharmaceutical practices in San Francisco. Like later statewide acts in California and states across the nation, the law confined retail sales of "poisons" to registered pharmacists. All poisons had to bear prominent warnings, reinforced orally on sale. The law banned sales of the most dangerous, "Schedule A" poisons unless the pharmacist recorded each sale together with the buyer's name and address and "the purpose for which it is stated by the purchaser to be required." As listed in 1872, Schedule A poisons included such deadly agents as arsenic and cyanide, while cotton

---

[125] "An Act to Amend . . . Section 2222 . . . Prohibiting the Sale of Poisons . . . ," 1909 *Wyoming Laws*, ch. 138, § 3 (Act of Feb. 27, 1909), p. 186; 1913 *Wyoming House Journal*, p. 429 (Feb. 20, 1913) (noting passage of House Bill No. 243, which amended existing antidrug laws, by a vote of 53 to 0); 1913 *Wyoming Senate Journal*, p. 448 (Feb. 22, 1913) (noting passage in the Senate of House Bill No. 243 by a vote of 27 to 0).

[126] Arizona Narcotic Control Act, 1931 *Arizona Laws*, ch. 36, §§ 3, 4, 7 (Act of Mar. 25, 1931), pp. 62–63, 67; "An Act to Amend . . . An Act to Regulate the Sale of Cocaine and Other Drugs . . . ," 1919 *Texas Laws*, ch. 150, § 1 (Act of Mar. 31, 1919), pp. 277–78; Gibson & Jung, *Historical Census Statistics*, tbl. E-7.

root and chloroform typified items in Schedule B. A few substances sometimes abused as recreational intoxicants also appeared—"opium and its preparations" in Schedule A and chloral hydrate in Schedule B.[127]

In a succession of new and broader "pharmacy" and "poison" laws enacted over the next several decades, recreational intoxicants generally emerged in Schedule B, then advanced to Schedule A, and finally joined the growing list of substances banned unless prescribed. Hence in the statewide poison law of 1880, chloral hydrate joined opium in Schedule A, while opium, if smoked in a den, advanced to the banned list in 1881. Having grown suddenly notorious in the 1880s, cocaine made its first appearance in Schedule A of the pharmacy law of 1891, while "chloral" retreated temporarily to Schedule B. The 1907 poison act restored chloral hydrate to Schedule A while removing from that list both cocaine and eaten opium, which the law now banned unless prescribed, together with three opium derivatives—morphine, heroin, and codeine. And making its first appearance anywhere in the California codes, "Indian hemp" effectively joined Schedule B. The law restricted its sale to pharmacies and required warning of its "poisonous" nature, but did not impose the recording requirements of Schedule A. Days later the California legislature placed "cannabis indica" on a different list in parity with better-established recreational intoxicants. The state's pure drugs act of 1907 deemed "mislabeled or misbranded" any drug offered for sale without disclosure of "the quantity of any morphine, opium, cocaine, heroin, alpha or beta eucaine, chloroform, cannabis indica, [or] chloral hydrate."[128]

By 1907, therefore, "Indian hemp" or "cannabis indica" had taken its place alongside other banned drugs and banned drugs in waiting. As the laws of that year and the next several years made clear, drugs deemed merely *poisonous* deserved the added distinction *banned unless prescribed* once their recreational abuse loomed large. Consider the drugs demanding disclosure under the 1907 pure drugs act. The first four—morphine, opium, cocaine, and heroin—all faced bans unless prescribed under the poison law of the same year. All except heroin had achieved recreational notoriety in other states years before. Chloral hydrate, likewise the subject of statewide bans elsewhere, met that fate in California under the poison law of 1909. Two years later, the legislature banned alpha- and beta-eucaine. In its annual report for 1911, the California State Board of Pharmacy

[127] "An Act to Regulate the Practice of Pharmacy in the City and County of San Francisco," 1871–1872 *California Statutes*, ch. 454, §§ 1, 7 (Act of Mar. 28, 1872), pp. 681, 683–84.
[128] "An Act to Regulate the Sale of Certain Poisonous Substances," 1880 *California Statutes,* ch. 94, § 3 (Act of Apr. 16, 1880), pp. 102–03; "An Act . . . Relating to the Sale and Use of Opium," 1881 *California Statutes*, ch. 40 (Act of Mar. 4, 1881), p. 34; "An Act to Regulate the Practice of Pharmacy and Sale of Poisons . . . ," 1891 *California Statutes*, ch. 85 (Act of Mar. 11, 1891), pp. 86, 90; "An Act to Regulate the Sale of Poisons . . . ," 1907 *California Statutes*, ch. 102, §§ 7–9 (Act of Mar. 6, 1907), pp. 124, 126; "An Act for the Prevention of the Manufacture, Sale or Transportation of Adulterated, Mislabeled or Misbranded Drugs . . . ," 1907 *California Statutes*, ch. 186, § 6 (Act of Mar. 11, 1907), p. 230, 231–32.

explained that lawmakers had expanded Section 8 of the poison law, which listed those substances banned unless prescribed, to include "additional habit-forming drugs which have, of late, come into use by drug habitués."[129] Here the board expressed a motivating principle: drugs used recreationally by "drug habitués" deserved the stamp *banned unless prescribed.*

Arguably, this principle should have nabbed cannabis in 1911. Though some modern observers doubt the drug's addictive potential, early reports of hashish and marijuana often and rather casually deemed them "habituating" or "addictive." Cannabis nonetheless eluded the expanded ban of 1911, most likely by flying beneath public notice. Recreational use of hashish in New York, Persia, and other faraway places had captivated California readers of the nineteenth-century. Between 1880 and 1900, the *San Francisco Chronicle* and *Los Angeles Times* printed a collective twenty-one articles on the topic, most in the *Chronicle.* Then the *Chronicle* lost interest, producing just two stories on recreational cannabis between 1900 and passage of the state's 1913 cannabis ban, which itself went unreported. Those two stories addressed hashish use in the Middle East and marihuana use in Mexico. The latter article, relating the scary "effects of smoking the marihuana weed" and the Mexican government's efforts to ban the drug, would be significant but for its August 1907 printing—too late to have prompted the appearance of cannabis in the poison and pure drugs acts of March 1907 and too early to have prompted the drug's 1913 ban.[130]

Coverage in the *Los Angeles Times* proved denser but still too sporadic and ill timed to supply a probable motive for anti-cannabis lawmaking. Between 1900 and passage of the 1913 ban, the paper printed eight stories on recreational cannabis—two concerning hashish in Egypt or India and six touching cannabis use among Mexicans or Mexican Americans. Of these six, two appeared in late 1907 or 1908, unable to affect the March 1907 acts and unlikely to have spurred the 1913 ban. A third story dealt prominently with morphine, not cannabis, adding only a single sentence about "E. Rodriguez, who was detected trying to smuggle some marihuana to prisoners in the East Side Jail . . . ." Of the remaining three articles, one appeared in March 1905 and another in February 1906. Though they surely could have influenced the 1907 lawmaking, only the latter concerned marihuana use in the United States. It consisted of three short,

---

[129] "An Act to Amend . . . 'An Act to Regulate the Sale of Poison . . . ,'" 1909 *California Statutes,* ch. 279, § 4 (Act of Mar. 19, 1909), pp. 422, 424; "An Act to Amend . . . 'An Act to Regulate the Sale and Use of Poisons . . . ,'" 1911 *California Statutes,* ch. 583, § 1 (Act of Apr. 25, 1911), p. 1106; California State Board of Pharmacy, *Report of the California State Board of Pharmacy for the Fiscal Year Ending June 30, 1911* (Sacramento: Superintendent of State Printing, 1912), p. 22.

[130] "Bar Smoking of Marihuana," *San Francisco Chronicle,* Aug. 4, 1907, p. 50; "The Hashish Drug of Greece," ibid., Feb. 8, 1908, p. 6. For examples of reports deeming cannabis drugs addictive, *see* "Local Hashish Eaters," *San Francisco Call,* June 24, 1895, p. 1 ("In Turkey, Egypt, and Arabia high and low are addicted to the [hashish] habit . . . ."); "Bar Smoking of Marihuana" (writing of a young American "addicted to the use of" marijuana).

page-sixteen paragraphs describing Decorso Gomez's crimes and mentioning drugs only once: "Gomez is said to 'go crazy' at times, and the Mexicans say he smokes a 'loco' weed, which unbalances his mind."[131]

That leaves a single story that genuinely might have influenced the 1913 cannabis ban—an October 1911 account to which I'll return.[132] Ultimately, however, the rarity of these reports belies the notion that public fear of pot-crazed Mexicans drove anti-cannabis lawmaking in California. So little did the public and press fret about cannabis that its ban seemingly escaped notice altogether. I have discovered no press account of the 1913 amendments to the poison law hinting at the act's anti-cannabis component. Some force besides public panic about marijuana abuse must have driven legislators to act.

The Lure of Completeness

As in Wyoming, that force likely was a legislative urge toward completeness. Having outlawed a handful of recreational intoxicants in 1907, the California legislature predictably stood poised to ban each new mind-numbing euphoriant as it came along. Wyoming's lawmakers expressed that urge with their 1903 law targeting certain specified drugs and any other drug "the natural effect of which is to induce delirium." The Watch and Ward Society's 1912 Model Law likewise banned several named drugs along with "any other narcotic or hypnotic drug"— where *hypnotic*, a synonym of *narcotic*, emphasized a drug's soporific qualities.[133]

A readiness to ban all comers had rational roots. Lawmakers seeking to suppress recreational intoxicants and their mind-numbing pleasures had to guard against substitute euphoriants. That concern helped prompt New York City's cannabis ban of July 1914, adopted four weeks after the state's ban on opium, morphine, and heroin took effect. In reporting the cannabis ban, the *New York Times* called the substance "Cannabis indica, which is the Indian hemp from which the East Indian drug called hashish is manufactured." The paper's emphasis on hashish suggests officials did not act out of fear of migrant Mexicans and their marijuana. A brief editorial the next day stressed instead the completeness principle: the city's action was "only common sense. Devotees of hashish

---

[131] "Delirium or Death," *Los Angeles Times*, Mar. 12, 1905, p. V20; "Arrested a Bad Mexican," ibid., Feb. 12, 1906, p. I16; "Murder 'Bug' in the Drug?" ibid., Aug. 4, 1907, p. V13; "Hasheesh," ibid., Nov. 17, 1908, p. I3; "The Road Is Open," ibid., May 16, 1912, p. II7 (telling of E. Rodriguez).

[132] *See* "Would Prohibit Sale of Weed," ibid., Oct. 19, 1911, p. I16.

[133] "Model Law," § 3, *in* Chase et al., *The Dope Evil*, p. [30]. On the definition of *hypnotic, see Webster's Academic Dictionary* (1895), p. 279, which offers as a first definition, "Tending to produce sleep; soporific," but also offers the meaning, "an opiate; soporific; narcotic," when the word is used as a noun.

are now hardly numerous enough here to count, but they are likely to increase as other narcotics become harder to obtain."[134]

This substitution risk also troubled Dr. Hamilton Wright, appointed in 1908 as one of three members of a national opium commission. Advocating unsuccessfully for a federal cannabis ban in 1909, Wright reasoned that addicts deprived of their opium and chloral "will feel that they must adopt something to take the place of the[ir] 'dope' . . . . Hasheesh, of which we know very little in this country, will doubtlessly be adopted . . . if they can get it." Wright repeated this rationale in a 1911 letter to Henry J. Finger, a longtime member of the California Board of Pharmacy. Wright told Finger he "anticipated some time ago that in event of our securing Federal control of the sale and distribution of morphine and cocaine, the fiends would turn to Indian hemp . . . ."[135]

If this simple urge toward completeness triggered California's 1913 cannabis ban, two stray facts fall in place. First is the ho-hum housekeeping attitude taken by lawmakers in passing the law and by the press in reporting it. Both houses of the legislature acted unanimously and with no apparent debate. And though scattered news reports may have eluded my search, the press appeared indifferent toward the 1913 law and unaware of its anti-cannabis component.[136]

The second stray fact is the striking synchrony of four far-flung state legislatures, all choosing early in 1913 to join an anti-cannabis bandwagon with only Massachusetts aboard. On three successive Tuesdays, lawmakers introduced the relevant measures—in California on January 28, in Maine and Indiana on February 4, and in Wyoming on February 11. Legislative gears cranked quickly in Wyoming and Indiana, slowly in Maine and California, both mixing and spreading dates of final passage.[137] But the rat-a-tat start dates suggest lawmakers

[134] "Muzzles the Dogs All the Year 'Round," New York Times, July 29, 1914, p. 6; "Topics of the Times: Sanitary Code Amendments," ibid., July 30, 1914, p. 8. For the text of the ordinance, see "Health Board Balks New Drug Evil Scheme," Pawtucket Times, July 29, 1914, p. 16 (reprinting the New York City ordinance, apparently in full); The Code of Ordinances of the City of New York (New York: Brooklyn Daily Eagle, 1917), vol. 32, ch. 20, art. 8, § 126, p. 116 (incorporating the new ordinance into the city's Sanitary Code).

[135] Musto, American Disease, pp. 31–32 (describing Wright's appointment and early role); "Nations Uniting to Stamp Out the Use of Opium and Many Other Drugs," New York Times Magazine, July 25, 1909, p. 4 (quoting Wright); Hamilton Wright to Henry J. Finger (July 11, 1911), "Records of U.S. Delegations to the International Opium Commission and Conferences of 1909–1913," Record Group 43, Entry 40 (Correspondence between Hamilton Wright and Henry J. Finger) (National Archives), quoted in Dale H. Gieringer, "The Forgotten Origins of Cannabis Prohibition in California," Contemporary Drug Problems, vol. 26, no. 2 (Summer 1999), pp. 237, 253, 278 n.75. On Finger and his interactions with Wright, see ibid., pp. 250 to 253. Dr. Gieringer, author of the richest history of California's early anti-cannabis laws, was my guide to many sources.

[136] See 1913 California Assembly Journal, pp. 2141–42 (Apr. 25, 1913) (reporting unanimous passage of A.B. 907); 1913 California Senate Journal, p. 2912 (May 11, 1913) (same). Gieringer writes simply, "The 1913 law received no attention from the press or public." Gieringer, "Forgotten Origins," p. 238. Two of my research assistants, Helen Kim and Alethea Sargent, hunted for contemporary commentary on California's 1913 cannabis ban and discovered none.

[137] See 1913 California Assembly Journal, pp. 285, 288 (Jan. 28, 1913) (reporting Assemblyman Sutherland's introduction of A.B. 907); 1913 Maine Legislative Record—House, p. 270 (Feb. 4,

in each state had stood poised at their legislative gates, ready to mend their antidrug defenses as soon as the session opened.

Yet even if lawmakers stood poised to act once the cannabis threat came in view, the question remains: What brought it in view? Especially in Wyoming and California, no clear answer emerges from legislative histories and news reports and other documentary evidence. Still, many events *could* have brought cannabis to lawmakers' minds. Perhaps the plainest was passage of Frank Chase's 1911 anti-cannabis law in Massachusetts. The Bay State's new law could have roused lawmakers elsewhere to question antidrug codes that left cannabis unscathed. As legislators in Maine, Indiana, Wyoming, and California met only in odd-numbered years, they had the better part of two years to catch the news from Massachusetts and resolve to act.

Or these legislators and Chase himself could have heard about the Foster bill, a failed federal bid to outlaw opiates, cocaine, chloral hydrate, *and* cannabis, introduced in Congress in April 1910 by Representative David Foster of Vermont. The Foster bill died early in 1911, a victim of the pharmaceutical industry's impassioned resistance and Foster's refusal to allow over-the-counter sales of low-dose proprietary remedies.[138] Even in failing, however, the bill's prominent vetting of a cannabis ban could have caught the notice of lawmakers countrywide.

A second national cannabis alert followed just over a year later. Hamilton Wright, whose role in conceiving national narcotics policy made him the antidrug czar of his day, heeded his own warning that drug addicts deprived of their usual dope might turn to hashish instead. In mid-1912 he joined arms with New York Congressman Francis Burton Harrison in crafting what later became the Harrison Narcotic Act of 1914. Wright served as principal draftsman and chief negotiator with the drug trades, while Harrison shepherded the bill through Congress. Their first effort, which Harrison introduced in the House in June 1912, targeted cannabis together with opium, morphine, and cocaine. Like the Foster bill, this original Harrison bill offered no shelter to low-dose proprietary remedies. Predictably the bill died where it dropped, in the House Ways and Means Committee, when the drug trades turned against it in force. A second attempt in January 1913 met largely the same fate. Pressed by Harrison to find terms with the National Drug Trade Conference, a legislative watchdog for the

1913) (reporting Rep. Clark's introduction of Maine's anti-cannabis bill); 1913 *Indiana House Journal*, pp. 667–70 (Feb. 4, 1913) (recording introduction and House passage of Rep. Sands's amendment to H.B. No. 277, adding the words "cannabis indica"); 1913 *Wyoming House Journal*, pp. 261, 265 (Feb. 11, 1913) (recording Rep. Hopkins's introduction of anti-cannabis bill). The bills became law in Wyoming on February 26, Indiana on March 6, Maine on April 12, and California on June 11.

[138] On the Foster bill and its fate, *see* Musto, *American Disease*, pp. 41–50.

trade groups, a reluctant Wright rolled back his draft's offending provisions in a May 1913 compromise. Casualties included the cannabis ban, which trade groups deemed needlessly restrictive of harmless cannabis ointments and corn cures.[139] State lawmakers perhaps followed and anticipated these events, for many acted quickly to fill the breach. Four states banned cannabis in 1913, two more in 1915, another two in 1917. By decade's end, eleven had entered the anti-cannabis ranks.

Yet another possible trigger of the 1913 surge in anti-cannabis lawmaking was the head-turning 1912 monograph, *An Essay on Hasheesh*. Distinguished by both its author, a Columbia University pharmaceutical chemist, and its publisher, the reputable Medical Review of Reviews, Victor Robinson's literary romp had the imprimatur of science and the titillation of pulp. Rather too candidly Robinson told of experimental injections of family, friends, a student, and himself. Cannabis sent Robinson "float[ing] into the outside air" and "sail[ing] dreamily along, lost in exquisite intoxication." And then there was sex. Like Dr. John Jones, who marveled two centuries before of opium's power to excite *"Venereal Fury,"* Robinson reported that on testing hashish, he grew "sensual unto satyriasis. The aphrodisiac effect is astonishing in its intensity. . . . Hot and blissful I float thru the universe, consumed with a resistless passion" and enchanted by visions of "dancing maidens with their soft yielding bodies, white and warm. I am excited unto ecstasy." Happily, he noted, cannabis cured not only impotence but gonorrhea too.[140]

Robinson's homage to cannabis hardly prolonged the drug's lawful sale. The cannabis of his description did not merely brighten a meal or lighten a conversation, as might moderate drinking. Rather, it supercharged the passions, displacing reason with base pleasure and loosing reality's earthly bonds. Again and again we have seen that absent a morally legitimate claim of need, such mindless euphoria disqualifies the substance that kindles it from moral use and lawful sale. Like Dr. Jones's paean to opium, Robinson's *Essay on Hasheesh* made the moral case for a ban.

---

[139] David T. Courtwright, *Dark Paradise: Opiate Addiction in America before 1940* (Cambridge: Harvard University Press, 1982), pp. 104–05 (tracing the early history of the Harrison Act); Musto, *American Disease*, pp. 45–48, 54–61 (describing trade group influence and resulting negotiations); *Congressional Record*, 62d Cong., 2d Sess., p. 7947 (June 10, 1912) (reporting introduction by Rep. Harrison of House Resolution 25239); *Congressional Record*, 62d Cong., 3d Sess., p. 1812 (Jan. 20, 1913) (reporting introduction by Rep. Harrison of House Resolution 28277).

[140] Victor Robinson, *An Essay on Hasheesh Including Observations and Experiments* (New York: Medical Review of Reviews, 1912), pp. 32–34 (supplying cannabis-based formulae for drugs to fight gonorrhea and impotence); ibid., p. 66 ("float[ing] into the . . ."); ibid., p. 68 ("sail[ing] dreamily along . . ."); ibid., p. 69 ("sensual unto satyriasis. . . ."); ibid., p. 71 ("dancing maidens . . ."); John Jones, *The Mysteries of Opium Reveal'd* (London: Richard Smith, 1700), p. 189. Robinson's essay also appeared in 1912 in the pages of the *Medical Review of Reviews. See Medical Review of Reviews*, vol. 18 (1912), pp. 159–69, 300–13.

And unlike the opium of Dr. Jones's day, cannabis could stake no claim that "medicine would be a cripple without it." Medical authorities of the early twentieth century assigned cannabis comparatively few curative roles, chief among them treating corns. "Not many drugs are used for both the brain and the feet," Robinson mused, "but with cannabis we have this anomaly: a man may see visions by swallowing his corn-cure." Even if lawmakers regarded corn cures highly, the law could spare them from broader bans by either exempting low-concentration ointments or permitting sales by prescription. All six of the first statewide anti-cannabis laws, as well as forty-two of the remaining forty-four, took one tack or the other or both.[141]

Any of these texts—Foster's failed 1910 bill or Chase's 1911 anti-cannabis act or Harrison's failed 1912 bill or Robinson's raucous 1912 essay—could have fixed lawmakers' gaze on the long-neglected specter of hashish, hovering just offshore. Moved to craft more complete drug bans, lawmakers in several states acted at once to splice cannabis into existing lists of forbidden agents. In California this completeness principle amply explains the state's 1913 ban.

Yet doubts nag. For a number of stray facts force into view in California a competing narrative, one that gives more solace to those who seek a racial account of early anti-cannabis laws. So let us look more closely at the origins of California's 1913 law, a story best told through its characters' eyes.

California's 1913 Anti-Cannabis Law—The Lawmakers

By any measure the 1913 law was well born. Both Assembly sponsor William Angus Sutherland and Senate sponsor Edward K. Strobridge were broadminded Republicans of broad influence and reformist views, cozily allied with Progressive Governor Hiram W. Johnson. Both were prolific lawmakers. In the 1913 session that gave rise to the state's first anti-cannabis law, Sutherland introduced fifty-six other bills, Strobridge at least forty-five. Sutherland claims paternity of the anti-cannabis law that concerns us, as his bill, introduced in the Assembly on January 28, survived the legislative gantlet into law. Strobridge's apparently identical Senate bill, though launched five days earlier, ultimately yielded to Sutherland's

[141] Thomas Sydenham, *Medical Observations Concerning the History and the Cure of Acute Diseases* (1676), *reprinted in The Works of Thomas Sydenham*, vol. 1 (R.G. Latham ed., London: Sydenham Society, 1848), p. 173; Robinson, *Essay on Hasheesh*, p. 32. The Massachusetts anti-cannabis law of 1911 spared use authorized by a doctor's prescription, as did the Wyoming and Indiana acts of 1913. California's 1913 act exempted corn remedies, while Maine's and Vermont's laws exempted both ointments for external use and sales prescribed by a physician. 1911 *Massachusetts Acts*, ch. 372, §§ 1, 3 (Act of Apr. 29, 1911), pp. 359–60; 1913 *Wyoming Laws*, ch. 93, § 1 (Act of Feb. 26, 1913), p. 101; 1913 *Indiana Laws*, ch. 118, § 1 (Act of Mar. 6, 1913), p. 306; 1913 *California Statutes*, ch. 342, § 6 (Act of June 11, 1913), pp. 692, 697; 1913 *Maine Acts*, ch. 211, §§ 3, 6 (Act of April 12, 1913), pp. 300–02; 1915 *Vermont Acts and Resolves*, no. 197, § 1 (Act of Mar. 12, 1915), p. 336.

measure. Neither man seemed deeply invested in the anti-narcotics bill he sponsored. Perhaps neither man even understood that the law he championed would extend the state's antidrug dragnet to "hemp" and "loco-weed." It seems instead each played power broker for the law's true progenitor, the California Board of Pharmacy.[142]

As "Gov. Johnson's right-hand man in the lower house," Sutherland held sway as the Assembly's chief powerbroker. He was, in the words of the *San Francisco Chronicle*, "the man looked to to do things in the lower house." His role as go-to man likely explains why the Board of Pharmacy tapped him to sponsor a bill proposing a series of amendments to the state's poison law. One such amendment extended a rule forbidding possession of drug paraphernalia to "extracts, tinctures, or other narcotic preparations of hemp, or loco-weed."[143]

His power to one side, Sutherland seemed an unlikely parent of the pharmacy board's bill. Though he practiced law for fourteen years before entering the Assembly, he seems rarely or never to have soiled his soles in the criminal courts. His Fresno-based practice instead consigned his Stanford legal training to the causes of bankers, big growers, and others with the power to pay. His move to Sacramento apparently broadened Sutherland's mind. His legislative interests traversed the legal landscape and extended beyond law to commerce, public works, utility regulation, and ownership of real property by noncitizens,

---

[142] "At the Parting of Their Ways," *Los Angeles Times*, Sept. 26, 1912, p. I 2 (reporting that Sutherland served on the Progressive Party's platform subcommittee and read the platform to the party's convention); "The Political Watchtower," ibid., Oct. 11, 1912, p. II 12 (deeming Sutherland a Bull Moose candidate for the Assembly); "Many Will Attend Convention of Bell," *San Francisco Chronicle*, Nov. 30, 1912, p. 11 ("Sutherland says that he is a Republican and will remain a Republican."); 1913 *California Assembly Final History*, p. 518 (reflecting fifty-seven bills introduced by Sutherland); 1913 *California Senate Final History*, p. 19 (reflecting forty-six bills introduced by Strobridge). My conclusion that the two men's bills were identical or nearly so rests on a comparison of the law finally enacted, which grew from Sutherland's Assembly Bill 907, with Senate Bill 630, which Strobridge introduced on January 23, 1913. *See* 1913 *California Senate Final History*, p. 249 (setting out the title of Strobridge's measure); California Senate Bill No. 630 (Jan. 23, 1913). If modified by the series of eighteen amendments to Sutherland's Assembly bill adopted on April 14, Strobridge's bill would accord with the final act almost word for word. 1913 *California Assembly Journal*, pp. 1514–16 (Apr. 14, 1913) (reprinting eighteen amendments to Sutherland's bill). Strobridge's bill died in committee without amendment. 1913 *California Senate Final History*, p. 249 (reporting January 27 transmission to committee as the end of S.B. 630's history); 1913 *California Assembly Final History*, p. 537 (noting A.B. 907's passage by both houses and final gubernatorial approval on June 11). On the Board of Pharmacy's role behind the anti-cannabis act, *see* Karl M. Anderson, "Urges Revision of Criminal Procedure," *San Francisco Chronicle*, Jan. 29, 1913, p. 2 (Sutherland's bill "carr[ied] out some of the ideas of the State Board of Pharmacy.").

[143] Lou Guernsey, "Three Hundred Bills Ready to Introduce," *Los Angeles Times*, Jan. 12, 1913, p. I 5 ("Gov. Johnson's right-hand man . . ."); Karl M. Anderson, "Minimum Wage Bill Confronts Solons," *San Francisco Chronicle*, Mar. 31, 1913, p. 3 ("the man looked to . . ."); "Plan Submitted to Abolish the Legislature," ibid., Apr. 24, 1913, p. 3 (deeming Sutherland "the real leader of the House"); Karl M. Anderson, "Proposed Increase of Tax on Some Corporations," ibid., Jan. 16, 1913, p. 3 (noting Sutherland's chairmanship of the Revenue and Taxation Committee); "Deny a Deficit of State Cash," *Los Angeles Times*, Jan. 21, 1913, p. I 6 (identifying Sutherland as co-chair of the Joint Committee of the Senate and Assembly).

which he opposed. The storm of bills he sponsored in 1913 included many related to crime and criminal trials, as well as a noncriminal measure that hints of a broader interest in substance abuse and treatment. That bill, providing for construction of a hospital for alcoholics and drug addicts, suggests Sutherland contemplated a medical remedy for much drug use then punished as crime.[144]

A deeper search for Sutherland's attitudes toward cannabis abuse confronts this frustration: no evidence I've seen suggests Sutherland knew the pharmacy board's bill included an anti-cannabis clause. The bill's critical language followed four and a half pages of dense type and lay tangled in terms addressing opium-smoking paraphernalia:

> The possession of a pipe or pipes used for smoking opium (commonly known as opium pipes) or the usual attachment or attachments thereto, *or extracts, tinctures, or other narcotic preparations of hemp, or loco-weed,* their preparations or compounds (except corn remedies containing not more than fifteen grains of the extract or fluid extract of hemp to the ounce, mixed with not less than five times its weight of salicylic acid combined with collodion), is hereby made a misdemeanor . . . .

Little wonder the *Chronicle*, in reporting Sutherland's introduction of this measure, referred only to its impact on "smoking opium and opium smoking paraphernalia" and said nothing of hemp or locoweed. As Sutherland introduced twenty-three other bills the same day, he perhaps read this one as carelessly as the *Chronicle* reporter. And if, as the *Chronicle* claimed, the anti-cannabis bill "carr[ied] out some of the ideas of the State Board of Pharmacy," Sutherland perhaps didn't write the bill at all.[145]

Senate sponsor Edward K. Strobridge, a Hayward fruit grower, may well have shared Sutherland's ignorance of the new law's anti-cannabis command. Yet Strobridge's record, which reveals a moralizing lawmaker intent on protecting innocent youth, supplies better grounds than Sutherland's to suspect a commitment to rid the state of recreational cannabis. When the Senate weighed a bill enabling local authorities to close bars between 1 a.m. and 5 a.m., Strobridge implored his colleagues "to protect the young men and women who go wrong

---

[144] "Urge Passage of the Anti-Alien Land Bill," *San Francisco Chronicle*, Jan. 28, 1911, p. 3; Anderson, "Urges Revision of Criminal Procedure" (noting several of Sutherland's bills bearing on crime, sentencing, and criminal procedure and reporting as well his proposal for an addiction-treatment hospital); 1913 *California Assembly Journal*, pp. 287–88 (Jan. 28 1913) (noting Sutherland introduced A.B. 906 to establish a state hospital for inebriates near Stockton and A.B. 908 to govern the commitment of inebriates to the state hospital).

[145] "An Act to Amend . . . 'An Act to Regulate the Sale and Use of Poisons . . . ;'" 1913 *California Statutes*, ch. 342, § 6 (Act of June 11, 1913), pp. 692, 697 (emphasis added); Anderson, "Urges Revision of Criminal Procedure."

in the early-morning hours." He introduced a measure calling for athletic and military training in high schools and physical culture and manual training in the lower grades. He offered bills to distribute free textbooks to schoolchildren and "to establish a State Censor Commission to censor moving picture films." He drew headlines by revealing the crumbling, unsafe conditions at the Whittier Reform School, where engineers had condemned the facility after a falling chimney killed a boy inmate. Strobridge introduced an "urgency measure" that provided for the immediate nighttime removal of the boys by chartered train. And turning to the girls' side of the Whittier School, he worried the young women endured the "auto flirtation" of passing motorists.[146]

As a moralizing crusader saving youth from corruption, Strobridge could have claimed J. Frank Chase's West Coast mantle. Perhaps he, like Chase, expressed his concern for youthful morals by adding cannabis to the state's anti-narcotics law regime. Yet if the legislation reflected "the ideas of the State Board of Pharmacy," as the *Chronicle* suggested, the board perhaps sought Strobridge's sponsorship to tap his vast legislative influence and access to the governor's ear, not because of any pointed interest Strobridge had in the topic.[147]

Whether we choose Sutherland or Strobridge as our guide, therefore, our hunt for the motives behind the state's 1913 cannabis ban leads us to the gates of the Board of Pharmacy.

California's 1913 Anti-Cannabis Law—The Pharmacists

For all that appears, very few Californians realized an anti-cannabis clause lay tucked in the folds of the 1913 poison bill—and it seems all who noticed were pharmacists. The most influential among them were the seven members of the state's Board of Pharmacy, all appointed by the governor to four-year terms. In 1912, two of the seven hailed from the Southern California towns of Santa Barbara and Pasadena and one from Fresno in the state's Central Valley. All the

---

[146] *See* 1913 *California Senate Final History*, p. 172 (noting Strobridge's introduction of S.B. 251 to supply free textbooks to schoolchildren); ibid., p. 343 (and of S.B. 1126 to establish a State Censor Commission); ibid., p. 450 (and of S.B. 1733 to remove boys from the Whittier State School); Lou Guernsey, "California to Embark in Insurance Business," *Los Angeles Times*, Apr. 10, 1913, p. I 2 ("to protect the young men . . ."); "New Measures in the Senate," *San Francisco Chronicle*, Jan. 30, 1913, p. 3 ("physical culture and manual training . . ."); Lou Guernsey, "Move Whittier Boys to the School at Ione," *Los Angeles Times*, Apr. 3, 1913, p. I 7 (describing Strobridge's "urgency measure"); "Whittier School Will Be Moved," *San Francisco Chronicle*, Mar. 25, 1913, p. 7 ("auto flirtation").

[147] If we may trust the *Chronicle*, Strobridge secured the chairmanship of the Senate Finance Committee, "the most important committee of the Legislature," as a reward for supporting the governor's preferred candidate in the 1910 election for U.S. Senator. The *Chronicle* flayed Strobridge as one of the governor's "Subservient Tools." "Hiram Finds Jobs for Relatives and Subservient Tools," *San Francisco Chronicle*, Oct. 31, 1914, p. 9; Anderson, "Urges Revision of Criminal Procedure" (noting Sutherland's bill "carr[ied] out some of the ideas of the State Board of Pharmacy").

rest lived or practiced in the Bay Area—two in San Francisco, one in Livermore, another in Alameda. Even the Santa Barbara member, Henry J. Finger, was born in San Francisco and started his career at a Redwood City drugstore. And the Bay Area was home to both outgoing board president J. O. McKown of Livermore, and incoming president George M. Sutherland, a longtime Alameda pharmacist with no apparent family tie to Assemblyman William A. Sutherland. Even the board's base by law was in San Francisco.[148]

The Bay Area's dominance of the Board may matter, for the specter of marijuana abuse and pot-crazed Mexicans rarely shadowed life near the Bay. My searches have turned up only one reference to nearby marijuana use before introduction of the anti-cannabis bill in January 1913. First printed in one or another San Francisco newspaper, that account appeared in July 1904 in the far-off Logansport, Indiana, *Journal* under the whimsical headline, "Canary Bird's Food Is Convicts' Dope." San Quentin officials reported inmates were growing hemp from the seed they bought for their caged birds. "Mariguana is a common-looking weed and nothing new to California," the *Journal* noted. But "[t]he variety at the prison is the Mexican brand," which can make a smoker "really drunk" after several strong puffs. After a few more puffs, it "overthrows his mind and he becomes a lunatic. He will run backward, imagining that all sorts of beasts are pursuing him." Hoping to repel the new drug threat, the warden declared "war on the deadly mariguana weed" and ordered guards to inspect the grounds, "inside and out, and dig out every weed found."[149]

Intriguing as this account was, it likely did nothing to prompt the 1913 anti-cannabis law. There was, after all, nothing menacing about the story—the marijuana-smoking prisoners proved not murderous but whacked out, walled in, and readily forgotten. By the time the anti-cannabis measure arose nearly nine years later, the episode probably had fallen from view. Meanwhile, amid a dearth of marijuana reports, the San Francisco press brimmed with accounts of old-hat opium raids and cocaine rings. Completely lacking was evidence of public concern about cannabis and its depredations.

---

[148] "An Act to Regulate the Practice of Pharmacy . . . ," 1905 *California Statutes*, ch. 406, § 5 (Act of Mar. 20, 1905), pp. 535, 537, (establishing the Board of Pharmacy and specifying its size and office location); "Old Sam Sing Beholds a Holocaust for His Good," *San Francisco Chronicle*, May 10, 1912, p. 18 (listing members of the Board of Pharmacy); "Opium Ashes Spirited Away," ibid., Feb. 7, 1914, p. 1 (same). Concerning Finger's life and tenure on the Board of Pharmacy, *see* "Prominent Pacific Coast Pharmacists," *Pacific Drug Review*, vol. 27, no. 12 (Dec. 1915), p. 26; Dale H. Gieringer, "The Origins of Cannabis Prohibition in California" (2006), *online at* https://www.researchgate.net/publ ication/242120559_The_Origins_of_Cannabis_Prohibition_in_California, pp. 16 & n.65, 17 & n.66. I am grateful to my research assistant Alisa Philo, whose sleuthing ruled out any likely family bond between the two Sutherlands.

[149] "Canary Bird's Food Is Convicts' Dope," *Logansport Journal*, July 17, 1904, p. 6. Though the Logansport report is datelined San Francisco and likely was reprinted from a San Francisco newspaper, the *Journal* did not specifically credit its source, and I've not found this article in the *San Francisco Chronicle*, the *San Francisco Call*, or the *Oakland Tribune*.

Hence we should seek the motives behind California's 1913 cannabis ban in the views of the pharmacists who apparently wrote it. Sadly, the board's members did not leave a thick trail of their views. In the tradition of their trade, they spoke not in sentences but in scribbles, leaving only shards of evidence, perhaps a half-dozen in all. Though few and scattered, these shards generally compel the conclusion that the 1913 anti-cannabis clause aimed at the low-lying threat of hashish and not at marijuana, smoked by Mexicans or otherwise.

The pharmacy press, including independent publications and trade group broadsides, supplies a natural portal to the druggists' views. The independent *Pacific Drug Review*, based in San Francisco and Portland, dropped a small hint in January 1913 when it reported results of a poll taken of its members by the California Pharmaceutical Association. Asked generally if the state's poison law needed changing, pharmacists overwhelmingly voted no, with 45 favoring change and 118 opposing. Some druggists—how many is not stated—supported change because they "favor[ed] the restriction of cannabis indica, contending that its sale should be restricted to the same extent that cocaine and morphine are."[150]

Two months later, as Sutherland's and Strobridge's bills coursed through the Assembly and Senate, pharmacy board member C. B. Whilden of San Francisco assured readers of the *Pacific Drug Review* that only one proposed change to the poison law affected pharmacists: the bill "takes Indian hemp and its preparations (except such as are used in corn remedies) out of Schedule 'B' and places it in the narcotic section, because of the increase in the use of 'hasheesh,' a detrimental preparation of hemp." To the Retail Druggists' Association of San Francisco, however, neither increased hashish use nor any other threat justified the changes proposed in Sutherland's and Strobridge's bills. The druggists opposed both bills with the cryptic comments, "Present poison law sufficient. . . . Sufficient penalties already provided."[151]

Among those who believed most fervently that the old poison law was *not* sufficient was Board of Pharmacy member Henry J. Finger. A longtime Santa Barbara druggist, Finger was named to the original pharmacy board in 1891 and served off and on till 1922. In 1911 he secured a seat on the three-person American delegation to the first International Conference on Opium held at The Hague. Outspoken and willing to offend, Finger hardly seemed a diplomat. But

---

[150] *See* "Result of California Referendum," *Pacific Drug Review*, vol. 25, no. 1 (Jan. 1913), pp. 7, 8 (noting poll of the members of the California Pharmaceutical Association and "favor[ed] the restriction . . ."); "Results of C.P.A. Referendum Voting," *Drug Clerk's Journal*, vol. 2, no. 3 (Dec. 1912), p. 32 (recording vote).

[151] C.B. Whilden, "Selling of Drugs by Grocers," *Pacific Drug Review*, vol. 25, no. 3 (Mar. 1913), p. 89; "Retail Druggists' Association of San Francisco," *Pacific Pharmacist*, vol. 6, no. 11 (Mar. 1913), pp. 278–79. My thanks to Dale Gieringer, whose research led me to several sources expressing pharmacists' views. *See* Gieringer, "Origins of Cannabis Prohibition" (2006), pp. 9–10 & n.34.

if his appointment raised eyebrows, it also secured him prestige at home and a respectful if not warm acquaintance with fellow delegation member Hamilton Wright.[152]

His concerns about cannabis abuse trace at least to July 1911, when Finger expressed them in a letter to Wright:

> Within the last year we in California have been getting a large influx of Hindoos and they have in turn started quite a demand for cannabis indica; they are a very undesirable lot and the habit is growing in California very fast; the fear is now that it is not being confined to the Hindoos alone but that they are initiating our whites into this habit.

"We were not aware of the extent of this vice at the time our legislature was in session," Finger continued, "and did not have our laws amended to cover this matter, and now we have no legislative session for two years (January 1913)." In response, Wright urged Finger to "have your legislature do something in regard to the control of Indian hemp." Months later the combined concerns of Wright and Finger found expression at The Hague in the American delegation's recommendation, rejected by other nations, that the convention classify cannabis together with cocaine and opium as menacing drugs.[153]

Other Californians shared Finger's aversion to Hindus. In January 1913, journalist Frederic J. Haskin stamped "Hindus the Most Objectionable of All" immigrant groups—the most illiterate and least assimilative and dirty to boot. A year earlier San Francisco minister A. Wesley Mell, a secretary of the American Bible Society, called Hindu priests "the most dangerous men in this country today," for they "seek here to propagate the heathen faith of India." Neither Haskin nor Mell nor any contemporary observer I could find joined Finger in linking California's reviled Hindus with use or cultivation of cannabis or any other drug. Still, the association between *Indian* hemp and Hindus from India may have proved hard to resist. Declaring "the foremost users of the hemp plant in one form or another are the Hindus," a *Los Angeles Times* article of December 1917

---

[152] "Opium Ashes Spirited Away" (identifying Finger as a pharmacy board member from Santa Barbara); Gieringer, "Origins of Cannabis Prohibition" (2006), pp. 16–18 & n.65 (supplying a biography of Finger and detailing his work on the Board of Pharmacy); Musto, *American Disease*, p. 50 (describing Finger's relations with Wright).

[153] Henry J. Finger to Hamilton Wright (July 2, 1911), "Records of U.S. Delegations to the International Opium Commission and Conferences of 1909–1913," *quoted in* Gieringer, "Forgotten Origins," pp. 251, 253; Hamilton Wright to Henry J. Finger (July 11, 1911), ibid.; "The Proceedings of the International Opium Conference at The Hague," *Pacific Pharmacist*, vol. 6, no. 9 (Jan. 1913), pp. 219, 221 ("The American delegation also unsuccessfully advocated restrictive regulations in regard to Indian hemp drugs."); Musto, *American Disease*, p. 51 (discussing the convention's rejection of the American delegation's proposal).

may have expressed a belief already widespread when the 1913 anti-cannabis law took form.[154]

There's no sure way to assess Finger's role or the force of his anti-Hindu feeling in drafting the legislature's 1913 addition of "hemp" and "loco-weed" to California's list of banned intoxicants. In December 1915, the *Pacific Drug Review* named Finger "the original author of the pharmacy and poison laws of California." But as the *original* California poison act, which dates to 1880, and the original pharmacy act of 1891 said nothing about cannabis, this attribution doesn't help us. And Finger was notably absent from the Board of Pharmacy in 1907, when the poison law first made "Indian hemp" a regulated substance in California.[155]

Still, Finger was a longstanding member of the seven-person board that apparently solicited lawmakers Sutherland and Strobridge to spirit its 1913 bill through the legislature. As he likely helped shape that bill, the views he expressed to Wright are telling. On two points they are clear: the drug Finger had in mind was the hashish of the East, not the marijuana of the South—and that the group he feared was not Mexicans. Whether we should take seriously Finger's frets of Hindus peddling hashish is less clear. Like Dr. Dale Gieringer, who researched this lawmaking episode in depth, I have found no evidence despite broad searches that *anyone* in California shared this concern in the years before the state's cannabis ban. The nearest evidence—an 1895 article in the *San Francisco Call* worrying about "Arabs and Armenians or Turks" growing twenty acres of hemp near Stockton and selling hashish in San Francisco—is too far afield in time and ethnicity to help.[156]

But let's accept what other readers of this evidence may think plain: Henry Finger, an influential member of the Board of Pharmacy, deemed "Hindoos . . . a very undesirable lot" and feared they had "started quite a demand for cannabis indica" and therefore crafted and promoted the 1913 amendment that added

[154] Frederic J. Haskin, "Immigration: The Influx from Asia—Hindus the Most Objectionable of All," *San Diego Union*, Jan. 3, 1913, p. 4; "Live Church News of the World," *Fort Wayne Journal-Gazette*, Apr. 1, 1912, p. 5 (quoting Mell); Don Marlin, "The Romance of Hemp—Marihuana," *Los Angeles Times*, Dec. 9, 1917, p. IX 10.
[155] "Prominent Pacific Coast Pharmacists" ("the original author . . ."); "An Act to Regulate the Sale of Certain Poisonous Substances," 1880 *California Statutes*, ch. 94 (Act of Apr. 16, 1880), p. 102; "An Act to Regulate the Practice of Pharmacy and Sale of Poisons in the State of California," 1891 *California Statutes*, ch. 85 (Act of Mar. 11, 1891), p. 86; "An Act to Regulate the Sale of Poisons . . . ," 1907 *California Statutes*, ch. 102, § 9 (Act of Mar. 6, 1907), pp. 124, 126. Concerning Finger's life and tenure on the Board of Pharmacy, *see* "Prominent Pacific Coast Pharmacists"; Gieringer, "Origins of Cannabis Prohibition" (2006), pp. 16–17 & nn.65–66, 68. Finger lost his seat to a 1904 scandal involving accusations of favoritism and bribetaking in awarding pharmacy licenses. He secured reappointment in 1909. *See* ibid.
[156] "Local Hashish-Eaters: Arabs Near Stockton Growing Indian Hemp and Making the Drug," *San Francisco Call*, June 24, 1895, p. 7, *quoted in* Gieringer, "Origins of Cannabis Prohibition" (2006), pp. 7–8.

"hemp" and "loco-weed" to California's list of banned intoxicants. Still, Finger's 1911 letter to Hamilton Wright states his true concern: "[T]he fear is now that [the cannabis habit] is not being confined to the Hindoos alone *but that they are initiating our whites into this habit.*"[157]

We have seen before such official complacency with non-whites' indulgence in a foreign vice, combined with distress when whites embrace that vice. That lesson dates to the beginning of antidrug lawmaking in this country and San Francisco's first-in-the-nation opium den ban of 1875. "[T]here are numbers of these places kept for Chinese only," a committee of the Board of Supervisors reported. But what was truly distressing was discovery of "eight opium-smoking establishments kept by Chinese, for the exclusive use of WHITE MEN AND WOMEN," where "young men and women of respectable parentage" were hazarding their virtue.[158] Again and again in this study we've seen that whatever the race of the source, the law sprang into force when lawmakers' own offspring—and those of their friends and constituents—were at risk.

California's 1913 Anti-Cannabis Law—The Inspectors

Two final players figured in the making of California's 1913 anti-cannabis law. As inspectors deployed by the Board of Pharmacy, both men enforced the state's poison law, one on the streets of Northern California, one on the streets of the south. Their different postings altered the focus of their concern.

On the beat in the north was yet another Sutherland—Frederick Alexander Sutherland, an energetic and enterprising chief inspector. This Sutherland lacked any traceable family bond to Assemblyman William Angus Sutherland or Board of Pharmacy president George M. Sutherland. But his experiences patrolling San Francisco, where the Board of Pharmacy met, and Sacramento, where the Assembly met, likely helped define the drug-related concerns of all three men in the years leading to the 1913 lawmaking.[159]

---

[157] Henry J. Finger to Hamilton Wright (July 2, 1911) (emphasis added).

[158] "The Opium Dens," *San Francisco Chronicle*, Nov. 16, 1875, p. 3.

[159] Evidence that Inspector Sutherland was no relation to Assemblyman Sutherland or Board president Sutherland took an unexpectedly dramatic form: Early in 1915, Inspector Sutherland accused various officials of the Board of Pharmacy, including president George M. Sutherland, of malfeasance of duty. In the course of an investigation that ultimately rejected the inspector's charges, the Board president denied a press report that Inspector Sutherland was his cousin and had secured his post with the Board president's aid: "We have the same name, but there our likeness ends," the Board president insisted. "As a matter of fact, when Sutherland came to work for this Board his name was not Sutherland, but Frederick Alexander Brown.... [H]e went into court and had his name changed from Brown to his mother's maiden name of Sutherland, for reasons of his own." "Charges Rife in Opium Scandal," *San Francisco Chronicle*, June 6, 1915, p. 32. *See also* "Opium Charges Fail; Board Is Exonerated," *Los Angeles Times*, June 16, 1915, p. I 6 (reporting that Inspector Sutherland's charges had been rejected). Aided by my research assistant Alisa Philo and both Sonia Moss and Kevin Rothenberg of the Crown Law Library, I have tried and failed to find evidence of a family connection

Celebrated for his industry and vigilance, Inspector Sutherland was a darling of the local news corps. In one or another account of an opium raid or cocaine bust, his name dotted the daily press. The *San Francisco Call* chalked to his credit "the most successful series of raids ever conducted in the United States." His 1912 marriage to Rose Mentor, a San Francisco druggist and one-time target of his undercover sleuthing, became page-two news. Later a bribery scandal and other missteps would bring him down, but early in 1913, when the anti-cannabis law took form, Sutherland was a minor media star.[160]

His celebrity permits us to track his raids across the Bay Area and beyond. Conducted mostly in concert with local police forces, these sorties were notable mostly for the utter absence of cannabis in any form, whether hashish or marijuana, either targeted or seized. Not once have I seen Sutherland's name linked with these substances. Nor have I encountered any Bay Area police raid before the 1913 lawmaking that sought or secured cannabis. Dr. Gieringer likewise reports that Sacramento police arrest logs for 1913 through 1916 mention opium, opium pipes, morphine, and cocaine, but say not a word about cannabis or hashish or marijuana. Instead the opium and morphine haunts of big-city Chinatowns supplied Sutherland's daily bread, while the cocaine trade supplied his butter. Speaking to a reporter for the *San Francisco Call* in November 1911, Sutherland ruled out a role for any other drug: "There are three drugs used by these 'fiends.' There is opium, morphine, which is an alkaloid of opium, and cocaine...."[161]

The same was not true for Sutherland's colleague and counterpart, Fred C. Boden, also a Board of Pharmacy inspector, said by the press to have "charge of the crusade in the southern part of the State against the drug traffic." Boden shared Sutherland's drug-fighting zeal and unstoppable energy. Even before his arrival in Los Angeles in July 1911, the local press heralded the "fearless inspector" whose tireless enforcement of the poison law on the streets of San Diego had left violators quaking. "Consternation reigns in the ranks of a certain class of local physicians," the *Los Angeles Times* wrote, for Boden had hauled into a

---

among any of these Sutherlands. Census and genealogical records suggest any such connection is unlikely.

[160] "Detective Wins Case and Fair Apothecary," *San Francisco Call*, Feb. 14, 1912, p. 2 (telling of Sutherland's courtship and marriage and crediting Sutherland with "the prosecution of the most successful series of raids..."); "Arrested Woman, Will Marry Her," *San Francisco Chronicle*, Feb. 14, 1912, p. 2 (telling of Sutherland's courtship and marriage); "Opium Scandal Grows Worse," *Los Angeles Times*, June 12, 1915, p. I 4 (reporting allegations that Inspector Sutherland had taken protection money from a San Francisco hotel keeper); "Opium Charges Fail; Board is Exonerated," ibid., June 16, 1915, p. I 6 (predicting Inspector Sutherland's dismissal for insubordination after charging colleagues and superiors at the Board of Pharmacy with misconduct); Associated Press, "Opium Probe Ends in Exoneration of Accused," *San Diego Union*, June 16, 1915, p. 1 (similar).

[161] *See* Gieringer, "Forgotten Origins," p. 260 & n.105; "Official Lives as Criminal to Gain Evidence," *San Francisco Call*, Nov. 27, 1911, p. 3.

San Diego court two doctors who prescribed opium and morphine in unlawfully large quantities. "Inspector Boden says he is after other doctors and that surely he will land them."[162]

Boden debuted in Los Angeles with "the biggest round-up of Chinese opium dealers ever made" in that city, netting twenty-nine "denizens of Chinatown." For the next fourteen months, before he traded public service for a private detective agency, the local press made familiar fare of his busts. Physicians, pharmacists, and addicts, from high society and low, fell before his restless and watchful eye. Though almost all the professionals and some of the addicts were white, Chinese users and dealers dominated the ranks of his arrestees. And while some Chinese dealers dealt cocaine, virtually all his targets used or sold either opium or morphine. Not one of his Los Angeles arrests concerned cannabis, for when Boden left service in September 1912, cannabis still lay beyond the poison law's ban. Four years later, after he traded back his private badge and resumed his Board of Pharmacy post, Boden finally made his first local cannabis arrest when he spotted the seven-foot "marahuana" stalks sprouting in Jesus Ersilch's Pasadena backyard.[163]

The law's expanded reach possibly owed something to Boden's advocacy— and to his fear of marijuana abuse among Mexican Americans. In October 1911, Boden claimed a fleeting page-sixteen headline in the *Los Angeles Times*: "Would Prohibit Sale of Weed." "In view of the increasing use of marihuano or loco weed as an intoxicant among a large class of Mexican laborers," the *Times* declared, Boden had "formulated an appeal to the State authorities asking that the drug be included in the list of prohibited narcotics." The Board of Pharmacy inspectors were "anxious for authority to inaugurate repressive measures without delay."[164]

Boden apparently said nothing of raging, pot-maddened Mexicans, for the *Times* wrote here only of the drug's euphoric effects. Marijuana "was cultivated in Mexico as an intoxicating agent," the paper said—and users preferred the male plant's leaves for their "stronger narcotic effects" delivering a more sustained "exaltation of the mind." Yet even if narcosis and not violence was his worry, Boden focused that worry on Mexicans.[165] And while his remarks may stand alone in linking California's early anti-cannabis law to fear of pot-soused Mexicans, his words demand attention, for Boden may have had the ear of a board member

[162] "The Road Is Open," *Los Angeles Times*, May 16, 1912, p. II 7 ("charge of the . . ."); "Physicians Are Frightened," ibid., Feb. 1, 1911, p. I 15 (all other quotes).
[163] "Hop Heaven Gets Boost," *Los Angeles Times*, July 11, 1911, p. I 13 ("the biggest round-up . . ." and "denizens of Chinatown"); "Boden with Burns," ibid., Sept. 19, 1912, p. II 9 (reporting Boden's move to a private detective agency); "Odd Crop Failure," ibid., July 7, 1916, p. II 3 (describing Boden's marijuana raid at the Ersilch home).
[164] "Would Prohibit Sale of Weed," *Los Angeles Times*, Oct. 19, 1911, p. I 16.
[165] Ibid.

with power to shape the new law. Hence we must consider a lawmaking rationale rooted in ethnic panic.

California's 1913 Anti-Cannabis Law—The Mexican Menace?

The "State authorities" Boden hoped to convince of the need for a cannabis ban were likely his superiors, the seven members of the state Board of Pharmacy. One or more board members probably wrote the 1913 amendments to the state's poison law, together with the new cannabis ban. Though the 1913 act contained many other provisions consuming six pages of text, and though the addition of "hemp" and "loco-weed" to the roster of banned substances occupied only part of a single long sentence, this provision was among the most important in the bill. Board members would not have let it slip into law without their approval. As the poison law gave the board a hand in the act's enforcement, its members had a powerful incentive to help shape any new amendments.[166]

The board member Boden knew best was possibly Henry J. Finger, based in nearby Santa Barbara. It's not likely, however, that Boden's views deepened Finger's anxiety about cannabis. Finger's letter complaining about "Hindoos" and their use of *cannabis indica* was dated July 2, 1911, fifteen weeks *before* Boden's October 18 statement to the *Los Angeles Times*. Prompted by Hamilton Wright to "have your legislature do something in regard to the control of Indian hemp," Finger *already* was eyeing January 1913, the start of the next legislative session, as the board's next chance to extend the poison law to ban cannabis. Moreover, Finger's letter and its handwringing about "a large influx of Hindoos," who have "started quite a demand for cannabis indica" and "are initiating our whites into this habit," hardly reflects Boden's concern about "the increasing use of marihuano or loco weed as an intoxicant among a large class of Mexican laborers."

Nor does it appear Boden's views circulated broadly in the California press. Though the *Daily Courier* of Oxnard, north of Los Angeles, reported his remarks, the *Los Angeles Times* never again did so. And though Boden hailed from San Francisco, the *San Francisco Chronicle* and *San Francisco Call* and

---

[166] Anderson, "Urges Revision of Criminal Procedure" (claiming the anti-cannabis act "carr[ied] out some of the ideas of the State Board of Pharmacy"); "An Act to Amend . . . 'An Act to Regulate the Sale and Use of Poisons . . . ,'" 1913 *California Statutes*, ch. 342, § 6 (Act of June 11, 1913), pp. 692, 697. The poison law of 1907 made it the duty of the district attorney, "at the request of the board of pharmacy," to conduct prosecutions arising under the law. The 1913 amendments to this law strengthened the Board's hand buy authorizing it to "employ special counsel to assist the district attorney in such actions and prosecutions." "An Act to Regulate the Sale of Poisons . . . ," 1907 *California Statutes*, ch. 102, § 6 (Act of Mar. 6, 1907), pp. 124, 125; "An Act to Amend . . . 'An Act to Regulate the Sale and Use of Poisons . . . ,'" 1913 *California Statutes*, ch. 342, § 3 (Act of June 11, 1913), pp. 692, 694.

Oakland Tribune all neglected his fears. Computer-aided searches of newspapers throughout the state have turned up no other reference to Boden's comments. Looking farther afield to Maine, Indiana, and Wyoming, the other anti-cannabis states of 1913, I have found no hint of Boden or his concerns.[167] And the Massachusetts cannabis ban of 1911 was on the books in April of that year, long before Boden's October remarks. That is, despite intensive searches I've found no repetition of Boden's alarum in any news outlet likely to have influenced the course of early anti-cannabis lawmaking.

Still, the story found legs, if only sporadically. It turned up in both the *Washington Post* and *New York Sun* in November 1911 and in the *American Practitioner*, a New York–based medical and surgical journal, in April 1912. Nine months later, in January 1913, the *Pacific Medical Journal* reprinted the *American Practitioner*'s version of the story. Yet the California Board of Pharmacy, as Dale Gieringer reports, said nothing about marijuana—or cannabis, hemp, hashish, or loco weed—in its minutes or biennial reports.[168]

Other evidence likewise tilts against the conclusion that ethnic hatred gave rise to the state's 1913 cannabis ban. Cannabis had been on the state's watchlist of drugs of concern since the inclusion of "Indian hemp" in the 1907 poison act, which confined the drug's sale to pharmacies and required warning of its "poisonous" nature. Once California lawmakers started cannabis up this regulatory ladder, the drug's advancement to banned status in 1913 was perhaps foreordained, a natural step completing the code's coverage of recreational intoxicants. Because the 1907 act took form during a 1905-to-1909 hiatus in Henry Finger's membership on the Board of Pharmacy, it probably owed nothing to his concern about "very undesirable . . . Hindoos" flowing into California and the demand they had stoked for *cannabis indica*. And Boden's 1911 cry for "repressive measures without delay" might have seemed alarmist and abrupt to lawmakers from the Bay Area and elsewhere in the state, where the specter of pot-maddened Mexicans had not crept into view.

More direct refutation of Boden's role in spurring action by the Board of Pharmacy lies in the pages of the *Pacific Drug Review* of March 1913. Addressing his audience of druggists, pharmacy board member C. B. Whilden explained the rationale of the 1913 cannabis ban. As a member of the board that probably authored the legislation, Whilden could state its intent with insider's knowledge.

---

[167] "May Stop Use of 'Loco' Weed among Mexicans," *Daily Oxnard Courier*, Oct. 19, 1911, p. 1; "Charged with Looking for Opium without Warrant," *San Francisco Chronicle*, Oct. 18, 1911, p. 2 (identifying Boden as "a prominent Elk of San Francisco").

[168] *See* "War on Crazing Drug," *Washington Post*, Nov. 6, 1911, p. 6; "War on the Loco Weed," *New York Sun*, Nov. 5, 1911, § 2, p. 2; "The Loco Weed," *Pacific Medical Journal*, vol. 56, no. 1 (Jan. 1913), p. 52, *reprinted from The American Practitioner*, vol. 46, no. 4 (Apr. 1912), pp. 182–83; Gieringer, "Origins of Cannabis Prohibition" (2006), p. 21 (reviewing these events and identifying sources).

And as his words appeared even as the legislature was weighing Assemblyman Sutherland's anti-cannabis measure, Whilden could comment with the unusual authority of one who speaks in the present tense. In justifying the legislation, he said nothing of marijuana or Mexicans. Instead, as I noted earlier, he said the pending action proposed to ban "Indian hemp and its preparations . . . *because of the increase in the use of 'hasheesh,' a detrimental preparation of hemp."* This rationale, wholly consistent with the completeness theorem, stands opposed to any claim that fear of Mexicans or their marijuana drove the 1913 legislation.[169]

Then, too, we have the lessons learned in each of the *other* states explored in this chapter, where anti-cannabis laws took form absent any discernible immigrant-fueled panic. We saw instead that two other forces triggered anti-cannabis lawmaking: a concern for the morals of youthful users tempted by the drug's euphoric effects and an urge toward completing the criminal code's prohibition of recreational intoxicants. In Massachusetts, Maine, Vermont, and Indiana, the impulse to protect youth, especially white youth, was most prominent. In Wyoming the lure of completeness figured larger.

In California both forces seem to have shaped the drug law regime. We have known since the earliest days of American antidrug lawmaking that Californians fretted about the threat drugs posed to the morals of "WHITE MEN AND WOMEN." This concern, voiced by the San Francisco Board of Supervisors in 1875, emerges here again in Henry Finger's 1911 letter to Hamilton Wright expressing Finger's distress about the spread of the cannabis habit: "[T]he fear is now that it is not being confined to the Hindoos alone but that they are initiating our whites into this habit."[170] And the decades-long evolution of California's pharmacy law, in which Schedule B drugs advanced to Schedule A before joining the growing roster of banned substances, reflected the completeness principle at work.

Seen in this light, Inspector Boden emerges not as an oracle revealing the thoughts of his superiors on the Board of Pharmacy but as a law officer who spoke with the biases that so often afflict those who patrol the streets amid a turbulent immigrant population. Though Boden's biases would drift north in time, they appear not to have moved the lawmakers whose 1913 cannabis ban achieved completeness in the narcotics code and shielded the morals of California's whites from an insurgent cannabis threat.

Still doubts nag. For the 1913 law itself, in outlawing not merely "hemp" but also "loco-weed," lends some comfort to those who argue ethnic fear spurred the cannabis ban. A common slang for the cannabis plant, *locoweed* hints at the drug's Mexican roots and suggests the possible force of Inspector Boden's

---

[169] Whilden, "Selling of Drugs by Grocers," p. 89 (emphasis added).

[170] "The Opium Dens," *San Francisco Chronicle*, Nov. 16, 1875, p. 3 (quoting committee report accompanying San Francisco anti-dens ordinance); Henry J. Finger to Hamilton Wright (July 2, 1911).

warning about Mexicans' use of "marihuano or loco weed."[171] Moreover, as we've learned over the course of this history, *some* early antidrug laws surely had roots in racial hatred. Bans on opium dens enacted after the 1883 miscegenation hoax concocted by the young men of New York's Church of the Transfiguration, an episode traced in Chapter 5, very possibly reflected anxiety to protect white girls from the wiles of Chinese men. And as we saw in Chapter 6, Louisiana's anti-cocaine law of 1898, the nation's sixth statewide ban, was the work of a white supremacist who perhaps framed the law as a means of racial oppression.

In the realm of anti-cannabis lawmaking, Richard Bonnie and Charles Whitebread offer a compelling case that media-fanned fears of marijuana-crazed Mexicans prompted passage of a few anti-cannabis laws, such as a 1929 Colorado act that hiked some cannabis penalties only days after a Mexican marijuana smoker confessed the murder of his stepdaughter.[172] These laws came too late to explain what gave rise to the nation's first anti-cannabis laws. But like Louisiana's 1898 cocaine ban, they show that when lawmakers are of a mind to oppress, antidrug laws offer a ready tool.

Ultimately, we cannot—and perhaps we need not—discern with certainty the forces impelling California's 1913 anti-cannabis law. My aim throughout this history has been to expose the essentially moral nature of the impulse to ban nonmarital sex, drunkenness, and drug intoxication and the common threads running through these regulatory schemes. The history of California's 1913 anti-cannabis law displays the vitality of these old moral forces even as racial hatred crept into view.

Reefer Madness

One last artifact of California history spotlights how fear for youthful morals—*not* of run-amok Mexicans—helped fuel anti-cannabis lawmaking. In 1939, two years after the Marihuana Tax Act committed the federal government to warring against the cannabis trade, G&H Productions of Beverly Hills released the feature film *Tell Your Children*. Now better known as *Reefer Madness*, a source of

---

[171] Though I believe both Boden and California's lawmakers used *locoweed* as slang for cannabis, the cattlemen of the old West more often applied the term to other plant species. Said to grow in foot-high bushes with white or purple flowers, locoweed proved irresistible to horses and cattle and disastrous to both. "Loco Weed," *Los Angeles Times*, Mar. 21, 1887, p. 5 (reprinting item from the *Colorado Live Stock Review*). The weed's botanical identity is uncertain. *Oxytropis Lamberti, Asragalus legum*, and *Astragalus mollissimus* all appear in a 1902 homeopathy manual as "'Loco-weed' or 'Crazy-weed' . . . producing the loco-disease in animals." John Henry Clarke, *A Dictionary of Practical Materia Medica*, vol. 2 (London: The Homœopathic Publishing Company, 1902), pt. 1, pp. 702–03.
[172] Bonnie & Whitebread, *Marihuana Conviction*, p. 72.

midnight guffaws for toked-up collegians, *Tell Your Children* offered the nation's parents a portent of pot's perils to their youth.[173]

The film's scrolling prologue warned of "the frightful toll of the new drug menace which is destroying the youth of America." Among the drug's ominous effects was "the loss of all power to resist physical emotions," not unlike the "resistless passion" of which Victor Robinson had written in 1912. Then came "acts of shocking violence," calling to mind the murderous rampages Harry Anslinger conjured in his 1937 "Assassin of Youth." "[T]he dread *Marihuana*," the prologue concluded, "may be reaching forth next for your son or daughter . . . or *yours* . . . or *YOURS!*"

What followed was a marijuana melodrama set in Anytown, USA, where the scrub-faced youth of Lakeside High shuttled from malt shop to tennis courts to backyard courtships over cookies and cocoa. Boys and girls fell into impromptu readings of *Romeo and Juliet* and snuck kisses behind mom's back. Then a criminal duo lured the youth to a nearby flat and hooked them on hand-rolled reefers. The first symptom was giggling, even in class. Then came sex and murder, suicide and insanity. At last two children lay dead; two others had blood on their hands. Assessing the carnage, the high school principal delivered the film's moral peroration: "We must work untiringly," he intoned, "so that our children are obliged to learn the truth. Because it is only through knowledge that we can safely protect them. Failing this, the next tragedy may be that of your daughter. Or your son. Or yours . . . or yours . . . or *YOURS*."

Tell Your Children committed many sins. Overacting was one, overwriting another, sermonizing a third. More gravely, the film lied in charging rampant murder and insanity against marijuana's moral ledger. Marijuana is likelier to soothe than incite, likelier to tranquilize than derange.[174] Allegations of social

---

[173] *See* Samantha Brandfon & Brian Perron, "Movies," in *Encyclopedia of Drugs, Alcohol & Addictive Behavior*, vol. 3 (Pamela Korsmeyer & Henry R. Kranzler eds., Farmington Hills, Mich.: Macmillan Reference USA, 3d ed. 2009), pp. 83, 86 (supplying basic production information). Though Brandfon and Perron trace the film to 1936, it likely was not released till 1939. A scene in the film shows a movie marquee featuring "Terry Rooney in 'Any Old Love.'" The marquee was a prop made for the film *Something to Sing About*, shot in mid-1937. And an item from the June 15, 1938, edition of *Variety* (at page 2) reported that producer George Hirliman "is readying 'Tell Your Children' for an early start." The March 25, 1939, edition of *BoxOffice* said the film was completed some "four months ago." Broad searches of U.S. newspapers show no other trace of the film till late July 1939, when it appeared in widely separated cities almost in tandem. *See* "Mission," *Albuquerque Journal*, July 28, 1939, p. 12; "'Outside These Walls' Coming to Paramount," *Logansport Pharos-Tribune*, July 29, 1939, p. 7. I thank Kevin Rothenberg for his ingenious sleuthing in dating the film's release. A screenplay is online at http://drugpolicycentral.com/bot/pg/propaganda/reefer_madness_movie_script.htm.

[174] As this book goes to press in 2023, there is no scientific consensus concerning the likelihood that cannabis consumption will trigger psychosis. A coauthor of a widely cited 2017 report by a committee of the National Academy of Sciences, Engineering, and Medicine explained that the report documented only an association between marijuana use and schizophrenia, not causation. "We do not yet have the supporting evidence to state the direction of this association," she said—meaning the association might result from a tendency toward cannabis use among persons suffering from or predisposed to schizophrenia. Aaron E. Carroll, "The Reasonable Way to View Marijuana's Risks," *New York Times*, Jan. 14, 2019 (quoting Dr. Ziva Cooper). More recent evidence, however, published

separation and sexual licentiousness had better footing in fact. They are, after all, the source of the moral unease that greets recreational intoxicants. A tuned-out toker is like Reverend Beecher's drunkard, "alone with his boat and bottle," or Dr. Kane's opium smoker, no longer perceiving "the real and unpleasant crudities of daily life." And sex is both template and metaphor for the reasonless pleasure that defines this class of substances. A horny toker recalls a drunken Lot, an opiated Dr. Jones, or a cocainized Dr. Hazen traveling with a woman not his daughter. All have abandoned the empire of reason, which "ought like a king in control to restrain the impulses of the lower flesh," and have surrendered to their basest appetites. It's this aspect of *Tell Your Children*, as Figure 7.8 suggests, that promoters thought worth flogging. Marijuana "[s]ows the seeds of lust in youthful brains," a movie promo proclaimed, and "[t]akes the brakes off young morals . . . ." Or as another promo put it, "Inhaling Desire/Exhaling Lust."[175]

Yet there's one sin *Tell Your Children* did not commit. The film did not engage in race-baiting. The evil duo of "Mae Coleman" and "Jack Perry," who plied the youth of Lakeside High, were white—indeed Mae looked blond. The "boss" who supplied their wares and delivered their marching orders likewise was white. All the child addicts were white. In fact it seems everyone onscreen was white. Only the malt shop piano player, with his olive skin and dark hair and habit of sneaking out between sets for a toke, roused ethnic suspicion. But his name, Hot-Fingers Pirelli, suggests Italian heritage, not Mexican. And though his demonic laugh hinted at evil intent, he played no part in the drama and never spoke. Rather it seems he represented the dread drug itself. That drug, we learn, sometimes was brought "into the country," though we're not told from where. As the drug—so we're taught—"grows wild in almost every state in the Union," nothing suggested a Mexican provenance.

That G&H Productions allied with the Federal Bureau of Narcotics in making *Tell Your Children* seems doubtful. At least one source, citing no authority, claims the Bureau produced the film, while other sources with seeming expertise attribute the film vaguely to religious backers. In 1944 the Federal Trade

---

in May 2023, found that as many as 30% of cases of schizophrenia in men aged twenty-one to thirty could be prevented by avoiding cannabis use disorder. Carsten Hjorthøj et al., "Association Between Cannabis Use Disorder and Schizophrenia Stronger in Young Males Than Females," *Psychological Medicine* (May 4, 2023), p. 6, *online at* https://www.cambridge.org/core/journals/psychological-medicine/article/association-between-cannabis-use-disorder-and-schizophrenia-stronger-in-young-males-than-in-females/E1F8F0E09C6541CB8529A326C3641A68.

[175] Lyman Beecher, *Six Sermons on the Nature, Occasions, Signs, Evils, and Remedy of Intemperance* (Boston, T.R. Marvin, 4th ed. 1828), p. 31; H.H. Kane, *Opium-Smoking in America and China: A Study of Its Prevalence, and Effects, Immediate and Remote, on the Individual and the Nation* (New York: G.P. Putnam's Sons, 1882), p. 61; St. Augustine, "On the Plagues of Egypt and the Ten Commandments of the Law: Preached in Carthage at the Shrine of Saint Cyprian," in *The Works of Saint Augustine*, vol. III/1 (Edmund Hill trans., Brooklyn: New City Press, 1990), Sermon 8.8, pp. 244–45; "Civic," *Linn County* (Mo.) *Budget-Gazette*, Aug. 30, 1939, p. 4 ("Inhaling Desire . . .").

Figure 7.8: "Tell Your Children" (1939 Advertisement).

Commission announced the film's producer had agreed to stop claiming—falsely—"that the Bureau [of Narcotics] cooperated in producing it."[176] Still, the film marched in cadence with Anslinger's "Assassin of Youth." The school principal recalled the case of "a young boy. Under the influence of the drug, he killed

---

[176] Steven B. Duke & Albert C. Gross, *America's Longest War: Rethinking Our Tragic Crusade Against Drugs* (New York: G.P. Putnam's Sons, 1993), p. 285 (stating *Reefer Madness* was "produced by the Federal Bureau of Narcotics"); Kevin Murphy & Dan Studney, "Reefer Madness History," *online at* http://web.archive.org/web/20060328163318/http://www.reefer-madness-movie.com/history.html. ("Reefer Madness . . . was financed by a small church group . . . ."). On the FTC's 1944 order, *see* "Reefer Pic Be-fogs Public; FTC's Edict," *Variety*, Jan. 19, 1944, p. 11. My thanks to Kevin Rothenberg for finding this article.

his entire family with an axe." And the film concluded precisely where "Assassin of Youth" began: a young girl, tormented by the guilt of having hooked her friends on pot, hurled herself through a window to her death, her body sprawled on the sidewalk below.

Such deaths never haunted the lawmakers who wrote the nation's earliest anti-cannabis laws. But concern for youthful morals—for the clarity of their minds and purity of their bodies—weighed heavily on their thoughts. *Tell Your Children* was guilty of melodrama, but as a reflection of the motives that drove state lawmakers, it told a good measure of truth.

8

Monogamy's Demise?

We arrive at last at our starting point: the San Francisco Bay Area, scene of the first shot in our nation's war on drugs. The setting no longer is Chinatown, the year no longer 1875, the drug in contention no longer the smoked opium of the Orient. Instead we travel to Oakland, San Francisco's grittier sibling across the Bay, where in 2017 the city council struggled to manage a metastasizing marketplace for newly legalized recreational marijuana.

Ballot measures in November 2016 had doubled from four to eight the roster of states that erased all penalties for sales or possession by adults of smallish amounts of marijuana. Today the tally stands at twenty-three. These new laws apply not merely to *medical* marijuana, already legal in a large and growing contingent of states now numbering thirty-eight. Nor do they merely *decriminalize* marijuana for personal use, deeming violations mere infractions—a tack taken in eight states where voters and lawmakers wish to ban the traffic without locking up the users.[1] Rather, the twenty-three renegade states go where no state had gone before: they legalize for adult *recreational* use and commercial sale an intoxicant other than alcohol.

Colorado and Washington were first to act. In November 2012, when voters in these two states opted to legalize recreational marijuana, 101 years had passed since J. Frank Chase first moved Massachusetts lawmakers to ban nonmedical cannabis. After a century of rough consensus around recreational pot, outlawed everywhere in this country and in most places on earth, change came quickly. In 2014 voters in Alaska, Oregon, and the District of Columbia lifted their bans. Two years later, legalization fervor swept up voters in Maine, Massachusetts, Nevada, and the biggest marketplace of all, California. Three more states followed in 2018 and 2019, seven others in 2020 and 2021, and five more in 2022 and 2023.

The resulting pattern of states, shown in Figure 8.1, tells a familiar tale of red-and-blue America.[2] Liberalism's blue armies have seized the entire West Coast,

---

[1] These eight are Hawaii, Louisiana, Mississippi, Nebraska, New Hampshire, North Carolina, North Dakota, and Ohio. In tallying states permitting medical marijuana, shown in Figure 8.1, I do not count those states that authorize medical use only of cannabidiol (CBD), a less psychoactive component of the cannabis plant than tetrahydrocannabinol (THC)—or those that authorize only very low-THC medical products. As of September 2023, these states include Georgia, Indiana, Iowa, Kansas, North Carolina, South Carolina, Tennessee, Texas, Wisconsin, and Wyoming.

[2] My thanks to Brett Diehl, Akansha Dubey, Alba Holgado, Sydney Kirlan-Stout, Jenny Moroney, David Oyer, and Nathan Tauger, who canvassed state cannabis laws and helped assemble this map.

Beware Euphoria. George Fisher, Oxford University Press. © Oxford University Press 2024.
DOI: 10.1093/oso/9780197688489.003.0009

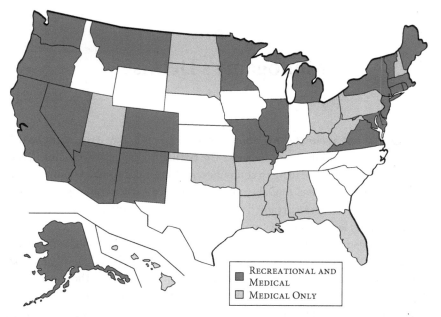

Figure 8.1: Those states that have legalized marijuana for medical or recreational purposes (September 2023).

a few Far West havens, three Great Lakes states, and a Northeastern stronghold that seems destined to grow. Of twenty-three states now permitting recreational marijuana, only Missouri and the libertarian bastions of Alaska and Montana voted Republican in the 2016 and 2020 presidential polling. In four other red states, Arkansas, North Dakota, Ohio, and Oklahoma, voters have *rejected* bids to legalize. And South Dakota voters, after briefly breaking rank in 2020 to legalize recreational use, recanted and rejected such a measure in 2022.

It's no shock liberal and libertarian states, with laxer moral codes and greater tolerance for human foibles, should be first to lift longstanding moral strictures. But why have they acted now, a century into the war on cannabis? And what can this timing teach us about the themes, moral and racial, of America's drug war today? It's these questions that lead us to Oakland, which in 2004 became the first city in the United States to license a medical cannabis dispensary.[3] Oakland's motives may not be typical, but in this deep-blue bubble on a deep-blue bay, they may prove transparent.

---

[3] Otis R. Taylor Jr., "Onerous Pot Shop Rules May Cost Oakland," *San Francisco Chronicle*, Nov. 18, 2016, at D1.

To Oakland

Six months before voters ratified Proposition 64, the 2016 ballot measure that legalized recreational marijuana in California, the Oakland City Council unanimously approved a "Dispensary Equity Permit Program" to govern the existing marketplace in medical cannabis and the recreational market hovering on the horizon. The equity program would have reserved half of all marijuana dispensary licenses for businesses at least half-owned by persons who met one of two criteria: either they had lived for two years in one of six East Oakland police beats with a high rate of marijuana-related arrests, or they had served time in the last decade for marijuana offenses committed in Oakland. The program's purpose, as the *San Francisco Chronicle* reported, was to offer "reparations for a U.S. drug policy that disproportionately punished people of color."[4]

The proposed equity program soon met a hailstorm of criticism. In favoring residents of only six police districts, the program excluded the vast majority of Oaklanders, including many Black and Brown persons, scattered among the city's fifty-one other police beats. The incarceration criterion excluded those ex-cons whose marijuana offenses never triggered confinement or took place outside Oakland or more than ten years earlier. Marijuana entrepreneurs who did not meet the program's strict demands complained their permit applications would languish in administrative logjams. Both purveyors and consumers worried that reserving half of all dispensary permits for a slender class of applicants could drive viable cannabis retailers to cities and towns with less onerous rules.

Then there were legal headaches. Even if Oakland officials smiled on ex-convicts in awarding dispensary permits, state authorities could invoke past convictions to deny such applicants an essential operating license. *Other* applicants could complain the program discriminated against them. And when critics tired of trashing the proposal, they turned their ire on the city council itself, which withdrew the equity program but couldn't coalesce around an alternative. Scorned for its "Highly Ridiculous" indecision, the council voted four to three to pack off the equity program to the city administrator for a rewrite and directed that Oakland's Department of Race and Equity review the rewritten proposals.[5]

---

[4] Rachel Swan, "Oakland Pol Backs Expunging Pot Crimes," *San Francisco Chronicle*, May 19, 2016, p. D1 (outlining the equity program); Rachel Swan, "Seeking to Light the Way for Minority Pot Moguls," ibid., May 16, 2016, p. A1 ("reparations for a . . ."). For the text of the Equity Permit Program, *see* Oakland Municipal Code, tit. 5, ch. 5.80, § 5.80.045 (May 17, 2016).

[5] Swan, "Seeking to Light the Way for Minority Pot Moguls" (noting Oakland's fifty-seven police districts); Otis R. Taylor Jr., "Clumsy Council Is Killing Oakland's Buzz," *San Francisco Chronicle*, Nov. 4, 2016, at D1 (anticipating "a logjam for permits"); Rachel Swan, "Oakland Pot Event Supports Diversity," ibid., Oct. 25, 2016, at A1 (quoting claim that dispensary owners are moving to other cities); Rachel Swan, "Oakland's Proposed Equity Pot Permits Run Afoul of State," ibid., Oct. 4, 2016 (noting the possible difficulty in gaining a state license); Robert Selna, "Oakland's Inequitable

One criticism, however, no one uttered. Neither councilmember nor pot pur-veyor nor cop nor casual observer—*no one* whose views cluttered the public record complained of the oddity front and center in Oakland's Equity Permit Program: it reserved passes to take part in a highly regulated and potentially lu-crative industry for persons convicted of and imprisoned for violating the legal regime that went before. The program would not merely overlook and excuse violations of old anti-cannabis laws, but would reward them. Or in the term embraced by many of the program's supporters, it would pay *reparations* to those victimized by the old legal regime. As the publisher of the African American *Oakland Post* put it, "I want to make sure we grandfather in the blacks and browns who spent time in jail over the green."[6]

Oakland City Councilwoman Rebecca Kaplan offered perhaps the most full-throated justification of the reparations program. Writing to her constituents and supporters in October 2016, she stressed a single rationale in urging support of Proposition 64: "[T]he 'war on marijuana,' has disproportionately targeted people of color, especially African Americans.... That is why we must tax the pot instead of locking people up." Kaplan put the point more plainly when she told the *San Francisco Chronicle*, "[I]t's been black people who've been locked up—had their freedom taken away, their families taken away, their jobs taken away—for something that white people mostly don't get punished for." In June 2016, a widely reported study had concluded that African Americans in California faced ticketing for marijuana offenses at four times the rate of whites. Because of "the ongoing suffering caused by people having a record and thus being denied access to jobs and other opportunities," Kaplan said, it's important to ensure access to the cannabis marketplace for those wronged by the war on marijuana. She there-fore proposed expanding the equity program to reach certain applicants living outside the six specified police beats and those ex-cons whose past marijuana convictions happened outside Oakland or did not lead to incarceration.[7]

Pot Permits," ibid., Sept. 25, 2016, at E5 (citing discrimination against applicants who don't fit the program's narrow criteria); Otis R. Taylor Jr., "Oakland Council Looking Highly Ridiculous," ibid., Oct. 7, 2016, at D1 (calling the plan "absurd"); Rachel Swan, "Oakland Council Calls for Pot Shift," ibid., Nov. 15, 2016, at A1 (reporting on proposed rewrite).

[6] Rachel Swan, "New Roadblock for Oakland Pot Entrepreneurs," ibid., Nov. 2, 2016, p. A1 (quoting publisher Paul Cobb); Otis R. Taylor Jr., "Brooks' Handling of Pot Permits Has a Bad Smell," ibid., Mar. 17, 2017, p. D1 (reporting that Councilwoman Desley Brooks "insists it's about equity, reparations for people of color disproportionately affected by marijuana arrests and convictions"); Tiffany Onyejiaka, "Is It Time for Marijuana-Related Reparations?" Ozy.com, Apr. 5, 2018. I thank my research assistant David Oyer for helping to confirm the lack of public complaint about the equity program's rewards for ex-convicts.

[7] Email from Oakland City Councilwoman Rebecca Kaplan to supporters (Oct. 26, 2016); Swan, "Oakland Pol Backs Expunging Pot Crimes" (quoting Kaplan); David Downs, "'Racial Injustice' Lurks in California Pot Enforcement, Study Finds," *East Bay Express*, June 2, 2016 (reporting on study conducted by the American Civil Liberties Union of California and the Drug Policy Alliance); Letter

Ultimately, the equity program survived, if in altered form. In March 2017, the city council voted to retain the program while broadening the qualifying criteria. Applicants had to be low-income Oaklanders either convicted of a cannabis offense committed in the city after November 5, 1996, or residing for ten of the previous twenty years in any combination of twenty-one Oakland police beats plagued by frequent marijuana arrests. In the first phase of the recreational marketplace's rollout, at least half of dispensary permits would go to equity applicants. In the second phase, set to begin when an Equity Assistance program was established and funded, equity applicants could seek zero-interest business loans as well as technical help and waivers from city permitting fees. In both phases, those with a record of marijuana crimes in Oakland would have a leg up entering the city's cannabis trade.[8]

Though it stood first, Oakland does not stand alone in privileging one-time cannabis convicts in the new marijuana marketplace. Ordinances in San Francisco, Sacramento, Los Angeles, and Portland, Oregon, grant special priority or assistance to would-be marijuana entrepreneurs branded cannabis criminals under the old regime. In Massachusetts, which launched the first statewide marijuana equity program, voters endorsed "full participation" in the cannabis industry by persons "from communities . . . disproportionately harmed by marijuana prohibition and enforcement"—later deemed to include those with past drug convictions and their spouses and children. As Boston city councilman Tito Jackson explained, "The people who got locked up should not get locked out of this industry."[9]

---

from Councilwoman Rebecca Kaplan to "Colleagues and Community" (undated) ("the ongoing suffering . . .").

[8] "Ordinance Amending Oakland Municipal Code Chapter 5.80, Medical Cannabis Dispensary Permits . . . ," Ord. no. 13424 C.M.S., § 5.80.045 (as amended Mar. 28, 2017), pp. 10–12, *online at* https://library.municode.com/ca/oakland/ordinances/code_of_ordinances?nodeId=823836.

[9] San Francisco Police Code, art. 16, §§ 1604(b)(4)(B) & (D), 1606(a)(1) (offering priority permits to those arrested for or convicted of a cannabis-related crime between 1971 and 2016—and to the parents, siblings, and children of such persons—if other conditions are met) (eff. Jan. 5, 2018); City of Sacramento, Cannabis Opportunity Reinvestment and Equity Program, §§ (6)(a)(i), (8)(a) (offering priority permits and other assistance to those arrested for or convicted of a cannabis-related crime in Sacramento between 1980 and 2011—and their immediate family members—if other conditions are met) (Aug. 9, 2018); Los Angeles Municipal Code, art. 4, § 104.20(a)–(c) (offering priority permits to those arrested for or convicted of a cannabis-related crime before Nov. 8, 2016, if other conditions are met) (as amended eff. July 2, 2018); City of Portland, "Social Equity Program Details" (2018) (providing a fee reduction and other financial support to those convicted of marijuana-related offenses before July 1, 2015), *online at* https://www.portlandoregon.gov/civic/article/698824; Massachusetts Question 4, § 5 (amending *Massachusetts General Laws Annotated*, ch. 94G, § (4)(a)(4)) (2016); Massachusetts Cannabis Control Commission, "Guidance for Equity Provisions" (Apr. 2, 2018) (providing training and other operational assistance to those with "a past drug conviction" and their spouses and children if residency conditions are met); Janie Har & Bob Salsberg, "Jurisdictions Aim to Help Minorities Enter Pot Industry," (Santa Ana) *Orange County Register*, June 1, 2017, at 9 (quoting Councilman Jackson).

Illinois lawmakers agreed. "[I]n the interest of remedying the harms resulting from the disproportionate enforcement of cannabis-related laws," they offered grants and low-interest loans and an edge in licensing to cannabis business applicants who faced—or whose family members faced—arrests for or convictions of certain cannabis crimes. As legalized cannabis hit the market in that state early in 2020, Governor J. B. Pritzker said the point of legalization was *not* to make marijuana more widely available: "The defining purpose of legalization is to maximize equity." And when New York joined the cannabis bandwagon in 2021, lawmakers gave licensing priority to applicants who had—or whose close relatives had—a marijuana-related conviction. "[T]his legislation is intentional about equity," the Assembly majority leader announced. "Equity is not a second thought, it's the first one, and it needs to be, because the people who paid the price for this war on drugs have lost so much." Of the twenty-three states that now permit recreational sales, at least eighteen provide for social equity in licensing. At least fourteen favor cannabis retailers prosecuted and convicted during the war on cannabis.[10]

At a national level, too, drug law reformers have cast marijuana legalization as the means of righting past racial wrongs. Representative Barbara Lee of Oakland, named co-chair of the Congressional Cannabis Caucus in 2019, condemned our "discriminatory marijuana laws": "When you look at who's in prison, who's in jail, whose lives have been shattered by marijuana charges—who is it? It's black young people; it's brown young people." Lee dedicated herself to "build[ing] an industry that is equitable" and "empower[ing] communities of color that have been disproportionately impacted by the failed war on drugs." The next month she and Senator Cory Booker, a 2020 presidential candidate, reintroduced their "Marijuana Justice Act" to end federal marijuana prohibition, cosponsored by at least five other presidential candidates. Though the act would not have undone state cannabis bans, it would have withheld federal funding for prison building and other law enforcement activities from any state where non-whites were likelier than whites to suffer marijuana-related arrests or incarceration and would have steered withheld funds to "communities most affected by the war on drugs." Noting the crush of candidates joining the cannabis crusade, the *New York Times*

[10] Illinois Public Act 101-0027 (Act of June 25, 2019), §§ 1–10 (defining "Member of an impacted family" and "Social Equity Applicant"); ibid., § 7-1(h) ("in the interest of remedying…"); ibid., § 7-15 (providing low-interest loans and grants); § 15-30(c)(5) (giving "social equity" applicants an advantage in licensing); National Public Radio, "Morning Edition," Jan. 3, 2020 (broadcasting Pritzker's statement); Luis Ferré-Sadurní, "New York Gives Green Light to Purple Haze (Other Strains, Too)," *New York Times*, Apr. 1, 2021, p. A12 (quoting Democratic majority leader Crystal D. Peoples-Stokes). The fourteen states giving a leg-up in licensing or other special assistance to retailers with old cannabis prosecutions are Arizona, Delaware, Illinois, Massachusetts, Michigan, Minnesota, Missouri, New Jersey, New Mexico, New York, Rhode Island, Vermont, Virginia, and Washington.

declared legalization "a litmus test for candidates' commitment to equal treatment for all races in policing and criminal justice . . . ."[11]

How have we arrived at this remarkable juncture? An antidrug legal regime that originally targeted white users and their often-white suppliers at last
is condemned as a tool of racial oppression. In search of the forces driving this
twenty-first-century racial dynamic, let us examine the consequences of the *last*
century's drug war.

Increasingly Severe Penalties

Time and again twentieth-century authorities learned the same lesson: prohibitions
don't work as planned. Even when bans *reduce* use, as did national alcohol prohibition, consumption runs rampant.[12] That's the natural consequence of banning
things many people want and will pay to get and other people are willing to sell.
Prohibitions' ills therefore include law enforcement's responses when bans fall
short. Time and again the chief responses have been increasingly severe penalties
and increasingly invasive policing.

William Blackstone, the eighteenth-century chronicler of English law,
explained the first phenomenon. When crimes are hard to detect, penalties must
rise to preserve the law's deterrent force.[13] Blackstone's criminals were rational
calculators who multiplied the costs of detection by its likelihood and weighed
the resulting risk against the expected fruits of crime. Blackstone could have had
modern drug transactions in view. Private sales between consenting adults are
very hard to detect—and with punishment so uncertain, only the prospect of

---

[11] Congresswoman Barbara Lee Press Release, Jan. 9, 2019 ("discriminatory marijuana laws" and
"build[ing] an industry . . ." and "empower[ing] communities . . ."), *online at* https://lee.house.gov/
news/press-releases/congresswoman-barbara-lee-named-co-chair-of-bipartisan-cannabis-caucus;
Tal Kopan, "Lee Leads Panel for Changes in Marijuana Law," *San Francisco Chronicle,* Jan. 23, 2019,
p. A1 ("When you look . . ."); Senator Cory Booker Press Release, Feb. 28, 2019, *online at* https://
www.booker.senate.gov/?p=press_release&id=892; "Marijuana Justice Act" (116th Cong., 1st Sess.)
(HEN19298, 2019), §§ 3–4, pp. 5–8, 10, *online at* https://www.scribd.com/document/400749867/
Marijuana-Justice-Act-116th-Congress; Trip Gabriel, "2020 Democrats Find Common Cause in
Pot," *New York Times,* Mar. 18, 2019, p. A10.

[12] As I noted in Chapter 3 at page 138, Wayne Hall documents evidence of plummeting drinking
beginning around 1917, as state and federal prohibitions took force, and of an upward trend beginning around 1920 that wiped out most but not all earlier gains. *See* Wayne Hall, "What Are the
Policy Lessons of National Alcohol Prohibition in the United States, 1920–1933?" *Addiction,* vol. 105
(2010), pp. 1164, 1166–69.

[13] William Blackstone, *Commentaries on the Laws of England* (Oxford: Clarendon Press, 1769),
vol. 4, p. 16 ("[I]t is but reasonable that among crimes of different natures those be most severely
punished, . . . which a man has the most frequent and easy opportunities of committing, which
cannot be so easily guarded against as others, and which therefore the offender has the strongest in-
ducement to commit . . . .").

harsh punishment can divert a would-be dealer's desires from the siren call of easy money.

This dynamic of increasing severity in response to failing bans has played out across time and place and in many illicit drug markets. Early drug bans imposed penalties paltry by today's standards. When New York's 1907 Smith Act first made unprescribed cocaine sales in that state a crime, violators faced at most a year's confinement and a $1,000 fine.[14] Still, the law had bite because it targeted mainly institutional sellers—the druggists who dominated the early market in nonprescription cocaine. With highly visible and immobile storefronts that made them easy marks for the cops, pharmacists found little cover from the law. The Smith Act therefore proved a highly effective deterrent despite its one-year sentence cap.

As New York's illicit cocaine traffic diffused into the nonmedical community, violators more easily dodged detection. Sellers now traded on street corners and trolley lines, in cafes and pool halls—and in private homes, where cocaine dealers such as "Professor" John Coey, featured in Chapter 6, stashed their wares. As dealers and buyers grew harder to spot, lawmakers acted in seeming confirmation of Blackstone's maxim and toughened sentences. Just six years into the Smith Act's tenure, in the face of informed reports "that the victims of cocaine are becoming more and more numerous and that some action should be taken to stop the indiscriminate sale," New York lawmakers hiked the maximum penalty for unprescribed cocaine sales to seven years.[15]

Consider, too, the progression of drug-law penalties in Massachusetts. The state's first broad narcotics ban, which J. Frank Chase helped present to the legislature in 1910, made unprescribed sales of opium, heroin, or morphine a misdemeanor punishable by up to a year's confinement. Seven years on, the report of a Massachusetts Special Commission appointed "to investigate the use of habit-forming drugs and the effectiveness of the laws pertaining thereto" proposed a harsher antidrug regime. Warning "that the drug habit is so prevalent in this State that comprehensive legislation is necessary to deal more effectively with the subject," the commission concluded that "[t]he unlawful selling and delivery of narcotic drugs should be made a felony, and the penalties for other violations of narcotic drug laws should be substantially increased . . . ." The commissioners' new penalty scheme, which lawmakers embraced and enacted some four months

---

[14] "An Act to Amend the Penal Code, in Relation to the Sale of Certain Drugs," 1907 *New York Laws*, ch. 424, § 1 (Act of June 5, 1907), pp. 879–80.

[15] "Stricter Cocaine Law Favored by Judges," *New York Tribune*, Dec. 3, 1912, p. 4 (quoting Judge Edward Swann: "that the victims . . ."); "An Act to Amend the Penal Law, in Relation to the Sale or Possession of Cocaine or Eucaine," 1913 *New York Laws*, ch. 470, § 2(g) (Act of May 9, 1913), p. 988 (deeming unprescribed sale a felony).

later, raised the maximum penalty for unprescribed sales or possession to three years' confinement.[16]

In boosting antidrug penalties to combat stubbornly high drug use, New York and Massachusetts presaged a twentieth-century dynamic driving up penalties in state after state. This dynamic drove Congress too. The earliest example of mounting Congressional severity when regulating substance abuse—and perhaps the example most obnoxious to contemporary observers—addressed not narcotics but alcohol. By early 1929, the Volstead Act banning sales of intoxicating drinks had been in force nine years. Deemed scandalously ineffectual, the act sparked derision on the right for its leniency and on the left for its bid to enforce a misguided ban. Moonshining and whiskey running thrived in defiance of massive federal funding to quash the illegal trade. With public sentiment tilting decidedly toward prohibition's repeal, juries often stood doggedly against conviction.[17] Calculating criminals of Blackstone's imagination saw little in the law to deter their traffic.

Congress responded in March 1929 with the "Increased Penalties Act," later known as the Jones Act. The new law jacked the maximum sentence for making or selling intoxicating drinks from six months' confinement and a $1,000 fine, as the Volstead Act prescribed on a misdemeanor first offense, to five years' *felony* imprisonment and a $10,000 fine—*and* authorized trial judges to impose the maximum penalty on each count of a multicount indictment, effectively removing any ceiling from the law's penalty scheme. Lawmakers thundered their approval with votes of 65 to 18 in the Senate and 283 to 90 in the House. The public was of an entirely different humor. As the *Cornell Daily Sun* said, "Both laymen and professional men in all strata of the national body politic are uniting in vigorous opposition to this drastic measure."[18]

Though public outrage at the Jones Act helped fuel a firestorm that soon brought prohibition down, Congress seemed emboldened. Hence when it later

[16] "An Act to Regulate the Sale of Morphine and Other Narcotic Drugs," 1910 *Massachusetts Acts,* ch. 271, §§ 1, 3 (Act of Mar. 22, 1910), pp. 207–08; "An Act Relative to the Sale and Distribution of Narcotic Drugs," 1915 *Massachusetts Acts,* ch. 187, § 11 (Act of Apr. 20, 1915), pp. 167, 172; "An Act relative to the Sale and Distribution of Certain Narcotic Drugs," 1917 *Massachusetts Acts,* ch. 275, §§ 13, 14 (Act of May 23, 1917), pp. 254, 259–60; Frank G. Wheatley et al., *Report of the Special Commission to Investigate the Extent of the Use of Habit-Forming Drugs* (unpublished manuscript) (Boston, 1917), pp. 4, 7, 20, 22.

[17] Howard Padwa & Jacob A. Cunningham, "Alcohol Bootlegging and Smuggling," *in Drugs in American Society: An Encyclopedia of History, Politics, Culture, and the Law* (Nancy E. Marion & Willard M. Oliver eds., Santa Barbara: ABC-CLIO, 2014), pp. 24–27.

[18] National Prohibition Act, Pub. L. 66-66, ch. 85, tit. 2, § 29, 41 Stat. 305, 316 (Act of Oct. 28, 1919), *repealed by* Liquor Law Repeal and Enforcement Act, Pub. L. 74-347, ch. 740, 49 Stat. 872 (Act of Aug. 27, 1935); "An Act to Amend the National Prohibition Act . . . ," Pub. L. 70-899, ch. 473, 45 Stat. 1446 (Act of Mar. 2, 1929) (Increased Penalties Act); "Dry Penalties Bill Passed by the Senate," *New York Times,* Feb. 20, 1929, p. 1; "Dry Penalties Bill with 5-Year Term Passed by the House," ibid., Mar. 1, 1929, p. 1; [Editorial], "Echoes of the Jones Act," *Cornell Daily Sun,* Mar. 30, 1929, p. 4.

became clear that the 1914 Harrison Act and 1937 Marihuana Tax Act had failed to suppress the traffic in opium, cocaine, and cannabis, lawmakers responded with succeeding rounds of get-tough antidrug laws that extended almost till the close of the century. Here several legislative episodes stand out.

First was passage of the 1951 Boggs Act. Plugging for his namesake bill, Louisiana Congressman Hale Boggs boldfaced a 77-percent spike in narcotics arrests between 1948 and 1950. "The most shocking part about these figures," he said, was "an alarming increase in drug addiction among younger persons." Boggs inserted into the Congressional Record an article quoting the New York attorney general's allegation that between 5,000 and 15,000 of New York City's 300,000 junior and senior high school students were drug addicts. The solution to this run-amok traffic, Boggs insisted, was toughened penalties. "Short sentences do not deter," he said, quoting Commissioner Anslinger.[19]

Existing sentences under the Harrison Act and Marihuana Tax Act were not precisely *short*. Both laws imposed maximum five-year prison terms on violators. Neither law, however, prescribed minimum terms or supplied stepped-up sentences for second or third offenders. The Boggs Act repaired these perceived shortcomings. Though the maximum penalty on a first offense remained five years, the law dictated a minimum two-year term. On a second offense, it imposed five to ten years; on a third offense ten to twenty years. Fatefully, for the first time in federal anti-narcotic lawmaking, the Boggs Act established mandatory-minimum penalties that dictated a floor below which judges had no discretion to sentence. On a conviction for a second or later offense, the act stripped the sentencing court of power to suspend the prescribed minimum sentence or impose probation instead.[20]

Yet lawmakers soon deemed the Boggs Act too feeble to contain the booming narcotics trade. Only five years later, with passage of the Narcotic Control Act of 1956, Congress imposed on drug sellers five to twenty years for a first offense and ten to forty years for a second. Adults who distributed drugs to minors risked ten to forty years even on a first offense —or, if the drug was heroin, ten years to life or even possibly death. Except in cases of first offenders convicted of possession only, the law denied judges discretion to suspend sentences or impose probation and even denied parole eligibility, an incentive to reform in prison once offered almost all federal offenders.[21]

---

[19] *Congressional Record*, vol. 97, pt. 6 (82d Cong., 1st Sess.), pp. 8197–99 (July 16, 1951) (statement of Representative Boggs).

[20] "An Act to . . . Impose a Special Tax upon All Persons Who . . . Deal in . . . Opium or Coca Leaves . . . ," Pub. L. 63-223, ch. 1, § 9, 38 Stat. 785, 789 (Act of Dec. 17, 1914) (Harrison Narcotic Act); Marihuana Tax Act of 1937, Pub. L. 75-238, ch. 553, § 12, 50 Stat. 551, 556 (Act of Aug. 2, 1937); "An Act to Amend the Penalty Provisions Applicable to . . . Certain Narcotic Laws . . . ," Pub. L. 82-255, § 1, 65 Stat. 767, 768 (Act of Nov. 2, 1951) (Boggs Act).

[21] Narcotic Control Act of 1956, Pub. L. 84-728, ch. 629, §§ 103, 105–107, 70 Stat. 567, 568–571 (Act of July 18, 1956).

Fourteen years later, at the prompting of President Richard Nixon, Congress yet again overhauled the nation's drug laws. Nixon warned lawmakers in 1969 that "several million American college students have at least experimented with marihuana" and other drugs and that "[p]arents must also be concerned about the availability and use of such drugs in our high schools and junior high schools." The Controlled Substances Act of 1970 responded to such concerns by giving federal anti-narcotic laws a whole new cast. The law divided regulated drugs into five schedules according to their medical usefulness and perceived danger and addictiveness. Though Congress authorized the FDA to move substances from one schedule to another, lawmakers' initial assignments of various drugs to particular schedules have survived the passing decades largely unchanged. In by far the most notorious designation, Congress classed marijuana together with heroin and LSD as a Schedule I drug with "a high potential for abuse" and "no currently accepted medical use in treatment in the United States." Relentlessly derided by drug war critics, this classification has destabilized the whole framework of federal narcotics enforcement and especially its anti-cannabis components. For marijuana's Schedule I designation, under review as this book goes to press, pits federal law against the thirty-eight states pictured in Figure 8.1 that have legalized cannabis for many medically sanctioned uses.[22]

At the same time the Controlled Substances Act achieved a rare liberalization of antidrug penalties by scrapping almost all the mandatory-minimum sentencing terms imposed in the get-tough fifties. Lawmakers voiced regret at having withheld sentencing discretion from judges, and they worried rigidly steep penalties might prompt prosecutors not to charge and jurors not to convict. Moreover, as the Senate Judiciary Committee explained in its report on the proposed legislation, "severe drug laws, specifically as applied to marihuana, have helped create a serious clash between segments of the youth generation and the Government" and have "contributed to the broader problem of alienation of youth from the general society." Liberalization at the state level took even greater strides as a dozen states representing almost a third of all Americans decriminalized possession of small amounts of marijuana between 1973 and 1978.[23]

Perhaps predictably, however, this rollback in sentencing severity heralded a fierce legislative blowback. In the mid-eighties, facing a surging traffic in crack cocaine and other drugs, lawmakers sought to quell the trade with toughened

[22]   Richard Nixon, "Special Message to the Congress on Control of Narcotics and Dangerous Drugs" (July 14, 1969); Comprehensive Drug Abuse Prevention and Control Act of 1970, Pub. L. 91-513, tit. 2, §§ 202(b)(1), 202(c), 84 Stat. 1236, 1247, 1249 (Act of Oct. 27, 1970) (defining Schedule I drugs; Emily Dufton, *Grass Roots: The Rise and Fall and Rise of Marijuana in America* (New York: Basic Books, 2017), pp. 49–51 (recounting the drafting of the Controlled Substances Act).

[23]   H. Rep. No. 1444, 91st Cong., 2d Sess. (Sept. 10, 1970), p. 11; S. Rep. No. 613, 91st Cong., 1st Sess. (Dec. 16, 1969), pp. 1–2; Dufton, *Grass Roots*, pp. 61–70 (tracing decriminalization in the 1970s).

sanctions. The Anti–Drug Abuse Act of 1986 created a fresh array of mandatory-minimum sentencing rules triggered by dealing in specified weights of banned substances. A first-time offender caught with just five grams of crack now faced a mandatory-minimum five-year term. As we've seen so often before, lawmakers embraced this hard-hitting measure over the barest opposition: only two senators and sixteen representatives voted no.[24]

Meanwhile, the United States Sentencing Guidelines effectively imposed a mandatory-minimum penalty scheme on almost all serious federal drug offenses. Authorized by the Sentencing Reform Act of 1984, the Guidelines took effect in 1987 and gained force in 1989 after the Supreme Court turned back constitutional challenges. The Guidelines designate for each crime a series of penalty ranges escalating with the gravity of the defendant's past record. Till 2005, when the Supreme Court made the Guidelines merely advisory, the lower figure in the defendant's sentencing range operated as an effective mandatory-minimum sentence, below which a federal judge could not sentence without issuing a written explanation subject to appellate review. Even under today's "advisory" Guidelines, judges typically must justify in writing sentences imposed beneath the Guidelines range.[25]

These 1980s law changes generated vastly longer sentences for federal inmates. A convict entering federal prison in 1986 served an average of 20.7 months; one entering in 1997 served 46.9 months—a 127-percent hike. Much or most of this increase traces to harsher sentences for drugs and weapons offenses, both often subject to mandatory-minimum sentencing provisions, and to the abolition of federal parole by the same law that authorized the Sentencing Guidelines. And these figures understate the *real* increase in sentence severity. For the proportion of federal offenders sentenced to prison, as opposed to probation or other intermediate sanction, grew steadily. In the five years before the Guidelines took effect, prison sentences accounted for 55 to 57 percent of all sentences of either imprisonment or probation. In the first eleven years afterward, that proportion grew by stages from 58 percent in 1988 to 79 percent in 1998.[26]

[24] Anti–Drug Abuse Act of 1986, Pub. L. 99-570, tit. 1, subtit. A, § 1002, 100 Stat. 3207, 3207-2–4, (Act of Oct. 27, 1986); "H.R. 5484—Anti–Drug Abuse Act of 1986" (recording votes), Congress.Gov, *online at* https://www.congress.gov/bill/99th-congress/house-bill/5484/all-actions?overview=closed#tabs.

[25] Sentencing Reform Act of 1984, Pub. L. 98-473, tit. 2, ch. 2, 98 Stat. 1837, 1987 (Act of Oct. 12, 1984); *Mistretta v. United States*, 488 U.S. 361, 367–68, 412 (1989) (upholding the Sentencing Guidelines against constitutional challenge and noting a judge must "give 'the specific reason' for imposing a sentence different from that described in the guideline"); *United States v. Booker*, 543 U.S. 220, 258–65 (2005) (deeming the Guidelines to be merely advisory to avoid constitutional conflict); *Chavez-Meza v. United States*, 138 S. Ct. 1959, 1963 (2018) (noting a judge who sentences outside the Guidelines range "must state 'the specific reason for the imposition of a . . . different' sentence").

[26] William J. Sabol & John McGready, *Time Served in Prison by Federal Offenders, 1986–97*, p. 4 tbl. 1; ibid., p. 5 tbl. 2 (Bureau of Justice Statistics Special Report, NCJ 171682 (1999), *online at* https://www.bjs.gov/index.cfm?ty=pbdetail&iid=868); Bureau of Justice Statistics, *Sourcebook of Criminal Justice Statistics—1998*, p. 408 tbl. 5.22 (1999) [hereafter *1998* (or other year) *Bureau of*

With more and longer prison terms came more crowded prisons. Here the figures are gloomily familiar to any reader of the day's press. Between 1980 and 2012 the total federal prison population grew ninefold—from 24,252 to 217,815. Among federal drug inmates, the increase was even more dizzying—a twenty-one-fold surge from 4,749 in 1980 to 99,426 in 2012, accounting in the end for just under half of all federal inmates. Drug offenders made up a smaller share of state prisoners—only 17.4 percent in 2010—and state drug offenders multiplied at a more leisurely (but still startling) rate, rising about twelvefold from 19,000 in 1980 to 237,000 in 2010. Altogether, with over 1.5 million federal and state prisoners and another 700,000 jail inmates, the United States has by far the highest incarceration rate of any major nation—one and a half times Russia's and almost six times China's.[27]

Even as toughened federal drug laws filled federal prisons, the state-by-state trend toward marijuana decriminalization faced the determined resistance of a national "parent movement." Galvanized by a late-seventies leap in adolescent marijuana use and buoyed by Nancy Reagan's fervent support, parents' groups drove permissive states into retreat. By 1983, all but one of the twelve states that had decriminalized pot possession in the 1970s had reversed course.[28]

Increasingly Invasive Policing

Increasingly severe sentences and the specter of mass incarceration are just two results of the drug regime's failure to reduce use to politically palatable levels. A third consequence is the inclination of police to act with mounting zeal and disrespect for individual privacy.

Justice Statistics Sourcebook], *online at* https://www.hsdl.org/?view&did=711233 (supplying imprisonment and probation tallies). On the abolition of federal parole, *see* Sentencing Reform Act of 1984, §§ 218(a)(5), 235(a)(1), 98 Stat. 2027, 2031.

[27] *See 2003 Bureau of Justice Statistics Sourcebook*, p. 519 tbl. 6.57 (supplying federal inmate counts for 1980); E. Ann Carson & Daniela Golinelli, *Prisoners in 2012* (Washington, D.C.: Bureau of Justice Statistics, 2013), p. 43 tbl. 10 (breaking down federal inmates by crime of conviction); The Sentencing Project, *Fact Sheet: Trends in U.S. Corrections* (Washington, D.C.: The Sentencing Project, 2018), p. 3 (noting state drug inmate count for 1980); E. Ann Carson & William J. Sabol, *Prisoners in 2011* (Washington, D.C.: Bureau of Justice Statistics, 2012), p. 10 tbl. 10 (breaking down state inmates by crime of conviction); Lauren E. Glaze & Diane Kaeble, *Correctional Populations in the United States, 2013* (Washington, D.C.: Bureau of Justice Statistics, 2014), p. 2 tbl. 1 (supplying U.S. prison and jail populations); E. Ann Carson, *Prisoners in 2016* (Washington, D.C.: Bureau of Justice Statistics, 2018), p. 3 tbl. 1 (stating state and federal prison populations); Roy Walmsley, *World Prison Population List* (London: Institute for Criminal Policy Research, 11th ed. 2015), p. 5 tbl. 2, p. 9 tbl. 3, p. 12 tbl. 4 (listing national imprisonment rates).
[28] Dufton, *Grass Roots*, pp. 85–106, 123–58.

More invasive crime detection emerged at the very outset of our history of prohibition, long before modern police forces took form. Recall England's short-lived gin ban, the topic of Chapter 2, which prevailed with uneven success between 1736 and 1743. Authors of the Gin Act knew enforcement depended on the complicity of insiders. Hence they enticed and rewarded drinker-informants— private persons who posed as thirsty patrons and then testified against their suppliers in court, all for the statutory spoils of five pounds per conviction. As Lord Bathurst said in debates on the Gin Act's repeal, informants had become "detested as the oppressors of the people." At least four fell to mob violence.[29]

This basic policing model has endured through the long history of prohibition enforcement. Over time, of course, professional police agencies mostly displaced private informants. Sometimes officers pose undercover as addicts craving a fix or dealers turning dope. Sometimes they recruit and pay civilian informants to play these roles. Alongside such undercover techniques, officers have adopted methods involving less stealth and more brute force. Raids on opium dens and cargo ships became standard fare among state and federal law enforcers in the late nineteenth century, as did seizure and destruction of drugs and other contraband.

Still there remained at the end of the nineteenth century a reticence among courts and law enforcers to invade private homes and conveyances. We encountered in Chapter 5 an 1887 ruling of the California Supreme Court hinting that the state lacked power to punish certain private vices, such as smoking opium at home among friends. As one justice wrote, "Every man has the right to eat, drink, and smoke what he pleases in his own house without police interference."[30] Because the court decided the case on other grounds, these words lacked the force of law. But they expressed the spirit of a time when the community was willing to wink at certain private vices rather than tolerate police intrusion into private spaces.

This solicitude for private refuges did not survive the twentieth century's repeated assaults on substance abuse. The anti-opium and anti-cocaine laws of the late nineteenth and early twentieth centuries tended to target opium dens and coke-selling pharmacies and other institutional sellers that operated at fixed locations in the public marketplace. With no ready way to hide from authorities, these entities quickly yielded much of their newly banned markets to street dealers and small-time smugglers and home-based producers, whose mobility or privacy allowed them to elude detection even as police surveillance intensified. In the end, however, the law followed where the traffickers scurried.

---

[29] *Hansard's Parliamentary Debates* (Lords), vol. 12, p. 1323 (1743) (remarks of Lord Bathurst). On the role of informants, see Chapter 2, pages 66–67, 74.

[30] *In the Matter of Sic, on Habeas Corpus*, 73 Cal. 142, 145 (1887); *id.* at 150 (Paterson, J., concurring).

On the East Coast, officers raided the New York apartments of doctors who dealt cocaine from home; on the West Coast, they seized cannabis plants from Los Angeles backyards and rooftop gardens.

National alcohol prohibition sped the erosion of old norms that had kept the law's prying eyes out of private spaces. Of *dwellings*, it's true, the Volstead Act was jealously protective. As adopted in 1919, the law exempted possession of liquor "in one's private dwelling" if used only by "the owner . . . and his family . . . and . . . his bona fide guests." And the law forbade warrants "to search any private dwelling occupied as such unless it is being used for the unlawful sale of intoxicating liquor, or unless it is in part used for some business purpose . . . ." Two years later, Congress strengthened the home's protections, making it a crime punishable by a $1,000 fine—and a year in prison on a second offense—for a federal agent to search a "private dwelling" without a warrant. But *cars* and *persons* were different matters. The House rejected as too sweeping an earlier version of the 1921 law that would have punished federal agents who searched "the property or premises of any person" without a warrant. The Judiciary Committee complained this proposal would "prevent the search of the common bootlegger and his stock in trade though caught and arrested in the act of violating the law. But what is perhaps more serious, it will make it impossible to stop the rum running automobiles engaged in like illegal traffic."[31]

Here legislators had the nature of Volstead Act violations in view. Moonshining, like pot growing today, was often a backwoods operation, easily scattered or disowned if the evidence was not seized when found. And rum running required only a drive over the Canadian border. "It is impossible to get a warrant to stop an automobile," the House committee warned. "Before a warrant could be secured the automobile would be beyond the reach of the officer with its load of illegal liquor disposed of." Hence the language Congress enacted in 1921, punishing federal agents who violated homes but not cars or other property, aimed to spare the enforcement techniques that had the most bite.

Four years later, the Supreme Court relied on this legislative history in granting police broad powers to stop and search private cars on the open road. A pullover on a highway spanning Grand Rapids and Detroit gave rise to the foundational Fourth Amendment case, *Carroll v. United States*. Revenue agents had found concealed in the car's upholstery sixty-eight quarts of whiskey and gin. Defendant George Carroll claimed the warrantless car stop and liquor seizure violated the Constitution's guaranty against "unreasonable searches and seizures," rendering evidence of the liquor inadmissible against him.[32]

---

[31] National Prohibition Act, §§ 25, 33, 41 Stat. 305, 313, 315; An Act Supplemental to the National Prohibition Act, Pub. L. 67-96, ch. 134, § 6, 42 Stat. 222, 223–24 (Act of Nov. 23, 1921); *Carroll v. United States*, 267 U.S. 132, 146 (1925) (quoting report of the House Judiciary Committee).
[32] *Carroll*, 267 U.S. at 143–47, 160.

Writing for the Court, Chief Justice William Howard Taft noted Detroit's border with Canada made the city one of the hottest hubs for running contraband spirits into the United States. He stressed that Congress, when drafting the 1921 amendment to the Volstead Act, had distinguished "between the necessity for a search warrant in the searching of private dwellings and in that of automobiles and other road vehicles in the enforcement of the Prohibition Act." The Fourth Amendment "does not denounce all searches or seizures, but only such as are unreasonable," Taft wrote. And on "reason and authority," if an officer has probable cause to believe a car contains contraband, the search and seizure are valid even without a warrant.[33] That is, the *Carroll* Court declared the law's readiness to enforce prohibition even when a legal principle must be newly fashioned for the purpose.

Succeeding decades in the war on drugs gave rise to scores of Fourth Amendment rulings granting greater license for police stops, searches, and seizures. Not all rulings went the government's way—now and then the Supreme Court slapped back police efforts to leverage the drug war into expanded prowess on the streets. Taken together, however, law enforcement's victories in the Fourth Amendment realm dominated defeats, and the drug war gave courts grounds to declare greater and more invasive police powers. One principle behind these rulings, the Supreme Court said, is the public's "compelling interest in detecting those who would traffic in deadly drugs for personal profit."[34]

Of all police tactics turned against the drug war, the one that roused the greatest public outcry was perhaps "stop and frisk," embraced most notoriously by New York City police between about 2003 and early 2014. By stopping street-corner clusters of young men and frisking them for weapons, officers sought to disrupt gang banging, drug dealing, petty thieving, and brawling before such disorder could gather force and spread. Together with "broken-windows" policing, also pioneered in New York, stop-and-frisk tactics traded on the theory that targeting small-scale criminality could forestall bigger crimes.

Critics challenged stop and frisk's constitutionality and lamented its community costs. Longstanding Supreme Court case law demands that officers who pat-frisk for weapons have a reasonable suspicion that criminal activity is afoot

---

[33] Ibid. at 149.

[34] *United States v. Place*, 462 U.S. 696, 703 (1983). Two anti-government rulings are *Kyllo v. United States*, 533 U.S. 27, 40 (2001), requiring warrants to gather evidence of "grow houses" using thermal imagers aimed at suspects' homes, and *Riley v. California*, 573 U.S. 323, 403 (2014), requiring warrants to search cell phones seized from suspects. For analyses of Fourth Amendment decision-making responding to the imperative of enforcing alcohol or drug prohibitions, *see* Kenneth M. Murchison, "Prohibition and the Fourth Amendment: A New Look at Some Old Cases," *Journal of Criminal Law & Criminology*, vol. 73 (Summer 1982), p. 471; Steven Wisotsky, "Crackdown: The Emerging 'Drug Exception' to the Bill of Rights," *Hastings Law Journal*, vol. 38 (July 1987), p. 889; Susan F. Mandiberg, "Marijuana Prohibition and the Shrinking of the Fourth Amendment," *McGeorge Law Review*, vol. 43 (2012), p. 23.

and that the subject is armed and dangerous. In a 2013 opinion declaring stop and frisk as then practiced in New York unconstitutional, a U.S. District Court found officers often acted with no basis for suspicion beyond the bunching of young men on street corners. Moreover, a *weapons frisk* is supposed to be just that—a pat-down of a subject's outer clothing that proceeds no further unless an officer feels a weapon or drugs or other contraband. The court concluded New York officers routinely reached into pants pockets and sometimes patted down buttocks and groin, converting a minimally invasive weapons frisk into a publicly humiliating search for concealed drugs.[35] The consequences, as stop and frisk's opponents complained, went beyond technical constitutional violations and extended to poisoned cop–community relations.

The court's ruling suppressed the bulk of New York City police stops. After rising from about 161,000 a year in 2003 to a peak of over 685,000 in 2011, stops dropped to around 200,000 by 2013. The November 2013 election of New York Mayor Bill de Blasio on a platform opposing stop and frisk effectively killed the practice, if not the complex of police attitudes that had sustained it. Yet stop and frisk continued to inform the public's view of antidrug law enforcement in general and anti-cannabis law enforcement in particular. For while the tactic purportedly targeted gun concealment, only 0.15 percent of those stopped proved to carry a weapon. Meanwhile, eleven times as many stops yielded drugs or other contraband—still a tiny percentage, but enough to help define stop and frisk in the public's mind as an antidrug program. Indeed, marijuana possession, which accounted for 16 percent of arrests after a stop, was the most common arrest offense. Marijuana possession arrests in New York City leapt from fewer than a thousand per year in the early 1990s to almost 60,000 in some stop-and-frisk years.[36] Anti-cannabis laws, therefore, have borne the freight of the public's suspicions about stop and frisk.

But the aspect of stop and frisk that *most* soured the public's taste for anti-cannabis laws was not the image of untethered cops or humiliated young men or strained community relations or even crossed constitutional lines. Rather, the vilest aspect of stop and frisk in the public's view was the cops' seeming fixation on young men of color. Between 2004 and 2009, 73.2 percent of those stopped by New York police were thirty-four or younger, 89.5 percent were

---

[35] *Terry v. Ohio*, 392 U.S. 1, 30 (1968); *Floyd v. City of New York*, 959 F. Supp. 2d 540, 625, 631, 636, 638, 641, 648, 651, 653, 655 (S.D.N.Y. 2013).

[36] New York Civil Liberties Union, *Stop-and-Frisk Data, online at* http://www.nyclu.org/content/stop-and-frisk-data; *Floyd*, 959 F. Supp. at 558 (reporting "hit rate" in frisking for weapons); Report of Jeffrey Fagan, Ph.D., filed in *Floyd v. City of New York*, No. 08 Civ. 01034 (S.D.N.Y.) (2010), *online at* https://ccrjustice.org/files/Expert_Report_JeffreyFagan.pdf, p. 64 tbl. 15 (stating percentage of stops yielding guns and other contraband); New York Civil Liberties Union, *NYPD Stop-and-Frisk Activity in 2012* (2013), p. 17 (reporting that 16% of arrests after stops were for marijuana possession, making that crime the most common arrest offense); Jesse Wegman, "The Injustice of Marijuana Arrests," *New York Times*, July 29, 2014, p. A20 (reporting surge in possession arrests).

male, 51.5 percent were African American, and 30 percent were Latino.[37] Stop and frisk therefore was multiply suspect: officers often acted with too little evidence of criminal activity; their "frisks" often extended without legal basis to full outer-body searches; and these abuses fell hardest on Black and Brown men. Nor did the poison of stop and frisk affect New Yorkers alone. Rather, the practice became a nationwide symbol of the racial injustices wrought by antidrug law enforcement.

The Impact of Racially Disparate Enforcement

Nor was stop and frisk the only such symbol. Instead, it was one of several reviled rules and practices that, taken together with increasingly severe punishments and invasive policing, fed a broad public perception of racially disparate and overly aggressive enforcement of antidrug laws.

The Anti-Drug Abuse Act of 1986 supplied rich fodder for such claims. Spooked by crack wars terrorizing America's inner cities and by reports of the "instantaneously addictive" drug's peculiar appeal among teens, Congress enacted what became perhaps the most vilified sentencing scheme in our long history of antidrug lawmaking. The act decreed that the penalty for trafficking in a given quantity of crack cocaine should match that for trafficking in a hundred times as much powder cocaine. Proponents of this 100:1 ratio claimed crack's greater addictive power, its lower "per hit" price, and its role in fueling street combat justified longer sentences for sellers. While it's true smoked crack addicts more readily than snorted powder cocaine, the two drugs are chemical equivalents. After the crack wars subsided in the mid-1990s, what remained was a penalty scheme that treated similar crimes disparately—and triggered far longer sentences for the African Americans who typically dealt crack than for the whites and Latinos who typically dealt powder cocaine.[38]

Despite loud and repeated calls for reform from judges and academics and commentators, Congress clung stubbornly to this imbalanced regime.

---

[37] Report of Jeffrey Fagan, p. 22 tbl. 3.

[38] Dufton, *Grass Roots*, pp. 189, 196 (noting reports crack was "instantaneously addictive" and alarmingly popular among teens); Anti-Drug Abuse Act of 1986, 100 Stat. 3207-2-4, tit. 1, subtit. A, § 1002; Charisse Jones, "Crack and Punishment: Is Race the Issue?" *New York Times*, Oct. 28, 1995, p. A1 (summarizing arguments for and against the crack–powder sentencing disparity); Associated Press, "U.S. Prisons Remain Quiet," ibid., Oct. 23, 1995, p. B9 (noting lawmakers' concern with crack's low cost, fast onset, and greater addictive potential); "Crack vs. Powder Cocaine: What's the Difference?" RehabCenter.net (Aug. 6, 2018) (comparing speed of onset and addictiveness), *online at* https://www.rehabcenter.net/cocaine-vs-crack/; Danielle Kurtzleben, "Data Show Racial Disparity in Crack Sentencing," *U.S. News & World Report*, Aug. 3, 2010 (online). For an excellent account of this statutory scheme's adoption, *see* David A. Sklansky, "Cocaine, Race, and Equal Protection," *Stanford Law Review*, vol. 47 (1995), pp. 1283–97; ibid. at 1291 & n.34 (addressing addictiveness).

Lawmakers killed a 1995 proposal by the U.S. Sentencing Commission to equalize penalties for trafficking in equal weights of crack and powder cocaine. And when the Commission returned in 1997 with a proposal to reduce the 100:1 ratio to between 2:1 and 15:1, Congress failed to act.[39]

For another quarter-century the problem festered. In 2007 the Commission modestly reduced the crack–powder disparity and once again called on Congress to achieve a more comprehensive solution. A handful of stout lawmakers on both left and right proposed more equitable sentencing schemes. Yet even as mounting discomfort with the racial inequity of the crack–powder disparity tested the public's faith in the fairness of the federal justice system, few Washington power holders dared moderate a federal sentencing provision. Not till 2010 did lawmakers work substantial reform with the Fair Sentencing Act signed by President Barack Obama. Even that measure did not penalize crack and powder offenders equally, but merely shrank the existing imbalance: those who trafficked in a given quantity of crack faced sentences as harsh as those who trafficked in eighteen times as much powder cocaine. At last, in the closing days of 2022, Attorney General Merrick Garland snatched the issue from Congress, which was then debating further reform, and ordered federal prosecutors to seek sentencing parity between crack and powder offenders.[40]

Standing alone, the crack–powder disparity might not have strained the public's tolerance for the drug war. The outrage it incited required another ingredient: knowledge that 79 percent of those sentenced for trafficking in crack were African American, while 70 percent of those prosecuted for trafficking in powder cocaine were white or Latino.[41] Hence another factor testing the public's tolerance for the drug war has been the relentless recording of law-enforcement data, which has left racially disparate practices and penalties little place to hide.

---

[39] *Amendments to the Sentencing Guidelines for United States Courts*, 60 Fed. Reg. 25075–25077 (1995); "An Act to Disapprove of Amendments to the Federal Sentencing Guidelines . . . ," Pub. L. 104-38, § 1, 109 Stat. 334 (Act of Oct. 30, 1995); United States Sentencing Commission, *Special Report to the Congress: Cocaine and Federal Sentencing Policy* (Apr. 1997), p. 2, *online at* https://www. ussc.gov/sites/default/files/pdf/news/congressional-testimony-and-reports/drug-topics/19970429_ RtC_Cocaine_Sentencing_Policy.pdf.

[40] United States Sentencing Commission, *2007 Federal Sentencing Guidelines Manual* (Washington: U.S. Sentencing Commission, 2007), app. C (supp.), p. 223, Amendment 706 (Nov. 1, 2007) (amending base offense levels for crack cocaine offenses); ibid., p. 225 (predicting an average sentence reduction for crack offenses of 12.4% and calling on Congress to do more); Neil A. Lewis, "Justice Department Opposes Lower Jail Terms for Crack," *New York Times*, Mar. 20, 2002, p. A24 (noting legislation proposed by Republican Senators Orrin Hatch and Jeff Sessions to reduce the crack–powder drug-quantity disparity to 20:1); Fair Sentencing Act of 2010, Pub. L. 111-220, § 2, 124 Stat. 2372 (Act of Aug. 3, 2010); Merrick Garland, "Memorandum for All Federal Prosecutors" (Dec. 16, 2022), pp. 4–5, *available at* https://www.justice.gov/media/1265321/dl?inline (last accessed Dec. 19, 2022); David Nakamura, "U.S. Attorney General Moves to End Sentencing Disparities on Crack, Powder Cocaine," *Washington Post*, December 16, 2022.

[41] Kurtzleben, "Data Show Racial Disparity."

All the law-enforcement trends noted here come with an overlay of cross-racial data. We saw that mandatory-minimum sentencing laws and the rigid penalty structure of the federal Sentencing Guidelines helped drive the number of federal inmates confined for drug crimes in 2016 to 81,900. Adding cross-racial data reveals that 37.9 percent of federal drug inmates that year were African American and 38.6 percent Latino, though these groups made up only about 12.3 and 17.1 percent of the nation's population. Likewise we saw that car stops and searches, assisted by police-friendly Supreme Court rulings, have snagged vast numbers of suspected drug runners. Cross-racial figures reveal that in jurisdictions across the country, police search minority drivers far more often than whites. Of drivers stopped by police in 2011, only 2.3 percent of whites faced searches, as against 6.3 percent of African Americans and 6.6 percent of Latinos.[42]

Drug war opponents and other justice system critics billboard such numbers as evidence of racial profiling by police and prosecutors and perhaps even judges. The charge implies authorities are arresting, prosecuting, and imprisoning minorities in greater numbers than whites because they see dark skin as evidence of culpability and as part of a composite image of the prototypical bad actor. African Americans speak of the crime of driving while Black and recount DWB arrests in cities across America. The system's failure to defuse such charges by either righting the present imbalance in stops, searches, arrests, and sentences or justifying that imbalance in racially neutral terms prompts deepening resentment. Like the crack–powder sentencing disparity, racially disparate car stops have become a festering wound, an emblem of the system's unfairness.[43]

The New Jim Crow

Though all these allegations of racial injustice in antidrug law enforcement have floated for decades in the public's consciousness and discourse, they lacked till 2010 a powerful voice to join the factual strands into a compelling case for drug-law reform. Here Professor Michelle Alexander and her defining work, *The New Jim Crow*, have proved stunningly influential. Alexander contends the congeries

---

[42] E. Ann Carson, *Prisoners in 2016* (Washington, D.C.: Bureau of Justice Statistics, 2018), p. 20 tbl. 15 (breaking down federal inmates by crime of conviction and race); U.S. Census Bureau, Population Division, "Annual Estimates of the Resident Population by Sex, Race, and Hispanic Origin for the United States, States, and Counties: April 1, 2010 to July 1, 2013" (2014); Lynn Langton & Matthew Durose, *Police Behavior during Traffic and Street Stops, 2011* (Washington: U.S. Department of Justice, 2013), p. 9 tbl. 7 (breaking down drivers searched by race), *online at* https://www.bjs.gov/content/pub/pdf/pbtss11.pdf.

[43] Sharon LaFraniere & Andrew W. Lehren, "The Disproportionate Risk of Driving While Black," *New York Times*, Oct. 25, 2015, p. A1 ("As the public's most common encounter with law enforcement, [traffic stops] largely shape perceptions of the police.").

of American drug laws, together with the rigid penalty schemes prevailing in the federal system and many states, have conspired to create a criminalized underclass of nonviolent drug offenders. Because dealing drugs offers young minority men a rare route toward economic gain, they gravitate toward the drug trade and are sucked into the system. Racially skewed policing practices concentrate patrols in "high-crime" neighborhoods, Alexander says, and focus suspicion on non-white faces, snagging minority dealers in enforcement dragnets while their white-skinned brethren swim free. Enveloped in the specter of mass incarceration, one in three Black men will spend part of his life in prison—except in the District of Columbia, where the figure is three in four. Nor does the blight strike only the imprisoned. Left behind in their communities are broken families, single mothers, and a generation of fatherless boys adrift amid bad influences, starting the cycle over again.[44]

The system's tendrils hold minority men in underclass status, Alexander alleges, even after their return from prison to the community. Those released on parole remain under justice system supervision, shackled by long lists of shalls and shall nots. Parole conditions demand regular supervisory meetings and forbid former inmates to see certain people, visit certain places, travel certain distances, and ingest certain substances. On a mere probable-cause finding of having breached any of these conditions, a parolee can land back in prison to serve the remainder of his paroled term. Those former inmates who manage to steer clear of the law still confront barriers to successful reentry. Many face denial of federal housing and education and low-income assistance and find potential employers unwilling to look past their criminal history. Those ex-cons who aspire to fight such constraints at the ballot box often find the polls closed to them by laws denying felons the vote.[45]

Skillfully argued and thickly sourced, Alexander's systemic indictment challenges the fundamental legitimacy of the nation's drug laws and their enforcement. In the face of her fierce assault, the recent movement to legalize recreational marijuana offers a tepid response. Though nearly one-third of all drug possession arrests concern marijuana, fewer than 1 percent of state and federal prison inmates are serving time for that crime alone. In October 2022, when President Joe Biden pardoned all 6,500 federal offenders convicted of cannabis

[44] Michelle Alexander, *The New Jim Crow: Mass Incarceration in the Age of Colorblindness* (New York: The New Press, rev. ed. 2012), p. 6 (noting the U.S. incarceration rate is the world's highest); ibid., pp. 6–7 (citing estimate that three in four young African American men in the District of Columbia will serve time); ibid., p. 9 (noting one in three young African American men will serve time "if current trends continue"); E. Ann Carson, *Prisoners in 2013* (Washington, D.C.: Bureau of Justice Statistics, 2014), p. 9 tbl. 8 (showing rates of current imprisonment by race), *online at* https://www.bjs.gov/content/pub/pdf/p13.pdf.

[45] Alexander, *New Jim Crow*, pp. 1–2, 53, 94–95. The 1998 amendments to the Higher Education Act of 1965 denied student loan eligibility to those convicted of drug crimes. Higher Education Amendments of 1998, P.L. 105-244, 112 Stat. 1581, *codified at* 20 U.S.C. § 1091(r).

possession, not one person walked free. Still, the charge of racially biased enforcement lodged by Alexander and others has fronted perhaps the most potent challenge to our anti-cannabis laws. As Biden explained when announcing his move, there are "clear racial disparities around prosecution and conviction."[46]

Other evidence, it is true, complicates Alexander's account of the drug war as an instrument of racial oppression. In *Locking Up Our Own*, Professor James Forman Jr. chronicles the supporting role of African American judges, politicians, and opinion makers in the crackdown on crime that fed today's massive prison population. One episode in Forman's history, retelling a 1975 attempt to decriminalize possession of small amounts of marijuana in the District of Columbia, presents a modern-day photo negative of the early drug bans I've recounted here. In that majority-Black city, a white city councilman's decriminalization proposal met defeat at the hands of Black community leaders who feared *their youth* and especially their young men would stray from the narrow path their elders had laid out for them. The white participants in the debate overwhelmingly favored decriminalization. The African American voices, in contrast, largely echoed the views of Black Councilman Douglas Moore, who said white kids, unlike Black kids, had good schools and "a lot of opportunities to think. . . . It would . . . be a social crime to depenalize marijuana so as to make it possible for more black children who cannot think already to keep them from thinking."[47] Taken together with the history of America's earliest antidrug laws, Forman's account suggests lawmakers of any race will act to protect the moral welfare of their community's youth.

Two generations later much the same dynamic played out in a first-round cannabis debate in New Jersey. Black lawmakers helped kill a 2019 legalization bill

---

[46] "Arrests for Drug Abuse Violations: Percent Distribution by Region, 2019," *in* U.S. Department of Justice, *2019 Crime in the United States* (Washington: Criminal Justice Information Services Division, 2020). As of 2004, the latest year for which I've found figures, only about 0.74% of state and 0.36% of federal inmates were confined for cannabis possession alone—and many such offenders probably won reduction of more serious charges in the course of plea bargaining. Christopher J. Mumola & Jennifer C. Karberg, "Drug Use and Dependence, State and Federal Prisoners, 2004." BJS Special Report (Oct. 2006, rev. Jan. 19, 2007), NCJ 213530, p. 4, *online at* https://www.bjs.gov/content/pub/pdf/dudsfp04.pdf. Other researchers, using 1997 data and excluding inmates with other aggravating factors, concluded that "nonviolent, small-quantity (i.e., 10 ounces or less) marijuana possessors who were not involved in drug distribution represent two-tenths of 1% of all drug prisoners and 0.06% of all prisoners." Eric L. Sevigny & Jonathan P. Caulkins, "Kingpins or Mules: An Analysis of Drug Offenders Incarcerated in Federal and State Prisons," *Criminology & Public Policy*, vol. 3, no. 3 (July 2004), pp. 401, 421. On Biden's pardon, *see* Michael D. Shear & Zolan Kanno-Youngs, "President Issues Federal Pardons over Marijuana," *New York Times*, Oct. 7, 2022, p. A1.

[47] James Forman Jr., *Locking Up Our Own: Crime and Punishment in Black America* (New York: Farrar, Straus and Giroux, 2017), pp. 21–25 (summarizing the position of those supporting decriminalization); ibid., p. 38 (quoting *Reform of Marijuana Laws: Hearing on Bill 1-44 before the Commission on the Judiciary and Criminal Law*, D.C. City Council (July 16, 1975, morning session), p. 44 (statement of Doug Moore)). For similar statements by other African American leaders and writers, *see* Forman, *Locking Up Our Own*, pp. 32–33 (quoting writer Orde Coombs); ibid., pp. 38–39 (quoting Judge John Fauntleroy).

that white governor Phil Murphy had made a centerpiece of his election campaign. State Senator Ronald L. Rice of Newark, a leading opponent, worried that "[i]n urban communities, neighborhoods will struggle against the spread of 'marijuana bodegas' disguised as dispensaries." Senator Shirley Turner warned of increasing use among teens. And Senator Nia Gill pointed to events in Colorado, where even after legalization, marijuana arrest rates among African Americans were double those among whites.[48]

Yet Professor Alexander and others who decry the racial injustice of the drug war proved persuasive to the Oakland City Council. Recall the reasoning of Councilwoman Kaplan, who reduced Alexander's history to a sentence: "[I]t's been black people who've been locked up—had their freedom taken away, their families taken away, their jobs taken away—for something that white people mostly don't get punished for." This history of uneven enforcement demands two responses, Kaplan said. First "we must tax the pot instead of locking people up." As a *San Francisco Chronicle* columnist wrote a few weeks before the November 2016 election, "A central argument for marijuana legalization has been that people of color are disproportionately subject to pot-related arrests . . . ." Second we must pay reparations for the ravages inflicted by the drug war on communities of color. Those "disproportionately targeted" by the war on marijuana, Kaplan said, should have a better chance to flourish in the new marijuana marketplace.[49]

Polling results confirm that Kaplan, in headlining racial justice and tax revenues, felt the electorate's pulse. Asked in October 2016 why they supported California's ballot proposition legalizing recreational marijuana, prospective voters stressed increased revenues (23 percent) and the "broken" criminal justice system, "overrun with non-violent marijuana users" (22 percent). All other rationales lagged.[50]

Across the country in the District of Columbia similar views prevailed. In February 2014, the same D.C. Council that in 1975 had rejected marijuana decriminalization voted overwhelmingly to embrace it. One witness argued before the council that criminalization had amounted to "a war on the District's black neighborhoods and black residents." Here Michelle Alexander's work "played a crucial role," Professor Forman reports, "with various witnesses citing *The New Jim Crow*." That fall, with a legalization initiative on the November ballot, the

[48] *See* Nick Corasaniti, "New Jersey Ties Legalizing Pot to a Debate on Racial Fairness," *New York Times*, Nov. 29, 2018, p. A1; Nick Corasaniti, "Effort to Legalize Pot Collapses in New Jersey," ibid., Mar. 26, 2019, at A21 (quoting Senator Rice); Nick Corasaniti & Jesse McKinley, "What Blocked Legal Pot in New Jersey?" ibid., Mar. 28, 2019, at A1 (noting concerns of Senators Turner and Gill).
[49] Email from Oakland City Councilwoman Rebecca Kaplan to supporters (Oct. 26, 2016) ("we must tax . . ." and "disproportionately targeted"); Swan, "Oakland Pol Backs Expunging Pot Crimes" ("[I]t's been black . . ."); Joe Garofoli, "Try Social Justice for the Best Buzz of All," *San Francisco Chronicle*, Oct. 10, 2016, p. C1.
[50] *USC Dornsife College of Letters, Arts, and Sciences/Los Angeles Times Frequency Questionnaire* (Greenberg Quinlan Rosner, Oct. 22–30, 2016), p. 16.

president of the D.C. chapter of the NAACP said the group saw the measure "as a step toward ending discriminatory drug policies." Rallied by the slogan LEGALIZATION ENDS DISCRIMINATION, 65 percent of D.C. voters chose to lift the ban on recreational use.[51]

Likewise in New York City. Announcing his decision in May 2018 to halt prosecutions for marijuana possession and smoking, Manhattan District Attorney Cyrus Vance Jr. lamented that "black and Hispanic individuals in neighborhoods of color continue to be arrested for marijuana offenses at much higher rates than their similarly situated counterparts in predominantly white communities." The *New York Times*, too, declaring support of recreational legalization, alleged "[m]arijuana has been essentially legalized for middle-class, white residents, who are rarely arrested on minor pot charges, while smoking it is still being punished in communities of color." African Americans suffered arrest for low-level marijuana offenses at fifteen times the rate of whites in Manhattan and Staten Island, the editors said, and seven times that of whites in Queens. They condemned the criminalization of "Smoking Marijuana While Black."[52]

Emily Dufton, who has studied how grassroots activism shaped modern marijuana lawmaking, sums up the evidence simply: "[S]ocial justice has become the most powerful incentive to transform marijuana laws in American history."[53] So we encounter this historical irony: though it's *not* true racial animus gave rise to our earliest antidrug laws, it *is* true the desire to rid our culture of a racialized drug war has proved perhaps the greatest force in undermining the legitimacy of our antidrug laws. Alexander's *New Jim Crow* and arguments like hers have so shaken public support for our drug laws that the most vulnerable of them— cannabis bans—have begun to crumble.

The irony dissolves, however, if we examine these events in light of the moral framework that undergirds our drug laws. Since its inception almost a century and a half ago, our antidrug legal regime has stood on the ancient conviction that to disable one's reason in pursuit of pure pleasure offends morality. Any legal regime that stands on so high-minded a moral principle must be moral all the way to the ground. If instead it rests—or even *appears* to rest—on rotten moral timber, the structure may topple. The widespread belief in the early twenty-first century that police, prosecutors, and courts have enforced our drug laws unevenly against Black and Brown persons has sapped our antidrug laws of moral legitimacy. A certain secular moralism now demands equal justice. As presidential

[51] Forman, *Locking Up Our Own*, pp. 219–20 (quoting council witness); Dufton, *Grass Roots*, pp. 234–35 (quoting NAACP chapter president and campaign slogan and noting vote margin).

[52] Manhattan District Attorney's Office, "District Attorney Vance to End the Prosecution of Marijuana Possession and Smoking Cases" (May 15, 2018); [Editorial], "New York's Small Step on Pot Isn't Enough," *New York Times*, June 21, 2018, at A20 ("Marijuana has been . . ."); [Editorial], "Smoking Marijuana While Black," ibid., July 17, 2017, at A18.

[53] Dufton, *Grass Roots*, pp. 230–31

candidate Senator Kirsten Gillibrand said early in 2019, "legalizing marijuana is an issue of morality and social justice."[54]

The Medical Ban and Its Undoing

Anti-cannabis laws proved especially vulnerable to this secular moralist attack in part because the Controlled Substances Act of 1970 already had breached longstanding moral norms by outlawing medicinal marijuana. From Augustine onward the moral aversion to reason-depriving pleasure has given way to the excuse of necessity. Alcohol and drug bans almost always have provided for medically necessary use. That was true of the English gin ban of 1736, which exempted spirits used in the "making up of medicines for sick, lame, or distempered persons." It was true of Maine's first-in-the-nation alcohol ban of 1851, which called for appointment of a city or town agent to sell "intoxicating liquors, to be used for medicinal and mechanical purposes and no other." It was true as well of the national Volstead Act of 1919, which said a person may "purchase and use liquor for medicinal purposes when prescribed by a physician" as long as the physician "believes that the use of such liquor as a medicine . . . is necessary."[55]

Likewise, in banning eaten opium, *all fifty* states preserved the possibility of medical use. They did so, too, in banning cocaine. So did Congress in effectively banning both opium and cocaine with the 1914 Harrison Act. Only in the case of smoked opium, thought too sooty for medical purposes and too hard to dose with precision, did states enact outright bans. Of the twenty-four states and territories that banned opium dens, only four allowed the possibility of a medical excuse to visit a den.[56]

Even in banning cannabis, states overwhelmingly preserved the potential of medical use. By 1937 all fifty states and territories had outlawed most cannabis sales. *Forty-five* exempted either all medical uses or all those sanctioned by a doctor's prescription. Of the remaining five states, three permitted over-the-counter sales of cannabis-laced ointments for external use—the corn remedies that in the early twentieth century ranked among the most common medical cannabis preparations. Only two states, Alabama and North Dakota,

[54] Senator Cory Booker Press Release, Feb. 28, 2019, *online at* https://www.booker.senate.gov/?p=press_release&id=892. I thank Nick Standish for suggesting to me this line of analysis.

[55] "An Act for Laying a Duty upon the Retailers of Spirituous Liquors . . . ," 9 Geo. 2, ch. 23, § 12 (1736); "An Act for the Suppression of Drinking Houses and Tippling Shops," 1851 *Maine Laws*, ch. 211, §§ 2, 3 (Act of June 2, 1851), pp. 416, 417; National Prohibition Act, tit. 2, §§ 6, 7, 41 Stat. 305, 310–11. Daniel Okrent notes that during national prohibition only twelve states banned medicinal alcohol outright. Daniel Okrent, *Last Call: The Rise and Fall of Prohibition* (New York: Scribner, 2010), p. 200.

[56] *See* Harrison Narcotic Act, § 2(b), 38 Stat. 785, 786. On state opium dens laws, *see* Chapter 4, pp. 179–83.

banned cannabis outright with no medical savings clause. As Alabama did not outlaw cannabis till 1931 and North Dakota not till 1933, they hardly served as trendsetters. Even the federal Marihuana Tax Act of 1937, in imposing crippling taxes to shut down the recreational cannabis trade, permitted doctors to prescribe or dispense the drug. Only in 1970, when the Controlled Substances Act classed marijuana as a Schedule I drug with "no currently accepted medical use," did the ban extend beyond the drug's recreational use.[57]

So the thirty-eight states that have revived medicinal marijuana have done nothing revolutionary. They perhaps have acted boldly in the face of an abiding federal ban. But seen through the long lens of history, they have restored the law to an old status quo in which medical use almost always eluded broad-based bans. Indeed, these states have conformed anti-cannabis laws with today's bans on opioids and cocaine, which typically permit legitimate medical use. Physicians deploy morphine for end-of-life care and oxycodone for pain management, and they perform surgeries with the anesthetic aid of fentanyl, all in complete conformity with federal law. And cocaine, classed in Schedule II with drugs that "ha[ve] a currently accepted medical use," retains its traditional role as a topical anesthetic.

Hence when Californians voted in 1996 to authorize marijuana's medical use and sale, they touched off a trend waiting to happen. Alaska, Oregon, and Washington trailed by only two years. Maine followed a year after that, and Colorado, Hawaii, and Nevada another year later. By 2012, when Colorado and Washington voters approved their historic laws permitting recreational pot, eighteen states had authorized medical marijuana or were in the process of doing so. By then, nearly three-quarters of Americans favored legalizing medical marijuana.[58] Today, as the map in Figure 8.1 shows, the trend has swept across three-quarters of the nation.

---

[57] *See* "An Act to Suppress the Use and Prohibit the Possession . . . of Marihuana . . . ," 1931 *Alabama General Laws*, no. 26 (Act of Feb. 11, 1931), p. 42; "An Act Defining Marihuana as a Habit-Forming Drug . . . ," 1933 *North Dakota Laws*, ch. 106 (Act of Mar. 6, 1933), p. 158; Marihuana Tax Act of 1937, §§ 5, 6(b)(1), (2), 50 Stat. 551, 553. Though the Marihuana Tax Act spared medical marijuana use when prescribed, Mark Eddy writes that the act "caus[ed] all medicinal products containing marijuana to be withdrawn from the market and [led] to marijuana's removal, in 1941, from *The National Formulary* and the *United States Pharmacopoeia*, in which it had been listed for almost a century." Mark Eddy, *Medical Marijuana: Review and Analysis of Federal and State Policies* (Washington: Congressional Research Service, 2005), p. 3, *online at* https://digital.library.unt.edu/ark:/67531/metacrs8244/. Eddy doesn't explain why the act triggered this result.

[58] ProCon.org, "Legal Medical Marijuana States and DC," *online at* http://medicalmarijuana.procon.org/view.resource.php?resourceID=000881; Russell Heimlich, "Favor Legalizing Medical Marijuana," Pew Research Center (2010), *online at* http://www.pewresearch.org/fact-tank/2010/04/09/favor-legalizing-medical-marijuana/ (reporting 73% of Americans support medical marijuana when prescribed). Louisiana gave statutory approval to medical marijuana in 1991, but did not establish a regulatory framework to enable medical distribution till 2015. "An Act . . . to Authorize Physicians to Prescribe Marijuana for Therapeutic Use . . . ," 1991 *Louisiana Acts*, vol. 2, act 874 (Act of Aug. 21, 1991), pp. 2655–56; Associated Press, "Louisiana's Medical Marijuana Program Slow to Take Shape," nola.com, Oct. 8, 2017.

Medical legalization has eased the tension between our post-1970 legal regime and our time-honored moral accommodation of medicinal drug use. At the same time it has undermined *all* anti-cannabis laws, including those against recreational use. Voters debating whether to support full legalization can see the sky hasn't fallen over the thirty-eight states permitting medical use. When Colorado and Washington voters went to the polls in 2012 to weigh in on recreational use and sales, they had lived with legalized medical marijuana for over a decade and had witnessed a blossoming of medical dispensaries. Proponents of legalization argued that if sale and use of medical marijuana had loosed no wave of cannabis-related crime or traffic fatalities or social disorder, there was no cause to fear recreational sale and use.[59]

The average voter likely found this argument compelling, for in the eyes of many, medical marijuana *was* recreational pot. Polls show large majorities of Americans believe marijuana has legitimate medical uses. And most every medical marijuana law requires buyers to secure a doctor's certificate and forbids doctors to issue certificates absent a genuine medical condition. Still, most people believe *most* medical marijuana is not for the sick. Only 29 percent of Americans surveyed by CBS News in 2012 believed officially sanctioned medical marijuana was "being used to alleviate suffering from serious medical illnesses." Not long before, the *New York Times* reported that on the Venice Beach boardwalk, hawkers dressed in green were offering ten-minute medical evaluations for $35. Arguing against a 2014 medical marijuana initiative in Florida, a contributor to the *Ft. Lauderdale Sun-Sentinel* said the Florida proposal "is not really about compassionate care; it's about getting high." And when comedian Jimmy Kimmel sent a reporter onto the streets of Los Angeles in 2016 asking passers-by if they had a medical marijuana card and why, their answers were revealing—and hilarious. "What medical condition do you have?" the reporter asked a young woman. "The condition is, um, children, jobs, life," she answered.[60]

---

[59] Norimitsu Onishi, "Marijuana Only for the Sick? A Farce, Some in Los Angeles Say," *New York Times*, Oct. 8, 2012, p. A16 (numbering medical dispensaries in Los Angeles at 500 to over 1,000); "Marijuana Dispensaries in California," *in* Ballotpedia, *online at* http://ballotpedia.org/Marijuana_ dispensaries_in_California (estimating between 500 and 1,000 medical dispensaries in California); Brooke Edwards Staggs, "Legalizing Marijuana Has Little Effect on Crime, Except in California," *Daily Democrat*, Feb. 23, 2017, *online at* https://www.dailydemocrat.com/2017/02/23/legalizing-medical-marijuana-has-little-effect-on-crime-except-in-california/ ("In California, the study indicates that legalizing marijuana helped lower violent and property crimes by 20 percent.").

[60] Michael Dimock et al., "Majority Now Supports Legalizing Marijuana" (Pew Research Center, Apr. 4, 2013), Q88, p. 6 (reporting results of a March 2013 poll showing 77% of respondents believed marijuana has legitimate medical uses), *online at* http://www.people-press.org/2013/04/04/major ity-now-supports-legalizing-marijuana/; Fred Backus, "CBS News Poll: Marijuana and Medical Marijuana after the 2012 Election," SCRIBD.com (2012), p. 2, *online at* https://www.scribd.com/ document/114941164/Marijuana-and-Medical-Marijuana-after-the-2012-Election; Onishi, "Marijuana Only for the Sick?" (telling of Venice Beach coupons); Barney Bishop, "Amendment 2 Not about Relief, It's about Getting High," *Ft. Lauderdale Sun-Sentinel*, Aug. 1, 2014, p. 17A. The Jimmy Kimmel clip is online at http://www.thecannabist.co/2016/04/19/jimmy-kimmel-medi

Such allegations of medical feigning and fraud supplied a potent argument for recreational legalization: if the so-called medical trade is just a shill for recreational abuse, the glut of medical dispensaries in some states is both proof we'll survive all-out legalization and evidence the barn doors are already open, spilling medical pot into the recreational marketplace. That marijuana has genuine medicinal value is largely beside the point. Hundreds of scientific studies have turned up at least a dozen symptoms and maladies that seem treatable with cannabis or its components—the nausea and vomiting of chemotherapy; cancer-related pain, anxiety, and depression; the anorexia of HIV disease; the spasticity and insomnia of multiple sclerosis; the seizures of Dravet syndrome; nonspecific chronic pain and resulting insomnia; post-traumatic stress; social anxiety; the symptoms of Tourette syndrome; and perhaps even traumatic brain injury. Some medical marijuana statutes take pains to limit medical use to the genuinely ill. New York's 2014 law, for example, demanded patients suffer from a "severe debilitating or life-threatening condition[]."[61] In this realm, though, the perception of voters and lawmakers is what counts. The knowing laughter of Jimmy Kimmel's audience as folks squirmed when asked to justify their medical marijuana cards—one man said he has "suspect glaucoma"—betrayed widespread suspicion there's no healing going on here.

Still we shouldn't assume the fifteen states that have embraced medical but not recreational marijuana have launched themselves down an icy slope toward full-scale legalization. Some euphoric drugs, including morphine and cocaine, have been available only by prescription for more than a century with no sign this line

---

cal-marijuana-conditions-video/52277/. My thanks to Matthew Miller, who canvassed an enormous array of public opinion polls on legalized marijuana.

[61] In 2017 a committee of the National Academy of Sciences, Engineering, and Medicine reviewed scores of existing studies and found "conclusive evidence" that oral cannabinoids are effective in treating chemotherapy-induced nausea and vomiting; "substantial evidence" that cannabis or oral cannabinoids are effective in treating chronic pain in adults and patient-reported multiple sclerosis spasticity symptoms; "moderate evidence" that cannabinoids are an effective short-term treatment of the sleep disturbance associated with obstructive sleep apnea syndrome, fibromyalgia, chronic pain, and multiple sclerosis; "limited evidence" that cannabis or oral cannabinoids are effective in treating HIV-related weight loss, social anxiety, posttraumatic stress, and symptoms of Tourette syndrome; and "limited evidence" that cannabinoids are associated with better outcomes after traumatic brain injuries. Committee on the Health Effects of Marijuana, *The Health Effects of Cannabis and Cannabinoids: The Current State of Evidence and Recommendations* (Washington: National Academies Press, 2017), pp. 88–97, 101–04, 115–24. *See also* Orrin Devinsky et al., "Trial of Cannabidiol for Drug-Resistant Seizures in the Dravet Syndrome," *New England Journal of Medicine*, vol. 376 (2017), p. 2011; Han Zhang et al., "Association of Marijuana Use with Psychosocial and Quality of Life Outcomes Among Patients with Head and Neck Cancer," *JAMA Otolaryngology—Head Neck Surgery* (Aug. 2, 2018), *online at* https://jamanetwork.com/journals/jamaotolaryngology/article-abstract/2688527?guest. For New York's medical marijuana law, *see* "An Act . . . in Relation to Medical Use of Marihuana . . . ," 2014 *New York Laws*, vol. 1, ch. 90, §§ 3360(7)(a)(1), 3361(1) (Act of July 5, 2014), p. 744. Again I thank Matthew Miller, who assembled a huge array of sources on marijuana's medical efficacy.

will waver. Medical marijuana marketplaces have given less liberal states a taste of the brave new world already on view in the twenty-three states with legalized recreational sales. Perhaps today's medical-only states will progress in due course toward full legalization with dispensaries thick as Starbucks. The lessons of this book, however, suggest three grounds for caution in predicting these more traditional states are on a fast path toward a recreational free market.

First Caution: The Challenge of Rebranding Pot

Advocates of full-scale legalization commonly claim marijuana does less harm than alcohol. Marijuana wreaks less havoc on health, they say, and fuels far less violence.[62] True as these claims may be, they misapprehend our moral coming to terms with alcohol.

That moral accommodation has had very little to do with *harm*. If harm reduction mediated the marketplace in recreational drugs, cigarettes would be banned, and marijuana and even Ecstasy likely would have hit store shelves long ago. Surely some drugs—fentanyl, say, which has killed many thousands—do enough harm to merit a ban. But the primary principle mediating the marketplace in recreational drugs has not been a drug's harms or risks but its intoxicating power. And our moral accommodation with alcohol has required us to limit that power.

We saw this lesson in Chapter 3. As drinking emerged from the legal dormancy of prohibition, those who hoped to revive open sales sought to *rebrand* alcohol by stressing its necessity as a social lubricant and urging both tradespersons and private hosts to render the drug nonintoxicating. Hence in 1933, the year of prohibition's demise, Alma Whitaker warned the "hostesses of the United States" that "the cup that cheers . . . positively should not inebriate." "Two cocktails is the absolute limit," she said, because "[w]ines and spirits should be strictly a social lubricant."[63] Whitaker expressed a broad social consensus favoring laws and norms that constrain alcohol's intoxicating force while embracing its social utility. Both law and custom therefore require innkeepers and householders to serve alcohol in moderate amounts and at reasonable hours, preferably with food and mostly in company, to supply seating and other social amenities, and to refuse service to those already drunk. Bottled drinks, moreover, mustn't contain

---

[62] Philip M. Boffey, "What Science Says About Marijuana," *New York Times*, July 31, 2014, p. A22 (citing "the clear consensus of science that marijuana is . . . less dangerous than the highly addictive . . . alcohol" and declaring marijuana's "effects are mostly euphoric and mild, whereas alcohol turns some drinkers into barroom brawlers, domestic abusers or maniacs behind the wheel").

[63] Alma Whitaker, *Bacchus Behave! The Lost Art of Polite Drinking* (New York: Frederick A. Stokes Company, 1933), pp. 3, 4, 7, 17.

too much alcohol. Consider how unthinkable it would be for an ad to boast of a beer's power to leave you smashed.

Sex, too, has undergone a clever rebranding, boosting its moral credentials by stressing its necessity even when procreation is not in view. The twentieth-century, post-Freudian concept of a "healthy sex life" exploits the very old moral indulgence of euphoric activities that serve a medical need. The notion of a healthy sex life so deeply pervades today's culture that it seems part of the background noise of our existence, not a *concept* that once had to rise up and take hold. Yet the phrase seems to appear no earlier than the first decades of the twentieth century, when physician Havelock Ellis repeated a patient's reference to "the need of healthy sexual intercourse" (1905) and psychiatrist Auguste Forel explained how to achieve "a healthy sexual life" (1908) and education writer Thomas Walton Galloway and sociologist Maurice Parmelee taught the precepts of a "healthy sex life" (1913 and 1918). Soon, mentions of a "healthy sex life" were legion and included even a claim of "the *necessity* for a healthy sex life."[64]

A *healthy sex life* invokes *health* in two ways. Like a healthy appetite, a healthy sex life is robust and vigorous. And like a healthy diet, a healthy sex life enhances the health of the organism. This sense of the term is critical, for the notion that one's sex life can be medically healthful offers a moral license to indulge. Though some early commentators spoke of a healthy sex life as cleansing the genito-urinary tract, others alluded to the psychic benefits of regular sexual expression—and to what one observer termed "Professor Freud's dictum that with a healthy sex life there can be no neurosis." Indeed Freud's work informed and supported the concept of a healthy sex life. That the sexual impulse, long suppressed, would erupt in strange dreams or troubling tics or disabling neuroses, as Freud's work predicted, surely seemed plausible to those who wished to indulge.[65]

[64] Havelock Ellis, *Sexual Selection in Man* (Philadelphia: F.A. Davis Co., 1905), p. 227; August Forel, *The Sexual Question: A Scientific, Psychological, Hygienic and Sociological Study for the Cultured Classes* (C.F. Marshall ed., New York: Rebman Company, 1908), p. 333; T.W. Galloway, *Biology of Sex for Parents and Teachers* (Chicago: D.C. Heath and Company, 1913), p. 49; Maurice Parmelee, *Personality and Conduct* (New York: Moffat, Yard & Company, 1918), p. 150; Bernard Benard, *Sex Conduct in Marriage* (Chicago: Health and Life Publications, n.d.), p. 28 ("the necessity for a healthy sex life"). I thank Rachael Samberg for her heroic research in tracing the lineage of this concept.

[65] E. Swift, "Health Talks," *New Journal and Guide* (May 1, 1926), p. 5 ("A mixed diet, plenty of fresh air and water and healthy sex life will keep the genito–urinary tract clean and save us from many troubles and such dread diseases as syphilis."); [William A.] White, "*A Thousand Marriages: A Medical Study of Sex Adjustment*, by Robert Latou Dickinson and Lura Beam," *The Psychoanalytic Review*, vol. 20 (Jan. 1, 1933), p. 354 ("Professor Freud's dictum . . ."); *Birth Control: Hearings before the Committee on the Judiciary, House of Representatives* (73d Cong., 2d Sess.) (Washington: United States Printing Office, 1934), p. 52 (Jan. 18, 1934) (statement of Smith Ely Jelliffe, M.D.) ("My experience of 40 years' study of medicine, especially in nervous and mental disease, and I believe practically all disease, save the infectious disorders, leads me to the sincere conviction that there is no really healthy life without a corresponding healthy sexual life."); Sigmund Freud, *The Interpretation of Dreams* (Joyce Crick trans., New York: Oxford University Press, 1999 (1899)), pp. 119–23, 125, 140–44 (describing the consequences of repressed sexuality).

Sex's moral rebranding under the guise of a healthy sex life has succeeded stunningly. There has been since Freud's day little dissent from the view that regular sexual expression enhances adults' psychic health. And the class of relationships perceived as enabling a healthy sex life has expanded slowly toward the limit of all affective, consensual relationships. Here the lead story has been the moral rebranding of same-sex relationships, which just a generation ago were clawing their way into moral respectability.

Observers of the modern scene commonly but mistakenly suggest the rapidly growing acceptance of same-sex marriage somehow assures similar acceptance of recreational marijuana. They overlook how radically gay sex has changed in the last four decades, in both reality and public perception. Forty years ago the specter of AIDS was gathering over a gay male community notorious for shadowed couplings at roadside rest stops and bus stop restrooms. Even as the AIDS threat checked anonymous sex and fostered monogamous bonding, the struggle against the disease exposed to public view a long-hidden LGBTQ community of long-term couples and lifelong friendships like those in every American hamlet. The fight for civil unions and later for same-sex marriage, far from challenging traditional morality, represents the ultimate rebranding of gay relationships as being much like other relationships. All serve timeworn moral needs for affective bonding, parenting, and lifelong mutual support.

The question now is whether marijuana too can shift its moral valence—whether its intoxicating force and aphrodisiac power and stoner image are inherent in the substance or instead are artifacts of a fading counterculture that no longer defines the drug. If pot's purveyors are wise, they will aim to reshape public perceptions by rebranding their drug not as a euphoriant or an agent to disable the mind or an aid in casual sex—in short not as a stoner drug.[66]

Those policy wonks and social engineers who favor legalization seem to grasp this challenge. In Colorado, where the recreational marketplace is most developed, lawmakers have imposed packaging and labeling rules that aim to dissuade consumers of marijuana candies and baked goods from eating too much. Lizzie Post—whose 2019 book, *Higher Etiquette*, is cannabis culture's answer to Alma Whitaker's *Bacchus Behave!*—stresses that cannabis highs "are not often foggy-headed, sleep-inducing hours of feeling checked out." Instead, she says, a smoker's aims may be to "foster motivation and creativity" and connect socially over "deep and meaningful conversations." Cannabis marketers, however,

---

[66] Jessica Bennett, "In Colorado, a Rebranding of Pot Inc.," *New York Times*, Oct. 5, 2014, p. ST1 (reporting on a conference of marijuana entrepreneurs asking, "How can the pot industry shed its stoner stigma?"); Max Berlinger, "Where There's Smoke, There's Business," ibid., Jan. 10, 2019, p. D2 (telling of new, cannabis-themed magazines that "are helping the archetype of marijuana smokers as shaggy-haired, bloodshot-eyed burnouts evolve into one of cultured, luxury-designer-wearing members of the creative class").

have shown less savvy, often trumpeting their products' psychoactive punch. Some Colorado dispensaries persist in naming themselves "Reefer Madness," "Altitude," and "The Stone." They peddle products styled "Head Banger," "Exotic Blowout," and the ubiquitous "Shatter," a form of high-octane butane hash oil. One of the most popular brands of cannabis-infused chocolates, inevitably called "Mile High," promises to take you to "peak elevation." Even Kaviar, a cannabis firm with an uptown vibe, can't resist reprinting adoring press reviews marveling that its joints "bubble all the way to space" and "launch[] your mind into a hazy bliss, leaving you completely stoned."[67]

The problem extends beyond marketing strategies. There is also the very real difficulty of titrating cannabis doses. Those who drink bottled beverages stamped with their exact alcohol content can limit precisely their alcohol intake. Cannabis users, even if not *aiming* to intoxicate, often can't calibrate consumption and achieve a predictably mild effect. Hoping simply to relax and ease conversation, they easily can overshoot and cloud their minds.

Calibrating doses is especially hard for users of marijuana edibles—those deceptively innocent cannabis-infused brownies, gumdrops, and lollypops—as their psychoactive kick can trail ingestion by an hour or two or more. By the time the drug hits the brain, the consumer long since has lost capacity to temper its effects. As one marijuana entrepreneur said, "[I]t's notoriously hard to control the titration in your stomach." Because smoked marijuana hits faster, a smoker can better measure the drug's impact.[68] Still, it seems unlikely a pot smoker ever will achieve a drinker's degree of dosage control. With consistent branding and pouring, an evening Scotch or glass of wine will leave a regular drinker without noticeable impairment night after night. A marijuana smoker can slip readily past a social buzz toward obtuseness.

The difficulty of dosage control is especially fraught because the cannabis products on dispensary shelves today pack a far harder punch than their Woodstock-era forebears. "This is not your grandfather's weed," says one Colorado police chief. The magic ingredient in today's psychoactive baked goods

[67] *Colorado Revised Statutes Annotated* § 12-43.4-202, (3)(a)(VII), (3)(c)(III), (3)(c.5)(I), and § 12-43.4-404, (4)(a), (8) (2017) (prescribing packaging and labeling requirements); Lizzie Post, *Higher Etiquette: A Guide to the World of Cannabis, from Dispensaries to Dinner Parties* (New York: Ten Speed Press, 2019), p. 15 ("are not often . . ."); ibid., p. 87 ("deep and meaningful . . ."; ibid., p. 144 ("foster motivation . . ."). Most ads are quoted from *Westword*, a Denver weekly. *Westword*, vol. 42, no. 45 (July 11–17, 2019), pp. 60–61 (page insert) ("Headbanger"); *Westword*, vol. 42, no. 46 (July 18–24, 2019), p. 43 ("Altitude"); ibid., p. 48 ("Reefer Madness"); ibid., p. 52 ("Kaviar"); ibid., p. 53 ("The Stone"); ibid., p. 58 ("Exotic Blowout"). *See also* iloveincredibles.com (advertising Mile High mint chocolate bars).

[68] Maureen Dowd, "Pot Rules," *New York Times*, June 8, 2014, p. SR11 (quoting Justin Hartfield, founder of Marijuana.com); Roni Caryn Rabin, "Edibles May Pose Special Risks," ibid., Apr. 2, 2019, p. D4 (quoting the director of the National Institute on Drug Abuse on the quick impact of smoked marijuana and the sluggish effects of edibles).

often is not simple marijuana, but butane hash oil or BHO. Running butane through dried cannabis flowers produces a highly concentrated cannabis extract bursting with the psychoactive chemical THC. The THC content of some butane hash oils runs to 80 or 90 percent, compared to less than 4 percent in yesteryear's marijuana. Not only does BHO get "you waaaaaaaaaaaaaaaaay fucking higher," in the words of one online commentator, and "render[] you pretty much useless," it also proves hard to taste in cannabis edibles. Such sweets are a recipe for overdose disasters, especially among novices. Unaware that eaten cannabis can linger in the system before lightening the mind, first-timers may keep eating till they've eaten far too much.[69]

Even if wise policy and careful warnings can deter such mishaps, there's no assurance marijuana can mimic alcohol in claiming to serve as a necessary social lubricant. For centuries folks have praised alcohol's conversational virtues. With the "enlivening aid" of a pint of beer, wrote a 1710 correspondent to *The Tatler*, a bashful man "thinks clearer, speaks more ready," and "express[es] himself upon any subject with more life and vivacity [and] more variety of ideas." The virtues of cannabis as a conversational aid are more dubious. Writing in *Popular Science Monthly* in 1878, Charles Richet, a future Nobelist in physiology or medicine, described a typical hashish smoker: "With the air of a tragic actor he will tell you that it rains, or that the wind blows." More recently, writer Andrew Sullivan contrasted the conversational virtues of ordinary marijuana and BHO. He and a friend "usually kick off long, digressive conversations with weed. But dabbing it"—vaporizing and inhaling BHO—"made me want to go to bed to escape all the sounds and sights around me. It ended the conversation."[70] One challenge of those who would rebrand marijuana, then, is persuading skeptics it can enliven and enrich conversation without dumbing it down or snuffing it out.

---

[69] "More News," *Denver Post*, Aug. 27, 2017, p. 1A (quoting Greenwood Village Police Chief John Jackson); "Butane Hash Oil," Vice.com (July 18, 2013), *online at* https://www.vice.com/en_us/arti cle/gqwz3y/butane-hash-oil (source of quotes); Joe Mozingo, "Blowing Up," *Los Angeles Times*, Feb. 6, 2014, p. A1 (describing the production of BHO); Anna Wilcox, "10 Strongest Dabs You Can Buy Right Now," *Herb*, Aug. 31, 2016, *online at* https://herb.co/learn/strongest-dabs/ (listing products with THC concentrations between 75% and 97%); "Colorado Marijuana Study Finds Legal Weed Contains Potent THC Levels," NBC News (Mar. 23, 2015), *online at* https://www.nbcnews.com/ storyline/legal-pot/legal-weed-surprisingly-strong-dirty-tests-find-n327811; Kenneth L. Davis & Mary Jeanne Kreek, "Marijuana Damages Young Brains," *New York Times*, June 17, 2019, p. A19 (noting the average THC content of marijuana seized in the early 1990s was about 3.7%); Rabin, "Edibles May Pose Special Risks" (reporting on the danger of eating too much).

[70] *The Tatler*, no. 252 (Nov. 18, 1710), *in The Tatler and the Guardian* (Edinburgh: William P. Nimmo & Co., 1880), p. 442 (reprinting unsigned correspondent's letter); Charles Richet, "Poisons of the Intelligence—Hasheesh," *Popular Science Monthly*, vol. 13 (1878), pp. 482, 483; Andrew Sullivan, "The Abyss of Hate Versus Hate," *Intelligencer*, Jan. 25, 2019, *online at* https://nymag.com/ intelligencer/2019/01/andrew-sullivan-the-abyss-of-hate-versus-hate.html. My thanks to Don Herzog for pointing me to Sullivan's essay.

Second Caution: The Danger to Youth

A second challenge is persuading concerned parents that legalization won't ease their kids' access to cannabis. As we've seen again and again in tracking the history of America's earliest drug bans, lawmakers respond to nothing more quickly than a drug's threat to youthful morals and health. Here the rollout of Colorado's recreational marketplace in 2014 supplied an object lesson for policymakers in copycat states. For the rollout's most disheartening aspect was the persistent allure of cannabis edibles among youth.

It's not that Colorado lawmakers failed to foresee the risk. From the beginning, the law banned sales to those under twenty-one and required childproof packaging of recreational edibles. Yet a stubborn drip of news stories about kids on cannabis nagged at the public consciousness. Here I'll set aside the distressing rise in hospital admissions of droopy toddlers laid low by mislaid cannabis baked goods. Troubling as they are, these tales don't concern *recreational* intoxication. Accounts of *older* kids snacking on marijuana edibles mounted a stiffer challenge to the industry's image. Such tales emerged in January 2014, the debut month of Colorado's recreational marketplace. At Olathe High School, far west of Denver, a fourteen-year-old passed around spiked brownies, dispatching one classmate to the emergency room. In March a suburban Denver middle school suspended twelve students who munched marijuana candies and expelled the two who supplied the drug. And in April a Greeley fourth-grader made a playground sale of his grandmother's marijuana to three classmates. The next day, one of the three brought *his* grandmother's cannabis edibles to school.[71]

As such stories peppered the press, Colorado lawmakers reacted quickly. In May 2014, they directed state regulators to devise rules requiring every marijuana edible to bear "a standard symbol indicating that it contains marijuana and is not for consumption by children." At a signing ceremony in the lobby of Aurora's Children's Hospital, Governor John Hickenlooper declared the law "critical to . . . our constant goal of protecting our children." Two years later, lawmakers acted again, this time forbidding "edible marijuana products that

---

[71] Jack Healy, "Snacks Laced with Marijuana Raise Concerns," *New York Times*, Feb 1, 2014, p. A1 (reporting the Olathe events); Trevor Hughes, "Colo. Kids Eat Parents' Pot-Laced Goodies," *USA Today*, Apr. 4, 2014, p. 6A (telling of the suburban Denver middle school); Jack Healy, "After 5 Months of Sales, Colorado Sees the Downside of a Legal High," *New York Times*, June 1, 2014, p. A14 (relaying the Greeley events); Associated Press, "4th-Graders Try to Sell Pot; Schools Warning Parents," *Denver Post*, Apr. 24, 2014, p. 4A (same); Tom McGhee, "Marijuana Edibles—Lawmakers Are Given a Taste of a Possible Packaging Problem," ibid., Apr. 11, 2014, p. 1A (collecting stories of child consumption and describing legislative backlash). For Colorado's packaging and labeling requirements for retail marijuana products, *see* Colorado Department of Revenue, *Retail Marijuana Rules* (2017), Rule 1004, pp. 158–62 (eff. July 1, 2013), *online at* https://www.colorado.gov/pacific/sites/default/files/Complete%20Retail%20Marijuana%20Rules%20as%20of%20April%202014%202017%20with%20DOR%20Disclaimer_1.pdf.

Figure 8.2: Cannabis edibles purchased in Denver's recreational dispensaries (October 2015).

are shaped in a manner to entice a child"—those resembling fruits, animals, or humans—or that include "additives . . . designed to make the product more appealing to children." At the same time, lawmakers authorized restrictions on marijuana ads directed to persons under eighteen.[72]

Such rules may slow but surely will not stop the flow of recreational pot to kids. Printed warnings can't protect children too young to read or too headstrong to take heed. And as I discovered on a tour of Denver dispensaries in October 2015, "child-resistant packaging" does not strip cannabis edibles of their allure or put them past a child's grasp. The platter of cannabis treats pictured in Figure 8.2, a child's sweetshop fantasy, contains some 528 milligrams of THC or about fifty-three standard doses. Though *small* kids might have trouble footing the bill—this

[72] "An Act Concerning Reasonable Restrictions on the Sale of Edible Retail Marijuana Products," 2014 *Colorado Laws*, ch. 236 (Act of May 21, 2014), pp. 870–71; John Ingold, "Children's Hospital Seeing Rise in Marijuana Ingestion," *Denver Post*, May 22, 2014, p. 4A (describing bill signing and quoting governor); "An Act Concerning a Prohibition on Edible Marijuana Products That Are Shaped in a Manner to Entice a Child," 2016 *Colorado Laws*, ch. 361, §§ 1, 2 (Act of June 10, 2016), pp. 1508–09; "An Act Concerning Rule-making Authority for Medical Marijuana Advertising Directed at Underage Persons," 2016 *Colorado Laws*, ch. 299 (Act of June 10, 2016), pp. 1213–14; Alicia Wallace, "Edibles Can't Look Like Candy," *Denver Post*, Sept. 28, 2017, p. 1A.

array of goodies set me back about $145, or $2.75 per dose—bigger kids and teens could carry the cost with ease. Even toddlers could outwit the childproof packaging, which typically yielded to a pair of scissors. Kid-pitched ads, some with rhyming morals—"For those underage, it's just not OK. Their brains are still growing, so keep it away"—mount a feeble defense against peer pressure to consume. It's true dispensaries police access with rigor; not one admitted me without first demanding a photo I.D. But as every big kid knows a young adult with an I.D., parents have cause to worry their kids can get stoned on sweets for a song.[73]

Though some studies suggest such fears are unfounded, others bear out parental concerns. Healthy Kids Colorado Surveys reveal a slightly *declining* rate of marijuana use among Colorado middle and high schoolers between 2009, when medical dispensaries began to proliferate, and 2017. Other surveys, including those conducted by the Centers for Disease Control and Prevention, have yielded similar statewide results. A very different story appears from a localized study of emergency-room and urgent-care visits to Aurora's Children's Hospital and its satellite clinics, clustered mainly around Denver, Boulder, and Colorado Springs. Near those cities, clotted with cannabis dispensaries, marijuana-related hospital visits among youth aged thirteen to twenty leapt from 161 in 2005 to 777 in 2015, rising steeply after 2009. Marijuana-related calls to Colorado's regional poison center likewise jumped. In 2009, sixteen such calls concerned persons aged nine to seventeen. That figure almost doubled in 2010 and doubled again to sixty-three in 2015, the year after recreational dispensaries opened their doors. Then, too, Colorado's school resource officers describe a striking rise in marijuana offenses. In one Colorado survey, 89 percent of officers reported increased marijuana use among students since recreational legalization. "I've written more marijuana tickets in the last two years than I ever wrote while out on patrol," said one school officer in 2017. And across the country in New York, just as legalized dispensaries began to proliferate in 2023, the *New York Times* headlined worries about "Kids Buying Weed from Bodegas" and "More and More Teenagers . . . Coming to School High," leaving some classrooms in disarray.[74]

[73] John Ingold, "Friendly Ad Campaign to Warn of Risks Is Praised," *Denver Post*, Jan. 22, 2018, p. 1A (quoting ad); *see* Robert J. MacCoun & Michelle M. Mello, "Half-Baked—The Retail Promotion of Marijuana Edibles," *New England Journal of Medicine*, vol. 372 (2015), p. 989 ("Even if consumption by minors is not intended by manufacturers, the packaging of edibles brings to mind the tort-law concept of the 'attractive nuisance': a hazardous condition that is foreseeably likely to attract children . . . ."). My thanks to Lu and Richard Koeppe, Denver residents who supported my Colorado-related research. Lu Koeppe helped me shop for and display the marijuana treats pictured in Figure 8.2. And Richard Koeppe briefed me for years on local press coverage of the developing cannabis marketplace.
[74] Healthy Kids Colorado Survey, "Colorado Youth Marijuana Use 2017," *online at* https://drive. google.com/file/d/1M3XdmqznZDl2y6D7Hz6iDGwTFTHSGrtP/view; Centers for Disease Control and Prevention, *Youth Risk Behavior Surveillance—United States, 2017* (Atlanta: Center for Surveillance, 2018), tbl. 111 (showing that in 2017, 19.6% of Colorado high schoolers had used marijuana in the past thirty days); Centers for Disease Control and Prevention, *Youth Risk Behavior Surveillance—United States, 2009* (Atlanta: Center for Surveillance, 2010), p. 78 tbl. 41 (showing that in 2009, 24.8% of Colorado high schoolers had used marijuana in the past thirty days); Magdalena

Nor can parents shrug off adolescent use as a harmless foible. For alongside stories of pot-sickened children, the press has run items reminding parents that young and developing brains are peculiarly vulnerable to cannabis intoxication. One in six youths who use marijuana will grow addicted, said one study. Another study, widely publicized though later questioned, suggested teens who use marijuana heavily till adulthood and become dependent on the drug will suffer an I.Q. loss averaging eight points. A third study associated adolescent cannabis use with thinning of the prefrontal cortices and, perhaps relatedly, attentional impulsiveness. Frequent use by teens predicts lower educational attainment, higher adult unemployment, and lower adult income. Accounts of Ivy-bound youth sidelined by pot, seemingly the stuff of anecdote and fearmongering, are too rooted in research for prudent parents to ignore. Yet the cannabis industry keeps whispering in children's ears. In 2021, despite years of handwringing about kid-friendly edibles, Wrigley and Hershey and other candy makers sued a raft of cannabis companies for making pot-infused lookalikes of Skittles and Reese's Cups and Almond Joys.[75]

Cerdá et al., "Association of State Recreational Marijuana Laws with Adolescent Marijuana Use," *JAMA Pediatrics*, vol. 171 (2017), pp. 142–48 & tbl. 3 (presenting survey data showing the percentage of tenth- and twelfth-graders who reported marijuana use in the past thirty days dropped between 2010–2012 and 2013–2015); George Sam Wang et al., "Impact of Marijuana Legalization in Colorado on Adolescent Emergency and Urgent Care Visits," *Journal of Adolescent Health*, vol. 63 (2018), pp. 239–41 & fig. 1; John Ingold, "Pot Sending More Teens to ER," *Denver Post*, May 19, 2017, p. 2A; George Sam Wang et al., "Marijuana and Acute Health Care Contacts in Colorado," *Preventive Medicine*, vol. 104 (2017), pp. 24, 28, fig. 2; Tom McGhee, "Jury Is Still Out on Legalization's Effect on Marijuana Smoking among Kids," *Denver Post*, Dec. 28, 2014, p. 21W (reporting survey of school resource officers conducted by the Rocky Mountain High Intensity Drug Trafficking Area); David Migoya, "Police in Colo. Find Use on Rise," ibid., Dec. 24, 2017, p. 1A (quoting officer); Ginia Bellafante, "Kids Buying Weed from Bodegas Wasn't in the 'Legal Weed' Plan," *New York Times*, Feb. 24, 2023; Ashley Southall, "More and More Teenagers Are Coming to School High, Teachers Say," *New York Times*, May 27, 2023, at A13.

[75] On addiction risk and I.Q. loss, *see* National Institutes of Health, "Regular Marijuana Use by Teens Continues to Be a Concern" (Dec. 19, 2012), *online at* https://www.nih.gov/news-events/news-releases/regular-marijuana-use-teens-continues-be-concern; J. Cobb Scott et al., "Association of Cannabis with Cognitive Functioning in Adolescents and Young Adults," *JAMA Psychiatry*, vol. 75(6) (2018), pp. 585–95 (suggesting "previous studies of cannabis in youth may have overstated the magnitude and persistence of cognitive deficits associated with use"); Matthew D. Albaugh et al., "Association of Cannabis Use During Adolescence with Neurodevelopment," *JAMA Psychiatry*, vol. 78(9) (Sept. 2021), pp. 1–11; on educational, employment, and income deficits, *see* sources cited in Judith S. Brook et al., "Adult Work Commitment, Financial Stability, and Social Environment as Related to Trajectories of Marijuana Use Beginning in Adolescence," *Substance Abuse*, vol. 34 (Mar. 7, 2013), p. 298; Edmund Silins et al., "Young Adult Sequelae of Adolescent Cannabis Use: An Integrative Analysis," *Lancet Psychiatry*, vol. 1 (Sept. 2014), pp. 286, 288, 291 (analyzing studies suggesting "daily users [of cannabis] before age 17 years had odds of high-school completion and [university] degree attainment that were 63% and 62% lower, respectively, than those who had never used cannabis"); Olivier Marie & Ulf Zölitz, "'High' Achievers? Cannabis Access and Academic Performance," *Review of Economic Studies*, vol. 84, no. 3 (July 2017), pp. 1210, 1213 (documenting "solid causal evidence" that denial of legal cannabis had "a large and positive impact on student performance"); Keith Humphreys, "These College Students Lost Access to Legal Pot—And Started Getting Better Grades," *Washington Post Wonkblog*, July 25, 2017, *online at* https://www.washingtonp

Third Caution: The Lessons of Alcohol Prohibition

There is one more cause for caution in predicting a marketplace in recreational cannabis will conquer the land: not one of the commonly heard arguments for legalizing recreational pot concerns what recreational cannabis *does*. No prominent pro-cannabis spokesperson has argued that what marijuana does to the brain is something the public should want. Some have deemed a stoner a better spouse or bar mate than a raving drunk, but few have claimed the community is ripe for a new legal intoxicant. On the contrary, one gets the sense from thoughtful commentary supporting legalization that marijuana's impact on the brain is a slightly embarrassing, even if benign or comical, encumbrance on an otherwise sound policy preference. Of *High Times* magazine's top-ten reasons for legalizing marijuana, not one so much as hinted the drug would *get you high*. So too at the *New York Times*, where editors advocated for legalization without uttering one good word about intoxication.[76]

Once before in this history we've seen an epic law change driven largely by forces other than the public's views of the regulated substance. Consider again America's embrace of the Eighteenth Amendment and national alcohol prohibition in the early twentieth century, for prohibition's fate may help forecast the course of today's movement to legalize cannabis. At the turn of the twentieth century, as told in Chapter 3, the statewide prohibition movement of the nineteenth century had stalled and retreated. By 1904 only three widely scattered states banned all alcoholic drinks. Then four forces, all largely distinct from the public's opinions about alcohol, conspired to revive the movement and fuel its victory. In the South, where all but one state of the old Confederacy embraced prohibition by the end of 1918, many voters and lawmakers aimed to keep down a restive population of African Americans who had the economic wherewithal to keep and patronize saloons and who, whites feared, threatened rape and rebellion when drunk. In some Southern, Midwestern, and Plains states dominated by old-stock white Protestants, voters and lawmakers shuttered their bars to

ost.com/news/wonk/wp/2017/07/25/these-college-students-lost-access-to-legal-pot-and-started-getting-better-grades/?utm_term=.4a38ce22e96f; Ryan S. Sultan et al., "Nondisordered Cannabis Use among U.S. Adolescents," *JAMA Network Open* (May 3, 2023) (finding that low or moderate cannabis use among youth aged twelve to seventeen nearly doubled the likelihood of slower thoughts, difficulty concentrating, truancy, and low grade point average), *online at* https://jamanetwork.com/journals/jamanetworkopen/fullarticle/2804450?guestAccessKey=0bdfa224-c61f-4586-b27e-640b4da7b939&utm_content=weekly_highlights&utm_term=051423&utm_source=silverchair&utm_campaign=jama_network&cmp=1&utm_medium=email; Valeriya Safronova, "Big Candy Takes on THC Treats," *New York Times*, May 23, 2021, p. ST1.

[76] Russ Belville, "The Top 10 Reasons to Vote Yes on Marijuana Legalization," *High Times* (Nov. 3, 2016), *online at* https://hightimes.com/news/the-top-10-reasons-to-vote-yes-on-marijuana-legalization/; [Editorial], "Repeal Prohibition, Again," *New York Times*, July 27, 2014, p. SR1. I thank David Oyer for leading me to these sources.

ward off western migration by swarms of swarthy Catholics and Jews from the hard-drinking countries of Southern and Eastern Europe. And in the Far West, beyond the likely reach of these migrants, newly enfranchised women saw prohibition as a victory over mostly male saloons and the drink that drained their household budgets and turned their husbands drunk and mean.

Take together all these forces—racism, nativism, and women's suffrage—and add to them an abiding suspicion in all quarters of the saloon in its pre-prohibition form, and *still* it's unlikely the nation would have tipped toward prohibition in the 1910s. Only the pressures of war overcame the resistance of those Eastern and Northern states that had tried prohibition in the nineteenth century and later happily abandoned it. Seized with the fervent patriotism of war fever, the public willingly dropped alcohol to spare scarce grain and deny trade to brewers bearing German names. As the count of prohibition states tripled from ten at the war's start to thirty-two at its close, what had seemed stubbornly unlikely suddenly seemed unstoppable.

Unstoppable—but hardly permanent. For national prohibition collapsed after less than fourteen years. It would have folded faster, probably much faster, had its undoing required a mere majority vote and not a constitutional amendment ratified by three-quarters of the states. The lesson of alcohol's demise and fast revival is that the public had erred in endorsing prohibition while focusing on all the wrong things. Prohibition had ceased to be primarily about alcohol and had become instead the means of putting down Southern African Americans, holding immigrants at bay, expressing women's growing might, and needling a wartime enemy. Later, with prohibition in effect, many one-time supporters regretted their victory and wanted back the pleasures of the social cup. By September 1922, after less than three years' experience with prohibition, 61.4 percent of Americans surveyed favored modification or outright repeal.[77]

America's experience with alcohol prohibition may offer the mirror image of today's movement to legalize marijuana. Rather than banning a substance long licensed for sale, we are licensing for sale a substance long banned. Rather than focusing on problems incidental to the substance's overuse, we are focusing on those stemming from its overly rigorous ban. Rather than stopping trade as a means to repress a minority race, we are opening trade to sap one source of that race's oppression. And rather than banning sale of something the mainstream wants and deems moral in moderation, we perhaps are opening sale to something the mainstream still finds morally unsettling.

---

[77] "Final Returns in 'The Digest's' Prohibition Poll," *Literary Digest* (Sept. 9, 1922), p. 11 (tallying 922,383 ballots). I discuss the *Literary Digest*'s prohibition polls and their methodological constraints in Chapter 3, pages 141–42.

If all these statements prove true, the current trend toward legalizing cannabis could follow the same course as national prohibition: after great initial enthusiasm and a sense of inevitability, the public may find that an agglomeration of short-lived forces has joined briefly to push the nation past the bounds of mainstream morality. In that event, the current trend toward legalization could stall out—and even retreat.

Looking Ahead

It's the usual privilege of historians to know the ending before setting to work. But having written this book in the midst of what may be epic change, I've grown less sure where the story ends. So with you I'll watch as our cannabis revolution unfolds. Here in closing I'll venture just one prediction and one hope.

My prediction is that wherever the nascent trend toward legalizing recreational cannabis comes to rest, the resulting law regime will not overstretch the bounds of mainstream morality. We have seen before that in this realm of euphoria regulation, a law that offends mainstream morals cannot long hold. As mainstream morals vary from place to place, we cannot expect everywhere the same cannabis regime. But everywhere we can look for a vestige of the old moral aversion to pleasures that disable the mind. That aversion, which has mediated marketplaces in recreational drugs throughout this long history, is not dead. It may not be your moral aversion or mine, and it may be harder to discern in some places than others. But it has not vanished from our culture.

So we must ask: If the moral precepts that for centuries have shaped attitudes to sex, alcohol, and drugs remain robust today, why do we hear so little of them? Why do we hear so little of the old aversion to appetitive, pleasure-seeking, mind-disabling conduct? Today nobody—at least nobody with a prominent public platform—speaks of barnyard beasts, suspended reason, or Augustine's "impulses of the lower flesh." Where has this old moral argot gone?

One answer is that it's not gone away—it's gone secular. We no longer hear that drunkenness "deprive[s] a man of the Image of God," as Increase Mather alleged. Nor would anyone today echo Matthew Scrivener in defining a sot—or stoner— as one who "boweth down his Reason to his Senses, and hangs down his Head to the Earth, after the manner of Beasts." But while spiritual and bestial imagery is gone, the underlying concerns of abandoned reason, self-indulgence, debasement, and dissipation endure, voiced by those who dare raise a doubt against the roiling currents of change.

Consider David Brooks of the *New York Times*, who dissented from his paper's editorial opposition to the federal marijuana ban. "I just don't think it's the way we want to spend our minds," he said, noting that "effects on the teenage brain are really pretty significant." Writing in January 2014, just days after recreational cannabis went legal in Colorado, Brooks recalled how his own teenaged toking with friends had turned his mind against legalized marijuana. Fun as their frolics were, Brooks and his friends gave up smoking—and not because it could addict or cause car accidents or lead to more serious drugs. Rather they aspired to become "more . . . coherent and responsible people," a process that "usually involves using the powers of reason, temperance and self-control—not qualities one associates with being high."[78]

Reason, temperance, and *self-control.* Here Brooks uttered the trifecta of moral virtues that stand in contrast to the appetitive, pleasure-seeking, mind-disabling temptations of wanton sex, excessive drink, and euphoric drugs. Yet Brooks invoked no saints, appealed to no creed, summoned no bestial imagery. He allowed he was making a "moral" argument, but seemed almost embarrassed to say so: "Many people these days shy away from talk about the moral status of drug use . . . ." Yet the kind of morality threatened by mind-numbing euphoria never required a spiritual footing. Instead it exalted self-command and the rational control of the lower appetites. The old moral argot may survive, therefore, in quietly secular tones.

Having heard my prediction, let me close with my hope: I hope the long lens of history lends depth and texture to our current legalization debate. Demonizing our antidrug law regime, so deeply flawed in so many ways, by alleging it sprouted from racist soil makes calls for its undoing seem too evidently right. There *are* grounds for its undoing, for we cannot abide a criminal market in which sellers battle for contested turf, blighted communities let police run amok, onlookers lose faith in a feckless system, and bad guys pocket all the profits.

But let us remember that moral impulses gave rise to our drug bans, and evil is not always begotten by evil. Parental anxiety over children's moral health is a worthy impulse, however badly it has played out.

---

[78] David Brooks, "Weed. Been There. Done That," *New York Times,* Jan. 3, 2014, p. A19.

Index

For the benefit of digital users, indexed terms that span two pages (e.g., 52–53) may, on occasion, appear on only one of those pages.
Tables and figures are indicated by *t* and *f* following the page number[*]

[*] My thanks to Jack Gleiberman, one of my research assistants, who compiled this index.

Lake, Henry, 103
Lallemand, Ludger, 110–11
Lamneck, Arthur P., 140
Lathrop, George Parsons, 5, 7, 12, 13, 123, 126, 167, 223–24
Latimer, Dan, 1–2, 227–28
laudanum. *See* opium: medicinal uses of
League of Nations Advisory Committee on Traffic in Opium and Other Dangerous Drugs, 343
Lee, Barbara, 430–31
Lee, Fong, 216
Lee, Jesse, 98
Lee, Leroy, 98
Lee, Wing, 249
Lemnius, Levinus, 43
Lewis, Andrew R., 287–91
Lewis, Michael, 135
LGBTQ community, 455
Licata, Victor, 338–41
  mug shot of, 340*f*
Livingston, Rose, 331
loco-weed, 400–1, 405–7, 412–13, 415–19
London, 44–45, 53–56, 58–59, 60–62, 73–74, 125, 151
Lonsdale, Lord, 57
Louisiana, 164
  cocaine prohibition in, 269*t*, 314–16, 452–64
  New Orleans, 164, 230, 306–13, 315–16, 318, 343
  opium prohibition in, 190*t*, 193*t*
LSD, 264, 435
Lynch, John, 261
Lynch, Thomas F., 252

MacNichol, Alexander, 132–33
Madden, John, 111
Maguire, Barney, 248
Maguire, Delia, 248
Maher, John F., 317, 320–21
Mahoney, James, 211–12, 217–18
Maine, xiv
  alcohol prohibition in, 115–14, 116–17, 129–30
  cannabis prohibition in, 346*t*, 351–54, 363–67, 416–17, 418
  cocaine prohibition in, 269*t*
  legalization of medical cannabis in, 450
  legalization of recreational cannabis in, 425
  opium prohibition in, 190*t*, 193*t*
Mallerau, Beatrice, 320–21
Manaton, Doctor, 302

mandatory minimums. *See* penalties for drug possession: mandatory minimum
Marihuana Tax Act of 1937. *See* cannabis prohibition in the United States: Marihuana Tax Act of 1937
marijuana. *See* cannabis
marriage equality, 455
Marshall, Orville, 191
Martinez, Cora, 209–10
Maryland, 194–96
  alcohol prohibition in, 12–13
  cannabis prohibition in, 346*t*
  cocaine prohibition in, 269*t*
  opium den ban in, 180*t*, 183–84
  opium prohibition in, 190*t*, 193*t*, 194–96
Massachusetts, 113–14, 179–81, 195
  alcohol prohibition in, 107–8, 113–14, 185, 188, 363–64
  Boston, 17, 105–7, 164, 181–83, 262, 320, 331, 429
  cannabis prohibition in, 346*t*, 347, 351–52, 354–60, 366–67, 368, 372
  Chelsea, 356
  cigarette regulation in, 380–81
  cocaine prohibition in, 302–6, 315, 316–17, 357–58
  legalization of recreational cannabis in, 429
  Lowell, 106, 209–10
  opium den ban in, 179–83, 180*t*, 357–58
  opium prohibition in, 185–86, 195, 357–58, 363–64, 369–70, 432–33
mass incarceration. *See* incarceration
Masters, Frederick J., 1–5, 8, 12, 13, 123, 126, 151–52, 164–65, 166, 167, 199, 210–11, 212, 223–24
  An Opium Smoker, 10*f*
  A San Francisco Opium Den, 3*f*
Masterson, Hugh, 327
Mather, Cotton, 42, 45, 46–47, 80
Mather, Increase, 17–21, 40, 45, 46, 62, 101–2, 117–18, 178, 464
Mather, Richard, 24
Mathews, Mary, 242
McCauley, Clark R., 47–49
McCumber, James, 161, 191–92
McEntee, John, 232–33
McFarland, S. F., 191
McGirr, Lisa, 139
McGowan, P. F., 323
McKown, J. O., 408–9
McLellan, William, 216
MDMA, xv, 264, 453